THE BEST OF
COUNTRY MUSIC

THE BEST OF COUNTRY MUSIC

by

JOHN MORTHLAND

A Dolphin Book
Doubleday & Company, Inc.
Garden City, New York
1984

Designed by Virginia M. Soulé

Library of Congress Cataloging in Publication Data

Morthland, John.
  The best of country music.

  Includes index.
  1. Country music—United States—Discography.
I. Title.
ML156.4.C7M67   1984   789.9′136452

ISBN: 0–385–19192–8
Library of Congress Catalog Card Number 83–14238
Copyright © 1984 by John Morthland
All Rights Reserved
Printed in the United States of America
First Edition

For further copyright information about the contents of this book, see page 435.

To Lester Bangs
1948–1982

CONTENTS

INTRODUCTION

In the last decade or so, country music has boomed. Once a grass-roots form viewed with scorn outside the South and the Southwest, it has now entered the American mainstream. No matter where you might be in the nation, you will almost certainly find at least a couple of country stations on your radio dial—one of the biggest is in New York City, of all places. Country singers now appear regularly in stadiums and posh urban nightclubs as well as on the old circuit of state fairs, honky-tonks, schoolhouses, and small-town auditoriums. They command their own television specials, and are used to endorse products intended for a mass market. Pop singers attempt to shore up faltering careers by putting some country in their sound, and country singers join this crossover trend by putting some pop into their own sounds. There are more country albums on the market than ever before; for the novice in particular, the sheer number of albums is bound to seem bewildering. This book puts those albums in perspective.

It is, by its very nature, a highly subjective book. Rather than attempt to evaluate all country albums available, I'm limiting myself to extended discussions of what I believe to be the 100 most significant albums, with brief mentions of hundreds more that should be of interest to those who wish to dig deeper.

The discussions of albums are divided into sections that begin with the earliest recorded examples of country music and continue right up into the eighties—more than half a century's worth of sound, of change. The music goes from the log cabin in the southern hills through the advent of radio and other mass media, the onslaught of World War II and the subsequent increasing urbanization of America, and winds up in Las Vegas. I did this because I wanted to leave the reader with something more than a cut-and-dried argument for one man's favorite albums; I wanted also to leave him or her with a critical history of country music. I wanted to show country music in the context of the world it came out of and the world it went into, to show how it shaped that world and how that world shaped it. I wanted to have things both ways: If you wish to use the book as a simple consumer guide, you can dip into it anywhere you please, but if you wish to read it from beginning to end, be my guest.

In choosing the top 100 albums, I relied almost entirely on quality, or at least my version of quality; that's why, in addition to several albums each from predictable big names like Jimmie Rodgers, the Carter Family, Bob Wills, Hank Williams, and Merle Haggard, an occasional obscurity like Harry Choates or Jimmy Murphy pops up. Quite simply, they made great music even if it wasn't wildly popular. Of necessity, criteria change as the music does.

Strong melodies remain a constant, as do vocal (or instrumental) techniques, the little fillips singers (or musicians) bring to their styles that make them unique, that connect them to something primal in all of us. Because country began as a form of folk expression, the best artists, even today, carry with them a sense of history, of tradition, that is palpable—as the saying goes, it's "as old as the hills." It's best when that sense isn't undercut by too much nostalgia or sentimentality, both cheap and easy emotions; since both are integral to the form, however, it becomes a question of how well the artist walks the line. As conservative as country music is, tradition doesn't count for everything, either; innovators who extend the tradition, taking the best of the old and mixing in some of the new, are essential to the music's growth, and to its ability to stay up with the times. Finally, singers needn't have lived their songs, but it helps a lot when it *sounds* like they did; it creates a persona the audience identifies with, it personalizes the music, turns it into a form of self-expression that maintains the vital link between the earliest country music and the latest.

In prewar country music, I lean toward a more raucous, unfettered band sound, musicians pushing against each other and against the boundaries of their idiom; this usually comes when they admit outside influences from blues and pop to mix with their country roots. In postwar country, when producers began taking over, the emphasis shifts to a lean, tight band sound that complements the singer; in general, the more production stands out over the voice, the less interested I am. And in both cases, I don't hesitate to reward an artist who, rather than challenging or defying the idiom, simply does it as well as anyone else around, with both commitment and conviction—just so long as that personal stamp is also on the music.

In recent years, the country song has become almost as important as the singer. It's hard to pinpoint what makes for a great song beyond the fact that it connects directly to the listener, that a thought or experience is shared between performer and audience without encumbrances. It is a definite advantage if a compelling story is told, but that's not essential; country may once have been primarily story-songs, but since that's no longer true, I'll settle for a simple truism or two in the lyric. And I have to admit that I'm a sucker for the puns, wordplays, and outrageous metaphors, corny as they can get, that country writers thrive on.

When in doubt, I also put weight on historical significance; some artists who *were* wildly popular are not necessarily to my personal tastes, but I have to give them credit for their important roles in the evolution of the music. These choices were all made easier by the fact that more often than not, the music I consider best is widely recognized as such by others, and sells accordingly. Still, the choices *must* remain subjective, no matter how much my tastes coincide or don't with those of the audience, and that being the case, I should also point out that my own background is steeped in rock 'n' roll and blues (and, to a lesser extent, in jazz) as much as in country; though this may seem blasphemous to the diehard country fan, I regard it as an asset, and am happy to let it shade my judgments. After all, your top 100 would be just as subjective no matter how much we happened to agree on, and I hope there will be many arguments about my choices—that's half the fun of being a fan in the first place.

I chose to leave out, except where they apply directly to country music, such closely related forms as Cajun and gospel. I tried also when possible—to limit my selections to in-print domestic album releases. Why rave on about LPs that are impossible, or nearly impossible, for the average fan to obtain?

The answer is that ignoring some such albums would leave unconscionable holes in the history of country music. Out-of-print albums by major stars can often be found in bargain bins or specialty stores. In many cases Europeans are much more diligent than Americans in keeping alive older forms of country music. So are the small, independent, domestic labels, which have a virtual corner on the market for bluegrass and pre-bluegrass forms simply because the major American companies ignore that music. These "indies" usually dub their albums off the original 78 rpm recordings, so the sound leaves much to be desired, but they're the only place you'll find the music at all. Some of them are so localized that you can't even find their products outside their immediate vicinities, not even in the usual specialty stores and mail-order houses; this has undoubtedly led to some omissions on my part, but I'm confident that you'll find this book offers a thorough overview.

Which brings me to my final point. The country boom has been a mixed blessing. It's introduced many people to a part of their heritage they'd been missing too long, but it's also diluted the music badly. I'm no reactionary, but the saccharine, homogenized, overproduced songs full of glib generalities I hear most often on the radio today have little to do with the rowdy good spirits, hard truths, and high, lonesome cries that first drew me to the music. And the former is winning out. In their rush to capture the mass market, artists and record companies are throwing out much of what is best in their music.

I suppose that part is inevitable—if the music stayed raw and feral, it wouldn't attract a mass audience to begin with—but a side effect has been that the grittier country music is not only going unrecorded most of the time, but the stuff that *has* been recorded in the past is not being kept in print. It was astonishing, and depressing, to look through the catalogs of the major labels and see how much they've deleted, including relatively recent material. Lawyers and accountants run record companies these days, and their bottom-line logic dictates that it's not profitable enough to even press and distribute older music anymore—why go to all that trouble to make thousands of dollars when there're millions to be had out there in the crossover market? And that part bothers me deeply, because while I'm the first to concede that more consumers will prefer a Kenny Rogers, I think those who've just discovered country music and want to explore it in depth should have the chance to hear prime Ernest Tubb as well. So I hope this book enhances the appreciation of those already well versed in country music, and adds to both their knowledge and their pleasure; but for those new to the idiom, who are in the great majority, I hope this gives them the urge and the guidance to look back past the obvious toward the rich, variegated, and uniquely American body of work that made today's boom possible.

That music is not going to be around much longer, so get it while you can. And happy hunting.

THE BEST OF
COUNTRY MUSIC

OVERVIEWS

Because mass interest in country music is so recent, there have been very few attempts at compiling albums that provide comprehensive overviews of the music, or of aspects of the music. Part of the problem is that such albums must draw on material from numerous record companies, which usually creates all sorts of licensing headaches. The few albums that have been released, however, show that these problems are hardly insurmountable. Presumably, there will be more such compilations in the future.

The Smithsonian Collection of Classic Country Music (Smithsonian Institution)

This is the Big One, folks—143 cuts, spread out over eight records, spiffily packaged in a blue-denim box with lengthy accompanying booklet written by album compiler Bill C. Malone, whose *Country Music USA* (University of Texas Press, 1968) is still the reference book all writers, myself included, start their careers by stealing from.

Songs are arranged almost, but not quite, chronologically. The first, and earliest, is A. C. "Eck" Robertson's "Sallie Gooden," (usually spelled "Goodin"). It's almost certainly the first country performance ever recorded, and though the popular fiddle tune was subsequently cut by dozens more, none have matched this flashy Texan for friskiness and sheer unpredictability. The last, and most recent, song is Willie Nelson's "Blue Eyes Crying in the Rain," itself a classic piece of back-to-the-roots minimalism that in 1976 put Nelson's long-shaky career on solid ground for good. So these two cuts are, in their insistence on directness and simplicity, not as far apart as you might have expected. But what's in between them fluctuates wildly, pointing toward several conclusions.

Country music typically takes two steps forward followed by one back. The problem is in determining what constitutes a step forward and what constitutes a step back—especially since the various forms of country music don't naturally follow each other in neat order, but overlap, or coexist side by side. In these records the traditional sounds of Robertson are followed by the traditional-sounding "The Little Old Log Cabin in the Lane," by Fiddlin' John Carson, which is followed by the "Tin Pan Alley country" of Vernon Dalhart, which is followed by the traditional songs "Goodbye Sweet Liza Jane" by Charlie Poole with the North Carolina Ramblers and "Soldier's Joy" by Gid Tanner and His Skillet Lickers. Jimmie Rodgers, meanwhile, perpetuates both traditional and nontraditional country music.

Later, honky-tonk, which started as a stripped-down version of western swing, is generally perceived as having been "taken too far" by rockabilly (which is consequently conspicuous in its absence). Industry powers responded to honky-tonk with the Nashville Sound, which was a big step away from the roots but is still widely perceived as the "real" country music of its time. An infusion of honky-tonk later trimmed the Nashville Sound down some, but not enough for the so-called outlaw movement (also largely ignored here), which simultaneously simplified *and* complicated the music by putting new themes to old music and old themes to new music, too. But outlaw posturing yielded to the safer, more tranquil countrypolitan music of Kenny Rogers, which is said to have finally reconciled country music unequivocally to the modern, urban world or to have finally destroyed country music once and for all (which may be the same thing anyhow). This most recent step is not documented here at all.

Which is odd, because the next important point to be made is that country has always strived for mainstream commercial acceptance. Today's purists (which I suppose I sorta am) forget this too easily. If we say that country music recordings originated in 1922 to fill a grass-roots need, then we have to concede that it took only two years (Dalhart's two cuts are from 1924) for the music to be co-opted, watered down, and restyled for mass consumption. There was undoubtedly resistance to this, as there is today to Kenny Rogers and his ilk, but sales figures don't lie now or then: The country audience approves, by and large, of this commercialization whether it comes from within or without. Acceptance of country music by the American mainstream, after all, also means acceptance of country music fans, who have always been people on the outside trying to get in. A few rebel, God bless 'em, but this urge to fit in is perhaps the strongest single impulse behind the music.

In a sense, country music peaked with Hank Williams, and since then has had nowhere to go but down. Williams, and the other country stars of his generation, grew up when traditional music was still thriving. Those who have come in his wake have their roots elsewhere, and however faithful they try to be toward traditional country music, it just ain't the same. The ones who've struggled hardest with that dilemma (Haggard, Nelson, Jones) usually make the best music.

Finally, country music doesn't all sound the same. That should be a given, but believe it or not, there are still people out there who will insist that it *does* all sound the same. Malone's compilation should set them straight. It has its flaws, such as the exclusion (unless you count one Johnny Cash cut) of rockabilly. And I'm still trying to figure how a native Texan, even a scholar like Malone, could suppress his Lone Star chauvinism enough to give western swing only a fraction of the attention he gives bluegrass. But at the same time, I'm glad he cut the album off before the slickest of the modern slickies take over. They're definitely the beginning of the end.

Country & Western Classics: Duets (Time-Life)

Duets exist in all forms of American popular music, but nowhere so prominently as in country. Why?

I figure it's because country music is always striving to project an image of togetherness, of family, of belonging. Duets do that, as they are usually siblings or spouses singing together. Nowadays unrelated male and female stars sing together for maximum commercial impact, and the possibilities in "cheating songs" are thereby opened up—but for every such song by a George and Tammy or a Conway and Loretta, there's another in which they swear undying love.

As Charles K. Wolfe writes in the accompanying booklet, duet singing didn't come out of folk traditions—how could it when the earliest country music was primarily instrumental?—but out of the church. The earliest documented country duet act is Reuben Puckett and Richard Brooks, who first recorded on January 29, 1925, which means duets have been around almost as long as the country recording industry has. But until the thirties, they were few and far between. Mac and Bob (with "When the Roses Bloom Again," 1927) and the earthier Hugh Cross and Riley Puckett ("Red River Valley," 1927) were regarded in their day almost as novelty acts, and the latter was only a temporary alliance to begin with. (Mac and Bob were a working team for years.) Darby and Tarlton were an even bigger anomaly; peers of Jimmie Rodgers, they're more important for their bluesy songs and picking than for their singing.

Brother teams of the thirties were the first true generation of duets, and Wolfe traces their rise to technology—improved mikes and amplification made it easier to sing softly and thus clearly and still be heard over the instruments, while radio created a need for "professional" entertainment, a designation that seemed to fit singers more than instrumentalists. There were other reasons too. Radio also created the need for "listening" (vocal) music as opposed to "dance" (instrumental) music, and the success of Jimmie Rodgers and the Carter Family contributed to the popularity of vocal music in general.

Brother duets sang in close harmony, and their repertoires consisted mainly of sentimental songs or traditional ballads; they usually backed themselves with just a guitar and a mandolin. Karl and Harty ("I'm Just Here to Get My Baby Out of Jail," "The Prisoner's Dream," and, to a lesser extent, the much-later "I Hide My Face and Cry") were one of the most influential, because they were *so* soft and precise, while teams like the Allen Brothers ("Just Because") and the Monroe Brothers

("What Would You Give in Exchange for Your Soul?") were more funky. But no team combined both worlds so well as the Delmore Brothers. With songs like "Broken Hearted Lover" and "Blues Stay Away from Me," Alton and Rabon Delmore matched smooth phrasing and precise harmonies to classic country voices and material. Other teams followed using only slightly different styles, including the Blue Sky Boys and especially the Louvin Brothers (whose 1955 "When I Stop Dreaming" is one of the last and best efforts in the genre), but already brother duets were yielding to honky-tonk music and/or husband-and-wife duets.

Lulu Belle and Scotty rose to prominence in the mid-thirties singing poppish material like "Remember Me" and "Have I Told You Lately That I Love You," while Wilma Lee and Stoney Cooper came along about a decade later with religious and mountain-oriented songs like "This World Can't Stand Long" and "The West Virginia Polka." But Lulu Belle and Scotty proved more the wave of the future than Wilma Lee and Stoney.

That's because as the honky-tonk joined the radio as a prime outlet for country music, it became necessary to record more modernistic songs; Lulu and Scotty were certainly not honky-tonkers, but they *were* a step closer, and eventually their love songs were giving way to cheating songs like "Slippin' Around" (1949) by Margaret Whiting and Jimmy Wakely. A new morality had a foothold in country music, and the style of duets began changing. Where the more traditional husband-and-wife teams usually featured the man singing a harmony underneath the female lead, the new men and women usually swapped lines (or verses) and sang harmonies only on the choruses. The apex of both these movements came in 1962, when Carl and Pearl Butler hit with the magnificent "Don't Let Me Cross Over."

Contemporary duets follow from that, but are even more explicit. Since the singing partners aren't necessarily married, they can work with a wider variety of songs, though domestic strife and happiness remain the two biggest themes. But that leaves much latitude, as shown by George Jones and Melba Montgomery ("We Must Have Been Out of Our Minds," 1963), David Houston and Tammy Wynette ("My Elusive Dreams," 1967), and Conway Twitty and Loretta Lynn ("After the Fire Is Gone," 1971).

So duets mirror the evolution of country music from its isolated, rural beginnings to a somewhat confused place in contemporary society. All of which makes me wonder what to make of the biggest new fad in duets as I write this—men who aren't kin. The trend was launched by the Willie-and-Waylon duets of the seventies, but really took hold when Willie Nelson started cutting with all his old friends and influences (Roger Miller, Johnny Bush, Ray Price, Merle Haggard, Webb Pierce).

George Jones has done albums with Johnny Paycheck and with Merle Haggard. Moe Bandy and Joe Stampley record together. So do Gary Stewart and Dean Dillon. It's not unprecedented, for this album includes the team of Red Sovine and Webb Pierce singing "Why Baby Why" (1955) and could have included even better examples, such as Tom T. Hall and Dave Dudley lurching amiably through "Day Drinking" (1970). These are really "buddy songs," the musical equivalent of certain Burt Reynolds movies. And come to think of it, that might be why they're becoming popular now.

Country & Western Classics: The Women (Time-Life)

In 1935, with "I Want to Be a Cowboy's Sweetheart," Patsy Montana became country music's first female million-seller. There were a few noteworthy women singers before her, and many more after, but Patsy was the first with a high profile both as a woman and as a country singer.

She fronted the Prairie Ramblers on the WLS Barn Dance in Chicago from 1934 to 1952, and was the show's undisputed star most of that time, perhaps the nation's best-known yodeler. She was also the first to tailor songs specifically for women, and as "I Only Want a Buddy, Not a Sweetheart" suggests, she had something of an independent streak. This doesn't mean she had the firmness of a Patsy Cline or a Loretta Lynn—Patsy Montana was much more coy, cute, and precious—but it was a start. Ironically, until Kitty Wells came along in 1952 with "It Wasn't God Who Made Honky Tonk Angels," few women followed Montana's lead, perhaps because her "message" was stated so indirectly that few took it seriously.

In its earliest days, country music had little room for female singers. Entertainment *(especially* music, which was often seen as sinful to begin with) was simply not "woman's work." As the booklet accompanying this three-record set explains, women sang harmonies, did comedy, and very occasionally got a solo spot, usually on a religious number; it helped if the woman was part of a family group, because that meant there was someone onstage to help "protect" her. Today, women have taken center stage in greater numbers, and they have much more latitude in terms of what they sing about. But because the industry wisdom is that women are the main buyers of records, country is still more a man's world.

Yet the first country record by a female, fourteen-year-old Roba Stanley's "Little Frankie" (a tame version of "Frankie and Johnnie") came in 1924, just two years after the first country record by a man, so women were there almost from the beginning. As sides by Lulu Belle and Zora Layman indicate, though, they were usually more pop-oriented, and when a woman had something to complain about, her only viable avenue was through satire. Most country women had to fudge on their femaleness or their countryness (or both) even for quite a while after Patsy Montana. Stereotypical roles were so forcefully delineated that even in a case like the Carter Family, A.P. was seen as the leader though he sang little and played no instrument. The real driving forces were Sara and Maybelle, who devised a new form of music, and "Single Girl, Married Girl" (1927), with Sara taking the lead, *is* both uncompromisingly country and uncompromisingly female.

But look at what's happening in the late thirties and early forties, right after Montana and the Carters. The Coon Creek Girls are country, but full of poppish sentiment. The Dezurik Sisters are pure gimmick in their yodeling, while the Girls of the Golden West are but one step above it. Louise Massey is basically a pop singer with country backing, while Judy Canova is even closer to pure pop. Cousin Emmy was the Barbara Mandrell of her day, a singer and multi-instrumentalist who did nothing well, but everything slick.

Still, not everyone fit the mold. Cindy Walker, with the haunting "Till the Longest Day I Live," is almost a prototype for Patsy Cline, and had Cindy continued as a singer rather than limiting herself to songwriting, country might have come around to women stars much sooner. Texas Ruby, with "Don't Let That Man Get You Down," verges on honky-tonk; she is husky, bluesy, and not to be crossed. Molly O'Day and Wilma Lee Cooper have the fatalism and steely resolve of the traditional mountain singer, regardless of sex, and Rose Maddox puts her jokes across and makes her stories stick through sheer exuberance. But until Kitty Wells, these women stayed in the minority.

After Kitty, possibilities multiplied. Goldie Hill's "I Let the Stars Get in My Eyes," although it is an answer song like "It Wasn't God Who Made Honky Tonk Angels," points a finger at nobody but the singer, but at least she wasn't led astray; whatever she did, she did herself. Jean Shepard's "Satisfied Mind" expresses strength of attitude new to country women, even if it's couched in terms both vaguely spiritual and sexually neutral. Brenda Lee and Wanda Jackson could rock with the big boys. Patsy Cline (represented here with "Walking After Midnight," "I Fall to Pieces," and "Crazy") said what was on her mind, but it was clear only to those listening close; the rest must have thought they were hearing the usual. Then Loretta Lynn stepped out with songs like "Don't Come Home A'Drinkin' " that were impossible *not* to hear loud and clear.

And that's the way it's remained for the last two decades or so. Some argue that a new, independent country woman has taken over, a contention this album aims to support, but the music doesn't quite bear that out. Instead, there's a little of everything, and no one type dominates. True, women are now stars in their own right, rather than components in a male package show. But what is independent about the stance of Tammy Wynette on "Stand By Your Man"? ("Your Good Girl's Gonna Go Bad" is atypical of her material.) There's new frankness about what women can say or do in Barbara Mandrell's "The Midnight Oil" and Jeanne Pruett's "Satin Sheets," but still no implication that cheating is as justifiable for a woman as for a man. Tanya Tucker's "Would You Lay with Me (In a Field of Stone)" and Jessi Colter's "I'm Not Lisa" are unabashedly erotic, though for different reasons, and they have nothing else in common. Dolly Parton can get incensed about being considered a "Dumb Blonde," but the album ends with Emmylou Harris's garbled "Boulder to Birmingham," and it's a telling fact that though Emmylou is seen as the symbol for the supposed new country female, she is, underneath it all, as passive and docile as they come. But she is clearly feminine and she is clearly country, at least, and in a field so conservative, that in itself may be a step up.

Folk Music in America (Library of Congress). This extraordinary set, compiled by Richard K. Spottswood, consists of fifteen albums, each of them on a particular theme *(Songs of Love, Courtship and Marriage, Songs of Migration and Immigration, Songs of Death and Tragedy, Songs of War and History, Songs of Humor and Hilarity*, etc.). It's not all country music by a long shot, but most of it is at least related, and the variety (different styles, different eras, different themes) is staggering. Each of the fifteen albums can also be obtained separately.

Supplementary Albums

60 Years of Country Music (RCA). This is a noble idea, as one label attempts to document its long-time involvement in country music. RCA was the first to record country and still maintains one of the biggest Nashville offices, so the problem was less what to include than what to leave out. They begin with string-band music and move through Jimmie Rodgers and the Carters, yodelers and singing cowboys, western swing, brother duets, Cajun, bluegrass, honky-tonk, and the Nashville Sound (more or less invented at RCA), and on up to the stars of today. And it's indeed a long way from "Arkansas Traveller" (recorded June 1922 with Eck Robertson on lead fiddle and Henry Gilliland on second fiddle) to Ronnie Milsap's "It Was Almost Like a Song" (recorded by singer and band in late February 1977, background voices added nearly a month later, a string section including viola, cello, and harp added the next day, along with a flute overdub). The other major labels—at least Columbia and MCA—should put out similar albums of their own.

EARLY STRING BANDS AND BALLADEERS

In the beginning, there were the songs from England, Ireland, and Scotland—long narratives about tragic love (usually), blissful love (occasionally), natural disaster, adventure, combat, human frailty, the supernatural. They were without rhythm, and were sung *a cappella* in a high, stiff, mournful voice; they were handed down orally from one generation to the next. When the first white settlers came to America, they brought these songs with them. And that was the start of country music.

The songs hung on longest in the American Southeast, especially in the more inaccessible mountain regions, but Americans are not a people big on tradition, so they set about changing them. They shortened the songs, and sentimentalized the lyrics. Rather than describing events in flat, detached voices, they identified with events in some way, expressed their emotions toward the events. In many cases, they downplayed the sex in the songs and gave increased attention to the violence. They downplayed the supernatural, and played up the religion. Finally, they began changing the words entirely, but keeping the old melodies, and soon our native American ballads were being sung interchangeably with traditional ballads.

At first, instrumentalists were rare in Anglo-Scots music, though there were some bagpipers. Then, around 1510, the violin was invented in Europe, and began spreading to the rest of the world. On the British Islands, it was welcomed because it made a droning sound similar to that of the bagpipe. It traveled easily—was small, light, and sturdy—so it was the instrument settlers most often brought with them to the New World. In the American South, whites started playing the fiddle in the seventeenth century. Again, many of the tunes they played were traditional jigs and reels from Scotland or Ireland; there were maybe a thousand in all, and some passed into America unchanged while others were altered. There were different fiddle styles in different parts of the country, too, just as there were different English dialects and accents.

Fiddlers were in demand at most group events, whether related to work (barn raisings, hog-killings, quilting bees) or purely social (wakes, weddings, shivarees). They were strictly amateur musicians, payed off with respect and admiration rather than money. At the same time, though, religious zealots said they were agents of Satan, and labeled their instrument "the devil's box," because of the all-night country dances and house parties they played. Many people thought there was something unsavory about musicians, which probably explains in part some of the guilt feelings that worked their way into country music.

Country dances were eventually replaced by fiddlers' contests, which sometimes lasted several days. They began around 1736 and peaked in popularity around 1865. By then, the banjo was challenging the fiddle for supremacy as a country instrument. The banjo was originally of African descent, and was popularized as a white instrument by minstrel shows, in which white musicians blackened their faces with cork. When the five-string banjo came into use around 1830 (it was supposedly invented by a Joe Sweeney of Virginia, though he probably only popularized it), the instrument backed up the fiddle at country dances. Unlike the original four-string banjo, a rhythm instrument used mostly by jazz orchestras, the five-string banjo could be picked. The fifth string was a drone string, and the new banjo was played by ringing that string with the thumb while brushing the other four strings with the fingers. (This became known as the frailing, or claw-hammer, style, and remained dominant for more than a century.)

The guitar was first used in America as the instrument of cultured northerners, who favored it to play their parlor songs; it was a link to European cultures, and didn't begin filtering down to the lower classes until around 1880, but it caught on quick. By 1894, the Sears catalog was offering seven guitar models; by 1909, it was offering twelve. Black railroad workers introduced the guitar into the mountains, and as soon as whites picked it up, they began altering their music to fit it. The guitar offered ideal rhythmic accompaniment for singers, and soon the ballad style (in which the singer repeats a line, pauses, repeats another, pauses again) was fading. Singers adapted their voices to the sounds and stylistic possibilities of their instruments, and they started singing country music in harmony as they had in church.

Fiddle, guitar, and banjo made up the basic southern string band, but there were variations. The dulcimer, which has strings that are plucked with the fingers or struck with padded hammers, came from Germany, and was originally the most popular instrument in the mountains. But it made such a thin sound that it was quickly phased out. The mandolin, another string instrument only slightly less delicate, was passed down from classical orchestras beginning about 1900. The harmonica and piano were sometimes used by bands in the southern lowlands, though rarely in the mountains.

As the music evolved, so did the songs. As late as World War I, folklorists were still finding people in the mountains who sang the pre-Elizabethan ballads unaccompanied. (Many with demonstrably English origin became known as Child ballads, after the folklorist who collected them.) But other influences had been seeping into the highlands all along. Mountain people learned new songs and styles, as well as other aspects of American culture, from visitors such as preachers and circuit riders, salesmen, railroad workers. Many were exposed to a myriad of new influences by the people and places they encountered while soldiers during World War I. Even the Sears catalog, which could be found in any country home, was an influence. Medicine show and vaudeville performers introduced mountain dwellers to commercial songs from Tin Pan Alley; so did radio and the phonograph. Southern musicians sometimes even learned a new (commercial) song from a professional performer and passed it back into oral tradition.

By the time there was a record industry, country music was already a mixed bag of styles and influences. The old traditional songs and styles dominated, of course, but that was only the backbone, the framework; there was also room for native American ballads, Tin Pan Alley and parlor songs, church music, minstrel and medicine-show tunes. There were regional variations, but radio was already minimizing them. Nashville did not yet dominate or define what country music was; it was simply another region, the "Grand Ole Opry" simply another local radio show. If there was any country music center at all, it was probably Atlanta, where recording activity was high.

The recording industry was still young when Texas fiddler Eck Robertson cut the first commercial country record ("Sally Goodin" b/w "Arkansas Traveller") in 1922. In 1923, Okeh Records executive Ralph Peer recorded Georgia's Fiddlin' John Carson at the urging of an Atlanta record salesman. Peer pronounced Carson's singing "pluperfect awful" and didn't even assign the record a catalog number until the client bought up five hundred copies and sold them out virtually overnight. Then Peer realized he had something.

In the twenties, a wave of nostalgia sweeping the increasingly beleaguered nation created a demand for more Gay Nineties tunes, urban and rural. Record companies rushed to fill it, and since traditions died harder in the rural South, finding country performers who knew the old songs was no problem. It wasn't called country music then, but the various labels given it by record companies—old-time tunes, familiar tunes, old-time southern songs, hill country melodies, songs from Dixie and several others—reveal the orientation. To this day, country music is wed to nostalgia, to a longing for supposedly simpler times in the past. But the music didn't get a name until 1925, when a string band recorded for Peer in New York. After the session, he asked the group its name. "Call us anything you want," one of them replied. "We are nothing but a bunch of hillbillies from North Carolina and Virginia." Peer called them the Hill Billies and, until the forties, when the derogatory implications could no longer be ignored, the name was applied to all country music.

Anthology of American Folk Music, Volume One: Ballads
(Folkways)

MEDIEVAL WOMAN DEFEATS DEVIL DESPITE HUS-BAND'S PRAYER is how Harry Smith summarizes Bill and Belle Reed's version of "Old Lady and the Devil." Buell Kazee's "The Wagoner's Lad" becomes LOCAL GIRL'S PROTEST THAT WHIP NEEDS FIXING FAILS TO HALT WAGONING BOY FRIEND'S DEPARTURE, while Uncle Eck Dunford's "Old Shoes and Leggins" becomes MOTHER HOSPITABLE, BUT GIRLS FIND SHODDY OLD-STER'S ACTIONS PERVERSE. The Williamson Brothers and Curry's "Gonna Die with My Hammer in My Hands" (better known as "John Henry") becomes JOHN HENRY VOWS TO DEFEAT MECHANI-ZATION; QUESTIONS CAPTAIN, WARNS SHAKER AND SON. WIFE STRONG TOO. William and Versey Smith's "When That Great Ship Went Down" (also known as "The Titanic") becomes MANUFAC-TURERS PROUD DREAM DESTROYED AT SHIPWRECK. SEG-REGATED POOR DIE FIRST, and the Carter Family's "Engine 143" becomes GEORGIE RUNS INTO ROCK AFTER MOTHER'S WARNING. DIES WITH THE ENGINE HE LOVES.

In 1953, Harry Smith, notorious experimental filmmaker, folklorist, and bohemian-about-New York, put together the three two-record boxed sets known as *Anthology of American Folk Music*. Most of the entries in this first volume are white mountain singers doing traditional Anglo-American and American ballads, and to convey the outright *weirdness* of these songs in his accompanying booklet, Smith hit on the inspired idea of reducing the contents of each one to a newspaper headline. The headlines dramatize the mystery, insanity, fatalism, and supernatural events of fantasy *and* real life in the rural South. Thus does he dramatize, for example, the violence of "The Old Lady and the Devil," in which a sprightly, happy-go-lucky melody and matter-of-fact singing almost obscure the fact that the devil has vowed to take a member away from this family, and the woman has thus "picked up a hatchet and split out his brains."

Nearly all these songs detail ghastly murders or suicides, inexplicable losses, catastrophes, betrayals, or flat-out impossibilities (ZOOLOGIC MISCEGENY ACHIEVED IN MOUSE FROG NUPTIALS, RELATIVES APPROVE, reads the condensation of Chubby Parker's "King Kong Kitchie Ki-Me-O"). The impossibilities are accepted at face value nonetheless because they are perceived as being no more unlikely than what already happens in everyday life. Most of the songs were recorded in the twenties; none were recorded later than 1932. This makes them among the oldest recordings available of American traditional music, and much of country music we know today derives from them. If the relationship sometimes seems tenuous, try to use as much imagination as these singers do. Coley Jones' wheezing, pinched "Drunkards Special" is not only still performed by country (and blues) singers, but it's a clear forerunner of the modern cheating song. The Carolina Tar Heels' "Peg and Awl" and Kelly Harrell's "My Name Is John Johanna" contain the roots of contemporary hard-time songs, while the courtships (however perverse) of "Old Shoes and Leggins" or "The Wagoners Lad" lead to the modern love song.

Even at this stage, it's possible to see modernization—or at least outside influences—entering the music. Frank Hutchison's "Stackalee" is a much more modern song than the Nelstone's Hawaiians' "Fatal Flower Garden," even if it was recorded three years earlier. "Stackalee" shows how English influences were already being written out of American mountain music by the time record companies began documenting it. And look at the difference in sophistication between Burnett and Rutherford's "Willie Moore" and the Carter Family's "Engine 143." In the former, the lead voice rises and falls crudely, a whining fiddle echoing the banjo. The Carter Family's singing and picking are both smoother: They were more conscious of the show-biz possibilities in their music. They reflected a trend toward less harsh, more flattened-out vocals that had begun when instruments were added to country music and singers began experimenting with harmonies. Charlie Poole and His North Carolina Ramblers, represented here with "White House Blues" (McKINLEY SWEARS, MOURNS, DIES. ROOSEVELT GETS WHITE HOUSE AND SILVER CUP), represent this process even more clearly. Perhaps the most popular string-band performer of the twenties, and virtually the only one who was a professional musician with no other means of support, banjo player Poole pioneered the technique of singing to a full string band, and served as a bridge between the era of string bands and the era of vocal stars.

Yet most of these sides belong to solo performers, for at this point

most country music was still made by people who entertained their
families and friends on their own and gave no thought to making a
living at it. Clarence Ashley's rolling banjo on "House Carpenter," Buell
Kazee's forceful banjo and vocal on "The Butcher Boy" and "The Wagoners Lad," Frank Hutchison's bluesy swagger on "Stackalee," and
G. B. Grayson's rudimentary voice and fiddle on "Ommie Wise" all
summon up the danger, exhilaration, and uncertainty of life in the
remote mountain hollows of the South.

Ernest V. Stoneman: *Ernest V. Stoneman and the Blue Ridge Corn
Shuckers* (Rounder)

Ernest V. "Pop" Stoneman, who first recorded in 1924 and who was
still appearing before audiences right up to his death in 1968, was the
foremost practitioner of the string-band music centered in Galax, Virginia, a brand of country music unique because it was so purely "white."
He devised a new way of playing autoharp even though it wasn't the
instrument he favored (at least not on records). He was also one of the
first to perceive country music as an industry in which one could potentially earn a living wage, and he was an avid collector of American folk
songs. Finally, he's widely recognized as the only country musician to
have been as comfortable in the recording studio in the era of stereo
albums as he was in the era of the phonograph cylinder.

But the Galax connection is perhaps the most significant in his
checkered career. He was born in 1893 in a log cabin near Monarat,
Carroll County, in the Blue Ridge Mountains of Virginia. He learned
harmonica and autoharp in his teens, and later mastered guitar and
banjo. He worked frequently in the mines and mills of the region, but
he was working as a carpenter when he first heard local millworker
Henry Whitter's record, "The Wreck of the Old 97" b/w "Lonesome
Road Blues."

Stoneman thought Whitter was awful because he "sang through his
nose so bad." Convinced he could do better, he wrote to Columbia and
Okeh for auditions. In September 1924, he traveled to New York, where
he cut a demonstration disc for Columbia, which then passed on him.
But over at Okeh, Ralph Peer was interested even though he thought
Stoneman sang too fast on the demo. Ernest, who believed that songs
should tell a story and be easily decipherable, agreed; when he returned
in January 1925 to record for real, he slowed down. "The Sinking of the
Titantic," his first release, was one of the biggest hits of the decade.
Between 1925 and 1929, Stoneman went on to record more than two
hundred sides for a variety of labels and using several groups (despite
the album's title, these sides are not all with the Blue Ridge Corn
Shuckers).

These fourteen sides were cut for Victor between 1926 and 1928, and are representative of his overall output. Stoneman was a favorite of Peer's because he learned new songs right away and was thus available to do "cover" versions of the current hits, and he was also adept at finding traditional material that had not yet been copyrighted by anyone else. But he also did a number of religious songs like "Sweeping Through the Gates" or "I Know My Name Is There," British songs and ballads like "The Raging Sea, How It Roars," humorous sketches like "The Savingest Man on Earth," (which has Uncle Eck Dunford declaiming a story over Stoneman's weirdly tuned banjo), sentimental ballads from turn-of-the century Tin Pan Alley, novelty songs from the same source like "All Go Hungry Hash House," older pieces out of minstrelsy.

Stoneman was well known for picking out melodies note-for-note on autoharp when everybody else (including the man who invented it) thought it could play only chords. But on these sides, he sticks to guitar, banjo, and harmonica. His guitar work is particularly stark—just basic chords are strummed, with no embellishment or concern for melody. He's joined by some of the Galax area's other leading musicians, most of whom he introduced to recordings, including, especially, the fiddler Kahle Brewer, whose precise playing was simplicity itself. Brewer's fiddling had an ancient, melancholy air to it, but like all other Galax picking, it derived solely from white music. Virtually alone among country players, Galax musicians showed no influence from blues, jazz, or ragtime. One need only listen to this version of "Ida Red" for confirmation. This well-known country song has been done by several generations in a variety of styles, but the wheezing harmonica and whirling fiddle make this the sternest and most severe version.

Listening to these sides, it's sometimes hard to hear just how Stoneman improved on Whitter and others. It's hard to understand a word he's singing on "Sourwood Mountain," for example, and while the song is indeed slower than breakdown tempo, it's not slowed down by much. The harsh, anarchistic harmonies on religious numbers like "The Sinless Summerland" (particularly the creaking voice of his wife, Hattie Stoneman), are certainly no "cleaner" than other mountain music of the day.

Ernest Stoneman was not one to hold his money very long, and when the Depression halted his musical career, he had nothing to fall back on. In the thirties, he and Hattie moved to Washington, D.C., where he did carpentry work at a naval gun factory. Meanwhile, they'd begun raising a family that grew to thirteen kids, most of whom learned Ernest's music as they were growing up. In 1957, when he recorded an album for Folkways as "Pop" Stoneman with the Stoneman Family,

Ernest launched a second career in music. By adding more contemporary material to their old-timey and bluegrass selections, the Stonemans were able to find regular work at folk festivals, coffee houses, and on television shows, as well as on the Grand Ole Opry (which they joined in 1962) and even at such incongruous venues as San Francisco's Fillmore West, the nation's first psychedelic ballroom.

You might wonder what that gig was like. Well, I was there, and mostly I remember everything being out of synch—their hyped-up arrangements and between-songs patter, totally at odds with the material, was more appropriate to Las Vegas or network TV, which of course was totally at odds with the crowd. It felt weird, but when I listen to music as austere and just plain alien as the music on this album, I think that to most people Pop Stoneman must have seemed weird even in his own time.

Uncle Dave Macon: *Uncle Dave Macon, 1926–39: Wait Till the Clouds Roll By* (Historical)

Uncle Dave Macon, the singer and banjo player who didn't turn pro until he was fifty, broke nearly every rule of traditional music—and it made him one of the most popular performers traditional music ever saw. He considered himself an entertainer first and musician second, so he often ignored his roots; yet because he was one of the oldest Opry members, his roots went deepest. Of the various Uncle Dave compilations in print, this one offers the most range.

He was born in 1870 at Smart Station on the Cumberland Plateau, in south-central Tennessee. His father was a wealthy farmer who'd been a Confederate Army officer. When Dave was thirteen, the family moved to Nashville, and Mr. Macon bought the downtown Broadway Hotel. The hotel catered to entertainers—mostly circus performers and vaudevillians—who gave Dave his taste for show biz. He learned banjo from a circus comedian named Joel Davidson, and in 1886 his mom bought him his first banjo. Later that year, when his father died, the rest of the family left the city for Readyville. In 1889, Dave married Matilda Richardson and bought a farm just up the road in Kittrell Community. But in addition to farming, he founded the Midway Mule and Wagon Transportation Company, and for the next twenty years he hauled freight over the twenty-mile stretch between Murfreesboro and Woodbury. He gave that up when cars and trucks made carriages obsolete (he refused to learn to drive), and that's when he began turning toward music. His first public appearance was in 1921, when he raised $17 at a benefit to buy the local Methodist Church a new door, but he didn't turn pro seriously until 1923, when he began touring the Loew's theater circuit.

By then, Uncle Dave (as he now called himself) had been playing banjo about thirty years. He'd lived in the country, where he learned traditional tunes, and he'd lived in the city, where he learned vaudeville and pop hits. In 1923 he added Fiddlin' Sid Harkreader to his act; in 1924 they went to New York to record for the first time. Uncle Dave joined the Opry in 1925, before it even officially had a name or regular time slot. A fastidious man who never toured without taking a black satchel containing a pillow, a nightcap, a checkered bib, and a bottle of Jack Daniels, Uncle Dave would twirl his banjo over his head onstage, stomp about and crack jokes, talk to his audience like they were one-on-one. None of this worked as well on radio or on records as it did in person.

His recording peak was 1925–30, when he averaged twenty sides per year, about half his career output. All but three of these sides come from that period. Yet this album (which is rife with discographical errors) may give us no more idea than the others of what Uncle Dave was really like. It's a frustrating fact that he never recorded much of his best-known material, traditional or otherwise. That includes his theme of "Uncle Dave Handles a Banjo Like a Monkey Handles a Peanut" (which, perhaps you can tell, is not the purest piece of traditional music around) as well as such crowd-pleasers as "Bully of the Town," "Mountain Dew," or the autobiographical "Cannon County Hills." What the album does reveal is an eclectic showman's repertoire and a banjo style that owes plenty to tradition.

According to Charles Wolfe's study of Uncle Dave's recorded output, about one sixth of his songs were original (or so Macon claimed) and another one sixth gospel or sacred numbers. More than half came from nineteenth-century Tin Pan Alley or minstrel shows. Only the remaining handful were "folk" or "traditional" in the strictest sense. Yet Uncle Dave seemed to have learned even the Tin Pan Alley tunes through oral tradition, and he played them as though they were no different from his real folk songs. And the traditional material he did record, particularly sides in 1927 with the Fruit Jar Drinkers and in 1928 with Sam McGee, are among the most influential early string-band sides.

The Fruit Jar Drinkers were Sam (guitar) and Kirk (fiddle) McGee and Mazy Todd (fiddle). They're heard here on the traditional quadrille "Sleepy Lou" and on "Hop High Ladies, the Cake's All Dough," another traditional fiddle tune for which Uncle Dave wrote new lyrics. In early 1927, Uncle Dave and Sam McGee recorded Dave's variation "The Death of John Henry." The banjo lines Uncle Dave plays here are among his most complicated, and his singing, often little more than functional, has rare urgency.

The 1928 sides feature Sam's six-string banjo-guitar, an instrument few others tackled. "I'm the Child to Fight" is doggerel, while "Buddy Won't You Roll Down the Line" has topical overtones. Uncle Dave had numerous other songs in both categories, but McGee's contributions make these among his most popular.

The songs on which Uncle Dave is accompanied only by his own banjo are usually novelties—"Never Make Love No More," "Arcade Blues," and "She Wouldn't Give Me Sugar in My Coffee." He often introduces them with a joke, anecdote, or dedication, which is his way of attempting to simulate how he did them live, and these are indeed the sides that give the best picture of Uncle Dave. Whatever formats he used for recording, live he usually performed alone (or with only a second instrumentalist, like his son, Dorris, or McGee). He played banjo in a three-finger "rapping" style that was traditional in origin and then bastardized by the minstrel-show influences. He was playing that style when he first surfaced, and he was playing it in his last public performance, just a couple of weeks before he died in 1952. Even that late in the twentieth century, he was still making nineteenth-century music accessible to the country fan, and in 1966 it got him elected to the Hall of Fame.

Gid Tanner and His Skillet Lickers: *The Skillet Lickers, Volume II* (County)

Gid Tanner and His Skillet Lickers was country music's first supergroup, put together by a producer drawing from a pool of musicians who played with each other in various configurations. James Gideon Tanner, a burly, red-faced, wisecracking chicken farmer from Dacula, Georgia, north of Atlanta, was the only old-time fiddler in the region who could give Fiddlin' John Carson a run for his money. Though Tanner considered himself a comedian first, he was invited in 1924 by Frank Walker of Columbia to come to New York to record. He brought with him banjo player-guitarist George Riley Puckett, blind almost from birth but already a radio star in Atlanta. Pleased with their recordings of old-time and vaudeville songs, Walker went to Atlanta in 1926. This time he insisted they add Clayton "Pappy" McMichen, an auto mechanic fifteen years Tanner's junior, who played fiddle in a jazzy modern style. McMichen then brought in fiddler Bert Layne, his brother in law from Arkansas, and Fate Norris took over on banjo. Musicians came and went from early sessions in a procession that has long confused discographers. But those first sessions did establish that Walker had assembled a hit band. They recorded mostly traditional tunes, including "Watermelon on the Vine" and "Bully of the Town" from this album; over the years, the latter (coupled with "Pass Around the Bottle and We'll All Take a Drink") sold an astronomical two million copies.

On those two songs, and on "Shortening Bread" (1927), Richard Nevin claims in his liner notes, the group sound was established—McMichen plays lead fiddle while Tanner plays unison harmonies or seconds him. Layne plays low baritone and rarely joins on the unison passages. The best example is "Bully of the Town," on which it's easy to discern all three fiddles as Tanner and McMichen zigzag in and out of each other with their contrasting styles.

Norris, who'd worked the streets as a one-man band before joining the Skillet Lickers, played a steady, frailing banjo that anchored the sound. Puckett's innovative guitar style was built on single-note bass runs that influenced the next several generations. Because he often played too fast, and rarely even brushed his treble strings, a few musicians had trouble playing with Puckett, but most welcomed him and his unorthodox style. He also usually sang lead in a voice smooth and strong; the shrill high "harmony" voice belongs to Tanner, who played the cutup to his more sophisticated sidemen.

On the fourth session, Lowe Stokes joined on fiddle. Stokes, who began as a McMichen protégé and wound up influencing his teacher, took lead. McMichen played just above or just below him in close harmony, while Tanner played fills, usually just above the lead. On songs like "Rocky Pallet," "Ride Old Buck to the Water," and "Liberty" the absence of a low fiddle part is dramatic, and though Puckett and McMichen were both considered tops in their styles, it was probably Stokes who most shaped the group sound. Once he joined, the emphasis moved away from dance music and toward fancy harmony fiddling, and when Stokes lost his hand in a 1931 barroom brawl, the band finally broke up. To some extent, the addition of Stokes left Tanner out in the cold, but he apparently agreed with Walker that it was good business. On "Night in a Blind Tiger," Layne is apparently back as third fiddler, Norris is gone, and Tanner is playing banjo.

"Night in a Blind Tiger" demonstrates how the group struck a balance between Tanner's primitive style and entertainer's instincts and the more modern leanings of the others. The song is a comedy "skit" of the type that Walker had convinced them to start doing in 1927. At that time they cut "A Corn Licker Still in Georgia" and it sold 250,000 copies. In all, there were seven records (fourteen sides) detailing the adventures of these moonshiners who played music on the side.

The skit undoubtedly comes from the minstrelsy and medicine-show experiences of rural musicians. "Blind Tiger" centers on McMichen, who wins a fiddling contest and goes to a speakeasy to celebrate. He has to prove who he is to get inside, though, and once he's there he's confronted by other musicians (Layne, Stokes, Puckett, Tanner) who claim he didn't deserve to win. The barkeep listens to each one play and can't tell who's best. When the local sheriff comes to see what's causing all the fuss, he's enlisted as a judge. He can't decide either, but decides they're all real good and they should drop by the station to play a little tune anytime they're free. Everybody sings a chorus of "Sweet Adeleine" and goes home happy. The skit may not be too far from the truth; Skillet Lickers recording sessions were known among Atlanta musicians as woolly affairs, with local bootleggers stopping by the studios periodically to make sure the booze never ran out, and the personnel on some sides was reportedly determined by who was in good enough shape to play.

"Dixie" has smart-stepping cadences that feature Puckett's most fluid lines; his guitar seems to bob among the other instruments. "Run Nigger Run," known today as "Run Boy Run," dates from slave rebellions of the 1830s, when plantation owners banned fraternizing among blacks and hired patrollers to search after curfew for slaves who left the grounds. Like "Dixie," as Nevins points out again, it shows how ready this band was to tamper with tradition in rearranging material. In the end, then, Tanner's traditionalism was no longer controlling the group.

Gid Tanner and His Skillet Lickers: *The Kickapoo Medicine Show* (Rounder)

In the five years they were together, the Skillet Lickers recorded eighty-eight sides, eighty-two of which were released. But in their entire careers, Tanner, McMichen, and Puckett participated in some seven hundred recordings, either as solo artists or as members of a group. Most of those sides were cut either before or after the Skillet Lickers, but some were spin-off recordings made while the core group was still together. Conventional wisdom, which is perpetuated by this album's liner booklet, holds that the music these men made apart was never as good as the group's music, and certainly in many cases this was true. But this album presents them in various pairings—the original Skillet Lickers, the 1934 version of the Skillet Lickers that Gid put together for one session three years after the originals broke up, the fiddle-guitar team of McMichen and Puckett, the McMichen-Layne String Orchestra, and groups fronted by Gid as either singer or instrumentalist—and the cuts featuring spinoff groups are in nearly every instance the equal of those with the classic group sound.

The original group is here with the traditional "Nancy Rolling"; the blackface-derived "Never Seen the Like Since Gettin' Upstairs," with Gid's background shouts nearly drowning out McMichen's own uninhibited singing; "You Gotta Quit Kickin' My Dog Around," on which

Gid plays keening fiddle but misses his usual support from McMichen, and "Don't You Hear Jerusalem Moan," which doesn't spoof religion in a safe, cute way, but instead shoots it an upraised middle finger.

The latter two, both from 1926, are the Skillet Lickers with Puckett but without McMichen, which means that Gid's own fiddling is more prominent. It makes a difference—north Georgia fiddlers were wilder than their counterparts from neighboring states, and Tanner was one of the wildest. He sounded raw, but he played with an unfettered glee McMichen never displayed. This is evident in Tanner's earliest recordings, such as the anarchistic "New Dixie" he cut in 1926 as Fate Norris and the Turner Boys, and it's evident in the re-formed 1934 group, with which he played banjo (as on "Mississippi Sawyer") or fiddle (as on "Cumberland Gap on a Buckin' Mule") while his son Gordon also played fiddle. There's also his boasting "I Ain't No Better Now," a tall-tale rewrite of the pop hit "Yes Sir! That's My Baby" from 1934, but Tanner as fiddler comes through best (despite the horrendous recording quality) when he spins out the fleet, rhythmic short-bow lines of "Prettiest Little Girl in the County."

McMichen's rolling style was seductive in its own right ("Farmer's Daughter," "Never Seen the Like Since Gettin' Upstairs," and "Paddy Won't You Drink Some Cider"), but for sheer excitement he pales next to Tanner. McMichen is best heard (with Layne) on the 1928 "Rake and Ramblin' Man," an ancient broadside that was also cut by the Carter Family, the Carolina Tar Heels, Wade Mainer, and the solo Riley Puckett. For rakishness, though, Tanner tops McMichen with "You Gotta Stop Drinking Shine," a sardonic blues he plays in a most unorthodox banjo style while singing in a tone that makes clear he has no intention of stopping for even a day. He's *all* attitude here, and, again, his denunciation of the Church was much more blatant than was normally allowed.

Had Tanner and his cronies been based in central Tennessee instead of north Georgia, they would undoubtedly be in the Hall of Fame by now. But ultimately, Walker couldn't hold his group together. Tanner was too old-timey, McMichen too pop, and Puckett too far-out. Puckett went on to enjoy a long solo career, while McMichen led his Georgia Wildcatters until he retired in 1955, by which time he was playing Dixieland. And Gid Tanner? When the group broke up, he went back to chicken farming, playing on the porch of his house and drinking that shine. Music had always been primarily a hobby with him anyhow.

Charlie Poole and the North Carolina Ramblers: *Charlie Poole and the North Carolina Ramblers* (County)

Charlie Poole was an innovative banjo player and vocalist. He was father to a whole musical movement in the hills of North Carolina. He was a key transitional figure between string bands and vocal stars. He was an archetypal country-music rambler, seemingly doomed to die young and somewhat fascinated by that very idea. Yet Charlie Poole is largely slighted in most studies of country music, as well as by the Nashville establishment.

In his lifetime he recorded some 110 sides with the North Carolina Ramblers, and more under different banners. Twelve of his best performances with the Ramblers are collected here, and point to Poole as one of the most resourceful and imaginative bandleaders of his time.

He was born in Alamance County, North Carolina, in 1892, and was a textile worker most of his life—when he wasn't on the road, that is. In 1911 he married for the first time, and in 1913 he fathered a son, but it wasn't enough to keep him home. He traveled as far away as Montana, returning to his family only once in a while. In 1917 in the coal-mining country of West Virginia, he met crippled fiddler Posey Rorer, and the pair began working together. When they went back to Spray and Leakville, in Poole's native north-central North Carolina, they added guitarist Norman Woodlieff.

The trio remained in the area until 1925, when they got jobs with an auto manufacturer in Passaic, New Jersey. On July 27, 1925, they went into New York City to cut four sides, including this album's wheeling, vibrant "Don't Let Your Deal Go Down," which remained their most popular song until they broke up. When the Ramblers recorded again in September 1926, Roy Harvey had replaced Woodlieff on guitar, and that completed the lineup that proved most influential. (In 1928, Lonnie Austin replaced Rorer on fiddle; later, Odell Smith took the spot.)

The repertoire was remarkably eclectic for a mountain group of the twenties, probably due to Poole's steady traveling. The Ramblers recorded sentimental pieces like this album's "Sweet Sunny South" and Anglo-American dance tunes like "Shootin' Creek" and "Mountain Reel." They recorded bluesy—if not outright blues—songs like "The Deal" (as that first big record came to be called informally) and "White House Blues" (a ballad about the assassination of President McKinley that later became a bluegrass staple), minstrel or "coon" songs like "Take a Drink on Me" and W. C. Handy classic blues like "Ramblin' Blues" (sometimes known as "If Beale Street Could Talk"). They recorded their version of "Frankie and Johnnie" (here called "Leaving Home") and their variant of "I Ain't Got Nobody" (here called "Took My Gal A-Walkin' ").

Harvey played long, melodic bass runs on guitar, while Poole played banjo in a clean, finger-picking style that he supposedly had to concoct after a childhood baseball injury; it's an up-picking style that utilizes the thumb and three fingers, and it's a clear forerunner to the Earl Scruggs bluegrass style. Rorer's fiddle played above or behind the other two, fleshing out their arrangements most of the time, though he was also a daring soloist. Harvey and Poole split lead vocals, though Poole was a superior singer. As early as "The Deal," in which his voice slips and slides through both the lyrics and the other instruments, he is clearly aiming for a "professional" singing style that could stand on its own.

"He Rambled" (a/k/a "Didn't He Ramble"), which could easily be Poole's life story, captures the various elements of the trio's style. The fiddle intro quickly sets the tone, and the vocals, tracing the adventures of a ne'er-do-well with a mixture of admiration and admonition, show evidence of both folk tradition and more formal vocal techniques. The roots of bluegrass are apparent in the guitar line, and Poole's banjo licks kick the song along forcefully.

The guitar-banjo interplay crucial to their sound shines through also on "Sweet Sunny South," where both instruments are bass-heavy but weave deftly in and out of each other without one ever crowding the other. Though the two men are capable of a dense and blurry sound (as on "Mountain Reel"), it's the clarity and precision of their work on "Sweet Sunny South" and others like "The Letter That Never Came" (held together by Poole's clipped, blues banjo) that make them one of the most accessible of the early string bands.

For the second half of the twenties, Poole and the North Carolina Ramblers toured throughout the upper South and into Ohio. They also recorded prolifically in various combinations (sometimes bringing in outside help, too) for several labels. But no matter what side projects the three individuals took on with other people, they always saved their best stuff for the North Carolina Ramblers sides with Columbia. They also resisted Columbia's efforts to get them to expand into a more conventional quartet. They laid the foundation for the next couple of generations of string bands in that region, particularly the bluegrass bands that came along a couple of decades later, and they would probably be regarded as pioneers if they had been based in one of country music's commercial centers.

As for Poole, his drinking increased with his popularity. But when the Depression hit, his record sales were wiped out and he lost his taste for music. In 1931 he was hired to do some background music for a movie. He bought a train ticket to California and a few jugs of liquor so he could go on one last king-hell binge with his local drinking buddies. It turned out really to be his last: It triggered a heart attack that left him dead at thirty-nine. His deal had gone down after all.

Nashville—the Early String Bands, Volume II (County).

Until the mid-forties, recording was rare in Nashville. In 1928, Victor made a foray into town to see what was available and wound up cutting sides on the Binkley Brothers, the Dixie Clodhoppers, Dr. Humphrey Bates' Possum Hunters, DeFord Bailey, the Crook Brothers, and Theron Hale and Daughters. But most Nashville musicians had to go to Atlanta or New York to record. Yet because of the Opry and the flourishing radio scene, there was no shortage of talent, most of it firmly rooted in nineteenth-century rural forms but not oblivious to more recent developments in pop, ragtime, and blues. The first of them are gathered on this top sampler of early Nashville music (with accompanying booklet by Charles Wolfe, from which I've borrowed extensively).

The Crook Brothers String Band (represented by "Jobbin' Gettin' There" and "Going Across the Sea" from 1928) were in most respects a typical hoedown band, with Tom Givan's rolling banjo underpinning their sound. The big difference was that they boasted two lead harmonicas—by Herman and Matthew Crook. (Matthew quit in 1930 to join the Nashville police; Herman is today the only Opry member to have been there since the first show.) Uncle Dave Macon's "Over the Road I'm Bound to Go" (1928) finds him bellowing over his fast, chunky banjo lines in equally typical fashion. But on "Bake That Chicken Pie" (1927) he's backed by Mazy Todd and Kirk McGee on keening fiddles. Theron Hale and Daughters were more genteel, calling to mind nineteenth-century parlor music. When they appeared on the Opry, which wasn't regularly, they favored slow, sweet tunes with graceful twin fiddles on top, but as "Jolly Blacksmith" (actually "Flop-Eared Mule") and "Hale's Rag" (both 1928) hint, they could cut loose when they wanted. Blind Joe Mangrum had similarly lofty ambitions; he was more partial to Italian waltzes than to breakdowns, and was always urging Opry management to let him slip some semiclassical tunes onto the show. With Fred Schreiber backing him on an accordion more reminiscent of the European continent than of the British Isles, he cut this bastard version of the perennial "Bill Cheatham" that could have been a starting point for western swing. But the real stars here are DeFord Bailey, Uncle Jimmy Thompson, and Sam and Kirk McGee.

Thompson was a hardy buzzard with full beard whose wife (Aunt Ella) used to buck-dance while he fiddled. On October 28, 1925, he accepted George Hay's invitation to play some of his favorite fiddle tunes on WSM. Response was so great that within a month it was a regular show that in 1927 became dubbed The Grand Ole Opry. When he made his first appearance, flaunting a repertoire of more than a thousand tunes that covered most of the last century, Uncle Jimmy was a sprightly seventy-eight years old. "Karo" (yet another version of "Flop-Eared Mule") and "Billy Wilson" (both 1926) demonstrate just how eclectic he was all along. Thompson was born in Tennessee, but spent much of his life farming in Texas. He played a swirling, swinging fiddle that had a gypsy-like shriek to it, and was much less choppy than the style of Tennessee fiddlers. Thompson had simply combined the styles of both his home states.

Though guitarist Sam McGee died in a 1975 accident on his farm, his banjo-playing brother Kirk remains on the Opry today. Sam was the first guitarist to broadcast on WSM, and also experimented with electric guitar a few times before Opry brass banned it. He was known as "Flat-Top Pickin' Sam McGee," and is credited with having created the finger-picking style, which drew heavily on blues and ragtime. He also played something called the banjo-guitar, which alternately rolls and stabs through his version of "Brown's Ferry Blues" (1934). "Old Master's Runaway" (1927) was also known as "Year of Jubilee" or "Year of Jubilo" and has one of the most infectious melodies of any Civil War-era fiddle tune.

DeFord Bailey was the only black man on the Opry. At the time it was common to hear blacks and whites playing the same music, and DeFord's harmonica reels and breakdowns were issued as both "race" and "hillbilly" records. He learned harmonica as a child while staying in bed for a year with infantile paralysis, and went on to become one of the first Opry stars. In the thirties he was the main attraction in touring Opry package shows, known to fans and fellow musicians alike as "the Harmonica Wizard." Then the Opry began sanitizing its image, and suddenly DeFord became an issue. At first he was condescendingly labeled "our little mascot" by Opry promotion. In 1933, Judge Hay fired him, ostensibly because he failed to learn new tunes. But later "the Solemn Old Judge" tipped his hand when he wrote in his Opry memoirs, in terms both commonplace and degrading, "Like some members of his race, and other races, DeFord was lazy." Bailey went to work full-time in his shoeshine parlor after that, and wouldn't play in public for decades. In the seventies, when the Opry sought to remove blatant stigmas from its image, a wary rapprochement with Bailey was achieved. He died in 1982.

In axing him, the Opry gave up a most imaginative country harp player. The snorts and sighs of Bailey's "Muscle Shoals Blues" (1927) are almost orchestral in range; he gulps and groans for air throughout the song, and it's amazing to hear all that sound coming from one man. "Pan American Blues" (1927), his calling card, is even more breathtaking. As a child in central Tennessee, Bailey hung out under a train trestle at Thompson's Station on the Tennessee Central Line. He learned to duplicate the sounds of the train so closely that years later a railroad engineer came to the Opry to congratulate him—and to correct a minor error he was making on the whistle pattern for crossings.

This album captures the sound of Nashville long before anyone dreamed of a Nashville Sound. All of these musicians worked day jobs for a living. They made music for fun.

Anthology of American Folk Music, Volume Three: Songs
(Folkways)

The banjo started out a black instrument and was usurped by rural whites. Through the end of the nineteenth century, the fiddle was common to both races, though blacks came to associate it with plantation days and largely gave it up. The guitar, which wasn't popularized until the turn of the century, was first mastered by blacks, though by the time the recording industry was revving up, numerous whites had devised their own guitar styles. Bluesmen and country singers had shared a common pool of songs, and of motifs, since the mid-seventeenth century. When it comes to American music, there's no such thing as racial purity, and this two-record boxed set is invaluable for the way it mixes blues and country to reveal relationships between blacks and whites.

Though country's deepest roots are in England and blues roots are in Africa, black and white musics in America remained close from the days of minstrelsy right up to the time that radio and the phonograph came along. Henry Thomas, a black Texas pre-blues songster who played guitar and pan pipes, offers one good example here of what they might have sounded like with his "Fishing Blues," which was later covered by several country artists. Thomas recorded in a country dance style that was, roughly speaking, the black equivalent to Uncle Dave Macon; by way of comparison, check out the two Uncle Dave cuts here, "Down Plank Road" and "Roll Down the Line." The repertoires of the two men, in fact, had at least five songs in common, and probably more.

But that wasn't unusual. Three of the songs on *Volume One* of the Folkways anthology—Williamson Brothers and Curry's "John Henry," Frank Hutchison's "Stackalee" and Furry Lewis' "Kassie Jones"—were commonly sung by both blacks and whites. (Macon and Thomas, for example, also did "John Henry," and bluesman Mississippi John Hurt does a variant called "Spike Driver Blues" on this album.) In his book *Blacks, Whites and Blues* (Studio Vista, England), Tony Russell lists a couple dozen more.

Similarly, on five consecutive songs here, Smith points out what he calls a "folk-lyric complex," or pool of lyrics, out of which the songs have been constructed. In this case, he cites "800 frequently heard couplets dealing with prison," some of which turn up in Ramblin' Thomas's

"Poor Boy Blues" (black blues), Cannon's Jug Stompers' "Feather Bed" (black jug band, though the song uses the melody of "Lost John," which is usually associated with country whites), Dock Boggs' searing "Country Blues" (white banjo song, possibly the melodic source for "Junker's Blues," a city blues popular two and three decades later among blacks), Julius Daniels' "Ninety-Nine Year Blues" (black blues), and Blind Lemon Jefferson's "Prison Cell Blues" (black blues).

Though Charley Patton was the bluesman most influential to blacks, it appears that Blind Lemon Jefferson, a Texan like Patton, was the greater inspiration for whites. Jefferson is represented here with "Rabbit Foot Blues" and "Two White Horses" in addition to "Prison Cell Blues." He first recorded in April 1926; the next month he cut "Jack O'Diamonds" with a slide, a device—usually a knife or bottleneck, brushed along the guitar strings to make a whining noise—derived from Hawaiian guitar. (Hawaiian guitar was a fad in America in the twenties, especially among whites, though the Hawaiians may themselves have originally derived it from blacks.) Jefferson also popularized the technique of playing melodic guitar phrases at the ends of lines. Five months after Jefferson, Frank Hutchison became the first country performer to record in an equivalent style. Like most whites, he played stiffer and faster, without the instrumental slur or improvisational skills of the bluesman, and though Hutchison (who's not included on this volume but is on *Volume One)* was a guitarist like Jefferson, you can also hear echoes of the style in such late-twenties banjoists and singers as Clarence Ashley ("The Coo Coo Bird"), Buell Kazee ("East Virginia"), Bascom Lamar Lunsford ("I Wish I Was a Mole"), and Dock Boggs ("Sugar Baby" as well as "Country Blues").

The interaction cuts both ways. Richard "Rabbit" Brown, represented here with "James Alley," was one of the first bluesmen to master twelve-bar blues chord patterns, according to Smith, but there's also a lot of country banjo in his easy-rolling guitar style. (The *real* attraction remains his otherworldly voice.) The Carter Family had a black guitarist travel with them to learn the new tunes they found so he could later teach them to Maybelle, and her driving guitar style in turn gives the trio a hint of the sound of a black group like the Memphis Jug Band, heard here on "K.C. Moan," a work song adapted by several white performers. Culturally united by class (rural poor) if not race, most of the performers here embrace musical miscegenation of the highest (and most casual) order.

Mountain Blues (County)

Musicians and musicologists agree about little, but they do agree that blues is not just a form. It's also a feeling. In the earliest days of the record industry, this was especially true—by the thirties, blues had become faddish enough that the term was attached to all manner of records strictly as a merchandising tool. The word "blues" sold more records.

But most of the sides on this extremely well-programmed anthology are from the twenties, when the term had a more literal meaning. Many of these are blues in form as well as in feel. But this album has hidden virtues as well, for it manages to showcase nearly every early string-band blues style extant, region by region.

Sam McGee's "Railroad Blues" is a good example, since it's white blues but also delineates a central Tennessee country style. McGee was one of the first musicians in the region to pick up guitar, and probably the first to exploit its possibilities as a solo instrument. His "flat-top" style enabled him to play rhythm and melody simultaneously, and he's often cited as the only true bluesman on the Opry. Yet most of his recordings suggest more that he assimilated black guitar styles into his own country sound. This cut is different—on this one, quite simply, Sam McGee plays the blues—supple, finger-picked guitar lines, rising and falling, as his voice scats along to the notes he picks, the verses linking classic blues lines from all over the place. He sounds like Blind Blake almost as much as Blind Blake does, and the style became widely imitated, though never matched, by generations of Opry-oriented pickers.

The sense of discovery, of falling for a new music and then urgently seeking to make it one's own, is nearly palpable on the best of these sides, and not only McGee's. Later, the country industry would water down and transform the blues into something softer and safer; but for now, country musicians who best felt the blues could use the borrowed form to express their own feelings in their own way. They didn't have to slavishly imitate blacks, but neither did they glibly ignore blacks.

Frank Hutchison, who originally hailed from West Virginia, provides another good example. He played slide in a style cleaner and quicker than that of black guitarists, but it's hard to imagine him having ever come up with "Cannon Ball Blues" had he not been acutely aware of current trends and techniques in black music. His slide lines are more insistent than those of the purely Hawaiian-derived white players, his voice cuts across the beat rather than coming down on the beat *or* on the offbeat. Among other white steel players, only Jimmy Tarlton of South Carolina, represented here by a warm, yearning version of "Careless Love," can equal Hutchison—and Tarlton's range might be more attributable to the fact that before he picked up the guitar or steel he had mastered banjo and several other instruments.

From throughout the Southeast other string bands checked in with other styles. Lowe Stokes and His North Georgians here play a string of traditional verses going under the title "Left All Alone Again Blues." Stokes, who recorded also with Gid Tanner's Skillet Lickers, played a pop-influenced break-down fiddle similar to Clayton McMichen's. On this cut, the band is made up of two fiddles and a guitar, which makes it right in the local tradition of twin lead fiddling. It's not blues, but it's awfully bluesy, thanks especially to Stokes' frail, vulnerable vocals.

Over in Mississippi, where the Leake County Revelers were so popular they once sold 200,000 of a single record and on another occasion helped get Huey Long elected governor of their neighboring state of Louisiana, the fiddle also dominated, but twin fiddles were unusual. Here the emphasis was more on sheer speed (which "Leake County Blues" doesn't necessarily indicate) and repetition (which it does). With their "Carroll County Blues," W. T. Narmour (fiddle) and S. W. Smith (guitar) have more the "songster" style of a Mississippi John Hurt, who they discovered in their mutual home town of Avalon. Doc Roberts, who came from Kentucky, played a fiddle as lyrical as it was bluesy on "Cumberland Blues," while Dick Justice ("Brown Skin Blues," which combines two Blind Lemon Jefferson songs) and Clarence Green ("Johnson City Blues") are two obscure musicians who played simple guitar blues of the type favored by black country bluesmen.

Then there's the Carolina Tar Heels, who on the salacious "Farm Girl Blues" put most of the emphasis on Garley Foster's harmonica, so the overall sound was softer and more somber. Or Dock Boggs, the West Virginia coal miner who played an absolutely unique style of banjo that involved him picking melodies note for note as he sang. The style limited him somewhat, but blues is a limited style anyhow, one in which nuances convey the true meaning and feeling. "Down South Blues," which Boggs learned from a 1923 record by the classic city blues singer Clara Smith, is all nuance, an intense banjo performance with dark, wailing vocals. More than anyone here, Dock Boggs demonstrates just how much white blues can function as form or feeling or both.

Supplementary Albums

The Allen Brothers: *The Allen Brothers* (Old Timey). Lee and Austin Allen emerged from south-central Tennessee to become the first successful brother duet singers in country music. They first recorded in 1927, and sounded bluesy enough that Columbia released an early single on its "race" (black) music line. The horrified Allens promptly sued for $250,000 and switched labels. Nonetheless, the error was excusable enough. The Allens were a guitar-and-banjo team that added kazoos and the like to create a jug-band feel, and much of their material came from black sources. Though best known for "Salty Dog Blues" (not included here) and "Hey Buddy, Won't You Roll Down the Line" (which is), they also specialized in boozer's laments like "Jake Walk Blues" and "Fruit Jar Blues." But as material like "Ain't That Skippin' and Flyin' " (a version of "Molly and Tenbrooks") shows, they were well rooted in tradition, and as material like "New Deal Blues" indicates, they had a social bent as well. With their emphasis on vocals and modern instrumental soloing, they were one of the key transitional acts into the Jimmie Rodgers era.

Anthology of American Folk Music, Volume Two: Social Music (Folkways). For the purposes of this two-record boxed set, "social music" means primarily church music or party and dance music. The Carter Family's "Little Moses" is a chilling example of the former, while Prince Albert Hunt's Ramblers' "Wake Up Jacob" is a thrilling example of the latter. Then there's Bascom Lamar Lunsford's take on "Dry Bones." Once again, the mix between black and white is both even and revealing.

Ballads and Songs (Old Timey). These are mostly traditional songs done by well-known names from the earliest days of recorded country music—"Rose Conley" and "Handsome Molly" by Grayson and Whitter, for example. There are also more obscure performers like Ephraim Woodie (who?), and some of these recordings run into the late thirties. With other cuts like "Frankie Dean" ("Frankie and Johnnie") by Darby and Tarlton and "Black Jack David" by Cliff Carlisle, it's one of the better primers around.

The Blue Ridge Highballers: *Blue Ridge Highballers* (County). This is the most popular square-dance band from the Virginia-North Carolina border region, and when you hear the torrid fiddle of Charley La Prade on these 1926 cuts, you'll understand why.

Dock Boggs: *His Twelve Original Recordings* (Folkways). If Uncle Dave represents the jovial, vaudevillian side of country banjo, Dock Boggs is of the dark, dread-filled mountain blues. He was from the coal-mining region of Virginia, and devised a style of "duets" between voice and banjo that none of his peers approached. His clawhammer banjo was heavily influenced by older black styles, and his voice was a sort of controlled bellow. He was also tortured by the too-typical struggles between music and the church, between alcohol and family life, and though he may have at times leaned toward a professional music career, he in fact spent most of his life in the mines. These twelve sides were cut in 1927 and 1929, and represent his entire output until his rediscovery during the folk boom. They are split about equally between songs drawn from the folk tradition and material he must have learned from records and radio. They express directly the ambivalence and doubt he fought all his life, and are indispensable.

Dock Boggs: *Dock Boggs* (Folkways). These sides were cut in 1963 by New York folkie Mike Seeger, but working with strong stuff like "Oh Death," Dock more than lives up to the reputation he gained from his Brunswick sides of the twenties. If anything, his age—sixty-seven at the time—added credibility to these performances, but there was a timeless quality to everything he did.

Dock Boggs: *Dock Boggs, Vol. 2* (Folkways). These 1964 recordings show off his range a little more, with added emphasis on original material, and they also better isolate his idiosyncratic banjo style.

Dock Boggs: *Dock Boggs, Vol. 3.* Closer conceptually to *Vol. 2* than to *Vol. 1,* and Boggs still isn't running out of probing, individualistic interpretations of material that might otherwise be overly familiar.

Burnett and Rutherford: *A Ramblin' Reckless Hobo* (Rounder). Their shimmering fiddle and (usually) banjo duets made the team of Leonard Rutherford and Dick Burnett one of the most influential to come out of south central Kentucky. "A Short Life of Trouble" is one of the most convincing explanations why. They could have been from the 1820s almost as easily as the 1920s.

The Carolina Tar Heels: *Can't You Remember the Carolina Tar Heels* (German Bear Family). This collects sides from various 1927–31 Tar Heel configurations. Most are not available domestically, or are saddled with poor sound in their American versions, and for a group with interplay as complex as this group's could get, that makes a difference. The Tar Heels were one of the first string bands to integrate the ragtime craze into mountain music.

The Carolina Tar Heels: *The Carolina Tar Heels* (Old Homestead). The big news here is the propulsive three-finger banjo style of Dock Walsh, the central figure in one of the few early string bands to eschew fiddle. But his choice of sidemen (guitarist Clarence Ashley, Gwen and Garley Foster on guitar and harmonica) wasn't bad either on these 1927–30 sides. Some clumsy interpretations of black music, but more often they stick to the white mountain music they do best.

The Carolina Tar Heels: *The Carolina Tar Heels* (Folk-Legacy). Recorded in 1964, this features Dock Walsh's son Drake (on fiddle and guitar) joining Dock (on banjo and vocals) and Garley Foster (on harmonica, guitar, and vocals) from the original group. The repertoire includes a few new songs as well as the more typical traditional ballads, including the ever-popular boast "I Was Born About Four Thousand Years Ago."

Fiddlin' John Carson: *The Old Hen Cackled and the Rooster's Going to Crow* (Rounder). Ralph Peer may have been a little harsh to pronounce Carson's singing "pluperfect awful," but it *is* kinda hard to take. That's because it's as crude as his scratchy, sawing fiddle, and these recordings are certain to separate the diehard fan from the casual observer.

A Collection of Mountain Songs (County). Let's hear it for the Tennessee Ramblers doing "The Preacher Got Drunk and Laid His Bible Down." For the Carolina Tar Heels doing "Your Low Down Dirty Ways," for Burnett and Rutherford doing "All Night Long Blues," and especially for Byrd Moore and his Hot Shots with country's most aching version of "Careless Love."

Vernon Dalhart: *Ballads and Railroad Songs* (Old Homestead). Dalhart was born Marion Try Slaughter in 1883 in northeast Texas, and before moving to Dallas in his teens, he punched cows between the towns of Vernon and Dalhart. In 1910 he moved to New York, where he sang in churches, mortuaries, and vaudeville while trying for parts in light opera and grand opera. His recording career began in 1917, and when he recorded "The Wreck of the Old '97" in 1924 (first for Edison, then for Victor), he gave a shot in the arm to the commercial country music industry. Because he was by then as much a New Yorker as a Texan, Dalhart has also been cited as the first country music sellout; there's no disputing that he opened industry doors for other country singers, but he also glommed onto their music to revitalize his own sagging career, and his wispy tenor is insignificant enough that one suspects it was the songs, as much as the singer, that sold his records. In 1982, when crossover had all but conquered country music, Dalhart was, appropriately enough, elected to the Hall of Fame.

Vernon Dalhart: *The First Singing Cowboy on Records* (Mark 56). By 1930, Dalhart was washed up as a commercial force, and in 1933 he stopped recording almost entirely (though he attempted a comeback unsuccessfully in the late thirties). But before then, he'd sold millions upon millions of records, and if the railroad song was always his forte ("Wreck of the Old '97" alone sold about six million in its fifty versions), he also recorded numerous "event" songs and cowboy songs. This puts the emphasis on the latter, and has more of a country feel. But it's still thin compared to similar music by genuine country singers of the era.

A Day in the Mountains—1928 (County). The subtitle to this anthology is "Old-Time Music and Humor," which explains the orientation. Most of these are two-part records that attempt to emulate aspects of a medicine show with musicians taking various speaking parts while popular fiddle tunes of the day are weaved into story lines that deal primarily with hunting and drinking. Most prominent are groups associated with Gid Tanner, but Stoneman's Blue Ridge Corn Shuckers get almost as much attention.

Early Country Music (Historical). An offbeat, invigorating and revealing mandolin album. John Dilleshaw was an early influence on Bob Wills, and his two cuts from 1928 are among the first to flaunt black finger-picking guitar styles (his guitarist is uncredited). The Golden Melody Boys are more obscure, and more peculiar. But the capper is Joe Evans, who has the first side to himself with three different lineups. Evans, who was apparently black but shared much with white hillbilly pickers, breaks out into tears as he talks his way through "New Huntsville Jail" in a parody that is truly bizarre. As usual with this label, even the atrocious sound can't undermine the extraordinary music.

The East Texas Serenaders: *The East Texas Serenaders, 1927–36* (County). This quartet (which sometimes expanded to a quintet) played a more rhythmic brand of string-band music that combined northern ragtime and Tin Pan Alley influences with the traditional tunes of the Southeast and the fiddle breakdowns of the West. Along with Prince Albert Hunt's Texas Ramblers, they thus helped pave the way for Bob Wills and western swing.

Echoes of the Ozarks, Vol. 1 (County). Arkansas musicians of the twenties recorded less frequently than others in the South because they lived in such a remote region. For the same reason, they had fewer pop influences. One result is that these bands often sound thinner, sketchier, than their counterparts in Georgia, Mississippi, Tennessee, or the Carolinas. But purists often prefer them for their unadulterated country ways. Major exceptions: Pope's Arkansas Mountaineers, represented here with five cuts, all several steps above the others in sophistication. Diamonds in the rough: the Morrison Twin Brothers String Band for "Dry and Dusty" and The Carter Brothers and Son for "Give the Fiddler a Dram."

Echoes of the Ozarks, Vol. 2 (County). Much of this is even cruder than its predecessor: Arkansas vocalists sound uncannily like Cajuns singing in English. Fiddlers are shriller, too, but that's usually okay. Milton Pope (of Pope's Arkansas Mountaineers) was apparently the man who discovered Reaves White County Ramblers, a family group heard best here on

"Rattler Treed a Possum" and "Drunkard's Hiccoughs." The Ramblers augmented the usual fiddle-guitar lineup with an organ. Dr. Smith's Hoss Hair Pullers, a "big band" of four singers and four musicians, raises the roof on "Where the Irish Potatoes Grow." These bands are joined by three lesser groups.

Echoes of the Ozarks, Vol. 3 (County). Fiddlin' Sam Long's "Echoes of the Ozarks" b/w "Seneca Square Dance" (1926) is believed to be the first recording from the Ozarks. The frantic Carter Brothers and Son have four more cuts here.

A Fiddler's Convention in Mountain City, Tennessee (County). What's this—live recordings from the famous 1925 convention? No way, of course, but all the musicians represented on this anthology were actually at the convention. And the programming is just right. Fiddlin' John Carson romps through "Don't Let Your Deal Go Down" and slides through "Hell Bound for Alabama." Three more sides preserve the best of the primitive (and clumsy) mountain jazz of the Hill Billies, who shouldn't be listened to in much bigger doses anyhow.

Folk Music of the United States: Anglo-American Songs and Ballads (Library of Congress AAFS L20). Field recordings (all made 1941–46) of songs identified with strictly American traditions, though some are variants on English ballads. These range from fiddle tunes from the deep South to cowboy songs from out West.

Folk Music of the United States: Anglo-American Songs and Ballads (Library of Congress AAFS L21). At first glance this seems to be more of the same, even including some of the same singers, particularly Bascom Lamar Lunsford. But there are also cuts explaining banjo tuning and fiddle tuning, and in general this seems to have been assembled more for instructional purposes, with a wider variety of styles represented.

Folk Music of the United States: Child Ballads Traditional in the United States (I) (Library Of Congress). Field recordings of English ballads that passed into popular tradition in the New World. They were recorded between 1935 (Aunt Molly Jackson with "Lord Bateman") and 1946 (Jean Ritchie with "The Two Sisters"). Music like this is where country music begins.

Folk Music of the United States: Child Ballads Traditional in the United States (II) (Library of Congress). More of the same. These performances are all by nonprofessional singers who learned the songs orally. They were recorded between 1936 and 1950; two of the songs were collected in California, one in Arizona, and two more in Wisconsin, which certainly gives the lie to the popular notion that transmission of Child ballads was largely limited to the deep South.

The Georgia Yellow Hammers: *The Moonshine Hollow Band* (Rounder). This group is often compared to the Skillet Lickers, which is legitimate up to a point. They have more of the Skillet Lickers' bounce than the flat-out drive of a north Georgia fiddler like Earl Johnson, and the repertoires are also similar. But the Yellow Hammers don't have quite the range of the Skillet Lickers, though their spirit is just as infectious and their vocals are often superior.

Addie Graham: *Been a Long Time Traveling* (June Appal). Addie Graham (the producer's grandmother) sings about turn-of-the-century hard times in eastern Kentucky with the certainty of one who lived it all and never forgot. Harsh realities come forth unremittingly in song after song—"Lonesome Scenes of Winter," "The Indian Tribes of Tennessee," "Wouldn't Mind Working from Sun to Sun," "We're Stole and Sold from Africa," "Hungry and Faint and Poor"—getting the picture yet? But even the religious songs are open and somewhat worldly in a way folklorists would have us believe people of that time and place weren't, and this is riveting stuff. Though recorded in 1978, she sings nearly every song in a haunting *a cappella* voice guaranteed to drive away the *nouveau* country fan. But that's okay, too.

Grayson and Whitter: *The Recordings of Grayson and Whitter* (County). Henry Whitter was a Virginia guitarist who was the second country musician to record, after Eck Robertson, though his first recordings weren't released until after the success of Fiddlin' John Carson. His chief claim to fame as a solo artist seems to be that he was so bad, he inspired Pop Stoneman and several others to demand auditions themselves, on the grounds that they could do it much better. But these sides, cut in 1928–30 with blind fiddler and singer G. B. Grayson, are full of energy and the musicianship can't be faulted. This has one of the most vehement versions of "Ommie Wise," and such songs as "He Is Coming to Us Dead," "Short Life of Trouble," "I Saw a Man at the Close of the Day," and "Dark Road Is a Hard Road to Travel" also pack punch.

Sarah Ogan Gunning: *Girl of Constant Sorrow* (Folk-Legacy). From Kentucky coal country and the sister of Aunt Molly Jackson, Gunning sings strident labor (and other topical) songs *a cappella*. But she also performs love songs and traditional Appalachian ballads in a style as haunting as it is harsh. This 1965 album sounds like it could easily have been done three decades earlier.

Kelly Harrell and the Virginia String Band: *Kelly Harrell and the Virginia String Band* (County). There are three volumes of Harrell available on import from Bear Family, but I'd stick with this one. It's plenty. Harrell is a cult artist whose music seldom matches his reputation. He was also a solo singer, a rarity in those days; he was given sidemen when he entered the studio, as he had no regular band. Most often, the sidemen were jacks-of-all-trades who didn't know country music that well. Here, he's with a string band that's compatible, but not much more; often, he didn't even have that much. His vocals are strangely detached and remote-sounding, though, and while I can see how that would be a source of fascination to some (especially when he's singing more melancholy songs), it quickly wears thin. Harrell is much closer to the roots than a Vernon Dalhart or a Carson Robison, but this is still recommended primarily as an example of country music groping toward mainstream commerciality.

Hell Broke Loose in Georgia (County). To this day, the Georgia fiddlers sound like the wildest of the bunch, much more limber and forceful than their counterparts in other states, and with a better sense of humor, too. These guys play for keeps, but it's party music they're playing. This anthology brings together some of the obvious ones—Gid Tanner's Skillet Lickers, Fiddlin' John Carson with Earl Johnson as the Virginia Reelers, Earl Johnson and His Clodhoppers without Carson—and some less obvious, like Bill Helm's Upson County Band. But if you think the more obscure ones deserve to stay that way, then one listen to the fiddle-guitar-mandolin interplay of the Shores Southern Trio on "Goin' Crazy" ought to set you straight.

Roscoe Holcomb: *The High Lonesome Sound* (Folkways). Like the title says, Holcomb has a piercing voice; yet for one so high, it also has a fair amount of grit. As he was the first to admit, his phrasing was influenced strongly by the Texas bluesman Blind Lemon Jefferson. These sides were recorded in 1964 by urban folkies, some of whom also accompany Holcomb.

Frank Hutchison: *The Train That Carried My Girl from Town* (Rounder). Those attracted to Hutchison solely for his blues tendencies will be disappointed, because he wasn't strictly a blues performer. He also recorded typical country ballads and traditional fiddle pieces, and this album correctly documents that aspect of his music too. If his blues could be stiff, his country could be delightfully loose.

Earl Johnson and His Clodhoppers: *Red Hot Breakdown* (County). This north Georgia fiddler's style may *sound* anarchistic, but it's really more of a finely controlled raucousness. He drew attention playing first with his brothers Albert and Ester (who both died in 1923) and then as second fiddler in Fiddlin' John Carson's Virginia Reelers. But these impassioned 1927 recordings show why it was imperative that he soon go out on his own, fronting a group that also included two guitars and a banjo.

Buell Kazee: *Buell Kazee* (June Appal). College-educated, formally trained in music and a preacher, Buell Kazee brought new sophistication to mountain music (which wasn't always appreciated) when he first recorded in the late twenties. Yet he wasn't exactly what you'd call "slick," either. He played banjo in the frailing (or "thrashing") style of downward strokes and sang with a vulnerable voice that suggested how deeply immersed he was in his religious calling. These folk-era recordings, compiled after his death in 1976, capture the full range of this archetypal Kentucky banjo stylist, and it's a good thing, too, because with the exception of a ripoff Folkways LP of mostly-talking, it's all there is on Kazee.

The Kessinger Brothers: *The Kessinger Brothers, 1928–30* (County). Clark Kessinger was *the* hotshot fiddler from the West Virginia area, with a smooth style that had its share of rhythmic and melodic quirks; he applied much of the technique of concert violinists to his own hillbilly background and became hugely influential among fiddlers already keeping one eye on the charts (such as they were). His nephew Luches Kessinger provided sympathetic support on these sides, which jazzed up traditional melodies and paved the way for men like Fiddlin' Arthur Smith.

Clark Kessinger: *The Legend of Clark Kessinger* (County). Recorded in 1964, but Kessinger still has some of the speed and sure touch of his earliest sides. He was recorded too often after his rediscovery, however, so this is the only one of his folk-era albums that can be recommended.

Bradley Kincaid: *Mountain Ballads and Old-Time Songs* (Old Homestead). Kincaid is an oddity—a soft, sentimental singer whose diction made him sound more like a budding folkie than like a genuine traditional singer. But his country roots are beyond challenge, and when he left the mountains for Chicago in the pre-World War I years, his radio shows brought country music to a new audience of college students and urban sophisticates.

The Leake County Revelers: *The Leake County Revelers* (County). This Mississippi group plays with such fleet, light swing that you almost want to believe they had more to do with the origins of Bob Wills than did Texas fiddle bands. You'd be wrong, of course, but good guess anyhow.

Bascom Lamar Lunsford: *Smoky Mountain Ballads* (Folkways). Lunsford is a North Carolina lawyer who in 1928 founded the Asheville Mountain Dance and Folk Festival, and continued running it through the seventies. He is also a spare, striking banjo player, best known for "I Wish I Was a Mole in the Ground," which is included on this ten-inch mini-LP recorded in 1953, when the folk revival was just heating up.

Bascom Lamar Lunsford and George Pegram with Red Parham: *Music from South Turkey Creek* (Rounder). A quarter century or so later, Lunsford is still pulling traditional songs from his seemingly limitless repertoire and infusing them with his mountain spirit and his mountain smarts. Pegram and Parham are less magnetic on banjo and harmonica.

Uncle Dave Macon: *Early Recordings* (County). This rates extremely high within the confusing batch of Uncle Dave reissues, thanks mainly to seven sides from the pivotal 1927 sessions with the Fruit Jar Drinkers (Sam and Kirk McGee and Mazy Todd). But the 1935 "Just One Way," with the Delmore Brothers backing him, is more than a mere curiosity, too.

Uncle Dave Macon with the Fruit Jar Drinkers: *Go 'Long Mule* (County). These sides are mainly from early in his career, and the emphasis is on energetic, upbeat numbers with the emphasis on roots.

Uncle Dave Macon: *The Dixie Dewdrop* (Vetco). Another of those something-for-everyone Uncle Dave samplers, with religious numbers holding an edge.

Uncle Dave Macon: *Vol. 3, From Earth to Heaven* (Vetco). Some of his first and some of his last recordings; his instrumental work is best spotlighted here.

Uncle Dave Macon: *Uncle Dave Macon* (Folkways). Compiled by folkie Pete Seeger, this stresses Uncle Dave's treatments of traditional material.

Uncle Dave Macon: *Laugh Your Blues Away* (Rounder). These seventeen cuts come from test pressings of sides never before released, from 1945 sessions he made on his own, and from radio broadcasts. Because Uncle Dave and record companies never got along with each other, twelve of these seventeen cuts are all we have of him from the forties and early fifties. He's slowed down on banjo, with son Dorris on guitar taking up the slack, but his sense of humor is as keen as ever. And the 1930 sides (especially the alternate takes of "Mysteries of the World" and "Go On, Nora Lee") can rank with anything he ever cut.

Sam and Kirk McGee: *Sam and Kirk McGee from Sunny Tennessee* (German Bear Family). Why isn't this released domestically? Sam and Kirk McGee didn't record much in their prime, but what they did was both innovative and accessible. They've made it onto lots of anthologies, and appear on other albums as sidemen, but putting this much of their early work together is the only way to do them justice.

Sam and Kirk McGee and the Crook Brothers: *Opry Old Timers* (Starday/Gusto). Early sixties recordings, absolutely faithful to twenties and thirties styles, from a pair of throwbacks who never moved forward. The Crook Brothers, fronted by Herman Crook's harmonica, are the more archaic of the two, both in songs and in sound.

Minstrels and Tunesmiths (JEMF). These are very early (1916–23) commercial recordings by the kind of popular singers who influenced the first country recording artists. Many of the songs will be familiar— they were later recorded by country singers—though you'll recognize the names of few of the people singing them here. But the purpose of this album is to heighten contradictions like that, until it becomes apparent that country music never was purely a "folk" music transmitted orally, but also had at least some roots in commercial pop music. The instrumentation and vocal phrasing also indicate how little difference there was at one time between what sounded "country" and what sounded "pop."

Nashville—the Early String Bands (County). Another illuminating collection, this one of sides cut between 1925 and 1934. The stars are Sam and Kirk McGee with the weary "Salt Lake City Blues" and Sam McGee with "Chevrolet Car," which is *still* being rewritten today in various guises by rock, country, and blues singers. But Paul Warmack and His Gully Jumpers come perilously close to rocking out on "Robertson County," and there're guitars, fiddles, banjos, and harps from Dr. Humphrey Bate and His Possum Jumpers, the roguish Binkley Brothers' Dixie Clodhoppers, Uncle Dave Macon and His Fruit Jar Drinkers, and others.

Old-Time Ballads from the Southern Mountains (County). There are a couple of obscurities, but this excellent sampler goes mostly for such known talents as Blind Alfred Reed and Grayson and Whitter.

Old Time Fiddle Classics (County). Somewhat off-the-wall in its randomness, with a mishmash of styles and regions represented. But when you've got vibrant performances from the likes of Clark Kessinger, Earl Johnson, Lowe Stokes, Clayton McMichen, Arthur Smith, and others, who can complain about lack of organization?

Old Time Fiddle Classics, Vol. 2 (County). This has more obscure artists than volume one, and also less obvious sides by the more obvious artists. Among the former, the Red Headed Fiddlers "Paddy on the Handcar" stands out, while Eck Robertson's "Texas Wagoner" is a good example of the latter. Plus such unknowns as Robinette and Moore, Sharp, Hinman and Sharp, and Ted Gosset's Band.

Old-Time Mountain Guitar (County). Roy Harvey, from Charlie Poole's group, dominates this album, playing sparkling duets with both Leonard Copeland and Jess Johnson. But the inclusion of John Dilleshaw and the String Marvel's influential version of "Spanish Fandango" and Lowe Stokes' North Georgians' original "Take Me to the Land of Jazz" makes this more significant for those seeking out the roots of country swing.

The Original Bogtrotters: *The Original Bogtrotters, 1937–42* (Biograph). Early Virginia string-band styles, recorded (by the Library of Congress) late in the game. But these men aged well, especially Fields Ward with his finely controlled singing and Crockett Ward and Eck Dunford for their fiddling; Dunford's persistent drone gives this music most of its flavor.

Paramount Old Time Tunes (JEMF). This documents the activities of one of the first companies to dive into hillbilly (and blues) recordings, and they cut many different artists in every setting imaginable. Given the potential, this album tends to disappoint at first, but it'll grow on you. Maybe there're no revelations, but there's no filler, either.

Charlie Poole and the North Carolina Ramblers: *Charlie Poole and the North Carolina Ramblers, Vol. 2* (County). More transitional banjo and fiddle music that shows off a diverse and intelligent repertoire beginning with "Can I Sleep in Your Barn" from his first session and extending through novelties like "Monkey on a String," hot dance numbers, an early version of "Hesitation Blues" called "If the River Was Whiskey," the sprightly "It's Movin' Day," and including "One Moonlight Night" from his very last session.

Charlie Poole and the North Carolina Ramblers: *Charlie Poole and the North Carolina Ramblers, Vol. 4* (County). Mainly of interest because it contains both sides of Poole's first record, "Sunny Tennessee" b/w "Man That Rode the Mule," plus a couple of previously unissued sides.

Frank Proffitt: *Frank Proffitt* (Folk-Legacy). Proffitt is a versatile banjo player from North Carolina who accompanies himself on mostly traditional ballads, plus a few more he claims to have written. He has an oddly winsome voice, and is particularly fond of drinking songs. Recorded in 1962.

Riley Puckett: *Waitin' for the Evening Mail* (County). In his day, Puckett was known primarily as a vocalist; later he became recognized for his finger-picking guitar runs. This album puts the emphasis on Puckett the singer, and includes a seminal version of "I'm Ragged but I'm Right." As a singer, Puckett is curiously deferential, though his voice is ultimately as distinct as his guitar.

Riley Puckett: *Riley Puckett* (Old Homestead). Some duplication with the County set, but more diversified. More guitar, too, which is good, and poorer sound, which isn't. This blind singer-guitarist, who did several things well in several different contexts, remains one of early country music's most intriguing (and most overlooked) figures.

The Red Fox Chasers: *The Red Fox Chasers* (County). This North Carolina string band from the late twenties is best known for the sophisticated vocals of guitarist A. P. Thompson and harmonica player Bob Crawford at a time when singing played only a small role in string-band music.

Blind Alfred Reed: *How Can a Poor Man Stand Such Times and Live?* (Rounder). A West Virginia fiddler and singer who also paid attention to city slickers like Carson Robison and Vernon Dalhart, Reed is best known for the title song, which may be the ultimate Depression-era lament, and for "Always Lift Him Up and Never Knock Him Down," which may be the ultimate brotherhood song. Though a preacher who sang rigorously moralistic songs, he also cut such wryly frank songs as "Black and Blue Blues." His worn baritone and forlorn fiddle (he reportedly kept rattlesnake rattles in his fiddle to improve the tone) make him one of the most memorable country singers of the twenties.

Jean Ritchie: *Precious Memories* (Folkways). Ritchie is a college-educated Kentucky mountain woman who lived in New York and was popular with the northeastern folk crowd in the sixties. She usually sang mountain ballads unaccompanied, though sometimes she used a dulcimer or other instruments, and sometimes she sang with other people. She was widely recorded on a number of folkie labels, though this album remains her most appealing because in trying to communicate the way commercial string-band music entered into traditional mountain music, it provided links to both these worlds.

Carson Robison: *Just a Melody* (Old Homestead). Robison was originally from Kansas, though he was based in New York. Along with Vernon Dalhart, he was the first to conceive of country music as a pop vehicle; his music is just as schlocky as Dalhart's, too, but these eighteen sides are important if only for the influence Robison exerted. Some of them even feature Dalhart working with Robison, though I'll take the sides done with Buell Kazee any day.

Round the Heart of Old Galax, Vol. 1 (County). This volume features late-twenties recordings by Ernest V. Stoneman and bands; it has crude and otherworldly versions of familiar tunes like "Flop-eared Mule" and "John Hardy" and serves as a companion volume to Stoneman's Rounder album for those who still haven't gotten enough.

Round the Heart of Old Galax, Vol. 2 (County). Of the several albums in this series, this one takes the cake because of the extent to which it spotlights the inimitable Crockett Ward on fiddle (with his brother Wade on banjo and other instruments). Among the other musicians on this 1926 collection are Eck Dunford and both Stonemans, and a good number of these sides were never issued before.

Round the Heart of Old Galax, Vol. 3 (County). This anthology doesn't have quite the kick or the cohesiveness of the previous two, but the variety can be a virtue in itself, especially when it includes solo fiddle pieces from John Rector. Others featured are the Sweet Brothers, some Wards, and Emmett Lundy.

Hobart Smith: *Hobart Smith* (Folk-Legacy). Smith plays syncopated banjo in what he calls the "old-time rappin' style" and fiddles on a couple of tunes as well. Most of the songs he does on this 1963 album originate from 1900–3, and are a self-conscious effort by Smith (and the record company) to document his mountain heritage rather than the pop music he was playing when he was discovered by the folk revival movement.

Ernest V. Stoneman: *Ernest V. Stoneman & His Dixie Mountaineers, 1927–28* (Historical). Ten of his Edison recordings, with the usual sterling accompaniment from fiddler Kahle Brewer and other Galax stalwarts. Though the emphasis is on sentimental ballads, the real interest is in hearing the unique Galax-style treatments of such familiar material as "Kitty Wells," "Careless Love," and "Sally Goodin."

The Stoneman Family: *Old-Time Tunes of the South* (Folkways). Pop Stoneman and his wife, along with some of their kids, in the landmark 1957 set of traditional tunes. Pop plays autoharp and sings in a harsh voice; Mrs. Stoneman specializes in five-string banjo. Other cuts feature Vernon (harmonica) and/or J. C. (banjo) Sutphin, Louise Foreacre (banjo), and H. N. Dickens (banjo). Confusing, but worthy resurrections.

The String Bands, Vol. 1 (Old Timey). Virtually as soon as it went public, country music began cross-fertilizing with blues, jazz, and ragtime, and this compilation seeks to document that process in its formative stages. Hence such oddities as "Japanese Breakdown" by the Scottdale String Band, "Jackson Stomp" by the Mississippi Mud Steppers, and "Down Yonder" and "Nobody Loves Me" by Hershel Brown and His Washboard Band, mixed in with the more predictable fare from Charlie Poole and the North Carolina Ramblers, Gid Tanner and His Skillet Lickers, the Allen Brothers, and the Arthur Smith Trio. Lively, and often surprising, twists on early string bands.

The String Bands, Vol. 2 (Old Timey). Another potpourri from (mostly) the twenties, and fascinating as a random look-see into that era. A couple (Eck Robertson, Earl Johnson) too obvious and already anthologized in other places, but the Hackberry Ramblers (primal Cajun) is a gem, the version of "I'll Roll in My Sweet Baby's Arms" by Buster Carter and Preston Young may be the first recording of that favorite, and cuts by Darby and Tarlton, The Spooney Five, Bayless Rose, Uncle Bud Landress and the Three Stripped Gears are all both off-the-wall and worthwhile.

The Stripling Brothers: *Old Time Fiddle Tunes, 1928–36* (County). The pride of northwest Alabama, these guys are predictably close to the bluesy Mississippi fiddlers, but if anything a little more upbeat, a little flashier. Nowhere near as influential, though, and I wonder why.

Gid Tanner and His Skillet Lickers: *The Skillet Lickers* (County). The most tradition-oriented album available on Tanner and Co., with such gems as "Big Ball in Town" (which Bob Wills later stole for "Big Ball in Cowtown," but then Tanner stole it from the traditional "Roll on the Ground" to begin with), "Soldier's Joy," "Cotton Eyed Joe" (now the Texas dance anthem), and also the first installment of the "A Corn Licker Still in Georgia" skit.

Gid Tanner and His Skillet Lickers: *Gid Tanner and the Skillet Lickers* (Vetco). Although sound quality leaves much to be desired, "Dance All Night with a Bottle in Your Hand" and "Goin' on Downtown" are what this group was all about.

Gid Tanner & the Skillet Lickers: *Hear These New Southern Fiddle and Guitar Records* (Rounder). This has some of Tanner's most eccentric work ("Tanner's Boarding House" and "I'm Satisfied," both from his very last session) as well as some interesting sides by other permutations of the original group.

Gid Tanner and His Skillet Lickers: *A Corn Licker Still in Georgia* (Voyager). This represents all fourteen sides of the ongoing sketches recorded by Tanner and cohorts between 1927 and 1930. Individually, all seven records were immensely popular; together on album they have a little less impact because they're so formulaic—bits of humor, most of it having to do with making moonshine without getting caught, interspersed with bits of fiddle music. But the talk is revealing, the music is as good as any Tanner's groups ever cut, and, as an added bonus, some of these tunes were never recorded in any other form. So it's an important album no matter how you look at it.

Texas Farewell (County). This anthology spotlights several of the most important Texas fiddlers to record in the twenties. The more predictable high points include two sides each by the East Texas Serenaders and by Eck Robertson, but relative obscurities like Oscar Harper's "Dallas Bound" are what give the album spice.

Traditional Country Classics, 1927–1929 (Historical). With Earl Johnson and His Clodhoppers ("Leather Breeches," "Red Hot Breakdown"), this has its share of fiddle-band pyrotechnics. With Ernest Stoneman, Grayson and Whitter, Charlie Poole's North Carolina Ramblers, and Burnett and Rutherford, it has its share of well-known (maybe too much so) performers and songs. So it's the obscure, oddball stuff that really sticks—like George "Dad" Crockett's leering "Sugar Hill," as well as two aptly titled songs in "Georgia Wobble Blues" by the Carroll County Ramblers and "Lye Soap Breakdown" by Dilly and His Dill Pickles.

Traditional Fiddle Music of Mississippi, Vol. 1 (County). From the stomping, bluesy Floyd Ming and His Pep-Steppers to the clanging Carter Brothers and Son to the softer and more influential Narmour and Smith, this offers more diversity that Mississippi fiddle music is supposed to have. Less driving than the music from other states, perhaps, but often elusive.

Traditional Fiddle Music of Mississippi, Vol. 2 (County). This spotlights more Narmour and Smith, plus the path-breaking Leake County Revelers. For contrast, there's the more archaic Freeny's Barn Dance Band and the more modern Nations Brothers.

Field Ward and His Buck Mountain Band (Historical). "Those Cruel Slavery Days" is a folk curiosity—written and sung from the point of view of a slave, but always most popular among whites. "Ain't That Trouble in Mind" is the other high point, a simple but eerie song that's a nice counterpoint to such well-known fare as "John Hardy." Joining guitarist-singer Ward is Ernest Stoneman on harmonica, autoharp, guitar, and vocals. The abominable sound on these 1929 sides is the only thing going against them.

Wade Ward: *Uncle Wade* (Folkways). The foremost practitioner of the Galax-area style of banjo frailing, Ward is represented here both by cuts from his Library of Congress sessions in 1938 and by recordings made at the height of the urban folk era, 1958–64. He lost little of his rhythmic sense as he aged, it turns out, though the album is marred by inclusion of some of his fiddle tunes, which are nowhere near as dynamic.

Way Down South in Dixie—Kentucky Fiddle Band Music, Vol. 3 (Morning Star). The Blue Ridge Mountaineers (with fiddle, banjo, harmonica, and piano) are fast and funky, especially on "Old Flannagan." Green's String Band is smooth and slick, especially on "Glide Waltz." Doc Roberts, Asa Martin, and H. L. Bandy get most of the rest of the album. Sound quality, which is rough throughout the series, is particularly treacherous on this volume.

Wink the Other Eye—Kentucky Fiddle Band Music, Vol. 1 (Morning Star). For some reason, Kentucky supported more different styles and songs than any other state, even those much more populous, and a surprising amount of it was black-influenced. (In Jim Booker, Taylor's Kentucky Boys even had a black fiddler.) These recordings, originally made for Gennett (of Indiana) in the twenties and thirties, run the gamut from the fiddle-and-guitar or fiddle-and-banjo lineup used by most groups to the "big" (seven pieces) sound of Jack's String Band (on the title tune and on "Pretty Little Girl"). Richard Burnett and Leonard Rutherford are probably the best-known musicians here, but the highlight is "Gate to Go Through," by Jimmie Johnson's String Band, with the sizzling, syncopated fiddle of Andy Palmer.

Wish I Had My Time Again—Kentucky Fiddle Band Music, Vol. 2 (Morning Star). Doc Roberts (who played a black Kentucky style though he was white) and H. L. Bandy (a showman who did for fiddle what Uncle Dave Macon did for banjo) are the two stars on this set, though "Black Snake Moan" (the Texas blues of Blind Lemon Jefferson) is a shocker; it's done by Cobb and Underwood, which is actually Hack's String Band under a different name.

DaCosta Woltz and His Southern Broadcasters: *DaCosta Woltz and His Southern Broadcasters* (County). They weren't broadcasters at all, but with an unorthodox lineup of fiddle and two banjos and a large repertoire of novelty songs, Woltz's group was one of the more memorable to come out of North Carolina. These 1927 sides are all they ever recorded.

THE DEPRESSION YEARS

In the first week of August 1927, Victor (now RCA Victor) Records representative Ralph Peer arrived in Bristol, a town half in Virginia and half in Tennessee, to record rural talent from the surrounding mountain areas. Peer, who had previously held a similar post at Okeh Records, was one of the few industry execs familiar enough with "hillbilly music" to know just what he was looking for on this trip. Before he left town, he had cut the first sides ever by Jimmie Rodgers and by the Carter Family. Most historians agree that these sessions mark the birth of modern country music.

This does not mean that string bands went out of business as soon as Rodgers and the Carters came in. For that matter, some of the musicians whose styles are associated with this era recorded before the thirties—as in the case of Darby and Tarlton—or after—as in the case of the Louvin Brothers. (For our purposes, the era I'm calling the thirties began in 1927; because of their success and influence, Rodgers and the Carters provide a clear starting point.)

The thirties was a time of extraordinary growth and, for a while at least, diversification. (Not coincidentally, this was also true for other forms of American roots music.) Much of this was made possible by technology, particularly by the invention (in 1925) of the electrical recording process. The new equipment was portable, which meant that record companies could easily go into the field, where the performers were. In the past, record companies tended to record a disproportionate number of urban imitators or those with sufficient ambition, money, and time to make the trip to major cities (usually New York) and request an audition.

Rodgers and the Carters offer sharply contrasting images that help define the era. The former was a freewheeling ex-railroad man from the southern flatlands, while the latter were rigid, God-fearing mountain people. Rodgers cut all types of songs in many different styles, while the Carters emphasized traditional tunes in strict mountain style. Both— the Carters with their "worried man" singing his "worried song" and

Rodgers with his restless, rootless hobo songs and his personal history of TB and certain premature death—were very much products of the Depression. Rodgers had perhaps the greatest overall influence.

First, he was a bluesman; even when he didn't follow strict blues form, he did catch the blues feeling. He was not the first white bluesman—there had been many before him in the twenties, most of them funkier and closer musically to the blacks they imitated—but Jimmie was the first to devise a blues style pleasing to both whites and blacks. Nearly every male country singer of the thirties started out emulating Jimmie Rodgers, and as competition increased to see who could come up with the hottest blues licks, dobro became more important in country music.

His image was just as important. Again, the rambling man had always been a part of country music, but Jimmie made him into a sympathetic figure, even an icon. He also dabbled with cowboy images. Most important, Rodgers (apparently at Peer's insistence) downplayed his southern country roots in an attempt to make his potential audience as broad as his repertoire.

Meanwhile, the Carters were keeping the faith for purists. They weren't as successful financially as Rodgers, but their harmonies and adherence to traditional material paved the way for brother duets and for the next wave of string bands, which eventually blended together into bluegrass.

If any one thing linked Rodgers and the Carters, it's that both were primarily singers. This in itself was something new for country music, which in the past had put the emphasis on picking. This was another area in which new technology played a prominent role. As pointed out earlier, the new electrical equipment was able to pick up voices at lower volume, and was able to better differentiate between voices, so that the subtleties of harmony singing weren't lost. In the past, everything had to be loud to be recorded at all. Were it not for this new system—particularly the microphones—it would have been nearly pointless to even try capturing the vocal sound of the brother duets.

Radio was important in so many ways. At first, country music had been dispensed largely by phonograph record. But as the Depression deepened, radio became the primary medium. The differences were dramatic: In 1927, 104 million records were sold; by 1932 the figure had dipped to six million. The Grand Ole Opry on WSM in Nashville and the WLS Barn Dance in Chicago were the two biggest, but there were country radio shows everywhere—even in such unlikely cities as Milwaukee, Pittsburgh, New York, Philadelphia, Minneapolis-St. Paul, Kansas City, and St. Louis. As it spread to new regions, the music adapted to its new audiences; more pop influences began creeping in.

Still, many of the traditional string bands hung on, too, and they were able to do so without placing vocals above instrumental technique. As their styles matured, many of them delved further into jazz phrasing.

Aside from blues, brother groups, singing stars, and modern string bands, the thirties saw the creation of spin-off genres like western swing and singing cowboys. Since the traditional songs started becoming overly familiar to musicians and fans alike, a group of professional songwriters rose to supply new ones. The electric guitar made its first appearance, as did the jukebox. As this talk of new technology, radio, increasing record sales, and public images makes clear, country music was fast becoming a business. A business is most efficient when its products can be homogenized, and that began happening further down the line. But the thirties were truly boom years for country music.

Jimmie Rodgers: *My Rough and Rowdy Ways* (RCA)

Time has done much to distort our impressions of Jimmie Rodgers. We think of him as a father of country music when, in his day, he (and apparently most others) didn't think of him as a country singer at all; in fact, his image-shaping nicknames, America's Blue Yodeler and the Singing Brakeman, were both carefully chosen because they carried no "hillbilly" connotations—yet neither of those nicknames really stuck to him when he was alive as they have since he died. We think of him as one of the true superstars of his era, and while it is true that his popularity brought him enormous sums at a time when money in this country had never been tighter, it is also true that he was virtually unknown outside the South; national recognition, to the extent that it came at all, came posthumously.

My Rough and Rowdy Ways has been in print longer than any album RCA has ever compiled on Rodgers, and perhaps that is because the album (despite having only eight cuts not available now on *This Is*) embraces all these contradictions, throws in some notable oddities, and still manages to present a cohesive overall picture. In the end, Jimmie's greatest strength was his ability to take almost any kind of band playing almost any kind of material and make it his own. He really has no modern counterpart unless—and this takes a great leap of faith across several generations—you count Elvis Presley, who also had obviously country roots without being a mainstream country performer, and who also was actually more comfortable in the city, albeit a southern city, than in the country.

Rodgers was born in 1897 in Meridian, Mississippi, which was not exactly a teeming metropolis, but which was an important crossroads in the South; even had radio not been growing more pervasive, Jimmie would have been exposed to more ideas and musics than the average country boy of his age. Because his mother died of TB when he was four and his father was a railroad section foreman who wasn't always home, Jimmie spent his childhood being shunted back and forth among relatives in Mississippi and Alabama. He finally left school for good in 1911 to become a water carrier on the line where his father worked; in the past, only blacks had held this job and Jimmie hung out with them enough to learn the rudiments of his music.

Which meant the blues, or at least a songster-type variation on blues, for Rodgers was savvy enough to realize that making a living as a bluesman was unlikely. He simply integrated those blues into the white musics he was picking up from radio and from his travels and then added his own personal touch, the blue yodel. Music remained solely a diversion for him until about 1925, when his TB made it impossible for him to continue the hard work of the railroad man.

By then he was married to his second wife and was a father. Significantly, when he began pursuing music as a vocation, he went first to Asheville, North Carolina, a resort town where patrons would presumably expect pop music rather than hillbilly. Within another year, he was in Bristol recording for Peer.

Whatever his pop aspirations, railroads and blues remained a large part of everything he did. He could engage in such unabashed sentimentalism as "Mississippi Moon"—that may be what his audience most preferred at the time, actually—but his heart was with such songs as this album's "Jimmie Rodgers' Last Blue Yodel (The Women Make a Fool Out of Me)," "Blue Yodel No. 9 (Standin' on the Corner)," "Southern Cannonball," and "Travellin' Blues."

"Blue Yodel No. 9" (1930) has always attracted the most attention, because a then-young up-and-comer named Louis Armstrong accompanies Jimmie on trumpet while Satchmo's wife, Lillian, is on piano. Lil holds the groove while Louis blows real languid; Rodgers, meanwhile, swaggers through this Memphis blues rife with passion, insolence, and violence. That was an image based on his railroad days that he clearly encouraged.

"Southern Cannonball" features Jimmie's whining train-whistle sound as well as his blue yodel. "Last Blue Yodel," recorded at his deathbed 1933 sessions in New York, has surprisingly assertive vocals and nimble guitar, though who made a fool out of whom is open to debate. Rodgers, after all, took pride in being a rambling man who could get his back scratched in any town he went to, and evidence suggests that the main reason his marriage to Carrie Williamson lasted so long is that he spent most of his time away from her. "Long Tall Mama Blues," in which he boasts about having so many girls he can't make up his mind, might be closer to the truth.

As long as he could outlast his TB, Jimmie Rodgers liked to hint, he had it made or had a good time trying—and during the harshest years of the Depression, people liked more than ever to know that was still possible. So one can talk in musical terms about some of the other highlights here—the hokum sound of "My Blue-Eyed Jane," the way "The One Rose (That's Left in My Heart)" translates blues feel into pop form, the elegant vocal and band performances on "Travellin' Blues," which represents some of the seeds of western swing—but what really matters most is that Jimmie Rodgers' nasal tenor not only seemed to share the burdens of the common man, but it also seemed to offer him transcendence, even if only temporarily, just as surely as that railroad held out hope that one could move down the line and possibly start life over. Even his imperfections—his poor sense of timing, for example— were made to work for him, because they dramatized his drive to surpass the limits that seemed to be imposed on him. That is why in 1961 he became the first member inducted into the Country Music Hall of Fame, and that is also why the story persists that throughout the South during those years customers would walk into general stores and say, "Let me have a pound of butter, a dozen eggs, and the latest Jimmie Rodgers record."

Jimmie Rodgers: *This Is Jimmie Rodgers* (RCA)

More than anyone else, Jimmie Rodgers made early country music "respectable." His plaintive, flexible tenor carried Southerners through the Depression on a musical diet of railroad and rounder songs, double entendres, hobo and cowboy ballads, lullabyes and sentimental songs, and, above all else, the white blues and blue yodels that made up a small part of his repertoire but the largest part of his legacy. This album offers but a sampling.

When the tuberculosis-wracked Mississippian died at age thirty-six by drowning in his own blood while hemorrhaging at the Taft Hotel in New York City in 1933, he had 111 recordings in the can from a career that spanned just over six years. He had come to professional music late, but he was around long enough to become the music's first bona fide superstar, and to inspire succeeding generations of superstars like Gene Autry, Jimmie Davis, Hank Snow, and Ernest Tubb. There was a time when nearly every young new country singer coming up wanted to be Jimmie Rodgers, and the greatest irony in this is that Rodgers consid- ered himself a popular entertainer, and not a country singer.

Though a southern boy with working-class roots, he also had some of the cool and diffidence of the urban hipster. Yet it was his blue yodel, very much a country device, that Rodgers introduced to American popular music. It was neither the classic Swiss mountain yodel nor the Afro-American falsetto cry common in Jimmie's native Mississippi, but a self-styled cross between the two, and it set off a fad that lasted nearly two decades.

Rodgers did all this for Victor, which is now known as RCA Victor and is less enlightened about its music today than it was then. Which means that precious little of the vital music this man created is even available today. Not *too* long ago, it was all still in print here. More recently, there was a deluxe boxed set of his complete works available on import from Japan. In America today, though, there's but one album assembled more or less randomly, a "greatest hits" set that actually emphasizes some of his worst efforts, and this double album containing all of eighteen sides.

But make do we must. For one thing, this does preserve what's widely regarded as Rodgers' all-time masterpiece. "Waiting for a Train" was recorded in Atlanta in 1928 with a tight, bluesy jazz band Rodgers had stumbled across while barhopping the night before the session. They complement perfectly his own bluesy vocals, and unlike a surprisingly large amount of his material, this song tells a story. The song has the high, lonesome feeling that later became a country cliché, and is the obvious forerunner to several decades worth of bumming-around songs, right up to "Me and Bobby McGee." You could pick eighteen Rodgers selections from a hat and come up with a pretty diverse lot, so even this album does okay on that count. When Ralph Peer first recorded Rodgers in Bristol, Jimmie performed with just acoustic guitar and his own voice. The same was true for his second session, in Camden, New Jersey, in 1927. In concert, Rodgers always performed solo. Throughout his career, he would continue to record that way sometimes too, but overall he utilized as many different settings as he did types of songs.

Two of the four songs he cut at those Camden sessions are included here. "Blue Yodel No. 1 (T for Texas)" was originally cut because Rodgers, having scammed Peer into recording him again, had no other material with which to close out the session. It was received by the public as a novelty song, albeit one that sold like crazy, and it established Rodgers as a yodeler. The blue yodel differed from black blues in several important ways, but it did string together enough public-domain blues lines—Rodgers wrote virtually none of his songs, though he's credited with writing most of them—to create a strong blues feeling. Not too strong for the white masses to swallow, mind you, but stronger than the white mass market had been used to. After that, Peer made it a point to assign blue-yodel numbers to similar songs in addition to the titles Rodgers gave each; in all, there were thirteen blue yodels, one issued posthumously. This album also contains "Blue Yodel No. 4 (California Blues)," a swinging performance cut with the 1928 Atlanta jazz band, and "Mule Skinner Blues (Blue Yodel No. 8)," cut in 1930 in Hollywood and one of his last solo efforts, featuring his own stark and twisting guitar line.

Early in his career, Rodgers relied for many of his songs, particularly the sentimental ones, on Elsie McWilliams, the sister of his wife. She wrote, or co-wrote, or helped put together, such songs as "Daddy and Home," a 1928 solo song inspired, she said, by a conversation with Jimmie about his railroading father, and "My Old Pal," a very urbane sort of countryish ballad. Elsie wrote more for the genteel side of Rodgers, though she also had a hand in "Never No Mo' Blues" (her attempt at a blue yodel) and "My Rough and Rowdy Ways." Since she considered blues and blue yodels vulgar, it's ironic that she was phased out as his writer about halfway through Jimmie's career, right when he was moving away from raunchy stuff and into more poppish music, which Peer thought would sell to a larger audience.

It did, too. But since I have been stressing the slick side of Jimmie Rodgers, it's worth pointing out this album's version of "Frankie and Johnny," done solo in Dallas in 1929, and often used by Rodgers as a theme song despite its out-front reference to "making love," or despite his refusal to tie the song's conclusion up with a nice homily of the type country audiences wanted so badly even then. "In the Jailhouse Now No. 2" also gets pretty explicit for the type of audience Jimmie usually played to, and though he's known primarily as a singer, this one joins "Mule Skinner Blues" in showing just how funky he could be with a guitar. And if "My Carolina Sunshine Girl" suggests he was best as a jazz singer, "Peach Picking Time Down in Georgia" shows just how much he was at home with a hard-country band (and Clayton McMichen's fiddle lines come eerily close to emulating a blue yodel). Jimmie Rodgers may be cleaner, slicker, and more mainstream than those who romanticize him are willing to concede, but yes, he could get down. Indeed he could.

Jimmie Rodgers: *Train Whistle Blues* (RCA)

"If the people like you when you're nice," Jimmie Rodgers used to tell friends, "they'll accept you when you're naughty." This understanding contributed greatly to Jimmie's success, because he definitely liked to be both, and when he wanted to be naughty, he seemed to know whereof he spoke. "I know pretty mama when you are hanging 'round/ I don't see no fire but I'm burning down," he sings on this album's "Let Me Be Your Sidetrack," one of those songs stringing together bunches of blues stanzas, some of which may even be original. This song is punctuated by the most deliciously lusty yodeling Rodgers ever recorded. But somehow, the song never becomes threatening the way that a hard (black) bluesman would make it; Rodgers takes his sex with a wink and a self-satisfied smile, but there's also disarming courtliness and innocence to his style. While she would undoubtedly have some second thoughts, a mother might even let her daughter go out with this man.

Even back when everything Rodgers recorded was on the market in some form, *Train Whistle Blues* was my favorite of his albums, and though it's now been deleted, I'd still recommend sifting the cut-out bins and mail-order houses for this before plunking down good money on what RCA has preserved. Not only does this contain examples of every kind of song and setting he utilized, it usually contains one of the best examples he ever cut.

Consider, for example, his work alone on "Any Old Time," a 1929 performance with an "uptown orchestra" forced on him by Peer. This sluggish ork has almost as much trouble with Jimmie's unorthodox timing as Louis Armstrong did, but Rodgers' own vocal is remarkably open and bighearted, giving credence to reports that this was his favorite song (though, thanks to the unwieldy orchestra, not his favorite record).

Then there's "My Good Gal's Gone Blues," a 1931 side cut with the Louisville Jug Band. This is apparently another case in which Rodgers heard musicians he liked and decided on the spot to record with them; it's certainly the only side he ever cut with a jug band, and his shouted asides at the ends of lines (which he always planned in advance) have a more spontaneous feel to them. He's clearly elated to be working with these guys. His vocals have real bite. George Allen's scintillating clarinet plays off the blue yodels and either Cal Smith or Fred Smith lashes out on the guitar break.

"Down the Road to Home" sounds almost *too* simple and straightforward, but this is what the country audience liked about Rodgers as much as anything else, and it does show what the heart song evolved out of, just as "Lullabye Yodel" shows the roots of the country weeper. "Treasures Untold" shows how his voice sometimes strained to go just a tad higher on poppish songs, and his yodel here is more seductive than lonesome, but the real highlight is the swooning steel solo by the song's co-writer, Ellsworth Cozzens.

But it's the blues, blue yodels and blues variations, and train songs that make up the bulk of this album. Not only is that the way a good Jimmie Rodgers album should be, but among the songs nearly all his favorite sidemen are showcased. Guitarist Billy Burke, who worked with Rodgers more than anybody else, contributes an insistent riff to the title song, but that's balanced out by Joe Kaipo's delicate steel. "Blue Yodel No. 5," a song of sorrow and affirmation, kicks off with a guitar solo by Rodgers so taut it makes you wonder why he ever recorded with anyone else on guitar—until you hear Hoyt "Slim" Bryant's biting solo on "No Hard Times." "Jimmie's Texas Blues," another 1929 cut spiced with interplay between Burke and Kaipo, also flaunts more optimism than Rodgers usually expressed, and it's hard not to be moved when he declares, "I'm not singing blues/I'm telling you the hard luck I've had/ The blues ain't nothing but a good man feeling bad."

Finally, there're two cuts here from the May 1933 sessions in New York that proved to be his last. "Somewhere Down Below the Dixon Line" and "Mississippi Delta Blues" are both about homesickness for his native South; the latter paints a word picture as vivid as it is sentimental, even if lines about "darkies singing their melodies" don't exactly hold up well today. But by now, his TB was at such an advanced stage that after each take he had to rest several hours on a cot set up in the studio before he had the strength to get up and sing another.

When he did die, his coffin went back to Meridian on a train engineered by one Homer Jenkins, who had been a friend of Jimmie's from the Singing Brakeman's own railroading days. Jenkins announced his arrival by hitting his whistle a full mile and a half outside of Meridian, and there are those who swear that when the train pulled into the station downtown, that whistle was still getting lower and more intense.

The Carter Family: 'Mid the Green Fields of Virginia (RCA)

The Carter Family was the first family group—actually the first group, period—to become full-fledged singing stars. They pioneered a new approach to rhythm and to arranging, both built around Maybelle's guitar lines. The Carters did offer innovations, but amid the upheavals of the Depression years it was the traditional characteristics of their music that caught the public ear. This album assembles sixteen of their earliest recordings to document that faction of transitional country music that remained less commercial, more folk-oriented. Most of the Carter Family's songs came from the church or from traditional mountain sources, and for that we can thank Alvin Pleasant Carter.

A.P. was born in 1891 at Maces Spring, in Poor Valley, southwestern Virginia, in the shadow of Clinch Mountain. His father had once played banjo, but upon marriage had given the instrument up as being unchristian. Gospel music dominated A.P.'s childhood, but he also developed a taste for fiddle music. As a teen-ager he traveled around the South and up into the Midwest in search of work, but returned to the Clinch Mountains in 1911 to sell fruit trees. On a sales trip over the mountains to Copper Creek, he met Sara Dougherty (born 1898 in Wise County, Virginia), who, according to legend, was singing "Engine 143" and playing an autoharp at the time. They married in 1915 and began living in Maces Spring, where they were favorites with the neighbors because they were always happy to play a song or two on request.

Their wedding provided the first encounter between Sara's first cousin Maybelle Addington (born 1909 in Nickelsville) and A.P.'s brother Ezra (Eck). They married in 1926, when she was sixteen and he was twenty-seven. At that time, A.P. and Sara had been making music together informally for a decade, and they were now joined by Maybelle, who added her guitar and alto harmony voice to Sara's lead singing and A.P.'s errant bass voice. (Eck, while supportive, never joined in.) As a trio, they played church socials, schoolhouses, and ice-cream gatherings around Poor Valley whenever they were all in the area, which, because of work and family commitments, still wasn't all the time.

So they were still semiprofessionals at best when they traveled to Bristol seeking the audition with Ralph Peer. As the A & R man later recalled, "As soon as I heard Sara's voice, that was it. I knew it was going to be wonderful." The Carters wound up recording four sides on August 1 and two more on August 2. Of those, "Bury Me Under the Weeping Willow" and "The Poor Orphan Child" are on this album.

Those records sold well enough that the Carters were called to Camden, New Jersey, in May of 1928 to record a dozen more. Included here from those sessions are "Keep on the Sunny Side," a turn-of-the-century gospel song that became the Carter theme, and "Will You Miss Me When I'm Gone," a beguilingly crude performance with repetitive guitar line and striking melody.

The Carter style was there from the beginning. In addition to Sara's leads and Maybelle's alto harmony, Carter "bassed in" (as he described it) when the mood so struck him; his voice is often barely audible, a hovering presence more than anything else, but he had an unerring sense for when to boom out his harmony lines.

Even more than the vocals, it was Maybelle's guitar that defined the sound. With Sara playing chords on autoharp, Maybelle played melody on the bass strings of her guitar while adding rhythm by playing chords on the treble strings. Her bass runs not only provided the lead and fills, but they added "bottom" to the overall sound. It was a complicated style that required her to use a thumb pick and two steel finger picks, but the result was a bold, bouncy sound that created a new school of guitar playing, one that endures today among bluegrass and folk musicians. The style is best known through the group's recording of "Wildwood Flower" (not included here) at those 1928 Camden sessions, but it also powered the title tune of this album and nearly every other song the group subsequently recorded. Maybelle had learned the basic technique from her brothers while growing up, but she was the one to perfect it. It was apparent even before the group began thriving that Maybelle was a serious musician, because in 1926 she spent the then-outrageous sum of $125 for a Gibson L-5 guitar.

Her style necessitated a new approach to arranging the traditional (or traditional-sounding) ballads the trio sang. In the past, picking styles had been adapted to voices, leading to all manner of odd tunings and instrumental techniques. But A.P. incorporated this group's vocals into the instrumental sound, which often involved simplifying both melody and rhythm. Others were doing the same thing around the same time, but few got results like A.P. did. The Carter Family songs were reduced to three chords played in steady 4-4 time, and this simplification was undoubtedly another key to their success. Keeping the music simple meant keeping it down to earth, and it's hard to get much earthier than the Carter Family.

The Carter Family: *Country & Western Classics: The Carter Family* (Time-Life)

"Can the Circle Be Unbroken (Bye and Bye)." "Keep On the Sunny Side." "Lonesome Valley." "Wildwood Flower." "I'm Thinking Tonight of My Blue Eyes." "Worried Man Blues." "Hello Stranger." "Foggy Mountain Top." The Carter Family was about songs as much as it was about anything else, and this three-record boxed set puts together a staggering collection of songs.

Then it goes a step further by adding performances from post-family spin-offs like the Carter Sisters and Mother Maybelle, the A. P. Carter Family, Sara and Maybelle Carter, and even eighties Anglo-American country-rocker Carlene Carter (Maybelle's granddaughter). The original trio's 1927–34 tenure with Victor is given short shrift here to concentrate on their 1935–38 stints with the American Record Company's group of labels and with Decca (during which time they cut confident new versions of many of their Victor sides) and a few more cuts from 1940 with other labels.

When Ralph Peer decided to function as the Carter Family's manager after first recording them in Bristol, it was largely because he wanted publishing rights to the vast body of songs A.P. had worked into the group's repertoire. That A.P. had not really written most of these songs was of small concern, for he had altered them substantially, either by rewriting the lyrics or by combining several songs into one. At a time when traditional songs were fading and Tin Pan Alley or professional songwriters were taking over American music, the Carters pumped fresh blood into the old forms; in effect, A.P. codified and preserved lines and verses from folk-song tradition. In addition, he usurped turn-of-the-century parlor songs that *had* been composed and copyrighted but that had since been neglected. And yes, he did write some himself, though often it's hard to be sure what he wrote and what he pinched from other sources.

As a child, Carter had learned many ballads from his mother, Mollie; this album's "Sinking in the Lonesome Sea," which Sara says the group really learned from A.P.'s uncle, was but one of Mollie's favorites. A.P. collected the others from a variety of sources; concerts became an ideal vehicle for uncovering new songs. Though they seldom ventured far from Maces Spring, the group was often housed overnight by locals because it was too late to return home. On such occasions, A.P. would pump his hosts for their own childhood favorites.

A.P. also went on trips for the sole purpose of finding songs, usually taking with him the black guitarist Leslie Riddles of nearby Kingsport, Tennessee. (Riddles sometimes went along on tours, too.) A.P. would jot down the words while Riddles learned to play the song on guitar so he could teach it to Maybelle when he and A.P. returned home. (He is thus undoubtedly a major influence on Maybelle's own revolutionary guitar style.) Riddles also taught the family his own songs, such as "Cannon Ball Blues," done here in an atypically swinging fashion, and he introduced them to such black blues as Ma Rainey's "Jealous Hearted Me" (which in this version strongly resembles "Hesitation Blues") and "Hello Stranger," on which Sara and Maybelle swap lines in a style more based on black music than on white church music.

In tapping so deeply into folk tradition, the Carters were able to compile a sort of musical composite of the symbolic American "worried man," as he's called in one of their best-known songs: restless, resigned, uncertain, lonely, doomed. In the Depression era, he could have been Everyman, so these songs hit home even more. At the same time, the Carters were reassuring, comforting, to the same audience, because their songs of mother and home offered at least the hope of stability, of continuity. There was also a sort of native American surrealism in their work that could be grim (in "Worried Man Blues" a man wakes up by the river in shackles and chains with nary a clue as to why) and humorous too (in the first verse of "He Never Came Back" a man leaves his prospective bride momentarily to buy a ring and never returns; in the second verse, a waiter takes a man's order and then never returns with the meal).

Such bizarre juxtapositions sometimes meant that a story line made little sense even if the song was emotionally coherent all the way through. This could be an accidental by-product of the folk process: A.P. simply misheard lyrics when he first learned the song. But just as often it was intentional: A.P. sought a particular mood, and didn't mind mixing nonlinear images or verses to get it. This is where his boundless talents as an arranger, and as a song "rewriter," came in; "Can the Circle Be Unbroken (Bye and Bye)" had been recorded by several others first, but the version that has become the standard is the version A.P. created when he added new lyrics about death to the original.

After the trio split up, priorities changed somewhat. For example, Nashville (and even New York) production values became crucial to the records made by Mother Maybelle (who'd now taken up autoharp) and her daughters Helen, June (who later married Johnny Cash), and Anita. Carlene's surprising romp through A.P.'s "Foggy Mountain Top" has much of the snap of the original even if she used British new wave rock guitarists to get it. A.P., who returned to Maces Spring after his divorce from Sara, came closest to keeping the original sound in the 1952 sides he made with her and their kids, Joe and Janette. But that figures, for A.P. was always the Carter most resistant to change, and he was the one who in "Worried Man Blues" warned, "If anyone asks you/Who composed this song/Tell 'em 'twas I/And I'll sing it all day long." It was, and he did.

The Carter Family: *On Border Radio* (JEMF)

Even at their peak, the Carters weren't huge record sellers, and they didn't tour systematically. So it's almost certain that they reached their biggest audiences ever via their broadcasts on the 500,000-watt XERA radio station on the Mexican-American border at Del Rio, Texas. These transcriptions show the Carters at their polished, professional best—a group that never changed so much as it refined and continued to grow. But at the same time, there is a subtle effort to present themselves in a more commercial manner than they had before.

Though elected to the Hall of Fame in 1970, the Carters had always functioned largely outside the commercial country-music milieu. It's unclear why they made this decision, though A.P. in particular was a stern man, set in his ways, and though he was outwardly no more religious than many others who did enter the music business, it might have been a matter of personal principle that he refrained.

Their sporadic touring remained limited to states within easy striking distance of their Clinch Mountain base. They worked cheap, even by the standards of the day. But they did little to promote their concerts or records, and they never established ties with the Opry or the industry growing in Nashville. This meant they were never very susceptible to trends or outside influences; even when Jimmie Rodgers recorded with them, he adapted to their style rather than vice versa.

Though not careerists, they were professionals. Their shows were carefully planned for maximum impact, their material skillfully molded to suit their specific needs, and they were all business onstage or in the studio. There were personal tensions in the group—especially after A.P. and Sara separated in 1933, for they didn't divorce until 1939—but these were only temporary obstacles. The sides the Carter Family cut for Decca between 1936 and 1938 are usually cited as their most fully realized efforts, and these radio transcriptions come from the same period.

The Carters went to Del Rio in 1938, and thanks to the wattage of the "border blasters" (the Carters worked other pirate stations after XERA), they were soon literally blowing their competition off the airwaves. For the first time ever, their music was being heard outside the South; in fact, XERA could be heard clearly as far away as California, Canada, and the American Northeast.

A.P. outdid himself in choosing and arranging material during this period. The song themes remained the same as ever—mother, poverty, disaster, stymied love—but a surprising number of them derive from turn-of-the-century Tin Pan Alley sources. A song like "I Cannot Be Your Sweetheart" was probably inspired by a traditional ballad anyway, and when it's molded to the Carter style, it's very much of a piece with something like "Bonnie Blue Eyes" or "Who's That Knocking," which apparently derives from a British broadside *and* a native American ballad. Then there're tunes like Lem Martin's 1932 "Old Ladies Home," which is fairly up-to-date for the Carters but is still based on those turn-of-the-century sentimental parlor ballads. The programs are balanced out with several spirituals and religious songs, a pair of recent tunes from urban country pioneer Carson Robison, some songs that A.P. claimed to have written and probably didn't, some more he claimed to have written and probably did, snatches of guitar instrumentals from Maybelle, and even an occasional blues like "Sittin' on Top of the World." A.P. would weave fragments from here and there until he had a song, and then he weaved several such songs until he had a fifteen-minute radio show.

This was made easier by the help at his command. Anita had been the first daughter to join the group, then Janette, and finally, in 1939, June and Helen. The daughters were more pop-oriented, and June, Helen, and Anita sang solo or in a trio. But the real star among the girls was Janette (daughter of A.P. and Sara), who's heard here singing "The Last Letter," a commercial country song that sounds vaguely traditional, and is thus perfect for this new Carter radio audience. In most other respects, the Carters were the same as always only better. Maybelle's guitar solos were more sure-handed, and the vocal highlights are the duets which pit Sara's stark leads with Maybelle's haunting harmonies. Even A.P. takes a couple of leads, singing songs like "I Cannot Be Your Sweetheart" in a dour, tremulous voice that is unforgettable.

The Carters stopped recording in 1941, though they continued playing winters on the Del Rio pirates through 1942. In the process, they expanded their repertoire considerably; they simply didn't have enough folk songs and previously recorded tunes to fill out two radio shows a day. But as these transcriptions show, the Carter Family was able to reach out to a wider audience without compromising its traditional country sound.

Steel Guitar Classics (Old Timey)

Except for the fiddle, no instrument is more closely identified with country music than the steel guitar, and this collection of songs from the late twenties and early thirties shows how that came to be. The rise of the steel guitar in country music parallels that of the slide guitar in blues; indeed, the two terms describe basically the same technique. The source for both was the Hawaiian music of the late nineteenth century.

Guitars were probably first introduced in Hawaii by Spanish and Portuguese sailors, and later by Mexican cowboys, early in the nineteenth century. They were taken up by the natives, who used them in their rituals and dances. Though they used the same Spanish tunings as their predecessors, Hawaiians rested the guitar across their knees and fretted the strings with a hard object, probably a bone or piece of metal, to produce a whirring, whining glissando that has been likened to a cry in blues and country alike. Joseph Kekuku, a student at Kamehameha Boys School in Oahu, is credited with having discovered Hawaiian guitar around 1894, but more likely he perfected folk techniques he'd already seen on the islands. Early in the twentieth century, Hawaiian bands began touring regularly in American vaudeville troupes, and a new fad was born.

Within a couple of decades, Hawaiian guitarists were mainstays on the American record charts. Sol Hoopii's Trio, represented here with "Farewell Blues," was the best known, from his arrival here in 1916 to his decision in 1939 to become an evangelist. Hoopii's brand of Hawaiian guitar is airier, more open, less eerie than its American descendant; it can also be more gimmicky, though in passages at the end of this instrumental he plays in what we know today as the "chicken-pickin'" style, and the roots of Leon McAuliffe and western swing are especially apparent in his work.

Blind Lemon Jefferson introduced slide guitar to blues in 1926, and Frank Hutchison introduced steel guitar to country about five months later. Whites and blacks got somewhat different sounds—country musicians were stiffer, more rigid—using the same techniques, so it's appropriate that they'd give the technique different names. The next step was to get the sound amplified. At first, country musicians elevated the strings on conventional Spanish guitars to create the illusion of amplification. Then, in the mid-twenties, the Dopera Brothers, Ed and Rudy, manufactured the all-metal National guitar, which became most popular with blacks, and in 1929, they manufactured the wood and metal Dobro, which became most popular with whites. (The term "Dobro" became so common it's now used generically.) Aluminum resonator discs inside the guitars created amplification without electricity.

Cliff Carlisle, who was noted for his novelties and double-entendre songs throughout the thirties, claimed that his music was "a cross between hillbilly and blues—even Hawaiian music has sort of blues to it." There certainly was consistent interaction between the races during this era, but Carlisle's "You'll Miss Me When I'm Gone," which reduces steel almost entirely to a gimmick, and his "Pan American Man," a Jimmie Rodgers train-song lift complete with yodels, are not nearly so strong as the three sides credited to Jimmy Tarlton. "Slow Wicked Blues" is built on a forbiddingly prickly steel line and sounds improvised on the spot; the lyrics, as well, are more blues than country. "Sweet Sarah Blues" is an effortless mating of Hawaiian and blues, while "Country Girl Valley" has the feel of a traditional country ballad.

The records of Jimmie Rodgers had the greatest influence on steel players; Carlisle even played on some of Rodgers' sides. But one of his most devoted acolytes, Jimmie Davis, went much deeper into black blues than Rodgers ever did. The three sides here were supposedly cut with the black guitarist Oscar Woods, but Davis denies having ever recorded with a black bluesman; he denies having even been influenced by one. That's because after Davis became a politician and a born-again Christian in the forties, he went out of his way to obscure his early career.

And no wonder! The born-again Davis piously denounced all music with even a suggestion of sex, while many of his own early sides were double-entendre songs of unbridled carnality. From 1929 to 1933, when he recorded for Bluebird, that's virtually *all* he sang, though his output tapered off after he switched to Decca. But these three songs from the Bluebird years provide a telling cross section of his concerns. "Down at the Old Country Church" interpolates "When the Saints Go Marchin' In" with Davis preaching along to a steel guitar, going up in falsetto like a black country preacher. "Red Nightgown Blues" addresses itself to such issues as male rape and staying hard all night, and is decidedly single-entendre. But "Sewing Machine Blues" manages to tie everything—blacks, whites, blues, sex—together in one verse. "Gonna telephone to heaven/To send me an angel down," cries Jimmie Davis, "If you ain't got an angel, St. Peter/Send me a high-steppin' brown." The guitarist on all three of these sides sounds more menacing than he does menaced, which was always a key difference between black and white bluesmen—maybe Davis had to disavow the guitarist because in twice getting elected governor of Louisiana on a segregationist platform, he would have had trouble explaining Woods away.

The final two cuts here feature steel guitarist James Clell Summey (later known as the country comedian Cousin Jody), with the Roy Acuff band, then called the Crazy Tennesseans, in March 1937. While they were released under Acuff's name, both songs are Summey's show all the way, and are important for two reasons beyond their musical virtues. First, Summey's style is much "whiter" than that of steel guitarists from barely a decade earlier; after a brief period of heated interaction, the two races had begun pulling apart. And second, Acuff was the Grand Ole Opry's first solo singing star, but at this stage in his burgeoning career, he's still sharing the spotlight with his steel player. That's a measure of just how prominent the steel had become.

Darby and Tarlton: *Darby and Tarlton* (Old Timey)

Jimmie Tarlton was not the first country steel player, as he has often claimed, but he may well have been the best. If any one musician could be said to have laid the groundwork for future generations of steel players from western swing right up to today's pedal steel, it would probably be Tarlton. He and his partner, Tom Darby, began recording in 1927, the same year that Jimmie Rodgers made his debut, and before the team broke up in 1933, Darby and Tarlton had cut more than eighty sides. As the fourteen collected here indicate, they weren't influenced directly by Rodgers nearly as much as they were influenced by some of the same music that influenced him. They didn't attain his popularity, but they did have a style of their own, which is more than can be said for most white bluesmen of the Rodgers era.

John James Rimbert Tarlton was born in 1892 in Chesterfield County, South Carolina, to a family of textile workers who moved frequently around Georgia and the Carolinas. He was thus exposed to a variety of indigenous musics, white and black, in addition to those he learned at home from his parents, both of whom sang and played, but in differing styles. He grew up playing several instruments before settling on guitar when he was nine. A year later, after observing local blacks playing bottleneck guitar, he adapted that style. In 1912, at the age of twenty, he left home for good, riding the rails to California and New York, supporting himself with odd jobs along the way. In 1923 he met Frank Ferera, a Portuguese who played with Hawaiian bands, in California. Ferera taught him to play guitar with a steel bar instead of the knife he'd been using, and so his style began taking on more Hawaiian overtones. (From the late twenties until his death in 1973, Tarlton used an automobile wrist pin instead of the steel bar.)

He began working with Tom Darby of Georgia in 1926. Tarlton was the guiding force in the partnership, picking the songs and defining the sound, but Darby also had something of his own to offer. Graham Wickham's liner notes here point out that his guitar style is as black-derived as Tarlton's, and just as personal: "The index finger maintains the dominant rhythm, rather than the more typical thumb-based style, which was the case with most of the older country accompanists. The rhythm was complicated and often obscured by Jimmie's guitar, although the ensemble sound would be extremely different had any other guitar player accompanied Jimmie."

Their second release, "Columbus Stockade Blues" b/w "Birmingham Jail," was their first hit, and proved in the end to be their biggest as well; the former was still being sung by country stars well into the sixties. Both recycled traditional themes and lines, and while neither is included here, the follow-up "Birmingham Jail #2" offers a taste of that sound.

Darby and Tarlton changed very little after cutting their earliest sides; unlike Rodgers, they eschewed additional instrumentation and stayed in a strictly country mold. Though he swore he had developed his style before ever hearing black *or* Hawaiian steel players, Tarlton is heavily indebted to blues, in form and feeling. Unlike a Frank Hutchison, he does more than hit the right notes; he also plays with the soul of a bluesman. "Ooze On Up to Me," which is basically a Tarlton solo performance, could have been cut by any number of Delta bluesmen, while "Heavy Hearted Blues" has a much more improvisational feel to it than most other white music of the era, including that of Rodgers. On "Lonesome in the Pines," Jimmie plays with special attention to detail and nuance, while Darby sings in a full, deep voice; on "Lonesome Railroad," their other variant on the traditional ballad, Tarlton is the lead singer and the overall feel is thus mellower and more melancholy. In general, Tarlton showed as much knack for blues phrasing as a singer as he did as a guitarist. His clear, confident tenor modulated up easily into what was regarded as a yodel, but actually sounds more like a black falsetto. And when Darby sang lead (which was more often than not), Jimmie's parts weren't harmony as much as they were background: stark, crude, pointed, and usually contrasting sharply with the lead lines. Darby and Tarlton had little in common vocally with the brother duets of this era.

Technically, Darby and Tarlton evolved well past the average early white bluesman. At the same time, they never were as polished, or as diversified, as Rodgers. They were the other side of his coin, blues that couldn't be commercially harnessed, and in listening to this album, it's easy to see why.

The Delmore Brothers: *The Delmore Brothers* (County).

Of all the brother acts, none were more productive or more influential than the Delmores. While best known for their close harmony singing and their gospel inflections, they were both also inventive guitarists, greatly influenced by the black blues and ragtime of their era. Their recording career spanned roughly twenty years—years that saw country music leaving the hills of the South to begin edging into the urban centers of the North. Their earliest material was very traditional-sounding, if not always traditional. The twelve sides collected here are among their earliest, recorded between 1933 and 1941 for RCA's Bluebird label.

They were born in Elkmont, Limestone County, Alabama—Alton in 1908 and Rabon in 1916, to tenant-farming parents. Their mother, Mary (Aunt Molly) Delmore, could read and write music. Alton learned guitar and singing from her, and studied further at a singing school run by her brother. The whole family sang regularly in church.

Alton then taught Rabon guitar; by the time Rabon was ten, they were teaming up for local dances and contests. Alton had learned on a tenor guitar, which he played like one would play a tenor banjo, and that's the technique he taught Rabon. Alton then took up the Spanish six-string guitar. When the two played together, they carried traces of everyone from Jimmie Rodgers to jazzman Eddie Lang to blues and ragtime guitarist Blind Boy Fuller. On most sides, Rabon strums a fat, propulsive rhythm which somehow remains melodic as well, while Alton spins out leads such as the curling lines that introduce "Nashville Blues," or the long, fluid runs that add sparks to the sentimental "Happy on the Mississippi Shore." On such songs as "Back to Birmingham" or "Honey I'm Ramblin' Away," they challenge each other for the lead, and the result is a prototype for the kind of boogie-woogie guitar duets they specialized in years later. They were equally flexible as vocalists, influenced by nineteenth century shape-note singing and by the call-and-response of rural gospel quartets. On most songs, Alton sang lead, in a high voice, and Rabon sang harmony even higher.

In 1930 the Delmores won the annual fiddling contest in Athens, Alabama. They barely beat a group that sang a novelty song, which prompted Alton to write "Brown's Ferry Blues" in case he and Rabon ever needed one themselves. While the song is tongue-in-cheek, it also sounds like the work of somebody trying to sing his way out of bad farmlands in the Depression years. Even then, Alton, who did most of the songwriting, was driven, dogged. While he wrote his share of stock, tragic schmaltz like "Til the Roses Bloom Again," he was more in his element with wanderlust songs like "Blue Railroad Train," "Honey I'm

Ramblin' Away" or "Fugitive's Lament." The reverse side of that, of course, is his longing for home—not just on "Happy on the Mississippi Shore," but also "Gonna Lay Down My Old Guitar," a song of impending death, or on "Back to Birmingham," in which the singer vows to leave Arkansas not just because his lover waits for him in Birmingham, but also because the jails in Alabama are more fun. ("Oh the jails in Birmingham sure are gay," is how he puts it.)

In 1932 the Delmores joined the Opry and quickly became one of the show's most popular acts. Though some of their vocal parts were too complex for anyone else to touch—check out the intricacies of "Nashville Blues"—they always kept an ear on the commercial trends of the day. On several songs here, they break into blue yodels. "Brown's Ferry Blues" and "Gonna Lay Down My Old Guitar" were big songs for the pair, and they also recorded behind such other Opry stars as Uncle Dave Macon and Arthur Smith.

But their own relationship with WSM and the Opry lasted only until 1938. "The people here, they treat me fine/They give me beer, they give me wine," Alton wrote sardonically in "Nashville Blues" (1936). Opry management considered him a temperamental man, plagued by moodiness and fits of deep depression, as well as a problem drinker. But later in his life Alton began an autobiography which was finally published (in unfinished form) in 1977 by the Country Music Foundation; *Truth Is Stranger Than Publicity* even-handedly described the feudalistic Opry's tight-fisted money policies, and the iron grip it kept on its members. In retrospect, it appears that Alton's unwillingness to conform probably had more to do with his departure than did any of his personal problems. In ensuing years the Delmores worked at radio stations all over the South and as far north as Indianapolis. Like the characters in Alton's own songs, they now lived much of the time on the rivers and the rails, always, it must have seemed, just one step ahead of the poverty and isolation they thought they'd left for good when they fled the rocky farmland of Limestone County.

Fiddlin' Arthur Smith and His Dixieliners: *Vol. II* (County).
From Roy Acuff on down, they'll all tell you that Arthur Smith was not only the best of the early Opry fiddlers, he was the most flamboyant, and this album bears them out. A master showman, Smith knew his traditional fiddle tunes and happily played them on request. But he took great liberties with them, and on his originals he really cut loose. Then he played with blinding speed—every fiddler who's ever figured out that the way to grab a crowd is to give 'em a double-time version of "Orange Blossom Special" owes his livelihood to Fiddlin' Arthur Smith. (If only a few of them had a fraction of his taste and finesse, though.)

Smith is the most important transitional figure between mountain fiddling and show biz, and the blues was at the heart of everything he played.

He was born in 1898 in Bold Springs, Humphreys County, central Tennessee; his father, who played fiddle, died when Arthur was five, by which time he himself was already learning the instrument. The local style involved complex fingering, which Arthur learned from Grady and Jim Stringer of neighboring Dickson County. Where most fiddlers played accents with their bow, Smith did it with his fingers, which allowed him to play faster and to add more accents; "Fiddler's Dream," from his first recording session in 1935, is full of accents and the song seems to climb higher and higher, while "Smith's Rag" (from 1940) is another jumping, darting tune.

At sixteen Smith married a local guitarist who worked with him on both the farm and the bandstand, but at that time he wasn't getting far with either calling. So they moved to Dickson County, where he took a job cutting crossties for the N.C. and St. L. Railroad (known as the "Dixie Line"). That turned out to be one of the best things that ever happened to his music career, because he eventually moved to maintenance, which required him to travel the entire line, thus exposing him to different fiddling styles. He also met Harry Stone, another Dixie Line employee, who moonlighted as an announcer for WSM in Nashville. Stone, who would later become general manager of the station, raved about Smith to station manager George D. Hay, and the fiddler got a job on the then-new radio station. According to notes by Charles Wolfe and Barry Poss in this album's accompanying booklet, Smith's first documented appearance on the Opry was in 1927, though he may have guested a few times prior, and whatever future he saw in music, he didn't quit his railroad job until the mid-thirties.

When Smith joined the Opry, his style was apparently still being shaped, though by the time he recorded the first of these Bluebird sides, he had found his groove. By then he was touring with the Delmore Brothers, who joined him in the studio as either the Arthur Smith Trio or as the Dixieliners; Smith had first applied that latter name to Sam and Kirk McGee, who began working with him on the Opry in 1932, but who unfortunately never recorded with him.

Smith called his style simply "country fiddling," but it became known as "rolling notes" or "long bowing." The most prominent characteristic was the fingering method; on "Indian Creek," a tune popular among Humphreys County fiddlers who reportedly first heard it on a brass-band record, he nearly leaves his guitarists (Alton and Rabon Delmore) in the dust. "Sugar Tree Stomp" moves just as fast, but he makes it seem easy; there's no sense of strain in what he plays. On

"Blackberry Blossom," another from his first session, he plays a showy, repetitive line that he keeps extending just when it sounds like he's run out of gas. This became his signature tune, and one that influenced bluegrass fiddlers in particular. Along with "Indian Creek," it's also the number on which he makes unanticipated octave leaps that more traditional fiddlers would have avoided. As he shows on "In the Pines," the novelty "Pigs at Home in a Pen" and even "There's More Pretty Girls Than One, Part 2," all tunes originating from traditional fiddle lines, he has complete mastery of the form; he'd rather be doing the other stuff, is all. But "House of David Blues," a jazz standard, reverses the effect, for it seems to have snatches of a half-dozen barely remembered traditional fiddle tunes worked into it.

Smith's other specialty was precise, piercing noting. It's heard most ominously on "Chitlin Cookin' Time in Cheatham County," which is based on "St. James Infirmary," and on "There's More Pretty Girls Than One, Part 2." On "Freight Train Moan," he plays swirling, swooning lines in a lower register, then jumps upward. And though he's noted for his clean sound, Smith could also play as dirty as they come. His lines on "Peacock Rag" are so screechy they verge on dissonance, and for most of the song it sounds like two fiddlers battling. "The Girl I Love Don't Pay Me No Mind" is one of his more underrated performances, with a bluesy fiddle that shrieks, moans, and cries. Even as a singer, at which he was just competent though his vocal numbers were his biggest sellers, he blows the Delmores away on this one.

After the thirties, Smith left the Opry and played all over the country, putting his technique to work for radically different types of bands. He also enjoyed a songwriting career that lasted into the sixties. But he never again took control like he does here; at his best, Fiddlin' Arthur Smith sounded like some kind of slightly mad genius, and he was given as much berth as he wanted.

Roy Acuff: *Greatest Hits* (Columbia)
You'd never guess it from these early sides, but Roy Acuff (who in 1962 became the first artist elected to the Hall of Fame while still alive) isn't known as a recording star so much as he's known for his role in the Grand Ole Opry. In February 1938, after weeks of trying, the east Tennessee fiddler and singer finally got a shot on the Opry—as a substitute for Arthur Smith, who was on tour that weekend. During his performance of "Great Speckled Bird," his once and always showstopper, Acuff was so nervous he forgot the lyrics. But he was invited back, and if we are to swallow without question the legend he has since built, then the whole focus of the Opry changed that weekend from string bands to singers—solely on the strength of this one man's appeal.

Facts suggest otherwise. The Opry did begin as a showcase for fiddle bands, and there were few singers. But the trend was established before Acuff by the Vagabonds (a smooth singing group), the Delmore Brothers, and Pee Wee King (who fronted a big western band), among others. Acuff simply made it official; within a few years, his single-minded hustling and his live show made him the symbol of the Opry, the "King Of Country Music." As string bands died of attrition, the Opry became a vehicle for solo vocalists and performers; by 1943, Acuff had stopped doing his own fiddling onstage so he could concentrate on singing and showmanship.

As a recording artist, he wasn't important for long, mainly because too many of his songs were so similar melodically. Within a decade of his Opry debut, his records had lost their luster entirely; though he continued to record (and still does), his attitude seemed to be that he made his living on the Opry and on the road, and that the records just didn't matter except as souvenirs of his show. Yet his earliest records helped usher in a new era of country music. Their dominant traits were the use of dobro and the unabashed sincerity in Acuff's voice; when he sang a sad song, he wept openly, and as far as the country audience was concerned, you can't get more sincere than that.

Acuff has described his voice as "a country tenor without training, performing in the Old Harp singing style." His father was a preacher, first at the Maynardsville Missionary Baptist Church and later at the Fountain City Missionary Baptist Church. (He then went into law, where his preacher's skills undoubtedly came in handy before a jury; he eventually became a judge.) Roy also learned from his sister, who had taken opera lessons and who taught him to sing from the pit of his stomach.

But he never intended to be a singer. He mostly played baseball, though he also worked in the L & N yards, where he learned to imitate train whistles, a skill he would employ onstage in the future. He was good enough as a baseball player to get invited to the Yankees rookie instructional camp, but a series of sunstrokes (the final, and decisive, one suffered off the field, ironically) dashed those hopes. He took up fiddle seriously in 1930, a year spent mostly in bed recuperating.

Though Acuff was a pretty fair country fiddler, and though Dynamite Hatcher played a fine train-whistle harmonica, the instrumental star of his first band was Clell Summey on dobro, who provides the prickly notes that distinguish Acuff favorites like "Mule Skinner Blues" and "Fire Ball Mail." Rarely does Acuff let fiddle dominate, though "Wreck on the Highway" is an exception.

"Great Speckled Bird," the song that won Acuff his Opry spot, is one of the great mysteries in American music. The title is from the

Bible, Jeremiah 12:9: "Mine heritage is unto me as a speckled bird, the birds round about are against her; come ye, assemble all beasts of the field, come to devour." Acuff claims the song was common around east Tennessee, and that he bought the lyrics off a local gospel singer before adding four verses of his own. It won him his first recording contract (in 1936), and though the melody is common in traditional music, nobody has ever figured out just what the bird is, or what it represents. The controversy adds to the song's power and majesty.

Religious songs were crucial to Acuff's popularity. The upward soar of his voice on "Were You There When They Crucified My Lord" is a truly scarifying example of backwoods-church singing; he insisted his band members not learn close harmonies, because that would undermine the authenticity of his leads. Aside from church, he sang about little except mother and trains. His best-known train songs are "Night Train to Memphis" and "Wabash Cannonball." But neither of them can match "Fire Ball Mail" for conveying the country boy's excitement at the powerful new machinery moving through his turf: "Here she comes/Look at her roll/There she goes/Eatin' that coal/Watch her fly/Huggin' the rail/Let her by/The Fire Ball Mail," he sings with as much jubilation as he normally gave to spirituals.

Acuff's limited repertoire proved to be his saving grace. He was basically a musical conservative, and while new forms were gaining prominence in the thirties, he upheld the old-fashioned mountain values with real fervor. As war loomed against the Nazis, he came to be associated with Americanism itself. Though his band personnel began changing almost as soon as he made the Opry—most significantly, Beecher Kirby took over on dobro and high harmony—his sound didn't. As of 1983, he still played the Opry every weekend; Roy Acuff seized his moment, and he's not about to let go of it now.

The Louvin Brothers: *Tragic Songs of Life* (Rounder Special Series)

With Ira's pure Appalachian tenor leading the way, there was no finer brother duet than the Louvin Brothers, but they were born too late. By the time they released this album, their crowning achievement, in 1956, brother duets were out of style.

Brother harmony groups—Bill and Charlie Monroe, Bill and Earl Bolick as the Blue Sky Boys, Alton and Rabon Delmore—flourished from the thirties well into the forties, ultimately giving rise to bluegrass. It was the music Charlie and Ira Louvin grew up with. They were born to the Loudermilk family, Ira in 1924 and Charlie in 1927, in Rainesville, Alabama, and raised on a farm near Henegar. In 1943 they went to Chattanooga, Tennessee, where they won a talent contest that led to a daily radio show. World War II temporarily halted their partnership.

After postwar stops in several towns, they wound up in Memphis, where they did three radio shows daily and took what live dates they could get. In 1951–52, thanks to publisher Fred Rose, they recorded for Decca and then MGM.

On radio they were primarily a gospel group, brimming with wrath, jubilation, and salvation; Ira played mandolin and Charlie played guitar. For the MGM sessions, other musicians were added to augment the sound without altering it notably. Their sharp, high harmonies remained the focal point—especially Ira's astonishingly high tenor, which was full of pain and longing, and which he pinched up so that there was always tension between what he was saying and what he refused, or was unable, to say.

Though they recorded secular songs for MGM, the Louvins stood foursquare for the values of traditional and religious country music: mother and family, fear of God, hard work, reverence for roots, and a rural life that could be both simple and unpredictable. The MGM sides (since reissued on another Rounder album) included several atomic-bomb songs, which enjoyed a brief vogue in blues as well as country. Like most of their peers, the Louvins saw war in both mass (unquestioningly patriotic) and personal (tragic) terms, and as the supreme test of our devotion to God. The bomb was perceived as having a power almost as awesome as God's, a quandary they resolved by affirming that He meant for us to have it and use it in His name.

Soon after their last MGM session, they signed with Capitol. Their career was disrupted again when Charlie went to fight in Korea for thirteen months, but by 1955 they had finally landed on the Opry and launched a string of hits. The first was the incandescent "When I Stop Dreaming" (not included on this album).

Though they recorded both secular and sacred material for Capitol, the latter was probably still dearer to their hearts. The gospel intensity never left their music, and it's particularly conspicuous on this album, a collection of mostly traditional songs often associated with earlier brother duet teams.

Ominous winds blow and strange men walk through these sentimental, moralistic songs of mishap, loss, and reconciliation. The first notes of each song establish a mood of dread and resignation that grows larger as the stories unfold. The only possible exceptions are "Kentucky" (the spiritual home of brother duets) and "Alabam," which both celebrate the natural beauties while asserting a sense of belonging—but the suggestion of death somehow hangs over these, too.

The rest go right to the uneasy heart of American folk music. Ira's lead is as chilling as the harmonies of "Let Her Go, God Bless Her," the tone of which is set by the traditional verse, "Sometimes I live in the country/Sometimes I live in town/But sometimes I take a good notion/ To jump in the river and drown." In "A Tiny Broken Heart," a seven-year-old boy wails, knowing all the while adults won't understand, as the seven-year-old neighbor girl he loves is forced to move. It's unsettling if only because the child is so sure of himself you almost believe him. In "Katie Dear," a man kills himself because his lover's parents won't let them marry; the girl then kills her parents and herself with the same dagger. In "My Brother's Will," a dying man asks his brother to marry the girl friend he's leaving behind. But the brother had once loved the same girl, and been rejected so badly he'd vowed to remain single. He wrestles with his conscience, goes to see the girl, and finds she's been fickle and married another man anyhow. Will his brother understand? In "Mary of the Wild Moor," a woman spurned by her father comes to his house with her child and he continues to refuse her entry. That night, she freezes to death outside: The father then goes insane with grief and guilt, and the motherless child dies also. Betrayal runs through most of these songs like it was the only thing certain besides death. They're all spine-tingling performances, but none more so than "In the Pines." Here, they glide into high-harmony cries that approximate the sound of the cold wind blowing through the forest, conveying the desolation much more effectively than words could have.

Needless to say, this was all quite anachronistic in an era of "The Wild Side of Life" and "It Wasn't God Who Made Honky Tonk Angels," of "Blue Suede Shoes" and "Whole Lotta Shakin' Goin' On." Still, the Louvins and a large segment of the country audience wouldn't acknowledge that anything had changed; there were many successful singles and albums (sacred and secular) following this one before the brothers split for the last time in 1963. Charlie salvaged the more successful solo career of the two; Ira's fatal auto accident in 1965 ended rumors that they might yet reunite. No matter, for the traditions they had upheld were now completely in the past; the Louvins had proven themselves an impossible act to follow.

Supplementary Albums

Roy Acuff: *Country & Western Classics* (Time-Life). Acuff milked the same two or three melodies far too often to ever sustain a productive recording career, and after he left the Columbia labels (including Vocalion and Okeh as well as the parent company) for Capitol and then Hickory (and finally Elektra in the eighties), he churned out useless albums at an alarming rate. In other words, he didn't artistically warrant a three-record boxed retrospective like this one; at the same time, he's a significant enough historical figure to warrant more than a single album like Columbia's hits collection. This box attempts to reconcile those contradictions by emphasizing the earlier, superior sides, including many not previously collected by Columbia. One of those is the scandalous "When Lulu's Gone," which should capsize his Mr. Clean image once and for all, and, as usual, Time-Life throws in a few cuts never issued before in any form.

Roy Acuff: *On Radio* (Golden Country). These are 1953 transcriptions of songs like "Tramp on the Street," "Turn Your Radio On," and "What Would You Give in Exchange for Your Soul." Acuff is in supple voice, the band is loose but not sloppy, and the oldest material gives us a look at Acuff's roots that was previously hard to come by. As is this semi-bootleg album from a label that won't even give out its address.

Anthology of Country Music: Early Country Harmony, 1930's (ACM). Because the sound quality on Old Homestead (which distributes this) albums is always much worse than it needs to be, this one almost fails to serve its purpose of documenting the era of brother duets and other harmony teams. It could do quite nicely, thank you, without such lightweight examples as the Girls of the Golden West, but it's hard to knock the Delmore Brothers, the Blue Sky Boys, the Monroe Brothers, and Karl and Harty. And it's a real treat to hear Wade Mainer and the Sons of the Mountaineers on "Home in the Sky," the spiritual on which "Home on the Range" is based.

Anthology of Country Music, Vol. 2: Early Country Harmony, 1940's (ACM). The two cuts by the Bailes Brothers are particularly doughty, and the two by Johnny and Jack are unusually intense. The duet (from live radio) by Hank Williams and Little Jimmy Dickens is a major disappointment. Though cursed with the usual atrocious Old Homestead sound quality, this accurately reflects the ways Nashville was cleaning up country harmony at a time when solo stars were also emerging on a bigger scale.

The Armstrong Twins: *Hillbilly Mandolin* (Old Timey). Floyd and Lloyd Armstrong were based in Arkansas and recorded in the mid-forties, which might explain why they're so obscure: The golden era of brother duets was already passed. Indeed, they don't have a lot in common with the more traditional teams. The Armstrongs are influenced significantly by western swing and hillbilly boogie, and their songs are upbeat, not the dolorous material most brother teams recorded. This is a strange, scintillating variation on an old form.

Clarence Ashley: *Old Time Music at Clarence Ashley's* (Folkways). Family and friends—including Doc Watson, most significantly—jam at the Ashley farm on traditional and original songs associated with the Original Carolina Tar Heels. The songs and styles range from Eva Ashley Moore's chilling "The Haunted Woods" to such quintet numbers as "Sally Ann" and "Honey Babe Blues."

Clarence Ashley: *Old Time Music at Clarence Ashley's, Part 2* (Folkways). Along with its predecessor, this is one of the more enlightening and invigorating albums to come out of the folk revival. (Both LPs are from the early sixties.) The old-timey songs are presented as part of an ongoing tradition constantly renewing and revising itself, and are definitely not museum pieces.

Atomic Cafe (Rounder). This has some blues, rock, and gospel on it, but country musicians carry the day, so I'm including it anyhow. What we have here is an anthology of atomic-bomb songs, which enjoyed a brief vogue in the late forties and early fifties. But country stars contemporary at the time weren't nearly as attracted to the subject as were those of previous generations. The album works nearly every imaginable variation possible on the subject, from horror to joy to piety to sarcasm to boasting; it is not only an endlessly fascinating piece of Americana, but stands on its own on purely musical terms as well. It's downright infectious, if that's the word.

The Bailes Brothers: *Early Radio Favorites* (Old Homestead). Johnnie and Walter Bailes, who both sang and played guitar, joined the Opry at Roy Acuff's request. They came along just a few years after him and were very much influenced by him, especially later, when they added Shot Jackson on steel. They specialized in stern religious warnings, their best-known song being "Dust on the Bible." They sang with chilling fervor, and it's puzzling that so many revisionist Opry histories tend to downplay their importance.

Banjo Pickin' Girl—Women in Early Country Music, Vol. I (Rounder). This is a hard concept to make work, because it's no myth that there was little place for women in early country music, and the ones that did make it (mostly singing cowgirls) tended to be pretty innocuous. But this does make available two cuts each from Louisiana Lou, arguably the first woman to make it as a professional country singer; Moonshine Kate, who sometimes threatens to live up to her name; and the Blue Ridge Mountain Singers, a Carter Family ripoff that passes muster despite its lack of originality.

The Blue Sky Boys: *Bluegrass Mountain Music* (RCA Camden). The bluegrass reference is primarily a marketing device, but their RCA years were this team's most productive, and so this budget-line twofer is worth searching for even though it won't be easy to find. The performances are full of spirit, and the material offers a virtual primer of traditional music of the thirties and forties.

The Blue Sky Boys: *Presenting the Blue Sky Boys* (JEMF). Bill (mandolin) and Earl (guitar) Bolick hailed from North Carolina, and were one of the most popular brother duets of their time. Vocally, they resembled the Delmores as much as anyone, for they had similar close harmonies and, despite their traditional orientation, they did develop a willingness to delve into popular forms as well. Seemingly always at loggerheads with the record industry, they retired and then changed their minds several times. In 1951 it looked like they would make retirement stick, but by the mid-sixties they were appearing before urban folk audiences. This is a reissue of the smooth and satisfying album they cut at that time (1965) for Capitol.

The Blue Sky Boys: *The Sunny Side of Life* (Rounder). An appropriate title for a batch of songs by the brother team that sounded sweet even with the saddest material. Still, this is the best in-print album capturing their 1936–47 Bluebird career, when they were at their commercial peak.

Jerry Byrd: *Master of Touch and Tone* (Mid-Land). Byrd was one of the giants of postwar electric steel, his strengths obvious from the album title alone. As the pedal steel came in, though, he immersed himself deeper in Hawaiian steel styles. Eventually he put his money where his mouth was, giving up Nashville and the country scene to move to Hawaii, where he found both a sensibility and a group of sidemen that he fit in with.

Cliff Carlisle: *Cliff Carlisle, Volume 1* (Old Timey). Carlisle may not be the most original of the Jimmie Rodgers acolytes, but he's certainly the most faithful, at least as a singer. His guitar style is as Hawaiian as it is blues, however, making this a fine example of the kind of currents joining together in the country music of the thirties.

Cliff Carlisle: *Cliff Carlisle, Volume 2* (Old Timey). Musically, no difference to speak of—but there're fewer hobo, railroad, and double entendre songs on this album; in their place is some sacred material that, somehow, doesn't ring quite as true.

The Carter Family: *From 1936 Radio Transcripts* (Old Homestead). Many of these songs were recorded elsewhere by the Carters, but not in versions this crisp and mature. Mostly for completists, who will be willing to suffer through the bad sound.

The Carter Family: *The Original Carter Family in Texas* (Old Homestead). The same applies here, though Carter's solo on "Out on Old Saint Sabbath" is particularly haunting. Old Homestead wound up issuing a slew of these, but be careful or you'll get sick of them fast.

The Carter Family: *In Texas, Vol. 6* (Old Homestead). This mixes radio transcripts with some of the long-unavailable Decca studio sides to create perhaps the most desirable album of this whole series. With the usual muddy sound, however.

The Coon Creek Girls: *Early Radio Favorites* (Old Homestead). Perhaps the first all-female group of instrumentalists and singers, the Coon Creek Girls were a string band with real mountain roots, but they had an ear for pop as well. These radio transcriptions from the late thirties offer ample evidence of both, and give a good idea of the range of material still holding forth commercially at that time.

Wilma Lee and Stoney Cooper: *Early Recordings* (County). Unless you count the Rich-R-Tone sides, which are *too* raw for most ears, these are probably the Coopers' finest efforts. They were cut for Columbia between 1949 and 1953. Yet the duo didn't achieve much popularity until they'd joined the Opry in 1957 and switched to Hickory Records. In an era of honky-tonking, the Coopers were a throwback to rigid mountain traditions, including stern religious training; they'd first met while singing together in a gospel group, the Leary Family. After they married in 1939 and split to form their own troup (The Clinch Mountain Clan), they recorded secular as well as sacred material, but Wilma's big, passionate voice was always most at home with songs like this album's "Thirty Pieces of Silver."

Wilma Lee Cooper: *Wilma Lee Cooper* (Rounder). Though Wilma Lee's voice has lost power with age, this set of pre-Nashville mountain music has more life in it than a month's worth of Music City releases on major labels. You have to hand it to a woman who records "Sinful to Flirt" and "Cowards over Pearl Harbor" in 1982.

The Delmore Brothers: *The Delmore Brothers* (Old Time Classics). After they left Bluebird, Alton and Rabon Delmore finished out the thirties recording for Decca. The style and orientation changed little. Their Decca sides have always been the least-known, and though anything on this evasive reissue label is hard to find, these twelve songs are worth whatever effort it takes.

Dirt Band and Various Artists: *Will the Circle Be Unbroken* (Liberty). Through much of the seventies, this L.A. group carried the banner for countryish folk-rock, acoustic branch. Their few attempts at country were usually painful—either entirely too stiff or entirely too cutesy. But in 1972, when they were still known as the Nitty Gritty Dirt Band, they put out this double album of bluegrass and string-band music with help from Mother Maybelle Carter, Earl Scruggs, Doc Watson, Roy Acuff, Merle Travis, and Jimmy Martin, and though it had its moments of boredom and in places comes on like an instant museum piece, more often the country stars set the tone, which makes a huge difference. So what if nearly all these songs are overly familiar, and if nearly all of them were done better the first time around? It's still a good introduction to the music of this time and place, and many of the originals are no longer available.

The Dixon Brothers: *Beyond Black Smoke* (Country Turtle). Carolina millhands Howard and Dorsey Dixon were disciples of slide guitarist Jimmy Tarlton. Which means that their thirties blues didn't come first-hand from blacks, but was passed along by him. So why do they sing and pick with a darkness and economy that most white bluesmen never approached? Added bonus: The original version of "I Didn't Hear Anybody Pray."

Dutch Cove Old Time String Band: *Sycamore Tea* (June Appal). This label has shown a real knack in the seventies and eighties for finding string bands that play traditional music with overdrive. Here's another of the best—a hint of swing, but nothing gimmicky or contrived, just the real thing, serene and seductive.

Woody Guthrie: *A Legendary Performer* (RCA). This was originally issued as *Dust Bowl Ballads,* and for my money is the best album ever assembled on Guthrie. It contains both parts of "Tom Joad," the song Woody wrote after seeing the *Grapes of Wrath* movie, and also the outlaw ballad "Pretty Boy Floyd." The Okie flight from the Depression-era dust bowl is described in songs like "The Great Dust Storm," "Talkin' Dust Bowl Blues," "Dust Can't Kill Me," "Dust Pneumonia Blues," "Dust Bowl Refugee," "Dust Bowl Blues," and "Dusty Old Dust." What happened to the refugees is chronicled in songs like "Do Re Mi." Some histories have asserted that Guthrie was part of a whole urban country movement when these sides were cut in 1940, but the other singers cited with him invariably turn out to be folkies with no true country roots. Guthrie had 'em, as you can hear on the eerie "I Ain't Got No Home in This World Anymore" (based on a traditional hymn) or on "Dust Pneumonia Blues" (which lifts the Jimmie Rodgers style almost intact). Like other country singers of the era, he wasn't above pinching the melody of a traditional song and putting his own lyrics to it, either.

Woody Guthrie: *Library of Congress Recordings* (Elektra). Cut by John Lomax in 1940, this three-record boxed set is probably the best introduction to Woody Guthrie, because it catches him performing traditional tunes as well as originals, and everything from gospel to western to murder ballads to Dust Bowl and topical songs. Between songs, Guthrie reminisces in his thick Okie accent about life from his rearing in Oklahoma to his later union activities. Too bad there's not more music, but Guthrie's storytelling powers offer sufficient compensation.

Woody Guthrie: *Dust Bowl Ballads* (Folkways). *Not* the same songs as on the RCA album that once bore the same title, though they are on the same subject. These were recorded perhaps a decade after the RCA sides, and are somewhat less bitter, a little more wry.

Woody Guthrie: *This Land Is Your Land* (Folkways). With versions of "Pastures of Plenty," the title song, "The Grand Coulee Dam," and "Goin' Down the Road," among others (but too few others, only nine songs in all), this could almost stand as a "greatest hits" sampler by the hobo, labor organizer, propagandist, and wandering minstrel who helped bring country to the city. Recorded in 1947, these songs grew out of a trip to Oregon, along the Columbia River, at the invitation of the Department of the Interior. Guthrie wrote and recorded new songs —most with just his own acoustic guitar, but a few with other people and instruments—most of his adult life, so there's plenty more out there to investigate in the way of labor songs, children's songs, political songs, cowboy songs, and folk and traditional songs. These albums barely scratch the surface of his prodigious and inspiring output.

Roy Hall and His Blue Ridge Entertainers: *Roy Hall and His Blue Ridge Entertainers* (County). These 1939–41 recordings (including the hit "Don't Let Your Sweet Love Die") are significant both for the influence they later had on bluegrass musicians and because they represent unfettered string-band music beginning to codify into a recognizable Nashville sound (if not Sound). Hall recorded "Orange Blossom Special" a full seven months before the Rouse Brothers (it was never released due to a conflict on publishing) and his version of "Wabash Cannonball" stands up well next to Acuff's, as it has a notably different feel. On his popular Roanoke, Virginia, radio show, Hall sang everything from the traditional "Lonesome Dove" to Johnny Bond's modern "I Wonder Where You Are Tonight."

The Home Folks: *Last Chance* (June Appal). This is one of the most curious of the modern string bands—modern in the sense that they're alive and well and recording today, that is, since they play an eclectic brand of mountain music that's been popular in southwest Virginia since before most of them were born. And though they are absolutely true to the original forms, they play with the clean drive and heel-clicking gusto of modernists. These traditional tunes have never before sounded so contemporary, and so right.

Aunt Molly Jackson: *Library of Congress Recordings* (Rounder). First arrested at age ten, married at fourteen, a mother of two at seventeen, and a widow at thirty-seven, Aunt Molly Jackson was a nurse, a midwife, and a union organizer to the coal miners of Kentucky. These songs on the miner's life are among the most incisive and bitter ever recorded. Sound quality, unfortunately, is atrocious, and given the number of songs she cut that aren't included here, there's too much talk and not enough music. Recorded by John Lomax in 1939.

Shot Jackson and Friends (Vetco). Veteran dobro master comes through with surprisingly engaging instrumental album that sounds very Hawaiian even though it's of recent origin. Sidemen all play guitars and steels (except Charlie Collins, who adds mandolin and fiddle), so it's harmonically interesting stuff.

Snuffy Jenkins and Pappy Sherrill: *Crazy Water Barn Dance* (Rounder). Jenkins was the architect of the three-finger North Carolina banjo style that inspired Earl Scruggs to invent bluegrass banjo, though Snuffy's own style is much less brittle. Sherrill plays a shuffling "wrist" fiddle (meaning he doesn't move his arm while bowing). They've been together since 1939—this album is named after their old radio show—and play a jazz-based brand of southeastern mountain music that developed pretty much parallel to Bob Wills and western swing though it has few musical similarities. For this seventies set, the team is joined by their usual sidemen (Greasy Medlin on guitar and quasi-blackface vocals, Dick Harmon on guitar, and Buddy Harmon on bass) for everything from traditional fiddle breakdowns to blues to country standards to pop tunes to novelties. They swing with ease, and the whole album is an unmitigated delight.

Grandpa Jones: *16 Greatest Hits* (King/Gusto). Jones is a banjo disciple of Uncle Dave Macon, though he added more modern influences and techniques (including tuning his ax a tone higher to get a brighter sound). A showman and an Opry institution in the late thirties and early forties, he was a struggling young musician in Cincinnati, where he hooked up with King Records. These aren't really his "greatest hits," because he had few hits. But they are a cross section of tunes closely identified with him, and are essential for fans of old-time country in transition.

Grandpa Jones: *The Other Side of Grandpa Jones* (King/Gusto). He's best known as a humorist, so the idea behind this album was to gather tragic country ballads he'd recorded over the years. His exuberant, frailing banjo style might not seem appropriate, but Jones is rooted in traditional music as much as he is in show biz, and the album is a qualified success.

Grandpa Jones: *Old Time Country Music Collection* (CMH). On this recent album of Grandpa's favorite songs by other people, certain familiar names crop up often—Uncle Dave Macon, Bradley Kincaid, the Delmore Brothers. But one of these songs goes back to the early nineteenth century, and others are from the Civil War to the turn of a century. Taken as a whole, they present a broader picture of country music than you might expect from an old-time banjo player. A good idea, done well.

Karl and Harty: *Karl and Harty With the Cumberland Ridge Runners* (Old Homestead). Karl Davis (mandolin) and Hartford Taylor (guitar) were an influential duet in their day (the thirties), but have been largely overlooked by history. Best known for their version of "I'm Here to Get My Baby Out of Jail," the Kentucky team was unusually smooth for this type of music, which probably explains both their initial popularity and their later obscurity.

The Louvin Brothers: *The Louvin Brothers Sing the Songs of the Delmores* (Golden Country). Question: With songs by Alton and Rabon Delmore and singing by Charlie and Ira Louvin, how could this go wrong? Answer: It can't, no way.

The Louvin Brothers: *The Louvin Brothers* (Rounder Special Series). Except for "The Get Acquainted Waltz," these are all sacred and/or atomic-bomb songs (from 1951) along the lines of "They've Got the Church Outnumbered," "The Great Atomic Power," and "Insured Beyond the Grave." The Louvins were so inventive, though, that you'll hear something new every time you listen. With a little more variety, this would be as haunting as *Tragic Songs of Life*.

The Louvin Brothers: *Songs That Tell a Story* (Rounder). These transcriptions from a short-lived 1952 radio show feature the bare-bones Louvin Brothers sound—guitar, mandolin, two stark backwoods voices, and a collection of religious songs like "Weapon of Prayer" and "Sinner, You'd Better Get Ready."

The Louvin Brothers: *The Family Who Prays* (Capitol). By Louvin standards, this is overproduced. But compared to other records coming out of Nashville at the same time (mid-fifties to early sixties), it is positively archaic. Though some instruments are added, the voices of Charlie and Ira still cut through effortlessly. All sacred songs, and all but one of them originals.

Lulu Belle and Scotty: *The Sweethearts of Country Music* (Starday/Gusto). Their smooth duets made them one of the most popular acts on the WLS National Barn Dance from 1933 through 1958. Though they sang a few traditional mountain ballads, Scotty Wiseman composed originals (including "Remember Me," revived by Willie Nelson, and "Have I Told You Lately That I Love You") in the same style. When they retired, Scotty went into education while Lulu Belle (Myrtle Cooper) went into the North Carolina state legislature. These are rerecordings made well past the team's prime, but since the early sides collected as *Have I Told You Lately That I Love You* (Old Homestead) has gone out of print, they must suffice.

J. E. Mainer's Mountaineers: *J. E. Mainer's Mountaineers, Volume 1* (Old Timey). This is string-band music as it sounded by the thirties—which is to say that this music was definitely made with a particular audience in mind. You can tell by the choice of material as well as the singing that Mainer was very conscious of radio as a tool for building a career, but he still relied largely on traditional music.

J. E. Mainer's Mountaineers: *J. E. Mainer's Mountaineers, Volume 2* (Old Timey). More transitional string-band music from Mainer and cohorts. Still not as sophisticated, or as polished, as what you might hear on the Opry at that time, but clearly a step in that direction when compared to earlier Carolina bands with similar lineups.

J. E. Mainer and His Mountaineers: *A Variety Album* (King/Gusto). This is thirties commercial string-band music, walking a fine line between folk expression and product, believing in the new material as strongly as in the traditional. And dabbling in a little of everything—novelty and sacred songs as well as commercial country and traditional songs. Though recorded two decades after his peak, the format is the same Mainer employed early in his career.

Wade Mainer and the Sons of the Mountaineers: *Wade Mainer and the Sons of the Mountaineers* (County). Wade is one half of the brother team that cut the perennial "Maple on the Hill." Away from J.E., he became a transitional figure between old-time string bands and bluegrass.

Wade Mainer: *Sacred Songs of Mother and Home—A Tribute to Wade Mainer* (Old Homestead). Today, J. E. Mainer seems to be better known than his brother Wade. But between 1935–41, when these sides were cut for Bluebird, banjo-playing Wade forged a winning combination of traditional sounds with commercial polish. This offers mostly duets with guitarist Zeke Morris, though on three sides J.E. and Daddy John Love sit in to make it a quartet.

Wade Mainer and Mainer's Mountaineers: *Wade Mainer and Mainer's Mountaineers: Sacred Songs Mountain Style* (Old Homestead). The band is augmented by Julia Mainer, a real backwoods shouter, and the sound is raw. Trivia buffs: "Beyond This Veil of Tears" comes from a poem by Ike Eisenhower.

Wade Mainer: *Wade Mainer* (County). Clyde Moody's guitar and harmonies contribute greatly toward the Mainer sound, which here in the late thirties and early forties is evolving ever closer toward bluegrass.

The McGee Brothers and Arthur Smith: *The McGee Brothers and Arthur Smith* (Folkways). This is from 1957, when all three Opry pioneers still had a fair share of fire in them. They stick exclusively to the old songs, and since none of these three were recorded as extensively as others from their era, this fills in some holes.

The McGee Brothers and Arthur Smith: *Milk 'Em in the Evening Blues* (Folkways). The McGees and Smith were a foot-stomping good combination, and it's too bad there aren't sides documenting their collaborations in the thirties. But these recordings from the folk revival years pass muster; if anything, Smith, in particular, grew more inventive with age.

The Monroe Brothers: *Feast Here Tonight* (RCA Bluebird). Charlie and Bill Monroe were one of the most original, and also one of the most popular, brother duets. They played faster and harder than most such groups, their bluegrass leanings already evident, but they sang much harsher, too. Bill is already turning the mandolin into a solo instrument here, and both his mandolin and voice threaten sometimes to overrun Charlie; even these earliest recordings make it clear which brother had the most ambition, though at this point Charlie is by far the more prolific writer. This double album features thirty-two gospel, traditional, standard, and original songs.

The New Lost City Ramblers: *The New Lost City Ramblers, Vol. 1* (Folkways). Mike Seeger, Tom Paley, and John Cohen went deeper into traditional music than any other folkie revivalist group. On this, their debut album (1958), they resurrected songs originally cut between 1925 and 1935, when mountain music was beginning to interact with the commercial record biz.

The New Lost City Ramblers: *The New Lost City Ramblers, Vol. II* (Folkways). Less meticulous than its predecessor, but no less faithful to the originators. Unlike most of their folkie counterparts, the Ramblers were not shy about injecting a little mountain anarchy into their music.

The New Lost City Ramblers: *The New Lost City Ramblers, Vol. V* (Folkways). By delving into the simplest and rawest traditional songs, the NLCRs inadvertently point to their biggest weakness, the relative slickness of their vocals (relative to the originals, that is, not to the other folkies). But this is perhaps the most relaxed of their Folkways albums, the one that seems to have been done for fun above all else.

The New Lost City Ramblers: *American Moonshine and Prohibition* (Folkways). Here's my kind of concept album. From "Al Smith for President" to "Goodbye Old Booze" to numerous odes to bootleggers, the Ramblers have done their homework in putting together this collection of broadsides from an era when country music dealt with *real* life and death issues.

The New Lost City Ramblers: *Songs From the Depression* (Folkways). Another topical album, this one on a more serious subject and thus with a more melancholy feel. As always, the Ramblers succeed as documentary *and* as music.

Molly O'Day and the Cumberland Mountain Folks: *A Sacred Collection* (Old Homestead). From the mid-forties until the rise of Kitty Wells, Molly was the most popular female singer in the Southeast; in 1952, though, she and her husband, Lynn Davis (who sings harmonies), gave up their careers to become ministers in the Church of God. She'd been singing gospel exclusively since 1950, and that music was the apt vehicle for her booming, exhortative voice. The proof is in this album, including the startling "Don't Sell Daddy Anymore Whiskey," which has a baby crying in the background all the way through.

Molly O'Day with Lynn Davis and the Cumberland Mountain Folks: *Radio Favorites* (Old Homestead). Molly was no slouch with the banjo, either, and she had a great ear for fresh material; she was the first to record Hank Williams songs, for example, and sang them with as much passion as he did. This album captures her on honky-tonkers and traditional (or traditional-sounding) songs as well as spirituals. Her lingering fascination with the cowgirl music of the previous generation (Patsy Montana's) is apparent, but her stern interpretations put her in a completely different league.

Red Clay Ramblers: *Meeting in the Air* (Flying Fish). This modern string band usually combines blues, jazz, ragtime, and country picking with shimmering vocal harmonies in a way that always knocks 'em dead on the folkie circuit but leaves hard-core country fans feeling left out. The trio's numerous albums are all highly regarded in their circles, but this tribute to the Carter Family is the only one to hold me. You, too, I bet.

Almeda Riddle: *Ballads and Hymns From the Ozarks* (Rounder). Her 1972 reworking of "Man of Constant Sorrow" into a cry for the California-bound dust bowl refugees of the thirties makes her sound like the female answer to Woody Guthrie. Not quite, because she hasn't got his boundless energy and imagination—but you have to admit, it's an intriguing idea.

Jimmie Rodgers: *The Best of the Legendary Jimmie Rodgers* (RCA). This leans way too heavily on his sentimental material to be very representative, or very enjoyable—particularly when the best blues and railroad songs are available elsewhere. Someone listening to this who thought it was really his greatest hits would undoubtedly wonder why all the fuss about this man. But if you're hooked by the other available albums, this offers a handful of new songs you'll also want to hear.

Jimmie Rodgers: *A Legendary Performer* (RCA). Again, much duplication with material on previously recommended albums. Notable mainly for "Whippin' That Old T.B." and "T.B. Blues," but neither is as cathartic as their titles might lead you to believe.

Jimmie Rodgers: *My Time Ain't Long* (RCA). With cuts like the title song, "That's Why I'm Blue," "Those Gambler's Blues," "Gambling Polka Dot Blues," and the two sketches with the Carter Family ("The Carter Family and Jimmie Rodgers in Texas" and "Jimmie Rodgers Visits the Carter Family"), this is an out-of-print album worth searching for.

Jimmie Rodgers: *The Short But Brilliant Life of Jimmie Rodgers* (RCA). Though a rather schizophrenic combination of hard blues and soft pop, this offers a substantial helping of prime Rodgers not available elsewhere. Like most of his albums, it's out of print.

Jimmie Rodgers: *Jimmie the Kid* (RCA). So is this one, which is one of the bluesiest albums RCA compiled on him, with four blue yodels in addition to material like "Desert Blues," "Memphis Yodel," and "Tuck Away My Lonesome Blues." Worth hunting for, and the remaining two

RCA compilations on Jimmie are unnecessary if you're able to find any of these.

Mike Seeger: *Old Time Country Music* (Folkways). Perhaps the most accomplished alumnus of the New Lost City Ramblers, Seeger turns in a focused set of revivalist traditional songs featuring winsome vocals and his own fiddle, banjo, dulcimer, guitar, harmonica, mandolin, and auto-harp.

Ricky Skaggs and Tony Rice: *Skaggs & Rice* (Sugar Hill). Right down to the cover art, this is a tribute to old-time brother duets. I really wasn't expecting miracles, not least of all because they aren't really brothers and that does make a difference in this form. But they do evoke the Monroes, Louvins, et al. faithfully enough, and there's no way they can be challenged on their picking. A little contrived, but only a little.

Jimmie Skinner: *Original Greatest Hits* (Power Pak/Gusto). Skinner was a forties and fifties bluesman with a dark, husky voice; he is proba-bly the most underrated of those who sought to follow in the footsteps of Jimmie Rodgers, and is today remembered mainly as a writer. These are sixties rerecordings of his best-known songs, but classics like "I Found My Girl in the Good Old USA" lose nothing through the update, and "Baby You Don't Know My Mind" is one of the all-time great rambling songs. I can't imagine why he wasn't more highly regarded as a per-former, but he remains one of my favorite cult artists.

Jimmie Skinner: *Jimmie Skinner Sings the Blues* (Vetco). Recorded for Skinner's own label long after he'd slipped from sight, this is predictably aged but unusually eloquent. Skinner was always less maudlin than most white country blues singers, and time didn't soften him. "Blues Are Out Early Tonight" shows how he learned to live with 'em.

Fiddlin' Arthur Smith: *Fiddlin' Arthur Smith, Vol. 1* (County). More Bluebird sides from the thirties, and ranking nearly as high as those on the other County LP. More emphasis on traditional fiddling with "Goin' to Town," "Bonaparte's Retreat," and "Lost Train Blues," but don't miss the dynamite twin fiddling of "K.C. Stomp" (with Tommy Magness from Bill Monroe's Blue Grass Boys) or the histrionic "I'm Bound to Ride."

Luke Smathers String Band: *Mountain Swing* (June Appal). The title describes it. This is mountain music as filtered through western swing—music with syncopation more than a strong beat per se, soloists playing strict lines that happen to sound improvised. New recordings by an old band.

Marion Sumner: *Road to Home* (June Appal). Here's why some folks object to the term "western swing," preferring instead something like "country jazz." Marion Sumner, who has played with Johnny and Jack, Roy Acuff, Kitty Wells, Don Gibson, and others, is clearly rooted in pre-swing fiddlers like Arthur Smith, but what he plays here is definitely jazz, though just as definitely *not* western swing. But that's what he calls his music, for lack of a better term. He has amazingly broad taste in songs, broader even than that of the original western swingers and an equally amazing storehouse of licks. He may well be America's best unknown fiddler.

The Tenneva Ramblers: *The Tenneva Ramblers* (Puritan). Talk about could-have-beens. This trio of Claude Grant on guitar, Jack Grant on mandolin, and Jack Pierce on fiddle is the group that performed briefly with Jimmie Rodgers as the Jimmie Rodgers Entertainers. And apparently they eased him out before those 1927 Bristol sessions because they felt *he* was the weak link in the group. Like Jimmie, they knew their traditional music, but they also understood they had to rework it into something more acceptable to the mainstream. Unfortunately, though they shared his orientation, they didn't have his inspiration.

Doc Watson: *The Essential Doc Watson* (Vanguard). Arthel "Doc" Watson is an American anomaly, a blind country songster more comparable in scope to Mississippi John Hurt or Henry Thomas than to other country performers. Though a singer and finger-picking guitarist most of his life, he didn't record until discovered by the urban folk crowd in the sixties. A down-home purist who also just happens to play pop and show tunes he learned off radio and records, he sounds as timeless as the North Carolina hills that nurtured him and his music. This presents him in a variety of settings, and offers a good sampling of his eclectic repertoire. It's a shame he was never recorded in his youth.

Doc Watson: *Doc Watson* (Vanguard). Mostly just Doc's voice and guitar, this music speaks to both the limits and the expansiveness of the American psyche. His best, especially late at night.

Doc and Merle Watson: *Ballads from Deep Gap* (Vanguard). Merle is Doc's son, and of the several albums they recorded together, this puts the most emphasis on mountain ballads. Doc plays with as much force and clarity as ever, and Merle fits himself in with grace and style. Their best together.

Doc Watson: *Doc Watson on Stage* (Vanguard). Always acutely aware of his image as a gen-u-wine American folk artiste, Doc liked to spoof it, but he played up to it, too. This was recorded at Cornell and at Town

Hall in Manhattan; the emphasis is on traditional ballads, but he also gets into some early commercial country music and even Hank Snow's "I've Been Everywhere."

The Watson Family: *The Watson Family* (Folkways). This 1963 album captures not just Doc, but his mother (who sings an ancient traditional ballad), his father-in-law (fiddler Gaither Carlton), his brother (Arnold, on banjo and French harp), his wife (Rosa Lee), and even a neighbor (who sings a local murder ballad concerning the death of her own husband). Though his own smooth, flat-picking style prevails, having the older family members along adds depth to what Doc does, demonstrates a convincing continuum, and confirms that no matter how impossible it is to classify him accurately, his music is of a piece with the entire country tradition.

SINGING COWBOYS

Singing cowboys helped put the western in country and western music, and they helped sanitize country music's image as well. Ironically, though, their music had little to do with real cowboys. Singing cowboys were pure Hollywood, an effective marketing device to help prop up a sagging western-movie industry.

True, real cowboys sang songs. Their music spread through the West in the 1880s, but cowboy singers weren't entertainers; they sang to provide themselves relief from the monotony of the range, to alleviate the agonies of hard work, and to help quiet the cattle. The words were usually taken from a poem in some small regional publication, and verses were added at will; some of the most popular songs (such as "Sam Bass") seem to have an endless number of verses. The melody was usually lifted from some Irish or English tune everybody already knew; there were said to be only three or four melodies in all of western music.

But real cowboys, and their music, were quickly absorbed into the domesticated West. In the years just before the Depression, there were a number of "cowboy balladeers" who helped place an image of the singing cowboy of the future into the public eye. Among them were Carl T. Sprague, Jules Verne Allen, "Haywire" Mac McClintock, the Cartwright Brothers, and Goebel Reeves. Even in their heyday, however, they were seen as little more than novelty acts, and few of them have any recordings in print today.

The old West had always been heavily romanticized back East and in the national press; the exploits, real or otherwise, of Buffalo Bill Cody and Wild Bill Hickock made good copy. The farther in the past the hard realities of the old West receded, the more fascinated Americans became with the myths. Hollywood westerns had helped spread those myths from the very first days of the film industry. Westerns thrived until the Depression, when the bottom fell out of the market. Something had to be done, and the Republic Studios decided (nobody has ever explained how) in 1934 that singing cowboys were the answer.

Gene Autry was groomed for stardom and dozens more followed in his footsteps, some successfully and many more not.

Autry began by singing songs from the Southeast before turning to Tin Pan Alley. Thus, the sound of what we think of as western music— the slow, happy songs with simple melodies and clippity-clop rhythms —was devised largely by men working in cubicles in New York City. These men knew nothing of the original cowboy songs, but they were pros who could turn out memorable melodies and hook lines, and it was better that way anyhow: Western movies were pure escapist fare, and bogging them down with reality would have been counterproductive. The most successful of the Tin Pan Alley writers was one Billy Hill, who wrote "Call of the Canyon" and "The Last Roundup" without setting foot off Broadway.

Musically, these songs had an airiness about them, especially rhythmically, that contrasted sharply with the pinched, constricted rural music of the Southeast; the singing was much smoother, too. But to the general public, all rural music was the same, and so the singing cowboys had a huge influence on the country music industry. Singing cowboys did much to popularize the guitar, and it was because of singing cowboys that country singers began wearing western costumes. Nashville stars went West to make movies of their own, in some cases to prop up fading careers and in others for the sheer ego gratification of seeing themselves on the big screen.

Singing cowboys did all this without really furthering any recording careers, too. Autry sold millions of records in his day, but few of them were with western songs. The Sons of the Pioneers were about the only western performers to build careers as recording artists (they appeared in many movies, too). Tex Ritter also eventually sold many records and won a spot in the Hall of Fame, but he did so by reversing the usual process—he started out a western star and then injected some country into his music.

But when you consider the impact of singing cowboys, record sales seem like a minor worry. Look at it this way: Think first of Gene Autry, and then think of the biggest country music stars of the same era. Who was more successful? Who made the most money, and reached the most people? Who is still remembered warmly today, is indeed still something of a national icon?

It's no contest, is it?

Cowboy Songs, Ballads and Cattle Calls from Texas (Library of Congress).

Few records sum up the differences between American myth and American reality more succinctly than this documentary album of authentic cowboy music. Except for "Colley's Run-I-O," a Maine lumberjack song included to illustrate how it permutated into "The Buffalo Skinners," a cowboy song, folklorist John A. Lomax made these recordings between 1941 and 1948. In many cases, the former cowboys explain first what they know about the origins of the song.

Lomax sought out the oldest former cowboys he could find and had them sing their songs just as they sang them when they were driving cattle across the range. These songs were usually sung around the chuck wagon at the end of a day's work and were never written down; verses thus vary wildly, as they always do when they belong to a strictly oral tradition.

Cowboys learned early on that the human voice had a soothing effect on cattle, which were skittish enough to stampede at any alien noise (gunfire, thunder, another animal). There were numerous nonverbal calls (some illustrated here) to get the herd moving, and also to stop it. While they were moving, the cowboy usually continued singing. "The Night Herding Song," sung here by Harry Stephens, has lyrics seemingly designed to reassure the cowboy as much as the cattle, but that didn't matter; it was only the sound that counted, and any words would do.

So the cowboys made up songs as they went. Or they sang old hymns and camp-meeting songs they'd known all their lives. Or they sang old Anglo-Scots ballads with lyrics changed to fit the occasion. "The Streets of Laredo," sung here by Johnny Prude, is one of our best-known cowboy songs. But it's an Americanized version of an eighteenth-century English or Irish ballad in which a soldier dies in a hospital of venereal disease—which is why he's buried by a drum and fife corps. (American cowboys sure weren't; the lyrics to this one just weren't changed enough.) The original song has nothing to do with drinking, gambling, or gunplay.

Because cowboy songs were primarily functional, the tune was always secondary to the words, and there was no incentive for a cowboy to sing "properly." As Stephens explains, "Well, some of them couldn't . . . couldn't hit any kind of a tune unless they'd pack it over their shoulder in a gunny sack, so they'd just have to say it." Nor was there usually any instrumental accompaniment; at most there might be a jew's harp or a creaky fiddle such as Jess Morris plays on his version of "Old Paint," but the guitar didn't reach the range until the very last days of the old West, and any instrument used had to be both durable and portable.

If Morris' story is to be believed—and his version of the song *is* the earliest anyone has traced—"Old Paint" derives from a black man who worked for his father. "The Zebra Dun," a story of a city slicker proving his mettle to cowboys by riding the meanest horse around, sung here by J. M. Waddell, also seems to have black origins. Yet there is nary a trace of black influence in any of the singing cowboys created by Hollywood. Though perhaps 30 percent of genuine old West cowboys were black or Mexican, white cowboys were notoriously racist, more so even than the American population at large. (Speaking of which, when did you see a black man in a western movie?)

None of these songs portray the West or the cowboy's life as being in any way idyllic. There is little or no romance; hard luck or death are simply accepted as part of the job. As Sloan Matthews sings on "The Cowboy's Life Is a Very Dreary Life," "You can talk about your farms and your Chinaman's charms / You talk about your silver and your gold / But the cowboy's life is a very dreary life / It's a-riding through the heat and the cold."

The contrast between these coarse, untrained voices and those of the Hollywood cowboys has led many to conclude that real western music had no impact at all on the music of the singing cowboys. I don't agree fully. When the genuine cowboy was domesticated, his ballads were simply lumped in with other rural folk musics. Oral traditions die hard, and though the impact might be slight, there is some.

There may be zero relationship between this music and that of Gene Autry or the Sons of the Pioneers, for example, but someone like Tex Ritter is a different story. He got a little of this pained, painful music into his own. Maybe only a little, but that's better than none at all.

Gene Autry: *Gene Autry's Country Music Hall of Fame Album* (Columbia).

Because of these songs and the thin, fanciful movies patched together around them, several generations of Americans find it difficult to remember there was ever a time when Gene Autry wasn't around, dispensing with the bad guys so he could strum his guitar and ride Champion off into the sunset.

Autry had a singing career before he became America's main man, but those early days now seem almost like a footnote. This album concentrates on later songs most closely identified with his movies—"Mexicali Rose," "South of the Border," "Home on the Range," "Red River Valley," "Back in the Saddle Again." All are innocuous, smooth, and pleasant, the melodies so simple they've become imprinted on our collective consciousness. But Gene Autry wasn't voted into the Hall of Fame in 1969 for that alone. He played a crucial role in the history of country music, for it was his image and songs that made the harder stuff more palatable to the mass audience. Along the way, he amassed a business empire that thrives today.

He was born Orvon Gene Autry in 1907 in Tioga, Texas, and raised on a ranch in Oklahoma. As a child, he studied saxophone; before he finished high school, he joined the Field Brothers Marvelous Medicine Show. In 1925 he took a job as relief telegrapher for the St. Louis and Frisco Railroad in Oklahoma. He passed some of the long night hours picking a guitar and singing songs he'd learned on cattle drives from his father's ranch, as well as pop and country hits of the day. His idol was Jimmie Rodgers.

According to legend, Will Rogers heard Autry singing one night at the telegraph office and urged him to head for New York. Autry went several times, recording a variety of songs for a variety of labels with little success. His style was a pale carbon of Rodgers'. But in 1931 he hooked up with Uncle Art Satherly, the artists and repertoire ("A & R") man for American Recording Co. Satherly wanted another Jimmie Rodgers for the ARC family of labels, and he connected when Autry sold a half million copies of "That Silver-Haired Daddy of Mine," an original that sounded enough like a southeastern ballad to fool plenty of people.

From there Autry was off to Chicago for the WLS Barn Dance; he'd already gained some radio experience on KVOO in Tulsa, and billed as "Oklahoma's Singing Cowboy," he built a following and a style of his own at WLS from 1931 to 1934. He sang in a soft, straightforward tenor that reeked of warmth and sincerity. Meanwhile, Republic Studios in Hollywood was planning to build a western star from scratch for the movies.

It's often said that Republic auditioned actors who could sing but couldn't ride and actors who could ride but couldn't sing before compromising on a singer and rider who couldn't act. Autry must chuckle every time he hears that story, because his first film appearance, a brief interlude in a 1934 Ken Maynard film called *In Old Sante Fe*, drew such wild response that he was quickly signed for a twelve-part serial called *The Phantom Empire*. In this one, he played himself—that is, he played an entertainer named Gene Autry who took care of the villains and then hoofed it on back to his Radio Ranch in time to warble for the folks out there in radioland.

When you've got a plot like that of *The Phantom Empire*, who needs a great actor? The story concerns the lost empire of Murania, which happened to be located under Gene's ranch. Queen Tika, the Muranian ruler, secretly lusted for the handsome radio star, but worried that he'd find the secret entrance to her civilization (it was through a gulley on the ranch). Meanwhile, some bad guys who'd discovered radium deposits on the ranch were also giving him trouble.

Well, a man's gotta start someplace. In fact, Gene followed the serial with his first feature, *Tumbling Tumbleweeds*, and his ingenuous, aw-shucks style was established. For the rest of the thirties, he turned out movies, all of them full of the obligatory old West horse chases, gunplay, and fistfights, but all of them incongruously set against contemporary or futuristic backdrops like that of *The Phantom Empire*.

It was because the songs for such movies needed to be more modern that Autry turned away from the Southeast and toward Tin Pan Alley for inspiration and material. His own vocal style didn't change much, but the arrangements did. All featured a simply strummed acoustic guitar and an accordion. A steel guitar, played by Autry's long-time collaborator Frank Marvin, was also used most of the time. But listen to the big vocal chorus of "South of the Border" or the violins *(not* fiddles) of "Someday You'll Want Me To," and you can see how much slicker this was than the country music of the day.

By 1940 urban America had discovered Autry, and he became associated with country music anyway. And country musicians, who smelled city-folk greenbacks in all this, not only didn't mind, but they became equally infatuated with the Autry image. Gene continued with his radio programs and movies while also mounting a stage show that featured horse tricks from Champion, comedians, Indian dancers, and rope tricks, as well as music. After taking his induction oath over nationwide radio, Autry spent World War II flying a supply plane in Burma and India. When he returned after the war, movie studios wouldn't meet his demands so he simply formed his own production company and began making his own movies (and soon TV shows). He tapped a lucrative new market in children's songs—"Rudolph the Red-Nosed Reindeer" alone has accounted for $9 million of his $25 million in record sales. He also invested well in real estate, radio and TV stations, hotels, ultimately even a baseball team (he owns the California Angels). By the early sixties, he was able to retire from show biz to concentrate on running those interests.

The moral of the story is that if you're a good guy, the same thing will happen to you. But watch out for those lost civilizations conniving under your backyard.

Gene Autry: *Back in the Saddle Again* (CBS Encore).

You're probably not going to believe this, but Gene Autry actually has musical roots. Before there were movie cowboys, before western songs had any impact, he was working in a distinct country music tradition. What he did in later years is connected to that tradition at least to the extent that his vocal style never changed. This album puts his evolution into perspective.

In his earliest incarnation, Autry was a Jimmie Rodgers devotee, plain and simple. He loved the Singing Brakeman so much that when Jimmie's TB became worse and it was obvious his days were numbered, why, Gene recorded a farewell tribute called "The Death of Jimmie Rodgers" just so he could be first on the market when the man actually did die. (It worked, too.) Though Autry recorded a few suggestive songs (like "Do Right Daddy Blues" in 1931), he zeroed in almost exclusively on the nostalgic, sentimental aspects of the Rodgers repertoire rather than on the rambler's and rounder's songs. The first four cuts here are from 1931–32, and are in that Rodgers vein; Autry could be a little bluesy, but he didn't perform blues.

On "Mississippi Valley Blues" and "Back to Old Smoky Mountain," Autry is joined by Jimmie Long, a singer, songwriter, and guitarist who had once been Gene's boss on the St. Louis and Frisco Railroad. Long had no show biz aspirations, and worked only briefly as a professional entertainer during the Depression, when he was laid off the railroad; as soon as his old job was available again, he went back to work. The high-harmony voice he provides on these two cuts owes more to southeastern conventions than to the kind of harmonies that became prevalent in western music.

Like "Why Don't You Come Back to Me" and "Moonlight and Skies," the other two songs from this phase, these songs are full of yearnings for things as they once had been. A primitive Hawaiian steel pines in the background as Autry reshapes words into blue yodels at the end of some lines; on "Moonlight and Skies," the steel itself sounds rather like a yodel.

It still does on "The Dying Cowgirl," which follows the melody of Rodgers' "Waiting for a Train." This is from the second phase of Autry's career. Once he began recording regularly and holding down spots on KVOO and then WLS, his material (much of which he still wrote himself) began changing. In essence, he grafted western themes onto what were still Rodgers-based country melodies. The prairies began replacing the mountains or the Delta in his lyrics, cattle and howling coyotes began replacing . . . people. The image of the solitary cowboy was already taking shape. On the pre-Hollywood western songs of 1933–35, guitars are still more prominent, though. On "Way Out West in Texas," they play complete runs, rather than simply providing rhythmic support. The steel is still there, and Autry is yodeling more than ever on songs like "Riding the Range" and "The Dying Cowgirl."

Autry was popular enough in the Midwest through his WLS Barn Dance spot that even if the movies had not beckoned, he would probably still have enjoyed a long and profitable career. But when the movies did beckon, he let them alter his music once again. Hollywood put the finishing touches on the Rodgers makeover. There were a few tasty flourishes like the blues guitar on "The End of the Trail," but on most of this music, violins are the most prominent instrument though even they are drowned out by yet more elaborate orchestrations. Vocal choirs back Autry, who is more and more a crooner.

Much as the music critic in me wants to, it's still hard to find fault with such quintessential Americana. The new songs from the late thirties and early forties may be romanticizations of Autry's earlier romanticizations of Rodgers, but they speak directly to our collective self-image of rugged individualism combined with good will and fair play. Autry's voice is still compressed just enough to evoke the image of a single man making his way across the vast plains. And the steel guitar has been integrated into the orchestral sound so skillfully that some western feel remains intact. Besides, these words and melodies have been pounded into our skulls since we were old enough to talk, and as some old galoot must have said at some time, "If you can't beat 'em, Hoss, join 'em."

Tex Ritter: *Blood on the Saddle* (Capitol).

Woodward Maurice "Tex" Ritter had a broader approach to western music than most of the singing cowboys because he was a scholar before he was a singer and a Broadway star before he was a movie star or a country music star. His work thus has some of the self-consciousness of the folk revivalist, but at the same time, he deals less with the romantic West of wide open spaces and the supposed freedom of the cowboy than with the more realistic West of death and disaster.

He was born in 1907 in Panola County, east Texas, and grew up preparing for a career in law and politics. But while a student at the University of Texas in Austin, he came under the influence of J. Frank Dobie, an expert on southwestern history; John Lomax, the folk ballads collector; and J. Oscar Fox, the glee club director and composer of

commercial cowboy songs. He attended Northwestern Law School for a
year, but went to New York as soon as the Depression hit; he was
determined to make his interest in southwestern folklore pay off for
him.

Oddly enough, when he arrived in 1930, New York was already
becoming something of a country music center, thanks mainly to the
growth of network radio. Ritter had a little radio behind him already,
and had also toured the South and Midwest with a musical troupe, so he
found work easily. In 1931 he got the featured role in *Green Grow the
Lilacs* (later transformed into *Oklahoma!*). In all, he appeared in six
stage productions. He also hosted the first western serial on radio,
WOR's "The Lone Star Rangers"; was the featured singer in the 1932
Madison Square Garden Rodeo; starred in another popular radio serial
called "Cowboy Tom's Roundup"; hosted the WHN Barn Dance radio
show; and even, billed as "The Singing Lecturer," spoke to college
students about western folklore. By the time he went to Hollywood in
1935 to pursue a movie career, he'd already picked up his nickname. In
the next nine years he would appear in eighty westerns.

Meanwhile, in 1933, he'd cut four sides for the American Recording Co. that threw training out the window and sought to match the
sound of authentic cowboy singers. In 1942, when he became the first
country or western singer to sign with Capitol, he began concentrating
more on a music career. By 1944 he had the top three records on the
country charts, and in 1953 he recorded the music for *High Noon*. His
Capitol sides were usually as country as they were western, and often
country-pop at that. But for this album, he attempted to get back the
feel of those primal ARC recordings.

Hence this recording of the title song, with its out-of-tune guitar
whanging away in an echo chamber and Tex braying the lyrics (about a
man who had his head bashed in by a bronco) like he was crumpled up
in pain, holding his wound. It's a gross and bizarre performance, over-
done to the point of burlesque, but then Tex always did consider it a
comedy song.

Most of the other songs are traditional western ballad variants that
didn't get recorded often, and they are grim: "Samuel Hall," with Ritter
taking the part of an unrepentant murderer being hung; the doom-
laden "Bury Me Not on the Lone Prairie;" "Little Joe the Wrangler,"
the story of a youth who leaves home because his stepmother beats him,
and who is then killed in a cattle stampede; "Billy the Kid," felled while
going after sheriff Pat Garrett, "who once was his friend"; "Streets of
Laredo," in which a dying cowboy blames his fate on cards and drinking; and "Sam Bass," the story of a free-spending horse racer who

becomes a bank robber and is shot down by the law when his sidekicks sell him out.

Instrumental backing is minimal, frequently just a bass and a guitar or two; Ritter delivers his tales in a charismatic *basso profundo,* and with enough flourishes and broad gestures to betray his previous experience on the stage.

His combination of folk tradition and professional acting polish was such a winner for Ritter that in 1964 he became one of the first living members inducted into the Hall of Fame. A few years later, he moved to Nashville and became one of the few western stars to achieve complete rapprochement with country music. He joined the Opry, ran (unsuccessfully) for the Senate, and played his role of elder statesman to the hilt. He even died with class: In 1974 he was killed by a heart attack in the Nashville police station while bailing out a friend.

Sons of the Pioneers: *Lucky U Ranch Radio Broadcasts, 1951–53* (JEMF/AFM)

The Sons of the Pioneers were the opposite of Gene Autry, who started out as a movie star who also sold records. They were recording (and radio) stars who also appeared in movies. The Sons triumphed through a combination of Bob Nolan's rich, evocative songwriting and creamy smooth harmonies that went *very* easy on the ear. And though twenty-one men have been members of the group since its inception in 1933, the Sons are still going strong today.

The original trio, which was inducted into the Hall of Fame in 1980, was formed in Los Angeles by a hustling young Ohio man named Leonard Slye. His original partners were Nolan (a Canadian) and Tim Spencer (who came from Missouri, and was the closest thing in the trio to a native Westerner). They called themselves the Pioneer Trio, but changed the name after two American Indian brothers, Hugh (in 1934) and Karl (in 1935) Farr, joined the group on fiddle and guitar respectively.

They were an immediate hit on L.A. radio, especially Slye. When Gene Autry left Republic in a 1937 contract dispute, Slye took his job. Republic changed Slye's name to Roy Rogers and began building a new superstar. After that, personnel changes became so routine that P-Nuts (as the group's fan club is called) can still argue all night as to which trio was the best. Rogers was always marginal as a singer; Nolan's quavering baritone was an acquired taste at best (though when he finally quit performing in the early fifties, RCA, then the group's label, insisted that he continue singing on the group's records, which he did most of the decade). Other singers who passed through inspire similar putdowns and praises.

I have trouble with this whole argument, because the Sons were a *sound* above all else, and to most ears, including mine, the various editions all sound pretty much the same. But this double album of transcriptions from their popular radio show provides a reasonable sampler of everything they did. The basic trio members are Lloyd Perryman, who played rhythm guitar and sang lead tenor on the "pretty" numbers; Ken Curtis, who sang lead in the trio passages and on "pop" songs like "Room Full of Roses;" and Tommy Doss, who sang baritone. The Farr Brothers were still there playing their jazzy instrumentals ("Blues in 'D,' " "Sweet Georgia Brown," "Honeysuckle Rose," "China Boy") that served as filler for the show. Frankie Messian provides accordion and Shug Baker bass. On the radio show, the Sons gave away a deed to an acre of land on the imaginary ranch every day, while also weaving together a wide variety of songs.

The best, though, came from Nolan's own pen. He wrote such western standards as "Cool Water" (not done here) and "Tumbling Tumbleweeds" (the group's theme, which served as the show's intro and outro and appears throughout the album). Nolan wrote about western landscapes like nobody else; on "Love Song of the Waterfall" he even gives the waterfall human attributes. (He wrote another song, not included here, from the point of view of a coyote.) "He's Riding Home," sung by Perryman, is about the end of a cowboy's workday and is also an apt metaphor for death (this performance, apparently dedicated to Hank Williams, must have been right after Hank's own death). He uses the rolling clouds, bright moon, and shooting stars to evoke emptiness after the death of an old friend on "This Ain't the Same Old Range," which alternates Perryman's lead with swelling harmonies that come and go like the wind on the plains. They use the same kind of harmonies on "Blue Prairie," which Nolan co-wrote with Tim Spencer. Though many of his songs became standards recorded by countless other singers, Nolan tailored everything he did specifically to the Sons' harmony style. He wrote frequently for the movies as well, and though he considered those songs mere hackwork, the two performed here ("Happy Rovin' Cowboy," which Hank Williams used as his radio theme, and "When Payday Rolls Around") don't really justify that judgment.

He wasn't the group's only writer, though. Tim Spencer penned "Room Full of Roses," here sung by Curtis, and the song went on to become a western *and* country standard, recorded by many others. Ken Carson's "Cowboy Jubilee" (Curtis sings lead again) is fluff, but it's effective fluff in the context of this group.

The Sons also drew from folk sources and from Tin Pan Alley. The group covered country material from the Southeast just as southeastern singers in turn often covered Sons material. And whatever they did, they put it through the Sons of the Pioneers pasteurizer and turned it into a precious little sing-along. But their harmonies helped pave the way for groups like the Statler Brothers, and their melodicism helped broaden the base of rural music. I may not be a P-Nut, but I know a sure-fire commercial success formula when I hear one.

Legendary Songs of the Old West (Columbia Special Products/ Publisher's Central Bureau).

These are not the "songs of the old West," but commercial western music. And this isn't the definitive collection it claims to be because only one label (Columbia and its affiliates) is involved. But never mind: This is the best introduction to western music available, with forty songs by sixteen artists, and defines the form loosely enough to include relevant western swing as well as the singing cowboys and western pop.

At one end of the spectrum are the four sides Tex Ritter cut for the American Recording Co. in 1933. Ritter was an unlikely combination of ethnomusicologist and recording artist, and "Rye Whiskey, Rye Whiskey," "Everyday in the Saddle," "Goodbye Old Paint," and "A-Ridin' Old Paint" are the closest thing to authentic cowboy music ever recorded commercially. Ritter sings crudely, with no regard for time or meter, and with a harsh accent laced with slurs and odd phrasing. He has only the most rudimentary instrumental accompaniment.

At the other extreme are the various configurations of Roy Rogers alone (three cuts), the Sons of the Pioneers without Roy (three cuts), and Roy with the Sons (four cuts). This is generally the blandest music on the album, but this compilation was put together with some care, so it includes a fair amount of previously unreleased material as well as some atypical performances. "Song of the Bandit" has unusual blues guitar runs, "Hadie Brown" swings fluidly, "Cowboy Night Herd" seems to bear at least some semblance of reality as a western song, and "When the Black Sheep Gets the Blues" milks its motifs imaginatively. All four are by Rogers with the Sons, and all but the last are previously unreleased.

Between Ritter and Rogers come all manner of western stars, some of them well known and predictable (Gene Autry, with seven well-chosen sides) and some not (Smiley Burnette, Ken Maynard, with one cut each). The Autry favors the mellower, orchestrated music of the forties only slightly, with three 1933 sides (especially "The Yellow Rose of Texas," with his original accompanist Jimmy Long) balancing the picture out.

Maynard ("The American Boy's Favorite Cowboy") was the first to sing on film *(Wagon Master,* 1930) and the first to use a western song as a movie title *(Strawberry Roan,* 1933). He was, to put it kindly, not a very good singer, and he recorded only once, in 1930, when he cut eight sides for Columbia. But they were traditional songs, done in a largely traditional style, and this alone makes him unique among singing cowboys. Burnette was Gene Autry's movie sidekick, and recorded mostly novelties like this album's "Minnie the Moocher at the Morgue."

Bob Wills' previously unissued "Rockin' Alone in an Old Rockin' Chair" (1936) is flaccid by the standards of his great band, but the 1941 "My Little Cherokee Maiden" and "Little Liza Jane" are up to snuff. The former especially puts emphasis on the western as much as on the swing (which Wills rarely did). The Sons of the West were a swing band admired for complex fiddle-steel arrangements, but you wouldn't know it from "My Prairie Queen," which could be any of a number of straight western bands. The Light Crust Doughboys' previously unreleased "Oh! Susannah!," with its banjo lead and hot soloists, offers further evidence of how western overlapped with western swing.

The Prairie Ramblers, the other swing group prominent here, are a more unusual case; they started as a Kentucky string band and followed their commercial instincts onto the WLS Barn Dance in Chicago, where they moved increasingly closer to western swing. Though founding member Tex Atchison left early (in 1937) for Hollywood, the group enjoyed a lucrative quarter century, ending in the mid-fifties. They recorded on their own (as they appear here on two cuts) and as backup for Patsy Montana (three cuts here, and the most obvious ones at that, which is unfortunate given the paucity of Montana material available domestically).

Most of the rest are more pop-oriented. This includes Louise Massey, best known for "My Adobe Hacienda" though her two sides here are more adventurous. "I'm Thinking Tonight of My Blue Eyes" takes its melody from "Great Speckled Bird," while "Ragtime Cowboy Joe" sounds more like Montana with the Ramblers than like Massey with the Westerners. Then there's Bob Atcher, who was born in Kentucky (in 1914) but grew up in North Dakota. He thus learned firsthand both the traditional country ballads of the Southeast and the cowboy songs of the West. He also recorded in both styles, but his tenor was so clear and proper that nearly everything he did came out sounding pop anyhow. He enjoyed a long stint with the WLS Barn Dance in Chicago, both as a solo act (here he sings "Cool Water") and as a duet with Bonnie Blue-Eyes (they do "You Are My Sunshine"), a role filled at different times by different women (one of whom, though she is unidentified by name, is heard here on "Seven Beers with the Wrong Man," a parody of "Seven Years with the Wrong Man" and its answer, "Seven Years with the Wrong Woman").

Nearly all the different elements that went into commercial cowboy music are thus represented in this four-record boxed set. If you were to own but one western album, this would be the best choice.

Supplementary Albums

Rex Allen: *Golden Songs of the Golden West* (Vocalion). The last of the singing cowboys, in that his *Down Laredo Way* (from the mid-fifties) was the last movie in that genre ever released. These are lush, somber recordings that don't stray far from cowboy themes despite the pop sound, and Allen's deep voice provides a macho tinge surprisingly absent from the genre most of the time.

Rex Allen: *Love Gone Cold* (Longhorn). The title song (by Johnny Bond) is the best thing Allen ever did, and as he expands his repertoire on these early-sixties sessions to include country standards by Floyd Tillman and Ted Daffan, among others, he reveals more vocal chops that his limited role as a singing cowboy suggested he had in him.

Rex Allen, Jr.: *The Best of Rex* (Warner Bros.). As a mainstream country singer, which he was during the late seventies, Rex Allen, Jr., was inconsequential. But when he then got romantic and nostalgic about the kind of romantic and nostalgic music that made his father famous, he became somewhat interesting, in a convoluted way.

Gene Autry: *Columbia Historic Edition* (Columbia). Given all they've got in the vaults, Columbia could have compiled a more imaginative Autry album, but this at least attempts to give a career overview by mixing western, country, and pop songs. Two have never appeared on record before.

Gene Autry: *South of the Border* (Republic). There is a "concept," if you will, behind this double album that good old Gene rereleased on his own now-defunct label. Take a bunch of Spanish-flavored songs like "Rancho Grande," "In a Little Spanish Town," "Vaya Con Dios," and "Mexicali Rose," mix 'em up with a few more Autry renditions of old favorites like "Down in the Valley" and "Back in the Saddle Again," and —ole!—you got yourself a fake Mexican music album and a fake western album wrapped up in one.

Gene Autry: *50th Anniversary Album* (Republic). This overlaps some with *Cowboy Hall of Fame* (also on Republic), but is the better deal if only because it's a double album. For the occasion, it's an apt mix of songs associated primarily with Gene ("Don't Fence Me In"), with other singing cowboys ("Cool Water"), and with pop music ("Harbor Lights"), as well as some obscurities like "Hills of Old Wyoming."

Gene Autry: *Favorites* (Republic). The bluesy Gene Autry; though he is no longer entirely convincing on this point, he's at least given good material like "Trouble in Mind" and "Blues Stay Away From Me."

Best Western Groups (Shasta). An anthology of oddities, among them the Three Ways, a group of singing and yodeling women that once included Mary Ford (of Les Paul fame). Much of this is a vehicle for various Jimmy Wakely groups and spin-offs, but there's also one standard from the Sons of the Pioneers and an obscurity by (post-Pioneers) Hugh Farr & the Foggy River Boys.

Johnny Bond: *The Best of Johnny Bond* (Starday/Gusto). Though western-based, Bond isn't easily pinned down. He once sang backups for Gene Autry and appeared in numerous movies, but he definitely wasn't a singing cowboy and you couldn't strictly call him a western singer, either, for he developed a much more expansive style than others with those roots. Some of his material was indebted to honky-tonk, and some of it had a rockabilly flavor. He was best known for his humorous recitations ("Ten Little Bottles"), and he cut the most influential version of "Hot Rod Lincoln." The woozy sensibility behind "Sick, Sober, and Sorry" or "Three Sheets in the Wind" will be familiar to any boozer, but "I Wonder Where You Are Tonight" is yet another change of pace. Droll as he can be, Bond has wide appeal.

Johnny Bond: *The Rare Johnny Bond Transcriptions* (German Cattle). These come from the mid-forties, feature a small band, and lean more toward the classic western sound, though Bond was too much the iconoclast to ever be neatly pigeonholed.

Wilf Carter: *The Wilf Carter Souvenir Album* (Canadian MCA). Known as Montana Slim, Carter carried yodeling into the fifties using a gimmicky "three-in-one" technique that relied on studio echo. This made him a popular recording artist as this double album of western songs attests, but undoubtedly a disappointment as a live performer.

Eddie Dean: *Sincerely* (Shasta). Dean began as a backup vocalist for Gene Autry and became a singing cowboy in his own right. He also wrote "One Has My Name" and "I Dreamed of a Hillbilly Heaven," both of which he sings here, though these recordings are from the mid-seventies and may be too country (and not enough western) for cowboy buffs.

Eddie Dean: *I Dreamed of Hillbilly Heaven* (German Castle). This includes the original recordings (from the forties and early fifties) of Dean's best-known hits, and is more desirable though much harder to find. Even back then, he showed a fair amount of pop influence, but he also had the great Speedy West there on steel to help keep him honest.

The Farr Brothers: *Texas Crapshooter* (JEMF). Sons of the Pioneers fiddler Hugh and guitarist Karl were the Joe Venuti and Eddie Lang of western music. This instrumental collection of traditional country tunes, pop standards, and Farr originals from 1934–35 and 1940 is jazzy enough to erase the distinction between western and western swing.

Pee Wee King: *The Legendary Pee Wee King* (Longhorn). Accordionist King and his western big band, the Golden West Cowboys, introduced western music to the Opry in 1937. He and vocalist Redd Stewart remained popular together for the next thirty years, with time off for a WW II army stint for Stewart. During that time, they also became songwriting partners, collaborating on such standards as "Tennessee Waltz." From 1952–56, King's group won all awards for western bands, and, in 1974, Pee Wee was elected to the Hall of Fame. All that said, I should quickly add that he is not for everyone; his northerner's notion of western music included pop *à la* Lawrence Welk, among other influences, and this very lack of country grit is part of the reason he was so popular. Furthermore, this album doesn't include many of his hits, which all went out of print from RCA years ago. However, these live transcriptions do capture him and his band near their early-fifties peak.

Pee Wee King: *Ballroom King* (British Detour). As the title implies, this is the big-beat side of King, leaning toward both early rock 'n' roll and back to western swing, and cut between 1947–56. At heart, he remains a straight western bandleader.

Harry McClintock: *Hallelujah! I'm a Bum* (Rounder). "Haywire Mac" was, among other things a railroad man, a miner, a cowboy, a hobo, and a seaman. He came along after the heyday of real cowboys, but before the advent of singing cowboys. Culturally speaking, that makes him a square peg in a round hole; judging from his songs and his writings (in various magazines), it was a role he relished. These sides, recorded in Oakland, California, in 1928–29 aren't all cowboy songs, for McClintock also wrote and/or sang hobo and rambling songs as well as novelties. But all give a taste for what it meant to live and work (and not work!) on the West Coast around the turn of the century.

Patsy Montana: *The Very Early Patsy Montana and the Prairie Ramblers* (German Cattle). Born in Arkansas and raised in California, Patsy broke in playing fiddle for Jimmie Davis, and her first recordings were quite sentimental, and quite ordinary. But by then, she had already worked out her own lusty version of a blue yodel. In 1933, when she joined the WLS Barn Dance in Chicago and was paired with the Prairie Ramblers, she came into her own as America's top female vocalist and a cowgirl not to be messed with. The Prairie Ramblers, meanwhile, evolved over the next sixteen years from a Kentucky String Band into a swing outfit. These are the highlights of those years together.

Patsy Montana: *The Cowboy's Sweetheart* (German Cattle). Again, most of these cuts are with the Prairie Ramblers, and combine polka and swing with old-time string-band music. They come from the thirties and forties. As time went by, Patsy became more tongue-in-cheek about her image; even as her material was becoming less sentimental, it was becoming more contrived. But her warmth, good spirits, and natural enthusiasm never waned.

Riders in the Sky: *Three on the Trail* (Rounder). These three eighties cowpokes are more up my alley than the Sons of the Pioneers and other singing cowboys they emulate. They really are selective about their covers, they write credible originals as well, and if their harmonies aren't executed quite as perfectly as those of the Sons, that's okay by me too; it just shows human qualities the Sons rarely showed. Finally, these guys are no dummies about what they're doing; they know as well as anyone that this music is not only obsolete now, it was obsolete when it was current, and their tongue-in-cheek approach offers a sign of affection as well as a touch of realism.

Tex Ritter: *The Best of Tex Ritter* (Capitol). Just as the title says, with most of the sides dating from the mid-forties, but two as recent as the sixties. Though cut with an eye on the pop market, Ritter himself is too earthy to be glossed over.

Tex Ritter: *An American Legend* (Capitol). "I Dreamed of a Hillbilly Heaven," indeed! Shortly before he died, Ritter rerecorded thirty of his best-known songs, adding spoken reminiscences about his entire career; it was all released in this three-record boxed set. These versions rarely flaunt the coarse vulgarity of the originals, but many of his classic songs are unavailable in any other form.

Marty Robbins: *Gunfighter Ballads and Trail Songs* (Columbia). Robbins, who hailed from Arizona, didn't learn his western music second-hand, and this ranks with Ritter's gems as the finest effort at cowboy music ever released by a Nashville artist. His warm, mellifluous voice is tailor-made for the likes of "Cool Water" and "Running Gun."

Marty Robins: *More Gunfighter Ballads and Trail Songs* (Columbia). This is only a notch below its predecessor (both albums are from the early sixties) only because Marty, singing songs like "I've Got No Use for Women" and "Song of the Bandit," is a little less convincing as the bad-ass.

Kenny Roberts: *Then and Now* (Longhorn). Roberts is one of the flashy forties-style yodelers more concerned with technique than with content; he's not very blue, in other words, but Lord can he do strange things with the form. This features his very first recordings (from 1946), a pair of 1962 yodel duets with fabled Elton Britt, and some 1964 (or thereabouts) sides backed by guitarist Sidney "Hardrock" Gunter.

Sons of the Pioneers: *Columbia Historic Edition* (Columbia). Among their earliest sessions, most of them featuring Len Slye (Roy Rogers) with Perryman and Nolan. For Roy Rogers fans, this is a must because these are the only recordings of the group with him that are widely available. And the Farr Brothers outdo themselves on the "Cajun Stomp" instrumental. Three songs never released before, and alternate takes of three more.

Sons of the Pioneers: Songs of the Hills and Plains (JEMF/AFM). This is the original group—Roy Rogers, Bob Nolan, and Tim Spencer, with the Farr brothers—from the mid-thirties in a series of radio transcriptions. The Pioneers sound is already there intact, and it's amazing how little it's changed since.

Sons of the Pioneers: *The Sons of the Pioneers* (JEMF). Nolan, Spencer, and Perryman, along with the Farr Brothers and bassist Pat Brady, in 1940 transcriptions that concentrate more on western songs than on the pop material they frequently performed on the radio during this time. It includes a large chunk of Nolan songs, many never recorded commercially, and ranks with their very best albums.

Sons of the Pioneers: Decca/Coral (JEMF/AFM). Lloyd Perryman, Tommy Doss, and Dale Warren, with the Farr Brothers and bassist Deuce Spriggins, in 1954 sessions featuring the previously unissued "Somebody Bigger Than You and I" and "Mystery of His Way," as well as the obscure Bob Nolan composition "Lonely Little Room."

Sons of the Pioneers: *The Best of the Sons of the Pioneers* (RCA). Because it leans on the hits, this one fails to show the true diversity of the group and of Bob Nolan's songs—too many slow ones here, for one thing. But if milestones are all you care about, here's "Cool Water," "Tumbling Tumbleweeds," "Riders in the Sky," "Room Full of Roses," and more from the early fifties, with Paul Craft singing lead.

Ned Sublette & the Southwesterners: *Western Classics* (Lovely). Here's an odd one. Sublette is a denizen of the downtown New York new-music scene, which is about as far as you can get from country. But in 1980 he returned to his native New Mexico, hooked up with a local band of old-timers he'd known since childhood, and cut this loose, respectful, and playful collection of standards like "Strawberry Roan," "The Buffalo Skinners," "Little Joe and the Wrangler," and "Rye Whiskey." Turns out he's a passable singer, too.

Jimmy Wakely: *Singing Cowboy* (Shasta). Though best known as a singing cowboy, Wakely scored his real hits with honky-tonk cheating songs. To further complicate matters, they were often sung with pop vocalist Margaret Whiting, for Wakely fancied himself a young Bing Crosby, though he also borrowed heavily from Gene Autry (one of his first employers). All but one of these fourteen sides are from his mid-fifties radio show, and indicate he also had a taste for jazz (but only a taste).

The Way They Were Back When (Shasta). From 1953 to 1958, Wakely hosted a CBS radio show which regularly featured great western swing stars. This album gathers a representative sampling of transcriptions from artists like Hank Penny, Merle Travis, and Wesley Tuttle; though nearly all these men use a touch of swing, and some are pure swing, the emphasis remains on western music.

WESTERN SWING

At first, the formula seems simple. Western swing, which rose to prominence in Texas (and the rest of the Southwest) on the shoulders of Bob Wills and the Texas Playboys beginning in the mid-thirties, was a combination of traditional fiddle music and the jazz of the day, first Dixieland and then big-band swing. Add to this influences from blues, pop, Mexican music, Jimmie Rodgers, and Hawaiian music, and you have the conventional wisdom for the evolution of this most unlikely offshoot of country music. Almost immediately, though, holes appear in the argument. Where does minstrelsy and the medicine show fit into all this? Why does Wills always get the credit for conceiving western swing when Milton Brown and His Musical Brownies, Roy Newman and His Boys, and Bill Boyd and His Cowboy Ramblers (to name just three) were playing the music regularly before Wills was?

Wills himself was a traditional Texas breakdown fiddler. Texas fiddlers were influenced somewhat by Mexican and Cajun musics, which automatically set them off from their southeastern counterparts. Texas fiddling was more rhythmic, more energetic, than it was back East, and this had to do with the social climate.

As in the hills of the Southeast, the square dance, or house party, was an institution in rural Texas; these would be held at someone's house, and neighbors would come from miles around. In the Southeast, where people lived closer together, such parties might last all night. But on the flat, endless prairies of the Southwest, celebrants had to come from so far away that the typical "platform dance," or "kitchen sweat," would last more like three days. Religion was more powerful in the Southeast, and house parties involved innocent forms of square dancing. But out West, where life was more wide open in every way, God seemed a little less threatening; booze played a more important role in the parties, for one thing, and touch dancing was common. Around the time that house parties moved to barns to accommodate larger crowds, banjos and guitars were added to complete the typical string-band lineup; meanwhile, in the urban areas of Texas, the dance hall was fast becoming the equivalent of a barn dance.

Two names best represent the Texas string-band era that paved the way for western swing. The East Texas Serenaders relied on ragtime for material and inspiration, making them forerunners of Wills even though their music had no real swing to it. Prince Albert Hunt didn't swing much, either, but he played fiddle with a rhythmic thrust that also hinted at the early Wills. Hunt lived in the black section of Terrell, near Dallas, and hosted daily jams with black musicians on the porch of his shanty. He also cut such songs as "Blues in the Bottle" with a harsh, bluesy accent. In 1931 he left his gig at a Dallas dance hall with his fiddle under one arm and a married woman under the other; outside, the woman's husband waited with a shotgun, and Hunt was blown away as soon as he went through the door.

Wills grew up in west Texas playing house parties with his father, known as Uncle John and regarded as the best fiddler in the region; in his own playing, Wills himself never deserted traditional fiddling. But he also picked up experience in medicine shows, and that is an influence that can't be overlooked. One of his earliest heroes was Emmett Miller, a blackface singer of the twenties and thirties whose yodels, jive talk, and swooping voice became an obvious element in Wills' style. So did Miller's use of drums and jazz-oriented backings (in 1928, Miller recorded with Tommy and Jimmy Dorsey and Eddie Lang; in 1929, he recorded with Gene Krupa). It seems apparent that this music, which was itself evolving into something inseparable from New Orleans jazz, influenced Wills at least as strongly as did black music directly. When Wills first arrived in Fort Worth in 1929, he was blacked-up and playing for a medicine show.

But he quickly fell in with guitarist Herman Arnspiger and singer Milton Brown, and the trio got a job on local radio plugging Light Crust Flour for Wilbert Lee O'Daniel and the Burrus Mill and Elevator Co. Known originally as the Aladdin Laddies, they were now christened the Light Crust Doughboys. O'Daniel proved to be a hard man to work for, and Brown left in 1932 to form his Musical Brownies. Wills left the next year, taking with him his banjo-playing brother Johnnie Lee as well as singer Tommy Duncan. They settled first in Waco; here, Wills began calling his band the Texas Playboys. At this point his music (like that of the Doughboys) was still the fiddle-band sound, but leaning toward what would become western swing. When he relocated in Tulsa in 1934, Wills settled on the dance-band format and began adding musicians. Significantly, Will and the Playboys worked dance halls exclusively, whereas the Doughboys and Brownies often played concerts.

Most important, then, was the two-four beat taken from Dixieland, which was then *the* hot music of the day. (As a white imitation of New Orleans jazz, it had also become the minstrelsy of its day.) That meant adding drums, unprecedented in any form of country music, and everything Wills added after that was meant in some way to accentuate the dance-band beat.

But there were many other influences. The fiddle-guitar duets of jazzmen Eddie Lang and Joe Venuti were tremendously influential on Texas musicians. There was classic blues (especially Bessie Smith, a Wills favorite) and pop (especially Bing Crosby). The polkas, schottisches, and waltzes of the Germans, Bohemians, and other central Europeans who settled south-central Texas adapted easily to the swing format; Adolph Hofner, for example, began in San Antonio in the thirties with a band that played western swing gigs one night and ethnic Bohemian dates the next, and he often sang in Czech, his first language. The beat and exuberant glide of Cajun music were also absorbed by Texas swing players. So was the heavily syncopated bass of *norteno* music from the Texas-Mexican border.

The Texas Playboys always resented being lumped in with "hillbilly" bands; they felt their competition came from the big bands, and they evolved accordingly. Other western swing bands, no matter how good, were never in the same league as the Playboys; most played swing music, but almost exclusively with string instruments, and they never grew to near the size (or depth) of the Playboys.

World War II almost killed off western swing. After the war, the action shifted to California, where all the emphasis was on sleeker, faster bands. Wills went along with that trend briefly, but soon went back to working with smaller groups that played funkier. Ironically, it wasn't even until after the war that the term "western swing" came into vogue; before that, it had been called "hot string-band music" or even country jazz. As the various names imply, this most eclectic of country musics never was easy to pin down.

Bob Wills and His Texas Playboys: *The Bob Wills Anthology* (Columbia).

Bob Wills knew what he wanted from the time he arrived in Tulsa with a small string band; he already had models in Brown, Boyd, Newman, and others, and his next step was simply to make it bigger and better. By the time of his first recording sessions, in September 1935, he'd put together an eleven-piece western swing band. On this double album of key hits and misses from prewar Wills bands (with two postwar cuts also), we can follow the evolution of his sound.

Six songs from the initial sessions are included here. The first three —"Osage Stomp," "Spanish Two-Step," and "Maiden's Prayer"—are all as much western as they are swing. Traditional fiddle dominates, for Wills (who was born near Kosse, in Limestone County, Texas, in 1905 and grew up on a farm near Turkey, in the western end of the state) never changed his childhood style; as the band got jazzier, he hired fiddlers like Jesse Ashlock to play the hot licks.

Still, even in this seminal stage, "Osage Stomp" provides soloists with a springboard the way a good jazz vamp should, and "Spanish Two-Step" has a pop melody so infectious that Wills later "turned it inside out" to create one of his biggest hits, "San Antonio Rose" (which is not included here, though "New San Antonio Rose," the 1940 big-band version, with lyrics added, is). After "Maiden's Prayer," yet another instrumental based on a traditional fiddle tune, are "Mexicali Rose" and "Old-Fashioned Love," two songs about equal parts pop and Dixieland. "Sittin' on Top of the World," which closes out the first side, is a blues equally popular among blacks and whites.

And there are the musics Wills would be building on for the rest of his life—traditional country reels and breakdowns, Spanish and Mexican motifs, white blues, pop, Dixieland. The basis is already there, too, for the instrumental attack Wills would quickly settle on—Smokey Dacus laying down a booming beat on drums, Leon McAuliffe adding a melodic steel, Wills providing bedrock country fiddling, the horns mixing in jazz, and pianist Al Stricklin offering an eccentric style based on who-can-say-what-all.

Then look toward the end of this album, at the 1940 "Big Beaver" or at "New San Antonio Rose." Both are sweet, melodic jazz-band performances, in the same league as Benny Goodman or the Dorsey Brothers, with string instruments nearly eliminated. The more horns he had, the "classier" Wills felt his bands to be.

The most crucial difference between the earliest and latest cuts here is that in 1938 guitarist Eldon Shamblin joined the band in place of Herman Arnspiger, who was too country for Wills' aspirations. Shamblin was a trained radio staff musician who knew more chords than the other Playboys, and he also had a sophisticated grasp of harmonics. He conceived the dual guitar leads for himself and McAuliffe on "Twin Guitar Special" and others.

But Shamblin and McAuliffe are just two among many stars in this band. Clearly, much of Wills' success came because he had the vision and charisma no other western swing bandleader could match, and thus was able to attract technically superior musicians. It was then up to him to mold them into a cohesive aggregation that had as much soul as it did chops; his bands not only had the most depth, they were invariably the most creative.

McAuliffe, for example, wasn't half the steel player that Bob Dunn (of Milton Brown's band) was. Leon played melody and kept it simple, but those bell-tone harmonics he played behind the fiddles on tunes like "Maiden's Prayer," "Silver Bells," and "I'll See You in My Dreams" fill out the sound skillfully without stealing anyone else's glory. And his "Steel Guitar Rag" became the measure by which all other steel players were judged; it may take a few listenings before you notice the wonderfully schizophrenic piano lines Al Stricklin plays on that song.

Or compare McAuliffe's work on the 1941 "Twin Guitar Special" with some of his first sides and see his progress, how much fleeter and more assured he became. Listen to "Blue Yodel #1" for how urbane a blues singer Tommy Duncan could be. For that matter, look at how Wills managed to continually replenish his ideas and surround himself with fresh new musicians for songs like "Brain Cloudy Blues." Shamblin was out of the band—this was recorded in 1946—and in Lester "Junior" Barnard, Wills was using Eldon's stylistic opposite. Where Shamblin was nimble and smooth, a jazz sharpie, Barnard was raw and meaty, a blues primitive. But either fit into Wills bands, because the leader always adapted his material to his musicians, rather than vice versa.

And that, again, comes down to Bob Wills alone. He is a singer, a fiddle player, and a bandleader, but most of all he is a catalyst with ideas and energy to burn.

Bob Wills and His Texas Playboys: *The Tiffany Transcriptions, Volume 1* (Kaleidoscope).

Popular belief has long held that while Bob Wills made some outstanding music in the postwar years, the fabled Tiffany transcriptions represent the last *sustained* excellence. The problem has been that with the exception of one early-seventies bootleg quickly pulled from the market, the transcriptions have been little more than a rumor for the last three decades. In 1982 a small northern California label finally hammered out a deal for the complete 220 (or so) sides and announced plans to reissue them all. This is the first album in the projected series, and it lives up to advance word.

After a disastrous army stint—he was discharged as unfit after seven months—Wills moved to California in 1943. Originally, he was based in the Los Angeles area, near the film studios. His music (which people were just starting to call "western swing") was by now as popular on the West Coast as it had ever been in Texas and Oklahoma. Wills toured regularly across the country, and sold more records than ever before in his career. He was becoming a wealthy man, and a respected musician and bandleader outside country circles.

But he remained restless, convinced that for all this, the music just wasn't the same. At one point he assembled a twenty-two-piece orchestra (which was never recorded), but as the forties wore on, he, like other bandleaders, was forced to trim down to a smaller unit. In June 1945 he moved to a ranch near Fresno, in the San Joaquin Valley of central California, and tried to set up a Tulsa-like base. It didn't work out, because he couldn't get the musicians he wanted. As his increased popularity required him to tour more, he was developing a stronger commitment to home and family. This left him constantly torn, and his drinking became a serious problem. Meanwhile, he was continuing to record for Columbia and then, starting in 1947, for MGM.

But the transcriptions he made in Oakland for Tiffany Music, Inc., were even more significant than his work for record companies. The Tiffany transcriptions were sent out to radio stations across the country; stations added local commercials and thus had complete programs. The music Wills recorded for these shows showed off his full range.

The bands differed during this period, but each was tight and well equipped to deal with the music at hand. Horns were de-emphasized, and fiddles and guitars picked up the slack. Brass and reeds still took solos and played fills, but they no longer made up a complete section because there weren't enough of them. The music remained jazz, but had a little more of the flavor of the string-oriented prewar bands. Fortunately, Wills never ran out of guitarists and fiddlers.

The strongest cuts on this album are the blues. "Blackout Blues" features Joe Holley with an appropriately woozy fiddle intro and Tiny Moore with a jagged solo on his electric mandolin (which sounded much like a guitar). Pianist Millard Kelso may not have had the overall imagination of an Al Stricklin, but as a strictly blues player, he was much more convincing. Tommy Duncan's vocals are masterful; he begins key lines by moaning so that he sounds like a kazoo, and Herbie Remington's steel molds itself to his voice.

But the standout musician of the lot is Junior Barnard, whose echo-laden guitar jolts the band. Barnard was easily the dirtiest musician Wills ever employed, and since Eldon Shamblin also appears on some of these cuts, the contrasts become apparent once again. While Eldon provides a firm underpinning for songs like "Straighten Up and Fly Right" before stepping out to a smart solo, Barnard lunges at his lines; he's always threatening to cross over into dissonance. His intro to "Cotton Patch Blues," another blues Wills wrote to conjure up his childhood days and early musical loves, wrenches the song from its foundation before the rest of the band even gets to it.

But this was not strictly a blues band by any means. "Mission to Moscow," with helter-skelter hot solos from Moore, Kelso, and Remington is pure exhilarating Wills-style jazz. "Little Betty Brown" is a square dance that takes Wills and the band straight back to his native Turkey, Texas, and "Nobody's Sweetheart Now" is Wills pop at its most jacked-up. "What's the Matter with the Mill" is an old Wills favorite which, in this arrangement with more aggressive fiddling and guitar, typifies the new musical era. "Jumpin' at the Woodside," a Count Basie tune that showcases Kelso's piano, is another successful update.

"I Hear You Talkin' " shifts the spotlight to Noel Boggs, who plays steel on the cuts that don't feature Remington. Boggs, who played also with Hank Penny, was (alongside Barnard) Wills' other "secret weapon" during this period. Like Barnard, he was much more a modernist than Wills; he easily made the transition from swing to a more complicated bebop-based steel style, and deserves more credit than he's ever gotten for helping Wills to keep up with changing trends.

The seeds of Wills' discontent can also be found here; for example, Tommy Duncan shares vocals with the comparatively colorless Dean and Evelyn McKinney. Duncan quit Wills in 1948, disgusted with his boss's escalating drinking binges and anxious to form his own group. Wills plays more fiddle here than he usually preferred, too. But those are minor quibbles. I seriously doubt if there are twenty more albums of comparable quality, but for now the Tiffany transcriptions are off to a rousing start.

Bob Wills and His Texas Playboys: *Country & Western Classics: Bob Wills* (Time-Life).

"You can change the name of an old song/Rearrange it and make it swing," Bob Wills pointed out on his hit "Time Changes Everything," and he spent a lifetime doing just that. In the process, as this three-record boxed set illustrates, Wills was able to become different things to different people. His greatest strength, perhaps, was that he usually managed to live up to the expectations of *all* these people.

Rich Kienzle, who compiled and annotated this overview of the Wills career, seems to favor the big-band Wills sides, which is definitely not my preference. But with both the cuts he includes and the liner notes he writes extolling them, he makes the case for Wills as a big-band leader above all else.

"Big Beaver," cited as one of the first Wills forays into big-band swing, is undeniably smooth, with sax and trumpet carrying the song in both the ensemble passages and the solo spots. Eldon Shamblin, who arranged this and many of the Texas Playboys' other most jazzy tunes, is the glue holding it together with his guitar. The previously unissued "Liebestraum" (yes, the Franz Liszt classical piece) is much the same; when Leon McAuliffe finally comes in with his chiming steel, he sounds almost out of place with the rest of these guys. The version of "San Antonio Rose" included here features both fiddles and horns, is clearly still in the experimental stage (McAuliffe's solo is real tentative), and was not even known to have existed until it was discovered when this album was being assembled. String instruments make no significant contribution to the Wills original ballad "My Confession," with Bob singing lead, while "Ten Years," another cut from the same session, combines Dixieland soloing with big-band riffing.

My guess is that Wills, who fiercely resented *any* implication that he was a "hillbilly musician," would agree with Kienzle that the big-band Wills is best. I suspect Wills aspired to be a Dorsey rather than, say, a Basie, because he considered that music more sophisticated (or more elevated in some other sense), and his work in this area is always professional and on a par with the music of the bandleaders he challenged. But no matter how much drive, that music has never had, to my ears, the sense of discovery, the thrill of breaking through, that can be found in the earlier music that's rooted about equally in country and in hot New Orleans jazz. Give me the winking, jubilant "She's Killing Me," with its darting solos from Jesse Ashlock on fiddle, Everett Stover on trumpet, and Al Stricklin on piano. Or the sassy "Fan It," with Wills jabbering away like a court jester, or the inspired improvisation of "Liza, Pull Down the Shades" (a joke that worked), or the hilarious instrumental theme, "Let's Ride with Bob," with Wills taking the role of a carny barker while the band puts out some of the most vulgar belching and droning it ever recorded.

"Let's Ride with Bob" was cut in 1942, well after the first successful big-band sessions, and indicates that whatever his personal preferences, Wills could be flexible—could jump back and forth without losing his touch, could rearrange an old song and make it swing. He specialized in old songs all along; by the time he got around to covering a song, it could usually qualify as nostalgia—if the song hadn't originally been too black for his audience to have heard it at all. Songs like "I Can't Give You Anything But Love, Baby," "I've Got the Wonder Where She Went (Blues)," and Bessie Smith's "Down Hearted Blues" (with Stover blowing a solo that reeks of backroom sex) all first appeared before Wills even *had* a band, but he always seemed to need a lot of time to get comfortable with a song (or lonesome for it) before he'd start using it himself.

No matter how far he strayed, he always came back to country. In 1935, just when he was beginning to master something else, he and Sleepy Johnson cut the fiddle and guitar duet on "Smith's Reel" that's included here. As late as 1947 he was still recording the traditional "Sally Gooden" (though overhauling it entirely, complete with jiving new lyrics). And the 1950 "Faded Love," one of his last major hits, was nothing but a variation on the traditional "Darling Nellie Gray" he'd been playing since he was a child.

Significantly, in the last few years before his stroke and coma in 1973 and his death in 1975, Wills himself seemed to be most nostalgic for the sound of the prewar band, the one that was as country as it was jazz. Wills got only belated recognition from the country music industry because he mostly scorned the "country" tag himself, because he never bothered with the Opry and Nashville politicking, and because he used horns and drums when they were taboo. He wasn't elected to the Hall of Fame until 1968, but more than anything else, that's a commentary on those who run the industry. Listen to this man and his music—how could his country credentials ever have been in doubt?

Milton Brown and His Musical Brownies: *Taking Off* (British String).

Milton Brown was not only playing western swing well before Bob Wills, but had he not died after a 1936 auto wreck, there's every reason to believe he would have matched Wills in popularity and staying power. Though the two bandleaders worked the same musical turf, this album demonstrates key differences between their approaches.

Brown didn't use drums or horns, while for Wills drums were what made the music go and horns were what provided the oomph. Wills adapted many traditional fiddle tunes to the swing-band format, while Brown only dabbled in traditional and western songs; he was committed to pop, blues, and jazz. And while Wills usually recorded his jazz and blues selections years after they were first hits (which means his versions had nostalgia appeal), Brown covered them right then and there, when they were still fresh in the public mind.

Brown was born in Stephensville, Texas, in 1903; his family moved to Fort Worth in 1908 and he finished high school in 1925. He was a police officer and then a cigar salesman before beginning his partnership with Wills and Herman Arnspiger in what became known as the Light Crust Doughboys. After quitting in 1932, he formed his first edition of the Musical Brownies, a quintet. He soon added a piano, which gave the music jazzier overtones. The turning point came when he added steel guitarist Bob Dunn late in 1934, after the Brownies had already cut their first sides for Bluebird.

Dunn was both a pioneer and a madman, a heavy drinker who was the first man in country music to amplify his steel and who made music to match his boozy, lurching disposition. He had toured with vaudeville groups for years before joining Brown. Feeling tied down by the constraints of the Hawaiian steel, he magnetized the strings and raised them high off the body of his standard, round-hole Martin guitar. He attached an electric pick-up to the guitar, connected it to a cheap, Val-U-Tone amplifier, and then he was, almost literally, off to the races. When the Brownies showed up for their Decca session early in 1935, they swung like nobody had before, and the impetus clearly came from Dunn. You can hear the results on the fourteen sides from 1935–36 that are included here. (Two more were cut in 1937, after Brown had died, with a substantially different band.)

As a soloist or a background player, Dunn is all over these records, a showoff with a cause; you get the impression he pushes so hard not because he craves the limelight but because he's so caught up in what he's doing that he can't stop. On "Chinatown My Chinatown," he plays a jumpy series of notes that are punctuated by yowls from beyond. In the background of the sweet, sedate "In El Rancho Grande," he plays notes that go BRAAANNNGGG like a spring had just popped loose. His solo on "Taking Off," which swing players everywhere tried in vain to emulate, begins with a long, repetitive line and then the notes start clustering and tangling each other up, but the momentum is ever onward. On "Some of These Days," Fred "Papa" Calhoun gets off a romping ragtime piano solo before Dunn steps in and takes the song over; his instrument almost quacks as he breaks up a typically smooth melody line with fast, dissonant bursts. He often used steel to try to recreate the sudden bursts of notes horn players used to give their own solos muscle. Dunn was at his best when he was playing fast, as on songs like "Sweet Georgia Brown," "Texas Hambone Blues," "Sweet Jennie Lee," and especially "Washington and Lee Swing," which the band takes at a jackrabbit pace while he keeps building his solo, upping the ante. Though he could play melody as well as any of the other swing steel men, he was not bound to it; he took solos like his steel was a musical jack-in-the-box, forever popping loose, bobbing about recklessly and then returning to its base. He had the best sense of humor in western swing, which made him the ideal foil for Brown.

But Dunn was not the whole show. Brown's own high-pitched voice was sweet and perky, echoing his idol Bing Crosby, but much more droll. Calhoun was the first piano player ever in a western band, and thus defined the style at least as much as Al Stricklin did; Calhoun's piano was more from the whorehouses and gambling dens than was Stricklin's, and his sure sense of rhythm usually provided Dunn with the launching pad he needed for his own solos. Calhoun always *hinted* at more than he actually played. Cecil Brower's fiddle had a sizzling gypsy flavor to go with its blues edge. When Cliff Bruner, another top bluesman, joined on second fiddle for the 1936 sessions, one would set up a drone behind the other's solos to fatten the sound, while the rest of the unit continued swinging with enviable compactness. But there was no doubt about the star picker in this group; Dunn was like a jolt of tequila that made everything go down with extra kick.

Milton Brown and His Brownies: *Pioneer Western Swing Band (1935–36)* (MCA).

"I got a job but I just couldn't keep it long/The leader said I played all the music wrong/And I stepped out with an outfit of my own," sings Milton Brown. "Got together a new kind of orchestree/And we all played the same goofus harmony/I must admit, we made a hit/Goofus had been good to me."

Brown was too aware of what he was doing to chalk his success up solely to luck. These twelve sides from 1935–36 ("Fan It" and "Goofus" also appear on the *Taking Off* LP) are further proof of that. But "Goofus" could be his own story, or an allegory for Life According to Brown, just the same. For even as this album puts more of an emphasis on Brown's fondness for pop and jazz standards, it shows what a squirrel he could be.

Because it was meant to be dance music, sheer escapism while

America was in the throes of Depression, western swing lent itself well to goofus, or hokum, as it is also called in "Easy Ridin' Papa." If Wills commanded attention because he was a huge man who looked like he took guff from nobody, Brown got by as a dandy, a scamp, on top of the world by his wits and his charm. His singing was smooth and clear, but it had impish qualities as well. Milton Brown liked to jive folks.

That meant novelty songs and double entendres, which he utilized more than any other swing group (though the Doughboys came close, and their "Pussy, Pussy, Pussy" is a landmark in the genre). Perhaps Brown's raunchiest was "Garbage Man Blues," which is unfortunately not included here. But there's no point complaining about its absence when we do have the likes of "Fan It," which *sounds* so blowsy and punch-drunk that the relative mildness of the lyrics hardly matters. "Somebody's Been Usin' That Thing" and "Yes Suh" are more of the same, though in these cases the reason is more clear; these are two more of Dunn's most crazed performances, and he can make almost any song sound obscene.

"Down by the O-h-i-o" was adapted by Brown primarily as a vehicle for introducing the band members, and features some of Brower's swiftest fiddle exotica as well as a deft (and surprising) boogie acoustic guitar break by Durwood Brown, Milton's younger brother, who was rarely featured in the band. By the time he gets around to bringing on Calhoun, Milton is so worked up all he can do is keep repeating the word "piano" over and over and over until he finally lapses into some semblance of scat. Then Dunn stumbles in like he's been wandering around a room trying to remember just where he is.

They even get away with the umpteenth version of "Hesitation Blues," thanks largely to Wanna Coffman's thumping, walking bass line and to the way Dunn pops off notes like he was behind the bar opening a round of longnecks. On "Sheik of Araby," Dunn demonstrates once again that formal training could never get in the way of his musicianship; even this most romanticized of pop songs becomes, for this nihilist, an exercise in brinkmanship, another test of how much he can get away with.

Brown and Wills remained friendly as the rivalry between their two bands grew. Today many Texas swing musicians praise Brown more highly than Wills, and there have been endless arguments about what would have happened had Brown not been cut down in his prime. Would he have expanded his band to include horns so he could compete head-on with Wills? Would that have been enough, or was his vision ultimately too limited? I do find it ironic that Wills, the man rooted in traditional fiddle breakdowns, pursued the big-band sound while Brown, the one who showed few roots in rural music, stuck by his small string band. And that Brown's music was nonetheless hipper, more urbane.

Brown's career came to an unexpected, and unnecessary, end in 1936 when his car blew a tire and flipped over as he was driving from Crystal Springs dance pavilion along Fort Worth's notorious Jacksboro Highway (also known as the Jaxbeer Highway because of the juke joints that lined it for miles). Due to shoddy medical treatment, he died of pneumonia in the hospital five days later. Though Brown was virtually unknown outside the Lone Star State, 3,500 people came to his funeral. His band members broke off into various splinter groups, one of which recorded ineffectually under the old name, but none attracted a fraction of Brown's acclaim, and no wonder: None had a fraction of his personality.

Western Swing, Volume 2 (Old Timey).

After the big two of Bob Wills and Milton Brown, western swing thinned out. There were a few others who made consistently hot records—most notably fiddler Cliff Bruner, with various groups—and more still who cut quite a few sides but rarely caught fire. There were one-shot wonders from all over Texas, and others from places more unlikely. Several get their due on this anthology, but cuts from Wills and Brown demonstrate once again why they dominated the field.

Leon McAuliffe recalls that Wills and the Playboys improvised "Liza Pull Down the Shades" in the studio and the instrumental has the loose, easy feel of something being made up as it goes along. But real pros know how to do that, and these are real pros. Smokey Dacus kicks it off on his cymbals, with the fiddles racing to keep up. McAuliffe's solo is repetitive and utterly simple, as though he couldn't think quite far enough ahead, but knew he'd latched onto a good thing anyhow. Bassist Son Lansford gets a short break, the fiddles and steel do a credible job of approximating a horn section, Al Stricklin's piano flirts with dissonance, and Wills jabbers happily throughout.

It's all atmosphere, and so is Milton Brown's "Garbage Man Blues," though this is at the other extreme; it's pure anarchy, probably cut at the end of a session at which the musicians had gotten well juiced. The rhythm section is a blur, the solos are all half-assed, Ocie Stockard's banjo plinks in all the wrong places and Brown is barely in control of himself. The song, loosely based on New Orleans pianist Luis Russell's "Call of the Freaks," is too blatant to qualify as double entendre, and if there's more dementia like this languishing in record company vaults, somebody should put it out quick; it's enough to give western swing a bad name, and that's good.

San Antonio groups make up much of the rest of this album. The best known is Adolph Hofner and His Texans, with Adolph's brother Emil making gimmicky but strangely effective background noise on his steel during "Brown Eyed Sweet." The Hofner brothers started out playing with Jimmie Revard and His Oklahoma Playboys, the first significant swing band in San Antonio despite their name. Revard personally preferred glossier big bands like those of Benny Goodman or Tommy Dorsey, but his own group excelled on slow grinds like "Blues in the Bottle." Eddie Whiteby does his best Satchmo imitation on the vocals, and the piano adds grit to a swinging steel and fiddle. Revard's "My Little Girl I Love You" features singer Curly Williams lamenting a girl friend who leaves her wig on the dresser, her peg leg under the bed, her glass eye on the window, and her false teeth on the chair; western swing had a way of getting into such subjects. "My little girl, you know I love you," Williams beseeches, "but you're scattered everywhere."

San Antonio groups were, if anything, more eclectic than most, Hofner's Czech and German influences being one instance. Another is *norteno* music from the border, for San Antonio has always had the state's largest Mexican population. Though often confused with *mariachi* brass bands, *norteno* is actually defined by close harmonies, a twelve-string guitar, and a swinging accordion. The Tune Wranglers picked up that feel so convincingly that Bluebird (their label) released some of their records on the Mexican music line under the name Tonos Hombres. But this was an aspect of their music they weren't overly proud of, and they played it down most of the time; "Up Jumped the Devil," a straight New Orleans dance-floor romp with broken syncopation and fluttering fiddle, is more typical of their output.

The Light Crust Doughboys get two instrumentals, "Gin Mill Blues" and "Weary Blues," both of them stolen by pianist Knocky Parker. The Doughboys were originally run by W. Lee O'Daniel, a legendary Texas huckster who started out claiming to hate country music. But he got the bug—and the bucks—from Wills and Brown. O'Daniel never sang or played an instrument himself, but when Burrus Mill and Elevator Co. fired him, he started a rival flour (Hillbilly) and band (the Hillbilly Boys) that he ultimately parlayed into the governorship of Texas and then a seat in the U.S. Senate. "Don't Let the Deal Go Down" was not only a favorite among swing bands, it might well have told O'Daniel's life story as well.

Little is known about the Rambling Rangers, who wandered into a Dallas studio seemingly off the street with a spaced-out steel player and a laconic singer to cut "Gettin' Tired." The Washboard Wonders weren't even from Texas, but from North Carolina, and their treatment of "Feather Your Nest" is pure hokum, but it fits here just the same.

There's no confusion about who Cliff Bruner was. Born and raised in the Houston area and a fiddler since he was four, Bruner had little interest in country music. He was a jazzman all the way, and one of the snazziest fiddlers swing produced. After his tenure in Brown's Brownies, he formed his Texas Wanderers (including Bob Dunn on steel and Moon Mullican on piano) in 1936 to record, among others, Kokomo Arnold's "Milk Cow Blues." Their version was so funky it became a swing favorite covered by numerous other bands. Five years later, Bruner was using a second fiddler for "Tequila Rag," which is taken at a quicker tempo and which anticipates the honky-tonk music on the horizon. Bruner pops in and out of the history of western swing all through his career, so it's appropriate that these two cuts should sum up beginnings and endings as succinctly as they do on this collection.

Harry Choates: *The Fiddle King of Cajun Swing* (Arhoolie).

They called him the Cajun Hank Williams, the Godfather of Cajun Music, but when it came time to bury Harry Choates at age twenty-eight, nobody stepped forward to pay for his coffin. He had done it all—the women, the rambling, the whiskey, the wild, swirling dance music that fused his own Cajun traditions with western swing—and these recordings stand as his last will and testament because, aside from a lousy reputation, there was nothing else left anyhow.

Cajuns are French-speaking people with roots in Acadia, that part of Canada now known as Nova Scotia. In the eighteenth century, the British forced a genocidal evacuation of Acadians; for many, the sudden and brutal exodus (memorialized by Longfellow in *Evangeline)* ended in what is now Louisiana, which was then French land as remote and as rich in resources as Nova Scotia had been. Though the earliest Cajun music was made with hand claps and kitchen utensils rather than with instruments, the French-based Acadian fiddle soon took over. By the 1920s, when Cajun music was first recorded, the accordion (brought by Germans passing through on their way to Texas) was dominant.

In the thirties the fiddle made a comeback, but with a difference. Governor Huey Long was building the roads that connected French bayou country to the outside world, and Cajuns were no longer practicing their traditional culture in splendid isolation; the new fiddlers played their waltzes and two-steps with hillbilly and blues inflections. Soon Cajun fiddle styles began creeping likewise into mainstream country music. Today country stars routinely use a Cajun song to spice up their shows, while among Cajuns, Jimmy Newman has come up with a Cajun sound for the Grand Ole Opry crowd and Doug Kershaw has come up with a Cajun freak show for the rock crowd.

Henry Choates was born in Rayne, Louisiana, in 1922, and grew up with the music itself. He spoke English with a thick Cajun accent and

Cajun French with a thick English accent; because his last name isn't French, there's still doubt as to whether he was even a true Cajun. Choates played accordion, guitar, and steel before settling on fiddle, but he never owned an instrument in his life; all his music was made on a $7.00 fiddle he borrowed from a friend and never bothered to return. By age twelve he was already a heavy drinker, and spent his teen-age years roaming the bayou country playing with various Cajun bands. In 1945, between belts of whiskey, he married a woman named Helen Daenen, fathered two children by her in quick succession, and then took off again.

He formed his first band right after World War II. It was not strictly a Cajun band, for just as western swing had borrowed some of its heavy beat and hot fiddle from Cajun music, so had the Cajuns been influenced by swing. Both were dance musics first and foremost; the Hackberry Ramblers had been playing Cajunized swing a decade before Choates went into a Houston studio in 1946 with Johnnie Mae Smirle on piano (she was one of his lovers, though he lost her to his banjo man), with Joe Manuel on banjo, and with B. D. Williams on bass. The song they cut, "Jole Blon" ("Pretty Blond"), had long been a Cajun favorite, first recorded by Amade Breaux around 1928. But Choates' reeling, maniacal arrangement was so popular that it became known as "his" song.

These sides, apparently cut between 1946 and 1949, add guitarist Eddie Pursley to the original band; in some cases, Ron Ray "Pee Wee" Lyons or Julius "Papa Cairo" Lamperez are on steel. "Jole Blon" isn't included, but there are such Cajun standards as "Allons a Lafayette" ("Going to Lafayette") and "Poor Hobo." Choates added flash to that typical heavily bowed Cajun shuffle stroke on fiddle. On "Grand Mamou" he wrings extra-high notes out of the classic fiddle line, and later he breaks into blues guitar lines on his fiddle. "Going high" was a Cajun trademark—most vocalists sang at the top of their range, and Choates translated this vocal cry to fiddle, standing on tiptoes as he played. On the flowing "Port Arthur Waltz" his playing is so full it sounds like two fiddles, and in other places he sounds like an accordion.

But it's more singular Cajun-swing fusions like "Draggin' the Bow," a charging instrumental, that are truly wondrous. "Harry Choates Special" is pure swing, obviously indebted to Wills, with each of the band members being called on for a solo break and then Choates dancing back into the groove with the inflections of a J. R. Chatwell or a Johnny Gimble. "Harry Choates Blues" is strictly jazz-based, with little relation to traditional Cajun music. The steel on these tracks is like a ghost, playing bell tones an octave or two above the melody, as Leon McAuliffe did with Wills. "Devil in the Bayou" is the musical equivalent to a monster movie, a jokey instrumental like the kind that turned up so often in the early days of rock 'n' roll.

Choates sings in a rough, whiskey-drenched moan, punctuating his voice and endlessly inventive fiddle lines with a lusty *eh-ha-ha* or *aai-eee* common among Cajun singers. His bawling vocals on "It Won't Be Long" are the perfect complement to what's been described as a "crying" fiddle style. I do not know what most of these songs are about, because they are sung in Cajun patois; even if I spoke French, I would have trouble, because Cajun is a bastardized oral language that has no dictionary and doesn't translate into "proper" French any better than it does into English. I assume his baby left him and he's feeling blue, because that's what most Cajun songs are about, and that's what he sounds like.

With such a vibrantly swinging band, Choates conquered Texas as easily as he had Louisiana—this despite the fact that he was notorious for failing to show up for gigs or for being too drunk to play. In 1951, when he was working out of Austin, Helen Daenen filed wife and child desertion charges against him, and when he failed to answer them in Jefferson County Court (east Texas), he was also charged with contempt. He was thrown in jail in Austin, and what happened next remains in dispute. The most common story is that he went into *delirium tremens* and was beaten comatose by jailers trying to quiet him down; another story holds that he was beaten after smart-mouthing a jailer. Newspaper reports quote the sheriff only as saying Choates had been "extremely nervous" and was thus transferred to a cell next to the jailer's office, where he could be "closely watched." He died only a half hour before the Jefferson County sheriff arrived to take custody of him, and no record of an inquest has ever been found. His family couldn't afford to bring the body home to Port Arthur, Texas, near the Louisiana border, so musician friends raised the money with a benefit concert. Thirty years later, local Cajuns raised enough money to buy him a grave marker.

Okeh Western Swing (Epic).

I am now in the ethically dubious position of recommending, as a supposedly unbiased critic, that you rush right out and buy an album which I compiled and annotated. I assure you that my motives are not financial; I was paid a flat fee for putting this double album together, and all royalties go directly into the coffers of Columbia Records, the parent company of Epic and the sponsor of this project. I include it here because it helps explain why major record companies are so often insensitive to the treasures in their own vaults; because it sheds more light on the myriad of forces that shaped western swing; because it contains several rarities previously unavailable; and because the music, every last track of it, is superb.

As a label, Okeh recorded much of America's best fringe musics from 1918 to 1969. In 1938 it was, along with Vocalion and the American Recording Co., swallowed up by Columbia; these twenty-eight sides actually come from all those sources. During the Depression, when Columbia went bankrupt, and again during World War II, many metal masters from which records were made were melted down so their copper bases could be sold for scrap. Superstars weren't affected, but much regional music was, including much of the western swing that co-producer Michael Brooks and I had hoped to include here. This practice was widespread among the majors, and companies that complain about their catalogs being pirated by indie collectors labels (which re-dub sides off old 78s, resulting in bad sound) have mainly their corporate forefathers to blame.

One of the ideas behind this album was to be more explicit about where western swing came from, for the standard explanations always seemed a little too pat, and probably also too romanticized, accompanied as they always were by rhapsodic prose about poor whites working alongside blacks in the cotton fields, and absorbing "soul" through something like photosynthesis. There may be truth in this notion in some cases, but western swing is also one of the first products of the radio boom when all forms of music were more accessible to listeners. Blacks and whites lifted freely from each other both firsthand and secondhand, especially in the years just before western swing surfaced. But the synthesis was made even more confusing because of blackface, which western swing buffs usually do their best to ignore.

However brutal the racial realities that created blackface as a form of mass entertainment, it was hugely influential, as the tracks by Al Bernard ("Hesitation Blues") and Emmett Miller ("Lovesick Blues") reveal. Miller is a particularly intriguing character, both because of his singular talents and because Wills was always more explicit in citing his influence than Wills biographers admit. Miller disappeared into anonymity as the medicine shows dried up. The last verified information about him is that in 1952 he was working at the Rainbow Room in Nashville's Printer's Alley, the notorious strip-club district.

When Brooks and I programmed the album, we wanted to add some pre-swing Texas fiddle music to show how it evolved, too. The likely choices were sides from the East Texas Serenaders or Prince Albert Hunt, but once we heard them, we changed our minds. Though both were excellent, they had little more than a suggestion of swing to them; their influence is apparent in a roundabout way, but how fiddlers made the jump from them to swing is not entirely clear. Could it be that this took place strictly in live performances, and wasn't documented because the record companies got there too late?

Time and again, the music here comes back to Wills. I hadn't heard of some of these groups when I began the project, and others I'd heard of without having ever heard their music. Yet it's amazing how many feature musicians at one time had spots in the Texas Playboys. And while the sides by each of the twenty-one other groups here are often every bit as exciting as the sides by Wills, most of these groups never came up with seven sides as good as the seven included here by Wills— and these seven represent a minuscule fraction of his output.

The career of John "Knocky" Parker, who takes the scintillating piano solo on the Light Crust Doughboys' "Knocky Knocky," offers more insight into the experiences and influences that shaped western swing. Raised on a cotton farm thirty miles outside Dallas, he used to go to town with his father on weekends. He remembers playing piano at age four with Texas country bluesman Blind Lemon Jefferson on "Deep Elm Street" (as one song calls it) in the heart of the Dallas ghetto. As a teen-ager, he took the Interurban into town on weekends to play dances there; since they always ended too late for him to get public transportation home, he'd spend the night with the families of the black musicians he'd been playing with. By the thirties he was playing with Blocky Simmons' Famous Blue Jackets, a group that never recorded, and then with the Doughboys. Both groups played pop and New Orleans jazz, but on the side Knocky had a duo with the pioneering electric blues guitarist T-Bone Walker at the Gem Hotel in Fort Worth. After he quit playing professionally, Parker taught college English and conducted workshops in stride and ragtime piano.

Western swing eventually broke down into the smaller honky-tonk combos; in its earliest form, honky-tonk was indistinguishable from western swing. Two prime examples here are "Give Me My Money" by the Blue Ridge Playboys, the group that spawned most of the major honky-tonk stars, and the later, tongue-in-cheek "Brown Bottle Blues" by Slim Harbert, who wasn't considered a swing artist at all. (Neither were the Sons of the Pioneers, represented here by "One More River to Cross," though the Farr Brothers on guitar and fiddle would have fit effortlessly into any of these groups.)

Yes, I am embarrassed by all the typos and discographical errors in the liners, even the ones that aren't mine. But this album includes every important western swing group except Milton Brown and His Musical Brownies, who never recorded for any of the Columbia labels. Having done its civic duty by releasing the record, Columbia pressed very few copies. But it remains the only western swing sampler available from a major label, which means it's the only one theoretically available outside specialty shops. I would recommend it enthusiastically even if it weren't "my" album. Honest.

How many shopping days are left until Christmas? I urge you to act now.

Supplementary Albums

Asleep at the Wheel: *Comin' Right at Ya* (Liberty). The first, and best, of the seventies western swing revivalists. The Wheel was formed in Paw Paw, West Virginia, but lived in Oakland, California, when their 1973 debut was released. By absolute standards they screw up tempos and blow a solo here and there. But the energy and good spirits are undeniable, as is their feel for the genre. They have three lead vocalists and, in Leroy Preston, a writer who can turn out what sounds like mainstream country standards ("Before You Stopped Loving Me"). He also has a dry, mordant sense of humor ("Hillbilly Nut") rare in seventies country. This is more than just a debt paid to the obvious influences of Wills, Williams, Mullican, Tubb, et al.

Asleep at the Wheel: *Texas Gold* (Capitol). By 1975 they've moved to Texas and expanded from six to nine pieces. This is their third album, and the first to capture their live sound. They're still covering Bob Wills ("Fat Boy Rag," "Trouble in Mind"), but they're also writing infectious material of their own in the same vein ("Bump Bounce Boogie"). And more important, they're assimilating influences the way Wills did rather than just assimilating Wills—check out Preston's interpretation of Amos Milburn's "Let Me Go Home Whiskey" or pianist Floyd Domino with "Roll 'Em Floyd," the Pete Johnson/Big Joe Turner medley. Or Chris O'Connell's plaintive cry on "Nothin' Takes the Place of You," Toussaint McCall's swamp-pop ballad. Finally, Preston's seriocomic "Tonight the Bartender Is on the Wrong Side of the Bar" assimilates honky-tonk well enough to send it up without insulting it.

Asleep at the Wheel: *Wheelin' and Dealin'* (Capitol). This may be a little wobbly by Wheel standards; "If I Can't Love You," a shuffling Jimmy Donley soundalike by Leroy Preston, and "The Trouble With Lovin' Today," a smart Leroy Preston soundalike by Kevin "Blackie" Farrell are the two best new ones. But Preston's jumping "Shout Wa Hey" is not far behind, and the three lead singers continue to grow; Chris O'Connell is singing with more power and clarity than any woman in country music, Ray Benson has his Ernest Tubb cum Cab

Calloway down cold, and Preston's droll hillbilly plaint works every time.

Asleep at the Wheel: *The Wheel* (Capitol). Personnel has changed frequently in this group (we're now up to 1977), but the core has remained stable—O'Connell, Preston, Benson, pianist Domino, steel player Lucky Oceans. They provide the glue even as the fiddlers, horn men, and drummers come and go. This might be their best album; it's certainly their broadest, with novelty ("Am I High"), mock gospel (Preston's incredible "Somebody Stole His Body"), rockabilly ("My Baby Thinks She's a Train"), Cajun ballad (Link Davis, Jr.'s "Red Stick"), and some more of the usual unclassifiable Preston originals ("I Wonder," "When Love Goes Wrong," "A Dollar Short and a Day Late" with Benson and Farrell, "Let's Face Up" with Farrell, "I Can't Handle It Now"). But the other key this time is how well they have integrated those fiddlers (Bill Mabry and Danny Levin, both sweet and swinging) and horn men (Taco Ryan and Link Davis, Jr., both good and greasy).

Beer Parlor Jive (British String). The continuing saga of Moon Mullican and Bob Dunn as the unsung stars of western swing. They both appear here with Cliff Bruner's Texas Wanderers ("Draggin' the Bow" and "When You're Smiling"), while Dunn is on the Milton Brown tracks and Mullican commiserates with the Texas Wanderers (minus Bruner and Dunn) on "Sundown Blues." Both back the elusive Buddy Jones on "Settle Down Blues," which establishes him as the best white blues singer of his era; in his tone and phrasing, Jones erased Jimmie Rodgers' sweet side and went straight for the gut. Adolph Hofner and His Texans tear into "Joe Turner Blues" with more flat-out aggression than they ever showed before, as brother Emil pours on some of his most jarring Dunn licks. A little duplication with other recommended albums, but these 1935–41 sides are too tantalizing to ignore.

Noel Boggs: *Noel Boggs and Friends* (Shasta). No doubt about it, Boggs took steel to new heights in the late forties and early fifties, playing patterns much more complex than did his peers. Like most great steel players, he has a tendency to want to do his biggest showing-off on schmaltz and pop standards, which mars much of his work on this label. This one leans heavily on boogie and blues, and Boggs steps out accordingly.

Bill Boyd's Cowboy Ramblers: *Bill Boyd's Cowboy Ramblers* (RCA Bluebird). Boyd wasn't one of the better western swingers, but he was one of the first, and his music represents an important step from fiddle band to small swing band. Texas Rose has an in-print album that presents him in poor light, so it's worth scouring the bargain bins for this out-of-print twofer instead.

Harry Choates: *Jole Blon—The Original Cajun Fiddle of Harry Choates* (D). This is closer to the Cajun mainstream, and thus doesn't swing as readily as the Arhoolie album, but it keeps up just the same.

Spade Cooley: *Columbia Historic Edition* (Columbia). Cooley was the Lawrence Welk of western swing, which I do not mean as a compliment. But Tex Williams sang with him for a while, and steel guitarists like Noel Boggs and Joaquin Murphy also passed through his bands; those who prefer to swing in more polite fashion should find this the appropriate music for doing so.

Spade Cooley & Tex Williams: *Oklahoma Stomp* (Club of Spades). Cooley is responsible for more unadulterated schlock than anyone else in western swing, but his best recordings are undoubtedly those he made when he was breaking Tex Williams in as his lead vocalist, beginning in 1942. Of the two albums documenting this liaison, this one shows the more self-assured Williams; the instrumentals boast more musicianship and less gimmickry than those on the companion album, too.

(Caveat: This label, which is an arm of Cooley's fan club, also offers a three-volume series *The Best of Spade Cooley's Transcribed Shows* and the three-volume *Mr. Music Himself* series, which is TV transcriptions. By the time Cooley hit TV, his music [except for the origins of some of the songs he covered] had virtually nothing to do with western and little more to do with swing; it was all mundane melody, much of it not even on a par with television theme music, and I'd recommend staying away from those sets entirely.)

Alvin Crow and the Pleasant Valley Boys: *Alvin Crow and the Pleasant Valley Boys* (Polydor). After Asleep at the Wheel, Crow led the "other" western swing revival band in Austin. His voice is thin and his band sounds more like a bunch of journeymen. But he's an ebullient fiddler with an entertaining notion of what makes for western swing, and of when to be serious and when to go for laughs.

Alvin Crow and the Pleasant Valley Boys: *High Riding* (Polydor). This one's a little jivier and a little more old-fashioned both, at least until you get to the dope-running song "(The Texas Kid's) Retirement Run." Both are out of print, but if you have a choice, go for the previous one.

Devil with the Devil (Rambler). With good-time strutters like "They Go Wild Over Me" and "I'm Wild About That Thing," the Tune Wranglers prove themselves masters of jive. Cliff Bruner's ultra-jazzy Texas

Wanderers aren't far behind with "The Right Key (But the Wrong Keyhole)" and "I Ain't Gonna Give Nobody None o' This Jelly Roll." On "Jig," a late edition of Bill Boyd and His Cowboy Ramblers puts Boyd's initial work to shame.

Four Giants of Swing: *S'Wonderful* (Flying Fish). Here's where the distinctions break down entirely between western swing and jazz. The four giants are Joe Venuti (the jazz fiddler) with Jethro Burns (once of Homer and Jethro) on mandolin, Curly Chalker (Nashville sessions ace) on steel and Eldon Shamblin (from the Texas Playboys) on guitar. The tunes are from Gershwin and Ellington, and if I worked in a record store, I wouldn't know *what* section to file this one in. But I'd always keep copies in stock.

Johnny Gimble: *Johnny Gimble's Texas Dance Party* (Columbia/Lone Star). "Produced in Texas by Texans," the credits boast, and with songs like "Lone Star Rag," "Texas Fiddle Man," "Texas Skip," and "Under the 'X' in Texas," you're not likely to forget it anyhow. But Gimble has a sense of humor about all this (right down to his description in "Bosque Bandit" of a musician as someone who's "too lazy to work, too nervous to steal"). He also has more drive, verve, and chops than any fiddler alive, and he evokes the spirit of Bob Wills every time he plays. What a pity that the best swing album of the whole seventies revival should have gone out of print so quickly. (Hint to Delta Records: Get on the case, fast!)

Johnny Gimble & The Texas Swing Pioneers: *Still Swingin'* (CMH). In 1979, Johnny Gimble, a Wills alumnus who carries on the sound and spirit of western swing today, gathered together various veterans from the music's golden era—banjo player Marvin "Smokey" Montgomery, pianist Frank Reneau, and guitarist Zeke Campbell of the Light Crust Doughboys, pianist Fred "Papa" Smith and fiddler Cliff Bruner of Milton Brown's Musical Brownies, fiddler J. R. Chatwell from the Hi-Flyers and Adolph Hofner's band (among others), and several more. Together, they created an autumnal album that swings with a lightness and sureness even the re-formed Texas Playboys could no longer match.

Johnny Gimble: *The Texas Fiddle Collection* (CMH). Texas chauvinists, unite! Gather 'round as Gimble, the most soulful fiddler alive, leads two different bands through a history of Lone Star fiddle styles. The earliest is represented in his rendition of "Sallie Gooden" and the latest is the electronic wizardry of "Breakdown on the Freeway."

Hartman's Heart Breakers: *Give It to Me, Daddy* (Rambler). Here's a real collectors album—the music is pretty ordinary small-group swing from North Carolina in the mid-thirties, but Betty Lou, the young-sounding lead singer, was the hillbilly Brooke Shields, and never failed to thrill the guys when she sang such lyrics as "We'll go up to Room 304/ Start on the bed and finish on the floor."

Hillbilly Jazz (Flying Fish). Modern folkies (David Bromberg) and swing devotees (Vassar Clements, Doug Jernigan) gather for a too-loose jam session that never really catches fire, but does throw off sparks.

Adolph Hofner: *South Texas Swing* (Arhoolie). In which San Antonio's favorite Bohemian western swinger connects on everything from "Maria Elina" to "Sam, the Accordion Man" to "Jessie Polka" to "Longhorn Stomp" to beer commercials. Recorded between 1935 and 1955, these sides include such esteemed pickers as J. R. Chatwell on fiddle, Emil "Bash" Hofner (Adolph's brother) on steel, and Curly Williams on guitar. Not the most dramatic Hofner set that could be compiled, but it all swings, even the polkas.

The Hi-Flyers: *The Hi-Flyers* (Texas Rose). According to leader Andy Scarborough, this group was the first to play "takeoff" solos, i.e., solos in which the musician departs from the melody, as in jazz. He claims the group was doing so in the twenties, though there is no recorded evidence backing him up. These sides are from 1937–41, and show the Fort Worth group to have one of the most relaxed swing sounds of the era.

Hot As I Am (Rambler). When it was first released, this was about the best anthology on the market. It was the only place you could find the Light Crust Doughboys' "Pussy, Pussy, Pussy." Or J. R. Chatwell's incendiary fiddle solo on the title tune. There're two more tracks from Cliff Bruner's Texas Wanderers, and three from the Tune Wranglers. Many of these have since turned up elsewhere, but as a sampler of swing from 1935 to 1941, this is still hard to beat.

Light Crust Doughboys: *String Band Swing, Vol. II* (Longhorn). For such a crucial group, the Doughboys are shockingly ill-served on reissues. Or are they? As a show band that never played dances, they were somewhat restrained, and though nearly all the western swing greats played with them at one time or another, the Doughboys weren't innovators, but imitators. (Remember, Wills and Brown had to leave them to launch western swing, and the Doughboys played catch-up.) Still, there's some grit here, and Ramon DeArmon sings with a sly touch.

The Light Crust Doughboys (Texas Rose). This package puts the emphasis on the gimmicky and the clever, but since they were never exactly path-breakers, that's probably the most sensible approach to the

Doughboys. Sound is pretty bad, but song for song, it's the best album available on a group that seldom lives up to its legend.

Leon McAuliffe: *Steel Guitar Rag* (Delta). McAuliffe works out on the damndest-looking steel guitar you've ever seen, one with four necks. Most (but not all) of these tunes are associated with Wills. Because McAuliffe has always been among the simplest of steel players, he hasn't slowed down much over the years, and while it's no virtuoso set, this is the best of the several solo LPs he's cut.

Roy Newman and His Boys: *Roy Newman and His Boys, 1934–38, Vol. 1* (Original Jazz Library). Pianist Newman is one of the great lost figures of western swing, having recorded in the style well before Wills. If anything, Newman's work showed *more* jazz influence, too, because his bands rarely cut country fiddle tunes; the Newman repertoire stressed jazz standards like "Black and Blue" and "Rhythm Is Our Business," along with down-and-dirty blues like Blind Lemon Jefferson's "Match Box Blues." The stars of the band included Jim Boyd (one of the first to record with amplified guitar), Holly Horton (a comical, controversial clarinet player roughly twice the age of everyone else in the band), and Earl Brown (one of the funkiest singers western swing produced).

Lucky Oceans and the Asleep at the Wheel Review: *Lucky Steels the Wheel* (Blind Pig). He was the Wheel's original steel player, and on this 1983 effort Lucky calls together some of his former colleagues plus the always-ready Johnny Gimble for a jaunty survey of prewar country swing styles. Lucky dominates, of course, but he's generous with his singers and sidemen, too, which gives this a much broader range than the usual steel player's solo album.

Operators' Specials (British String). A mixed bag of performers and styles from outside the swing centers of Fort Worth and Houston—which means lots of San Antonio bands like Jimmy Revard and His Oklahoma Playboys, the Tune Wranglers, and Adolph Hofner and His San Antonians. J. R. Chatwell's darting fiddle on Hofner's "Sometimes" is a swing landmark. But Buddy Jones once again supplies the most excitement, boasting with a cocky, strutting self-assurance that even Jimmie Rodgers himself never possessed so fully. On "Rockin' Rollin' Mama" (probably the first country song to use that phrase), Jones makes much of the fact that while his baby can chug all night, she comes home to him for the real thing; on "Mean Old Sixty-Five Blues" he looks forward to retirement because his pension will finance fighting and whoring. Sparked by singer/fiddler Cotton Thompson, electric guitarist Junior Barnard and pianist Millard Kelso, Johnnie Lee Wills and IIis

Boys also turn in some crack blues, much "blacker" in feel than Bob
Wills was.

Hank Penny and His Radio Cowboys: *Tobacco State Swing* (Rambler). Penny is one of the few worthwhile western swingers who didn't
come from the Southwest; he's from Alabama, and this collection of his
earliest sides (1938–41) reveals significant deviations. Most of all, he
unlocked some of the ramifications of swing and moved his music along
into something closer to bop, which is to say that he evolved alongside
jazzmen more than alongside country players, most of whom were
never able to get out of the swing era. For this, Penny can thank his steel
player Noel Boggs above all, though Hank's own steady rhythm guitar
work helped keep things moving, too.

The Prairie Ramblers: *Tex's Dance* (German Cattle). In which everybody's (meaning mainly Patsy Montana and Gene Autry) favorite
backup band from Kentucky evolves from a conventional (though
highly spirited) string band into a western swing unit, sort of. This
catches them at their eclectic peak, 1933–38.

Eldon Shamblin: *Guitar Genius* (Delta). With Shamblin fronting the
band, the jazz basis of even the most countryish Bob Wills material is
more explicit. But Shamblin is an austere guitarist who moves around
the music map without losing his singular touch, and after a while
individual cuts start sounding less like jazz, country, Wills material, etc.,
than like Eldon Shamblin stylings. His backup is so lightweight it's easy
to blot out entirely, which is the best way to hear Eldon's reflective,
graceful melodic lines.

Buddy Spicher and Buddy Emmons: *Buddies* (Flying Fish). Two of
Nashville's renegade pickers unite on fiddle and steel respectively to
turn everything from Michael Legrand to Bill Monroe to Clifford
Brown into an ambitious, artsy, modern swing hybrid.

Ocie Stockard and the Wanderers: *Ocie Stockard and the Wanderers,
1937* (Origin Jazz Library). Banjo player Stockard, who made his name
playing with Milton Brown, put together this group after Brown's
death. They recorded fourteen sides in one day and promptly dis-
banded. It was a peculiar brand of western swing, for there was no steel
guitar at all, and the top musician in the band was Harry Palmer, a
jazzman who played a wild and woolly trumpet, an instrument seldom
associated with western swing. The material is a little trite, but the band
is not.

Stompin' at the Honky Tonk, Western Swing in Houston, 1936–41
(British String). If western swing was forged in Fort Worth, it was pol-

ished to a shine in Houston, an urbane city which was visited more often by touring black jazz bands. How else to explain the unmistakable Ellington influence on a group like the Port Arthur Jubileers? Shelly Lee Alley (whose band was called the Alley Cats) was even classically trained. Bob Dunn's Vagabonds, who perform the title song, sound funkier than usual next to some of the more sophisticated groups here.

"Brother" Al Stricklin: *Bob Wills' Original Piano Player* (Delta). Stricklin is a great piano player not just because he's so unpredictable, but because he has a sense of humor and he knows when to lay out; some of his best moments on this mid-seventies album come when he's playing in support of another soloist. But his readings of "San Antonio Rose" and "Take Me Back to Tulsa," among others, show that he always did have ideas of his own about how Bob Wills music should sound, and as an added bonus, not everything here is Bob Wills music.

The Original Texas Playboys: *Live & Kickin'* (Capitol). In the mid-seventies, when the western swing revival reached unanticipated heights, Leon McAuliffe rounded up some of the vets and put them back on the road. The group consisted of himself on steel, Smokey Dacus on drums, Joe Frank Ferguson on bass, Al Stricklin on piano, Bob Kizer on guitar, Leon Rausch on vocals, and Jack Stidham and Bob Boatwright on twin fiddles. For this live album, Rudy Martin sat in on clarinet and sax. Austin country-rock queen Marcia Ball sang "Texas Blues." It's a mixed bag but this is the best of the three albums they cut for Capitol (probably because they were more comfortable on stage than in a studio). Ambitious choices in material don't hurt, though.

Texas Sand: *Anthology of Western Swing* (Rambler). Moon Mullican turns up twice here, grooving through "That's What I Like About the South" as pianist-singer in fiddler Cliff Bruner's band, and as pianist for the Sunshine Boys on "No Good for Nothin' Blues." Roy Newman and His Boys sound tight as ever on "Everybody's Trying to Be My Baby" and especially "Texas Stomp," while steel player Emil "Bash" Hofner gets off some raunchy licks for Jimmy Revard and His Oklahoma Playboys on "Old Waterfall." But the real highlights are two songs ("Texas Sand" and "Lonesome Blues") by the Tune Wranglers, an early, Mexican-influenced San Antonio group with melodic flair to burn, and the wonderfully eccentric "Betty Ann" by Jesse Ashlock, a Bob Wills alumnus playing a singing, old-timey fiddle in front of a modern (1947) band.

Hank Thompson: *The Best of Hank Thompson and the Brazos Valley Boys* (Capitol). Thompson is the last of the successful western swing bandleaders, though he's always worked with small bands. His first hit came in 1949 with "Whoa Sailor," and though he's perhaps best known for "Wild Side of Life" (1952) and "Six Pack to Go" (1960), his real forte is the humorous wordplay ("Humpty Dumpty Heart," "Waiting in the Lobby of Your Heart," "Blackboard of My Heart") or the flat-out silly novelty ("Squaws Along the Yukon"). There's something about the man himself that's just a little out of whack, which does wonders for songs most others wouldn't go near.

Hank Thompson: *The Best of Hank Thompson, Vol. 2* (Capitol). The subtitle here makes note of Hank's "all-time novelty hits," which means there's an overlap between this and its predecessor on songs like "Squaws Along the Yukon," "Humpty Dumpty Heart," "Whoa Sailor," and "Rub-a-Dub-Dub" (too "novel" to be a good novelty song even by Hank's sometimes-dubious standards). And I don't believe "Oklahoma Hills" was ever meant to be a novelty song. But the rest of these, like *Vol. 1,* come from Hank's prime years of 1949–61, and they swing lightly while exuding good cheer and a sublime sense of the absurd.

Hank Thompson: *A Six Pack to Go* (Capitol). As he chortles, chuckles, and lurches his way through the likes of the title song, "Hangover Heart," "Bubbles in My Beer," "Wild Side of Life," and "Warm Red Wine," Thompson makes alcoholism seem like more fun than baseball or sex. Actually, his label assembled this from various fifties and sixties singles and key album cuts, so he can't be held fully responsible—or get all the credit—for this laugh-a-minute album of small-band swing.

The Tune Wranglers: *The Tune Wranglers, 1936–38* (Texas Rose). Because they hailed from San Antonio, these seminal western swingers leaned more heavily on Cajun and Mexican influences. But they added a healthier dose of Hawaiian music than most other bands, and though they never made much of an impression outside their south Texas base, they stomped with more exuberance than many of their better-known peers. More bad-boy feelthy humor, too.

Western Swing (Old Timey). Much of the Wills here is found on other albums, and there's too much Billy Boyd and His Cowboy Ramblers. But on "You've Got to Hi-De-Hi" and "French Two Step," the Hackberry Ramblers pull off the elusive Cajun-swing fusion that only they and Harry Choates (represented here by "Rubber Dolly") ever mastered.

Western Swing, Vol. 3 (Old Timey). "What's the Matter with the Mill" is Wills at his shouting best, but his other two cuts are no letdown, either. The San Antonio groups (Adolph Hofner and His San Antonians, Jimmie Revard and His Oklahoma Playboys) acquit themselves handsomely, and there's intriguing esoterica in the Bar-X Cowboys and the Night Owls. You might want to listen closely to "Everybody's Truckin' " to see how often the Modern Mountaineers say "truckin' " and how often they say "fuckin' "—for 1937, this stuff gets pretty explicit, though of course it wouldn't mean a thing without that rhythm track.

Western Swing, Vol. 4: The 1930's (Old Timey). One of the most resourceful anthologies in this series. The Modern Mountaineers, led by J. R. Chatwell's sizzling fiddle, once again explore further ramifications of the F-word on "You Got to Know How to Truck and Swing" and nearly top it with "Gettin' That Lowdown Swing." Hank Penny and His Radio Cowboys get progressive on "Mississippi Muddle" and on the nonsensical "It Ain't Gonna Rain No Mo'." The Crystal Springs Ramblers get funky on "Down in Arkansas" and the Washboard Wonders come from deepest left field (actually, North Carolina, not exactly a swing bastion) on "It Ain't Right." Plus Ted Daffan's Texans with the original "Worried Mind."

Western Swing, Vol. 5: The 1930's (Old Timey). Western swing produced its fair share of one-hit wonders, but few outdid Buddy Jones. On "Settle Down Blues" and "Mean Old Lonesome Blues" he resurrects the ghost of Emmett Miller via Jimmie Rodgers. Nothing else here is quite that spectacular, but Milton Brown and His Brownies are irrepressible as always—and they even got Jimmie Davis to sit in on the tragicomic "Honky Tonk Blues" (not the Hank Williams song). That was after Brown died, and before Davis was born again and quit singing about such matters.

Western Swing, Blues, Boogie and Honky Tonk, Vol. 7—The 1940's and 50's (Old Timey). As swing went West to California and merged into honky-tonk and boogie around the rest of the country, it became harder to tell the players without a scorecard. *Vol. 6* of this series is forgettable though it tries to demonstrate this process; meanwhile, this volume moves even further from swing, the most notable exceptions being Bob Wills and His Texas Playboys with "Silver Lake Blues" and "C-Jam Blues" and Ole Rasmussen and His Nebraska Cornhuskers with "Sleepy-Eyed John." Tommy Duncan and His Western All-Stars check in with "Wrong Road Blues," one of the best of his post-Wills efforts. But the real attractions here are "Bustin' Thru" and "This Ain't the Blues," two of the celebrated jazz duets by steel guitarist Speedy West and guitarist Jimmy Bryant.

Western Swing, Blues, Boogie and Honky Tonk, Vol. 8—The 1940's and 50's (Old Timey). Is that a harmonica on "Boogie Woogie Blues" by Art Gunn and His Arizona Playboys and on "Out of Money, Out of Place, Out of Style" by Jimmy Walker? Is "Steelin' Home" by Noel Boggs and His Day Sleepers (great name!) too sophisticated to even qualify as western swing? Isn't Bill Nettles ("Too Many Blues," "High Falutin' Mama") really just a southeastern honky-tonker who took a trendy boogie-woogie injection? Yeah, but who cares. There may be very little western swing here, but among the obscurities are hot sides by such veterans as Hawkshaw Hawkins, T. Texas Tyler, and Tommy Duncan, and this is one of the most consistent albums in the whole series.

Billy Jack Wills and His Western Swing Band (Western). Billy Jack was Bob's brother; though not nearly as well known, he concocted a brand of western swing in many ways more advanced. There was a bigger beat, and the band moved into bebop (which Wills never figured out) and even something suspiciously close to rock 'n' roll. But all this was happening in northern California in the early fifties—wrong place, wrong time—and so was never recognized. These radio transcriptions of their most brash material should help change that.

Bob Wills: *Columbia Historic Edition* (Columbia). A mishmash with emphasis on western numbers, mostly from the early forties. But there'e're a couple of Wills faves that haven't surfaced on other greatest-hits collections, and "Lyla Lou" and "Away Out There" are issued for the first time.

Bob Wills: *24 Great Hits by Bob Wills and His Texas Playboys* (Polydor). Wills had his ups and downs with MGM, (which first released these sides) from 1947 to 1954, but this preserves most of the high points. These editions of the Playboys are bluesier than earlier ones, with "St. Louis Blues," a Wills favorite, providing a fine showcase for his fiddle as well as Louis Tierney's. Postwar themes surface in songs like "Bubbles in My Beer," which is somber stuff despite the carefree arrangement, and in weepers such as the bitter "Still Water Runs the Deepest" and "I'm Dotting Each 'I' with a Teardrop." On occasion, Wills even got angry; "The End of the Line" pulls no punches, with Johnny Gimble scatting along to his manic fiddle solo. Gimble brings some of the crazy energy of early Wills bands to this postwar group, as does Herbie Remington on steel. The capper here is "Faded Love," the 1950 ballad which has since become essential to the repertoires of every bar band ever to play in Texas.

Bob Wills, Tommy Duncan and the Texas Playboys: *31st Street Blues* (Longhorn). These are mid-forties radio transcriptions made with bands that may not have been Wills' best, but were among his last good ones. Junior Barnard gets lots more space here than on any other Wills in print, and the songs are an agreeable mix of the ultrafamiliar and the unpredictable.

Bob Wills and His Texas Playboys: *In Concert* (Capitol). Released in 1976, these are unspectacular but atmospheric small-band performances with an unidentified group apparently from the early sixties. Good variety, and though not essential, it's better than anything else I've heard from this era.

Bob Wills and Tommy Duncan: *Hall of Fame* (Liberty). Another double album in the label's "Legendary Master" series, these are also early-sixties sides, and virtually the last listenable music Wills made in the studio, even though much of it is actually remakes of early hits. Having Duncan back must have made a difference, because there's a spark on "Sittin' on Top of the World" that Wills had been missing for some time.

Bob Wills: *Keepsake Album #1* (Longhorn). Just Wills, fiddling on traditional tunes or some of his compositions, with Sleepy Johnson on guitar, Marvin Montgomery on banjo, and Luke Wills on bass. In such an informal "living room" atmosphere (the musicians sat in a circle with one mike above them, and everything was done in one take), "Faded Love" becomes a deep blues and other songs sound more country than they ever did with the Playboys. Cut in the mid-sixties, this is the only Wills album of its kind, a return to his childhood days of fiddling for fun, and it's a real find.

Bob Wills and His Texas Playboys: *For the Last Time* (Liberty). This double album (with booklet) contains the sides that the reunited Playboys were cutting (with Merle Haggard sitting in) in December 1973 when Wills suffered the stroke that left him comatose until his death in 1975. He is too weak to sing or play, but does more or less lead the band and gets off a holler here and there. As the first of many "Playboys reunion" albums, it does have a certain freshness to it, and the musicians are also spurred on by the presence of their leader. But musically, this will interest fanatics only.

Johnnie Lee Wills: *Tulsa Swing, 1950–51 Radio Transcriptions* (Rounder). Bob's brother comes on like an unpretentious Spade Cooley, light and mellow most of the time, and preferable to others of this ilk.

Smokey Wood: *The Houston Hipster* (Rambler). Smokey wasn't so much western swing as he was white jazz and boogie, period. He also seems to be a sterling example of the musician-as-bum-and-damn-proud-of-it; the liner notes dwell on his fondness for marijuana and his skills as a flimflam man almost as much as they do on his effervescent, delightfully unorthodox piano and singing. These sixteen sides from

1937 do indeed showcase a man who loves to flaunt convention, even the conventions of the form he chooses to work in. Unpredictable, irascible, full of humor and good spirits, Smokey Wood was an all-around, all-American smart-ass, and he made music to match.

BLUEGRASS

After the country music boom of the thirties, musicians felt there were two chief courses open to them. They could move closer toward modernization and commercialization (with honky-tonk) or they could try to hold back the clock. Bluegrass was the course purists took in an attempt to hold back the clock. When you listen today to classic bluegrass, with its roots deep in the old-time mountain string-band sound, it's hard to believe that this music was evolving parallel to honky-tonk.

At first, it wasn't even called bluegrass. It was just the music of Bill Monroe, identified largely with the three-finger banjo style of Earl Scruggs, until late in the forties, when a host of Monroe imitators appeared. Asked what kind of music they played, they would reply, "We play Blue Grass music," referring to the name of Monroe's band. Soon, all bands in that style became known as bluegrass; by the time he was voted into the Hall of Fame in 1970, Monroe was known as "Daddy Bluegrass."

Bluegrass has a harder edge than the mountain music it grew out of. It's often defined by the instruments that make up a classic bluegrass band—fiddle, guitar, mandolin, bass, and banjo. Occasionally, other instruments have been used—dobro, harmonica, accordion, second guitar. In a classic band the instruments are all acoustic, and the role of each is defined in fairly strict terms.

Until the mid-sixties, the guitar was a driving background instrument, used primarily for rhythm and to play short, snappy bass runs (as a sort of punctuation mark) at the end of solos from the fiddle, banjo, or mandolin. The fiddle and banjo, both of which were fading in mainstream country music, were the chief solo instruments; the mandolin was used as either a lead or a percussion instrument. The bass player provided simple rhythm patterns. This was all played at breakneck tempos, and despite the rigid structure, solos were often improvised, giving the music a spontaneous feel lacking in most other string-band music.

On top of this came the vocals. Though noted for its dazzling instrumental technique, bluegrass was originally a vehicle for the high, shattering voice of Bill Monroe, and all the top bluegrass groups used strident two-, three-, and four-part close harmonies. In the ideal blue-grass group, nearly everyone can sing, so there's a lead, a tenor, a baritone, and a bass.

At a time when the rest of country music was moving into the barroom and the bedroom, bluegrass clung steadfastly to the old moun-tain themes of death, tragic love, lonesome pines, log cabins, mom, and religion. The latter was especially strong, and there are bluegrass gospel superstars (the Lewis Family, Carl Story) who have been around seem-ingly forever although their music is incredibly dull by bluegrass stan-dards.

For bluegrass is a cult music, always has been. Even at the peak of its popularity, in the early fifties, there were no more than a dozen bluegrass groups signed to major labels. As the decade wore on, the music became increasingly in danger of extinction. It was saved in a most unexpected way: Bluegrass, the most reactionary of country music forms, became the darling of progressive urban intellectuals and polit-icos. To the urban folkie, bluegrass was authentic American folk music, the voice of the common man and one of the last bulwarks against mass-merchandised music. Where bluegrass had once been confined to the mountain areas of Tennessee, North Carolina, Virginia, and Kentucky, it was now playing New York and Boston. Before long, urban folkies were forming their own bluegrass bands (with predictably dismal re-sults, in most cases).

Meanwhile, a new generation of bluegrass musicians was also com-ing of age in the area around Baltimore and Washington, D.C. Unlike the urban folkies, they had authentic mountain family roots though they may never have lived in the mountains themselves. This meant they had firsthand contact with bluegrass culture but were also far enough removed from its sources that they felt free to take liberties with it. The best known of these groups was the Country Gentlemen.

By the late sixties these two new bluegrass factions had more or less united into something called "newgrass" (after New Grass Revival, one of the seminal groups). Newgrass could be electric, and could use such unlikely instruments as sax or flute. In newgrass, everything was pushed to the limit: The already fast tempos became even faster, the guitar runs more emphatic, the solos jazzier, the harmonies higher. Some (most notably David Grisman) pushed past the limits into a form of improvisa-tion that has only the most tenuous connection to the bluegrass they started with.

Needless to say, this infuriates the old guard still working in what was once the purest of musics. Most of them are old men and are simply being outlasted. But they still work with the new breed at the annual bluegrass conventions, and that's because they need each other badly. Bluegrass is *still* (or more so than ever) a cult music. Bluegrass fans are an unfathomably devout bunch. They fill those festivals year after year. They buy hundreds of albums on dozens of small labels seemingly without regard for quality; to the zealous and defensive bluegrass fanatic, it's all good. But there just aren't enough such fans, at least not relative to the rest of the country music market. Which is why major labels don't bother with bluegrass at all anymore.

Bill Monroe with Lester Flatt and Earl Scruggs: *The Original Bluegrass Band* (Rounder Special Series).

Bluegrass was almost entirely the creation of Bill Monroe, and he didn't develop it overnight. But it didn't come out of nowhere, either. Monroe gave it his personal stamp, but its antecedents go right back to his Kentucky childhood. They have been conscientiously traced by Monroe scholars, who are legion, and all are evident on this reissue of twelve late-forties sides that define the form.

He was born William Smith Monroe in 1911 on a farm outside Rosine, far from real bluegrass country. The youngest of eight children, he was cursed with poor vision and was a loner. But his mother, who died when he was ten, was an old-time fiddler and singer, and his extended family included others—especially his uncle Pendleton Vandiver, the fiddler celebrated in "Uncle Pen"—who played. Monroe has credited Uncle Pen with teaching him timing, and Bill's mandolin style (on songs like "I'm Going Back to Old Kentucky" and "Blue Grass Breakdown") is his attempt to emulate the uninterrupted flow of notes played by fiddlers. The other key figure was guitarist-fiddler Arnold Schultz, a local bluesman whose influence is clear on cuts like "Heavy Traffic Ahead" and "Blue Grass Breakdown." As a child, Monroe often backed Schultz at dances.

That's when Bill was playing guitar; he switched to mandolin when he began performing more with his brothers, because nobody else in the family played it. Bill's mandolin had only four strings instead of the usual eight because he played so loud.

In 1929, after moving North to find work in the oil refineries, he and his brothers Birch and Charlie began touring regularly; by 1934, Birch had left, and by 1936, when the Monroe Brothers recorded for Victor, they were already one of the most polished brother duets around. They drew heavily on bluesy traditional material, but because of their experience on Chicago's WLS National Barn Dance, they were no strangers to more commercial sounds. Their harmonies (Charlie sang lead, Bill tenor) were right out of the shape-note hymnals they'd learned as kids at Methodist and Baptist singing schools. But the two headstrong brothers clashed often, and by 1938 they'd gone separate ways. Both kept large followings.

Bill's group recorded in 1940 for Victor; he'd begun singing some leads and had been an Opry favorite for the last year with his rushing adaptation of "Mule Skinner Blues." On his first Victor sides, he proved to be a masterful weaver of voices, styles, instruments, and repertoire, but the sound wasn't quite there yet. It *is* there on the twenty-eight Columbia sides cut between 1945 and 1949. There had been a long gap between recordings, during which time Monroe had built one of the most popular live shows of the era, and when he went back into the studio, his constant juggling paid off.

At his first sessions, Sally Ann Forrester's accordion was still present, a throwback to the old days, but it was quickly dropped. Howard Watts (a/k/a Cedric Rainwater, later Hank Williams' bassist) had been added on string bass; he played in the four-four "cut time" (as opposed to the old two-four dance beat) that, on songs like "Little Cabin Home on the Hill" freed Monroe from having to worry so much about providing rhythm. Once a background instrument that added turnarounds at the end of verses, the mandolin was now taking over a lead role.

Fiddler Chubby Wise was from Florida, but his prior experience had been in western swing bands, an influence still apparent in cuts like "Heavy Traffic Ahead," "Molly and Tenbrooks," "Toy Heart," "My Rose of Old Kentucky," or "When You Are Lonely." The addition of Lester Flatt brought the sound more into focus, and then the addition of Earl Scruggs crystallized it.

Guitarist and lead singer Flatt came to Monroe in 1945 from, of all places, Charlie Monroe's band. With his trademark runs on the bottom strings, he brought more drive and syncopation to the band. He also provided a full, resonant tenor to create the "high, lonesome" sound. Flatt and Monroe co-wrote many of the group's songs, tailoring material specifically to their own strengths.

Scruggs came a short time later that year. Monroe had used a five-string banjo (by David "Stringbean" Akeman) since 1942, but Earl's fleet, three-finger style (derived from a western Carolinas tradition dating back to Snuffy Jenkins) threw the group into overdrive. He was as well steeped in blues as Monroe himself, and like his boss, Scruggs created new ways to use his ax as a lead instrument.

This meant the Monroe band was able to bring a more variegated sound to the old songs than anyone had before. There were no less than four pickers swapping breaks, and the vocal trio (tenor lead, baritone, and high tenor harmonies) was chilling. Monroe's live show featured comedians and individual instrumental spotlights, group members and a gospel quartet, even a baseball team to entertain before the music began; he traveled with his own circus tent because most towns didn't have a hall large enough to accommodate the crowds he attracted.

The shows featured slow blues like "Summertime Is Past and Gone" and hurtling breakdowns like "Blue Grass Breakdown," which is kicked off by Monroe's racing mandolin before Scruggs dives in, piling up notes almost to the point of atonality; he's that fast. There was the ancient "Molly and Tenbrooks," the story of a horse-racing grudge match that must have been a special pleasure for a Kentucky boy. And there was "Sweetheart You Done Me Wrong," on which Monroe's pinched, otherworldly high harmony seems to distill the very essence of both innocence and experience. It was, indeed, something new in country music.

Bill Monroe and His Blue Grass Boys: *The High, Lonesome Sound of Bill Monroe and His Blue Grass Boys* (MCA).

In the early fifties, when these sides were recorded, Bill Monroe's bluegrass got higher and lonesomer. There were reasons, many reasons.

The first was the departure from the Blue Grass Boys of Lester Flatt and Earl Scruggs. Scruggs had been the first to quit, in 1948, ostensibly because he was tired of Monroe's nonstop touring schedule. Flatt soon followed, and within the month the pair teamed up to make music very similar to Monroe's (how could it *not* be?). Even more insulting, from Monroe's point of view, their band included former Blue Grass Boys Howard Watts on bass and Jim Shumate on fiddle. Monroe felt bitter, betrayed, and the rivalry between the two groups reached such a peak that when Flatt and Scruggs signed with Columbia in 1950, Monroe promptly quit the label and went over to Decca.

Monroe's personal life was becoming as unsettling as his professional life, and he became nearly impossible to work for. He was tense, withdrawn, steely, suspicious. His temper, always near the surface even in the best of times, took over. Flatt and Scruggs were now getting some of the lucrative bookings that used to be his, so he could no longer pay sidemen as well as the competition did. After being badly injured in a 1953 auto wreck, he became even more moody. Band members were coming and going with increasing regularity.

Monroe responded to his growing isolation by putting it directly into his music. Though Jimmy Martin was with him for five years in the early fifties, Monroe sang more leads than ever before, and his voice moved up into a range that sounded unbelievably desperate and mournful. The series of singles he made for Decca during this period were gathered for this album years later.

Martin, who went on to form his own popular band, provided some stability for Monroe during these troubled years because his personality was almost the exact opposite. As lead singer when Monroe wasn't up front, he brought changes to the vocal sound, too. Martin could glide with sure pitch to and from sustained notes, so Monroe changed to such ornate parallel harmonies that he eliminated the need for a third voice. Meanwhile, his power had so increased that on cuts like "Memories of Mother and Dad," "I'm Blue, I'm Lonesome" and "When the Golden Leaves Begin to Fall," he nearly overwhelmed his lead singer's voice.

As if to spite Flatt and Scruggs, but also undoubtedly to focus attention on his strongest pickers, Monroe also changed the instrumental emphasis in the band. Martin, though a sure guitarist, was no match for Flatt, and he played backups most of the time. Banjo players like Jim Smoake, Rudy Lyle, Sonny Osborne, and Joseph Drumright stepped out rarely in comparison to Scruggs.

But the fiddle, an instrument more appropriate to Monroe's gloomy state of mind, was featured more often, and his bands during this period helped launch the careers of Vassar Clements, Red Taylor, Charlie Cline, and Gordon Terry. He experimented with twin fiddles, and even, on "My Little Georgia Rose," with three fiddlers.

His own mandolin playing grew fiercer and more expansive. On "My Dying Bed" he throws out licks like a shotgun discharging spent shells, while on "Whitehouse Blues," one of the album's flat-out breakdowns, his urgent singing is matched by mandolin passages so swift and high they seem to want to pass out of the human hearing range. The most tersely to-the-point mandolin he ever played appears on "I'm Blue, I'm Lonesome."

In 1949, Monroe began writing autobiographical or, as he labeled them, "true" songs. "Now come and listen to my story," he urges at the beginning of "My Little Georgia Rose," "A story that I know is true." Among his other "true" songs, this album includes "Letter from My Darling," "Memories of Mother and Dad," "On the Old Kentucky Shore," and "On and On."

Virtually all of them are taken at funereal tempos, and they make for a despairing body of work, brooding and preoccupied with death. Steeped as they are in archaic language, they fit right in with the tragic mountain ballads that were part of his original repertoire. Even "Sugar-Coated Love," the closest thing to an upbeat song here, isn't really upbeat; in it he merely concedes to having experienced pleasure at some point in the past. But his music remains as awesome as his misery. In this era only Hank Williams could match him for turning private desolation into art.

Flatt and Scruggs: *The Golden Era* (Rounder Special Series).

Flatt and Scruggs and the Foggy Mountain Boys took bluegrass to a mass audience. Building on Monroe's base, they quickly won over the country audience and landed both a spot on the Opry and their heralded radio show, the Martha White Flour Hour. But they went further by becoming the darlings of the urban folk set in the fifties, and pop stars (of a sort) in the sixties, TV and movie themes and all. By then, the music itself was scattered and hokey, but the early success, as these 1950–55 sides show, was no fluke.

Lester Raymond Flatt was born in 1914 in the Appalachian foothills of Overton County, Tennessee, and raised thirty miles south near Sparta. He came from a musical family, and was playing guitar and singing in a church choir by age seven. By the end of the thirties, he was married and playing regularly on the radio in various local groups while working in the mills around Covington, Virginia. In 1943 he joined Charlie Monroe's Kentucky Pardners, which led to a job the next year with Bill Monroe's Blue Grass Boys.

Earl Eugene Scruggs was born in 1924 in Flint Hill, North Carolina, also to a musical family. By the time he was ten, he was already playing banjo in the local style—hand-picking the strings with his thumb, index, and middle fingers. He worked locally throughout his teen-age years before "turning pro" when he joined the group of Lost John Miller in 1945 in Knoxville, Tennessee. Then came the offer from Monroe.

With the Blue Grass Boys, their styles gelled. Lester played his trademark bass runs and his melodies on the low guitar strings with his thumb, while brushing the high strings with his first finger to add a dash of rhythm. Earl's three-finger technique may have been common around his native Cleveland County, but elsewhere it was considered an innovation; he added even more syncopation, and did things with melody a banjo hadn't done before. He also used tunings previously foreign to the banjo.

The music they made on their own was an obvious variant on the sound of the Blue Grass Boys, but the differences stood out, too. They cut their first records for Mercury in 1948, and their two-year affiliation produced such classics as "Salty Dog Blues," "Roll in My Sweet Baby's Arms," and "Foggy Mountain Breakdown."

By the time they went to Columbia, they were set. As heard on these sides, the Foggy Mountain Boys used much less mandolin than Monroe, and much more banjo. But mandolinist Curley Seckler added buoyancy with his off-the-beat style, and the band swung. In 1951, Scruggs tuned one string down and then back up to give a sliding effect that accentuated the swing; he later devised Scruggs Pegs (as heard here on "Flint Hill Special") that did this automatically and the sound further set them off from the competition. Flatt's vocals grew more relaxed, more easygoing. Soon they were experimenting with snare drums, and when dobroist Buck Graves signed on shortly after Flatt and Scruggs joined the Opry in 1955, he brought yet another distinctive new ingredient to the mix.

It's Graves who adds the bluesy touch to "Randy Lynn Rag," which would otherwise be remembered solely as Scruggs' most turbo-charged performance. Utilizing his Scruggs Pegs at a mind-boggling pace, Earl charges high notes and hits them all, fiddler Paul Warren kicks out, and the band plays actual riffs behind Scruggs, an arranging technique seldom used in bluegrass.

There were also gospel numbers—"I'm Working on a Road," on which mandolinist Everett Lilly turns in shining harmonies, and "Brother I'm Getting Ready to Go"—and nostalgic, sentimental tunes like "The Old Home Town." But Flatt and Scruggs also staked out new turf early on. Though Earl seemed the more adventuresome of the two, it was Lester who wrote "I'm Gonna Sleep with One Eye Open," definitely racy by bluegrass standards. "Dim Lights, Thick Smoke (and Loud, Loud Music)" adapts honky-tonk imagery to their form.

These bluesy sides made the Flatt and Scruggs reputation in the South, but in 1954 they got support from an unexpected quarter. New York banjo guru Pete Seeger included a chapter on Scruggs' style in his instruction book, and Earl became a hero to urban folkies. The group first played New York City in 1954, and by 1957, owing to the added exposure, they were making more personal appearances than any other Opry act. They embraced their new audience enthusiastically, adding instruments to their records and cutting songs that had only the remotest connections to their mountain roots.

In the phrase of Little Richard, "They got what they wanted and lost what they done had." Between the time they did the theme for the "Beverly Hillbillies" TV series in 1962 and the time they landed the theme for *Bonnie and Clyde* in 1969 (with Earl's 1949 recording of "Foggy Mountain Breakdown"), they fell apart. Everything they did sounded cluttered, thanks to twelve-string guitars and vocal choruses. Scruggs began playing more guitar than banjo, and when he did play banjo, he sounded tired and hollow, all form and no function. On songs like Bob Dylan's "Rainy Day Woman" Lester sounded like he was singing with a gun at his head.

They played together for the last time at President Nixon's 1969 inaugural parade. Lester then retrenched, returning to Nashville and straight bluegrass music. Earl formed a group with his sons that was at first intriguing, but became tedious and rudderless. Many of their powerful early sides went out of print, and then it took ambitious reissues like this one to prove that the original excitement had been justified in the first place.

The Rich-R-Tone Story—The Early Days of Bluegrass, Volume 5 (Rounder).

He found them in Burlington, North Carolina, and Knoxville, Tennessee, in Bristol, Virginia, and Wheeling, West Virginia. Jim Stanton was an independent record man, and he went where the musicians were. Pretty soon, they began coming to him. By then, his Rich-R-Tone Records in Johnson City, Tennessee, was recording some of the rawest and richest bluegrass and mountain music of the postwar years. The best of it is right here on this anthology.

He grew up in Johnson City. In high school, Stanton started tagging along after a local jukebox operator on his route. Before long, he was working for the man, and then he got his own route. But as he explains in the excellent booklet accompanying this album, he always felt he could make records better than the ones he was stocking. In 1946 he started Rich-R-Tone, which flourished for nearly a decade before he went into custom recording.

Stanton was the ideal indie record man. He was beaming, easygoing, a real fan of the music he recorded. Johnson City was in the heart of bluegrass territory, and since the majors now ignored music indigenous to the region in favor of more commercial country musics, he stepped right in, cutting and pressing performances by local favorites one week and selling them out of the trunk of his car the next.

His policy was to sign people who'd already built radio followings. In doing so, he got a little of everything. Some was what we now think of as authentic bluegrass, and some wasn't; all of it had a similar feel. Sometimes, because he kept his ear so close to the ground, Stanton caught future stars on their way up; others had no aspirations toward show biz, performed locally after getting off their day jobs, and recorded mainly as an afterthought.

The Caudill Family of Whitesburg, Kentucky, offers pure old-time church music. Wilma Lee and Stoney Cooper were never considered a bluegrass group; they played a brand of string-band music that developed parallel to bluegrass, and they obviously kept up with the developments on that front, as the mandolin work by Bill Carver shows on their two wrathful sacred numbers, "Wicked Path of Sin" and "This World Can't Stand Long" ("This world has been destroyed before/Because it is so full of sin/For that very reason/It's gonna be destroyed again"). But they never made the transition fully, in either their vocal or their instrumental arrangements; when they left for Columbia Records (and a spot on the Opry), they delved deeper into pre-bluegrass forms.

The Stanley Brothers also went on to bigger things after recording first for Stanton. They're represented here by "Little Glass of Wine," which, with its frantic guitar (by Carter Stanley) and startling fiddle (by Leslie Keith) was their most popular number at the time; it's about halfway between commercial string-band music and bluegrass.

Both Cecil Surratt and His West Virginia Ramblers and Lambert and Curley Parker with Their Pine Ridge Boys have one cut in the string-band vein and one closer to mainstream bluegrass. Glen Neaves and the Grayson County Boys are so close to straight bluegrass on "The Old Swinging Bridge" that you hardly miss the bass, but "Black Mountain Rag" is a more standard breakdown.

Neaves is the type who never went far from home (the Galax, Virginia, area) but never gave up his music, either. Others are even more obscure. Buster Pack and His Lonesome Pine Boys provide the album's biggest charge with "Better Late Than Never," a bluegrass stomper full of heavily bowed fiddle, jabbing banjo, and driving, Monroe-style mandolin. Frank Hunter and His Black Mountain Boys are nearly as harsh, but not as purist, on "Long Time No See" and "Tennessee Boy."

Along with the Stanleys, the Bailey Brothers and Their Happy Valley Boys, and the Sauceman Brothers with Their Hillbilly Ramblers Quartet were the most enduring. The former even had a stint on the Opry before returning to their previous base in Knoxville. In 1947, when they added Wiley Birchfield, one of the unsung heroes of three-finger banjo picking, they made the move into bluegrass. Though the bluesy "Rattlesnake Daddy," with Charlie Bailey singing lead, is more in the Jimmie Rodgers mold, Monroe's influence is already apparent. The Saucemans, represented here with "Hallelujah We Shall Rise," were another of the first Tennessee groups (they were from Greenville) to incorporate Monroe's style into their own.

Stanton eventually ran into the same problems that plagued all indies, irregular distribution above all. He had little money for promotion and his artists had to move on to major labels if they were to make a go of it professionally. But before that happened, he'd done what only the indies can do: He'd tapped directly into the creative juices of his region. His was perhaps the most regional music of all, but that didn't stop Jim Stanton, because he knew his stuff.

The Stanley Brothers: *The Stanley Brothers and the Clinch Mountain Boys* (King/Gusto).

If Bill Monroe and Flatt and Scruggs are analogous to the kind of forest fires that give off bold leaping flames, then the Stanley Brothers are equivalent to the kind of smoldering, slow-burning fire that on the surface isn't as spectacular, but in the end lasts just as long and burns just as deep. Neither Carter's lead nor Ralph's tenor harmony voice could match Monroe for vocal pyrotechnics; neither Carter's guitar nor Ralph's banjo can touch the virtuosity of a Flatt or Scruggs. But their music is perhaps more timeless than any other in bluegrass, their sound more in tune with the mountains themselves. The Stanley Brothers never really left the Clinch Mountains where they grew up, and that is evident in their music.

Carter was born in 1925 in McClure, Virginia, and Ralph in 1927 in Stratton. It was coal country, and the farmland where they lived near McClure yielded few good crops. After interruptions for military service and a few not-so-lucrative gigs with other groups, they launched their musical careers for real in 1946. At first, they were a mainstream mountain string band, influenced by Wade Mainer, the Blue Sky Boys, and other commercial country groups of the thirties and early forties. But by the time they cut their first sides for Rich-R-Tone in 1948, they were moving toward the new sound of Bill Monroe, due in no small part to the urgings of their mandolinist, Pee Wee Lambert. In 1949, when they went to Columbia, they were committed to bluegrass, though still stumbling with the form. At this point, they offered a study in contrasts. Ralph had evolved a three-finger banjo style out of Scruggs, but still showed the influence of the old clawhammer style he'd grown up playing. Their material was equal parts traditional ballads, commercial string-band music and bluegrass originals.

In the early fifties they split briefly while Ralph pursued his original interest in veterinary medicine. Carter bided his time working in Monroe's band, where he picked up a few more tips. When they regrouped and signed with Mercury in 1954, they cut some of their most incendiary sides ever, but the overall output was still erratic. From there they went to Starday, a Nashville-based label whose scattershot approach to recording produced further unevenness. Finally, in the late fifties, they settled in with King, and found a consistent groove. Though they recorded often—probably too often—they kept coming up with sharp new arrangements, and Carter had now come into his own as a writer, so they were seldom short of material. And though there were a few attempts to fit them into the faddish collegiate folk-music mold, they mainly went their own way.

This is their first King album, and if no single cut stands out the way "Mule Skinner Blues" did for Monroe or "Foggy Mountain Breakdown" did for Flatt and Scruggs, it's still hard to find faults. The Stanleys were by now rock solid, and the only thing really missing here is one or two of the gospel songs they sang with such quiet conviction.

The sound is sparse, but stately—a reflection of Carter's own stern demeanor (for he called the shots in this duo). Carter's leads are deceptively relaxed; Ralph's tenor harmonies, once shaky, are now full and mature. The overall effect is one of dignity and great reserves—the proverbial still waters running deep.

More than other big bluegrass acts, the Stanleys made white mountain music exclusively; there was hardly a trace of blues or jazz in what they did. When somebody solos on an instrumental like "Clinch Mountain Backstep" or the bittersweet "Keep a Memory," there's little happening in the background beyond simple rhythm patterns. Though mandolin was de-emphasized after Lambert and then Curley Sechler came and went, Bill Napier gets his licks in on a few breaks here, and contributes tasteful ensemble work throughout. So does fiddler Ralph Mayo, whose predecessors included the likes of Benny Martin and Howdy Forrester; he has the chops of neither of these men, but he's always *right there* in the group sound. He's turned loose on the aptly titled "Midnight Ramble," as is Ralph on banjo, but what's most effective is the group mind, the way the musicians work together as a unit.

With moralistic pieces like "She's More to Be Pitied," the wistfulness of "How Mountain Girls Can Love," and the soft sorrow of "The Memory of Your Smile," this lays the groundwork for the team's voluminous King output. Though at the top of the bluegrass cult both at home and abroad, they never made the move to Nashville at the height of their popularity. When they got off the road, they returned to the sanctuary of their old Clinch Mountain home to recharge and gather inspiration; that sense of space, silence, and distance that the mountains produced thus stayed in their music right to the end. Carter, whose voice had been blunted by alcohol for several years, was killed in a 1966 auto wreck, and Ralph carried on without him. After so many years in the shadow of his brother, he did better than most of his fans expected, and he did so by clinging to the duo's original policy: In a form rife with overstatement, the Stanley Brothers proved that nothing succeeds like understatement.

The Country Gentlemen: *Yesterday and Today, Volume 1* (Rebel).
Newgrass begins with the Country Gentlemen. Over the years they took in many of the movement's top pickers, and cleared the way for countless other groups. When they finally split, each member formed influential spin-off groups. They were the first to step, however gingerly, outside the rigid traditions of the form, and though they took

more liberties as they grew, they never went too far. They combined the best of both worlds.

This is the first of a three-volume retrospective covering the peak years 1963–71 (prior to Rebel, they recorded for Mercury, Folkways, and Starday). The core of the group was Charlie Waller (guitar), John Duffey (mandolin), and Eddie Adcock (banjo), with a procession of bassists (the most enduring was Tom Gray). But the founder was banjo player Bill Emerson, who played in the Washington, D.C., area with Buzz Busby.

When Busby was injured in a 1957 auto wreck, Emerson had to patch a group together quick or lose a scheduled gig. Out of the fertile D.C. scene he came up with Waller and Duffey in no time. When he then left the group soon thereafter, Waller and Duffey went through several banjoists before agreeing on Adcock.

As a vocal trio, they emphasized the similarities, rather than the differences, in their voices, and as "The Fields Have Turned Brown," "The Long Black Veil," and "Get in Line Brother" all show, they had a satisfying blend. But as individual singers, they also stood out.

Waller was a smoothie with precise phrasing, and he sang more like commercial Nashville vocalists than like an unreconstructed Kentucky mountain man; this made sense because he was from Louisiana. Duffey was a "loud" tenor, more impressive on harmonies than on leads. He, too, had little of the flat inflection of the pure bluegrass singers, and that also made sense; his father was an opera singer, and the influence is clear in John's fluid voice and soaring style. Adcock, a soft baritone, never took leads, but gave the trio a firm footing.

Of the three, the star musician was Duffey. He sometimes relied too heavily on flash and technique, but he was much less excessive than most newgrass pickers, and Adcock's three-finger banjo playing was a tough foil. Waller was the most understated of the three.

What made the group so different was its attitude and its material. They were too far removed from the traditional environment and lineage to claim bluegrass as their own strictly by heritage. So there's a self-consciousness and calculated craftsmanship about their music that gave them room to poke a little fun at it, to take liberties with it. Waller's guitar runs on "Long Black Veil" (1967) are frequently out of place, from a traditionalist's viewpoint, but they are apt, and they flow directly out of the song's structure.

The background vocals on Duffey's "When They Ring Those Golden Bells" (1968) also have little to do with strict tradition; they lend the song a pop flavor. This tendency is even more pronounced on "Get in Line Brother" (1967), another admonitory Duffey song, this one sporting an unusually complex vocal arrangement.

The songs are a mixed bag. The Country Gentlemen took from and contributed to the urban folk movement of the early sixties. Again, they were self-conscious enough about it to lampoon "Tom Dooley" (1963)—commercial folk music, ech!—just so nobody would be confused as to which side they were on, but what the hey, the song deserves no better, right, and besides, what's a bluegrass set without at least one piece of low humor? Their version of Larry Sparks' "I Never Will Marry" (1963) was picked up by numerous citybillies and itself became something of a commercial folk song.

But who would expect a bluegrass group to turn Ernest Tubb's weeper "Are You Waiting Just for Me" (1967) into a strident, flat-out stomp? Or to take Carter Stanley's sentimental "The Fields Have Turned to Brown" (1971) as a straight blues? Nor is "Less of Me" (1970) an obvious choice, though it lends itself well to bluegrass interpretation, especially with Mike Auldridge's dobro adding flavor in the expanded, six-man group.

Jimmie Rodgers' "Blue Yodel #4" gets a speeded-up arrangement full of showy mandolin and banjo that manages to span several generations' worth of country music. Duffey's squalling lead vocal here keeps breaking into a semi-yodel throughout the song, before finally going all the way up at the end. And the Gentlemen bring all their influences together when they cover Jimmy Murphy's "Electricity" (1964), which likens the holy spirit to electricity in that both are strong and yet invisible. It's a double-edged song—both wry and serious, seemingly right in the tradition until you listen more closely—and it combines Rodgers' wit with the spirituality of a Monroe or a Stanley.

Duffey, who was more or less the group's leader, was also the first to leave; he was replaced by Jim Gadreau. Adcock was next, his spot going to none other than Bill Emerson. Later editions of the group grew progressively more pop. The last cut here is a bucolic arrangement of "Mrs. Robinson" (1969) that draws genuine folk roots out of Paul Simon, even. But you'll notice that they cut it as an instrumental only. Even at their most "outside," the group knew intuitively that bluegrass was not yet ready for the New Morality, and that is the way it *should* be.

Supplementary Albums

Red Allen, Frank Wakefield and the Kentuckians: *Bluegrass* (Folkways). Wakefield is an adventurous, though erratic, mandolin player, while Allen is a tradition-bound guitarist. The group also features banjoist Bill Keith, and provides some of the truest second-generation traditional bluegrass of the early sixties.

Mike Auldridge: *Mike Auldridge* (Flying Fish). On a par with *Dobro* and *Blues and Bluegrass,* his two harder-to-find albums on Takoma. As always, he's working with a group of folk and newgrass all-stars to create an acoustic music that leaves its roots behind fast. Still, the Seldom Scene veteran makes his dobro do things nobody else has matched.

The Bailey Brothers: *Have You Forgotten?—The Early Days of Bluegrass, Vol. 6.* (Rounder). Charlie and Daniel Bailey were the first to apply the close harmonies of brother duets directly to the bluegrass instrumental lineup. Which means that while they were later coming to the form, they became almost as influential as Monroe, Flatt, and Scruggs and the Stanleys. Even though they were favorites of Hank Williams, among others, they remained relatively obscure, a fact at odds with the open-minded approach they show on this album.

Kenny Baker: *A Baker's Dozen—Country Fiddle Tunes* (County). Because he practically invented bluegrass fiddle while playing with Bill Monroe, one invariably expects more from a Baker solo album. This one is mainly for pickers, but with its balance of originals and reworked traditional tunes, it has more drive and spirit than most of his solo work.

Byron Berline: *Dad's Favorites* (Rounder). About the only consistently listenable album made by this wide-ranging (but basically traditional) fiddler who seemed to get too much too soon and failed to live up to his promise.

Norman Blake and Red Rector: *Norman Blake and Red Rector* (County). Blake is a meticulous, flat-picking guitarist most popular among urban folkies, while Rector is an older man, a traditional (but adventuresome) mandolin player. Both have made several contemporary solo albums, but none stand up to this, which itself would probably have turned out better had they interacted more rather than just alternating choruses.

Boone Creek: *One Way Track* (Sugar Hill). Ricky Skaggs and cohorts in 1979. This is basically relaxed, straight-ahead bluegrass that at its best ("Daniel Prayed") stretches the tradition without defying it.

Hylo Brown: *Hylo Brown Meets the Lonesome Pine Fiddlers* (Starday/ Gusto). Guitarist/singer Brown, who once worked with Flatt and Scruggs, has an outlook similar to that of Doc Watson: He's a self-conscious folkie who doesn't let it get in the way of his music, and he respects the rules so much he knows just how to break them and make it work. The Lonesome Pine Fiddlers have always been popular inside bluegrass circles and unknown outside; without a front man (like Brown) to spark them, they're usually faceless and uninspired. The material here is strong, from spirituals and traditional songs to Jimmie Rodgers and George Jones to "The Ballad of Jed Clampett" and Brown originals; a drug song like "The Needle" brings bluegrass into areas it's always avoided. Brown molds it all into a traditional bluegrass sound, and sings with as warm a voice as this music has ever heard.

Vassar Clements: *The Bluegrass Sessions* (Flying Fish). Just what the title says, with credible sidemen, none of whom do much stepping out. But next to the overkill of most Clements albums, this one comes as a small relief.

Charlie Cline: *Country Dobro* (Adelphi). Cline has his roots in blue-grass, but the music on this album is looser, more relaxed, less pyrotech-nic. His terse, snappy lines don't have much to do with more traditional, Hawaiian-based songs, either. This is the best of his several modern albums, both because his group is more sympatico and his material is more rustic.

Connie and Babe: *The Early Days of Bluegrass, Vol. 10* (Rounder). Guitarist-singer Babe Lofton is the driving force behind this sometimes-group, mainly because he wrote such classics. But he's not even on many of the 1958 sessions, so then the group becomes Connie (Gately) and Joe (Drumright). These guys didn't play that much, but their best work is as memorable as that of some of the groups who made a living with bluegrass, which wasn't many.

Country Cooking: *Country Cooking* (Rounder). Just when it looked like newgrass had played itself out completely, this band came along in the early seventies with the two-banjo attack of Tony Trischka and Peter Wernick to take it one step further. These are all instrumentals, but are seminal.

Country Gazette: *All This, and Money, Too!* (Ridge Runner). A daring extension of bluegrass, and for once it works. The basic group of Roland White (mandolin) Alan Munde (banjo/guitar) Michael Anderson (bass), Joe Carr (guitar) is joined by various guests. These flings with contempo-rary western swing and rock are a lot more interesting than their more mainstream work, though they still need someone who can sing with conviction (vocals are shared by all but Munde).

The Country Gentlemen: *The Traveler and Other Favorites* (Rebel). Some gripping Americana here in "The Border Incident,"

"Buffalo Girls," "Amelia Earhart," and "Johnny Reb," as well as savvy choices like "Dark as a Dungeon." But would you believe a bluegrass arrangement of the theme from *Exodus?* And don't miss John Duffey's liner notes explaining that Dylan's "It's All Over Now, Baby Blue" ". . . deals with a person talking to his 'id' (one's inner self). . . ."

The Country Gentlemen: *Gospel Album* (Rebel). For obvious reasons, gospel songs bring out the best in good bluegrass groups. Though they didn't write some of the songs to which they lay claim, you can't fault this group for their choice of material.

The Country Gentlemen: *Sit Down Young Stranger* (Sugar Hill). Cut in 1980 with—gasp!—drums and everything, but Waller is as steadfast as ever, and he gets assistance from the likes of Doyle Lawson and Mike Auldridge. The best of their ultramodern albums.

The Country Gentlemen: *John Duffey, Charley Waller and The Country Gentlemen Sing and Play Folk Songs and Bluegrass* (Folkways). Recording for the New York revivalist label, the group predictably enough went for a more folk-flavored sound, particularly in their vocal arrangements. Eddie Adcock's charging banjo drives the band.

The Country Gentlemen: *Yesterday and Today, Vol. 2* (Rebel). A step below *Vol. 1,* with a tendency toward the precious in songs like "Aunt Dinah's Quilting Bee." But originals like "East Virginia Blues" and intriguing covers of John D. Loudermilk's "Warm and Windy" and Jimmy Skinner's "Doin' My Time" compensate handsomely.

The Country Gentlemen: *25 Years* (Rebel). This double album is a little too much Country Gentlemen at one sitting for my tastes, and the previously unissued cuts should probably have remained that way. More is not necessarily better, and some editions of the group were not necessarily as good as others, but this provides a retrospective overview that newgrass fans are bound to appreciate.

J. D. Crowe & the New South: *J. D. Crowe & the New South* (Rounder). Crowe is a Scruggs-based banjoist who first made his name with Jimmy Martin, but went on to become one of the newgrass pickers who held onto his roots and his common sense. The group, which includes Tony Rice on guitar and lead vocals and Ricky Skaggs on mandolin, fiddle, viola, and tenor vocals, is equally comfortable with "Sally Goodin" or Fats Domino's "I'm Walkin'."

J. D. Crowe: *The Model Church* (Rebel). Guitarist Doyle Lawson sings most of the leads on this tightly arranged gospel album featuring vocal trios and Crowe's syncopated, bluesy banjo breaks.

J. D. Crowe, Tony Rice, Doyle Lawson, Bobby Hicks, Todd Phillips: *The Bluegrass Album* (Rounder). Newgrass all-stars turn in a traditional set just to remind the folks they haven't forgotten how. And they don't even need overdubs to do it.

Crowe, Rice, Lawson, Hicks, Phillips: *The Bluegrass Album, Volume Two* (Rounder). Surprisingly, for an impermanent band, this is more cohesive than its predecessor, with a vocal blend that makes you wonder what they would do if they worked together all the time. They could be less predictable in choosing material, though.

The Dillards: *Back Porch Bluegrass* (Elektra). The Dillards arrived in L.A. from Salem, Missouri, in the early sixties and immediately galvanized the local folk scene with this, their debut album. Imagine—L.A. folkies with *real folk roots!* The star is Doug Dillard with his driving banjo, but Rodney Dillard (guitar, banjo, dobro), Mitch Jayne (bass), and Dean Webb (mandolin) have no trouble keeping up.

The Dillards with Byron Berline: *Pickin' and Fiddlin'* (Elektra). Around the time half of L.A. was using various Dillard members to add authenticity to mid-sixties folk-rock projects, the group added fiddler Berline and cut its most traditional LP yet.

Jim Eanes and the Shenandoah Valley Boys: *The Early Days of Bluegrass, Vol. 4* (Rounder). An original Foggy Mountain Boy and briefly one of Bill Monroe's Blue Grass Boys, Eanes played rhythmic guitar and sang in a smooth baritone that had almost as much to do with mainstream country as with bluegrass. (During the seven years between these 1951 and 1958 sessions for a North Carolina indie, he did pursue a career in Nashville as a country writer-singer.) He'd try anything, from Fiddlin' Arthur Smith's "Florida Blues" to his own Korean War weeper "Missing in Action" to "Lady of Spain" as a banjo instrumental, and his relaxed approach to such material was often a relief in the frenetic world of bluegrass picking.

The Early Days of Bluegrass, Vol. 1 (Rounder). Raw, early-fifties near-bluegrass from some of the earliest followers of Bill Monroe. Though "Old Grey Goose" is credited to Red Belcher and the Kentucky Ridgerunners, it's really a showcase for fiddler/singer Tex Logan. Two duets by the Lilly Brothers (Everett and Mitchell) are both sparser and slicker. Ronnie Knittel and Holston Valley Ramblers' "Holston Valley Breakdown" is inspired amateurism, but the real oddities are two by Hobo Jack, who turns out to be an affluent preacher from Cincinnati, and Phebel Wright's "Lint Head Stomp" ("lint head" being a pejorative for cotton-mill worker), a title Wright himself disavowed.

The Early Days of Bluegrass, Vol. 2 (Rounder). Like volume one, this album sports names that went largely unknown outside their immediate region. Most are from Kentucky, though many wound up in Ohio, where the factory jobs were. Frank Wakefield (teamed here with Buster Turner for two cuts and Marvin Cobb and the Chain Mountain Boys for another), Red Allen (two cuts under his own name), and the Brewster Brothers (one cut alone and one with the Four Brothers Quarter) are the best-known names, while L. C. Smith, Ralph Mayo, and the Southern Mountain Boys (with the delightful "Radio Boogie") and Estil Stewart and the Flat Mountain Boys (with the insistent "I Could Love You All the Time") are the new discoveries.

Flatt and Scruggs: *Country & Western Classics* (Time-Life). A three-record boxed overview of their career, which means, on the minus side, some of the dreck from their last years and, on the plus side, some of the epochal Mercury sides that are unavailable in any other form.

Flatt and Scruggs: *Columbia Historical Edition* (Columbia). Wouldn't you know it? The major company that actually owns vintage Flatt and Scruggs can't do half the job of packaging it that the specialty labels can. Confidential to completists: "You Put Me On My Feet" and "Who Knows Right From Wrong" are here released for the first time.

Flatt and Scruggs: *Don't Get Above Your Raisin'* (Rounder Special Series). More prime Columbia sides, and the title song is one of their most striking blues efforts. Not up to the *Golden Era* album, but catchy enough, and a must for devotees.

Lester Flatt and Earl Scruggs: *The Golden Years, Vol. 1* (County). Another reissue of Columbia sides, with much duplications of the Rounder LPs and somewhat inferior sound. This compilation is bluesier, and less bouncy, however, and might be preferable for those who usually find Flatt and Scruggs too cheerful.

Lester Flatt and Earl Scruggs and the Foggy Mountain Boys: *Blue Ridge Cabin Home* (County). This is even better, because it concentrates on Columbia sides generally unavailable on other reissues.

Flatt and Scruggs and the Foggy Mountain Boys: *Live at Carnegie Hall* (Columbia). Probably the best overall introduction to the sixties Flatt and Scruggs, as it catches them when they're just stretching out past the normal boundaries of bluegrass, but are not yet committing the excesses that later become commonplace.

Flatt and Scruggs with Doc Watson: *Strictly Instrumental* (Columbia Limited Edition). Since the bluegrass team was getting sluggish at the time of these recordings (1967), it's hardly surprising that Watson cuts right through them with his own clear, distinctive style. Though it was clearly not his intent, it becomes more his album than theirs—which, as far as I'm concerned, is all for the better.

Flatt and Scruggs: *The World of Flatt and Scruggs* (Columbia). This double album is not exactly a "greatest hits" package; it includes some hits and more misses, with the latter coming chiefly from their "progressive" phase. But this does provide the best overall sampler of their Columbia years.

Lester Flatt: *The Best of Lester Flatt* (RCA). This is the high point of Lester's return to bluegrass in the early seventies, after the acrimonious split between him and Earl Scruggs. Many of these songs are better known in their original versions by Flatt and Scruggs and the Foggy Mountain Boys, but the renewed vitality Flatt brought to them in the seventies can't be denied.

Lester Flatt and The Nashville Grass: *Pickin' Time* (CMH). The best post-Scruggs Flatt is on the out-of-print RCA "best of," but the best post-RCA Flatt (and he recorded often) is right here. Flatt had been back from extensive surgery several times when he recorded this in 1978, but he sounds more loose than he does tired.

The Greatest Show On Earth (Sugar Hill). Recorded live, this double album is a virtual primer on tradition-oriented newgrass. So it stands to reason that among cuts by the Seldom Scene and the Country Gentlemen, the real standouts would be the New South featuring the tradition-oriented Ricky Skaggs.

The Greenbriar Boys: *The Best of the Greenbriar Boys and John Herald* (Vanguard). Of the many bluegrass or old-timey revivalist groups to come out of the New York folk movement, the New Lost City Ramblers were probably the most proficient technically, but the Greenbriar Boys were the most fun. Singer and guitarist Johnny Herald brought both humor and sex appeal to a form that badly needed both, and in the group's second incarnation, mandolin player Frank Wakefield brought legit country roots.

David Grisman: *Early Dawg* (Sugar Hill). Mandolinist Grisman left the rest of the field so far behind so long ago that most of his albums don't even belong here. But this one, made up of tapes from 1966, does. The material is almost all traditional or bluegrass standards, and his Monroe roots are distinctive.

David Grisman: *The David Grisman Rounder Album* (Rounder). Recorded with newgrass all-stars (Vassar Clements, Bill Keith, Tony Rice, Jerry Douglas, and occasionally Ricky Scaggs and Buck White) after he went "outside," this shows both sides of Grisman. Relatively straight bluegrass cuts alternate with jazz excursions. While it's possible that fans of one will be uncomfortable with the other, thus defeating the purpose of this album, it will be their loss.

The Hillmen: *The Hillmen* (Sugar Hill). They weren't quite up to the Kentucky Colonels, but the Hillmen were a crucial bluegrass group in the L.A. folk scene; their eclecticism is best demonstrated by the fact that while Rex and Vern Gosdin went on to become commercial country stars, Chris Hillman became a rock star. This is a reissue of tapes from 1963–64.

John Hartford: *Aero-Plain* (Warner Bros.). Though he had several (now out-of-print) albums of his own in the late sixties, Hartford was best known as the man who wrote Glen Campbell's "Gentle on My Mind" hit. This 1971 album, recorded with acoustic-country stars like Vassar Clements, Norman Blake, and Tut Taylor, mourns the passing of traditional music, a loss symbolized by the Opry's move from the Ryman Auditorium to a suburban theme park.

John Hartford: *Mark Twang* (Flying Fish). Away from major labels since the early seventies, Hartford has been left free to indulge his musicianship and his riverboat-captain fantasies, both of which he does on this album. As usual, he plays mostly banjo, with a little guitar and fiddle as well—but on this album there are no overdubs and no sidemen. Hartford provides his own percussion with his feet, hands, and mouth.

John Hartford: *Nobody Knows What You Do* (Flying Fish). Hartford is so flip, his sense of humor so silly and obvious, that it's easy to overlook how flawless he is as a banjo player. This one has him back in a group context, and shows off his love for bluegrass a lot more than his other albums.

John Hartford: *Catalogue* (Flying Fish). Solo Hartford at his most whacked-out, even if most of the songs are rerecordings of material from his RCA and Warner Bros. days.

Jim and Jesse and the Virginia Boys: *Radio Shows* (Old Dominion). Jim and Jesse were a fine traditional bluegrass group caught between a rock and a hard place. They spent years trying to decide whether to stay purist or go for a commercial country audience. When they finally decided, by signing with Columbia for most of the sixties, they reduced themselves to things like pop-bluegrass albums of Chuck Berry songs.

Their musicianship never slackened, but their inspiration did. Before all that happened, though, they played regularly on an Alabama radio station where they did fancy versions of classic bluegrass with sparkling harmonies—"progessive," maybe, but definitely not what would come to be known as newgrass. These transcriptions from that show were made in 1962, and are the only "old" Jim and Jesse still on the market today.

Jim and Jesse: *All-Time Greatest Country Instrumentals* (Columbia Limited Edition). It's a shame that the only major-label album available by this transitional bluegrass group is an all-instrumental effort, because the changing vocal styles need to be documented as well. Still, the material is well selected and the performances stretch out just enough and then no more.

Bill Keith: *Something Auld, Something Newgrass, Something Borrowed, Something Bluegrass* (Rounder). Keith, who rose to prominence in the early-sixties band of Bill Monroe, devised the "chromatic" style of banjo playing, creating extended melodic lines based on scales rather than chords. It was the first advance on the instrument since the days of Earl Scruggs, and Keith's influence is wide. With this blend of sidemen from both the traditional (fiddler Vassar Clements) and the folk revivalist (vocalist and rhythm guitarist Jim Rooney, mandolinist David Grisman, guitarist Tony Rice) camps, he has created a primer of fancy, yet accessible, newgrass picking.

The Kentucky Colonels: *Livin' in the Past* (Sierra). Early (1961–65) and primitive live recordings of the band that invented L.A. bluegrass, sparked by the late Clarence White's concise flat-top guitar picking.

Doyle Lawson and Quicksilver: *Rock My Soul* (Sugar Hill). No young modernists have been more faithful to the unquestioning devotion and slightly desperate yearning of the bluegrass gospel masters. Divine, and a real find.

The Lilly Brothers and Don Stover: *The Early Recordings of the Lilly Brothers* (County). Only four of the sides on this reissue were even released when they were first recorded for a small indie in 1956–57. But the four-piece band produced driving third-generation bluegrass behind the classic voices of Bea and Everett Lilly.

The Lilly Brothers: *Bluegrass Breakdown* (Rounder Special Series). A reissue of 1964 bluegrass sides that sound older. Thanks to a regular gig at a Boston club, this version of the Lilly Band—Everett on mandolin and vocals, Bea on guitar and vocals, Don Stover on Banjo, Herb Hoover on fiddle, and Fritz Richmond on bass—was especially influential on urban folkies in the Northeast.

The Lilly Brothers: *The Lilly Brothers* (County). Gospel bluegrass from the early seventies, affirming faith and optimism rather than preaching fire and brimstone. Tempting.

Benny Martin: *Tennessee Jubilee* (Flying Fish). Martin, who made his name fiddling for Bill Monroe and for Flatt and Scruggs back in the formative days of bluegrass, is a self-effacing singer, but one with undeniable charm. Joined on this contemporary set by Flatt, John Hartford, and such other names as Buddy Emmons and Buddy Spicher, he romps through oldies pungent with nostalgia and originals full of optimism.

Jimmy Martin and the Sunny Mountain Boys: *Good 'n Country* (MCA). For a bluegrass singer, the post-Monroe Martin is incredibly good-natured—too much so, some would argue, because he seems to be addicted to novelty songs. I would say that when they are as charming as his version of Hylo Brown's "Grand Ole Opry Song," who cares if it's a novelty, and I would also point to his version of Jimmy Skinner's venomous "You Don't Know My Mind" as proof that he can handle the hard stuff, too.

Jimmy Martin and the Sunny Mountain Boys: *Jimmy Martin and the Sunny Mountain Boys Sing* (MCA). And what they sing is a goodly number of truck-driving songs, bluegrass style, including "Widowmaker," one of the most stirring songs of its type (trucker gives up own life to save school bus full of children—you'd be surprised just how many songs there are on this theme). But these aren't all trucking songs; there's room for covers of A. P. Carter and the Delmore Brothers, as well as for "Ocean of Diamonds," which develops a kind of imagery rare in bluegrass.

Bill Monroe and His Blue Grass Boys: *The Classic Bluegrass Recordings, Vol. 1* (County). Spottily programmed, but still the bona fide thing, these Columbia sides go back to the first session, when Sally Ann Forrester was on accordion, and show bluegrass coming to life.

Bill Monroe and His Blue Grass Boys: *The Classic Bluegrass Recordings, Vol. 2* (County). Most of the remaining Columbia sides, including the original version of "Blue Moon of Kentucky." Slimmer pickings, but these two together could supersede the Rounder album earlier discussed at length.

Bill Monroe and His Blue Grass Boys: *16 All-Time Greatest Hits* (Columbia). The single album containing the most cuts from the 1945–49

Columbia sessions, and thus a bargain, but docked a notch for cruddy reprocessed stereo. (The Rounder album has good sound; the County LPs are more iffy.)

Bill Monroe: *The Best of Bill Monroe* (MCA). A good cross section of fifties and sixties Monroe, but some cuts are rerecordings of the Columbia hits. Most noteworthy for the second version of "Blue Moon of Kentucky," on which he speeded up for the second verse; released in 1954, it was more influential than the original.

Bill Monroe: *Bill Monroe's Greatest Hits* (MCA). Nearly all from the sixties, and thus Monroe singing all the leads with none of the harmonies that made earlier work so galvanizing. There's some dubious material here, and a few deviations from strict form, but they are experiments, not cheap tricks; when Monroe alters his sound he does so slowly and carefully.

Bill Monroe and His Blue Grass Boys: *Bluegrass Special* (MCA). With material like "Blue Ridge Mountain Blues," "Columbus Stockade Blues," "Careless Love," and "I'm So Lonesome I Could Cry," this adds immeasurably to the music available from the period when Monroe was at his bluesiest and most mournful.

Bill Monroe and His Blue Grass Boys: *Bluegrass Instrumentals* (MCA). This captures various editions of the Blue Grass Boys from 1951–63, but Monroe and his mandolin, alternately swirling and punching, maintain a steady course throughout.

Bill Monroe and His Blue Grass Boys: *A Voice From on High* (MCA). A "greatest gospel hits" album covering much of the fifties. Needless to say, Monroe's strident, intense voice is well suited to the form.

Charlie Monroe: *Charlie Monroe on the Noonday Jamboree, 1944* (County). Two radio shows, complete with laxative commercials, featuring a version of the Kentucky Pardners that included Lester Flatt and was never recorded by Victor, Charlie's label at the time. Since it's live, it's lively, and right neighborly, too. This isn't quite bluegrass yet, but it's sure getting close.

Moore and Napier: *The Best of Moore and Napier* (Starday/Gusto). Charlie Moore played old-style clawhammer banjo and sang in a precise, resonant voice. Bill Napier started with the Stanley Brothers on mandolin before switching to guitar. In the mid-sixties, Moore and Napier made these smooth, mainstream bluegrass recordings as a team.

Tiny Moore and Jethro Burns: *Back to Back* (Kaleidoscope). Moore is the former electric mandolinist with Bob Wills and the Texas Playboys.

Burns is half the old country comedy team Homer and Jethro. Their current music is neither western swing nor bluegrass (nor comedy), but a fleet, jazz style that swings *and* sways, and is soulful enough to put technicians like Sam Bush (of New Grass Revival and solo fame) to shame.

Mule Skinner (Ridge Runner). Reissue of much-admired newgrass jam from the early seventies featuring Clarence White, Bill Keith, David Grisman, and the vastly overrated Peter Rowan and Richard Greene. Nearly all these songs come from the Bill Monroe repertoire, and this group's version of "Mule Skinner Blues" is a modern classic.

New Grass Revival: *When the Storm Is Over* (Flying Fish). If this group hadn't been clever enough to coin the phrase "New Grass," I bet they wouldn't enjoy near the respect they have. Of an inconsistent batch of rocking album releases, this is the one that does the most different things while remaining true to roots.

The Osborne Brothers: *The Osborne Brothers and Red Allen* (Rounder Special Series). Bobby (mandolin, tenor, and lead singer) and Sonny (banjo) had played in many of the major bluegrass groups before hooking up with guitarist and tenor/lead vocalist Red Allen in the Dayton, Ohio, area, where they were raised. Their 1956 MGM debut, "Ruby," featured twin banjos and a slow ending on an up-tempo song, both of which became key elements in their sound. "Once More" (1958) introduced the "high lead," in which both the tenor and baritone harmony lines are sung below the lead vocalist, and together the voices simulate the sound of a pedal steel. Though they were the first bluegrass group to use drums and a dobro together, it's the "high lead" that assures the Osbornes a chapter in bluegrass history. These sides, all cut between 1956 and 1958, also show some rockabilly influence, and because the Osbornes did experiment so much (though not always with results as good as these), they were in turn a key influence on newgrass groups.

The Osborne Brothers: The Osborne Brothers (Rounder Special Series). More from the MGM years, which ended in 1963. All these sides were cut after Allen left the group for purer pastures, and the Osbornes began playing with electric instruments, with special attachments to the old acoustic instruments, with pianos and the like. The "high lead" on the trio remains their chief selling point, along with some bizarre choices of material.

The Osborne Brothers: *The Best of the Osborne Brothers* (MCA). This double album includes rerecordings of early material as well as examples of the sixties country-bluegrass fusion that led to them being virtually the only bluegrass-based group besides Flatt and Scruggs to enjoy consistent chart success.

Radar Blues (King/Gusto). A trucker's anthology with emphasis on bluegrass, including Moore and Napier's winsome "Truck Driver's Queen," Reno and Smiley's straight-ahead "Interstate 81," the Stanley Brothers' "Rollin' on Rubber Wheels," and a reprise of Moore and Napier with the self-fulfilling prophecy "Guitar Pickin' Truck Driver." (Some of these songs have pretty tenuous connections to trucking, in case you haven't figured it out, but what the hey, a bandwagon's a bandwagon and better to jump on than be left behind.) Except for Hylo Brown's version of "Truck Driving Man," which is available on several other anthologies, the remaining highlight here is Red Sovine and Johnny Bond telling about "The Gear Jammer and the Hobo."

Reno and Smiley: *16 Greatest Hits* (Starday/Gusto). Don Reno was a three-finger banjoist who almost joined Bill Monroe before Earl Scruggs did, which would have made Reno the father of bluegrass banjo. He joined the Army instead, but when he got out, he did play with Monroe. Red Smiley was a nimble guitarist with a smooth, mainstream country voice rather than a bluegrass twang; he was also a gifted songwriter. They teamed up in the early fifties, and through the rest of the decade they were one of the most commercially viable bluegrass groups. That's because of their hilarious, carefully planned stage show, as well as their willingness to give bluegrass a beat and to deal in honky-tonk themes. But it's mainly because of the evolution of Reno's banjo playing, which got jazzier, more like guitar picking; he pulled off some of the wildest, most unlikely banjo lines ever, as showcases like this album's "Choking the Strings" and "Banjo Riff" will attest. This covers that whole decade, beginning in 1952 when they first signed to King, and the sheer *variety* of material recorded remains almost as impressive as Reno's hurtling, improvisational banjo style.

Reno and Smiley: *The Best of Reno and Smiley* (Starday/Gusto). This puts nearly all the weight on their urgent vocal style, and they pull it off. Reno and Smiley were as modern as classic bluegrass got, and they had the veritable something for everyone—traditional songs, knowing originals, weepers, novelties.

The Sauceman Brothers: *The Early Days of Bluegrass, Vol. 7* (Rounder). Like the Stanleys, the Saucemans were an important transitional group, inspired by Monroe and then left to find their own way from traditional mountain music to bluegrass. They never achieved a sound quite as individualistic, but this album documents their evolution from enthusiastic novices to slick, seasoned pros.

The Earl Scruggs Revue: *Live From Austin City Limits* (Columbia). I dunno. Ever since Earl split from Lester Flatt and formed an electric group featuring his sons, everything he's done has sounded like machine-gun banjo. Because this is live, that's even more the case—but it also provides a decent showcase for everyone in the group, and serves as a sampler, too.

The Seldom Scene: *Live at the Cellar Door* (Rebel). John Duffey formed this group to showcase his own voice and mandolin, as well as the clean guitar of John Starling and the stinging dobro of Mike Auldridge. This band doesn't modernize bluegrass so much as it integrates bluegrass with other forms. Recorded in 1974 before an adulatory audience in D.C.'s top folk club, this really does catch the atmosphere. But a little goes a long way.

Ricky Skaggs: *Sweet Temptation* (Sugar Hill). Mainly bluegrass with a couple of diversions, this catches Skaggs at his speedy, hypergrass apex. It works, too, especially his urgent vocals. Next stop: increased prominence via Emmylou, solo album on major label.

Ricky Skaggs: *Family & Friends* (Rounder). But mostly friends, because with the exception of some members of the White family (which Ricky married into), the friends are better pickers and singers. This 1982 bluegrass is simple, brisk, and warm, but not at all dragged down by its concept.

Larry Sparks: *The Best of Larry Sparks and the Lonesome Ramblers* (Rebel). In those transitional years between bluegrass and newgrass, Sparks held the line better than anybody. He broke in playing guitar for Ralph Stanley in 1967, but stayed with the Clinch Mountain Boys only long enough to establish himself as a young guitarist to be reckoned with. He then formed his own band, and these sides are among his earliest, recorded originally for both King Bluegrass and County; with efforts like "Wonder Where You Are Tonight," "Waltz of the Wind," and "Life of Sorrow," it's easy to see how he was able to fill Carter Stanley's shoes in the first place.

Larry Sparks and the Lonesome Ramblers: *Bluegrass Old and New* (Old Homestead). Sparks is ridiculously overrecorded, but can still be an eager and biting singer. And with banjoist Don Lilly providing the only real instrumental flash on these 1972 sides, the emphasis is definitely on singing.

Larry Sparks and the Lonesome Ramblers: *It's Never Too Late* (June Appal). Nearly a decade down the line and here's Sparks with some very low key, very reflective bluegrass, slow and bluesy and not particularly purist. Were Sparks not so young, you might even call it autumnal.

Springtime in the Mountains (County). Since all of these names are revered only in bluegrass circles, and not well known to the more general-interest country fan, the overall quality of this anthology is doubly surprising. It's subtitled "Classics of Early Bluegrass," and the title isn't fooling. Red Allen's achingly high lead on "Close By" is the sort of thing that justifies cults; while Richardson and Smith were together only briefly, I'm glad as many as four sides are included here, especially the no-nonsense "Let Me Fall" and "Lonesome Road Blues."

The Stanley Brothers: *Their Original Recordings* (Melodeon). A complete album of the verging-on-bluegrass Rich-R-Tone sides, this should appeal to bluegrass and old-timey fans alike.

The Stanley Brothers and the Clinch Mountain Boys: *The Columbia Sessions, 1949–50* (Rounder Special Series). By now, they can fairly be called a bluegrass group, though vestiges of the past remain. They're still not entirely comfortable with the new form, especially Ralph. But the trios alone make this worthwhile.

Stanley Brothers: *The Columbia Sessions, 1949–50, Vol. 2* (Rounder Special Series). Like its predecessor, this album has its ups and downs, but the impact of this music survives. Though lighter in tone than fully matured Stanleys, it's still somber stuff. The Stanleys later rerecorded many of these songs, as did numerous other groups.

Stanley Brothers: *16 Greatest Hits* (Starday/Gusto). Prolific as they were during their stints with Starday and King (which is the source of all this material), the Stanleys were also more consistent than they had any right to be. These songs were not "hits" because bluegrass groups rarely had hits, but they were crowd pleasers, and for good reason. Songs like "How Mountain Girls Can Love" or "Mountain Dew," as well as corn like "How Far to Little Rock," may have been quite familiar to even a casual bluegrass fan, but the Stanleys always invested them with fresh conviction that brought them back to life.

Stanley Brothers: *16 Greatest Gospel Hits* (Gusto). I can think of better sides that appear on other albums, but gospel music is always a litmus test for great bluegrass, and there's no doubt this is a great bluegrass team. "Rank Strangers" is a Stanleys' classic.

The Stanley Brothers: *The Best of the Stanley Brothers* (Starday/Gusto). These people have a way with album titles, don't they? Despite the similarities, though, there's little duplication between this and *16 Greatest Hits* or anything with a similar title.

The Stanley Brothers with George Suffler: *Hymns of the Cross* (King/ Gusto). Consistently strong gospel all the way through, but the two side-closers—Dock Boggs' chilling "Oh Death" and J. E. Mainer's "Building On That Rock"—are utterly transcendent.

Stanley Brothers and the Clinch Mountain Boys: *Hymns and Sacred Songs* (King/Gusto). This is their other recommended all-gospel set, with "Daniel Prayed" and "He Said If I Be Lifted Up" the two highlights. Both sport kinetic arrangements with high voices that seem to reach for the very heavens.

The Stanley Brothers: *Everybody's Country Favorites* (King/ Gusto). Some of their most enduring sides—"Sunny Side of the Mountain," "Tragic Romance," "Shackles and Chains," and more—originated on this album, and if you thought you never wanted to hear another version of "I'm a Man of Constant Sorrow" you were wrong; the version here is guaranteed to give you goosebumps at the least, and nightmares at most.

The Stanley Brothers: *The Stanley Brothers of Virginia, Vol. 1: That Little Old Country Church House* (County). This collection of fiery gospel standards from the early sixties, first recorded for Wango, is a cult favorite. For once, the cult is right.

The Stanley Brothers: *The Stanley Brothers of Virginia, Vol. 2: Long Journey Home* (County). George Shuffler on guitar is the only accompaniment Ralph and Carter get for this collection of secular songs from the same era. But he's all they need to get a surprisingly full sound. There are two more volumes of Wango sides in this series, but they're both thinner—the cult was right only up to a point.

Ralph Stanley: *A Man and His Music* (Rebel). Ralph plays and sings in enough distinct mountain styles to make this a virtual bluegrass primer. It's one of the first solo albums he made after Carter died, and one of the most diversified. Since then, he has recorded endlessly and unvaryingly, so be careful.

Ralph Stanley: *The Stanley Sound Today* (Rebel). Here it is 1981 and Ralph is still going strong; the "sound today" has altered some, but not appreciably, from the classic Stanley sound, and even the material ("Jimmy Brown the Newsboy," "Sitting on Top of the World") is compatible with just what he was doing two decades ago.

John Starling: *Long Time Gone* (Sugar Hill). With help from big-time hotcha stars like Emmylou Harris, Bill Payne, and the late Lowell George, Seldom Scene vet Starling recreates the quiet strength, but little of the actual sound, of classic bluegrass. The clarity and economy couldn't have been inspired by anything *but* bluegrass, and this is the most striking music to come out of the D.C. bluegrass scene in the eighties (even if it was recorded in 1977 for Capitol, which then rejected it).

Joe Val and the New England Bluegrass Boys: *Bound to Ride* (Rounder). Val is a no-nonsense mandolin player whose fiddleless groups feature crisp harmonies and an emphasis on ensemble playing rather than soloing. His prior albums weren't as consistent as this, but when he's on, he fronts the best bluegrass group in the Northeast today.

Frank Wakefield: *Frank Wakefield with Country Cooking* (Rounder). Wakefield is one of those southern pickers who made the transition from bluegrass to newgrass and is thus idolized by northern folkies. He's been way overrecorded, and is too often dazzled by his own technique, which can make his records disappointingly hollow affairs despite his undeniable talents. This is his best all-around, with two installments in his ongoing series of bluegrass-classical-jazz compositions, "Jesus Loves His Mandolin Player."

Paul Warren with Lester Flatt and the Nashville Grass: *America's Greatest Breakdown Fiddle Player* (CMH). Warren was a disciple of Fiddlin' Arthur Smith who cut his teeth with the Johnny and Jack Show before enjoying fifteen years with Flatt and Scruggs and, when that team broke up, seven more with Lester Flatt. Not only could he play faster than anyone around, but as these radio transcriptions (made during his tenure with Flatt) indicate, he could make that fiddle sing like nobody else, too.

Buck White and the Down Home Folks: *That Down Home Feeling* (Ridge Runner). Though perhaps overrecorded, Buck White's group can almost keep up the pace because of the variety of lead singers and songs. The former category includes his wife, Pat, and two of his daughters, Sharon and Cheryl. But the conception is clearly Buck's and this group injects some Texas-country flavor into their contemporary bluegrass. Like all their albums, this is modern, but rooted.

Buck White and the Down Home Folks: *Live at the Pickin' Parlor* (County). With special guests like Norman Blake sitting in, you know White and family aren't going to stick to the tried and true, and they don't. Instead, they weave everything from "Salty Dog Blues" to "Tumbling Tumbleweeds" to "If I Could Only Win Your Love" to Bob Dylan's "Nashville Skyline Rag" into one spirited, cohesive family outing.

Buck White: *More Pretty Girls Than One* (Sugar Hill). In which the connections between bluegrass and jazz become more explicit. And including an instrumental version of "Just a Closer Walk with Thee" that might make you a believer.

Mac Wiseman: *Sixteen Great Performances* (MCA). Having served apprenticeships with Molly O'Day, Flatt and Scruggs, and Bill Monroe in the late forties, Wiseman went solo. At first he was strictly a bluegrass performer, and his sleek Irish tenor graced some records today regarded as seminal in the development of early bluegrass. But his survival instinct was always stronger than his allegiances to bluegrass, and he expanded into more commercial forms. This album is basically bluegrass, including many of the songs that made him famous, but most are rerecordings, and the shadow of Nashville hangs over the singing. But it's the closest thing to a rootsy Wiseman album on the market.

HONKY-TONK AND HILLBILLY BOOGIE

Honky-tonk, the postwar sound that began in Texas, represented the end of traditional and the beginning of modern country. The music was made mostly on string instruments—bass, guitar, fiddles, steel—but those instruments quickly became electrified, and piano and drums were added to make the music more percussive. Vocalists sang in direct, intimate styles, aided only by a high harmony voice. The overall sound was smoldering, and usually quite bluesy. At first, honky-tonk sounded essentially like a small-band version of western swing; it replaced the big swing bands that had been torn apart by the war. But the lyrics were about liquor and failed love most of the time, or about some form of displacement; this was the music of country people moved into urban environments during World War II, and it mirrored the new situations they faced and the rootlessness and alienation they felt.

The phrase "honky-tonk" can be traced back to the turn of the century, when it was used in east Texas, Oklahoma, and Louisiana. What it actually *meant* has never been traced, but the phrase was particularly common among New Orleans blacks until it turned up in a song title in a 1918 Tin Pan Alley musical. After that, it began appearing regularly in jazz and blues titles.

In country music, the term applied first to the taverns that popped up around east Texas oil-boom towns during Prohibition. Soon, honky-tonks could be found nearly any place in Texas where there was enough of a population to support one; the honky-tonk became a community center, of sorts, for people not used to living in a community. Owing to their workingman clientele, they had a reputation for being dangerous places; musicians referred to the worst of them as "blood buckets" or "skull orchards." One went there to drink and find women, to drink and dance, to drink and fight, to drink and drink some more, to blow off steam however one could; honky-tonks had their own code, and it was different from the code of either work or home.

By the late thirties, the jukebox was an essential feature in any honky-tonk. But these places were so noisy you could hardly hear the records over the crowd. Guitarists, some of whom had already been experimenting with amplification, simply went electric to solve that problem. Live bands had to do the same; further, they had to supply a dance beat. This led to the introduction of the "sock rhythm" style of acoustic guitar, a chunky sound made by choking the strings immediately after striking them. This served as a dance beat when there were no drums, but drums soon became commonplace.

Ernest Tubb is usually credited with all these innovations, but it's more accurate to say that he popularized the sound throughout the Southeast after he left Texas to join the Grand Ole Opry in 1943. He certainly wasn't the first in Texas; if the origins of honky-tonk can be traced to any one source, it would probably be the Blue Ridge Playboys, an east Texas band of the thirties. They made music that evolved from swing into honky-tonk; they spawned most of the major early honky-tonkers and a fair number of western swingers, too. Floyd Tillman, Leon "Pappy" Selph, Moon Mullican, Ted Daffan, and Dickie McBride all worked with the early Playboys.

If the seeds for honky-tonk were planted in the thirties, the forties were the peak years. Most of America discovered the music in 1943, when Al Dexter sold 1.6 million copies of "Pistol Packin' Mama." The opening line was, "Drinkin' beer in a cabaret," and it's hard to get more explicit than that in defining what honky-tonk was about. *Newsweek* denounced the song as "obnoxious," calling it "naive, folksy, and almost completely devoid of meaning." It was banned from "The Lucky Strike Hit Parade," the influential radio (and later television) show of popular music, because the FCC wouldn't allow such overt references to alcohol. When the lyric was changed to "Singin' songs in a cabaret," the tune promptly shot to No. 1.

Unbelievably, there is no album of Dexter's music available today. Nor is there one for Ted Daffan and His Texans, who went over the million-seller mark with "No Letter Today." Daffan was a steel guitarist who used different singers to front his band, but he's best known as a writer. His "Born to Lose," originally the B-side of "No Letter Today," was ostensibly about a broken love affair, but for the millions of displaced working people forced to stay in cities like Detroit and Chicago in order to keep jobs, the song was received as a metaphor for modern life in general. So was his "Heading Down the Wrong Highway." Daffan also wrote "Blue Steel Blues," "I'm a Fool to Care," and numerous other honky-tonk standards.

Floyd Tillman was another of honky-tonk's most influential writers and singers. He was also a Texan, but by the mid-forties, the music had spread around the country. Out in California, Merle Travis was its leading exponent. Little Jimmy Dickens, who was from West Virginia but who was working at northern radio stations when he got the call to join the Opry, made his guitar crackle with a new urgency that presaged rockabilly.

Hillbilly boogie was just what the name implies—country musicians joining in the national fad for eight-to-the-bar boogie-woogie. It developed among country musicians in the Southeast more than in Texas, and its growth paralleled that of honky-tonk; it was treated as an up-tempo version of honky-tonk, and by about 1950 the two musics had become inseparable, though hillbilly boogie favored novelty lyrics where honky-tonk was usually sad.

The top of the charts in the early fifties was dominated by Hank Williams (from the Southeast) and Lefty Frizzell (from Texas). Both were classic honky-tonkers, though their styles differed considerably. But, in general, the infusion of boogie into honky-tonk meant increased emphasis on speed, on hot rhythms, and boisterous licks. Honky-tonk was setting the stage for rockabilly, which in turn nearly killed off country music in general and honky-tonk in particular. There were some exceptions—Webb Pierce, George Jones, and Ray Price were among the survivors—but not many. When Buck Owens and the Bakersfield sound emerged in the early sixties with a West Coast version of honky-tonk, they gave mainstream country music a much-needed shot in the arm. But when honky-tonk came back again in the mid-seventies, there was more than a twinge of nostalgia to it; though part of the back-to-the-basics movement, the revived honky-tonk of that era was frequently treated by country singers and fans as some sort of neoclassical movement.

Floyd Tillman: *The Best of Floyd Tillman* (Columbia).

Ernest Tubb is better known, but Floyd Tillman has as much claim to the title "Father of Honky-Tonk." Trouble is, he was always reluctant to demand it. Tillman was one of the first to play electric guitar, he was a driving force behind the group that spawned honky-tonk, and he was versatile enough as a writer to produce both the first blatant cheating song ("Slippin' Around" in 1949) and others that became pop as well as country standards ("I Love You So Much It Hurts," "It Makes No Difference Now," "I'll Keep On Loving You"). Yet he had no taste for self-promotion and record-company politics, and he never toured outside his Houston-area base. He became a country music star without an agent or manager (he handled both jobs himself) and without any ongoing relationship with Nashville.

He was born in 1914 in Ryan, Oklahoma, but was raised just across the Red River in Post, Texas. He began playing in country groups while in his early teens; even then, he deviated from form by using guitar to play jazzy leads rather than as a backup rhythm instrument. By 1935 he'd ventured to San Antonio, where he played in Adolph Hofner's swing band and polished his style of stinging, single-string guitar solos. A few years later, he united with Leon "Pappy" Selph to form the Blue Ridge Playboys; with this group, he helped popularize the electric guitar. He also wrote songs like "It Makes No Difference Now" and "I'll Keep On Loving You" that straddled the line between country and pop; Bing Crosby (Floyd's idol) covered the former, while Connie Boswell made a pop hit of the latter. This means that Tillman was a fairly consistent crossover writer nearly a decade before Hank Williams was. Soon, Floyd had a solo contract that resulted in hits like "They Took the Stars Out of Heaven" (1942) and "Each Night at Nine" (1943).

In the postwar years, when these recordings were made, Floyd's career soared. Tillman, as much as anybody, told it like it was becoming for displaced rural people struggling to establish new lives in the urban centers. His best-known song, "Slippin' Around," immediately connects the old and the new. The steel guitar is still heavily Hawaiian-influenced, and the fiddler plays a waltz. Tillman's flat, drawling baritone is an unlikely mix of Crosby and Tubb, but his song is about extramarital sex, and it offers no apologies, no moralizing, and no excuses. Though Tillman wound up with a hit, his record company was initially too leery of the song to even promote his version until Jimmy Wakely and Margaret Whiting had already scored a huge hit with their primmer duet version.

"I Love You So Much It Hurts" also cuts both ways. For much of the song, the backing is just mandolin and guitar, with a hovering fiddle in the background. But the piano is pop, romantic, and so are the lyrics; it's now been covered by everyone from Vic Damone to Ernest Tubb to Ray Charles. A mix of pop piano and mournful country fiddles carries "It Had to Be That Way," with Tillman's voice slithering and breaking all over the song. He had one of those classic "bad" voices that only country singers can build a career on; in his case, there was also a light, lazy warmth that proved captivating, and his manner of singing behind the beat (as on "I'm Falling for You") was later appropriated by Willie Nelson, a singer's singer.

On most of his postwar records, Tillman maintained that connection between old and new instrumental patterns, and in doing so, staked out his own sound while others got caught up in honky-tonk uniformity. He might use Texas twin fiddles on "I'm Falling for You," but he'd also call on western swing mandolinist Leo Raley to help out on something like "I Finally Saw the Light," one of his few full-throttle, up-tempo songs. With its melody similar to "Roll in My Sweet Baby's Arms," it sounds old-timey, but it also has swinging steel fills taken from blues by ex-Texas Playboy Herbie Remington, a gnarled guitar break, and that mandolin chipping away at the beat.

It's still as a songwriter that Tillman leaves his greatest mark. "I Gotta Have My Baby Back," with Remington's gloomy steel intro and Floyd's pleading, befuddled vocals, paints a full picture of barroom solitude with remarkably few words. "This Cold War with You" adroitly draws parallels between the era's leading political issue and two fighting lovers who won't talk to each other. And "A Small Town" does a reversal on prior country songwriting conventions by making small-town night life a symbol for the emptiness of small towns in general, and the city a symbol for hope and freedom. The spooky background fills on steel make that little burg seem like a ghost town rather than the idyllic setting it had previously been in country songs. This mid-seventies reissue album may have gone back out of print, but it's worth looking hard for. The more maverick his work became, the better Floyd Tillman sounded.

Ernest Tubb: *The Ernest Tubb Story* (MCA).

Ernest Tubb is the kind of country singer who separates the true fan from the fellow traveler: his voice is all wrong, and yet it is just right. As the man who popularized electric guitar and first brought honky-tonk to the masses, he is also one of the music's few living pioneers, as his 1965 induction into the Hall of Fame indicates.

So it's a crime that most of his important songs are available only in the form of rerecordings done in the early sixties to exploit the then-new stereo form. Most of these songs were first cut in the forties and early fifties, and didn't have drums (which he first used in 1949), pedal steel (he first used lap steel in 1941, though he didn't begin featuring it until 1946), and piano (which he began using sporadically in 1949.) Yet with the exception of some soulless vocal choruses, the full band rarely gets in Tubb's way, so overwhelming is his own vocal style, which hasn't changed much in forty-five years. And there's plenty to suggest that he, like many country singers, was eager to update old songs—as if modernizing somehow renewed their vitality. In 1945, for example, he also rerecorded, of his own volition, some previous hits so that he could have versions of them done with his new, bigger band.

Tubb was born in 1914 on a farm outside Crisp, Texas. The product of a broken home, he kicked around the state for most of his childhood. The one constant factor in his life was his love for Jimmie Rodgers; as a teen-ager, he practiced two years to perfect Rodgers' blue yodeling techniques. It paid off in 1939 when he finagled a meeting with Carrie Rodgers, Jimmie's widow, in San Antonio. She took him under her wing, resulting the next year in a recording session that produced a pair of tribute songs to his idol. They went nowhere, and for the next five years he recorded only a few more times, always unsuccessfully. Then, in 1941, he hit with "Walking the Floor Over You," which featured an electric guitar over his own acoustic, and which sold 400,000 copies in its first year before going on to top one million in sales.

Tubb has always claimed that he did his best singing from 1936 to 1939, and that his voice then changed because he had his tonsils removed. He has a point, as anyone who's heard his earliest sides can confirm, but as he is quick to add, the operation probably worked out for the better because it made him develop his own style.

And what a style it turned out to be. Tubb begins each song almost exactly a quarter tone flat, and from there he usually goes flatter. But it's never stopped him from projecting a warmth, graciousness, and magnanimity unparalleled in country music. There's a folksy, neighborly flavor to everything he does, and within his narrow confines, he's able to express an astonishing range of emotions.

On "I'll Get Along Somehow" he is stoic, while on "Slippin' Around" it's the very flatness of his voice that lends authority to the key phrases. Here, there's also just a suggestion of a chuckle as he mourns a situation he can't quite control. In "There's a Little Bit of Everything in Texas" that chuckle turns into a philosophical chortle as he boasts unabashedly about the wonders of his native state. On "You Nearly Lose Your Mind," a blues, he takes the role of been-there-before elderly sage, able to stand back and once again be amused, among other things, by his misfortunes. On "When the World Has Turned You Down" his voice drops to almost a whisper, and slip-slides through the lyrics, while on "Have You Even Been Lonely," he sounds like one man crying out from a desert island. "I Love You Because" ends on a triumphant bellow, while on "There's Nothing More to Say" he vents frustration by starting low and going lower. On "Let's Say Goodbye Like We Said Hello," he's conciliatory; unlike most honky-tonkers, Tubb was rarely defiant or bitter with the women in his weepers and cheating songs, and when he pleaded, which was often, there was still as much pride as self-pity in his voice.

He wrote or co-wrote most of his own songs, and wasn't big on metaphor. "Rainbow at Midnight," in which the rainbow becomes a symbol for eternal life and love, and "Driftwood on the River," in which he likens himself to driftwood floating aimlessly out to the safeness of the vast and empty seas, are about as close as he comes. His singing on the latter is sublime, an obvious precursor for everyone from the corner honky-tonker to (listen for yourself if you don't believe me) the midsixties Bob Dylan.

More to the point, though, is "I'm walking the floor over you/I still don't believe that it's true." Everything he's done since has been in this mold, and even with the added instruments, this version remains faithful to the original. This edition of his band, the Texas Troubadors, was one of the best. Tubb had originally added instruments slowly, as the times demanded. He first went to electric guitar in 1941 (after an aborted attempt the previous year). By the time he recorded again in 1943, after a long layoff due to a musicians union strike, he was fronting an electric lead guitar plus bass, fiddle, steel, and rhythm guitar. Jimmie Short was the first of his steady lead guitarists, but Billy Byrd (from the fifties and sixties band heard here) most deftly executes the rising, four-note fill that's as much a Tubb trademark as his voice. In 1946, Jerry Byrd's Hawaiian steel and Red Herron's hot fiddle became more prominent, but Buddy Emmons' pedal steel and Tommy Jackson's fiddle on this album are able substitutes. The originals are still the greatest, of course, but these will do.

Ernest Tubb: *Greatest Hits* (MCA).

Tubb never let up; still hasn't. Once his popularity spread from the Grand Ole Opry, he simply worked harder, staying out there on the road to your town three hundred nights a year, getting home in time to play the Opry more weekends than most regulars, and cutting his usual quota of hits as well. Yet his recording career has been made a shambles of by his dinosaur of a (former) record company.

Six of these eleven songs also appear on *Story*. The other five are prime Tubb, which makes the album essential. If we must have a rerecording of "Walking the Floor Over You," I suppose I'd rather have this swinging version, with its ringing steel fills and Billy Byrd's jazzy guitar, but we already have one elsewhere. Why must a man of Tubb's stature be represented so shoddily in the marketplace? Why can't there be albums of material the way Tubb first conceived it, and without cuts overlapping from album to album? The British, who are good at this sort of thing, have taken tentative first steps with their *The Country Hall of Fame* compilation, which features original versions of songs going back to his earliest days, but even that ultimately plays more to his range than to his strengths.

So we are left with this, which is great though it could easily be greater. The new cuts run from 1958 to 1963. By then, Tubb was one of the grand old men of country music. Honky-tonk had faded and then become respectable again, and men who'd cut their teeth on Tubb were now following him into the charts. (Grant Shofner, now known as Cal Smith, and Jack Greene, from Tubb's sixties band, later went on to solo stardom.) His Ernest Tubb Record Store, established in 1947, was as much a Nashville institution as the Opry itself. When the Opry went off the air at night, it was always followed by another live broadcast, this one from Tubb's store. In 1947 he headlined the first country show at Carnegie Hall.

Tubb's voice became even lower, but more velvety, having aged like Jack Daniels Black label. The Jimmie Rodgers influence had become increasingly a thing of the past, but when Tubb broke into a semi-yodel as he sang, "I've got half a mind to leaea-ea-ve you," he brought it all back home. He's now slipping into self-pity more often (as on "Mr. Juke Box," which is still a great song). But if you can get past that vocal chorus, which sings songs the way a child draws by connecting the numbered dots, you're once again under the boozy, woozy spell of Ernest Tubb.

He delivers his own definition of honky-tonk when he thanks his ex "a lot," declaring "I got a broken heart/That's what I got." The sardonic "Thanks a Lot" is from 1963, and features a Texas Troubadors lineup that some will argue was his best. Jack Drake played a booming bass, and guitarist Leon Rhodes was more expansive than Byrd; he drags out lines on his guitar the way Tubb does words with his voice. Buddy Emmons, whose steel guitar on the 1958 "Half a Mind" was still very much Hawaiian-influenced, was replaced by Buddy Charlton, whose work on the 1966 "Another Story" is more in the crying style of bent notes and prolonged phrases. (Emmons later got so deeply into the intricacies of pedal steel that he started building them.)

But some things never change, and Ernest Tubb is thankfully one of them. "Waltz Across Texas," from 1965, allows him to once again flaunt his Lone Star chauvinism even while he's getting all sentimental (as he also did more often in later years) over his girl. After listening to the song, it's hard to decide which he loves more, her or Texas, and there's nobody else in country music who could pull off that kind of conceit so gracefully.

I last saw Tubb in December 1981. In the seventies, emphysema had sucked some of the strength from his voice and MCA dropped him after thirty-five years without so much as a "Thanks/Thanks a lot." But there he was, inexplicably booked into a downtown Manhattan punk club, singing to the trendies with more vigor and enthusiasm than you'd dream possible from a man pushing seventy, and not altering his show a bit for this audience, either. They had to take Ernest Tubb the way everyone else did or not take him at all. The next weekend I was at the Grand Ole Opry in Nashville, and damned if he wasn't there, too. (The difference is that I'd flown in for the weekend; he came in on his bus, having played five more towns between his New York date and this night.) As I left through the backstage exit after the show, the bus was revving up out in the parking lot, ready to take the boss on to another one-nighter in Jasper or Bossier City or Lufkin or wherever else the friends and neighbors promised to come out and see him play. He lives for the road, and as his former sideman Jack Greene once declared, "I think Ernest will die right in the back of that damned bus."

The Delmore Brothers: *The Best of the Delmore Brothers* (Starday/ Gusto).

Among old-time country artists, the Delmore Brothers were virtually alone in growing and evolving with the music itself. These King sides are among their last, and while the brothers ended their career still rooted in the traditional forms they'd begun with, they had also modernized to the point where they were making some of the hottest hillbilly boogie around, cutting down guitar heroes half their age and helping to pave the way for rockabilly.

When World War II arrived, the Delmores were working on WLW

in Cincinnati. Alton was drafted and Rabon wasn't, so the latter stayed on as a solo act. By the time Alton returned, Rabon had been fired, and though WLW was willing to rehire Alton as a solo act, they wouldn't take back the duet. So the pair tried several other cities, finally settling in Memphis in 1945.

The move was reflected in their music. By now, they'd already cut their first King sides, which indicated how far they'd progressed from their original sound. But soon after hitting Memphis, the blues center of the South, the Delmores cut "Hillbilly Boogie," which is exactly what it says it is, and which was one of the first such songs to hit the country charts. They quickly began experimenting with amplification and with extra sidemen, including the unsung Zeke Turner on electric lead guitar, and later in 1945 they cut "Freight Train Boogie" with what amounted to a full country band. Wayne Raney, who became an integral part of their new sound, was on harmonica, but it's Alton's flat-top guitar lines that make this song move.

The third key record in this series is 1947's "Barnyard Boogie," which the Delmores labeled "the silliest thing we ever did play." But it's the sort of jump 'n' jive that Louis Jordan was cutting around the same time with his R & B combos, and these are the records that Memphis rockabillies grew up with and later drew on for inspiration. (The session that produced "Barnyard Boogie" also yielded "Mobile Boogie," which features the most torrid guitar duets they ever recorded, and whoever is responsible for it being left off this album should be fired at once.)

Also while at King, the Delmores developed the Brown's Ferry Four as an outlet for the religious songs Alton was writing. The gospel quartet consisted of the brothers plus, depending on who was around the studios that day, some combination of Rome Johnson, Roy Lanham, Louis Innis, Merle Travis, or Red Foley. (According to Travis, the Brown's Ferry Four sides were all cut in California in 1945 and Grandpa Jones, contrary to most reports, was not on any of them.) As always, Alton and Rabon also contributed to records by their friends, appearing in strong supporting roles behind Raney and Jones.

Finally, in 1949, the Delmore Brothers cut "Blues Stay Away From Me," which took them as deep into the blues as they'd ever been (a feat they tried to duplicate with "Trouble Ain't Nothin' But the Blues," which is included here, and "Blues You Never Lose," which isn't). The simple—but unforgettable—Turner guitar riff that opens the song was worked out with Henry Glover (King's black A & R man, who often produced country sessions) and Raney's mournful harp filled out the sound. It quickly became the team's biggest hit ever.

By then, they were long gone from their Memphis base, having left in 1946 to try several locations before settling in Fort Smith, Arkansas. They never repeated the runaway success of "Blues Stay Away From Me," which stayed on the charts twenty-three weeks, but they did make a decent living, and cut several more significant records before separating in 1952. On "Field Hand Man" (1950) they actually wax nostalgic about the punishing work of the sharecropper, an indication perhaps that they're beginning to weary of music and the highly mobile lifestyle it requires. "I'll Be There" (1952) is an out-and-out honky-tonker that deals bluntly with failed love in a way no previous Delmores song had; Glover wrote it for them.

Alton probably couldn't have had he wanted to. Boogie, with its drive and buoyant optimism, was right up his alley; honky-tonk, no matter how close a kin, dealt with more sordid matters. In Houston in 1951–52 he lost his taste for the music business. This was partly because he'd been cheated out of the ownership of "Beautiful Brown Eyes" just as Rosemary Clooney was making it a pop hit; next, his father and then his youngest daughter died within months of each other. When Rabon's never-stable marriage fell apart in 1952, he went to Detroit to work as a solo act while Alton stayed in Houston. Though they recorded together several times that year, Rabon died of lung cancer on December 4, and it's doubtful they would have been a working team again anyhow. Alton continued writing successful songs right up until his own death in 1964.

Merle Travis: *The Best Of Merle Travis* (Capitol).

Merle Travis is best remembered today as a guitarist, but in the years after World War II he did so many things so well that he was known as a guitarist, a songwriter, *and* a singer; a folkie, a honky-tonker, *and* a western swing bandleader. He fills all those capacities on this album.

Travis was born in 1917 in the coal-mining town of Ebenezer, Muhlenburg County, Kentucky. He took up guitar as a child and soon mastered a regional style of unknown origins. Travis uses the thumb and a thumb pick to play rhythm on the bass strings while at the same time playing melody on the treble strings with his index finger; it sounds like two guitars are being played at once. He was introduced to the style by Ike Everly (father of the Everly Brothers) and another local man named Mose Rager. They'd picked it up from Arnold Schultz, a black fiddler and guitarist who possibly learned it from black ragtime guitarists of the twenties and thirties. It is bluesier, more syncopated, than most country guitar styles, and it requires an exacting sense of timing and coordination.

"Travis-pickin'," as it came to be known, is most easily heard on some of this album's solo acoustic tracks—"Nine Pound Hammer," with its stinging fills, or the driving "Sixteen Tons." But Travis, who was ultimately elected to the Hall of Fame in 1977, had been inspiring country guitarists since well before he first recorded. Soon after making his performing debut in 1935, he began appearing on WLW in Cincinnati. He was heard there by Chet Atkins, whose style grew from attempts to imitate Travis. Rockabilly guitarists, especially Scotty Moore, relied on elements of Travis-pickin' to give their groups a fuller sound. Later, the style moved into folk circles via Doc Watson and into the modern Nashville mainstream via Jerry Reed.

Travis didn't record until after he'd been discharged from the Marines, when he moved out to California. He worked with several Los Angeles western stars before he was spotted by Capitol A & R man Lee Gillette while backing Tex Ritter in the studio. Probably thinking of the successful folkish records Ritter was making, Gillette suggested Travis cut an album of folk songs from the coal-mining regions of Kentucky. When Travis allowed as how he didn't really know any, Gillette told him that was okay, he could just write himself a fresh batch. Thus came the sides collected on *Back Home;* later, Travis recorded another album called *Songs of the Coal Mines,* and these earned him his reputation with urban folkies of the fifties and sixties.

Country fans still remember him best for such hits as "Divorce Me C.O.D." (1946), "So Round, So Firm, So Fully Packed" (1947), and such cuts from this album as "Sweet Temptation," "Three Times Seven," and "Fat Gal." All are a singular mix of western swing, western, and honky-tonk; all reveal a sly, tongue-in-cheek sense of humor. Perhaps it seems incongruous that the man who specialized in folk ballads about the hardships of miners would also write and record so many novelty songs. But even Merle's folk ballads (think of "Sixteen Tons") often had a head-shaking, eye-winking, ain't-life-weird? tone, and he adapted this easily to the postwar optimism of California.

What was more incongruous was the band he recorded with. Nobody else had one quite like it, for it included trumpet (usually Ginny Cushman) and accordion (Pedro DePaul) as well as the usual fiddles (Harold Hensley) and steel (usually Joaquin Murphy, but sometimes Leodie Jackson or Noel Boggs). It wasn't what purists would consider honky-tonk, but it was as much honky-tonk as it was anything else; mostly, it was great dance music.

The records were all arranged similarly. A muted trumpet played the intro, and solos were passed around among fiddles, steel, and Merle's own guitar. Merle was one of the first country guitarists to plug in, but his work on these sides was a natural extension of his earlier acoustic efforts. He had always played with a rolling sense of rhythm similar to that created by a banjo; on these records he lowered his profile, and bolstered the rhythm section more often than he soloed himself. But his solos, as on "Fat Gal," had a crackling sharpness that bounced off the steel guitar with authority. While the steel would drone in the background some of the time (as on "Follow Thru," the only song here Merle didn't write), it was also used as a solo instrument. Merle's version of "Steel Guitar Rag" (for which he and Cliffie Stone added lyrics to Leon McAuliffe's melody) defines the role; as played by Boggs, it has little less swing and a little more jump than the steel in a swing band. The fiddler's light touch offered contrast in the barroom dance-floor atmosphere of numbers like "I'm a Natural Born Gamblin' Man," and often added harmonies with the accordion that came out of Cajun music. But as he shows on "Sweet Temptation," accordionist DePaul sometimes had to play straight blues as well. Merle, who died in Oklahoma in 1983, presided over all this with good spirits and jaunty vocals, a mirror image of the wide-open West Coast scene. It may have been a long way from the dangers of Kentucky coal mines, but Merle made himself feel right at home.

Moon Mullican: *Seven Nights to Rock* (Western).

Thank Aubrey "Moon" Mullican, the King of the Hillbilly Piano Players, for Jerry Lee Lewis, Mickey Gilley, and anyone else who ever adapted the "pumping piano" of blues and boogie to country music. Moon was there first. Though he recorded some thirty years, this album concentrates on sides from 1946 to 1956, roughly the middle third of his career; though he cut such ballads as "I'll Sail My Ship Alone" (his only No. 1 hit) and "Sweeter Than the Flowers," this concentrates on the up-tempo stompers that paved the way for rock 'n' roll and that, in Moon's own words, "makes those bottles bounce on the table."

He was born in 1909 in the piney woods around Corrigan, Polk County, Texas. His first instrument was guitar; at age eight he learned to play blues from a black sharecropper on the Mullican farm named Joe Jones. When his father bought a pipe organ so the girls in the family could learn church music, Moon used it to teach himself blues and boogie keyboard. (Years later, when asked why he took up piano, he told an interviewer, "Because the beer keeps sliding off my fiddle.") At sixteen he left home for Houston, where he worked the whorehouses and honky-tonks until joining Floyd Tillman and Leon Selph in the seminal honky-tonk band the Blue Ridge Playboys; in 1936 he joined Cliff Bruner's Texas Wanderers. Over the next few years he'd work with Bruner, Tillman again, the Sunshine Boys, Jimmie Davis, Buddy Jones, the Modern Mountaineers, and others. This was the age of western swing, and put on the bandstand alongside knowledgeable jazz-based players, Moon himself began stretching out. Where before he had played fairly simple barrelhouse piano, now he was playing long, skittering jazz lines. But he also kept that straight-ahead boogie beat, nothing fancy about it, and added dashes from other sources such as the Cajun music popular in his native east Texas. During the war, he worked mostly around Houston with his group the Showboys, and had a radio show called "Jambalaya," which could have been a description of his music as well as his favorite dish. Later, while touring with Hank Williams, Moon cooked up some pidgin Cajun slang which Williams put to the tune of the traditional "Big Texas," and thus was the song "Jambalaya" written. (When he recorded it, Hank took sole writer's credits.) At his first King session, Moon cut a coy, raving version of the Cajun hit "Jole Blon" (using pidgin English instead of pidgin French) and made it a hit again under the name "New Jole Blon."

By 1946 boogie-woogie had moved out of the joints (both black and white) and had entered the American mainstream. Moon stayed right in the thick of it, but he was investigating other forms, too, most of them black. In 1950 he had his biggest year, with three records on the country charts—"I'll Sail My Ship Alone," "Mona Lisa," and "Goodnight, Irene," none on this LP. But that same year, he was also recording Roy Brown's "Grandpa Stole My Baby" (which is included here) in a shouting style similar to that of the New Orleans R & B legend who wrote it. Moon used a full horn section on that one, as he does on the title song and on "I'm Mad at You."

Not that he required horns to beef up his sound. On "Well Oh Well," everybody gets off stinging solos, especially guitarist Mutt Collins and the steel player (possibly Bobby Koeffer), with Moon himself driving it home on piano. During this period he could record a straight country number like "Southern Hospitality," a risque jump blues like "Pipeliner's Blues," or novelties like "Tokyo Boogie" and make each his own. He sang in a warm, shouting style that was soft enough to take the edge off black blues, but muscular enough to be heard over the fat dance beat his band was laying down.

While Moon may not have stayed atop the charts for long, the dancers never tired of him; a huge man with a huge appetite for food and drink, he was always happiest playing the barrooms. Once, he was driving to New York to become the first country artist to play Carnegie Hall. During a stop in Shreveport, Louisiana, he met some old drinking buddies and they disappeared together into the wilds of the bayou country for about two weeks. Moon blew the historic gig, and couldn't stop bragging about that for years. Besides, he was one of those artists who thrived without air play. In 1949, Hank Williams recommended him to the Opry. Though reluctant, Opry officials finally invited him to join. He stayed six years, and was the first Opry star to both sing and play piano.

These recordings show country and R & B merging into rock 'n' roll, but Moon held back a little too much to make the transition himself. Still, he kept right on jukin' until his death on January 1, 1967. Said his widow, Eunice, at the funeral, "I got him to quit drinking and he ate himself to death."

Hank Williams: *24 of Hank Williams' Greatest Hits* (Polydor).

Here's a moment of truth, for all the superlatives were used up long ago, and it often seems like there's nothing more to add about Hank Williams.

The first thing that *has* to be said is that his recording career is now an unmitigated *mess.* After he died, most of his records, made originally with a standard string band and occasionally a piano, were overdubbed with drums and piano. So were the remaining demos. But even later, MGM undertook to "modernize" Hank by adding whole violin sections, background choruses, and all manner of inappropriate instruments. This album's "Move It On Over," "Kaw-Liga," and "Jambalaya" are all in their Hank-with-strings versions, and I can't find words to express how *awful* they sound. Except, that is, for the voice and the actual songs, which seem able to survive anything.

Hank Williams makes such a great symbol that it's easy to forget how great a country singer he was. But "Your Cheatin' Heart," the first song on the album, counteracts that impulse. Hank was born (in Mount Olive, Alabama) in 1923, which is about when vocals began catching on in string-band music. He was thus heir to the entire country vocal tradition, and he approached it in a manner both innovative and respectful. A high, keening steel kicks the song off, while the fiddle echoes Hank's mournful voice most of the way through. When he sings "But sleep won't come/The whole night through," he sounds like a judge sentencing somebody to a penalty worse than death itself. But his other embellishments are just as memorable, and just as unique. He begins lines by breaking his voice high on the first word and then descending into a normal singing voice; this is the opposite of the standard country practice of breaking the voice at the end of the line. When he sings, "When tears come down/Like fallin' rain/You'll toss around/And call my name," his voice swells at the end of the first and third lines, while the last words of the other two lines are thrown away almost in disgust. When he drags out the word "heart" from the title, it's to further emphasize just how *serious* this matter is. His voice is all tension, and all spite; of course it was written to his notorious ex-wife Audrey, and it was recorded at his very last session, so close to his death that it's likely he never sang it before an audience.

Williams always claimed his vocal style was about halfway between Roy Acuff and Ernest Tubb, but he turned those two so far inside out that it's often hard to hear the similarities. Pick almost any song here, though, and it can stand as a primer on country singing. "Lovesick Blues," the one that made him a superstar in 1949 when he performed it at his Opry debut before an audience that demanded at least six encores, was popular most likely because of the semi-yodel on the title; this was hardly an innovation, was in fact a throwback, because hardly anyone yodeled anymore (let alone on a Tin Pan Alley song, which this was). But Hank did, and he made it work. "Lost Highway," often considered a theme song of his, is not here, but "Ramblin' Man," which is built around the same idea and to my mind is a superior performance, is included. Here, better than anywhere else, we can get a taste of what Hank must have learned from Rufus ("Tee-Tot") Payne, the street-singing Alabama bluesman Hank claimed as his only real influence, back when he was first learning music as a child. His voice, his whole being, seem to sag under centuries-old doom, the eternal curse, contained in these lyrics. This man was still in his mid-twenties when he sang them.

Then there's his songwriting. Today, because the Williams myth has hardened with time, it's guesswork to say what he wrote and what came from Fred Rose, the northern sophisticate who wound up in Nashville in time to become Hank's publisher, producer, co-writer, and mentor. The standard explanation is that Hank brought Rose anything from an idea to a few lines or pieces of imagery to a completed song, and Rose then polished it into shape. (This explanation fails to acknowledge the existence of one Paul Gilley, a college student who apparently sold Hank verses which Hank then put to music and claimed as his own, a practice common in Nashville.)

"I'm So Lonesome I Could Cry" (which supposedly originated with Gilley) is the one most often cited, and for good reason. It's a song that tries, more than his others, to be poetic, and it succeeds on a certain scale. "Did you ever see a robin weep/When leaves begin to die/That means he's lost the will to live/I'm so lonesome I could cry" does, indeed, produce the desired effect with phrase-making a little more ambitious than is usually found in country songs, and it is both tough and tender, infinitely sad but not maudlin. But for me, the song has always been equally impressive for the simplicity and preciseness of another, more typically country, verse: "I've never seen a night so long/When time goes crawlin' by/The moon just went behind the clouds/To hide his head and cry." I once watched the moon drift across the sky and behind a cloud while this song was on the radio as I rode in a semitruck through rural northern California at four in the morning; the driver and I had lapsed into silence a good half hour before the song came on, we remained silent for some time after it was over, and I never did ask him if he'd seen what I saw—but the song split my night so sharply I still get chills every time I hear Hank sing it, and if that's not what a good country song is supposed to do, I give up.

That's the most dramatic example, but not the only one. Whoever was writing these songs, in other words, could speak at different levels of complexity without sacrificing impact. Hank's deftness with commonplace imagery (a shackled heart, for example) and his ability to capture an emotion so succinctly and overpoweringly, seem to elevate the actual words he uses. Though his lyrics and delivery made women want to sleep with him, or mother him, they also had a take-me-as-I-am conviction that made men identify as well. He went straight for your heart every which way he could. If you've read this far, you already know about the songs on this double album; most of them you probably know in your gut.

Hank Williams: *24 Greatest Hits, Volume 2* (Polydor).

The good news is that the overdubbing here is a little less odious than on the preceding volume. The bad news is that the songs aren't quite up to the previous batch. Most of them are merely excellent, as opposed to great.

"You're Gonna Change (or I'm Gonna Leave)" shows Hank in fine and furry voice, while "I Heard That Lonesome Whistle Blow," on which he emulates the sound of the train whistle as he repeats the title line, is one of his minor (and often-overlooked) masterpieces. On "Long Gone Lonesome Blues" he makes every word in the hook line several extra syllables long, dragging the line out to excruciating length and exacerbating the effect by doing so in a sobbing yodel that renders the words nearly indecipherable. His gift for wordplay ("Well, you're just in time to be too late," or "You looked me up / I turned you down") comes across in "I Won't Be Home No More." "I Saw the Light" is his most optimistic (i.e., least death-obsessed) spiritual, and as personal as his secular songs.

But it's not as autobiographical as "Lost Highway," and that one was written (and originally recorded) by Leon Payne. Again, this very young man sounds like a very old man as he summons up the blues spirit to make the music's tiredest clichés fresh again. He's resigned to being stuck out there forever himself, he warns in a voice full of pain and remorse, but that doesn't make his warnings any less crucial for others who might be tempted to choose his path.

The lesser-known songs say pretty much the same things as the major ones; it wasn't subject matter that necessarily determined the quality of his writing. The first (and last, and always) point is his tortured relationship with Audrey Sheppard Guy, the fiery, luscious woman he married at an Alabama gas station in 1944 after meeting her at a medicine show. Hank had terrible relationships with all the important women in his life; his mother, a huge woman who was bad news in a barroom brawl, was extremely protective of him and at the same time determined to make him grow up fast. He was totally dependent on her, and totally resentful of her. Audrey's main problem was that she wanted to be a star, though her singing was painfully bad. She got her way with Hank primarily through judicious use of sexual threats and favors; neither party was particularly faithful to the other, but he seemed to need her more than she did him in this regard. Their classic love-hate marriage spilled out into nearly all his songs that dealt at all with the subject of men and women on this (and any other) album— "Mind Your Own Business," "You're Gonna Change," "I Just Don't Like This Kind of Living," "Why Should We Try Anymore," "Cold, Cold Heart," "I Can't Help It (If I'm Still in Love with You)," "Half as Much." All of them ask the same question—why do we keep trying to make this work?—but what's most significant is that everybody knew what and who these songs were about. That was something new in country music —living your songs as publicly as Hank did. When Audrey finally divorced him in 1952, his last year alive, which he spent in a hopeless and helpless daze, he retaliated by marrying a naïve, star-struck nineteen-year-old named Billie Jean Jones; in fact, he married her twice, once before a j.p. and once before a sold-out auditorium in New Orleans before a show (actually, there were two shows, so there was a sold-out wedding "rehearsal" as well).

Novelty songs take up more space on this album than on the other. Though he was a driven and self-destructive man, though he was said to never smile offstage, Williams was a practical joker with an acute sense of hillbilly humor, and the novelties are every bit as much a part of legacy as the honky-tonk blues. His humor could be as silly, and as down-home as "Howlin' at the Moon," in which his new girl has him acting like a hunting dog that just treed a good catch. But more often it was the philosophical, black humor of "Nobody's Lonesome for Me" or "I'll Never Get Out of This World Alive."

Finally, a word about Hank's band and the music they made with him. The Drifting Cowboys were Jerry Rivers on fiddle, Don Helms on steel, Bob McNett, and then Sammy Pruett on lead guitar and Hillous Butrum and then Cedric Rainwater on bass. But the Williams sound, which was primarily the work of Rose and Hank himself, came also from top-flight Nashville session players on the earliest records—Zeke Turner, the trenchant guitarist (he created that lovely hook line on "I'm So Lonesome I Could Cry"); Jerry Byrd, the Hawaiian steel guitarist; Tommy Jackson or Chubby Wise, the versatile fiddlers, and others.

Hank's sound, like his songs, was only cautiously innovative. In his lyrics, for example, he never mentioned alcohol (except in joking contexts); though it was the one constant in his life, alcohol as a song subject was still a commercial taboo. Everyone knew about it, but nobody said anything out loud. And if Hank's personal life was a constant challenge to polite Nashville society, he wasn't about to issue a similar challenge with his lyrics. He would write the same kind of songs everyone else was writing; he would just do it better than anyone else.

Probably Rose did a lot to rein him in there, and Rose certainly deserves responsibility for much of the sound of the records. He didn't use drums until Hank's last session, and he used electric guitar sparingly. But Zeke Turner, the first electric guitarist to accompany Hank on record, came up with the dead-string, or "sock rhythm," technique of damping the strings with the back of his hand after striking them. This produced a percussive effect that Pruett later streamlined, and it paved the way for rockabilly rhythms. Finally, it was Rose who got Don Helms playing in increasingly higher registers until pretty soon that steel's cry stood out more than anything on the records except Hank's own voice.

There were up to seven musicians (sometimes a mandolinist, or extra rhythm guitarist, or pianist) on Hank's sessions, but the sound they created was thin and tight. (That thinness is another forerunner of rockabilly.) Behind Hank's own voice, thin and cutting like a razor blade, they created a directness that complemented perfectly his naked sincerity. And that, more than any other single factor, is the main attraction on a Hank Williams record.

Hank Williams: *Country & Western Classics: Hank Williams* (Time-Life).

At this point, I should mention that the complete works of Hank Williams were released in Japan in a ten-record boxed set called *The Immortal Hank Williams,* which also includes one album of radio transcriptions. Each cut appears there as it was first released by MGM, which means some have string bands or drums overdubbed but none have orchestras. The set has apparently gone out of print, though even when it was in print it was hard to locate, and I still see copies of it in stores now and again. Unless you want (and are able to find) that collection, this three-record boxed set is the best Hank Williams you can buy. It contains forty cuts. "No, No Joe," a Luke the Drifter recitation, has never appeared on any prior Hank Williams album. "My Main Trial Is Yet to Come," which combines prison song and gospel song, and "The Log Train," a straightforwardly autobiographical song about Hank's father accompanied only by acoustic guitar, were not even known to exist, let alone to have ever been released, before this album was compiled. (Hank's father, Lon, a WW I shell-shock victim, went into a VA hospital when his son was seven and got out when he was seventeen; his marriage was through by then, and though father and son were on friendly terms, they were never close.) In all, there are only eleven songs here that don't appear on either of the Polydor compilations, and most of those are Luke the Drifter recitations; that was the pseudonym Hank used (though everybody knew it was him) to record grimly morbid morality stories that didn't fit either the Williams image or the jukebox format. Eleven songs is not good value for the price of this album, but at least all these are without the overdubs MGM later added.

In listening to this, I'm struck mainly by how inadequate criticism is in pinning down Hank's music and his power. Instead, I keep thinking of the way his songs were used in the movie *The Last Picture Show* both to orchestrate the isolation of those small-town characters and to reinforce the fact that even in what appear to be dead-end situations, lives and dreams go on, with people doing the best they can whether they understand or not what's happening to them.

Hank's music is mainly about limits, and you can take that several ways. Most obviously, "Honkin Tonkin'," "Hey, Good Lookin'," "Honky Tonk Blues," "Settin' the Woods on Fire" and others all aim for a good time on Saturday night, but it's nothing symbolic or metaphorical, and really not even anything special. That's all they *dare* aim for, because in the grinding, numbing poverty of the rural South that produced Hank Williams, release or escape could never be more than temporary.

Then there were the limits set up by the feudalistic system that was the Grand Ole Opry, which was the only show in town. The Opry resisted hiring Hank Williams at first because of his drinking, and then hired him only when he'd become so popular there was no choice. Still, the powers behind the Opry seemed to keep their fingers crossed that he'd fail, and they moved swiftly to fire him when he did. Once he was safely dead, the same people lionized him because now he was no threat. (He was elected to the Hall of Fame in 1961.) The fans represented still more limits. He had started out just like them, white working folks scraping to get by, and though they didn't begrudge him his success—they welcomed it, for it held out hope to them, too—they did not want him to ever rise above them, though he could hardly help it under the circumstances. It was a double bind, but one he could appreciate, for he knew all about double binds; his marriage, the bad back that hampered him all his life and probably caused some of his erratic behavior, the dependencies on drugs and liquor, all gave him plenty of experience in that department.

Hank was a child of the transitional South. You could hear it in his music, which echoed everything from traditional Appalachian string-band music to the most modern pop-oriented performers. You could hear it in his lyrics, which utilized both archaic language obsolete since he was a child and the latest slang. But most of all, you could hear it in the stories he told. Here was the postwar American South, hurtling from a rural to an urban culture, from agrarian to industrial, from underdeveloped to technological, from oral traditions to mass media. It was unsettling, disorienting. And here was a man who didn't speak to those issues directly, but spoke in terms of the turmoil in his personal life, and did so in a style that made it appear he was talking to each person in his audience on an individual basis. Of course these people would understand that one-to-one approach best, because that was the way their culture had always communicated best. And what this man was saying was that his life was a shambles, he had no control over anything, everything was going too fast, he was torn up from his roots and on a treadmill he couldn't escape.

Williams gave shape, gave a certain kind of proud and defiant dignity, to those fears. But he was frail, both physically and emotionally, and he had little education or training in dealing with the larger world around him. He could never really overcome those fears and obstacles, wasn't really equipped to even give it a very good try (and might not have bothered had he been able to). In articulating them so well, though, he took country music, as people then knew it, as far as it could go—and then those limits rose up again. His songs were being covered regularly by pop artists, which Hank loved because he craved both the money and the respectability such cover versions brought him. But he was never able to even consider going pop himself—he was too hillbilly. In a working-class South that had, since Reconstruction, gotten used to abuse and exploitation from the North, that was as big a victory as Hank Williams could win at the time, but it was a significant start; for better or for worse, he had brought the modern world into country music, and then he had brought country music into the modern world. That, as much as any other reason, is why 25,000 people came to his funeral in Montgomery, Alabama, after he died in the back seat of his car on his way to a January 1, 1953, gig in Canton, Ohio.

When Jimmy Carter was elected President in 1976, I remember the commentary, nearly all of it pure drivel, about how this meant the South was finally being integrated into the rest of the country. But Carter, though he did have traditional southern traits, was also a nuclear

engineer, a bureaucrat, and a technocrat who in most respects had been
integrated into the American mainsteam long ago, I thought. His ascendance wasn't the beginning of something new so much as it was the
culmination, or confirmation, of a process that had begun three decades
earlier with Hank Williams as much as anyone else. The best thing that
could happen for his legacy now would be if Time-Life undertook to
compile another volume or two that would restore the rest of his material; his work needs to be taken from the musical goon squad at his
record company and put into the hands of people who care about it.

Lefty Frizzell: *Remembering . . . The Greatest Hits of Lefty
Frizzell* (Columbia).

At his peak, Lefty Frizzell was the only serious competition Hank
Williams had. In October 1951, for example, Frizzell did something
nobody else has done before or since: he put four records in the Top 10
simultaneously. They were "I Want to Be with You Always," "Always
Late," "Mom and Dad's Waltz," and "Travelin' Blues," and all but the
first are on this album. But Lefty's stay at the top was mysteriously brief;
the big, steady hits stopped coming after 1952, though he did continue
to enjoy off-and-on success for some time.

Meanwhile, most of his hits are barely available in America. The
Greatest Hits album available through Columbia Special Products is
deceptive; the song *titles* are right, but the versions are almost all either
weak rerecordings or else originals marred by heavy-handed overdubs.
And this particular album was in print only briefly; but it was in print
into the eighties, at least, and is still relatively easy to find in bargain
bins.

Lefty was born William Orville Frizzell in 1928 in Corsicana, Texas.
His father was an itinerant oil driller, and during the Depression the
family moved frequently around Arkansas, Oklahoma, and Texas. In his
mid-teens, Frizzell was a Golden Gloves boxer. That didn't last long, but
his powerful left did earn him his nickname.

Around the time he was fighting, Lefty began singing publicly. It
was the honky-tonk era, but Frizzell was also an heir to the Jimmie
Rodgers tradition, and the music he played integrated Rodgers' railroad
blues into the small-band barroom sound then dominating Texas. Before he was old enough to legally drink, Frizzell knew his way around
the dangerous, makeshift clubs that grew on the edge of oil towns,
towns that went boom and bust, here today and gone tomorrow.

Which is not a bad description of Lefty's attitude, and hence of his
subsequent career. In 1950, after several years in the clubs of New
Mexico and Texas, he hooked up with promotion man Jim Beck of
Dallas. Lefty cut a demo for Beck of "If You've Got the Money I've Got

the Time" and by October of that year he was not only signed to Columbia, but the label had released the demo intact and it had climbed to No. 2. It's a classic, up-tempo honky-tonker's shout for freedom, freedom being defined as no more than a good time on Saturday night with no complications or repercussions.

"I Love You a Thousand Ways" followed a month later, and went further toward establishing the Frizzell vocal style. The words "you" and "true" get dragged out for several syllables each at the end of lines, while the word "days" becomes "day-yuz." Frizzell's phrasing and diction were so crude, yet so basic and natural, that they became a measure by which other country singers were judged. He always claimed that his slurring, sliding drawl was an attempt to compensate for his inability to yodel (à la Rodgers) after his voice changed.

Whatever the case, his resonant voice and unprecedented style served him especially well in 1951, for he had two other chart records ("Look What Thoughts Will Do" and "Give Me More, More, More," the latter included here) in addition to the four listed above. "Give Me More, More, More," along with "Mom and Dad's Waltz" and "Always Late," helps to further define Frizzell's range and his appeal.

"Give Me More, More, More" gets a slow, acoustic intro, with Lefty sounding a bit unsure of himself, but then he swoops confidently into the main part of the song. It has a simple, steady rhythm, as all his early records did; by emphasizing piano as much as string instruments, the arrangement gives his voice more of a rhythmic foundation off which to play. "Always Late" has a shimmering steel intro before Frizzell's voice again breaks all over the first line. Most of these recordings sound like just acoustic guitar and bass, with steel fills, so understated are the other instruments, but the solos all remain strong, assertive. "Mom and Dad's Waltz" is perhaps the most peculiar of the three; it's the type of pledge more common to the country music of a decade or so earlier, and it's eerie to hear this product of a broken home giving an almost erotic reading to lyrics about his everlasting devotion to his parents. On all three of these songs, his vocals are intimate, almost conversational, in tone.

As a writer, he had masterful control over moods, and his best songs were double-edged. "I Love You a Thousand Ways" is ostensibly a straightforward declaration, yet it's laced with guilt. (He claims it's the first song he ever wrote, and that it was written to his wife, Alice, while he was in jail.) "Saginaw, Michigan" wasn't written by him, but sounds like it could have been. Ostensibly a song of triumph and one-upmanship, it is full of deep hurts. He frequently used internal rhyming to make his lyrics stick, and his melodies seemed to generate their own momentum.

So what happened later? Lefty himself was always vague about his fall. He blamed it on "private problems at home" caused by "too much success too soon." Given the right material, he could still put it across. In 1959 he capitalized on the saga-song boom by recording "Long Black Veil," an "instant folk song" (written by Nashville pros) of endless guilt and remorse. "Saginaw, Michigan," from 1964, also has the feel of a saga song, and went all the way to No. 1, the last Lefty Frizzell song to do so. It is a cruel fact of the country music business that the honky-tonk life has a way of destroying honky-tonk music.

Lefty Frizzell: *Treasures Untold* (Rounder Special Series).

Though it contains only one chart record ("Look What Thoughts Will Do," from 1951), *Treasures Untold* adds considerably to the Frizzell legacy. That's because it sticks to his earliest work (1950–53), which had minimal production and thus let Lefty himself shine through, and also because the songs tend to be tougher. Some of Frizzell's best efforts weren't promoted as singles in the conservative country market, which was true also for any number of other explicit honky-tonkers. Something like this album's "My Baby's Just Like Money" ("Money goes from hand to hand / And my baby goes from man to man") was considered too coarse for an audience more comfortable with the cut-and-dried sentiment of "Mom and Dad's Waltz."

Frizzell, like Hank Williams, wasn't an innovator. Instead, he took the dominant form of his time and invested it with more passion than anyone else except Williams. His instrumentation wasn't different from that used by other honky-tonker singers, though perhaps his bands swing a bit more (not surprising, given his Texas roots). Lefty's major influence had been Jimmie Rodgers, but that was also true of virtually every other honky-tonker from Ernest Tubb on down. No, Frizzell stood above the rest because the songs he wrote were so well developed, because as a stylist nobody else could touch him, and because of the special warmth his records projected.

His songs were ambitious, aspiring to poetry in the same way as some of Williams' best songs. On "How Long Will It Take (to Stop Loving You)," Lefty piles up question after metaphorical question in a way that expands the song ever outward. "Look What Thoughts Will Do," "Time Changes Things," and "Waltz of the Angels" also use imagery more sophisticated than that of most country writers of this era; they suggest a mystical streak that manages to coexist nicely with both the gritty honky-tonk language and the country fatalism.

Lefty's voice, which deepened later in his career, was a relaxed, flexible tenor with a Spanish tinge. Even on the up-tempo numbers, he sounded like a man drowsing away a blistering afternoon under the shade tree, but as Ronnie Pugh's liner notes quote him, "I'm not really a lazy guy, but I get tired of holding high notes for a long time. Instead of straining, I just let it roll down and it feels good to me." He would break notes like a bluesman, and stretch words to their breaking points.

With such a singular style, there was no mistaking Lefty for anyone else—as soon as the song came over the radio, you knew it had to be him singing. This served him especially well because in the postwar years songs seemed to be written and sung to a specific person, rather than to a generalized audience. Frizzell's direct, distinctive drawl created an intimacy that gave listeners all the more reason to identify with him.

From late 1952 to early 1955, Frizzell didn't land one record on the country charts. The onslaught of rock 'n' roll usually gets the blame for his decline, but even Lefty didn't buy that explanation entirely, and it's true that he lived his songs. Money burned a hole in his pocket and he could drink for days on end; he had no business sense, and he was irresponsible. When he was out roaring, he would forget (or simply skip) concerts and recording sessions.

He was also burdened with increasingly cheesy production and with material that emphasized his sentimental streak almost exclusively. From the late fifties through the early seventies, he had a string of moderate hits (and a couple more that did even better). In 1975, just as he was attempting to launch a comeback, he was felled by a cerebral hemorrhage at age forty-seven; his body, after years of abuse, just gave out on him.

His influence has continued to grow. Even today it is far greater than his own commercial ups and downs might imply, which is why in 1982 he was elected to the Hall of Fame. Merle Haggard began his career aping Frizzell, and Willie Nelson's 1977 *To Lefty from Willie* repaid some old debts. You can hear the ghost of Frizzell in singers as young as Johnny Rodriguez, John Anderson, and even Hank Williams, Jr. But none of them has equaled the raw, offhanded beauty of the sides that Frizzell cut in his own youth.

Hank Snow: *The Best of Hank Snow* (RCA).
    The first two cuts here explain Hank Snow's importance and influence. "I'm Movin' On" dominated country music in 1950. The chugging beat establishes that this is a train song, and the fiddle and steel push harder than is usual on Nashville records from this era. There's real anger and determination in Snow's voice, which sometimes sounds too smooth for this type of song. Next up is 1951's "The Rhumba Boogie," which has an equally insistent beat, features Snow's own boogie guitar solo, and dispenses dance instructions along with a description of "Madame Lasonga teaching the conga in her cabana in old Havana."

That line sounds like something Carl Perkins or Chuck Berry might have written, and there are hints of rock 'n' roll in more than just Snow's wordplay. "I'm Movin' On" had enough drive to adapt itself nicely to Ray Charles, who was later covered by the Rolling Stones and thus countless bar bands. Or listen to "(Now and Then, There's) A Fool Such as I"—cloyingly sentimental, for sure, but Snow gives it such a clean, spare reading, and his enunciation is flawless. It's exactly the kind of sentiment that country music contributed to Elvis Presley's sensibility; we even know this particular song was an Elvis favorite by the way he spoofs it on the Million Dollar Quartet tapes, and he finally recorded it properly in 1961. (Dean Martin, another of El's idols, probably dug it, too.)

In serving as a godfather to rock 'n' roll, Snow came a long way both literally and figuratively, because he began his career in Canada as a Jimmie Rodgers imitator. He was born in Nova Scotia in 1914. His parents divorced when he was eight, and he went to live with his grandparents. He ran away frequently, finally returning to his mother in Liverpool. She had remarried, to a man who apparently hated Hank and beat him often. (Snow is active to this day in battered-children charities.) At age twelve, Hank went to sea as a cabin boy to escape his stepfather. At sixteen, he discovered Jimmie Rodgers and took up music. At twenty-two, he earned his first contract, with RCA in Canada. He first came to America in 1944, and spent the next two years shuttling back and forth between the two countries. In 1946 he landed a radio show in Wheeling, West Virginia, and came to America to stay. He made a couple of disastrous trips to Hollywood before settling in Texas in 1948. In 1949 he finally won a contract with American RCA; in 1950, at the urging of Ernest Tubb, another man who started out as a Rodgers imitator, Snow was given a spot on the Opry.

But by now he was no longer a Rodgers imitator. Early in his career, Snow had billed himself as the Yodeling Ranger and featured blue yodels on his records. But as he aged, his voice deepened and he could no longer yodel. No problem, though: he simply changed his billing to the Singing Ranger and carried on in the Rodgers spirit.

Snow was thus not only an influence on rockabilly; he also bridged the gap between older country styles and the Nashville Sound. At the center of his style is his mellow, resonant baritone, which seems to filter out through a stopped-up nose. It's a flexible voice that can adjust to up-tempo tongue twisters like "I've Been Everywhere" (a novelty song that speeds up with each verse, and seems to name every small town in the nation) as easily as to a waltz like "Let Me Go, Lover."

His guitar playing also left its mark. He may have begun in the bluesy Rodgers style, but he soon picked up the tempo and moved into fast boogies. He coaxed a robust sound out of an acoustic guitar, and it's apparent that while Elvis was listening to "A Fool Such as I," Scotty Moore was concentrating on hits like "Music Makin' Mama from Memphis" (in which the players pass around hot licks like a swing band) or "The Golden Rocket."

In all, you can glean a capsule history of nearly the entire pre-rock era from the records of this 1979 Hall of Fame inductee. "With This Ring I Thee Wed" is marked by Hawaiian steel, a sound nearly archaic by the early fifties, while "I Don't Hurt Anymore," a 1954 song that spent forty-one weeks on the country charts, is in a similar vein. Yet "Miller's Cave" and "I've Been Everywhere" have arrangements that are early examples of the Nashville Sound.

Always, though, the ghost of Jimmie Rodgers hangs over Snow's music. "I've Been Everywhere" is a modern rambler's song, albeit a humorous one, and "I'm Movin' On" and "The Golden Rocket" are descendants of Rodgers train songs. "Ninety Miles an Hour (Down a Dead End Street)" modernizes that very same imagery by using an automotive metaphor to describe an illicit affair. For Hank Snow, the more things changed, the more they remained the same.

Truck Driver Songs (King/Gusto).

These singers and songs may be obscure, but they are part of a noble tradition. Ted Daffan's "Truck-Driver's Blues," recorded by Cliff Bruner and His Boys in 1939, was the first trucker song. With its sympathetic portrayal of the hard-working man fighting loneliness, fatigue, and other bad conditions to get his job done, it set the tone. But the genre didn't really get rolling until after World War II, when trucks began taking over from railroads as the chief means of moving the nation's goods. In the early sixties the form produced its first superstar in Dave Dudley, who hit with the legendary "Six Days on the Road" in 1963 and continued to work that vein for the next decade, becoming an honorary Teamster in the process. (Shockingly, his records have all been allowed to slip out of print.) The other best-known song on the subject is Terry Fell's "Truck-Driving Man," which has a folkish simplicity and has been cut by nearly every male singer in the *Country Music Encyclopedia*.

The rugged individualist celebrated in early country music lived on in trucking music more than anywhere else. "Six Days on the Road" lionized a frenzied driver "takin' little white pills and my eyes are open wide," all the while dodging weigh stations (because the truck is overweight and he hasn't kept up his logbook) and seductive women (because he's true to his baby at home). Other songs deal with hazards of the road like speed traps and hazards of equipment like faulty air brakes. Women, usually dressed up or made up to the nines, are either an awful distraction or a welcome diversion. There're foxy waitresses, coffee, a quick meal, and amphetamines at the truck stops, and the rest of the time there's just that long white line. But truckers represent freedom, too; they are always on the move, and appear (however mistakenly) to be responsible to nobody but themselves.

In such a self-contained world, there's plenty of room for novelty songs, and that's what most trucker hits have been. Only Dudley and, for lesser periods of time, Red Simpson and Dick Curless have been able to build careers on trucking songs. But others (like Red Sovine) did quite a few trucking songs, and there has been a multitude of one-shots, by established stars as well as nobodies. A huge number of this last category were released by the Nashville/Starday labels of the sixties and, before that, from the parent company, King. These songs can be found on a series of anthologies, the most consistent of which is this King compilation of sides from the mid-forties to the early sixties.

For one-shots, these are inspired efforts. The other Starday/King anthologies feature (at least in part) such stars as Johnny Bond, Red Sovine, and the Willis Brothers, but the names here are almost *all* unfamiliar to even the diehard fan. Moore and Napier might be known to the bluegrass fan, a few people might recognize the name Jimmy Logsdon from his handful of mid-level hits for Decca and King, and the extra-alert might know Bob Newman as the man who wrote the *Hee-Haw* theme, "Phfft! You Were Gone." But even those are real longshots, and meanwhile, who *are* Tommy Downs, Swanee Caldwell, Cowboy Jack Derrick, and Coleman Wilson? None had enough success to warrant a line in the index of any of the standard encyclopedias or reference books, but all have what it takes to turn in a convincing trucker's performance.

Primarily, that's a deep—as in burly, manly—voice, because that's the way real truckers want 'em. The music, similarly, is usually up-tempo, because that's the only way to convey the feel of one of those big rigs hurtling down the highway. Caldwell's version of "Six Days on the Road" is a prime example; his voice may not be as husky as Dudley's, but it's close enough to put this heroic boast over, and his drawling diction is right neighborly. The band has almost as much thrust as the one that recorded behind Dudley. Caldwell's "Radar Blues, Part 1" is a talking blues with a similar beat.

Thanks to overdubbing, Newman's "Haulin' Freight" has the fattest sound of all, roaring like a truck engine while the splashing cymbals, whining steel, and grinding rhythm guitar make like a gear box. His "Lonesome Truck Drivers Blues" is equally dense (again due to overdubs), especially the fiddle and steel, but this one doesn't bluster like the other; it's more a sigh of exasperation that builds its moods with blue yodels.

With "Big Casey," Tommy Downs taps into a common trucker's theme, that of the gallant driver who gives up his own life to save a school bus full of children. Jimmy Martin did it best—i.e., did it most heroically—on "Widowmaker" (recorded for another label years after these and thus not here), but Downs tells his story well, too, and the band chugs right along with no instrumental breaks. On "Wild Catter," Downs takes the motif one step further, becoming an outlaw among outlaws—he's a wildcatter, which means company drivers avoid him, and he's hauling explosives, which means the other wildcatters avoid him. (He even has to drink his coffee alone at truck stops!)

Jimmy Logsdon has no such bad feelings, even when, in "Gear Jammer," he loses his job after getting ripped off when he stops to help a sexy blonde who turns out to be bait for a theft ring. A man who likes his highway straight and his women with curves, Jimmy simply chuckles and warns, "Keep your *truck* on the highway / And your *eyes* on it too!" His "Truck Drivin' Daddy" is yet another boaster.

Coleman Wilson, backed by acoustic guitar and with his mouth seemingly full of tobacco, mumbles and drawls his way through two hard-luck tales, "A Green Truck Driver's First Experience with Radar" and "Passing Zone Blues." Charlie Moore and Bill Napier pledge fealty to their "Truck Driver's Queen." And finally, saving the weirdest for last, Cowboy Jack Derrick does the same for his "Truck Driving Man." That's right, after getting an erotic thrill from the sound of a motor, Cowboy Jack gets *all* steamed up and deadpans "When my truck drivin' man comes back to town / I'll dress up in my silken gown." I mean, are you *sure* this one wasn't meant for Texas Ruby or someone like that? (Actually, this is more likely a demo that nobody listened to closely before throwing it on here; King was notorious for such haphazardness.)

Trucking songs have fallen on hard times; in the mid-seventies they mutated into CB songs and got trivialized beyond repair. But it's hard to picture them doing well in the antiseptic world of modern country music anyhow. Can you picture Alabama doing something that might get their hands dirty? Or the Barbara Mandrell of today cooing for a man who might not know which fork to use (as she did on "Tonight My Baby's Comin' Home," one of the best trucking songs from the early seventies)? I thought not, but if that sounds like your kind of man, look into the truckers anthologies, starting with this one.

Webb Pierce: *The Best of Webb Pierce* (MCA).

In the year after Hank Williams died on January 1, 1953, Webb Pierce was the most popular singer in country music, with six singles in the Top 30. He'd had three hits in 1952, and in 1954 and 1955, the years Elvis was turning country music upside down, Webb charted four and five times respectively. He was not only the man whose records introduced the pedal steel guitar to country music, but Webb Pierce was the honky-tonk hero who held down the fort when the going got tough.

This double album begins with "Wondering," his 1952 debut Decca hit (after some success on regional labels), and runs into the early sixties. It should be honky-tonk heaven, but unfortunately the versions here are rerecordings ordered by his record company to exploit new stereo techniques in the early sixties. The background voices (especially) sweeten things up way too much. But this is the only version of his hits that's distributed these days; the arrangements are close to the originals, and Webb's singing style, a tenor pushing against the top of its range, hadn't changed appreciably between the time he surfaced and the time he cut these sides. So you'll not be *too* disappointed.

When Willie Nelson decided to cut a duet album with Webb in the early eighties, eyebrows raised. Ray Price, Roger Miller, Ernest Tubb, Floyd Tillman, Johnny Bush . . . these Nelson collaborations made sense, for these were all fellow Texans who once worked with Willie or had been big influences. Pierce didn't seem to fit.

Listen again: Pierce is the secret ingredient in shaping Willie's vocal style. The similarities—Webb's pinched, yearning vibrato, the way he stretches a word at the end of one line and then snaps one off at the end of another to build momentum, his way of singing just behind the beat—are too close to be coincidence.

Pierce was born in 1926 near West Monroe, Louisiana. In his teens, he played on local radio before moving to Shreveport. When the Louisiana Hayride began on KWKH, Pierce was one of its first stars. His bands spawned such future names as Faron Young, Goldie Hill, Jimmy Day, Tommy Hill, and Floyd Cramer. But Pierce still paid the rent by working as a shoe salesman at Sears Roebuck.

His songs were about honky-tonks, heavy drinking, streets, jails, and cheating hearts. A few years later, he flirted with pop and rock. "In the Jailhouse Now" (1955) had a beat not unlike that of Memphis music, "I Ain't Never" (1959) was an up-tempo crossover hit, and "Tupelo County Jail" (1958), "I Don't Care" (1955), and "Love, Love, Love" (1955) all sport progressions like those of teen ballads from the fifties. (During these years he also cut songs like "Teen-Age Boogie" and "Bye Bye Love" that aren't included here.) But nobody—least of all Pierce—ever mistook him for a pop singer.

In 1952, after a few years slogging it on the Hayride and on the southern circuit of roadhouses and municipal parks, Pierce signed with

Decca. In 1953, when "There Stands the Glass" became his second straight No. 1 single, he moved to Nashville to join the Opry.

His reputation was built on songs like "There Stands the Glass," with the guitar and steel swapping crisp solos, and "Back Street Affair" (1952), one of the first cheating songs to pull no punches. With its bluesy piano intro and Webb's punchy vocals, the song was a crucial stepping-off point for Elvis and other rockabillys.

In 1954, Pierce's "Slowly" revolutionized the steel guitar in country music. The song as it appears here is nearly identical to the original. Webb gives it a dramatic intro, his voice coming through like that of a man falling off a cliff. Bud Isaacs steps in with a short, soft, sliding pedal steel solo that nearly everyone in Nashville was imitating within a year. Note-bending, in which notes glide up and down within a chord, became essential to country steel after those few seconds of crying, and for that you have to hook a pedal up to the steel. Until they learned about the pedals, steel players tried all kinds of tricks to ape the Isaacs style. When they finally found out how he did it, they made pedal setups out of coat hangers, old gas and brake pedals, you name it. The current instrument, with its legs and double necks, soon followed.

In Pierce's earlier records, even in these remakes, you can hear Isaacs and him working toward that sound. "I'm Walking the Dog" (the single that immediately preceded "Slowly") is one reference point. "That's Me Without You," from earlier in 1953, features Hawaiian-based steel, but already the sound it makes is "drooping" like a shroud being lowered over Pierce's voice.

"Slowly" clinched matters for Pierce, and with records like "More and More" (1954), he and Isaacs stepped out further. When rockabilly came in, Pierce was able to make a living while other country singers were packing it in. Pierce continued with his unadulterated honky-tonk ballads, with only a few exceptions, and even when he tried to get pretty, as in "Is It Wrong (for Loving You)" (1960), he was pure country.

And what did Nashville's most unreconstructed hillbilly do with his new wealth and fame? Quite simply, he did it all. He decked himself out in the most garish western suits money could buy. He embedded hundreds of silver dollars into his Pontiac, substituted six-shooters for door handles, mounted steer horns on the hood, and rebuilt the car seats into saddles. Finally, he ordered up a guitar-shaped swimming pool for his backyard. That item went on to become a country music cliché, a symbol for all that is corny about Nashville, but know this fact: Webb Pierce was there first.

Ray Price: *Greatest Hits* (Columbia).

"The sound they had going at the time in country was a two-four sound and a double-stop fiddle. I added drums to it, which had been done before, but not much, and a four-four bass and a shuffle rhythm and the single string fiddle," Ray Price explained in 1979. "We came up with it right there on the session, I don't know why or where from; that's just what I wanted. That's the way things happen, on the spur of the moment. Everybody at the session thought it was the funniest thing they ever heard. The new sound, and just the words: 'Crazy arms that long to hold somebody new . . .' They thought it was strange. It was— and it was on the charts forty-five weeks."

Price is describing the genesis of "Crazy Arms," the 1956 hit that launched a new sound in hard country just when the music needed one most. With the songs on this album, Price held on through the rest of the decade, while the unlikely bedfellows of rock 'n' roll and the Nashville Sound conspired to keep hard country off the radio. It worked for a few others as well, but to this day that rhythm is known in country music as the Ray Price Beat.

Price's career has been a study in stubbornness. He was, how you say, country when country wasn't cool, and then he was pop when pop wasn't cool. Such bullheadedness is the mark of a true Texas boy. Price was born in 1926 in Perryville and raised in Dallas. After leaving the service, he went to North Texas Agricultural College in 1946 to become a veterinary surgeon. But he began playing locally with his pickup band of fellow students, and by 1949 he was appearing on the Big D Jamboree in Dallas. Later that year, he quit college and split for Nashville.

Once there, he recorded for the local Bullet label and hung out with Hank Williams, then so deep into the process of flaming out that when he couldn't make gigs, which was most of the time, he let Price have his band. Price let Hank move into his Nashville duplex; then, unable to cope with Hank's escalating recklessness but wary of hitting a man already so obviously on the ropes, Price moved out of his own place. He had a pair of hits upon signing with Columbia in 1952, then hit a dry spell before clicking in 1954 with "I'll Be There," "Too Young to Die," "If You Don't Someone Else Will," and "Release Me," which is exactly the kind of "big" ballad Price liked best to wrap his pipes around. In the course of the song, his husky voice moves back and forth from a smooth plea to a desperate bleat, a style he would later polish even more. The fiddle provides the very definition of country eroticism, while the silent spots in the crying-steel solo approximate the rancorous pauses in a lovers' argument. There was one more follow-up hit before "Crazy Arms" broke.

Written by steel guitarist Ralph Mooney, whose manic solo does the song proud, "Crazy Arms" kicks off with a heavily bowed fiddle before Price eases into the first line: "Now blue ain't the word for the way I feel." Despite the awkward English, Price stretches out "word" and "way" to dramatic lengths, with a high harmony voice then joining him on the chorus. The rest of the song is almost as fanciful, and testifies to Price's ear for an offbeat honky-tonk lyric. (Since he didn't write himself, he needed one.)

"City Lights," in which the country boy is unable to forget his troubles in the flashing world of the big city, "Invitation to the Blues," one of the first hits Roger Miller wrote, and "Heartaches by the Number," which was a perfect country conceit, have all become honky-tonk standards. In the late fifties, when all were hits, they were so reactionary they were almost revolutionary. In true honky-tonk style, Price always saw himself as a passive victim of misfortune. Notice how in "Crazy Arms" none of his feelings come from the heart or the head—his arms keep telling him what to do. On "My Shoes Keep Walking Back to You" it's his footwear that does his thinking for him, against his will.

Price's records were always identifiable even before his taut vibrato cut through. Before he found his formula, he experimented with a western swing band, and the Ray Price Beat, as heard on hits like "One More Time," was basically an even-handed fusion of honky-tonk and western swing. Once he settled on it, all his songs began with the heavily bowed fiddle, which also took many of the breaks, while the steel guitar wriggled through the tune like a snake through the grass before stepping forward to exchange licks on the break. The walking bass was the final ingredient, and the guitar was almost superfluous. Over the years, his band, the Cherokee Cowboys, included such future stars as Willie Nelson, Johnny Bush, Roger Miller, Johnny Paycheck, and steel wizards Buddy Emmons and Jimmy Day.

Having made the airwaves once again safe for honky-tonk, Price went pop with a vengeance in the early sixties. By then his voice had mellowed even more, and by 1967 he was making a hit out of "Danny Boy," cut with a forty-seven-piece orchestra behind him. Purists were mortally offended, and Price didn't approach the form with near the imagination he brought to honky-tonk, but the pop balladeer had been in him all along. You can hear it clearly in cuts like "City Lights" and "I'll Be There" as well as in "Release Me." In 1963 he built a whole concept album around a then-struggling Willie Nelson's "Night Life." The song was as country as they come, but Price gave it a semioperatic reading that pointed to the direction he was headed vocally. Like the man says, "That's the way things happen."

George Jones: *16 Greatest Hits* (Starday/Gusto).

Today it's almost a cliché—albeit a true one—that George Jones is the greatest country singer alive, the last bastion of honky-tonk purism and the creator of a vocal style so tricky nobody can even pay him tribute by copying it. His earliest sides, sixteen of them collected here by his first label, show just how committed to the form he's always been. Jones first hit in 1955 with "Why Baby Why," a honky-tonker with steel licks right off a Hank Williams record and a nasal voice that mocked both the cuckolded male and the cheating woman in the song. Jones was then twenty-four. At a time when most men his age were singing rockabilly for kids, and country music was sweetening itself to hold on to the older folks, Jones bucked both trends by immersing himself in the very music everyone else was leaving behind.

He was born in 1931 in Sarasota, east Texas. As he grew up, Texas was changing from a predominantly rural to an urban and industrial state; World War II hastened this process. Like many other families, the Joneses soon moved to nearby Beaumont, where defense plants and oil fields created thousands of new jobs. Though now nominally city dwellers, these people didn't entirely desert their country ways.

In musical terms, this meant that a young man like Jones might recognize the modernizing influences urban life brought to country music, but that didn't mean he had to go along with them. During the three years covered by this sampler, George also cut a few sides (under the name Thumper Jones) approaching pure rockabilly. But those don't carry near the conviction of his honky-tonk sides.

Jones had a hand in writing most of them. He rarely writes today, and yet these originals still aren't as blatantly autobiographical as many of the songs others now provide him, and there are several possible reasons for that. One is that George was a conservative man working in a conservative form, and like most of the artists he grew up on, he was content to speak in honky-tonk generalities rather than being more specific; perhaps he had not yet found his own voice, only his subject matter. Also, his tumultuous private life was then still a private matter, and he was still young enough to be somewhat cavalier about it. As a writer, George knew how to hit nerves with cheating and hurting songs, but he had at that point not accumulated many years of hard living, so those songs didn't have to hit as close to home as they do today; he didn't have to let those themes swallow him up like they now do. Back then, he could ignore his drinking problem altogether, for example, probably because he didn't yet see it as a problem. Still, he was no slouch as a honky-tonk writer, and his best efforts develop their ideas impressively; on "Seasons of My Heart" he explains how no one emotion can dominate him any more than one season can dominate nature.

Nor do you hear the Jones voice of today on these tracks, for his style took years to develop. But you do hear the foundation, including the earliest influences—Bill Monroe, Roy Acuff (especially when Jones reaches for a wailing high note), Hank Williams (but of course), Lefty

Frizzell, and Floyd Tillman (particularly when he bends notes). At the same time, you can't say these influences are *all* you hear, for at no time does George "sound like" any of these men. Maybe he doesn't yet have a fully developed personal style, but it's significant enough that he was working on one right from the beginning, because most country singers, even many of the good ones, start out aping someone else.

His biggest trick was to drop from his normal tenor into a bass register when he wanted to admonish or tease, as on "Uh, Uh, No." (He does something similar today, only he slides down much less perceptibly, so that when he gets there it's a surprise.) On "One Is a Lonely Number," his voice pines like the Hawaiian-based steel licks, and there seems to be a frustrated sigh at the end of each line. The rise and fall of his voice on "Don't Do This to Me" echoes the waltz meter. On "Color of the Blues," a 1958 hit, his voice is deeper, more resonant, and he's breaking it (as on the word "blues" in the title phrase) with new sureness. On "What Am I Worth" he injects a glimmer of optimism into a most pessimistic song.

The band is a crack east Texas honky-tonk outfit, which means twin fiddles, jaunty steel solos (usually by Herbie Remington), some biting guitar leads (probably by Hal Harris), and fiddle-steel duets that add a touch more swing. There's a bit of rock influence still in songs like "Eskimo Pie," but most of the up-tempo material is more along the lines of the country boogie of "No Money Down" and the barroom shouting of "If I Don't Love You" or "Long Time to Forget." The spry young George Jones was as comfortable with these fast songs as he is with any other tempo; the George Jones of today best puts across his adult pain when he's singing slow songs.

Starday started out as a Houston label co-owned by H. W. "Pappy" Daily, who also managed Jones for years. Their relationship was always fraught with ambivalence; though George has always given Daily credit for recognizing his talent when others were passing on him, he has also noted ruefully that Pappy wound up with virtually all the singer's earnings. Despite the album's title, most of these early sides went nowhere; their importance was recognized only in retrospect. George quickly left Starday for Mercury, where he did start having steady hits, and while it's true his records got slicker, he also grew immensely as a vocalist. As for these, they're best summed up by the lyrics to an old song that George sings and claims (falsely) to have written: "I'm a rambler, a gambler/I've lived every life/I tell you folks/I'm ragged but I'm right."

George Jones: *George Jones* (United Artists).

Until his most recent triumphs, George Jones' years with United Artists were his most rewarding. During the period covered in this double album of hits (1962–66), he had only one No. 1 single ("She Thinks I Still Care," his first release for the label), but he was consistently high on the charts, and in 1962–63 he won several awards from trade papers, his only recognition from the industry until his long-overdue CMA plaudits in 1980–81. His brand of honky-tonk heartbreak rang true at a time when the rest of country music had gone limp. Most important, it was during this period that Jones truly freed himself from the conventions of the honky-tonk genre and originated the intensely personal style he's been refining ever since.

It's never been an easy singing style to describe, though it certainly starts with honky-tonk and the open, full-throated wail that honky-tonk singers employed to convey their joy, doubts, and pain. But with George that became just a starting point, and the variations he devised are chilling. His voice doesn't seem to start in his chest, as is usually the case; it seems to rise from the knots in his stomach, and is released from somewhere in the back of his throat. The words aren't always released through that wail, either; just as often, he seeps them out through clenched teeth. For everything he does let out, you get the sense he's holding back that much more; this means there's no catharsis, no letting-go in his music. Instead, there's tension and then more tension piled on top of it. If this is really how he sees life, and apparently it is, the wonder is not Jones' capacity for self-destruction at all; rather, it's his survival instinct, and why he'd bother to develop one in the first place.

One of his most disorienting tricks is to sound like he's modulating down when in fact his voice is going up. He often curls it upward to "worry" a lyric, as in "A Girl I Used to Know," which is fortified further by the nagging Jones vibrato. That leap upward is his personal equivalent to the black bluesman's falsetto cry. On the new, confident version of "Ragged but Right" he drops way down to signal contentment, or at least freedom from worry. Whenever he is feeling lighthearted, he'd go down like that; it's a wink done with the throat rather than the eye. At other times, such as on his version of "Faded Love" (Jones cut a great Bob Wills tribute LP during this period), he seems to want to swallow the words he's singing; he gets them halfway down, then changes his mind and lets them escape. He swoops in and out of different pitches, drags words out past their breaking point or snaps them off with a swift crackle. He can convey strange ambivalence, as on "She Thinks I Still Care," a song of both pride and self-pity. On other, equally complex songs like "You Comb Her Hair" he shows surprising tenderness for one who's been so battered around. And on "Where Does a Little Tear Come From" he sounds at one moment like an innocent young boy and at the next like a wizened old man.

That song expands outward and then turns back in on itself, explaining that the tear comes from the heart, the heart comes from the river, and, finally, the river comes from the many tears that have been shed. On the puzzling "You Comb Her Hair" all that comes through with certainty is George's longing for someone close but not quite attainable.

"Sometimes You Just Can't Win" expresses longings more tangible, but just as dark and desperate, as Jones tries to forget (and rationalize) a rejection that hurts more the harder he tries. By now he's become primarily a ballad singer, for slow songs give his voice the most room to work in. There are exceptions like "The Race Is On," a classic corny country metaphor likening a jilted lover's state of mind to a horse race, with various emotions dominating and then falling back. But more typical is "Open Pit Mine," a story-song about an Arizona copper miner who kills his unfaithful girl friend, and then kills himself.

It's a first-class country ballad, but I mention it in contrast to "The Race Is On" not just because of the respective tempos of the two songs. "The Race Is On" uses simile in a conventional way. "Open Pit Mine" contrasts sharply because it's not until we're well into the song that we realize Jones thinks of his life as being like that mine, an open sore that's picked clean and then deserted. It's an eerie realization but that's the whole idea—Jones wants it to haunt you as much as it haunts him. And it does.

Johnny Horton: *The World of Johnny Horton* (Columbia).
The title of this album is at least a triple entendre, because Johnny Horton's specialty was historical songs like "The Battle of New Orleans," "North to Alaska," and "Sink the Bismarck," but before he settled into that niche, Horton proved himself as a gutsy honky-tonker, and recorded other songs that were as close to rockabilly as they were to country. He was also silky enough to pass as a pop singer when he wanted. So why, since he died in a 1960 auto wreck, hasn't he been recognized as one of the most versatile country singers of his generation? Why, after a steady string of pop hits, is he relegated to a tiny corner of the country music world?

Perhaps his stirring brand of patriotism became quaint and dated— the historical songs were a fad, and are now a novelty—but it couldn't be his voice, a fluidly inventive instrument in its own right. He recorded over a small (but full-sounding) country band, and his vocals were always front and center. In the lower range he had a slight growl; in his upper range, a slight hic.

Horton made singing sound easy. He was born in Tyler, Texas, in 1929, and spent his childhood picking cotton under the muggy east Texas sun. He went to junior college in Jacksonville and in Kilgore,

Texas, and was a good enough basketball player to earn a scholarship to Baylor (in Waco). From there he went to the University of Washington in Seattle. Upon leaving college, he worked in the fishing industry in Alaska and California; in 1950 he began singing on KXLA in Pasadena, but soon moved to Cliffie Stone's "Hometown Jamboree" on KLAC-TV. In 1955 he returned to east Texas, joining the Louisiana Hayride in nearby Shreveport as "The Singing Fisherman."

His first hit, "Honky Tonk Man," came in 1956. It was not raw like most honky-tonk. Horton took the song at a languid, dreamy pace that made the dangers he sang about sound romantic, dashing. He was clearly out of the honky-tonk tradition, but he came along late enough that he could be reflective about that tradition; he fit into the Nashville scene so well because his voice was flexible enough to qualify as a producer's dream.

Horton toughened up for the 1957 hit "I'm Coming Home," the pledge of a sex-starved trucker with bulging pants and a slobbering tongue. With a crude, pulsing band playing double time behind him, Horton is all lust and anticipation. "The First Train Heading South," another song full of fancy fast picking and a grating guitar, is in the Johnny Cash vein, as are Horton's readings of "Rock Island Line" and "The Golden Rocket." "I'm Ready if You're Willing" has the swooning feel of Elvis singing something like "I Don't Care if the Sun Don't Shine."

So while he was working the country music joints, Horton was keeping apace of the rockabilly upstarts. But he didn't reach pop ears himself until 1959, when he was all over the airwaves, country and pop. His first No. 1 record that year was "When It's Springtime in Alaska," a ballad about a Klondike prospector killed in a knife fight. Next, Horton released "The Battle of New Orleans," first recorded the year before by Jimmy Driftwood, who simply took the melody to the traditional "The Eighth of January" and wrote original lyrics about the British Army retreating under ferocious attack by Stonewall Jackson's troops. Horton's youthful, rugged version was much shorter than Driftwood's, and much more successful.

It touched off a brief vogue for historical songs, or saga songs, that were a modern counterpart to the broadside traditions in early country music. Nobody capitalized better than Horton himself, though. He came back with the likes of "Johnny Reb," "Sink the Bismarck," "North to Alaska." All of them had militaristic, death-march drumming and a prominent banjo (played by Nashville sessionman Harold Bradley) that completed the link to the country music of three decades before. In places Horton's voice eased up into a sob, but more often he dipped down into a gruff, boasting rumble that must have been hell on the tonsils, but that spoke directly to the rough 'n' ready part of the American psyche that still has not stopped believing in the absolute righteousness of all our military actions; even today, in the post-Vietnam era, Horton's songs sound noble.

The softer side of Horton came through on B-sides and on album cuts. On "All for the Love of a Woman" he phrases with special care, delicately spitting out key words before his voice soars up into barrenness. His version of Hank Williams' "Lost Highway" is a smooth update, but no less final in its message. (Horton had more than musical ties to Williams; his manager at one point was Louisiana entrepreneur Tilman Franks, who also once managed Williams; when Horton died, he left as his widow Billie Jean Horton, Hank's own second wife.)

For all his success on the pop charts, though, and for all his ability to put across a pop lyric, Horton was never considered anything *but* a country singer who lucked into the right place at the right time. He worked the roadhouses with a small honky-tonk band, and his black-inflected east Texas accent was as thick as the Gulf Coast air in hurricane season. His fatal auto accident was a grisly one, occurring right after he'd completed a nightclub date in central Texas and was on his way back to Nashville. The owner of the club he'd just played had to identify the body, and was able to do so only on the basis of a toupee that came off Johnny's head during the wreck; everything else was too badly mangled to be identifiable. There were posthumous hits, but they charted country alone; for the late Johnny Horton, things had gone full circle.

Supplementary Albums

Moe Bandy: *Best of Moe Bandy* (Columbia). In 1974, Bandy released two singles in a row for a small Atlanta label that featured his anguished voice knifing through simple honky-tonk arrangements. They were called "I Just Started Hatin' Cheatin' Songs Today" (one of those lyrics that refers to numerous other song titles) and "Honky Tonk Amnesia" (one of those lyrics that refers to getting too drunk). At a time when Billy Sherrill ruled, they made everything else, even Willie or Waylon albums, seem a little excessive. Bandy was rightly hailed as the avatar of the new honky-tonk, and the miracle is that when he switched to Columbia late in 1975 he and producer Roy Baker didn't alter the sound very much at all. This album is compiled primarily from the three LPs he cut for GRC before graduating to Columbia. It is one of the great honky-tonk albums of the seventies, but if you ever see any of the GRC albums—*I Just Started Hatin' Cheatin' Songs Today, It Was Always So Easy (to Find an Unhappy Woman)* or *Bandy the Rodeo Clown*—don't pass them by, either. The second is a little long on filler, but the first is mean all the way through, and the third isn't far behind. With a biting voice like Bandy's, and songs coming from Whitey Shafer, Doodle Owens, and Dallas Frazier, the three albums together are like honky-tonk heaven. More recently, albums have begun to thin out into two-hits-and-some-filler, but they're still refreshingly free of heavy production.

Boogie with a Bullet (Dutch Redita). A sampler from the Bullet label, a curious Nashville indie that recorded blues and country from the mid-forties into the early fifties. Includes a couple of archetypal Roy Hall boogies, and a Chet Atkins instrumental much dirtier than anything else available by him. Also Leon Payne's original of "Lost Highway." And anyone who still believes Ray Price sold out when he went country-politan should hear his 1950 debut "Jealous Lies," which establishes once and for all that in his heart he was a crooner first and a honky-tonker second.

The Brown's Ferry Four: *16 Greatest Hits of the Brown's Ferry Four* (Starday/Gusto). Guest vocalists sit in with the incomparable Alton and Rabon Delmore in a great set of gospel quartets. These four voices weave, blend, and lock so seamlessly it's easy to forget that this was not an ongoing group, but just a few friends getting together in the studio once in a while.

Cowboy Copas: *16 Greatest Hits of Cowboy Copas* (Starday/Gusto). An Oklahoman who helped put the western in country and western, Copas came to the Opry in 1946 as featured vocalist in Pee Wee King's Golden West Cowboys. In the forties he had such hits as "Filipino Baby," "Tragic Romance," and "Signed, Sealed and Delivered," but he slumped through most of the fifties before returning with "Alabam" in 1960. Just when his career was back in high gear, he was killed in the 1963 plane crash that also took Hawkshaw Hawkins and Patsy Cline. These hits showcase an appealing baritone that, especially on the up-tempo songs, was a major influence on Johnny Cash.

Little Jimmy Dickens: *Greatest Hits* (Columbia). His overreliance on novelty songs sometimes hides the fact that Dickens could be an explosive guitarist and an authoritative singer. Unfortunately, because his image as an uppity nut dominates, much of his best work was either never a hit or was left off the album for the sake of symmetry. This is still a few notches above your basic country novelty album, but the dose or two of no-joking material included makes me hope somebody gets around to putting out an album with more of that, too.

Diesel Smoke, Dangerous Curves and Other Truck Driver Favorites (Starday/Gusto). A consistently listenable anthology, which is more than can be said for many of them, even if the only truly extraordinary cut here is Hylo Brown's friendly, urgent bluegrass workout on "Look at That Rain," which is unforgettable.

Buddy Emmons: *International Steel Guitar Convention/Recorded Live, Vol. One* (Mid-Land). Emmons can be the jazziest of the pedal steel stylists. Which, when he's doing athletic stuff like "Raisin' the Dickens," is truly stimulating. This modern steel album could use a little more of that and a little less cocktail jazz, but that's about all it could use.

Tennessee Ernie Ford: *16 Tons* (Capitol). He may be best known for his lugubrious heart songs and hymns, but Tennessee Ernie was actually one of the heppest hillbilly boogie singers of the early fifties. This is basically a "greatest hits" compilation, and in addition to the 1955 title song offers such romps as "Shotgun Boogie" (from 1950), "Anticipation Blues" (1949), and "Blackberry Boogie" (1952). They make his later about-face seem rather inexplicable.

Lefty Frizzell: *Columbia Historic Edition* (Columbia). Though his producers didn't always give him the best shake, it's probably fair to say Frizzell never sang a song poorly in his early years. This one has a few big hits also found elsewhere ("I Love You a Thousand Ways," "Always Late"). But it restores unjustly ignored hits from the early fifties ("I'm an Old, Old Man Trying to Live While I Can"), a previously unreleased novelty ("Cold Feet"), and a monstrous blues in "No One to Talk To (but the Blues)." They make this nearly as worthwhile as anything in print on Lefty, and besides, it's hard to get too much of him.

Lefty Frizzell: *Lefty Frizzell Sings the Songs of Jimmie Rodgers* (Columbia). Lefty may have had the heart of a honky-tonker, but he had the soul of a rambling bluesman. Tribute albums are a hallowed tradition in country music, which clings to the past like no other form, but none can touch Lefty's early-fifties tributes to Jimmie.

Lefty Frizzell: *The Legendary Lefty Frizzell—His Last Sessions* (MCA). Recorded in the mid-seventies after a long drought, this is deathbed Lefty. He sounds, in the words of one of his early songs, like "an old, old man," though he'd not yet reached fifty. But hard living had taken its toll, and when Frizzell moans, "I can't stand to see a good man go to waste/One who never combs his hair or shaves his face," it's shocking to realize he's talking about himself. Relatively spartan production increases the sense of loss on this unsettling double album.

Harmonica Frank: *The Great Original Recordings of Harmonica Frank* (Puritan). Frank Floyd was Sam Phillips' first stab at synthesizing something new out of a "white man who had the Negro feel." These sides were all cut in Memphis between 1951 and 1958, and were just too anachronistic for the market Sam was trying to reach. What we have here is an updated version of the ne'er-do-well medicine-show singer; Frank played guitar and harmonica and did blues and talking blues, but everything had a country feel to it, and songs like "Swamp Root," "Howlin' Tomcat," "The Great Medical Menagerist," and "Rockin' Chair Daddy" are some of the truest links we have left to an America (and a rootless, restless, wily kind of American) that is now a thing of the past.

Hawkshaw Hawkins: *16 Greatest Hits of Hawkshaw Hawkins* (Starday/Gusto). "Lonesome 7-7203," his first No. 1 hit, was released just two days before Hawkins was killed in that infamous 1963 plane crash. But he was one of the most diversified of the first wave of postwar country artists, with material that drew on blues, boogie, traditional, and, above all else, honky-tonk.

Johnny Horton: *Johnny Horton Makes History* (Columbia). On individual albums, various sides of Horton's personality were explored in greater detail. This out-of-print set concentrates on saga songs, from hits like "Battle of New Orleans" to flops like "O'Leary's Cow."

Johnny Horton: *Honky Tonk Man* (Columbia). This one, also out of print, zeroes in on the Horton who moved back and forth between rockabilly and honky-tonk as if he thought they might be one and the same—which, in his hands, they often were.

Bud Isaacs: *The Legendary Bud Isaacs* (Mid-Land). The man who brought pedal steel to public attention with his work on Webb Pierce's records, Isaacs can still bend a note or two, though his LP suffers from the same cheesy production values that mar most of the other steel albums in this series. Like all the Mid-Land albums, this is more for pickers than listeners, but not exclusively so.

George Jones: *The George Jones Story* (Starday). For some reason, George's old Starday albums seem to turn up in bargain bins more often than anything else by him (except maybe RCA albums from the early seventies, which are themselves reissues of Musicor sides). Though out of print, this double album with thirty songs offers the most comprehensive overview of his early years.

George Jones: *George Jones* (Starday). Though there's a certain amount of overlap among all the Starday albums (including the Starday/Gusto reissues) this is another out-of-print set worth scouting for, because it offers George's barking vocals on "Long Time to Forget" and his sorrow on "Color of the Blues" and "Don't Do This to Me."

George Jones: *Long Live King George* (Starday). "I Gotta Talk to Your Heart" is one of his gutsiest early ballads, and though many of this out-of-print album's best songs ("Seasons of My Heart," "Ragged But Right," "Why Baby Why") are available elsewhere, this one also offers worthwhile obscurities. Any George Jones on Starday will be full of a young comer's spirit and energy, and will offer a chance to hear that distinctive style in its most formative stages.

George Jones: *Good Old Bible* (Gusto). Jones sings the most mundane songs like they were God's own truth, so it follows that he would sing gospel the same way only more so. He means it, too, which you can tell by the amount of gospel he includes in his live show, and also by the warnings inherent in such Jones originals as "Take the Devil Out of Me," "Wandering Soul," and "Boat of Life." Or at the very least, he *wants* to mean it.

George Jones: *Golden Hits* (Gusto). A mind-boggling compilation from the United Artists and Musicor years, which means they could have been produced better. But it's hard to fault in any other way a set that includes "Things Have Gone to Pieces," "Tender Years," "Walk Through This World With Me," "Take Me," and six others of that caliber.

George Jones: *Greatest Hits* (Mercury). I could put together a better package from his Mercury years—where's "You're Still on My Mind," which is quintessential Jones and also charted higher than some of these selections?—but for "Tender Years" and "The Window Up Above" in particular, this is not to be missed.

George Jones: *George Jones Sings Country & Western Hits* (Mercury/ Wing). Here's another I see in bargain bins fairly often, and if it offers few revelations, it's a real pleasure to just kick back and hear George interpret other people's hits—Harlan Howard's "Heartaches by the Numbers," Leon Payne's "I Love You Because," Lefty Frizzell's "If You've Got the Money (I've Got the Time)," Don Gibson's "Oh Lonesome Me," and more. As you can see, the accent is on Texas music, and George has it down cold.

George Jones: *Trouble In Mind* (Liberty). In the early-eighties Liberty stumbled across a treasure trove of old George Jones (from his United

Artists days) in its vaults and began reissuing albums. This one was itself originally a patchwork effort that threw together sides from several other early-sixties albums, but the title song is George at his best. Covers like "Worried Mind" and "I Heard You Crying in Your Sleep" compare favorably, as do originals like "Lonesome Old Town" and "You Done Me Wrong." And if you can just blot out that obnoxious girl chorus, "Sometimes You Just Can't Win" reveals itself as a definitive Jones ballad, a lost masterpiece that may stop you dead in your tracks.

George Jones: *I Get Lonely in a Hurry* (Liberty). Another reissue of 1962–66 Jones; what with "The Race Is On" and his reading of Buck Owens' "Love's Gonna Live Here," this has more of an up-tempo feel than many Jones albums, but those ballads are as cutting as ever, too.

George Jones and Melba Montgomery: *What's in Our Hearts* (Liberty). George and Melba pull out all the stops here; among these guilt-wracked, doubt-ridden duets are "Let's Invite Them Over," one of Nashville's first mate-swapping songs, and "We Must Have Been Out of Our Minds," which is so exquisite you know they couldn't have been.

George Jones: *George Jones Sings Bob Wills* (United Artists). As long as the parent company is putting out so much old Jones material on Liberty, they ought to consider this out-of-print masterpiece. Jones has said in interviews that he didn't even consider Bob Wills a *true* country artist, but you'd never know it from the way he sings these favorites. The choice of material could have been less predictable, but you'll forget that quibble as soon as you hear George squeal, "Mother Nature does *won*derful things" on "Time Changes Everything."

George Jones: *Country & Western Classics: George Jones* (Time-Life). If you were to own but one George Jones album, I guess this three-record boxed set would be the one. But if you want only one George Jones album, even one triple album, you're reading the wrong book. This is the usual superb career overview from Time-Life, including some previously unissued sides, and it's the one place where you can follow style evolving over the years. But there's simply too much overlap between this and the early-Jones and late-Jones albums I recommend at length. It does, however, restore to the catalog some of the best mid-period Jones I also wrote about extensively even though it was out of print.

Loretta Lynn: *Here's Loretta Lynn* (Coral). Here's most of Loretta's very first album, recorded for a small west Canadian label and purchased by Decca (MCA) after she conquered Nashville. The songs (all originals) are a characteristic mixture of innocence, experience, humor, and harshness; Loretta's vocals are already clear and resonant as a bell, there's just a harmony voice instead of chorus, and the band is punchy and to the point. Though ostensibly still in print, this is usually hard to find—but worth the search.

Maddox Brothers and Rose: *1946–51, Volume 1* (Arhoolie). Natives of Alabama but thirties immigrants to the Promised Land of central California, the Maddox family first formed a band with eleven-year-old Rose singing lead in 1937, worked off and on during the forties as military duties of the various brothers allowed, and finally hit it big when they moved to Hollywood in 1951. Rose was a raucous, roaring singer, the brothers (Cliff, Fred, Henry, Don, Cal) and supplementary sidemen were hot pickers, and the group turned out to be the West Coast's leading purveyors of hillbilly boogie. They were also a show band, which means they'd do whatever was necessary to get a laugh, including breaking out laughing in the middle of their own records. This is real hot stuff—especially the clattering instrumental "Water Baby Boogie."

Maddox Brothers and Rose: *1946–51, Volume 2* (Arhoolie). Don't let their propensity for foolishness fool you; this band had some pickers in it, and they rarely gave much slack. And Rose may have sounded like she just wandered down out of the hills, but she took lip from nobody and held her own among these strong-minded men. She also sang songs (like "Hangover Blues") that were not only considered most unladylike then, but would be regarded in the same light today. The group had no hits, by the way, and (not coincidentally) no relation with Nashville, though starting in 1959 with Capitol, Rose ran up a string of hits on her own.

Maddox Brothers and Rose: *Rockin' Rollin' Maddox Bros. and Rose* (German Bear Family). Not really, but this *is* a weird kind of up-tempo, post-boogie country and western with some of rock 'n' roll's energy and humor. In truth, the cuts that are furthest from rock 'n' roll are the most fun, and pure fun is what this group rises or falls on. As to how they *really* feel about rock, hear their desecration of "I Got a Woman," here called "The Death of Rock and Roll," and damn funny in spite of itself.

The Man Behind the Wheel (Starday/Gusto). "Gears," a lengthy recitation about one woebegone trucker that's set to a breezy backing track, is probably Johnny Bond's greatest moment as a trucking balladeer; as always, he shows good humor as well as real empathy for his subject. Red Sovine's own finest moment is here, too, a recitation called "Big Joe . . . and Phantom 309," one of those stories in which a driver picks up a hitchhiker that turns out to be a ghost who gave his life on the highway years back, but still haunts the site where it happened.

Joe Maphis: *Honky Tonk Cowboy* (CMH). Joe Maphis, Barbara Mandrell's uncle, is from Virginia, though in 1951 he and his wife, Rosie Lee, moved to Los Angeles, where they became stars on the "Town Hall Party" TV show. Joe's blinding-fast, double-necked guitar style made him much in demand as a sessions player, too, both for country stars and for rockabillies like the Collins Kids, Ricky Nelson, and Wanda Jackson. His best sides, cut in the fifties for Columbia, are West Coast honky-tonk at its most aggressive, but are not available in any form. Of his several CMH albums, this is the one that comes closest to matching the Columbia sides.

Memphis Country (Sun). One of those Shelby Singleton Sun reissues that was put together without any thought, and survives such carelessness anyhow. Onie Wheeler's country-boogie "Jump Right Out of This Jukebox" is a lost classic, Jack Clement's "Ten Years" is one of his pop-hits-that-missed, and other obscure cuts shed new light on David Houston, Conway Twitty, Roy Orbison, and Texas Bill Strength.

Memphis Rocks the Country (Dutch Redita). Honky-tonk music that wishes it was blues or rockabilly, anything but straight country. Still, Memphis cut a tougher brand of country than Nashville, and this has its share—especially the peculiar rhythm experiments of Lloyd Arnold and Danny Williams, the George Jones-influenced country-rock of Tommie Pierce, and the priceless "Wino of the Year" by one Jim Waldrop.

Moon Mullican: *Greatest Hits* (Starday/Gusto). The other side of Moon Mullican's honky-tonk bravado was a maudlin streak deep enough to bring an Opry audience to tears. He didn't think much of it himself, and thus exploited it rarely; when he did, he often sounded like his heart wasn't entirely in it. But it was effective enough to bring him his hits while the boogie failed to crack the charts, and when you hear him creaking through "I'll Sail My Ship Alone" and "Sweeter Than the Flowers" you'll know why.

Red Murrell: *Hard Country & Swingin' Western Music* (German Castle). Like the title suggests, few men better demonstrate the affinity between Texas swing, western, and honky-tonk than this obscure forties singer and guitarist. He stakes out the middle ground between Hank Williams and Ernest Tubb so diligently that he can even record Tubb's "Walking the Floor Over You" the way Williams might have.

Willie Nelson and Webb Pierce: *In the Jailhouse Now* (Columbia). Pierce's voice isn't quite the instrument in 1982 that it once was, and because he doesn't phrase exactly like he used to, he and Willie don't sound as similar to each other as they once might have. But that's okay, because the differences do dramatize their respective styles, and they still work well together. This is certainly the funkiest of Willie's duet albums, and arguably the best.

Jimmy Newman (German Castle). Newman, who hails from Louisiana, sounds like a Cajun version of Lefty Frizzell on these early-fifties sides, which are far superior to the better-known sixties hits that presented an unhappy cross between Cajun and Nashville.

James O'Gwynn: *Star of the Louisiana Hayride, Vol. 1* (German Cattle). East Texas honky-tonk with a hard edge, similar to that of early George Jones, which should come as no surprise because in the second half of the fifties, when these sides were cut, O'Gwynn was working for Pappy Daily, who originally discovered and recorded George.

Gene O'Quin: *The Late Gene O'Quin—A Hillbilly At Heart* (German Castle). In the fifties O'Quin divided his time between radio and television shows in Dallas and Los Angeles. He sang sprightly honky-tonk and hillbilly boogie with a what-the-hell sense of humor and muscular arrangements featuring the intricate steel guitar of Speedy West.

Vernon Oxford: *If I Had My Wife to Love Over* (Rounder). In the Nashville of the seventies and eighties, Oxford is, as he claims, an odd man out—an unabashed hillbilly singer who wouldn't dare go far enough uptown to turn his back on songs like the one this album is named after. But he's not a *complete* oddball, as he also claims, because others broke through during this time singing similarly old-fashioned material. And the constant comparisons to Hank Williams are laughable —Vernon doesn't have a fraction of Hank's range, or of Hank's gift for improvising new vocal fillips. Let's just say that Oxford is one of the most well-meaning hard country singers around today and not try to make him into anything more. This 1978 album is Oxford at his most uncompromising, and the material (including three songs by Hank Williams and four by a Benny Williams) his most durable.

Johnny Paycheck: *Extra Special* (Accord). In the sixties, when he was unabashedly aping George Jones, Paycheck was also writing some of the most twisted, sick-o songs honky-tonk ever saw. You can often find them on his Little Darlin' albums, which still turn up in bargain bins, and you can get a taste from this budget-line reissue's "Billy Jack Washburn" and "There's No Easy Way to Die." This is when he was *really* an outlaw, instead of a caricature. Meanwhile, it's also worth noting that he's always had a classic country voice, and it can suck you into his personal descent like it was quicksand.

Johnny Paycheck: *The Outlaw* (Little Darlin' Special Products). In the late seventies, when Paycheck's outlaw career was peaking, Little Darlin' pulled itself out of bankruptcy long enough to issue some cheapy albums like this. It's pretty random, but does include "I've Got Someone to Kill," in which Johnny, thinking of his wife cheating on him while he's at the bar, interrupts a conversation by saying, "Pardon me/I've got someone to kill," puts down his drink, goes home, and does just that to her and him both. Cool, Johnny. There's also "Ballad of Frisco Bay" (modern prison ballad with extra-macabre twist), "Down on the Corner at a Bar Called Kelly's" (fed-up husband lays down law to wife), "Bayou Bum" (self-explanatory), and "The Loser" (ditto) and "I'm a Coward" (ditto again) from various out-of-print albums. All with a sparse country band that likes the beat.

Johnny Paycheck: *Bars—Booze—Blondes* (Little Darlin' Special Products). I tell you, that Johnny Paycheck was some guy. Half these songs were outtakes and they *still* cut most of what was coming out during the sixties. Who else would talk up a "Fools Hall of Fame," lament "The Pint of No Return," or boast "I Drop More Than I Drink"? I could listen to him doing this stuff all day.

Johnny Paycheck: *Greatest Hits* (Little Darlin'). I don't care what anybody says, the mid-sixties honky-tonk Paycheck was far and away the greatest, and his artlessness was much of the reason. Hell, his greatest hits weren't necessarily even his greatest songs, though the faint of heart shouldn't mess with stuff from this album like "A-Eleven" or "Jukebox Charlie," let alone "Motel Time Again" or "And I'll Be Hating You." The capper is "You'll Recover in Time," in which our hero is sitting in a padded cell, held down by a straitjacket, and fantasizing that the woman who left him is about to face the same fate. Hot damn! Little Darlin' Special Products seems to be getting old Paycheck back in print randomly, but they should put this one out there intact.

Webb Pierce: *Without You* (Coral). Cunningly disguised as a regular old Webb Pierce album, this is actually a greatest hits package covering the years 1952–55, and that was Webb at his absolute peak—wailing on songs like "Backstreet Affair" and "Your Good for Nothing Heart." If you can find this, snap it up.

Webb Pierce: *It's All Between the Lines* (Picadilly). Before he hit a stone-country stride in Nashville, Pierce was aching for a hit any way he could get it—which in the early fifties meant a more boogie-oriented sound reaching out for mainstream country. These are the sides he cut for a small Southern California indie at that time.

Ray Price: *Ray Price's Greatest Hits, Vol. II* (Columbia Special Products). This collects the rest of honky-tonk Ray's best work from the early sixties, as he approached countrypolitan—which means that the ballads here outnumber the shuffles, but with hurtin' songs like "This Cold War With You," "Night Life," "Another Bridge to Burn," and especially "A Way to Survive," you can hardly accuse him of having already gone soft. In fact, *this*—and not the later stuff—is my idea of country that doesn't give the word "crooning" a bad name.

Ray Price: *San Antonio Rose* (Columbia Limited Edition). On this tribute album to Bob Wills, Price displays the natural affinity he always had for western swing, makes explicit the link between his own shuffle and the Wills beat, and, by concentrating on atypical Wills material—mostly hurtin' songs—removes some of the "escapist music" stigma from swing's image.

Ray Price: *Night Life* (Columbia Limited Edition). Taking a then-still-green Willie Nelson's title song as his theme, Price fashions his own private desolation row out of a collection of honky-tonk nighttime ballads. This bleary-eyed 1963 album is morose and filled with misgivings, but it's one of the most successful concept albums of its day, and the slow ones point to Price's future direction.

The Roots of Rock, Vol. 10: Sun Country (British Charly). If nothing else, the Clyde Leoppard Band's "Split Personality" shows Sam Phillips and Sun had a flair for the novelty song. So, to a lesser extent, do "Peepin' Eyes" (Charlie Feathers) and "Drunk!" (J. R. and J. W. Brown, who weren't recording artists at all, but drinking buddies of Jerry Lee Lewis, appropriately enough). And records like Howard Seratt's "Troublesome Waters" show just how far afield Sam was willing to go in search of a different sound.

Arthur "Guitar Boogie" Smith: *Mister Guitar* (Starday/Gusto). This does not catch him at his absolute peak, but Smith was one of the country artists who did the most to make boogie commercially viable, and he had a huge influence on rockabilly guitarists. His only real hit was a 1963 novelty song thankfully not included here, but his trademark "Guitar Boogie" and his reworkings of standards like "The Double Eagle" are more dynamic anyhow.

Super Hits Country—The 1940's (Gusto). This valuable collection puts the emphasis on hillbilly boogie. It has the hit makers (Cowboy Copas, the Delmore Brothers) in abundance, but it also includes such rarities as the York Brothers (one of the more underrated brother duets) with "River of Tears" and even a cut ("Why Don't You Haul Off and Love Me") from the nonpareil country harmonica player Wayne Raney, whose own King album has been left out of print for too long.

Super Hits Country—The 1950's (Gusto). This label makes its money by rerecording old hits on once-popular singers who've faded, or on repackaging old material purchased from Starday, King, and Nashville. As a rule, the older the Gusto album, the better it will be. This one, which is made up of honky-tonk music recorded during the rise of the Nashville Sound, is a case in point. Jimmy Dickens' celebratory "Hillbilly Fever" appears on a Columbia rockabilly anthology, and George Jones' "Why Baby Why" appears on several other albums. But this is the only place you'll find Jack Cardwell's great "The Death of Hank Williams," which is journalistic in its detail and truly mournful (as opposed to maudlin, like most of the Williams tributes) in its tone.

That's Truckdrivin' (Starday/Gusto). Johnny Bond gets the best action here, with one mock-frightening story-song in "Highway Man" and some further mythologizing in "Johnny Overload," "Old Mack," and "Ridge Route."

Thunder on the Road (Starday/Gusto). The Willis Brothers and Red Sovine are not the most gripping singers around—for that matter, neither is Minnie Pearl, who has one cut here—but Johnny Bond is back for four more songs, and taken as a whole, the songs on this collection make a pretty good case for the trucker as outlaw.

Merle Travis: *Guitar Album* (Capitol). Travis plays a little of everything here—blues, pop, Tin Pan Alley standards, mountain music, honky-tonk, swing, and jazz. But he brings it all together so seamlessly that it becomes more than just a showcase for him; it is instead a compendium of country styles and influences.

Merle Travis: *The Guitar Player* (Shasta). Because these fifties radio transcriptions were originally done for Jimmy Wakely's radio show, the flavor here is more western than honky-tonk, though Travis does cut loose on a couple of numbers.

Truck Drivin' Man (Starday/Gusto). Mostly honking truckers ballads, with Joe and Rose Lee Maphis kicking things along on "Ridin' Down Ole 99" and Betty Amos raising some hopes with "18 Wheels A-Rollin'."

Truck Drivin' Son of a Gun (Starday/Gusto). Red Sovine cut his fair share of truckers' ballads, and most of them were quite forgettable. One real exception is this album's "Ten Days Out, Two Days In," which catches some of the reality behind the romantic image, but doesn't spare us the romance, either. Slim Jacobs gets right philosophical on "That's Truck Drivin'," and Johnny Bond kicks up some dust on "Thunder on the Road."

Ernest Tubb: *Ernest Tubb Sings Jimmie Rodgers* (Golden Country). Here's the earliest Ernest Tubb, when he was entirely under the sway of his idol. His voice is richer than after his 1939 tonsil operation, just as he's always claimed, but try as he may, Ernest couldn't ape Rodgers perfectly, and the nascent Tubb style is already poking through on this wondrous album.

Ernest Tubb: *Honky-Tonk Classics* (Rounder Special Series). After winning a lawsuit from MCA for releasing old George Thorogood demos, Rounder chose to take its award not in cash, but by getting rights to release old Decca material. MCA did its best to stop them from getting their hands on anything exceedingly desirable, which is why this album consists largely of ET obscurities rather than hits (even though MCA hasn't released ET hits in their original form for years). But these sides, taken from the years 1940–54, represent a gold mine anyhow; four have never appeared on LP before, and four more have never been on American LP. Among the highlights are "Blue-Eyed Elaine," Tubb's first Decca release, "I Ain't Goin' Honky Tonkin' Anymore," Tubb's first side to utilize electric guitarist Fay "Smitty" Smith (1941), the answer song to "Walking the Floor Over You," and "That Wild and Wicked Look in Your Eye."

Ernest Tubb: *The Country Hall of Fame* (British MCA/Coral). These are the originals, folks, including "Walking the Floor Over You" and "Mean Mama Blues" from the turning-point 1941 sessions. It's harder to find every day, though, and what's really needed is a systematic Tubb reissue series.

Ernest Tubb: *Ernest Tubb and His Texas Troubadors* (Vocalion). All right! Ostensibly, all of ET's Vocalion and Coral albums are in print, even though they're nearly impossible to find. If you ever do spot one, though, snap it right up, because it'll be the real thing, original versions of Tubb classics. I see this one more than any of the others, so I assume it's the most common. It contains a wonderfully drunken version of "There's a Little Bit of Everything in Texas," a shouting "Kansas City Blues," the undeniable "Drivin' Nails in My Coffin," and seven others from Tubb's absolute peak from the mid-forties to the mid-fifties. Good as the rerecordings are, they sound tame next to brazen, reckless sides like these.

Ernest Tubb: *Stand By Me* (Coral). This is a gospel album in the old Tubb style; you might find the idea of an Ernest Tubb gospel album a little comical, but anyone who sings like him *has* to mean what he's saying. If anything, his ability to parlay such a lack of "good" voice into an enduring career is enough to make you think that faith will indeed conquer all obstacles.

Ernest Tubb: *Greatest Hits, Vol. II* (MCA). Continuing in the grand Decca/MCA tradition of screwing up Tubb's recorded legacy, though this isn't as flagrant a violator as others. These are half originals and half remakes, and they run concurrent with songs on *Vol. 1* because the label didn't have enough sense to make the two volumes chronological. This is an older, more reflective Tubb, singing foreboding songs like "Warm Red Wine" and "Thoughts of a Fool." And don't forget "Pass the Booze": "Please put the bottle on the bar so I can pet it/And take my address down before I forget it."

Ernest Tubb: *Great Country* (Coral). Short on hits, long on soul.

Ernest Tubb With the Texas Troubadors: *I've Got All the Heartaches I Can Handle* (MCA). Is this 1973 album, his last for his original label, Ernest's Vietnam commentary? Well, it does include "MIA" and "The Last Letter." On the other hand, he's just as emotional about "Texas Troubador," a tribute to him written by Porter Wagoner, and "The Lord Knows I'm Drinking."

Ernest Tubb: *The Living Legend* (1st Generation). One side of this album is remakes of old Ernest Tubb hits, which is to say that it's remakes of remakes. The other side is new songs written strictly in the Tubb style by various seventies writers. For what it is, the first side is surprisingly comforting; the second is even better.

Ernest Tubb: *The Legend and the Legacy, Vol. 1* (1st Generation). The "tribute duets" album became a Nashville vogue in the late seventies. This one is the most uncompromisingly country of the batch, as no pop stars or fancy pickers were called in to help crossover sales (unless you count Charlie Daniels). Instead, it's just an autumnal Ernest in overdubbed duets with Willie Nelson, George Jones, Loretta Lynn, Johnny Cash, Merle Haggard, John Paycheck, and more. Welcome surprise: Conway Twitty gettin' down for real on "Jimmie Rodgers' Last Blue Yodel (The Women Make a Fool Out of Me)."

Charlie Walker: *Greatest Hits, Vol. 1* (Plantation). One of the most authoritative honky-tonk singers from the late fifties to the late sixties, Walker is also one of the very few who sounded good as ever when he rerecorded his original hits a few years later in an attempt to revive a sagging career. That's what this album is, and though I'd rather have the originals, I'm more willing to settle for this than is the case with most artists. The typical Shelby Singleton short change, though, with only eight tunes included.

Speedy West: *Speedy* (Steel Guitar Record Club). Speedy West was one of the most pyrotechnic steel guitar players, and in country/jazz guitarist Jimmy Bryant he met his match. This collection of Speedy's Capitol hits from the fifties shows them working through a tantalizing variety of music, all of it charging, swinging instrumentals that turned many heads when they were first released. Cuts like "Water Baby Blues" sound as complex—and as natural—to this very day.

Speedy West: *Steel Guitar* (Steel Guitar Record Club). This is a reissue of a mid-fifties Capitol album that was in itself basically a batch of singles. Bryant and West weave in and out of each other, or double each other, with spellbinding ease and intensity. "Speedin' West," which was used as the theme song of numerous California DJs, just won't quit, and "This Ain't the Blues" sure ain't. It's not exactly country, either, but a futuristic hybrid of the two.

Hank Williams: *I Saw the Light* (Polydor). In 1983, Polydor (which had bought up MGM several years earlier) began reissuing Hank Williams albums as they'd first appeared on the original label—which means sometimes with limited overdubbing, sometimes with none. Given his label's track record, the restoration of Williams to the catalog seems almost like a corporate oversight. That they should appear on a budget line is all the more encouraging, though. This is the only one of his gospel albums rereleased, but it was also by far the best of the several available earlier. It contains most of his best-known gospel (the title song, "When God Comes and Gathers His Jewels," "Wealth Won't Save Your Soul," etc.), as well as the more obscure, and more devastating, "Angel of Death."

Hank Williams: *Honky-Tonkin'* (Polydor). This one has a great faded cover, and intelligently shades over from out-and-out novelties to black humor to anger. Was that programming intentional?

Hank Williams: *Sing Me a Blue Song* (Polydor). Another of those compilations lacking a single novelty or upbeat song. They can really tear you apart when they come one right after another with no relief, but that was the whole idea, wasn't it? This one compensates with a couple of obscurities like "Blue Love (in My Heart)" and one of his rare stabs at western, "Singing Waterfall."

Hank Williams: *Moanin' the Blues* (Polydor). This one also offers minimum relief but maximum quality. Taken as a whole, the four 1983 reissues might be on a par with the two double albums of hits—these are certainly less tinkered-with—but the *real* Hank Williams retrospective has yet to surface in America outside the Time-Life box.

Hank Williams: *Hank Williams as Luke the Drifter* (MGM). Over the years, MGM released dozens of albums by Hank Williams, some of which still turn up in bargain bins, specialty stores, flea markets, and the like. Though they are now all out of print, the paucity of Williams material available and the man's stature make it worthwhile to pick out the cream of the crop anyhow. The Luke the Drifter recitations, which also appear scattered individually among various other albums, are an acquired taste, but they were meant to be that way when they were recorded. They deliver pithy moral statements that made them closer to the gospel music than to commercial C & W even if they have none of the actual sound of gospel music. They are also an obvious attempt by Hank to justify some of his own excesses.

Hank Williams: *First, Last and Always* (MGM). An offhand compilation of some of his more obscure tunes—but "With Tears in My Eyes," "The First Fall of Snow," and "There's No Room in My Heart (for the Blues)," are all worth hearing.

Hank Williams: *Hank Williams Sings Kaw-Liga and Other Humorous Songs* (MGM). I keep thinking that this should be better, but "Everything's Okay" is a fine mockery of country stoicism, and "Fly Trouble" must sound *awfully* ridiculous coming out of a barroom jukebox at about 3 A.M.

Hank Williams: *The Lonesome Sound Of Hank Williams* (MGM). Not the best album of bluesy Hank—in fact, the title is misleading, because this has its share of novelty, nostalgia, and western—but do hear "Sundown and Sorrow."

Hank Williams: *The Unforgettable Hank Williams* (MGM). From the opening "I Can't Get You Off My Mind" to the closing "Leave Me Alone with the Blues," with stops in between for the likes of "I Don't Care (if Tomorrow Never Comes)" and "Never Again (Will I Knock on Your Door)," this is the most bitter Williams album MGM ever compiled.

Hank Williams: *Hank Williams Lives Again* (MGM). One of the most durable single-album collections of hits; all that is missing is "I'm So Lonesome I Could Cry."

Hank Williams: *I'm Blue Inside* (MGM). Would that the label had the brains to have released *all* the Williams albums according to simple little concepts like this. It gathers blues with songs that at least have the word "blues" in the title, throws in a few more tearjerkers, and doesn't take the pressure off for a minute.

Hank Williams: *Lost Highway and Other Folk Ballads* (MGM). This attempts to do the same with the more traditional-sounding material, and isn't quite as big a success because whoever programmed it had seriously flawed notions about "folk" music. But it does get "Lost Highway" and "Ramblin' Man" both on the same album, which is where they belong.

Hank Williams: *The Collectors Hank Williams, Vols. 1–3* (British MGM). I'm lumping these three together because that's the way they should be heard. They're easier to find than the Japanese boxed set, but even the usually reliable specialty shops and mail-order houses don't always have them in stock, so they may be harder to acquire than most imports. They should thus be considered "last resorts" for the frustrated consumer, but they are still done the way Hank Williams reissues should be done. All the cuts appear as they first surfaced stateside—which means that some are demos (just voice and acoustic guitar), some are with string band, and some have the overdubbed rhythm instruments. But at least there's no overdubbed string sections and the like. They also cover a lot of ground, taking in most of the big songs without ignoring some of the more interesting esoterica. Would it be asking too much of American Polydor to put the series out over here?

Tex Williams: *Tex Williams* (German Castle). Williams was one of the stalwarts of the postwar California scene; he sang with honky-tonk and swing bands and had a mock-gruff voice that added extra humor to the novelty songs he favored all along. These fifties sides, like the records of Merle Travis, are essentially honky-tonk that swings.

Faron Young: *The All-Time Great Hits of Faron Young* (Capitol). Too bad these 1952–63 sides have gone out of print, because the early Faron Young captures the Hank Williams sound-alike sweepstakes hands down. He also had an ear for writers—Willie Nelson ("Hello Walls") and Don Gibson ("Sweet Dreams") were just two that he discovered.

ROCKABILLY

Rockabilly—white, southern rock 'n' roll—threw down the gauntlet, splitting country music down the middle and revealing a generation gap nobody had previously suspected. Until rockabilly, country music had always been for the whole family; everyone from the kids to the grandparents went out to see Ernest Tubb or Hank Snow, and presumably those men spoke to the values of everyone in the audience. But when rockabilly struck (when, for that matter, all rock 'n' roll struck) the old music suddenly looked and sounded pretty irrelevant, if you were young and feeling fenced in.

Rockabilly was invented in 1954, when Sun Records head Sam Phillips cut Elvis Presley singing "That's All Right" and "Blue Moon of Kentucky," backed only by Scotty Moore on guitar and Bill Black on stand-up bass. Once Elvis broke through, it seemed like every white boy below the Mason-Dixon Line was ready to rock along right behind him.

Elvis was the answer to Sam Phillips' famous hunch: "If I could find a white man who had the Negro feel, I could make a billion dollars." Elvis had been by the Sun studios to make custom recordings as a birthday present to his mom, and his voice had impressed Marion Keisker, the Phillips aide who ran the custom service. Sam was less impressed, but later agreed to try the kid out on a demo he was interested in having someone record. The kid couldn't hack it. Sam tried him out on some other things, which also didn't go well. So Sam tried him on anything, and the kid cut loose.

What busted out *then* was a possessed, feverish synthesis of all the southern musics that had come before it—gospel, country, R & B, pop, deep blues. Sam liked it, because it was different from anything else, much more ferocious than the countrified R & B that Pennsylvania singer Bill Haley had been causing such a stir with up north. That was simply a white western swing/boogie interpretation of black R & B, and though it had the big beat the kids went for, it didn't have the liberating energy, spirit, and invention that Elvis had, not really.

Actually, something similar to what Elvis was doing *had* been around for some time, it seems, in the honky-tonks of the South, but nobody had put it on tape. Several had come close, including Sam Phillips himself, with the up-tempo hillbilly boogie records he'd been cutting. But that stuff, exciting as it could be, was still safe; it fit into a pre-existing framework, could be played on the country radio stations. With rockabilly, nobody was sure at first *what* would happen—until local DJ Dewey Phillips (no relation to Sam) played the new Elvis single and Memphis listeners demanded that he keep playing it all night.

The rockabilly sound was the creation of Phillips and Elvis and the musicians they used. It always seemed to be the exclusive domain of Sun Records, because though many tried, nobody caught the sound like Sun did—not even the original Sun artists, once they moved to different labels, let alone the legions of country poseurs trying to play catch-up by cutting up-tempo honky-tonk or boogie and calling it rockabilly to cash it on a fad they prayed would soon pass.

It was remarkably simple music, for all the excitement it generated. In later years, instruments would be added, but primal rockabilly was made with only bass and guitars. The accent is on the second and fourth beats, and until drums were added, the rhythm came from just an acoustic guitar and a booming, stand-up bass slapped with the hand or a drumstick. Rhythms and song structures were blues-based, if not strictly blues, and vocalists swaggered through the songs using a variety of exaggerated hiccups, stutters, and slurs. A piercing guitar—blues with a twang, sort of—cut through everything. Put on a lot of echo and you have a sound that's the musical equivalent of a switchblade snapping open. "Rockabilly has to sound thin," Charlie Feathers once told writer Michael Bane. "You know, like it was getting ready to jump off the record."

But sound alone doesn't convey enough, because in rockabilly, attitude was everything. The music seemed to embrace all the contradictions and dark secrets of the white South, seemed to burst right out of the pages of W. J. Smith's *The Mind of the South*. This was music sung with a sneer and a swivel of the hips; it was unabashedly sexual, like the exotic, verboten blues, and thus it suggested miscegenation. Young whites just weren't *supposed* to go around singing the praises of bow-legged women, blue suede shoes, shakin' in the barn, and things like that.

Rockabilly was a celebration of and a way out of the insidious social system that had risen in the South since Reconstruction to contain the so-called white trash. There was a menacing air of violence about it, and of impulsiveness. These boys—or were they men, is that part of what they were trying to say?—went places Hank Williams and his generation didn't dare speak of. Rockabilly was the young white Southerner's every Saturday-night blowout wrapped up in about two minutes of explosive music, and even if life was restored to normal on Sunday and the old limits applied once again, rockabilly still signaled a whole new ball game in country music.

The Sun Box (British Sun).

With pitifully few exceptions, the memorable rockabilly records were made for Sun Records of Memphis. Yet Sun was a blues label before it was a rockabilly label, and this three-record boxed set offers a rare chance to look once again into the relationship between blues and country, this time as they had evolved by the fifties.

Sam Phillips, born in 1935 in Florence, Alabama, was the founder and guiding force behind Sun. A white man who loved black music, Phillips went into business first in 1950 as a custom recording service; mostly he recorded social functions like bar mitzvahs, but on the side he recorded such bluesmen as Howlin' Wolf and Joe Hill Louis, leasing the results to R & B labels like Chess in Chicago or Modern in L.A. In 1952 he founded Sun, his first real successes coming with city bluesmen like Junior Parker and Rufus Thomas (though Phillips' personal tastes ran more toward country blues). Slowly, Sun got into country music, which even then sounded different in Memphis than it did in Nashville, and finally in 1954, with the release of Elvis Presley's first record, Sun was in the rockabilly business. Thanks to artists like Johnny Cash, Jerry Lee Lewis, Carl Perkins, Roy Orbison, Billie Lee Riley, Warren Smith, Charlie Rich, and others, rockabilly became the label's legacy.

Phillips became at least as big a legend as his artists, though his exact role isn't always easy to pinpoint. Certainly most of his artists were strong-minded men who brought singular styles to his studio with them, but he was the one who recognized this in each of them, and he often had much to do with the finished results, prodding artists in directions they didn't necessarily want to go or refining their sound for them. Thus Junior Parker and His Blues Flames enjoyed great success recording in blues styles they felt archaic; Jerry Lee Lewis and Johnny Cash came to Sun playing country and were told to learn rock 'n' roll; Carl Perkins came playing rock 'n' roll and was told to play country.

There are certain consistencies in sound on these records from the earliest blues to the latest rockabilly. Phillips turned amps up on his blues guitarists almost to the point of distortion. That was what gave such awesome presence to songs like Jackie Brenston's "Rocket 88" (1951), Howlin' Wolf's "Howlin' for My Baby" (1951), Joe Hill Louis' "Treat Me Mean and Evil" (1952), or James Cotton's "Cotton Crop Blues" (1954), with Pat Hare's crushing solo. Many of these bluesmen played ringing, single-string solos that directly inspired Carl Perkins and lesser rockabilly guitarists. Likewise, it was the undeniable groove of these records that Presley went for and got on his up-tempo hits, that Perkins went for and got on "Dixie Fried." The jive of Joe Hill Louis' "Tiger Man" or Rufus Thomas' "Bear Cat" provided rockabilly with some of its vocabulary, as did Doctor Ross extolling the virtues of "The Boogie Disease." Junior Parker may have provided Presley with a crucial song in "Mystery Train," but Junior's lilting voice on "Feelin' Good" also offered Presley part of his vocal style (as did Johnny Braggs' effervescent lead tenor on the Prisonaires' "Just Walkin' in the Rain").

The ratty twenty by thirty-foot Sun studios offered another link between the two musics, mainly through the heavy use of echo and the loose atmosphere Phillips provided. But these are all rather tenuous connections, and it's hard to get any more specific. Because the best rockabillys didn't "take black music and make it their own," they didn't "usurp black music," they didn't "add their own sound to the black sound," as white bluesmen did in other eras. Rockabilly instead sought to capture blues intangibles—sense of self, purpose, feeling—and for the most part ignored blues structures. Aside from the shouting, declamatory vocal style, rockabilly was purely white music that lifted little *directly* from black blues.

In fact, though it's easy to hear the pieces falling into place here, it's harder to explain exactly how Sun got from blues to country to rockabilly. Consider the evidence on side three, labeled "Memphis Country." It starts with the minstrelsy of Harmonica Frank, sort of a white Doctor Ross, a one-man band playing black-derived Memphis country, which had more of a beat than Nashville country, owing to its stronger western swing influence and also to Memphis' heritage as a wide-open river town uninhibited by the Bible Belt morals that prevailed in Nashville. The most prominent such cut is "My Kind of Carryin' On," by Doug Poindexter and the Starlite Wranglers, a tough piece of country boogie with one of those amped-up guitar solos. It's good, but it's hardly extraordinary, and the fact that just two months later this band's guitarist (Scotty Moore) and bassist (Bill Black) left to join Elvis Presley in inventing rockabilly doesn't compute. There's barely a hint that the music will leap from one to the other, and though this is the music Phillips had been working toward for years—white people with the black feel, something that might catch the ears of both races—it must be that this is where vision, inspiration, experimentation, and hard work all entered into the picture together. That took Elvis *and* Sam, but when they found what they were looking for, they knew it.

So did everybody else. Dozens of bop-crazed white boys came to Phillips in addition to the big six (Elvis, Perkins, Cash, Lewis, Orbison, Rich). Some, like Charlie Feathers (with the country "Defrost Your Heart") and Sonny Burgess (with the rockabilly "Ain't Got a Thing" were a little too unpredictable even for Phillips to mold and market. Some (like Billie Lee Riley with "Flyin' Saucers Rock 'n' Roll" and "Red Hot") seemed to have everything and still didn't last. There were men like Ray Harris ("Come On Little Mama") who got by on sheer spirit, and men like Jack Earls ("Slow Down"), Malcolm Yelvington ("It's Me Baby"), or Hayden Thompson ("Love Me Baby") who nearly made it simply by sounding as similar to Elvis as they could. As this essential set shows, they were all in some way the children of Sam Phillips, but they were also the bastard offspring of Howlin' Wolf and Ike Turner.

Elvis Presley: *The Sun Sessions* (RCA).

They said that on his first records Elvis "sounded black." But since even a perfunctory listening is enough to confirm that this is a white boy singing, I think they meant something more like he "sounded alien," the implication being also that he thus "sounded threatening." Elvis sounded like anything *but* a white country singer. Country music is slow to accept and absorb anything new, and certainly the Sun rockers—which are the songs people mean when they refer to Presley's early days—are unlike anything that preceded them in *any* music. You could not call what Elvis did the "progressive country" of its day, as you later could the music of Willie and Waylon. You couldn't call it "moderniza-tion," the way Ernest Tubb or Hank Snow modernized Jimmie Rodgers. Born in 1935 in Tupelo, Mississippi, Elvis Presley was a complete origi-nal at age nineteen.

Before Elvis, country artists appropriated blues forms in the most limited sense. They made blues over in their own images, but they rarely sang improvisationally like a bluesman; neither did they slur, moan, whoop, mutter, gasp, hiccup. To present all that in one persona, let alone in one song, was too complicated for a music that meant to express emotions as being cut and dried. But Elvis did it anyhow; he wanted it all, and to him that meant he had to give his all. Which meant that he had to embrace (or embody) country conventions along with his bopcat moves, and that's the kind of tension that fuels the Sun sides, even the schmaltz.

So Elvis is both the rebel and the loving youth devoted to home and family. He is an anarchist and he upholds the status quo. He seeks release and he seeks security. He is pious and he is profane. As a shy, poor white Southerner, he has scores to settle with those who have done him wrong, but he also wants to be accepted as one of them.

The sound—Elvis' oozing, crystalline tenor, Scotty Moore's twanging boogie guitar, Bill Black's thumping slap-back bass, producer Sam Phillips' use of reverb and echo to give it all muscle—is as timeless, as out of nowhere, today as it was then. His transformation of Arthur "Big Boy" Crudup's "That's All Right," the first song of El's career and of this album, has a rhythm that jumps and rolls, Scotty playing high notes above the voice before breaking into machine-gun riffs for his solo, Elvis sneering good-bye to his girl before breaking into scat. It's so compressed, it jumps out at you so quickly (just as Charlie Feathers said), that the thrill is unmatched by anything else in popular music; the performance is full of innocence, discovery, spontaneity, even though these four men worked a long time to get it.

But if that performance is cataclysmic, the expansive version of Bill Monroe's "Blue Moon of Kentucky" on the flip side confirms Elvis' notion of his place in the white country mainstream he has just rendered obsolete. At its most extreme, this affirmation turns into the acquiescence of something like "I Love You Because," complete with hokey clippity-clops, an embarrassing attempt at old-line crooning. *This* is the Elvis who first came to Sun to cut sentimental ballads as a gift to his mother.

But that side of Elvis, as obvious as it later became, was initially ignored, and why not? It was no departure from Dean Martin *or* Slim Whitman, while the up-tempo, blues-based songs he was cutting offer new revelations every time out. Each seemed to be built on the one before it, so that "Good Rockin' Tonight" confirmed the power of "That's All Right," and "Milkcow Blues Boogie" expanded on them both.

"Good Rockin' Tonight" takes on all comers—Elvis is confident, poised, but not really posturing. He's ready for anything, but mostly he's ready for good rocking tonight. There's a hint of danger in the invitation, but that's part of the fun, and he welcomes it. The band is rumbling, Scotty bearing down to play call-and-response choruses with himself. "Milkcow" feels at first like a setup; when Elvis halts the opening slow vamp to start the song over, we feel we're hearing for the first time ever the calculation that went into the music, because he *can't* just talk like that off the top of his head. (Can he?) But he makes you forget it instantly when he begins singing, first feeling hurt and a little insane, then getting philosophical and resigned, winding up just plain pissed off.

Then there's the final two singles Sun released, "Baby Let's Play

House" and "Mystery Train," where Elvis is more than just sure of himself—he's *so* in control it seems like he could handle anything. "House" is brasher and faster than anything he's ever done; the hiccuping intro is a device that will be slavishly copied by every ducktailed singer to step before a microphone. But most important, Elvis teases himself a little while he's laying down the law to this girl; there's a bigheartedness not so apparent on his other rockers. Finally, on the whitehot, all-stops-out "Mystery Train," he challenges the funeral train that's carrying away his girl and he whips it; what is supposedly a song of loss and defeat becomes instead his ultimate triumph.

Each of these songs gives us a man testing himself and his world, seeing how far he can go, which automatically sets him off from previous generations of country singers who weren't concerned with how far they could go, but only with how they could fit in; who didn't want to conquer, but only wanted to succeed. Perhaps Elvis is not sure where all this is leading, but he's certain that it's got to be better than what he's leaving behind. The Sun B-sides and songs left in the can until RCA released them while Elvis was in the Army are less galvanizing, but often just as telling. His leap into falsetto on "Blue Moon," which he learned in the Pentecostal Church as surely as he did the shouting techniques, the matter-of-fact cool behind "You're a Heartbreaker," the way his voice on "I Don't Care if the Sun Don't Shine" veers from suggestiveness to cuteness—all of these round out the picture of Elvis as we will later know him. The clues were there all along, but everyone was rocking too hard to look closely.

Elvis Presley: *Worldwide 50 Gold Award Hits, Volume 1* (RCA).

As soon as Elvis defined and then conquered rockabilly, he moved to escape it. After all, the best rockabilly records (his) on the best rockabilly label (Sun) were barely heard outside the South at that time, and Elvis was trying to get to everybody. And if that meant taking some of the sting out of rockabilly, replacing it with something that was more accommodating to more people, well, Elvis would be happy to do that; it's the direction he'd been headed all along. In the process, Elvis became the Dave Kingman of American music: He hit maybe .200 to .250 and struck out more often than he did anything else, but when he connected, it was all over. This four-record boxed set begins with "Heartbreak Hotel," his first RCA release, in January 1956, and closes with his version of Eddie Rabbitt's "Kentucky Rain," from January 1970, when Elvis was still undergoing rejuvenation thanks to his comeback TV special and initial Vegas triumph. It has more home runs than it does strikeouts, though some of the whiffs are as memorable as the homers.

"Heartbreak Hotel" was an attempt to beef up the Sun sound without otherwise tampering. Chet Atkins was added on second guitar and Floyd Cramer on piano, but the rest of the band was Elvis' own—D. J. Fontana is now fully integrated into the sound as drummer, Bill Black's walking bass issues its lugubrious warning, and Scotty Moore plays both elegant fills and some solos that hurt. There are enough durable riffs to constitute a whole second set of hooks on top of those Elvis sings, and the echo might as well have been added by Sam Phillips himself. It was a success, Elvis' first national hit.

Thus Elvis now belonged to everybody, not just to young white Southerners struggling to reconcile their ideas of upward mobility with the social realities of the era. His television appearances—and every one should be considered a success, no matter how severely he was mocked and ridiculed—made this even more true. Elvis' rockabilly, which had previously been a sort of controlled chaos, now emphasized control above all else, for that was the most essential ingredient in pop music.

He still made some outstanding rockers, though none seemed to have as much at stake as the Sun rockers. "Jailhouse Rock" (1957) is the very best, for the swagger and the *appearance* of abandon are there all the way through, and Elvis also stays at the very edge of his voice for the entire song; it's always on the edge of fraying, but never does, and the effect is thrilling. Numerous others are nearly as strong. The trashy, tacky instrumental backing on "Hound Dog" is inseparable from his own vocal, one of the rare occasions when the band drives Elvis rather than vice versa. "Too Much" has a swinging groove he fits himself into easily. The confidence and abruptness of "Teddy Bear," the Little Richard goofs on "Hard Headed Woman," the raucousness of "Wear My Ring Around Your Neck" are all testimony to a man who knows exactly what he wants—he wants to rock—and how to do it.

Supposedly, Elvis lost this when he went into the Army, but the evidence indicates that he repeated it as often as he wanted upon his return in 1960. "I Feel So Bad" (1961), one of the best blues he ever recorded, strips him bare, with the band's weird offbeat and the piano framing his own, puzzled, forlorn vocals. "Little Sister" (1961) retains as much of the original Sun feel as anything he did on RCA, and though the rockers were blunter and sillier after that, "Return to Sender" (1962) offers a pleasing gait and a rare sax solo, while "(You're the) Devil in Disguise" (1963) shows he could still get it up for a while. The five-year tailspin that followed, built around terrible movies and their soundtracks, didn't affect just his ability to rock, after all, for the ballads from this era are every bit as bad.

But no more plentiful than they were in the pre-Army days. It's another piece of misinformation to suggest that all he cared about in the post-Army years was drecky ballads, so that's all he did with any feeling. The drecky ballads had been there all along, and were never an accident or the result of a lapse in taste or of an attack of apathy and *ennui*. They were a crucial part of his (and Colonel Parker's) marketing strategy and desire not to just enter the mainstream, but to *be* the mainstream. I'd argue that he cared most about the dreck—that he perfected it—*before* he went into the Army—probably with "That's When Your Heartaches Begin" (1957), which is the first time he sounds to me like he's projecting his own ballad style rather than simply digging in somewhere between Johnny Braggs (of the Prisonaires), Slim Whitman, and Dean Martin.

What was most important about the comeback, which was built around exquisite ballads, was that it allowed Elvis for the first time ever to act like an adult. "If I Can Dream" was written specifically for the 1968 TV special, the purpose of which was to show that Elvis hadn't lost interest, that he was as full of passion as ever; and in this way, he *was* the same. But because he was now singing a song that spoke, however marginally, to social issues, he was clearly *not* the same as ever, too. Coming on the heels of all those insipid, juvenile soundtracks, "In the Ghetto," "Suspicious Minds," "Don't Cry Daddy," and "Kentucky Rain" were modern, not just in their arrangements and instrumentation, but because they presented him as a mature adult man in mature adult situations. No wonder he could put more heart and soul into them —even if he soon tired of that stance as quickly as he tired of everything else. It's also significant that the last song in this collection was written by Rabbitt, then a struggling young songwriter, now a country superstar crossing over regularly to pop. The bathos of these songs—even the ones that mean to be pop songs—is more country than pop.

By now reams have been written about Elvis, and when I try to sort out my own thoughts, I'm not sure I have anything truly original to add. I certainly disagree with those who claim he remained a vital artist his whole career, and write his shortcomings off to bad material or just a bad day (week) (month) (year). Their logic often approaches that of Professor Irwin Corey, and while it's always fascinating to watch them squirm as they try to prove their thesis, they remind me of the Mets announcer who raves about how Kingman shows a "major league swing" as he fans on three pitches for the fourth straight time in the game. But I can't agree either with those who claim Elvis lost it, or threw it away, when he left Sun, or when he went into the Army, or whatever. Nothing here has the immediate impact of the Sun sides, but the best of it has as much staying power. It's easiest to think of these songs as old friends I'm always comfortable with, shortcomings and all, and if I like to be challenged by my friends sometimes, there are more times when I'm just plain glad to have them around. In the end, I agree most with Nick Tosches, who once wrote, "I think Elvis Presley will never be solved."

Johnny Cash: *Superbilly* (Sun).

Of all the major Sun artists, Johnny Cash was probably the most country, the least rockabilly. Yet he fit right into Sam Phillips' stable of mavericks, a singer who sounded like nobody else, as this collection of greatest hits attests.

Cash was born in 1932 on a farm near Kingsland, Arkansas. When he was three, the family bought twenty acres worth of New Deal land near Dyess, Arkansas (a region so remote it didn't get electricity until 1946), and farmed cotton. As a family, they all listened to and sang gospel music and the songs of the Carter Family. By the time Cash entered high school, he was singing songs he'd written himself; upon graduation, he joined the Air Force and spent four years in Germany, where he taught himself guitar and fronted a combo that played American military bases.

When he was discharged in 1954, he went to Memphis for radio announcers school, paying for classes with a variety of odd jobs. There he met guitarist Luther Perkins and bassist Marshall Grant. The trio began rehearsing together with the vague notion of someday recording; mostly, they played gospel songs, Hank Snow hits, and Cash originals.

In June 1955 they got an audition with Phillips and played him Cash's "Hey, Porter," a stirring anthem to Dixie. Phillips was impressed, but wanted more pop-oriented material. That night Cash wrote him "Cry, Cry, Cry," one of the most bitter songs he's ever written.

Both those sides are on this exemplary package of twenty sides. Cash had his influences—Hank Williams, Ernest Tubb, Hank Snow, Tex Ritter, Jimmy Skinner—but his own inimitable sound was there from the beginning. He took the walking bass from honky-tonk and swing bands (Memphis was the western swing capital of the Southeast) but got rid of the fiddles and steel and instead boosted the electric guitar. Perkins played simple ascending triplets that led right up to Cash's quavering baritone then descended again; he used the palm of his hand to deaden his guitar strings, while Cash put a piece of paper between the strings and fret board of his acoustic guitar to accent Luther's percussive licks. The sound was both ominous and primitive, as rough as a sharecropper's hands, and it focused all attention on Cash's voice, which was so earthy and faraway it seemed to spring like an apparition out of the southern soil itself.

The sound was orchestrated early on. Jimmy Van Eaton was soon added on drums (Fluke Holland played them in the road band, though). Later Sun sides often had a piano and background singers. When he took over as Cash's producer, Jack Clement put flutter echo on both the voice and the instruments; this thickened the sound considerably. But Luther Perkins was always able to get nuances of emotion and meaning by altering the tone of his guitar—check out the doomy lines on "There You Go"—and the basic form proved so durable it's still there today.

"Folsom Prison Blues," all bass and dead-string guitar, was a successful country follow-up to "Cry, Cry, Cry," but Cash didn't crack the pop market until "I Walk the Line" sold a million in 1956. Once again, Sam Phillips' faith and patience had paid off, and he now had himself another rockabilly star, competing for the big bucks of the pop market rather than the small change of the country field.

Cash wasn't entirely comfortable in that role. As "Katy Too," "Rock Island Line," and even "Get Rhythm" (which he wrote for Elvis) show, Cash had trouble with fast songs. He liked the form enough to write several hit rockers for others; he just couldn't sing them too well himself. In 1956 he became the first Sun artist to join the Opry (which rejected Elvis, and refused to acknowledge the existence of Jerry Lee). He also reportedly wanted to sing more religious material than Sam Phillips would allow, which perhaps explains why in so many of his early lyrics he sounded like he was testifying anyhow: "I keep a close watch on this heart of mine," "I see that train a-comin'/It's rollin' 'round the bend," and "I taught the weeping willow how to cry," all of them opening lines, are the unyielding declarations of a man who's a preacher at heart.

As a writer Cash also evoked the American landscape in songs like "Hey, Porter" and "Big River" with the love and stunning clarity of a true native son. His favorite themes were lost love, trains, and prison, and he made lasting contributions with each. "Home of the Blues" was his version of "Heartbreak Hotel," and "Folsom Prison Blues" (written after he saw the B-movie *Inside the Walls of Folsom Prison)* became the definitive train song. He has written—or put his personal stamp on—so many train songs they fill several albums. And when he needed more pop hits in the Sun days, Jack Clement was always around to write him such tales of everyday teen trauma and triumph as "Ballad of a Teen-Age Queen." Clement also gave him "Guess Things Happen That Way," his most haunting and melancholy pop hit. Johnny Cash was perhaps never cracked up to be a teen idol, but while he was at Sun, he sure did make the best of it.

Carl Perkins: *The Sun Years* (British Sun).

Carl Perkins has always prompted mixed feelings. He not only could have been a contender, goes the conventional wisdom, he might have been the next Elvis; at the same time, this argument continues, he didn't have Presley's charisma, drive, vision, or sex appeal. Contradictory as this position remains, it receives support from this three-record boxed set of almost everything Perkins recorded for Sun, including a healthy number of demos, alternate takes, and previously unissued sides. Perkins' music was of his own conception, not something he whipped up in the wake of Presley's success; he was the only rockabilly (until Buddy Holly) equally talented as a singer, writer, and instrumentalist, and he was the first to take a record ("Blue Suede Shoes") to the top of the country, pop, and R & B charts simultaneously. But something—personal problems, unforeseeable disasters, changing public tastes—always intervened.

Perkins was born in 1932 on a tenant farm near Tiptonville, in northwest Tennessee; his family members were the only white sharecroppers on the farm, and he grew up immersed equally in gospel, blues, and country. By 1954, when the family moved to Bemis, Tennessee, Carl had already been playing for years with his brothers Clayton (bass) and Jay B. (rhythm guitar), and his influences—John Lee Hooker, Muddy Waters, Arthur "Guitar Boogie" Smith, Merle Travis, B. B. King, Bill Monroe—were already apparent in his music. In the mean juke joints of nearby Jackson, Tennessee, the Perkins Brothers Band honed its driving honky-tonk music spotlighting the boogie and single-string blues runs of Carl's guitar.

Later that year, they got a hearing with Sam Phillips. Carl was anxious to record in the new rockabilly style, but Sam felt there wasn't yet room in the field for anyone else but Elvis. He required Perkins to keep doing honky-tonk songs, and on his earliest recordings (things like "Turn Around," one side of his first single, in 1955) he phrases like a huskier Hank Williams, which is not a style to take lightly. For those early recordings, sidemen like Bill Cantrell (fiddle), Quinton Claunch (guitar), and Stan Kesler (guitar) augment the band (which had previously added drummer W. S. "Fluke" Holland as a regular member) to fill out the honky-tonk attack. But already Carl is stepping out as much as he can get away with; his solos on "Honky Tonk Gal" and "Gone, Gone, Gone" are something more than up-tempo hillbilly boogie; they're right on the edge of becoming the shattering guitar lines of his later rockabilly hits, which finally began coming soon after Phillips turned Elvis over to RCA in 1955. Late that year Perkins cut his first unadulterated rockabilly, and it looked like he'd pick up where Elvis left off.

"Blue Suede Shoes" was written after Carl observed a young clotheshorse at a Jackson dance. On the three versions heard here, you can follow him as the lyrics get revised (always becoming more teen-oriented), and the guitar fills get worked out, and Carl's solo, which technically didn't change much from first take to last, becomes angrier, more fluid, sharper—until finally it rocks and rolls both. The flip side, "Honey Don't," is heard in a rough demo and then in a denser final version, and the whole session had a feel that was exploratory but confident. (Thanks, reportedly, to the large bottle of whiskey that got emptied that night.) Early in 1956 "Blue Suede Shoes" made Perkins suddenly as big as Elvis; just as suddenly, it was over.

On the way to New York to perform "Blue Suede Shoes" before a national TV audience, the band was in a Delaware auto wreck that left them all badly injured, especially Jay B. Carl watched from his hospital bed while Elvis sang "Blue Suede Shoes" on national TV a few weeks later. Carl's career was on hold for months while Jay recuperated. Even then, Carl didn't exploit his rockabilly triumphs exclusively; he continued cutting honky-tonk and hillbilly boogie as well, and it's clear that all this music—music of rebellion *and* music of restraint—coexisted in his soul.

By any standards, his rockabilly is exceptional. As a writer, Perkins experimented with the rhythmic and melodic properties of words as much as with their literal meanings, but he also exulted in the language of rock 'n' roll more than anyone else of his generation except Chuck Berry. Songs like "Perkins Wiggle," "Boppin' the Blues," "All Mama's Children," "Put Your Cat Clothes On," and "Pink Pedal Pushers" were crucial in creating that language.

He also wrote the book on rockabilly guitar—blues and boogie with a twang. The shotgun solo of "Everybody's Trying to Be My Baby," the jagged lines on "Her Love Rubbed Off," and the momentum of "Right String Baby (but Wrong Yo-Yo)" have been chased by generations of rockers. When Perkins combined them all on one magnificent solo, as on "Somebody Tell Me," the result was so far ahead of its time that the song was never even released until this album. (Is that because the solo was considered one big mistake?) He sang rockers with wit and abandon, playing his voice off against his guitar, and on a ballad like "Only You" he offers one of the most deeply moving transformations ever of black material into white country blues.

"Dixie Fried" is a touchstone for the whole rockabilly moment. The band is swaggering, menacing, and Carl plays switchblade guitar. His voice is full of both warnings and fellowship, and the lyrics celebrate a roughhouse juke-joint Saturday-night blowout led by a character who "jerked out his razor but he wasn't shaving." He is ultimately thwarted, in jail, but even that is symbolic of how the rockabilly moment itself was shot down. "Dixie Fried" is thus the last word on the hell-bent country-boy ethos, but in a market dominated by northern teens, it didn't fare well. No wonder Perkins ultimately felt more secure in country music. There were other factors, of course—notably Carl's deepening alcoholism after Jay's death of cancer in 1958. But Carl's rockabilly, in the end, was just too harsh for most. Surprisingly, the country music he cut after following Johnny Cash to Columbia in 1958 didn't find much of an audience, either. But he seemed more comfortable in that niche, and most comfortable of all playing sideman to Cash, which he did for a decade beginning in 1967. Was his rockabilly, in the end, also too harsh even for Carl Perkins himself?

Jerry Lee Lewis: *The Sun Years* (British Sun).

Jerry Lee Lewis. The Pumping Piano. The details are etched in the brain. Born in 1935 in Ferriday, Louisiana, just across the river from Natchez, Mississippi. Grew up with his cousins Mickey Lee Gilley (who belatedly became a country star by aping Jerry Lee's style) and Jimmy Lee Swaggart (the TV evangelist) almost as brothers, and started playing piano, in a style no one had ever heard before, the first time he sat at one. At thirteen got his first taste of public acclaim playing at the opening of a Ford lot. Went professional, playing mostly drums at first, in the toughest joints of the toughest part of the South. In 1954 was turned down all over Nashville, a city with which he has continued to enjoy a heatedly adversary relationship. In 1956 went to Memphis for a Sun audition. Jack Clement (Sam Phillips was out of town that day) liked what he heard, but advised Jerry Lee to play more rock 'n' roll, less country. Nevertheless, when he heard Jerry's tape of "Crazy Arms," the Ray Price hit, Phillips also saw the potential, and released it in December 1956. It charted slightly, and Jerry Lee came to Memphis to stay, doing Sun sessions work until April 1957, when the cataclysmic "Whole Lotta Shakin' Goin' On" was released. It went on to sell six million. In November 1957 the demonic "Great Balls of Fire" came out and did nearly as well. In 1958 Jerry Lee began his first tour of England, taking with him his thirteen-year-old wife, Myra Gale, who was also his cousin. The ensuing scandal drove him back to America after only three gigs, and the heat was on here as well; Jerry Lee's three singles from that year sold disappointingly, and only partly because they were a cut below his previous work. He wouldn't chart again until 1961, when a pair of singles got lukewarm action, and then the unofficial blacklist continued until 1968, when he became a straight country singer (on record, if not in his live shows).

But the simple facts do little to prepare the uninitiated for the sheer explosive power of the 155 sides on this mammoth twelve-record boxed set of virtually everything known to exist from Jerry Lee's Sun days—the original sides, the alternate takes and outtakes, previously unreleased material, and even revealing between-takes studio chatter.

As a singer Jerry Lee was influenced equally by R & B shouters like Roy Brown and by what he's called "the only three real stylists there ever was before me," meaning Jimmie Rodgers, Al Jolson (yes, *that* Al Jolson), and Hank Williams. But Jerry Lee had an audacious leer, a reckless cockiness, in his voice that none of them dared. As a piano player he was influenced by country boogie men like Moon Mullican and by Opry star Del Wood, but more important were the black musicians he and Mickey and Jimmy used to hear when they snuck off to Haneys Big House, the nightclub on the "other" side of Ferriday. When Jerry Lee played country boogie, his right hand rocked and his left hand rolled with untamed urges previously alien to country music. And in all his music, as in his very soul, the war raged between his Pentecostal upbringing and his will to out-devil the Devil himself. For that, one need only hear the studio argument occurring between takes of "Great Balls of Fire," a legendary debate heretofore available in shorter form on a bootleg album called *Bopcat Beat.* Before one take, Jerry Lee is raving that he can't possibly play such an obviously blasphemous piece; before another, he is announcing that he sure wouldn't mind "eatin' pussy" right now.

After all these years, "Whole Lotta Shakin' " still never fails to churn the adrenaline. There's the momentum of the bass line on piano, the gradual acceleration, the rhythmic pulse Jerry sets up and then speeds up or slows down, toying with the music, with the listener, with the girl, his piano solo full of the pulsating glissando and trills that became his trademark, even (for once) a rugged Roland Janes guitar solo that struggles to match Jerry's piano. Finally, there are Jerry Lee's declamations at the end, as he tells his baby how to shake; you can almost *see* him putting his hands on her young body. Here is a man establishing complete control over his world, if only so he can later tear it apart himself.

Jerry Lee didn't write much, though when you hear the originals of the songs he covered—and "Whole Lotta Shakin' " is the prime case in point—you know he should probably get some of the writer's credits if only because he so fully overhauls songs. He gets such a fat, surging sound that it's easy to forget a record like "Great Balls of Fire" contains only piano and drums (the perfectly sympathetic Jimmy Van Eaton), but that is indeed the case.

Jerry Lee loved it all, played it all—country ballads, rhythm and blues, teen tunes, standards. In that respect, he was the rock 'n' roll equivalent to the southern minstrel, and the material was never as important as what he did with it. Early in his career, he rocked up old songs—"You're the Only Star in My Blue Heaven," "Silver Threads (Amongst the Gold)," "Old Pal of Yesterday"—for the old people, to affirm that they, too, were part of his heritage. Though he recorded little straight blues, the pounding, stinging treatment he gives "Deep Elm Blues" or the gleeful prurience behind "Big Legged Woman" leaves no doubt as to his feelings about that music. "Slippin' Around," the pivotal Floyd Tillman cheating song, becomes here a song of affirmation, a celebration of cat-and-mouse games among the sexually insatiable; Jerry Lee was a master at interpreting pop-wise country writers like Tillman and Hank Williams. But as his version of "Little Queenie" confirms, he could also out-Chuck Berry Chuck Berry when he was so moved. He could use dirty R & B ("Sixty Minute Man") as simple warmups, and could convert harmless teen ditties ("Pink Pedal Pushers," "Milkshake Mademoiselle") into something well beyond what the writer originally had in mind. There are touches of brilliance in the most unlikely, as well as the most likely, places—the offhand genius behind his version of "Matchbox," the old-time religion of "When the Saints Go Marchin' In," the vanity of "Lewis Boogie" (a rare original), the intro to "Drinking Wine Spo-Dee-O-Dee," the manic intensity of "Ubangi Stomp" or "Good Rockin' Tonight." After the British debacle, he seemed to turn a little more often toward country material again, but the very titles—"I'll Sail My Ship Alone," "I'm the Guilty One"—told of his defiance and his bitterness. And he never stopped rocking with equal vehemence during this period.

Jerry Lee left Sun in 1963. Because his output was so huge, and his legend writ so large, we tend to forget how few hits he really had. Collections like this remind us that no matter how great they were, hits don't always tell the whole story, for while some of these records stand out above the rest, there's not a truly bad one in the bunch. This set is more than a document of one of the most sensational careers in rockabilly; it's also a document of the most productive. Jerry Lee gives no ground, and this boxed set is forever.

Buddy Holly: *The Complete Buddy Holly* (MCA).
Buddy Holly was the only major rockabilly star never to place a single on the country charts. He was one of the few who didn't come from the deep South; he hailed instead from west Texas, where influ-

ences were significantly different (broader, if anything). His sound was
so much closer to mainstream rock 'n' roll or pop that purists sometimes
question whether he should be considered rockabilly at all, and second-
generation rockabilly might indeed be a more accurate term. But as this
six-record boxed set shows, Buddy Holly was his own man, which is
more than can be said for most second-generation rockabilly stars, who
chose to imitate Elvis slavishly rather than do something of their own.
When Holly died in the infamous 1959 plane crash that also took the Big
Bopper and Richie Valens, he left behind a sound and a body of songs
that continue to have impact in both rock and country.

He was born in 1936 in Lubbock, Texas, and was the youngest of
four kids. Polite, quiet but cheerful, just a little awkward, he took up
guitar at age twelve. At first he didn't seem too serious about music, but
by 1954 he and his hometown friend Bob Montgomery were cutting
demos. They make up the first side of the first album here, and could
best be described as western music with a heavy beat; Buddy and Bob
called it western bop, which also isn't bad. But either Buddy was uninspired by the form or he hadn't blossomed yet as a songwriter, for
nearly all these originals were written by Montgomery, and are western
genre pieces with little teen appeal. They are significant in that they
reveal Buddy's allegiances to (and also discomforts with) traditional
country or western forms.

Then Elvis happened. Where Buddy's first influences had been the
country music usuals—Hank Williams, Jimmie Rodgers, Bill Monroe—
now his adenoidal voice took on more Presleyesque hics and catches,
and he was changing band members to get closer to the Presley sound.
At first, record companies turned him down because he was *too* close to
Elvis, but finally Decca signed him and in 1956 sent him to Nashville to
record. If anyone doubts Holly's rockabilly credentials, they should hear
his uncompromising versions of "Don't Come Back Knockin'," "Midnight Shift," and "Rock Around With Ollie Vee" from Nashville (in all,
there were three sessions there that year, but no real hits).

Still, it *was* a different type of rockabilly, and as Holly defined his
sound in 1957, the differences became more apparent. He favored a
graceful, loping Tex-Mex beat, a beat with seemingly as much open
space in it as Texas itself. Instruments gelled rather than jarring. Buddy's rockabilly was not about busting loose and it's hard to imagine him
ever—ever—singing songs with any of the hoodoo overtones of the Sun
artists; his music didn't suggest a trace of Saturday-night honky-tonk
brawls. Buddy was concerned almost exclusively with young love, and
what it meant to move from adolescence into adulthood. He was an
Everyteen, mirroring the dreams and frustrations of anonymous, small-
town kids everywhere.

That's what's behind his biggest hits, which began with the release in 1957 of "That'll Be the Day," his third single. By now he was recording in Clovis, New Mexico, under the loose supervision of Norman Petty. (Holly was so clear about what he was doing in the studio that he didn't really need a producer per se.) His band, known as the Crickets, had pretty much stabilized with Jerry Allison on drums, Joe Mauldin on bass, and Niki Sullivan on guitar in addition to Buddy's vocals and guitar. Records were soon being released under both his name and the name of the Crickets, on Coral and Brunswick, (both labels were Decca subsidiaries, the parent company having dropped Buddy after the Nashville sessions failed to produce a hit).

"That'll Be the Day" is quintessential Holly, as tough as the Nashville sessions. There's plenty of sneer in his voice, which was capable of great range on any song, and Buddy's solo is a prime example of clanging, buzzsaw rockabilly guitar. On "Peggy Sue," another of his biggest hits, he sings in several voices, all of them nasal and country-based. There's a true, pleasing country lilt to songs like "Maybe Baby," and if he alters his phrasing just a little, it's easy to picture a song like "Listen to Me" on the country charts. There are traces of country phrasing in even Buddy's most poppish arrangements, such as "It Doesn't Matter Anymore," while "Well . . . Allright," one of his most exotic efforts, has some of the pacing, the ebb and flow, of a western ballad. "Rave On" is Johnny Cash in overdrive, and "True Love Ways" could just as easily have been sung by Elvis himself.

Like Elvis, Buddy wanted it all. His sound would change slightly when band members changed—when Tommy Allsup joined in 1958 from a western swing band, for example, the Crickets accommodated his guitar style rather than making him change it—but Buddy himself continued to control the overall sound. Later in 1958 he moved to New York, where he took an apartment with his new Puerto Rican wife, Maria Elena. It was a bold move for a young man out of the west Texas plains, but it enabled Holly to more easily pursue the softer, more poppish flavorings he sought. This involved orchestrations and the kind of session musicians you couldn't find in Lubbock or Clovis.

The recordings in this set come in several forms. Many, of course, are completed records. Others are demos, with just voice and guitar; still more started out as demos, but Petty overdubbed them with the Fireballs (a rock 'n' roll band of small repute) after Buddy died. Nearly everything Buddy did holds interest, but the 1959 demos he made alone in his New York apartment are especially intriguing. They suggest that if he hadn't died prematurely, he might have invented folk-rock a good five years before Bob Dylan ultimately did so. But he did die, in a chartered plane after a gig in Clear Lake, Iowa, in the middle of a winter tour in the bitterly cold Midwest. Later, that crash became known in song as "the day the music died," but Buddy's sound kept coming back, in artists as diverse as the Beatles of the mid-sixties and the Waylon Jennings of the mid-seventies. (Waylon played bass for Buddy on that final tour, and his first record, a hilariously inept version of "Jole Blon," which Buddy produced, is included in this set.) Holly's influence has been that pervasive.

Supplementary Albums

Sonny Burgess: *The Legendary Sun Performers* (British Charly). Burgess dyed his hair red to match his red suit and red Cadillacs. He also sang about a "Red Headed Woman," but it was no gimmick; that song and its flip side, "We Wanna Boogie," comprised his first Sun single, and it was one of the toughest fusions yet of country, R & B, and raving redneck mania. The rest of this album, including several previously unissued cuts, shows that Burgess must be considered one of the Sun singers whose failure to click had nothing to do with his ability.

Johnny Burnette/The Rock 'n' Roll Trio: *Tear It Up* (Solid Smoke). Burnette, his brother Dorsey and guitarist Paul Burlison (the man who accidentally discovered feedback guitar when his amp malfunctioned) were the real thing, Memphis working-class boys who took to rockabilly itself rather than to Elvis. The original trio recorded barely a year before splitting, and these seventeen sides are both their legacy and the basis for their cult (which is among the most rabid in a field known for rabid cults). Johnny's vocals were sometimes artificially hyped up, but ballads like "You're Undecided" and rockers like "Train Kept A-Rollin' " and the title song bear out the cult. Burlison was definitely an original, and though they weren't very successful in their day, these guys turn out to be among the most influential rockabillys.

Johnny Burnette's Rock and Roll Trio: *Johnny Burnette's Rock and Roll Trio and Their Rockin' Friends from Memphis* (Rock-a-Billy). Not really. Guitarist Paul Burlison, the sole surviving member from the original trio, gathers together (in 1980) a bunch of the old rockabilly gang and finds that, however good their intentions, most of them can't get it up anymore. But there's one exception, and it's a stunner: On "Gone and Left Me Blues," Charlie Feathers goes further into Hank Williams' heart of darkness than anyone's been in years.

Johnny Cash: *Get Rhythm* (Sun). Despite obnoxious overdubs, an outrageously short playing time, and "Sugartime," this contains such dark-horse Cash as "Mean Eyed Cat" and "New Mexico." Of all the non-hits packages, this is the best-rounded.

Johnny Cash and the Tennessee Two: *Original Golden Hits, Vol. 1* (Sun). Shelby Singleton's Sun reissue program is a shambles. The only two cuts here not also available on the recommended *Superbilly* album are "Next in Line" and "Don't Make Me Go," neither of which is exactly essential. It's a great album, but for an overview of the Sun era, why not go with *Superbilly* and get nearly twice as much for the money?

Johnny Cash and the Tennessee Two: *Original Gold Hits, Vol. 2* (Sun). The four cuts here not already available on *Superbilly* are "Come in Stranger," "I Just Thought You'd Like to Know," "Just About Time," and "Thanks a Lot." Otherwise, see above.

Johnny Cash and the Tennessee Two: *Original Golden Hits, Vol. III* (Sun). The duplication with *Superbilly* material begins thinning out here, but so does quality. You might want this solely for Cash's version of "Doin' My Time," but once you've got that, you're at the point of diminishing returns with this whole series. Except . . .

Johnny Cash and Jerry Lee Lewis: *Sunday Down South* (Sun). *Not* duets, as the title might imply, but one side each of Cash and Jerry Lee singing gospel. The Killer's tastes run more toward the folkie, oddly enough, and his version of "When the Saints Go Marching In" *does* have Cash on harmony, as well as another Elvis-like voice that must be Charlie Rich.

Johnny Cash and Jerry Lee Lewis: *Johnny Cash and Jerry Lee Lewis Sing Hank Williams* (Sun). It's hard to go wrong with songs like these, and worth noting that after all these years Jerry Lee's resigned version of "You Win Again" is *still* one of the best Hank Williams covers ever. Again, these aren't duets.

Chess Rockabillies (British Chess). Right, Chess Records of Chicago, the blues titan. The label didn't record much rockabilly, but there's some good music and some good fun mixed up in here. In the first category are Rusty York with "Sugaree," Johnny Fuller with "All Night Long" (black rockabilly), Dale Hawkins with "Lovin' Bug," and Gene Simmons with "The Shape You Left Me In." In the latter category we have Mel Robbins' "Save It," a Jerry Lee rip. These sides are more properly called country-rock than rockabilly, but let's not split hairs.

Chicken Rock (British Eagle). Another of those rockabilly-based anthologies seemingly put together with no rhyme nor reason except that most of the artists and songs are impossibly obscure. Still, this one has some depth, as well as lots of jive talk, with monster-rock overtones.

Eddie Cochran: *Eddie Cochran* (Liberty). Cochran was one of the first rock 'n' roll heroes; he was born in Minnesota and country music was his first love. His family moved to a Southern California suburb when he was a teen-ager, and that's where he launched his career, as part of a rockabilly duo with Hank Cochran (no relation), who later moved to Nashville and became one of the top country songwriters of the sixties. When they split, Eddie's own music went toward a hard rock 'n' roll sound, but in both his phrasing and his chunky guitar work, he retained some of those early country and rockabilly influences, and songs like "Cut Across Shorty" have been covered by country stars while rock singers covered the likes of "Come On Everybody" and "Twenty Flight Rock." Eddie himself cut "Milk Cow Blues" and "Blue Suede Shoes," so you know *he* never felt like he left the fold entirely. His best-known song remains "Summertime Blues," a perennial teen anthem, and Eddie's talents seemed so limitless that there's no telling what would have happened had he not been killed in a 1960 auto wreck while touring England with Gene Vincent. You'll find all the hits and then some on this double album in the "Legendary Masters" series.

The Collins Kids: *Introducing Larry and Lorrie* (Epic). These fifties schoolkids have won a huge cult following among rockabilly fanatics even though their music is less rockabilly than it is up-tempo hillbilly boogie with adolescent vocals. An acquired taste for sure, and the Collins Kids are probably best heard a little at a time on the Epic anthologies, but there's no accounting for cults.

The Everly Brothers: *Original Greatest Hits* (Barnaby). The sons of a semipopular Kentucky C&W duo, Don and Phil Everly combined brother-duet harmonies with pop-rockabilly songs and mainstream sheen to stake out a corner of the charts all their own. They were the last of the brother duos, a pair of high tenors, and their biggest hits were teen ballads of innocent, ideal love, many of them from the crack Nashville writing team of Felice and Boudleaux Bryant. They make up the bulk of this double album, which is out of print but still turns up, in various forms on various labels, here and there. "Bye Bye Love," their first hit, in 1957, sets the tone, while "Bird Dog," "Wake Up Little Susie," "All I Have to Do Is Dream," and " 'Til I Kissed You" keep up the pace.

The Everly Brothers: *End of an Era* (Barnaby). An out-of-print twofer like its predecessor, this one includes the rest of the important material from the prime years 1957–59. Because the Everlys so personified wistful teen love and pop-rockabilly, it's easy to forget that their earliest records were released country, and the Everlys were not promoted as a pop act until the first couple of singles crossed over on their own; then the material became increasingly teen-oriented, too. But during their tenure on Cadence (which Barnaby eventually bought), the Everly Brothers also recorded traditional country standards in the brother-duo mold like "Kentucky," "Barbara Allen," "I'm Here to Get My Baby Out of Jail," and "Who's Gonna Shoe Your Pretty Little Feet," and this album collects that material (most of it from a Cadence set called *Songs Our Daddy Taught Us*). Warning: Nearly all the Everly Brothers Cadence material (reissued by Barnaby and by several import labels) is worthwhile if you can find it, but avoid the Warner Bros. albums—even the ones that claim to be "greatest hits"—because they're really clumsy rerecordings except for a song or two. Exception, if you can find it: The 1968 *Roots*, a modernization of their Cadence sound and style that really did enhance their standing as country singers. It's now also out of print.

The Everly Brothers: *The Everly Brothers* (British Ace). This import will have to serve as the alternative if you can't scare up the out-of-print American twofers. It features twelve of their earliest sides, with emphasis on rock 'n' roll, and is in pristine mono.

Charlie Feathers: *Rockabilly's Main Man* (British Charly). Probably the most representative early Feathers album, though it doesn't include the one *essential* Feathers cut ("One Hand Loose," available on *King-Federal Rockabillys*). To hear him tell it, Feathers invented rockabilly for Elvis, and most of these sides, cut for Sun from 1955–59, do have the heavy echo and walking bass of Sun rockabilly. But they're up-tempo honky-tonk and hillbilly boogie that manages to fall into the cracks between country and rock 'n' roll. Which is where Feathers wants to be anyhow, because he's too far into his own private muse to let himself get lumped in with either camp—for verification, consider here his weird version of "I Forgot to Remember to Forget" or his forbidding, bluesy remoldings of Autry Inman's "Uh Huh Honey," Roy Acuff's "Mound of Clay," and Hank Locklin's "Send Me the Pillow That You Dream On."

Charlie Feathers: *Rockabilly Rhythm!* (Cowboy Carl). Time didn't mellow Feathers; if anything, the combination of time and failure intensified his brooding and his determination to disturb. These 1973 sides have a smaller band and a fatter sound than he's used since, but he's still chasing—and being chased by—ghosts.

Charlie Feathers: *Charlie Feathers* (Feathers). Stark, defiant, crazy stuff. Charlie Feathers, circa 1979: "Ain't it downright disgusting/The

shape that I'm in/I've been through hell, Lord/And I'm going again."
To which he later adds, "Time took my soul, Lord/Now it's after my
mind."

Charlie Feathers: *Volume Two* (Feathers). More of the same, only not
quite as peculiar—except for "Wide Muddy River," which is only the
most peculiar thing he's ever done, sort of a redneck Van Morrison, if
you see what I mean. These two albums don't rate high with Feathers
connoisseurs, but I'm hooked.

Sonny Fisher: *Texas Rockabilly* (British Ace). Fisher, who hailed from
east Texas and worked mostly around Houston, was a subtle, insinuating
rock shouter who handled a back beat too skillfully to be considered a
country singer cashing in. He moved easily from a deep growl to a high
yip, and worked well with guitar whiz Joey Long, who led Fisher's
band, the Rocking Boys. Long is best known as a blues guitarist, and is a
genius at breaking up songs with wicked rock riffs and slicing solos. In
fact, he still plays regularly around Houston today, which is more than
can be said for Fisher. This eight-song, ten-inch EP offers some of the
bluesiest Texas rockabilly around.

Bill Haley and His Comets: *Greatest Hits* (MCA). All the major hits by
the first white man to hop up western swing and boogie-woogie enough
to get it called rock 'n' roll. Many were doing it better around the same
time, but his "Rock Around the Clock" was the first to break through
nationally.

Bill Haley: *A Tribute to Bill Haley* (British MCA). The English version
of Haley's greatest hits, and, as usual, they do it better. This has more
songs, better selection, and better sound than its American counterpart.

Bill Haley: *Rockin' Rollin' Bill Haley* (German Bear Family). Haley
for gluttons: A five-record boxed set that exhausts the Decca years (as
well as all but the most diehard listeners).

Bill Haley and His Comets: *Rock the Joint!* (English Roller
Coaster). Haley's 1952–53 sides for Essex, the small Philadelphia indie,
that immediately predated his rock 'n' roll breakthrough. They're a
little more country-rooted than the Decca sides, but basically in the
style that made him famous.

Roy Hall: *Boogie Rockabilly* (Swedish Rock & Country). More boogie
than rockabilly, but it don't stop shakin'. Hall, who played piano in
Webb Pierce's band is—at least as far as anyone can ascertain—the man
who conceived "Whole Lotta Shakin' Goin' On" before Jerry Lee
mauled it into shape. Oddly enough, Hall doesn't play piano on it at all.

Most of the other songs are in the same vein, with crackling guitar and gleeful vocals. Hall should have gone further on his own than he did.

Dale Hawkins: *Chess Rock 'n' Rhythm Series* (Chess). Here's a cultist, elitist LP for you. Dale Hawkins had one enduring record in "Susie Q" and several lesser hits like "My Babe." With his Jerry Lee-like vocals and the chopping guitar of James Burton, the Louisiana man built a rabid cult. That's who this reissue, which includes alternate versions of "Susie Q" and "My Babe," plays to. This is fine for collectors, but I'd think that if the albums's producers were that interested in turning people onto their man Dale, they would have instead offered more of his other material (he did great stuff that didn't make it onto this LP) and left the obscurities to a companion volume, bonus EP or the boot-leggers. Since now even this album is out of print, the argument is academic. But since Chess has started a new reissue series, I hope they do better by Hawkins next time.

Ronnie Hawkins: *Arkansas Rock Pile* (British Roulette). Hawkins (no relation to Dale) was the greasiest rockabilly of all, a leering, slobbering second-generation singer best known for "Mary Lou" and "Thirty Days" (both 1959). But he really hit his stride in the early sixties, when his band was made up of the five men who would later back Bob Dylan and then become late sixties and early seventies rock heroes in their own right under the name The Band. With this group, Hawkins cut a menacing "Who Do You Love?" and other raunch. He's still rocking, based in Toronto and turning out new albums and new sidemen regu-larly. Little of his best work (including this album) is still in print, however, except for isolated cuts on anthologies, and the deficient Ac-cord LP.

Ronnie Hawkins: *Premonition* (Accord). This is the sole Hawkins still in print, including the salacious "Odessa," and a rather haphazard selec-tion of hits and covers. At nine songs, it's disgracefully skimpy, but at least you'll be able to find it in the stores.

Hillbilly Bop, Memphis Style (British Meteor). Meteor was a Memphis company, which means that even if it didn't get the best artists (they invariably went to Sam Phillips at Sun first), it was closer to the source than most labels. Meteor made rawer, less commercial records than Sun, which makes it a cult favorite at the least. And there are numerous fine sides here, including two each by Charlie Feathers and Junior Thompson. But my vote goes to Steve Carl with the Jags, who do "Curfew," a dread-filled song even if you don't hear a word they're singing. Style hit: "Charcoal Suit," by Brad Suggs with the Swingsters.

Bluesy hit: "Lonesome Rhythm Blues," by Wayne McGinnis with the Swingteens.

Buddy Holly: *A Rock and Roll Collection* (MCA). Unless you splurge on the complete works, you're going to have trouble patching together a representative selection of Buddy Holly. This double album offers more quantity than anything else still in print, and though the obvious hits are all accounted for, there was evidently also a fair amount of consideration involved in picking which non-hits to include.

Buddy Holly/The Crickets: *20 Golden Greats* (MCA). The only single-album hits compilation of Holly available, and a good buy though the overlap with *Collection* is substantial. If you go for one or the other, which is what you should do, *Collection* probably still gets the edge.

Buddy Holly: *The Great Buddy Holly* (Coral). "That'll Be the Day" and an intriguing cross-selection of non-hits, including key records from the Nashville sessions. I don't know why MCA chose to keep this in print while deleting others, but I'm not complaining.

Buddy Holly: *For the First Time Anywhere* (MCA). Here are ten 1956 Holly classics, as he originally recorded them (i.e., sans overdubs). Other versions of these songs are available on numerous other albums; but when you get to hear them the way Buddy first heard them, you see both that his rockabilly had more crackle and his pop was more concise.

The Million Dollar Quartet: *The Million Dollar Quartet* (British Sun). In December 1956, in the midst of a Carl Perkins session that included the then-unknown Jerry Lee Lewis on piano, a then-very-well-known Elvis Presley (who'd already graduated to RCA) dropped by his old stomping grounds, the Sun studios. Johnny Cash was there for a while too, and the four of them got to jamming, mostly on gospel tunes they all knew. Behind the board, an alert Jack Clement rolled the tapes for about two hours. For the next quarter century or so, that jam was one of the great legends (and mysteries) of rockabilly. Then bootlegs began seeping out, culminating with this album that Charly (which *is* British Sun) swears is a legal reissue because it was a Perkins session to begin with. (RCA successfully argued that it has worldwide exclusive rights to anything Elvis sings on when it suppressed this bootleg in the States, so it's unclear why the label tolerates this import.) Meanwhile, what about the music? Well, it's the same thirty-minute slice that turned up on all the bootlegs (leading to speculation that the rest of the tapes have never been found), Johnny Cash is nowhere to be heard (he recalls he left to take his wife shopping when they started playing), and it all sounds very ordinary and unspectacular. I *still* wouldn't give my copy up for anything.

Imperial Rockabillies (British United Artists). Another anthology with better material than you'd anticipate, but Imperial did have better connections in the South, particularly in Louisiana, than did most L.A. labels. Bob Luman's "Red Hot" is the best try, and Bill Allen's "Please Give Me Something" is the dark-horse favorite. But it takes the black New Orleans shouter Roy Brown, with "Hip Shakin' Baby," to show how it's really done.

Wanda Jackson: *Only Rock 'n' Roll* (French Capitol). Jackson was the raunchiest of the female rockabilly singers; performances like "Let's Have a Party" were about as raw and wild as the form got, and she belted others like "Fujiyama Mama" that proved it was no fluke. Plus, she got to tour with Elvis. This double album contains most of her significant rockabilly sides.

George Jones: *White Lightnin'* (British Ace). These are the supposed rockabilly sides George cut, some under the name "Thumper" Jones, early in his career. "Rock It" is the only out-and-out rocker here, though, and while George handles it fine, he's obviously happier singing up-tempo country fast enough to fool Pappy Daily into *thinking* it's rock. For his part, Pappy adds lots of echo. Though this ten-inch album has won a large cult for the "rockabilly George," I don't consider these sides his best early work; they are fun, though, and George shouldn't be as ashamed of them as he says he is.

Benny Joy: *Rock-A-Billy With Benny Joy* (Dutch White Label). Joy is not exactly an original rockabilly guitarist and singer, but he's talented enough to be good for an album side. That would be side one here, with a pair of atmospheric sax and guitar instrumentals in "Money Money" and "Rebel Rock," and a thumping piece of bombast in "Crash the Party." And "Ittie Bittie Everything" shows he sure does know his way around a fast one.

Jukebox at Eric's (British Eric). The people who put together this rockabilly compilation apparently had two criteria: the record must be very rare and it must be very weird. Especially very weird.

King-Federal Rockabillies (King/Gusto). Since King turned out all manner of postwar country music, it stands to reason the label would have some rockabilly in the vaults, even if none became hits. In fact, the elusive Charlie Feathers did his best work here on "One Hand Loose," a casually brilliant performance that dwarfs his other early sides. He's got three other cuts on this album, while Mac Curtis has a total of five, all of them proficient rockabilly, none of them truly outstanding. Also included is Hank Mizell's "Jungle Rock," which became a freak hit in 1976, two decades after it was first released.

Sid King and the Five Strings: *Gonna Shake This Shack Tonight* (German Bear Family). Like many Texas rockabillys, King was as concerned with establishing a groove as he was with busting out. But he had his lingo down too cold for it to have been an accident, and, besides, it was a damn good groove.

Sleepy LaBeef: *Downhome Rockabilly* (Sun). Depending on your point of view, Sleepy had been a rockabilly cult hero or a rockabilly has-been (never-was?) for some two decades when this album was released in 1979. But its sweaty barroom feel makes it the first he's done to suggest just what his supporters hear in him.

Sleepy LaBeef: *Electricity* (Rounder). On which this living rockabilly legend finally delivers the goods the way his word-of-mouth rep has always sworn he could—resourceful material, rockin' band, and a charged baritone that ties it all together.

Jerry Lee Lewis: *Original Golden Hits—Volume 1* (Sun). There's so much prime Jerry Lee available on Sun reissues, and so little overlap among albums, that even the true fan will cringe at paying for them all, but this is definitely the one to start with. It includes his first record ("Crazy Arms"), a couple of the big hits ("Great Balls of Fire" and "Whole Lotta Shakin' Goin' On") and two of the very few songs he ever wrote ("Lewis Boogie" and "End of the Road").

Jerry Lee Lewis: *Original Golden Hits—Volume 2* (Sun). Hits thin out, but quality doesn't. "High School Confidential" was perhaps his best piece of purely teen material, and the movie that went with it is a cornerstone in the fifties teen exploitation genre. "Money" reveals some of the roots of surf music, and the rest of the cuts are nearly all country or R & B standards on which Jerry Lee puts his personal stamp.

Jerry Lee Lewis: *Rockin' Rhythm and Blues* (Sun). After you've heard this one, you'll understand why they call him "the Killer." Song for song, this is as gutsy as any Lewis repackaging on the market, and Jerry Lee outdoes the original R & B versions of many of these. The highlight is his salacious reading of "Big Legged Woman," on which he leers, swoons, and chuckles his way through explicit sexual metaphor after explicit sexual metaphor before averring, "I'm gonna tell you tell you, mama/What I'm talkin' about/I'll bet my bottom dollar/There ain't a cherry in this house." At the end of the song, he drunkenly declares, "It's a hit!" It wasn't, of course.

Jerry Lee Lewis: *Ole Tyme Country Music* (Sun). Like the R & B set, a modest concept with immodest results. These songs may be old, but the arrangements are state-of-the-art Killer, and "Deep Elem Blues" is something even more ferocious than that.

Jerry Lee Lewis: *Original Golden Hits—Volume III* (Sun). Here's where material in general starts thinning out, though "Lovin' Up a Storm" is a primo Jerry Lee rocker and "As Long as I Live" an apt statement of purpose.

Jerry Lee Lewis: *The Golden Cream of the Country* (Sun). This relies on country hits of the rockabilly era, or of the very recent past, and though they're more rocked-up than his Smash sides were a decade later, they suggest both his heritage and his future direction.

Jerry Lee Lewis: *A Taste of Country* (Sun). The real highlight here is "Am I to Be the One," an Otis Blackwell rocker with a harmony voice that sounds like Elvis but is probably Charlie Rich.

Jerry Lee Lewis: *Monsters* (Sun). Random collection of rockers, most available on other reissues, but this is still recommended for the hardcore.

Jerry Lee Lewis: *Nuggets* (British Charly). The subtitle is "16 Rare Tracks by Jerry Lee Lewis," and most are curiosities more than anything else. "I Get the Blues When It Rains" and "In the Mood," for example, are both sides of an instrumental single he once released under the name "The Hawk." "The Return of Jerry Lee" uses snippets from numerous Jerry Lee hits to make humorous commentary on his British tour debacle; it's in the style of those oldies in which an interviewer asks a question and is answered musically by a line from a song. "It Won't Happen with Me" finds the Killer swearing he'll never be washed up like those other pop stars (some of whom he names). It did happen with him, though.

Rare Jerry Lee Lewis, Volume 1 (British Charly). Some more rare than others, little of it superlative, but Jerry Lee fanatics like myself go for albums like this anyhow.

Jerry Lee Lewis: *Golden Rock & Roll* (Sun). Unlike the other Sun sets of "20 Originals," this concentrates not on the hits but on some of the obscurities. So instead of "Great Balls of Fire" and "Whole Lotta Shakin' " we get "The Return of Jerry Lee" and "Lewis Boogie." There'e also unlikely covers such as "When I Get Paid" or "Hong Kong Blues" (Jerry Lee does Hoagy Carmichael). Plus, it must be conceded, a little filler and self-cannibalization like "Whole Lotta Twistin'." Still a good deal as a supplement to the various "greatest hits."

Bob Luman: *The Rocker* (German Bear Family). Luman was a would-be Elvis clone who had one hit before being drafted, just like his idol, in 1960. Whether he would have lasted longer is open to question; rockabilly was largely a thing of the past even by 1960, and Luman never had the command of the form that his rabid cult gives him credit for; he was better at the rockin' country he recorded after he got out of the service, but as a sort of unintentional rockabilly swan song, these sides hold some fascination. A young James Burton on guitar is the star of the set. (A second volume, however, is too much, though one is available from the same label.)

Janis Martin: *That Rockin' Gal* (German Bear Family). She was known as "the female Elvis Presley," and cut a song to him called "My Boy Elvis." With the exception of Wanda Jackson, who had a little more bite, Janis Martin was the only female rockabilly worth talking about.

Janis Martin: *That Rockin' Gal Rocks On* (German Bear Family import). Her deep, sassy voice was definitely the female counterpart to male rockabilly surliness, and Janis Martin phrased like running a line of jive came pretty natural to her. These are the last of the thirty sides she cut between 1956 and 1959, when, at the age of eighteen, she had a child and went into retirement.

Mar-Vel Masters, Vol. 1 (Cowboy Carl). Mar-Vel was one of those legendary rockabilly/hillbilly boogie labels that thrived through the fifties despite little action outside its home base. Established in southern Indiana in 1949 and active through 1966, the label's music isn't nearly as intoxicating as its mystique, but of the several anthologies available, this is the best. It runs the gamut from swing to boogie to rock, and exhibits profound respect for the trashy novelty song.

MCA Rare Rockabilly (British MCA). This really is mostly rockabilly, unlike most of those British compilations, and if you can't locate a Roy Hall album, you'll definitely want this for his "Whole Lotta Shakin' Goin' On," "Three Alley Cats, Diggin' the Boogie," and "Offbeat Boogie." (Well, maybe it's not really rockabilly in the *strictest* sense.) And by the way, that guy Donny Young, who sings "Shaking the Blues," is known today as Johnny Paycheck.

MCA Rare Rockabilly, Volume III (British MCA). This *is* boogie as much as rockabilly, and the whole series of Decca rockabilly (for that's the label these originally appeared on) has hit the point of diminishing returns. But there's more Roy Hall here worth checking out as well as such curiosities as Jerry Kennedy (better known today as a producer and executive) singing "Teenage Love Is Misery," the York Brothers singing "Everybody's Tryin' to Be My Baby" (could somebody tell me how writer's credits on this wound up with Webb Pierce and Johnny Mathis?) and Moon Mullican doing "Moon's Rock." (We won't mention Red Sovine trying to rock on "Juke Joint Johnny.") In general, Decca was less lame than most of the majors about co-opting rockabilly.

MCA Rare Rockabilly, Vol. IV (British MCA). Most of the rockabilly is gone, and what's left is up-tempo country and hillbilly boogie. Patsy Cline's "Got a Lot of Rhythm in My Soul" doesn't fall into either camp, though, while Webb Pierce's boogie arrangement of Jimmie Rodgers' "California Blues" is about as good as the latter got.

The MGM Rockabilly Collection (English MGM). Thanks mainly to Andy Starr, who at his best is a genuine Arkansas/Texas wildman, these sides represent more than just another attempt by a major label to catch lightning in a bottle (and after the storm is mostly over at that). Bonus, just for laughs: "Rockin' and Rollin' with Granmaw," by Carson Robison, who should know, since he was sixty-six when he cut it.

The MGM Rockabilly Collection, Vol. 2 (English MGM). This is more diverse, and more spotty, with too many examples of attempted cash-in by a major label. But Conway Twitty's "Long Black Train" is one of the best Elvis imitations ever, as well as pretty fair Conway Twitty, and there's some interest in hearing unfamiliar material from familiar names like Marvin Rainwater, Arthur Smith, and Don Gibson, as well as a take on "Long Gone Lonesome Blues" by black bluesman Jimmie Newsome.

Ricky Nelson: *Ricky Nelson* (Liberty). There are those who'll argue that soft-voiced Ricky Nelson, far from being a suburban wimp, was really an Everyteen, the last, and best, of the second-generation rockabilly singers. I say he had a great band, especially guitarist James Burton, and access to the best teen material of the late fifties and early sixties, which was much more appropriate for him than the likes of "Milkcow Blues." Unless you're a glutton or a James Burton completist, you can find everything you ever wanted to know about Ricky in this double album from the label's "Legendary Masters" series.

Roy Orbison: *The Original Sound* (Sun). Before Orbison hit his stride as a big balladeer, Sam Phillips sought to mold him into an Elvis-style rockabilly shouter. It's not so much that his voice didn't fit as that his heart wasn't in it, but he was always blessed with tight bands and records like "Rock House" and "Oobie Doobie" are nothing to be ashamed of.

Roy Orbison: *The All-Time Greatest Hits of Roy Orbison* (Monument). In the early sixties, Roy established himself as one of country-rock's most awe-inspiring balladeers, turning out hit after grandiose hit. These records—"Running Scared," "Only the Lonely," "It's Over," "Crying"—were full of paranoia and bathos, but Orbison made them work anyhow by squeezing the most out of his full, expanding voice, and by utilizing string arrangements that were not just decoration but contributed to the buildup of the songs. When he and they hit a crescendo simultaneously, the results were more bloodcurdling than anything else of its era. He also turned out a few convincing rockers like the casually seductive "Pretty Woman," but it was definitely the ballads that earned him his nickname "the Voice." This double album collects all the major hits and a few of the interesting misses, and though it's not exactly rockabilly, it is a dramatic and singular rockabilly-based music.

Carl Perkins: *Original Golden Hits* (Sun). If you want only a single album of Carl's top rockabilly, this is it. When his output is condensed down to the eleven most power-packed songs, it can sound even more impressive than it does spread out through the boxed sets.

Carl Perkins: *Blue Suede Shoes* (Sun). Again, you won't find anything here that's not on Charly's boxed set, but for an inexpensive Perkins sampler that covers his country as thoroughly as his rock, this one comes through.

Elvis Presley: *Elvis' Golden Records, Vol. 1* (RCA). If you've got the four-record *Gold Award Hits* boxed set, you won't need this; but if you want just one album of his earliest hit singles for RCA, this is it.

Elvis Presley: *Elvis: Golden Records, Vol. 2* (RCA). This is the one with the famous "Fifty Million Elvis Fans Can't Be Wrong" banner. They're not, yet, but they're getting close. Again, if you have the *Gold Award Hits* set, pass on this, which is more for the budget-minded. The next two volumes are more for the diehard only, and I wouldn't recommend them to anybody except to say that if you want that much Elvis, skip those two and these two and splurge on *Gold Award Hits, Vol. 1*.

Elvis Presley: *World Wide Fifty Gold Award Hits, Vol. 2* (RCA). The way most of these songs got to be gold records was that they had the good fortune to appear on the B-side of *good* records that deserved to go gold. Maybe ten good sides from his early RCA days, but the rest nearly renders the whole "gold" concept meaningless. Casual fans will be happy to settle for just *Vol 1*.

Elvis Presley: *For LP Fans Only* (RCA). There's so much crap out on Elvis that several writers have made whole careers out of just sorting through that stuff. But there's no doubt that this is one of the essential rockabilly albums; RCA released it while Elvis was in the Army, and in addition to a big chunk of the Sun sides, which at that point were not available on album (which is no longer the case), this included some of his better RCA rockers, particularly his version of Big Boy Crudup's "My Baby Left Me."

Elvis Presley: *A Date with Elvis* (RCA). Another Army album, with Sun and RCA rockers interspersed. Like *LP Fans Only*, it's in reprocessed stereo, so if you're buying it for the Sun sides, better stick to just *The Sun Sessions* LP discussed earlier; by the time RCA got around to putting that out, they had wised up enough to leave everything in its original mono.

Elvis Presley: *Elvis* (RCA). Some of his most vital RCA rockers (including two Little Richard covers) and very little schlock.

Elvis Presley (RCA). More early RCA rockers, and still no warning that this man will ever go soft. After these four albums, the rocking Elvis Presley appears on RCA albums less frequently and with diminished power. Some of the sound tracks *(King Creole, Loving You)* have cuts hinting at the primal force of the early Elvis, but only a few; these four albums are all the additional fifties Elvis you need.

Elvis Presley: *Elvis Sings the Wonderful World of Christmas* (RCA). I've always been surprised that country, a pious and sentimental form, hasn't produced more great Christmas music. But this is a good Christmas album and a good Elvis album, with all that piousness and sentimentality held in check by a handful of Christmas rockers that show Elvis hasn't forgotten.

Elvis Presley: *Elvis Is Back* (RCA). This is his first post-Army album, and rocks out hard enough and often enough that you might suspect it was recorded in the pre-Army days and left in the can until now. But you'd be wrong (and too cynical to be a very good fan). The fact is, he was happy to be a civilian again, and feeling his oats.

Elvis Presley: *How Great Thou Art* (RCA). It took people a long time to figure out how much of a role gospel played in Elvis' music, but the house-shaking Pentecostal sounds of his youth were there from the beginning. This 1967 set is the best of his gospel albums, thanks in no small part to his epic reading of the title song. By now, the initial Elvis-backlash panic had subsided, and albums like this made his roots explicit while at the same time doing wonders to flesh out his image. Which is not to suggest that he took no liberties with this music; in the end, he took it just as seriously as the rest of his music, meaning he had no compunctions about sticking the 1960 pop hit "Crying in the Chapel" on here with the true gospel just to help jack up sales. He sang it like a true gospel song, anyhow; like I said, it really was all the same to him.

Elvis Presley: *The TV Special* (RCA). After years of stupefying movies and sound tracks, at a time when acts like the Beatles, the Stones, and Jim Morrison ruled, Elvis put everything on the line for his 1968 Christmas TV special—and he delivered. It was the first time in too long that he concentrated on making music, and even a studio orchestra cannot hide the majesty of these performances, which proved that El could still rock with the best of them—especially when the orchestra took five and it was just him and the original trio (Scotty and Bill) holding the stage. By the way, the *complete* trio-only material, only a little of which made it onto this record, can be found (if you're lucky) on a bootleg called *The Burbank Sessions* (Audifon).

Elvis Presley: *From Elvis in Memphis* (RCA). Along with the 1968 TV special, this marked Elvis' return to the Real World. The key is Memphis almost as much as it is Elvis; get him away from all those windup L.A. session men and those silly movie tunes and put him back among some soulful pickers working with contemporary country, soul, and rock songs and you'd better believe it makes a difference. Elvis is more than up for the occasion; his voice is full, eager, and poignant.

Elvis Presley: *From Memphis to Vegas/From Vegas to Memphis* (RCA). When you're hot, you're hot. Half this double album marks Elvis' return to the stage in Las Vegas after his TV special triumph; this live album goes heavy on rockers, as if to announce that he had never really left the fold, and the orchestra doesn't often get in the way of the crack rock band he'd assembled around guitarist James Burton. The other album sounds like a very good follow-up to *From Elvis in Memphis,* which was a tough act to follow; still, he may sing "Stranger in My Own Home Town" here, but that's thankfully not the case at all. Later, this was broken down into two single albums, *Elvis in Person at the International Hotel, Las Vegas, Nevada,* and *Back in Memphis.*

Elvis Presley: *Elvis Country* (RCA). I've always been partial toward this 1971 effort of El's to show the big boys how country is *really* glossed up, even when it's done with a small group like the one he used in the old days. The concept (conceit?) doesn't always work, but I'm fascinated by his choice of the traditional song ("I Was Born About 10,000 Years Ago") that ties all these country standards together. Bill Monroe's "Little Cabin on the Hill" is precisely the kind of song missing from his repertoire for too long, while "Whole Lotta Shakin'," "The Fool," and "It's Your Baby, You Rock It" kick up their heels pretty good, especially among such countrypolitan overkill as "Tomorrow Never Comes." One of the few truly experimental albums Elvis ever made, and largely a success.

Elvis Presley: *A Legendary Performer, Volume 2* (RCA). This sampler delivers where *Volume 1* held back. We get an unreleased 1954 Sun master on "Harbor Lights" as well as previously unreleased versions of "Blue Suede Shoes," "Blue Hawaii," and "Baby What You Want Me to Do." None are revelations; all are welcome additions to the legacy, which, in view of previously unreleased movie sound-track stuff like "Cane and a High Starched Collar," still needs all the help it can get. "How Great Thou Art" and "If I Can Dream" are savvy choices, too.

Elvis Presley: *This Is Elvis* (RCA). Double-album sound track from the posthumous movie bio, and not only is the choice of material generally good, but there are bonuses like live tracks from the Dorsey TV show and the Milton Berle show that were previously available only on bootlegs. Plus the kind of interviews and snippets of aural memorabilia that turn up on the *Legendary Performer* albums, too. (For the record, those TV-show bootlegs have become almost impossible to find, but a bootleg label called Golden Archive did at one time have albums out called *The Dorsey Shows, From the Waist Up* (El's performances on the Ed Sullivan shows), and *The Rockin' Rebel, Vols. 1 and 2* (miscellaneous live stuff from the early years).

Elvis Presley: *Elvis' Greatest Shit* (Dog Vomit). I simply cannot help but give this Elvis bootleg a listing to itself. It appeared in 1982, and was not as well distributed as other Elvis bootlegs, so I have no idea how you'll ever find it. But it's a revelation in its own right, gathering together as it does a batch of the worst songs he ever recorded, most of them from the movies, including such paradigms of the pop form as "Yoga Is as Yoga Does," "Song of the Shrimp," "He's Your Uncle Not Your Dad," "Confidence," "The Walls Have Ears," a "Do the Clambake" medley, "Dominic the Impotent Bull," "There's No Room to Rhumba in a Sports Car," and oh so many more. The revelation, for me, is that I'd always assumed I knew just how lame El could be, but once I heard this, I realized I'd had no idea. And words fail me when I try to describe it beyond that. But I would like also to note the packaging, including a copy of an allegedly real drug prescription signed by Dr. Nick. I've gotten threatening looks from people who saw me carrying this on the street, but whoever put the album together is an Elvis fan through and through, and so is anybody who listens to it as often as he does to the Sun sides. As the great man himself declares at one point in the album, "Hot damn tamale."

Rare Rock 'n' Roll, Vol. 1 (English MCA/Coral). Cultural confusion reigns on this anthology in which rockabillys like Roy Hall and Billy Lee Riley rub elbows with rockabilly-influenced blues and R & B shouters like Danny Oliver ("Sapphire" sounds like a country Little Richard) while fending off people who don't belong here at all (it takes more than a title like "Baby Let's Rock" to convince me that Bob Wills ever did anything even remotely close to rockabilly or rock 'n' roll).

Charlie Rich: *20 Golden Hits* (Sun). Charlie Rich was the Sun sophisticate, an Arkansas farmboy who swore by Stan Kenton, Count Basie, and Dave Brubeck. He had only one hit ("Lonely Weekends" in 1960) for Phillips International, the Sun subsidiary. Still, he made lots of jazz-flavored records that didn't chart but today sound as good as ever. If you were going to limit yourself to one Rich album, this would be the one—but you'd be missing out on too much of this man's singular gifts if you limited yourself to just one. (Be sure to avoid Sun's *Best of Charlie Rich*, which offers half these songs at the same cost.)

Charlie Rich: *Lonely Weekends* (Sun). The title song is a must, of course. But there's also Charlie's brooding "Who Will the Next Fool Be," a blues covered by everyone from Bobby Bland to the Amazing Rhythm Aces, "Sittin' and Thinkin'," his tortured boozer's plea, and "Break-Up," which shows that, jazz phrasing aside, the man can handle a straight-ahead rocker as easily as the next guy. By the way, he wrote all four of 'em.

Charlie Rich: *Fully Realized* (Mercury). In the early sixties, Charlie cut *The Many New Sides of Charlie Rich* and *The Best Years* for Smash/Mercury. They both went out of print, but were repackaged together into this double album when Rich hit in the mid-seventies. It has since also been dropped from the catalog, but it's not that hard to find, and worth any effort. These represent the only sessions Rich ever did that he himself was satisfied with, and his pride in them is justifiable. The first one in particular presents us with a white soul singer of rare power, depth, and subtlety, from the novelty hit "Mohair Sam" to the tongue-in-cheek blues of "Down and Out" and "Everything I Do Is Wrong" to the overpowering "I Can't Go On," a piece of orchestral rock that would do Phil Spector proud. *Best Years* isn't quite as sturdy, but "You Can Have Her" is no-nonsense rockabilly, and both Rich's voice and piano are absolutely unique to country or country-rock. More than any other records, these back up the claims that Rich was simply too talented in too many ways to ever fit into an easy record-biz niche.

Billy Lee Riley: *Legendary Sun Performers* (British Charly). Billy Lee was the Little Richard of the label—everything he did was hard, fast, and loud. His two best-known records in that vein were "Flyin' Saucers Rock 'n' Roll" and "Red Hot" (first recorded for Sun by R & B singer Billy Emerson). Why he never made it is something of a mystery, for nearly everything else was in the same frantic mold and his stage show was legendary. If you think Riley didn't have the feeling, just listen to his secularization of the famous spiritual "I'm gonna slip on my boppin' shoes/Down by the riverside!"

Rock Rock Rock (Dutch White Label). This features some of the best known of the unknown rockabilly singers. Foremost is Herschel Almond, who checks in with "Let's Get It On," with its vicious, twisting guitar, "I Love You Baby," which starts raucous and descends delightfully into pure noise, and the ominous "Looking for a Woman." The other outstanding cut is the insinuating, accusatory "What I Learned About You" by Jeanne Caine, one of the few women to sing rockabilly convincingly.

Rockabilly Stars, Volume 1 (Epic). This is very patchy, though *Volume 2* is much worse. You'd think CBS could find enough real rockabilly in its vaults to do things right, but I guess not, and commercial considerations dictated that the label also include recent rockabilly-inspired cuts or cuts by former rockabillys in addition to real rockabilly and the hillbilly boogie that so often finds its way onto these compilations. Among the cuts making this worthwhile are the early "The Sun Keeps Shining," an appropriately bright-sounding effort from the Everly Brothers' first session in 1955; the real winners in the kiddie sweepstakes, however, were the Collins kids, Larry (who was eleven when the team signed to Columbia in 1955) and Lorrie (who was thirteen). Much of their material was boogie, the novelty being that it was done by kids, but "Party" rocks out smartly. Finally, there's Charlie Rich's unaccompanied version of "I Feel Like Going Home," the existence of which Billy Sherrill had until now been denying ever since the pair cut it in 1972; a version with full Sherrill treatment was released as a B-side in 1973, but it can't begin to touch the impact of just Charlie's voice and craggy piano on this moving ballad of pride and defeat. Neither can anything else Rich cut with Sherrill. Or anything else on this album, though there are also performances from Little Jimmy Dickens, Carl Perkins, Link Wray, Ersel Hickey, Bob Luman, Johnny Cash, and others.

Rockabilly Stars, Volume Three (Epic). This has more real rockabilly on it than either of its predecessors, but the highlights are still the cuts that fall between the cracks—stuff like Little Jimmy Dickens "Hillbilly

Fever" (cut in 1950 with a honky-tonk band and a beefy guitar solo that's pure rockabilly years ahead of its time), the original, oh-so-cool finger-poppin' version of "Tobacco Road" (by John D. Loudermilk, who wrote it), and the dry country humor of white-blues throwback Jimmy Murphy.

The Roots of Rock, Vol. 4: Cotton City Country (British Charly). Primarily pre-rockabilly Sun country, though a few later tunes turn up as well. Most of the strongest cuts, oddly enough, are by country singers about to become rockabilly singers, e.g., Carl Perkins with "Sweethearts or Strangers," Jerry Lee Lewis with "It All Depends (on Who Will Buy the Wine)," and Johnny Cash with a previously unissued take of "Come in Stranger."

The Roots of Rock, Vol. 5: Rebel Rockabilly (British Charly). Ray Harris freaks out on "Lonely Wolf," one of those totally off-the-wall cuts that not only couldn't have come from anywhere except Sun, but probably couldn't have come even from Sun except on those weird occasions when conditions were just right. Nothing else here is quite that startling, though it does offer some surprising names (Narvel Felts, Gene Simmons) along with lesser-known songs from Sun stalwarts (Jerry Lee, Billy Lee Riley, Sonny Burgess, etc.). Together, they give an accurate picture of the rockabilly underbelly.

Jack Scott: *Jack Scott Rocks* (Dutch Rock 'n' Roll). Scott is another rockabilly whose cult has always been bigger than his talent. But "The Way I Walk" has certifiable bopcat style, and "Leroy" tries hard, too. Of the many Scott collections on the market, this is the biggest (twenty tracks) and the best.

Warren Smith: *Legendary Sun Performers* (British Charly). Like many others in Memphis, Smith was ultimately more comfortable with country than with rockabilly; even here, his roots show. But the touch of restraint he thus brought to songs like "Rock 'n' Roll Ruby" or "Red Cadillac and a Black Moustache" actually benefitted the finished records, and "Ubangi Stomp" is a full-blown rockabilly fantasy springing to life. Plus, "Tonight Will Be the Last Night" is Memphis country at its tautest and most economical.

Starday-Dixie Rockabilly, Volume 1 (Gusto). These fifties sides were released only regionally in most cases, and the accent is on Texas and Louisiana. Sonny Fisher is the best of the lot, but "Groovey" Joe Poovey and Rudy "Tutti" Grayzell are fascinating if only because they are so totally obsessed with the language of rockabilly. You'll find the complete hepcat's glossary in such songs as "Ducktail," "Ten Long Fingers (on 88 Keys)," and "Jig-Ga-Lee-Ga."

Starday-Dixie Rockabilly, Volume Two (Gusto). I'm as fascinated by this album as I am by its predecessor, and for the same reasons. Link Davis, Thumper Jones (really George Jones under a *nom du rock),* and Benny Joy are all passable rockabilly singers, but Sonny Fisher, who has a real feeling for the blues, is the only one here with anything approaching inspiration. Yet the slavishness with which these men approach every rockabilly vocal fillip, and their determination to work every bit of slang they can into their lyrics, attest to the power the music initially hit with, and to the way it fired imaginations and made converts overnight.

Sun Rockabillies, Volume One (Sun). None of these sixteen sides were released in the fifties, when they were originally recorded. (Does that make "failure" the "theme" of this album?) I have no idea why, since so many of them kick and scream as well as the performances that did find their way onto record. Junior Thompson, for example, is one of the toughest rockabilly singers never to have a record released by Sun (most of his good stuff is on Meteor; this album includes "How Come You Do Me"), and Smokey Joe Baugh does a passable Big Joe Turner imitation on "Listen to Me, Baby." Hayden Thompson pulls out all the stops for "Fairlane Rock," while about half of side two, especially the opening cuts by Ray Smith and Edwin Bruce, sounds like tributes to Jerry Lee.

Ten Years Collector Records (Dutch Collector/White Label). Has anybody out there figured out where these Dutchmen keep *finding* all these obscure rockabilly records? Certainly their collectors-mania willingness to issue anything has resulted in a bunch of unnecessary albums, but this is one of their most consistent *and* one of their most unique, and the artists, as usual, are virtually unheard of except by those who've found their work on other Collector anthologies. The Lonesome Drifter does a pretty good Jerry Lee (especially on "Eager Boy") and Billy Wayne and the Jackson Boys leave better-known rockabillys in the dust.

Transfusion (British Pacific). Anthology of rarities including weak Conway Twitty, strong Al Downing. Nervous Norvus lives up to his name, while Vince Taylor and the Playboys' "Brand New Cadillac" is about as close as the British ever came to getting rockabilly right. But the real capper is Robbie Robertson's monstrous guitar solo on Ronnie Hawkins' version of "Little Red Rooster" (a/k/a "The Rooster Song," a Louisiana swamp blues).

Conway Twitty: *Greatest Hits* (Polydor). As a rockabilly singer, Conway wasn't all that much different than as a country singer. In fact, though rockers turn up on the odd anthology, his hits are almost all ballads that keep his hic intact but don't have the sense of dynamics—of buildup, and of tension and release—that his later work has. Still, a teen balladeer this blue will never go unrewarded, and besides, Conway was much more in tune with real blues than was the average teen balladeer.

Gene Vincent and the Blue Caps: *Rock 'n' Roll Legend* (French Capitol). With his limp (a result of a Korean War accident) and his leer (a result of an overactive libido), Gene Vincent of Norfolk, Virginia, was one of the few rockabillys fit to wear Presley's black leather jacket. He was also a closet schlockmeister. He got his break by winning a contest to find an Elvis sound-alike; the result was the 1956 hit "Be-Bop-a-Lula," which many people (including Presley's mom) thought at first was Elvis. Vincent was more overtly sexual than Elvis—especially with his lyrics—and his vocal style consisted of a series of slurs, moans, hics, and humping noises that went far enough to get him busted at least once for public lewdness. Gene racked up a good string of hits through the rest of the fifties, but when rock went limp he was unable (or unwilling) to make the transition into pop or country like Elvis, Jerry Lee, Perkins, Conway, and the rest. So he fell into limbo, continuing to work Europe and mount the occasional U.S. comeback right up to his death in 1971. His guitarist, Cliff Gallup, proved almost as influential as Gene himself to future rock generations. This four-record set tells you everything you ever wanted to know, and then some, about Vincent, from the hit singles to smut like "Woman Love" to schmaltz like "Over the Rainbow."

Gene Vincent and His Blue Caps: *The Bop That Just Won't Stop (1956)* (Capitol). As usual, the Europeans have it all over us in the rockabilly department, though by concentrating on his most productive year and including a couple of previously unissued songs, this qualifies as the best single-album reissue domestically. Unless you're a Gene Vincent fanatic, this should be all you need.

THE
NASHVILLE
SOUND

The Nashville Sound was country music's response to rockabilly. If the kids were going to desert country entirely, the reasoning went, then the music would be softened up to attract new listeners from outside, as well as to hold on to the older fans who'd been country all along. Like country people, country music was moving to the suburbs—out went the fiddles and pedal steels and high harmony voices, and in came string sections and vocal choirs. The music became so easygoing and free of any kind of tension that if it weren't for the lead singers, you could hardly tell it was country—and sometimes even the singers went bland, removed the nasal twang from their voices.

At least that's what the Nashville Sound meant when it rose to prominence in the fifties. Through the sixties, as Nashville was growing into a recording center to rival Los Angeles and New York, the term came to apply not to a specific sound so much as to a specific way of making records. At a time when public taste seemed to change daily, those who made their livings by meeting that public taste were now attempting to impose some sense of order on it.

The Nashville Sound was really the creation of a small number of people. In the mid-fifties a group of Nashville's most advanced pickers used to jam at the Carousel Club in Printer's Alley. Among them were guitarist Chet Atkins, bassist Bob Moore, guitarist Hank "Sugarfoot" Garland, pianist Floyd Cramer, drummer Buddy Harmon, guitarist Grady Martin, and saxophonist Boots Randolph. (Notice there's not a fiddler or a steel player in the bunch.) The music these men eased into had a relaxed flow to it, a soft and loose beat that was a little like jazz; it swung, but ever so gingerly.

Meanwhile, an industry was growing in Nashville. Record companies found it convenient to open branch offices there, where the talent was, and next they opened studios. Society bandleader Owen Bradley had been hired in 1947 to run the Decca (known today as MCA) operation, and in 1952 he also opened the town's first recording studio. Atkins, who'd become an all-purpose troubleshooter at RCA after his own solo recording career failed to take off, began heading up that label's operations in late 1957. Both men would have been called producers, had such a term existed then, and both went on to become top-ranking officers within their respective companies.

Basically, they took the soft sound Atkins was getting with his jamming buddies and put it on record. There were superficial differences between their styles. Atkins, who was a fan of pop and classical music as well as country, used lots of strings and horns on his records; Bradley favored background vocal choirs (from the Jordanaires or the Anita Kerr Singers.) Both wound up making lush records that sounded as much like pre-rock pop as like country. Atkins did his most fully realized work with Jim Reeves, and Bradley with Patsy Cline.

With the success of the Nashville Sound, studios began popping up all over town. In the late fifties, Nashville had two full-fledged recording studios. By 1970 there were dozens. This period also marked the rise of the sideman. In recording towns like L.A. and New York, each studio had its own sidemen to play on the records recorded there. But in Nashville, a floating pool of sidemen functioned like hired guns, moving from studio to studio, recording behind anybody and everybody. They'd known each other for years, having played together at the Opry, in local clubs, or in road bands. They could anticipate each other's moves.

Their job was to work out a backing track—more like a cushion, actually—that neatly framed the lead singer without calling attention to itself. There was no flashy soloing on Nashville Sound records, though occasionally a picker was called on to take a short, sympathetic break. Since they had worked together so much in the past, these sidemen were able to improvise arrangements quickly, by ear, without use of sheet music. (These are known as "head arrangements," and are common in other forms of music, too.) Once the sidemen had put down the basic track, the producer could "sweeten" it by overdubbing strings, horns, background choruses, or whatever else he wanted.

This stepped-up output created the need for more new songs. Enter the professional songwriter, another new breed, who operated under a code nearly as strict as the sideman's. For example, as women were perceived to be the major buyers of country records, the rule for a songwriter was to "always put the woman on a pedestal." Love songs went best with the smooth, polished sound of the records; but if a man lost his woman, it was always strictly his own fault. The sentimentality that was once applied to mom or the little cabin in the hills now became identified almost entirely with relations between the sexes. These songwriters felt less nostalgia for the old days, even if they did still uphold simple values. They presented an idealized view of life, but when it went wrong, they weren't ashamed to cry in their beer.

What all this meant is that music in Music City U.S.A. was being taken away from musicians and turned over to producers. The producer chose the song and the pickers, and told the singer how to sing it. Once overdubbing became more feasible, it wasn't unusual for a singer to come to his own session and be presented with a finished track; all that was left was for him to put his vocals on, and then the record would be ready for release. For the producer, who thus knew exactly what he'd be getting before each session even began, this system was efficient and economical. It also had most of the properties of an assembly line, and pretty soon the music started sounding like it; every record coming out of Nashville seemed to be exactly the same—bland, gutless, lacking in personality and character.

There was minor rebellion. Thanks to pressure from Texas and Bakersfield, honky-tonk made something of a comeback in the early sixties. Once again, it was acceptable to highlight steel or fiddle on a country record. So different singers and producers began getting different sounds, and now the whole idea behind building a career was to find a successful formula and stick with it. Records were still being made the same way, though, by a small group of session men and producers working out head arrangements in the studio and then overdubbing the rest later. So the Nashville Sound was now actually several sounds; the term now referred to just about every record coming out of Nashville, and what it really described was not what the records sounded like, but the system that was used to record them. And once again, it all started sounding the same.

Not that this bothered record companies. The country music industry enjoyed unprecedented growth during this period. The Nashville Sound had achieved its goal: Older fans appreciated the new "sophistication," while many who in the past had scorned country now found it more palatable (i.e., less "hick") than before. The country audience (like country producers) seemed to *want* to know in advance what it would be getting, seemed to discourage invention and innovation in its performers. Records and singers were now crossing over to the pop charts with regularity, rather than every once in a while, and that's where the really big money was.

This whole rigid system peaked under Billy Sherrill, the head of CBS Records in Nashville and a producer who devised the lushest sound yet during the late sixties and early seventies. Sherrill didn't push fiddles and steel aside entirely, he simply dwarfed them with orchestras and background voices. Somehow, it was soothing and bombastic at the same time, and that was the whole idea. Country music was now inextricably a cultural force in the modern world, though getting there turned out to have fostered so much resentment that a whole new generation of rebels would soon step forward.

Patsy Cline: *The Patsy Cline Story* (MCA).

The Nashville Sound may have been invented for Patsy Cline, but that was only one of her accomplishments. Though preceded on the charts by Kitty Wells and others, Patsy was the first woman singer to achieve full-fledged stardom on her own, building a solo career rather than appearing as the female attraction on a male star's package show. That career was cut short by a plane crash, but the high points fill this double album (although some of these songs have the original vocals but new backing tracks).

"I Fall to Pieces" and "Crazy" provide the cornerstones. The first has an austere intro of chiming guitar, with piano and faint steel in the background. Patsy sounds both incredulous and sorrowful as she describes her inability to cope without her man; the breathy vocals build with the song, putting different emphasis on each word as the background singers creep in. Unlike most country singers, Patsy can stretch words without breaking her voice, and both her phrasing and breath control on the song are incredibly precise. On "Crazy" she's given backing of a lilting piano, strings, and guitar; the vocal chorus deepens the record this time rather than cutting her off, and a Texas blues guitar plays razor-sharp fills around her devastated phrasing.

She recorded when the Nashville Sound really was a sound, and Patsy's sure, smooth, and supple voice provided a perfect pop foil. She sounded like a softer Kay Starr, or a Patti Page with wisdom and experience. Patsy was the inspiration for Loretta Lynn, but today her records sound more like the roots of Crystal Gayle, Loretta's pop-star sister. Patsy's records sold both pop and country, and had she not been a robust, outgoing southern woman, she would likely have been considered strictly a pop singer.

She was born Virginia Patterson Hensley in 1932 in Winchester, Virginia. In 1948 she made her first trip to Nashville, but went home discouraged after only a few club dates. In 1957 she won an "Arthur Godfrey Talent Scout" show singing "Walking After Midnight." Her subsequent record of the song, a light, shuffling beat punctuated by clenched little sobs of pain from the singer, went onto the pop and country charts. Though she opted for country by basing herself in Nashville, she made it clear she was not your average "girl singer."

She'd caused something of a scandal in her small hometown, and seemed to carry the stigma with her to Music City. Though basically an irrepressible optimist, there were bouts of surliness and the kind of aggressive behavior considered unladylike by her peers. She was not above drinking and carrying on in public, and her love life could be turbulent. She wore her makeup loud and her sweaters tight. When she didn't like someone, she might just tell them so. She was also friendly and helpful toward every new "girl singer" (as they were then known) who came to town.

All of this came out in her music. The songs added up to a persona not wholly unlike that of other country women: Patsy Cline's inchoate yearnings for a better life, in the end, defined that as meaning "a good man." But she clearly had a much more complex understanding of the possibilities and the limits involved. And if she could not always say exactly what she felt, she did always manage to get it between the lines.

She could be pensive and resigned, as on "She's Got You." On "Strange," she faces her seemingly unreal predicament philosophically, and something similar happens on "Your Cheatin' Heart." Her reading of the song has none of Hank Williams' vengeance; instead, there's an almost cosmic sense of regret that suggests she's not really taking things *too* personally, but feels both partners are acting out roles in some eternally recurring play. But she can still wail about "When tears come down," and at the end, she gets right sassy.

On "Leavin' on Your Mind" she's seductive, though she seems to realize it's in vain; she doesn't want this man to leave, but figures he will anyhow, so what she's most emphatic about is the need to get it over with right now. "So Wrong" is another incredulous triangle song with Patsy wondering again how she could get herself into such a jam, while at the same time knowing the answer to her own question and being both awed and amused by it.

She also had a much firmer grasp of irony than most Nashville singers, and she liked having the last laugh, as she does literally on "Imagine That." This is one of her most underrated performances, a catalog of what she does most convincingly. Her voice breaks all over the first line to emphasize her wistfulness, but when she sings "I can't help it," she isn't crying out in frustration. She's making a simple and straightforward statement about a bad situation, attempting to work things out without soliciting fake sympathy. But she also knows it won't work, so the song drips with sarcasm.

Patsy Cline sang country torch songs, the opening "Heartaches" being a perfect example. Pop touches dominated her records—the background voices on "She's Got You"; the way her voice swells up with the strings on "Leavin' on Your Mind" or "Wayward Wind"; the organ playing where the fiddles should be on "South of the Border"; the way violins and understated swing on "San Antonio Rose" win out over the steel guitar. But it worked both ways. "Foolin' Around" is ostensibly a pop song, but it's a country music motif that prevails. "A Poor Man's Roses" announces itself with a grandiose violin section, but it's really the female version of "Mansion on the Hill," with Patsy choosing love over wealth. "Sweet Dreams," a posthumous hit, made a pop single out of a country song, and her voice takes a quirky catch not found in other singers of either style. In the end, Patsy Cline created a pop-country continuum that was the white equivalent to Billie Holiday's pop-blues fusion.

She was country because she called herself country, even if it meant she had to say one thing and mean another in order to survive in what was still strictly a man's world. At the height of her crossover popularity, she joined the Opry when she could have been cracking New York and Las Vegas. She sang the songs of Willie Nelson, Don Gibson, Hank Williams, and Floyd Tillman. And she didn't strip the country soul from them so much as she gave them a new dimension. When she died young in a 1963 plane crash, country music lost one of its few genuine path-breakers. Her admission in 1973 to the Hall of Fame didn't come a bit too soon.

Don Gibson: *The Best of Don Gibson* (RCA).

If there was a time when Otis Redding was unquestionably the Mr. Pitiful of soul music, there was a time too when Don Gibson held the title of Mr. Loneliness in country music. He staked out that turf and explored it thoroughly in the late fifties and early sixties, and what makes the analogies to Redding even more apt is that Don Gibson was nothing if not a white soul singer. His voice brimmed with so much conviction that even when he was saddled with the densest background voices in the history of the Nashville Sound, he cut through them like a hot knife through butter. Gibson was one of the first to get the full Nashville Sound treatment, and as this album, which is out of print but not too hard to find, illustrates, his records to this day are among the few on which the singer sounds neither shackled nor *too* comfortable with the soft new pop intrusions.

So it's ironic that when Gibson first came to Nashville he was accepted only as a writer, and that today he is remembered primarily as a writer. His songs have been covered by artists as diverse as Ray Charles (who did the early-sixties version of "I Can't Stop Loving You" that introduced country music to a new audience after Kitty Wells had had a 1958 country hit with the same song) and Ronnie Milsap (who made "(I'd Be) A Legend in My Time" a country hit in the early eighties, about two decades after Gibson cut the original), Neil Young (who did an agonizingly slow version of "Oh Lonesome Me" in 1970), and Tracy Nelson (who turned in a fine interpretation of "Blue Blue Day" the same year), Faron Young (who gave Gibson his first hit as a writer with the 1956 "Sweet Dreams"), and Emmylou Harris (who gave him one of his last with her 1976 cover of the same song).

Gibson was born in 1928 in Shelby, North Carolina, the southwestern part of the state, which spawned a number of traditional country stars. A professional musician at fourteen, by the end of WW II he was in Knoxville, holding down spots on the WNOX Tennessee Barn Dance and on the Mid-Day Merry-Go-Round. From there he went on to Nashville, and Young's hit with "Sweet Dreams" led to a recording contract for Gibson. Though his mountain string-band roots held forth during the Knoxville years, his first Nashville records (such as "Give Myself a Party") were in more of a honky-tonk vein. But in 1958, Chet Atkins took over as his producer and the first record they cut together was the two-sided hit "Oh Lonesome Me" b/w "I Can't Stop Loving You," which soared to No. 1.

The latter set the tone for Gibson's ballads. There's a slack guitar intro before a fat, full band comes in. At first, the piano (usually Floyd Cramer) plays a repeated line over and over, then the guitar starts doing the same. They provide the kind of deceptively simple, catchy instrumental hooks that became a Gibson/Atkins trademark. The vocal choir is not as obtrusive as it would later become, but Gibson's own deep voice is pensive and melancholy, full of yearning.

Likewise, "Oh Lonesome Me" proved typical of his up-tempo songs. The intro is played on an acoustic guitar, but it's more emphatic, stroked firmly and quickly. It has almost a rockabilly feel—which makes Gibson the only artist at the time integrating that into the Nashville Sound, rather than running scared from it—while the echo on his voice and Atkins' jolting, bluesy electric guitar break accent the mood.

Acoustic guitar was more prominent than electric on many of Gibson's records, and when steel guitar was used at all, it was barely noticeable. Gibson's phrasing became surprisingly sophisticated for a man who began as a pure mountain vocalist. On "(I'd Be) A Legend in My Time," which was inexplicably never a hit for him, he compares favorably with Elvis as a ballad singer. On "It's My Way" and "It's a Sin" he croons and quavers like a more rootsy Marty Robbins, and the Latin-flavored guitar on the latter—and also on "I Think It's Better (to Forget

Me)"—suggest that perhaps Atkins wished to make Gibson into his label's version of Robbins, who was then one of Nashville's brightest stars. But Gibson was too morose, too blue, too lacking in Robbins' sweetness, ever to play that role.

But it's doubtful that a Marty Robbins could handle something as hard-edged and potent as Gibson's "Sea of Heartbreak," either. Though one of the few Gibson hits he didn't write himself, this is one of the most emotional pieces of singing to come out of Nashville during those years. The 1961 song, carried by propulsive piano and bass, climaxes Gibson's experiment with pop-rockabilly, and though the background voices are mixed high and all over the record, Gibson manages to overpower them by shifting back and forth from drawn-out to rapid-fire phrasing. Thus does he transform one of the oldest metaphors in music into something fresh and urgent once again.

But then it's a subject he seemed to know well, as his song titles alone indicate. Even his hymns ("God Walks These Hills with Me" and "Where No One Stands Alone") are about the need for companionship, and Gibson best summed up his own feeling with the ironic, self-lacerating words he wrote in "(I'd Be) A Legend In My Time." "If loneliness meant world acclaim," he sings as though he doesn't even recognize the irony, "Then everyone would know my name/I'd be a legend in my time."

Loretta Lynn: *Greatest Hits* (MCA).

When Loretta Lynn began singing professionally in 1961, country music had produced but two major female stars: Patsy Cline, with her bittersweet country-pop stylings, and Kitty Wells, with her hard-country admonitions. Loretta had trouble at first because she sounded so much like Wells. By the time she began recording for a major label (Decca, now MCA, in 1962), she was singing more like Cline, though her arrangements were mainstream country. But curiously, after a couple of records, she went back to her earlier singing influence, Wells, even as the music itself became slightly more poppish à la Cline. Meanwhile, the themes of her songs were also evolving, as she moved from "girl singer" songs to something more tough-minded and self-sufficient. This can all be traced on singles released from 1962 to 1967 and collected here.

Thanks to *Coal Miner's Daughter* (the title respectively of a hit single, an album, a best-selling book, and finally a top-grossing movie), her story is well known. She was born in the mid-thirties (she refuses to say when) and raised in Butcher's Hollow, Kentucky, a mountain area where contact with the outside world was minimal. At fourteen, she entered into a thankless and one-sided marriage; by the time she was eighteen, she had four kids and still knew virtually nothing about sex. Her husband encouraged her—coerced her, some would say—to start singing in local clubs, and in 1961, by which time they were living in Washington, she had a national hit on a tiny northwestern label. She went to Nashville and has enjoyed steady hits for the last two decades.

By the time Loretta became a star, she was well into her mid-twenties, sufficient time for a strong self-image to have formed. She'd already left her family and moved across the nation; however adept she'd been at presenting herself as a wholly innocent mountain girl, she *had* seen and experienced more than those women singers who'd never left their native regions until they began touring.

Yet in the beginning, probably because she was so anxious to please the Nashville people who'd taken over her career, her music reflected none of this; instead, she fit herself into the "girl singer" mold. "Success," her first Decca single, had a hard-country arrangement built around steel and fiddle, but Loretta's vocal is as smooth, as close to Patsy Cline, as she can get, with the echo ironing out some of the mountain harshness she can't remove herself. The story is a warning common in country songs: Girl from poor background marries man from rich background, watches helplessly as marriage is torn apart by his business.

By 1965, melodies (on songs like "Blue Kentucky Girl") are much more modern-sounding, while the instrumentation remains pure Nashville country. But on a song like "The Home You're Tearing Down," Loretta phrases with an exaggerated backwoods twang she'd worked hard to hide just a couple of years earlier. The combination finally gives her a winning formula for modern country, and within another year she's singing a whole new type of song. This was first hinted at, though, in 1964, with "Wine Women and Song" and "Happy Birthday," two sarcastic jabs at promiscuous husbands not unlike Mooney, Loretta's own. Here's where the Kitty Wells influence figured biggest.

Until Kitty's "It Wasn't God Who Made Honky Tonk Angels" in 1952, women in country music were a passive, pliable lot. Women performers worked solely under the guidance of men. Women in songs stayed home, took care of the kids and the household, and asked no questions or made no demands of their husbands. Women who did otherwise were considered tramps if their existence was acknowledged at all. But "It Wasn't God Who Made Honky Tonk Angels" asserted that "bad" women were often made that way by "bad" men. Wells deserted that stance after the one record. But Loretta was in her mid- to late teens when "It Wasn't God Who Made Honky Tonk Angels" hit, and it was a theme she well understood.

So in a song like "Don't Come Home A'Drinkin' (with Lovin' on Your Mind)," she warned her husband that he could drink or have her, but not both at the same time. The catch is that he can continue to have them both as long as he keeps them separate. Loretta is still very much committed to traditional ideas about marriage and family; she just wants to make them work better. And if that means tolerating double standards, she is willing to do so up to a point. For that matter, when she can no longer tolerate them, she'll take her anger out on the Other Woman (as in "You Ain't Woman Enough") rather than on the guilty man. This is not a very sisterly attitude, though in future songs Loretta will alter it. For now, her undeniable spunk and sass are still in the service of enforcing traditional roles—but that they are there at all is a big step forward for country music.

Loretta Lynn: *Greatest Hits, Volume II* (MCA).

Here's where Loretta's record company betrays her. *Volume II* includes hits from 1968 to 1973. Inexplicably, it ignores several top ten hits (including two that went to No. 1) from that period in favor of two songs that weren't hits at all. Three of the missing hits are included, however, on 1970's *Loretta Writes 'Em and Sings 'Em,* a sparkling collection of originals that is the equal of this but repeats one song from *Volume I* of her greatest hits and three more from here. The solution would have been to cover these five productive years solely with two comprehensive volumes of hits. That way we'd get "I Know How" (Loretta at her sauciest) and "You Wanna Give Me a Lift" (Loretta at her sassiest) from *Writes 'Em* and such uncollected hit singles as "Woman of the World," "Here I Am Again," and "Rated X," in addition to the hits already on this album such as "Wings Upon Your Horns," "One's On the Way," and "Coal Miner's Daughter."

But as those last three titles indicate, this one stands easily enough on its own. It offers a cross section of Loretta's triumphs as she climbed toward the CMA's Entertainer of the Year award (the first woman so honored) in 1972. It covers an era when she took up self-mythologizing on a larger scale. And often enough, her non-hits during this period are as good as anyone else's hits.

That includes relatively slight material like "Ain't It Funny," which contrasts the innocence of childhood with the worries of adulthood, or "What Sundown Does to You" and "Hey Loretta," two imitation-Loretta tunes that she actually transforms into vehicles almost as personal as the first-rate songs.

"Wings Upon Your Horns," in which the singer gives up her virginity to a man who then spurns her love, may be her best ever. Loretta claims that when she wrote this in 1969 she was thinking solely of the Bible—of Satan and angels—and that the erotic overtones escaped her entirely. (Yeah, sure, and her later "When the Tingle Becomes a Chill"

is about autumn turning into winter. . . .) But it's that very clash between the biblical and the purely carnal that makes this so powerful,
and she re-emphasizes it as often as she can—in the churchy arrangement, in her voice (which reeks of shame), and in her phrasing ("You're
the first to ever make me [long pause] fall in love and then not take
me.")

"Fist City" and "Your Squaw's On the Warpath" catch Loretta
making a crucial transition. The first is aimed at the Other Woman, and
is raucous and filled with neat internal rhymes; it's also so wildly over-
stated that nobody but Loretta could get away with it. The latter is full
of fire and angry threats, marred only by a cutesy male chorus, and is
aimed directly at the man who's wronged her. Both these songs declare
that there's now no turning back for country women in terms of what
they can and can't say.

Having made that point, she moved into other areas. And the more
blatantly autobiographical her songs became, the more she identified
with her female audience. "You're Looking at Country" (1971) uses a
dobro and vaguely old-timey arrangement to second its emotion; it's
both sly and proud, Loretta romanticizing the heritage she shares with
her fans. "Coal Miner's Daughter," her calling card from 1970, manages
to capsulize the hardships and deprivations of her childhood and make
them sound idyllic—in fact, it makes them sound *too* idyllic, but that is
how she makes the hardships and deprivations faced by her audience
that much more endurable. (It also suggests that anyone can rise above
such handicaps, a message crucial to this audience.)

This identification with the listeners is something all country singers pay lip service to, but if more could actually do it, you can be sure
more would. Sometimes Loretta strains too hard for effect (saying she
was "borned" a coal miner's daughter rather than "born"), but the
warmth, wit, and guilelessness of her singing always bails her out. In
"One's On the Way," she deals with the common plight of blue-collar
women (rather than their differences, as she would have done a few
years earlier). To the Topeka housewife who has to raise kids while the
husband's out drinking with old Army buddies, the D.C. social scene has
no relevance whatsoever, and feminism is a luxury only urban intellectuals can enjoy. Meeting the immediate needs of her family takes every
minute this woman has. But singing for these women is itself an intense
act of sisterhood, if not feminism, and Loretta is singing for these
women just as surely as these women are living for their husbands and
kids—despite the fact that with her wealth and fame, Loretta by now
probably has much in common with the society women she dismisses so
disdainfully. It's not easy to continue identifying with a working-class
audience when you've risen above it yourself. But Loretta succeeds in

her music at least partly because she succeeds in continuing to identify with precisely that audience.

Johnny Cash: *At Folsom Prison* (Columbia).

Recorded in January of 1968, this album marked Johnny Cash's return to the fold after nearly a decade of disenchantment; it is also one of the few albums in country music history that was considered an Event in itself. With this one, Johnny Cash lived up to his image(s)—all of them.

According to legend cultivated by Cash and his image-makers, the sixties were his dog years, nearly a whole decade lost to amphetamine psychosis. The truth is probably more complicated, for in spite of his monumentally self-destructive personal habits during this period, Cash managed to stay productive. Almost as soon as he joined Columbia, he put the teen ballads behind him and began stressing country songs. At the same time, he kept his youth appeal by acknowledging Bob Dylan and the folk-music crowd then growing on American campuses. He also broadened his base by reaching back deeper into his own roots. All this made perfect sense, for Cash had always had more than a little of the folkie in him, and the result, as writer Frederick E. Danker has noted, was an ambitious series of albums that proved successful both artistically and commercially. *Ride This Train* was his salute to the railroads, *Blood, Sweat and Tears* to the working man, *Bitter Tears* to the American Indian, and *Ballads of the True West* to frontier myths and realities. All four of these albums were uncanny in their ability to appeal to both folk-music and country-music devotees, but as much as Cash welcomed this, you can't say it was solely calculation; country music itself had once been folk music, and Cash was one of the few who remembered that.

His output may have been erratic (as it had been even at Sun, don't forget), but his best singles from this era—records like "Ring of Fire" (1963) and "Understand Your Man" (1964)—were also his best sellers. But as the decade wore on, the songs were increasingly lightweight, and Cash's performances increasingly desultory. "The One On the Right Is On the Left," "Everybody Loves a Nut," and "Boa Constrictor" were the kind of novelties that Cash had previously used as filler; in 1966 they comprised three of his four singles. Cash was losing interest in his own career.

It's hard to tell exactly what happened next. The legend (which led to his induction into the Hall of Fame in 1980) holds that when he fell in love with June Carter, he found the strength to kick pills "just like that," and immediately was born again. For a man as thoughtful, and as restless, as Cash, there was probably much more soul-searching, doubts that had to be defeated—but realities like that only confuse legend, and legend alone is what we're left with.

Until this album came along, that is. Because it added a new dimension to the legend, brought it to life in a way that everybody could see. At the time, young radicals saw Cash as a sort of modern-day Woody Guthrie, and he remained strong among working people as well. In that blood-filled year of 1968, Johnny Cash was undoubtedly the only man in America who could count among his friends both Richard Nixon and Bob Dylan, the two symbols of an ever-widening social gap. And now Cash was embracing yet another outgroup, prisoners, who struck a common chord in both the opposing factions. Were there no limits to his empathy? This was a p.r. man's dream.

But p.r. is manufactured, and some phenomenon—such as the rapport Johnny Cash enjoys with the inmates of Folsom Prison—can't be faked. From the opening cut, a version of his old favorite "Folsom Prison Blues," with the band bearing down harder than usual, this album is all rapport. Quite simply, Cash identifies with these inmates and they with him. His own prison experience was much less than his legend suggested, but he still knew, either instinctively or because it was important enough for him to have thought it out, about the regrets, casual violence, camaraderie, hopelessness, and stultifying boredom inside those walls. He carried that knowledge like it was a burden he'd been bearing forever, and the inmates could look at the lines and crevices of his "lived-in" face (as June Carter described it so perfectly) and hear his battered voice struggling to get down from baritone to bass, and they knew he was singing for them as well as to them.

How else would Cash know that he could sit on a stool with just his acoustic guitar and do "Dirty Old Egg-Sucking Dog" and "Flushed from the Bathroom of Your Heart," the two most intentionally silly songs Jack Clement ever wrote, and these men would roar with approval? How else could he make wisecracks about the condemned man in "The Long Black Veil" and draw appreciative laughter in return? That's called gallows humor, and it's not something convicts will freely share with just anyone.

June Carter is magnificent, a gutsy shouter in synch with the blues, on her duet with Cash of "Jackson." Cash's humor, like his singing, is always respectful, often nervous and self-effacing. His voice gets shaky in places and the band isn't always right there like it should be. But those are technical considerations, and this music isn't about technique. It's about presence, that intangible quality that only the best performers have—and usually because they're not performing so much as they're engaging in an act of communion. On this album, Johnny Cash is all presence.

Jerry Lee Lewis: *The Best of Jerry Lee Lewis* (Smash/Mercury).

This is the way it will be. If you are a country DJ and you refuse to play Jerry Lee records because you disapprove of his bigamous marriage to his thirteen-year-old cousin (for the divorce from his previous—second—wife had not been finalized when he married Myra Gale), or because you disapprove of his drinking and pill-popping and fighting and whoring and unreconstructed redneck ways, or because his language offends you, or simply because Jerry Lee plays real rock 'n' roll at a time when that music has been taken over by the Philly cream-cheese kids and then by a bunch of long-haired Britishers and psychedelic jerks, then Jerry Lee Lewis will cut some hard country sides for you. He will sing these drinking and cheating songs as truly as they can be sung, and if for no other reason than that, you will play them on your country station.

That's where these records came from, and how the Killer came to be a country star.

Sun Records virtually gave up on Jerry Lee after the Myra Gale scandal. Smash (Mercury's Nashville subsidiary) didn't seem to know what to do with the Killer after they signed him away from Sun. First they had him rerecord his old rockabilly hits, though that music was now out of fashion, then they had him cutting R & B and what-all else. His recording career continued to flounder. This could not help but effect his price for live shows, which also plummeted, but he stayed out on the road anyhow, playing all those southern tank towns, and if anything, the music grew more frenzied. The now-deleted *Greatest Live Show on Earth* is from this period; it combines Buck Owens with Chuck Berry and Little Richard (and Jerry Lee Lewis) and easily lives up to its title. Meanwhile, as if in defiance of those who had first scorned him, the sneer on Jerry Lee's face grew larger and meaner; his personal habits grew more self-destructive; paradoxically, his religious beliefs grew stronger at the same time. Enter Eddie Kilroy, a former rodeo rider who joined Smash just a few weeks before Jerry Lee was due to leave the label.

Kilroy convinced Smash to let him cut Jerry Lee country. He convinced Jerry Lee to try one more session. And he convinced country DJs to play the results, "Another Place, Another Time." And play it they damn well should have, for it is one of the most unforgettable performances of the late sixties. Though contractual agreements stipulated that Jerry Kennedy get credit, Kilroy actually produced it. The song is about loss, and though it concerns a woman, it could easily be his own career Jerry Lee is singing of, for his voice is that much older and wearier and more experienced. Though in the song he is cautionary, brooding, exasperated, defeated, he is also too stubborn to admit his true feelings, and so he tries to sound nonplussed. In 1968, exactly a decade after the British tour debacle, "Another Place, Another Time" went to No. 4 on the country charts, and Jerry Lee came in out of the cold, swearing that he had been country all along (which, in spite of the obvious compromise here, was also true).

Kilroy's production could be called Nashville Sound mainly because it was done in Music City with local pickers augmenting Jerry Lee's band, the Memphis Beats. The sound was much sparser than the sound of most Nashville music, and the beat was more pronounced, though it was still not as loose and slaphappy as the beat on Memphis country records. Jerry Lee's whiskey-drenched voice was mixed way up high; his piano, though now more melancholy, more sedate, still propels the band. When Kilroy left Smash and Kennedy then took over production chores, he tampered with this sound very little at first. Then, of course, he gave in to his natural inclination to schlock things up.

"What's Made Milwaukee Famous (Has Made a Loser Out of Me)," which finds Jerry Lee at the confessional of the bar stool, followed in 1968, and his crying vocal along with the steel and harmonica hooks and the piano trills carried it to No. 2. "She Still Comes Around (to Love What's Left of Me)," another classic Jerry Lee lament, reached the same heights that year, and there is no sarcasm or meanness in Jerry Lee as he speaks here of "the fool that lives in me," his voice eventually easing up into something close to a blue yodel. Finally, to cap off his comeback year, Jerry Lee cut "To Make Love Sweeter for You," a positive love song written by Kennedy and Glenn Sutton. Coming on the heels of three straight weepers, it carried him to No. 1 on the country charts.

Through 1970, the year of the last hit on this recently deleted album, the song titles continued to tell the story. "She Even Woke Me Up to Say Goodbye" equates his soul and psyche with a new day, but not a good one ("Just like the dawn, my heart is slowly breaking"), and once again conjures up that recent past when every day did in fact seem to bring new obstacles. On "Once More with Feeling" he tells his woman off in the most biting terms before suggesting they go out in style anyhow, while "All the Good Is Gone" is more direct and unequivocal. "One Has My Name (the Other Has My Heart)" is a typical triangle song handled atypically, philosophically, for there are some things that just don't slow Jerry Lee down.

His live shows had always remained as much rock 'n' roll as country, and soon he would again be recording rock 'n' roll alongside the country with no repercussions. Increasingly, though, as his personal life unraveled, with much help from himself, he grew bored with his material; though he made some fine records during the seventies, he made many more that were inconsequential, tossed off by rote, as if now that he had once again reached the top, there was nothing left to prove. By the beginning of the next decade, he was lying in a hospital bed, near death. He survived that, but his future seemed more uncertain than ever. For a brief period back there in the late sixties, though, Jerry Lee had sung and played as though something very real was at stake, and in doing so, he had seized the time once again.

Tammy Wynette: *Greatest Hits* (Epic).

As we all know by now, Tammy Wynette stands by her man (all five of them, thus far). But how does she stand by her man? Let us listen to her early hits and count the ways. They reveal surprises—namely, that Tammy did not begin as the symbol of female subordination she later became.

She was born Wynette Pugh in 1942 near Tupelo, Mississippi. When she was a child, her mother moved to Birmingham, Alabama, to work in defense plants, and Tammy was raised by her grandparents on a nearby farm. Her mother reclaimed her after the war, but at seventeen Tammy married for the first time. In three years she had three kids, the last one born after the marriage had broken up. The kids were sickly, so to keep up with medical bills, Tammy began supplementing her beautician's income by singing locally.

After moderate success, she tackled Nashville, where four record companies turned her down before Billy Sherrill at Columbia/Epic took an interest. In 1966 they released her first single, a version of Johnny Paycheck's "Apartment No. 9." A heartbreak ballad with crying steel and piano and a single harmony voice (possibly Tammy singing with herself via overdubs), this is much leaner than the records that made her famous. "Your Good Girl's Gonna Go Bad," a chugging honky-tonker in which she threatens to get back at her straying man by becoming a barfly, is quite out of character for the Tammy we've since come to know.

She and Sherrill were still searching for a style and image, and in 1967 they began finding it. In "I Don't Wanna Play House" Tammy overhears her little girl refusing to play house with the neighbor boy because the girl associates "playing house" with her father leaving. The throb in her voice pours on the shame, regret, and pain—Tammy becomes the eternally wronged woman, persevering in an unfair world where she must take the blame for someone else's wrongdoing. Sherrill's production has become more elaborate; the band swells on the chorus, and Tammy belts out the hook line.

Relatively speaking. Because unlike a Connie Smith or a Loretta Lynn, who can cut loose and soar, Tammy makes belting seem like hard work. Within Sherrill's frame of reference, this is for the better, because it makes her sound more vulnerable, more penned in. It's easy to see why he liked Tammy so much, why his formula peaked with her.

Her voice is very poppish, almost like a Patti Page voice. But that throb is an essential element, too, and much more pronounced than the tear in most country voices. At the same time, it was not strong enough to control a record; it rested snugly on Sherrill's banks of strings, his vocal choirs, and his smidgen of steel.

"I Don't Wanna Play House" was Tammy's first No. 1 single; it was followed to the top by "Take Me to Your World," in which a barmaid pleads for a knight on a white horse to rescue her from misery. "All I want is just to be your girl," she declares, and that turned out to be Tammy in a nutshell. Next came "D-I-V-O-R-C-E," on which everything clicked into place for the Wynette-Sherrill team. The hook—a woman and her husband, having always spelled out words they didn't want their little boy to understand, are finalizing their you-know-what —is the kind of clever gimmickery country thrives on; Tammy's anguish is palpable, no doubt because she was no stranger in real life to this particular legal process. Sherrill hits new heights in excess. The song is built around a rumbling piano line, a tactic he would return to frequently in the future. The band swells up bigger than ever on the chorus, the drummer kicks in harder, and Tammy turns on the tears and anguish.

If that song solidified Tammy's career, the follow-up guaranteed it. "Stand By Your Man" became as much of an anthem by proclaiming that nothing in life could be worse than a broken marriage, so a woman should pledge eternal fealty no matter what, because, "After all, he's just a man." At a time when feminism was just beginning to develop a broad base, Tammy spoke for the rest; she became a symbol, a source of strength, to all those women who clung to conventional male-female relationships.

Thanks to that image, she was voted CMA Female Vocalist of the Year three straight times from 1968 to 1970. On "Singing My Song" she marvels at how lucky she is to have a man she can serve: "I don't know what I do that's right/But it makes him come home at night." On "Too Far Gone" she assures her man she'll let him go if he wants and take him back anytime he wants, though it drives her crazy. On "Almost Persuaded" she's nearly picked up in a bar but manages to resist, and the thought of sinning becomes as evil as the sin itself.

Many claimed that Sherrill built Tammy's attitude from scratch as much as he did her sound, but that's absurd. This early in her career, Tammy was hungry, and looking for something that worked. Had "Your Good Girl's Gonna Go Bad" been a runaway smash (it did go as high as

No. 3), she might have become another Loretta Lynn. But she was clearly satisfied with what did click, and the reason she and Sherrill wrote songs together and worked so well together is that they already did see eye to eye. It may seem peculiar that someone who had endured so much marital strife would continue to place so much faith in marriage and family as a panacea. But country music, contrary to the tell-it-like-it-is image, is often not about what life is like, but what we'd like to believe life is like. As her autobiography *Stand By Your Man* (the book) makes clear in abundant detail, Tammy sees her life as a fairy tale, right down to the 1968 marriage to her idol George Jones. As the turbulent marriage, the 1975 divorce, and the subsequent marriages and affairs show, it's been more like a soap opera. Her earliest hits are most powerful precisely because they do capture both the fairy-tale and the soap-opera aspects.

Dolly Parton: *Best of Dolly Parton* (RCA LSP-4449).

To those whose image of country music comes strictly from the Johnny Carson show, Dolly Parton must appear to be the real thing. There she is with her gaudy costumes and her unfathomable figure, looking like a hillbilly Mae West but bubbling over with down-home innocence, energy, and charm. The songs this Dolly Parton sings today are appropriate to that image—campily innocuous fluff in which life is a carnival where nothing ever goes wrong, and each day is a fresh batch of cotton candy to be consumed.

But there's another country music of deep, dark mysteries that go back seemingly to the beginnings of time, a music of awful deaths and unspeakable human mishaps, of real courage and conviction, and that is the kind of country music that launched Dolly's career. You'd never suspect it today, but there are few modern performers whose roots go deeper in country tradition.

She was born in 1946, the fourth of twelve kids, on a farm in Locust Ridge, Sevier County, Tennessee. In this mountainous region in the eastern part of the state, folklorists were still collecting old English ballads as recently as the thirties. At age ten, Dolly was already appearing on local radio and TV; at age thirteen, she cut her first records for a small Louisiana label. In 1964, the day after she graduated from high school, she moved to Nashville and began writing songs. Her first ("Dumb Blonde" and "Something Fishy") were released by Monument in 1967, the same year she joined the Porter Wagoner show, at which time she also switched to RCA, Porter's label. These are her earliest RCA singles, covering 1968 to 1970, and only "Mule Skinner Blues" (1970) creased the country Top Ten, though later in 1970 "Joshua" (not included here) would become her first No. 1 single.

In later years Dolly stressed in interviews how vivid her imagination had been during her childhood; life was so hard, she said, that the few pleasures one had were usually in one's mind. That carries over into her early songs, where the range of themes is unusually broad, and the material almost always seems to come out of her imagination (as opposed to mid-period Dolly, which was autobiographical). Most country music, like the music Dolly made later in her own career, is made by stylists who milk a sound and a persona for as long as they can. Yet the Dolly of this period never stood still for more than a song at a time. Consider the roles she plays and the themes she stresses on these eleven songs, most of which she wrote, no two of which are alike.

There's a conventional hymn in "How Great Thou Art," but the rest concerns a lady mule skinner ("Mule Skinner Blues"); an unwed mother who is deserted by the man who fathers the child, which dies at birth anyhow ("Down from Dover"); an innocent mountain girl who spurns her boy friend to go to New Orleans, where she falls into life as a whore and pines in vain for her first love, who's since married ("My Blue Ridge Mountain Boy"); a satisfied woman looking back on her dirt-poor childhood, as happy to have it behind her as she is to have experienced it ("In the Good Old Days (When Times Were Bad)"); a wanderer who commits suicide after her dog and her lover are killed accidentally in separate events ("Gypsy, Joe and Me"); a there-but-for-fortune moralist ("In the Ghetto"); a woman demanding that her shortcomings be received no more critically than would be those of a man ("Just Because I'm a Woman"); a woman whose husband committed her to a mental institution so he could run off with his new lover ("Daddy Come and Get Me"); a woman of rapidly changing moods and unorthodox habits ("Just the Way I Am").

And there you have, in miniature, a history of women in country music, from the morbid American Gothic of the death songs, which are modern versions of traditional English ballads, to the proud defiance of the contemporary woman. Dolly identified with them all, so immersed was she in country music lore, and in so identifying, she upheld old traditions even as she helped pave the way for new ones. Of all the women singers, she was the best bridge between traditional and modern country music.

If there're any flaws here, they're in the production, which is credited to Bob Ferguson, but which has Wagoner's stamp all over it. Country as she was, Dolly's pop ambitions were also evident from the start, and were shared to some extent by her producers. Vocal choruses drown out the fiddle more often than they should, the steel guitar doesn't cut through as often as you'd like. Meanwhile, Dolly's melodies build from the traditional to the modern much like her lyrics, and she sings in a small, pinched soprano that's full of vibrato. The sameness of the productions not only fails to accent her voice, but sometimes it homogenizes the melodies. Dolly would later break from Wagoner, in part over production differences, and as atrocious as Wagoner's successors were, she had a point: Even back then she was one of those rare artists going too many different ways at once to benefit unqualifiedly from the Nashville production style. But the young Dolly Parton broke through that obstacle like she hardly even noticed it was there.

Dolly Parton: *Best of Dolly Parton* (RCA APL1-1117).

In the early seventies, Dolly Parton was writing and singing the most progressive "traditional" country around. She was also moving inexorably from country to pop. This album documents both impulses.

With songs like "Bargain Store," "Jolene," "Traveling Man," and "Coat of Many Colors," she pumps new life into some of the most overworked country conceits. Songs like "I Will Always Love You" and "Love Is Like a Butterfly" indicate clearly the direction she will soon be taking. "Touch Your Woman" strikes a happy balance between the two.

Significantly, Porter Wagoner is now getting sole production credit, and though he has an eye on the pop market, his arrangements and overall sound are meant to keep Dolly in with the hard-country crowd. That conflict between her ambition and his conservatism is what makes some of these records so memorable. They are constantly challenging each other, but it's the kind of healthy creative conflict that improves the finished product rather than making a jumble of it.

This is apparent from the first cut, "Jolene" (1973), a remarkable piece of songwriting in which this most desirable of country women pours on the humility in begging another woman not to steal her man. Her phrasing swoops and soars almost as a countermelody to the lines played on acoustic guitar, and Wagoner fleshes out the sound with a small country band.

She's equally impressive on the 1972 country hit "Touch Your Woman." Here, her voice shifts from insistence to contentment in one line. Or on "Lonely Comin' Down," a Wagoner composition in which her phrasing descends so delicately into vibrato that the shift is almost imperceptible until it's over. The mournful fiddle that hovers over this song without ever controlling it is another masterful touch from Porter.

Dolly's own compositions turn phrases and images so strikingly that at first it's puzzling to contemplate why so few other singers record them; the answer is probably that her own readings are so definitive it's hard to figure out any other way of doing them.

Sometimes, though, she does go overboard. "My Tennessee Mountain Home" is *too* precious to be revealing, a nostalgic song in which

Dolly seems to edit out memories that contradict the idyllic portrait she's painting. It simply doesn't ring true, especially given all those morbid songs from earlier in her career. But it's also typical in its way: As part of her evolution from hard country to pop, Dolly moved first from the side of country that dwells on death and fear to the side that wants to put a happy face on everything.

When that approach works, she turns in instant classics like "Coat of Many Colors," which is everything "My Tennessee Mountain Home" tries to be but isn't. The song is about a coat Dolly's mother fashioned for her out of scrap material, and also about the strength Dolly got from wearing it even though her classmates laughed. It's a sentiment that has a point, nostalgia that celebrates something besides itself, and there's no way she won't win you over with it. On "The Bargain Store" she again does the unlikely. She wins sympathy for her previous difficulties— remember, most women would kill to be in her place—and she also presents herself as confident and ready to try again. It takes a very special kind of person to pull off such a combination of humility and brashness.

Was Dolly "wrong" to go pop all-out? Well, listen to "Love Is Like a Butterfly." It's certainly one of her cornier similes, and the melody is about as mindlessly perky as she's ever been. In other words, it's intended to be an MOR hit, done in 1974, a year before "Bargain Store" and two years before she formally announced her crossover aspirations. You can picture how it would have sounded had she recorded it a few years later—you can tell right where the horns and string sections would go, where all the sweet background singers would chime in, everything. But here, it's all done through understatement, and again with a surprisingly small studio band. I wish there was someone with comparable restraint working around her today. Yes, Porter Wagoner held her back in some ways, but once she was free of him, she wasted no time overcompensating grotesquely in the opposite direction.

Porter Wagoner and Dolly Parton: *The Best of Porter Wagoner and Dolly Parton* (RCA).

At its peak in the late sixties and early seventies, few country music spectacles were more surreal than Porter Wagoner's syndicated television show. The sponsor was the Chattanooga Medicine Company, makers of Wine of Cardui and Black Draught elixirs and distributors of a wall calendar as common in rural southern homes as the Bible or the Sears and Roebuck catalog. The gangly star would stride out wearing the most dazzling Nudie suits, his peroxided pompadour swept up on his head, his eyes threatening to bulge out of their sockets; he'd give the crowd a grinning, winking, aw-shucksing howdy-do, and then launch into a hymn, a complicated cheating song, an updated public domain selection, or one of his harrowing story-songs about what he called (in his best-known modern murder ballad) "the cold hard facts of life." He could choose between wino's laments like "Skid Row Joe," morality plays disguised as auto-wreck ballads like "Carroll County Accident," or insanity tales like "Julie" and "The Rubber Room." All were delivered with unimpeachable sincerity before Porter introduced "Miss Dolly," who replaced Norma Jean on his show in 1967; she'd then do a couple of her own exquisite songs and they'd team up for duets. Along the way there was room to also spotlight Buck Trent's novel electric banjo (which sounded like an electric guitar), Mack Magaha's faithful old-timey fiddling, and the corn-pone humor of Speck Rhodes, one of the last of the baggy-pants, bass-playing country comedians.

It's long gone, of course, but this album of hit duets from 1968–71 preserves some of the flavor. Porter, a farm boy born in 1930 in West Plains, Missouri, had come to Nashville in 1955 and hit pay dirt with "Satisfied Mind." For nearly twenty years after that he turned out such finely polished gems as "Misery Loves Company," "In the Shadows of the Wine," "Sorrow on the Rocks," "Green, Green Grass of Home," "Big Wind," and others. He managed his money well, made some canny investments, and became one of the wealthiest men in Nashville while building a musical empire as an artist, producer, writer, publisher, and recording-studio manager. But when the times changed—when Dolly left him to go uptown with the rest of Music City—his records were coldly dropped from the RCA catalog. "This hillbilly crap's gotta go," you can almost hear the accountant bitching as he blue-pencils Porter's name from the corporate ledger book. All that remains in print now is this one album of duets, but it alone is enough to assure that Porter won't be entirely overlooked.

The harmonies are as carefully and as soundly constructed as Porter's d.a. haircut or Dolly's figure. As the liner notes gush, "Generally Dolly sings the melody (lead) and Porter sings tenor harmony. But the effect seems reversed, for Porter, whose voice is lower, sounds as if he's singing melody, while Dolly's high soprano seems to be carrying the harmony. It seems like we're getting four vocal parts out of two people!" Yeah, well, not exactly. When Dolly's voice breaks, Porter's glides, blending seamlessly into the background singers, as on "Tomorrow Is Forever." In other places they reverse the effect. When the two voices are given nearly equal prominence, as on "The Pain of Loving You" (melody courtesy "Wolverton Mountain"), they create the kind of mix that goes back many decades. And when he's singing strict harmony, as on most of "Just Someone I Used to Know," Porter doesn't sound like two voices so much as he sounds like a persistent, enveloping breeze blowing spookily through some Smokey Mountain hollow on the blackest night of the year.

They had a formula for their duet albums, every element of which also appears on this compilation. There was always a religious song like "Daddy Was an Old Time Preacher Man," which Dolly (with her aunt) wrote about her grandfather. Dolly soars with the first half of this, spewing out the word "hell" with a dread and venom that makes you wonder if today she can even feel the heat at all. Porter takes most of the second half with a droning fiddle behind him, and they shout the chorus (with quotes from various gospel standards) together. The drums and tambourines are unusually emphatic even for a gospel hand-clapper, the sort of touch that indicates how much closer to pop their duets were than the solo records of either. This was true from their first collaboration, Tom Paxton's "The Last Thing on My Mind," with its busy, squiggling guitar lines and echoey choruses, and is further heard in the Spanish-tinged horns of "Just Someone I Used to Know."

The pop leanings were even more prominent on their novelty songs spoofing marital strife. On "Better Move It On Home," he's out drinking while she's home cooking, and a stinging guitar and harried horns are used to convey their respective emotions. "Run That By Me One More Time" is funnier, a choice cut of cornball southern humor, with each incredulously berating the other for real and imagined shortcomings. That wine you think you smell is just after-shave, Porter declares. Look me in the eyes when you lie like that, an indignant Dolly fights back. By the end, Porter is swearing, "I oughta box yer jaws!" while Dolly snorts, "Oh, you'd hit yer mama before you'd hit me!" It's all true, it's all in fun anyhow, and my only regret is that they couldn't find room here for "Me and Her and the Mobile Home," which was the apex of this genre for them.

They do squeeze in one of Dolly's dead-baby specials, "Jeannie's Afraid of the Dark," about an only child who dies unexpectedly and whose parents continue leaving the light on in her room at night. Porter's recitation is his poker-faced best, and Dolly sings like she's expunging another of the morbid childhood fears that figured in so many of her early songs.

There are also more conventional heartbreak songs ("Just Someone I Used to Know"), don't-look-back songs ("Tomorrow Is Forever"), perseverance songs ("We'll Get Ahead Someday"), and music to match each mood. On most, Porter assumed a world-weary position while Dolly sounds like she can handle whatever comes her way even if she'd rather not have to. Porter and Bob Ferguson (who's listed as producer) had a nifty way of mixing Pete Drake's steel guitar as almost a third harmony voice. But the real show, hands down, is the empathy between

Porter and Dolly. When they had a piece of material like "Holding On to Nothin' "—the most dramatic, most urgent, and most sorrowful performance here—they made all the other duet teams sound like footnotes.

Tom T. Hall: *In Search of a Song* (Mercury).

"I had to learn that I was and would always be a 'hillbilly' in some imponderable part of my being. I have made the step back to my beginning, and there was to be a sadness and wonder in the journey," Tom T. Hall wrote in his autobiography about the songs on this 1971 album and others like it. "Although there were no words to describe it, there was an underlying notion of violence, compassion, and hatred in us mountain people."

At his peak, Hall was the best songwriter in Nashville because, more than any other, he spoke from, of, and to these mountain people without flinching. He saw the tiny details, the humor and the heartbreak in their lives. He made them more comprehensible because he didn't romanticize *or* trivialize those lives. He was a bridge between the stock Nashville writers who came before him and the progressives who followed, though neither faction produced anyone else who said so much on so many subjects with so little posturing.

Hall was born in 1936 in Olive Hill, Kentucky, the son of a preacher; his mother died when he was eleven, and at fourteen, Tom quit school to work in a garment factory. Soon he was leading his own little country band; when he joined the Army and went to Germany in 1957, he continued fronting a band, and began writing songs. On his release, he kicked around Kentucky, Indiana, and West Virginia until 1964, when he moved to Nashville because artists there had begun cutting his songs. By 1967, he was cutting them himself. In 1968, Jeanie C. Riley became an overnight sensation singing his "Harper Valley PTA"—a gleeful celebration of one headstrong woman's triumph over small-town conformity and hypocrisy—and Hall was marked as a man to watch.

He responded with a string of imaginative songs ("Ballad of Forty Dollars," "Homecoming," "A Week in a Country Jail") that got him dubbed "the Storyteller." He took his new role—the songwriter as journalist—so seriously that he began making trips out of Nashville just to observe, talk to the locals, and get song ideas. One such trip, which included a return to Olive Hill, inspired most of these songs.

They contain an undercurrent of ambivalence, as though Hall was sure of what he was seeing and hearing but not sure he should tell anyone else (which, he explains in his autobiography, *The Storyteller's Nashville*, was exactly the case). Though he felt deep kinship with these innately conservative people, he took liberal positions on the issues he raised, and writing these songs required him to confront his feelings on matters he'd dodged in the past. He did it anyhow, and no doubt because he was so concerned about not getting it wrong, his eye and ear for people and situations was never more incisive. These songs are filled with affection, understanding, and yearning, but because they are so unremittingly honest, they don't offer escape so much as they offer something like transcendence; they remove burdens from shoulders simply by holding these burdens up for everyone to see.

What's more remarkable is how slight the songs often appear to be at first. "Kentucky Feb. 27, '71" describes a visit to a farmer outside Olive Hill. The two men talk all afternoon, with the farmer explaining how it's impossible to make a living in these parts without working with your hands, how parents who did know hard work want to spare their kids such lives so you can't blame the kids for being lazy, and how those kids then move to the city anyhow in their quests for something new. Then he concludes, "I'm glad I met you Mr. Hall/But I guess there ain't no song here after all." And that's how bluntly and elegantly the song ends.

"It Sure Gets Cold in Des Moines" is, literally, a song about nothing, and while many a writer has tried the subject (what a challenge, after all!), Tom T. is the only one I know of to have succeeded. A snowstorm shuts down the city and confines him to his hotel, where he drinks because the restaurant is closed, watches a girl cry for no apparent reason and understands that "life is just like that sometimes" and putters around his room. Life goes on even when nothing "happens," this song says; it makes Hall country music's answer to rock ironist Randy Newman.

On "Trip to Hyden," he visits the site of a mining disaster in which thirty-nine were killed and only one survived. The average writer would milk this for drama, romanticize the town and the deceased, work up righteous anger over conditions in the mines. But Hall is moved by the mundane: Hyden's still just a little dot on the map, primarily. At the mine site there's no sign of death; it looks like every other mine site, now that everything's returned to normal. But townspeople gather around trying to be helpful because they mistake Hall for a real journalist and they hope to get their names in the paper, which seemingly has become something of an avocation for some of them; one person opines that the miners are worth more dead than they ever were alive. Throughout this song Hall doesn't use irony so much as he points out the obscene ironies inherent in the situation.

Other characters are delineated just as carefully. There's Clayton Delaney, an unknown local picker Hall used to tag after as a child, and who died at nineteen of alcoholism and TB. There's a hog farmer confined to a hospital bed who up and leaves one day against doctor's orders because nobody else could take care of his stock. There's the traveling musician himself, lonely and depressed, leafing through the Tulsa phone book in a vain (and comical) attempt to track down a former one-night stand whose name he can't remember. There's the woman preacher who pulls an Aimee Semple McPherson with her guitarist, and the mute girl who identifies her rapist by imitating him.

Hall tells all their stories in a pleasant baritone that has no outstanding characteristics. He often talks more than he sings, but he gets the job done. Most of the songs are up-tempo, which gives this vocal style added urgency; half the time he barely keeps up with the band. Though producer Jerry Kennedy proved elsewhere that he could be the penultimate Nashville hack, for Hall he came up with a smart dobro-and-harmonica sound quite appropriate to these talking blues. Later, Hall's concern for the common man degenerated into bathos, cloying sentimentality, and cheap liberalism, but on *In Search of a Song*, he found more than just some songs. He found (and illuminated) a whole world, populated by people who seem extraordinary because no human life scrutinized this carefully and compassionately could possibly then continue to appear ordinary.

Conway Twitty: *Greatest Hits, Volume 2* (MCA).

Conway Twitty is living proof that formulas can be benign rather than limiting, that an artist can exploit a fairly rigid form in a way that enhances him and it both. Twitty took the Nashville Sound, to paraphrase one of his best-known hits, about as far as it could go. On this album you can hear him stretching it out.

The world first heard of him as a rockabilly singer from Friars Point, Mississippi. Born Harold Jenkins in 1933, his name was changed in 1957 by an agent who supposedly took it off a map (Conway, Arkansas, and Twitty, Texas). The agent then dispatched him to Hamilton, Ontario, Canada (an industrial city near Toronto) to compete for the Elvis sound-alike dollars. While there, Conway wrote "It's Only Make Believe," which broke out of Columbus, Ohio, a year later. It became the archetypal Twitty ballad, and he rode it for nearly a decade. By 1965, however, the Beatles had rewritten the book on rock 'n' roll; tired of slogging it out on a circuit of nameless bars through the South and up into Pennsylvania and New Jersey, Conway switched to country music. In 1968, after three years' worth of records that did well enough to keep him going but not well enough to make him secure, he scored his first No. 1 country hit, "Next in Line." By early 1982 he'd had twenty-seven No. 1 country hits, more than anyone in history.

Twitty claims that he always wanted to be a country singer, but started in rock because it was easier. When he came to Nashville, he says, he was really coming home. Everyone who's ever switched to country from another field has said the same thing; it's part of doing penance, establishing your sincerity. But in Conway's case, you believe it, for he is quiet, guarded, undemonstrative—ill-suited, really, for any music but country.

So he fit himself easily into the Nashville system. On the hits from his first big period (1968-72) there was very little fiddle, only string sections and lots of background voices. The songs play heavily on the themes of guilt and regret. One in particular best sums up his dilemma. "How Much More Can She Stand" is, literally, about being possessed—by the Other Woman, by the very thought of her, even. Conway likens it to being in the devil's own grip, and he sings like a man possessed: "I try to stay at home, love only her, play with the kids and watch TV/But then my mind becomes unsure about the kind of love I need/My reasons for cheating, they're as good as lies can be/How much more can she stand, and still stand by me?" How much more tortured can a country boy be?

Two things distinguish his records. The first is his throbbing voice; typically, he'd begin a song with a low, raspy growl, and then both voice and band would build into a crescendo, Conway adding a few moans and sighs along the way. The second was steel player John Hughey, the only member of Conway's road band always to appear along with the session musicians on his records. Hughey has the most instantly recognizable steel sound in Nashville; he peels and bends notes like they were pretzels, or holds them so long that his whine seems to become the whole point of the record.

He's even stolen songs from the star, including this album's "(Lost Her Love) On Our Last Date," which was originally an instrumental (Conway's written lyrics for his version) in which Floyd Cramer's piano imitated a steel. In all, these sides from 1972 to 1976 make up a slightly more diversified compilation than does *Greatest Hits, Volume 1* precisely because Conway *does* deviate slightly—by giving Hughey more room, by using electric piano or even synthesizer for fills and coloring. These are conservative strides by a man who doesn't question his conservative form. But the demands of the Nashville Sound help give Conway focus, and what stands out then is the little things he does within those confines. He's learned to use his voice much more dramatically; a song like "You've Never Been This Far Before" swells and then goes back down, rather than just building through to the end. "After All the Good Is Gone" follows the chord progression of a fifties blues-rock ballad and has a melody reminiscent of "Crying Time," an apt fusion of the two musical forms Conway is best with.

Something else happens here. As he expands his pet themes of adultery and old loves he can't forget, Conway becomes a barometer for how far the Nashville mainstream can go with lyrics as well as with music. His virile voice and sensitive phrasing provide a combination female fans can't resist; he comes off the strong, silent type, an image he cagily reinforced by refusing to talk onstage for more than a decade. (His bass player handled all the between-songs patter, and Conway just sang.) In these highly suggestive songs of trembling hands, shaky legs, pounding hearts, and breaking voices, the Sensuous Man conquers Nashville.

Take the "You've Never Been This Far Before" controversy of 1973. Conway insisted that the song was about a woman who'd just left her husband, and was thus now available to a man who'd longed for her for years; she's nervous, though, because she's never been involved with someone outside the well-defined parameters of marriage; she's not quite sure how this particular game is played, and so the man is trying to reassure her. There's even plenty in the lyrics to support this interpretation—but none of it turns up until halfway through the song, by which time the tone has been set by the title phrase and the imagery implying that a virgin is being seduced. Similarly, "The Games That Daddies Play" concerns a young boy's appeal to his mother (a divorcée) that he needs to learn the facts of life. The first verse has overtones of incest; the kid might be asking her to show him how. The rest of the song makes clear that he's only asking permission to get the word from a father of a friend. It's a moral song after all, and like "You've Never Been This Far Before," it went to No. 1. Conway Twitty knows what he can and can't get away with.

Loretta Lynn and Conway Twitty: *Lead Me On* (MCA).
Listening to Conway and Loretta is like enduring the proverbial heaven-and-hell. If you don't believe me, look at how they describe it on the title song: (Loretta) "Lead me on and take control of how I feel/I can't do this on my own, 'cuz it's against my will." (Conway) "I need love warm and tender in a way I've never known." (Loretta) "If you want me, I'll go with you, but you'll have to lead me on."

In her solo recordings, Loretta is always the feisty woman fighting to right wrongs against her; in his, Conway is weak but sensitive, a combination creating such conflicts he's often driven to do things he knows he shouldn't. Pairing them is potentially combustible, and this album, from 1971, when both were near their creative peaks, realizes that potential like none of their other duet albums. It's hot enough that for years many fans assumed Conway and Loretta were married, like George and Tammy. (That mistake, by contrast, was seldom made about Porter and Dolly.) And it's not just that the love songs are steamy, though they are. Guilt is a palpable enough presence on many of these sides that it constitutes a third voice; it almost steps out of the grooves the way a cloud in the shape of a death's skull rises out of a whiskey bottle in antidrinking commercials.

When they sing together, their voices entwine so intimately that you can tell they were in the studio singing at the same time (as opposed to most of their other duet albums, where you can tell they usually overdubbed their vocal parts separately). That richness, that closeness, makes even something like "Never Ending Song of Love" (covered by dozens of other artists around this time) surprisingly fresh. But it's by alternating lines that they best set a song up, and then the harmonies drive it home; here, their (uncredited) producer makes a big difference, too. Loretta sounds much as she normally does on her own solo record-ings, but Conway's style is more subdued; rather than creating drama by swelling up, as he does on his own records, he levels off these lyrics, and the situation they describe then speaks for itself. This also helps keep his uneasy feelings right out front where they belong.

"How Far Can We Go" is a cheating song, of course; she's definitely married while he's apparently not. "We're doing the things only *sinners* do," Loretta wails early on, adding later, "We made a mistake one night and didn't quit." "I feel like a thief when I hold you tight," Conway responds at one point, then concedes, "We're taking the back road, going nowhere fast." There's a bit of irony in the soothing Spanish guitar that weaves through the voices, but the truth outs in the end, as the drummer pounds an insistent beat over and over while Conway and Loretta ask the title question over and over; it keeps reverberating well after the music's ended.

"When I Turn Off My Lights (Your Memory Turns On)" is another medium-slow one giving the singers plenty of room to phrase their laments: Each thinks of the other while sleeping with his/her own spouse. On "Playing House Away from Home," the cheating lovers give their spouses excuses and go to another town, where they can carry on as man and wife and nobody knows the difference.

"Back Street Affair" is covered with the most hard-country ar-rangement on the album—a whining fiddle as foil to Loretta's deepest Kentucky twang, full of vibrato, adding extra syllables to nearly every word. In this song, a woman falls for—which is tantamount to seducing —a man, not knowing he's already married. In the public eye, that makes her trash and him a victim. What they can't say publicly is that his wife was the first to cheat, so their behavior isn't as immoral or damaging as it may appear to be. The ending is basically optimistic and positive, with the two of them maintaining their dignity by clinging to the belief that because of the circumstances their affair is justifiable. One of the earliest cheating songs to hit, "Back Street Affair" now sounds dated in certain ways. In modern cheating songs, for example, it's not absolutely essential to maintain dignity like that, and there doesn't have to be a conclusion at all; they can just end with the situation still hanging.

On the less salacious side, "You're the Reason" has a nice shuffling feel behind it, and comes off wholesomely sexy. "You Blow My Mind," with its dobro and banjo arrangement, offers a welcome departure from the standard Nashville groove of the other tracks, and the food metaphors and playful vocals add a light touch to an album that deals mainly in weighty matters. (The novelty song would later become a Conway and Loretta tradition, culminating with "You're the Reason Our Kids Are Ugly," but that kind of material is generally better left to Porter and Dolly.) "Easy Loving," another of those songs-you-never-want-to-hear-again-by-anyone works this time because of the balance struck by Conway's sensuality and Loretta's sincerity. The album's final cut is the best contentment song of the bunch, though. It kicks off with a fiddle shouting for joy, and both singers have unusually buoyant vocal lines. The song declares ("I'm gonna get up and . . .") "Get Some Loving Done," and that's just what this album is about. And then some.

George Jones: *Anniversary—Ten Years of Hits* (Epic).

George Jones defies reason. Through the seventies and into the eighties, his life was one huge, well-documented ball of trouble. There was a failed marriage and related drinking and drugging binges that escalated until he had to be hospitalized. There were arrests on various charges. He missed gigs as often as he made them. He declared bankruptcy and switched managers repeatedly. He remarried. Yet through it all, as this double album reveals, he continued to grow as a singer. Where most artists find a winning style and then duplicate it on each new release, George has never stopped honing his, never stopped adding new twists. When he's healthy, he's the best singer alive, period.

By 1972, three years after his marriage to Tammy Wynette, he began recording with producer Billy Sherrill, the man who mixed "country cocktails" (as writer Dave Hickey aptly put it) out of large shots of melody and strings, with a dash of steel. But production isn't the only way in which these are unlike George's prior recordings, because these deal head-on with the impossibility of maintaining both the honky-tonk life-style and a decent home life in one's middle age. This is an issue Jones had never considered; before, he seemed to assume that he could go on forever living the honky-tonk life, or that, as he was powerless to rein himself in, there would always be someone else around to do so. Either way, he was not fully responsible for himself.

The bleakest songs here aren't about dashed hopes, but about the futility of having hopes at all. As his songs became more overtly autobiographical, he no longer even wrote them. Maybe he just couldn't find words, as Hank Williams could, to describe what he was doing to himself, and what was being done to him; maybe he didn't want to bother, and was satisfied to have others observing his dissolution write it down for him. But unlike the past, when he sang songs that mirrored his feelings without being specific about details of his own life, he's now often singing about himself in particular. He sings with stunning finality, so it's understandable that the hurting songs have more impact.

But until 1975, George's ideal marriage was as real to him as anything, and he celebrated his bliss as convincingly as he did his misery. On "Once You've Had the Best" (1973) Sherrill pours on the strings, bringing them to peak after peak, and each time George rises to the occasion, straining, and ultimately succeeding, at staying on top of the arrangement. When he sings "I go to pieces" on "Loving You Could Never Be Better" (1972), George's voice soars and swoops like an eagle zooming in on its prey.

Before his marriage failed, though, George was already singing about how and why it would. His chief device was to construct a series of misfortunes that are then made to look puny next to the singer's own woes. On "The Door" (1974) he recounts his war experiences, then declares they are trivial next to the sound of his wife leaving him. "A Picture of Me (Without You)" (1972) compares his desolation to a Sunday without church bells, or a river in which nothing flows. On "The Grand Tour" (1974) he guides a visitor around the house he once shared, and the rooms become symbols for the emptiness he feels knowing that the special meaning behind each object is now irrevocably lost. "These Days (I Barely Get By)" (1975), which George co-wrote with Tammy, sums it up; George salvages a drippy Sherrill intro as soon as he grabs hold of the words, which detail a day of setbacks. They are all mundane enough (his car broke down, etc.) that they could happen to anyone; they are the raw materials of country songs, and the list is so complete it's almost laughable until you hear George sing it. For there's a rub—one of these events, though it seems fitting, is *not* an everyday nuisance: At the bottom of everything is the fact that his wife left him, a fact which *does* trivialize all the others. A lesser country singer would simply turn all this into melodrama, thereby defusing the devastation. But when George cries, "I wanna give up, lay down and die," there's not melodrama so much as a frustration and desperation so blind he can only let it out in bits and pieces. "The Battle," a 1976 divorce song set to martial drum beats, gives the final details.

It was around this time that the Jones cult suddenly grew into a mass audience. He became recognized as the man who had bought the brutalizing dictum that to sing like Hank, you had to live like Hank. By now, even Sherrill had wised up to what it was people heard in George Jones; he stripped down his production, and the voice had more freedom to move around than ever before.

There were moments of mockery like "Her Name Is . . ." (1976), in which the guitar simulates the sound of Tammy's name instead of George singing it. But mostly, as his annihilation grew increasingly imminent, his voice moved beyond pain into a realm where pain was the only given in life. His expression of that ghastly thought was so complete that a listener might even find himself feeling guilty for finding beauty in George's music, but the beauty was there nonetheless. The listener was thus in a sense complicit with the horrible forces driving George, and even in country music, which had seemingly exhausted all the artistic possibilities in the themes of guilt and pity, this was an unprecedented situation. When he sang a gorgeous devotional ballad like Bob McDill's "I'll Just Take It Out in Love" (1978) or a statement of hope like "Someday My Day Will Come" (1979), George might have been indulging in wishful thinking. But for the few minutes each song lasted, you also believed the unbelievable.

"He Stopped Loving Her Today" (1980), from his "comeback" album, was yet another apex. Fresh from the detox ward, George sang a morbid song about a man who couldn't give up loving his ex to get on with his own life until she died. Sherrill's orchestrations, which had begun creeping back in the last couple of years, enhance the mood this time. And with "If Drinkin' Don't Kill Me (Her Memory Will)" (1980) and "Same Old Me" (1982) George seems more resigned than ever to his fate.

With "He Stopped Loving Her Today" the necrophiliacs, never far from the center of country music, gathered around to cash in, and the same people who had made a Nashville sport out of watching and waiting for George to die now gave him his first major CMA awards two years running. He responded to such stardom in the only way that, in his world view, made sense—by pushing himself further out onto his own lost highway, destined, like a country music Dutchman, to ride it forever. But when his health allowed, he sang his sorrowful songs with a majesty and conviction that made all others sound pale and insincere by comparison.

George Jones and Tammy Wynette: *Greatest Hits* (Epic).
For most country fans, the George and Tammy affair was too good

to be true, a storybook romance that took place on record as well as in real life. Step right up, folks, for the country music soap opera of the seventies, as contained within the grooves of this record. It has everything:

In 1968, George and Tammy are married (each for the third time). George, long recognized as the greatest country singer alive but too often more preoccupied with his drinking problem than with his music, has long been Tammy's idol. Recently, he's become a big Tammy fan, too, and why not? "D-I-V-O-R-C-E" and "Stand By Your Man" had just made her the most popular woman singer in country music.

By 1972, George had quit drinking and had moved to Tammy's label (Epic) and producer (Billy Sherrill). Both were already celebrating their union in their individual singles, but now they were also able to record duets together. Somewhere in there, George fell off the wagon— hard—and so the tone of duets turned from devotional to anguished. They separated in 1974 and were divorced within the year, but knowing a good thing when they saw it, they continued recording together. Now the music evolved from what-went-wrong? to bitter disappointment and self-pity and then to nostalgia.

There was nothing subtle about it. Their initial duet, "Take Me" (1971), pledged eternal love in a way only the most fervent could accept, and they followed that up the next year by reciting their wedding vows to music in "The Ceremony." By 1973 they were promising each other "We're Gonna Hold On," and reconcile they did. But the next year they cut "We Loved It Away," a song that explains their love was so strong it destroyed all obstacles, and there's a lingering sense that ultimately it destroyed even its two participants. By 1976 they'd checked out with the lachrymose "Golden Ring," which detailed the rise and fall of a marriage from beginning to aftermath.

Actually, they don't sing together all that often in these duets. More often, they alternate verses and sing a little harmony on the choruses, at which point Sherrill has this nasty habit of burying them both in background singers. The reason they don't sing together more often, I presume, is that Tammy is a much more limited vocalist than George.

You can also hear it on her own records; she'll go up for a high note, and just when it's obvious she's not going to make it, Sherrill sweeps in with a bank of violins that covers her trail. She's only comfortable in a medium-slow tempo that swells up into overkill; there, the break in her voice becomes so eloquent you can forget her shortcomings. George is perhaps *most* comfortable at a similar tempo because it allows him to stretch his voice out, but he can handle any tempo.

He's constantly compensating for Tammy, adjusting his style to her limits. Most of these sides, in fact, sound much like their marriage was:

George holds himself in check to keep Tammy happy, but when he can't stand it anymore, he just soars away from her, no contest. There's continual tension in their work together because George, the eternal down-and-outer, is trying so hard to believe in the kind of life Tammy believes in automatically, which is essentially a fairy tale. And try as he may—which, like a good husband, he really does—George just can't put such an idealistic face on everything.

But we cannot have such tensions in a modern Nashville album, even when it exists in real life, and so who better to preside over such a grand, glorious, potentially messy situation than Billy Sherrill, the man who perfected country schlock? Sherrill can smooth out the most prominent harsh spots, and he outdoes himself working with these two. Touches like the string section on the fifties-sounding ballad "Near You" are too much even by his standards. Sherrill almost manages to take the sting out of these songs, to make them palatable to the meekest of souls —but underneath the creamy smooth veneer he provides, the troubled heart of George Jones is still making waves. Thus does this trio manage to have things both ways.

Supplementary Albums

Bill Anderson: *The Bill Anderson Story* (MCA). He came to Nashville to be a writer (and he had some good ones in "Po' Folks" and "City Lights"), but wound up the utterly average artist, long on image though short on singing ability. They don't call him "Whispering Bill" for nothing, you know, though he's swift enough in the studio that production usually bails him out.

Eddy Arnold: *The Best of Eddy Arnold* (RCA). In the mid-forties, Arnold was country's brightest new star—smooth, plaintive, with few of the country inflections that made crossover so impossible back then. He could be considered the Southeast's answer to Gene Autry, and by the fifties, which is when he cut the earliest of these sides, he'd gone even further in that direction. He's a pop singer here, with polished phrasing and slick backup bands. Typically, his record company has made a mockery of his career on album, so that a man with literally dozens of hits is given a greatest hits album in which five of the twelve cuts never even charted for him (though it's fortunate that "Anytime," his most effective pop effort, is included).

Eddy Arnold: *The Best of Eddy Arnold, Vol. II* (RCA). Hard country fans soured on Arnold fast, and for good reason; once he figured out how to make that pop crossover, he ironed the last vestiges of country out of his voice much more thoroughly than he probably needed to. By the time he'd peaked, it was easy to confuse "the Tennessee Plowboy" with a mediocre cabaret singer. This collection is as spotty as the previous volume, includes more from the sixties, and thus documents the continuing bland-out.

Chet Atkins: *Country Music* (Time-Life). Chet may have invented the Nashville sound, but with no country voice cutting through his instrumentals, his own records sound more countrypolitan. This one is an exception, and somehow it figures that a weekly newsmagazine would do a better job of repackaging Atkins than RCA (his own record company) does. This contains "Canned Heat," a piece of fancy country picking from his first session, in 1947, and moves through jazz tunes right on up to his more recent pop stylings. It's balanced, but the scales are tipped slightly in favor of country, which is so obvious an idea that he and RCA never even thought of it.

Moe Bandy: *Greatest Hits* (Columbia). With the exception of one song, this ignores the early (GRC) Bandy material in favor of Columbia sides from 1976–81; it thus overlaps little with Bandy's *Best Of* discussed elsewhere. At the same time, there's a slight, but still perceptible, softening of both his stance and his sound. It always seemed likely that this might happen to a singer as specialized as Bandy is. But even with some of the sting removed, he still sounds refreshingly free of pretense on songs like "Barstool Mountain."

Moe Bandy & Joe Stampley: *Greatest Hits* (Epic). These two guys sound a little alike, and look almost identical. The sides herein, nearly all of them humorous story-songs, were culled from a pair of albums they cut together in 1979 and 1981, and most of them could provide plot lines for new episodes of *Smokey and the Bandit*. In fact, some of them are funny (and unusual) enough that they would be a big improvement over the original movies, though the stereotypical good-old-boyisms run so rampant that ultimately they're best taken one or two at a time.

Bobby Bare: *This is Bobby Bare* (RCA). With his two "greatest hits" albums out of print, this is where you'll find the best summary of Bobby Bare's sixties. There's a provocative mix on this double album, from the folk-flavored hits ("Four Strong Winds," "Long Black Veil," "Green, Green Grass of Home," "Detroit City," "The Streets of Baltimore," and much more) to "(Margie's at) The Lincoln Park Inn" (the most shocking of his infrequent cheating songs) to the unabashed patriotism of "Bless America Again."

Johnny Bush: *The Best of Johnny Bush* (Power Pak/Gusto). In the late sixties and early seventies, Bush was known as "the Country Caruso," a Texan with a booming baritone and a fondness for slow songs that showed it off impressively. Bush recorded some of Willie Nelson's greatest, and most obscure, songs long before *that* was fashionable; "What a Way to Live" was as desperate as country music got during those years. Nearly everything he did for Stop/Million during this period has since been reissued by Power Pak, and nearly all of it is recommended. (The three RCA albums which followed were only a cut below, but they're now all out of print.)

Johnny Bush: *Undo the Right* (Power Pak/Gusto). At his most abject, Bush sounded like he was singing from the bottom of a bottle, and he had an unremittingly depressing outlook on life. But he sang with such power and conviction that even the bleakest albums sound like triumphs. With the likes of "What Made Milwaukee Famous (Has Made a Loser Out of Me)," "Bottle, Bottle," "Life Turned Her That Way," "Apartment #9," and the title song balanced only by "Today I Started Loving You Again," this is one of the bleakest.

Johnny Bush: *You Gave Me a Mountain* (Power Pak/Gusto). The title song, which deals with loss and gain and the illusions of both, is Bush at his most dynamic; it starts with a rumble and builds slowly to a roar. "Darkness on the Face of the Earth," another of those Willie Nelson tunes it took Bush to rediscover, is almost as dramatic. Nothing else is quite that devastating, but with "Don't You Ever Get Tired of Hurtin' Me," "Mama's Hungry Eyes," "She Still Comes Around (to Love What's Left of Me)," and more in the same vein, Bush shows his usual impeccable taste in songs, and sings every one like it might be his last.

Carl and Pearl Butler: *Honky-Tonkitis* (CMH). Their out-of-print sixties sides on Columbia are the best, but these rerecordings are nothing to be ashamed of, and are much more easily found. Carl and Pearl were the first husband-wife team to get seriously into cheating songs and honky-tonk duets, and he in particular is a venerable barroom balladeer.

Johnny Cash: *Greatest Hits, Vol. 1* (Columbia). Early sixties hits like "Ring of Fire," "Understand Your Man," a rerecording of "I Walk the Line," and "Jackson" (with June Carter). Upon leaving Sun, Cash matured instantly. While these sides were recorded during his most troubled period, and include a few pieces of lame material, they do demonstrate the breadth of his concerns at that time.

Johnny Cash: *Ring of Fire—The Best of Johnny Cash* (Columbia). The title song is also available on *Greatest Hits, Vol. 1.* But "I Still Miss Someone" captures his sense of loss, yearning, and resolve as well as anything he's done, and this also has enough hymns to fill you in on that side of Cash without overdoing it.

Johnny Cash: *Blood, Sweat and Tears* (Columbia Limited Edition). The last of the "folkie" Cash albums remaining in print from the sixties, this is also the most satisfying, pinpointing at first a specific American workers' hero, John Henry and his legend, and generalizing outward to embrace all working men. Harlan Howard's poverty anthem "Busted," a 1963 country hit for Cash, came off this album too (Ray Charles turned it into a standard), and several other songs in the same vein establish a mood that's bluesy but not bathetic.

Johnny Cash: *Now There Was a Song!* (Columbia Limited Edition). Now *here* is a concept! Cash covers his favorite country songs, from sources both predictable (Hank, George, ET) and obscure (Melvin Endsley, Roy Hogshead), and in the process says more about the music than he does in most of his other, more popular theme albums from the sixties. Every cut is a gem, and though I doubt if many people consider this their favorite Cash album, I'd put it up against anything else he's done.

Johnny Cash: *The Unissued Johnny Cash* (German Bear Family). Cash cultists will prize this set if only for the German-language versions of "I Got Stripes" ("Viel Zu Spat") and "Five Feet High and Rising" ("Wo Ist Zuhase, Mama"). (Somebody must have gone crazy trying to translate that one, and Cash's diction will never win a Grammy, either.) All of this material comes from 1958–63, Cash's first years with Columbia, and finds him in transition between the teen traumas of his Sun output and the adult concerns of his new music. It adds little to the Cash mystique, and is thus for cultists only.

Johnny Cash: *The Johnny Cash Collection—His Greatest Hits, Vol. II.* (Columbia). Covering the period after *Folsom Prison* when Cash could seemingly do no wrong, this collates such novelties as "A Boy Named Sue" (1969) with such dead-serious songs as "Sunday Morning Coming Down."

Johnny Cash: *At San Quentin* (Columbia). This 1969 live album was intended to recapture some of the magic of the *Folsom Prison* album. It doesn't, though it is consistently fervent Cash; the most memorable songs it yielded were Bob Dylan's "Wanted Man," "San Quentin," and "A Boy Named Sue," the latter of which half the nation is probably *still* trying to forget.

Johnny Cash: *Greatest Hits, Vol. 3* (Columbia). In the late seventies, after coasting rudderless for too long, Cash began straightening out again. His novelty songs—"Oney," "One Piece at a Time"—showed wit rather than silliness, and his duets with Waylon Jennings—"There Ain't No Good Chain Gang," "I Wish I Was Crazy Again"—may not be wholly successful but they do show new signs of life for him. And "After the Ball" is almost a dance song.

Johnny Cash: *The Adventures of Johnny Cash* (Columbia). As "presented" (produced) by Jack Clement, that is, which automatically makes things a lot more adventurous. With the exception of "We Must Believe in Magic," which sounds ludicrous, this 1982 attempt to put Clement's style of glitz on top of the Cash beat is a lot more satisfying than most efforts to put Cash's style of glitz on top of the Cash beat.

Patsy Cline: *Country Great* (MCA). Trying to choose among the available Patsy Cline albums is always a problem because more often than not, while the vocals remain the same, the record company has erased the original band track and overdubbed a new one. Sometimes it's hard even to be sure when that's the case, because the new backing is occasionally sympathetic and Patsy's vocals, which of course are the originals, prevail anyhow. This album *sounds* like primo Patsy, and the material is fairly obscure.

Patsy Cline: *Here's Patsy Cline* (MCA). All the above applies also to this collection of bittersweet ballads.

Patsy Cline: *The Country Hall of Fame* (British MCA). Rest assured that these recordings are the real thing, and an acceptable mix between the ultrafamiliar and the esoteric. As with all the albums in this series, the compilers sought to present diversity more than anything else, but because Patsy rarely succumbed to ideas *too* far out, this becomes a blessing in her case.

Hank Cochran: *Make the World Go Away* (Elektra). Cochran was another of those sixties writers like Willie Nelson who got rich off cover versions but could never break through himself. In 1980, when this album was released, he was trying again as a singer, and failing again. Don't ask me why—he sings with a winning combination of vulnerability and experience, and the songs are among his best. A sleeper, even if it has gone out of print.

Floyd Cramer: *The Best of Floyd Cramer* (RCA). On a mid-fifties Don Robertson demo that caught the ear of Chet Atkins, the piano player "bent" notes a full tone in much the same way a steel player bends notes. Atkins liked the sound so much that he instructed session-pianist Cramer to duplicate it identically. Thus was born the slurring, slip-note "Cramer style" that is a cornerstone of the Nashville Sound. Here are twelve examples of Cramer doing same, including his calling card, "Last Date." And what happened to the guy who really invented the sound? Don't ask.

Dick Curless: *Hard, Hard Traveling Man* (Capitol). Curless was Maine's first (and probably last) national country star. He first struck in 1965, when "Tombstone Every Mile," the folkish trucker's ballad about a treacherous northeastern highway, became a local hit that was then picked up by a major label. He has a voice like an eighteen-wheeler revving up, and the song quickly became a national hit. For a while, only Dave Dudley surpassed him as the truckers' favorite. This is all trucker and/or traveling songs that easily evoke the lure of the highway; the hit single is the highlight, but he also rumbles as well as Dudley on "Six Days on the Road," and he's much more bluesy overall. Though Curless spent several years in Bakersfield when that city was at its peak musically, this album is a Nashville production that somehow evaded the sweetening machine.

Dick Curless: *Live at the Wheeling Truck Driver's Jamboree* (Capitol). Truckers are as faithful an audience as anyone could ask for, and they bring out the best in Curless. This 1973 album was the last in a distressingly uneven career, but the voice is as gravelly as ever, and in addition to the trucking tales you'd expect, he sings some R & B ("Sixty Minute Man," "Evil Hearted Me," "I'm Gonna Move to the Outskirts of Town") that fits him well. Classy little band, too—this live album makes up for lost time. But like all his work, it's now out of print.

Jimmie Davis: *The Best of Jimmie Davis* (MCA). Davis, who wrote "You Are My Sunshine" and parlayed it into the governorship of Louisiana, launched his career as a Jimmie Rodgers imitator with the dirtiest batch of songs any one person had ever recorded in country music. Then he found God, and switched to spirituals. Which music, when he rerecorded old sides for this album in the early sixties, did he concentrate on? Two guesses.

Skeeter Davis: *The Best of Skeeter Davis* (RCA). As one half of the Davis Sisters, Skeeter brought teen heartbreak into the country mainstream in the early fifties. Later, on her own, that little-girl innocence grew into an appealing openness and humanity that lasted her into the early seventies. But it's been a long time between hits, and this has slipped out of print.

Jimmy Day: *All Those Years Ago* (Mid-Land). Day is a Texas pedal steel player who's probably seen every barroom in the state; he's played with many of the Lone Star greats, and his last steady gig was with Willie Nelson. When Day left, Willie never bothered to replace him. So it's no surprise that he'd cut an instrumental album of songs associated with Ray Price, Roger Miller, George Jones, and Willie; and for all his technique, he's as lowdown as they come. Now if only those choral voices weren't there.

Jimmy Dean: *Greatest Hits* (Columbia). Though one of the few to reconcile honky-tonk, the Nashville Sound, and pop, the deep-voiced Dean is best known for "Big Bad John" (1961) and "P.T. 109" (1962), two hits that glorified President Kennedy while at the same time fitting neatly into the saga-song fad then sweeping country music. (After those, he's best known for the pork sausage that he sponsored.)

Dave Dudley: *Truck Drivin' Son-of-a-Gun* (Mercury). Dudley, whose peak years were 1963–70, had a deep, rumbling voice that made one think not only of semitrucks downshifting, but also of too many cigarettes and beers around 3 A.M. He was best known for his trucking songs, and this 1965 album has nothing but.

The Best of Dave Dudley (Mercury). This album, which is out of print though generally easy to scrounge up, covers the years 1963–69, and includes a healthy dose of trucker's songs while repeating only one from the above album. Here's where you'll find Dudley's breakthrough version of "Six Days on the Road" as well as genre pieces like "Trucker's Prayer." But Dudley didn't limit himself to trucking songs; this album's "What We're Fighting For" (written by Tom T. Hall) is a pro-Vietnam War song from 1965, before much of the nation realized we were fighting there. Unfortunately, this doesn't include the absolute best of his non-trucking songs, both from 1970, "The Pool Shark" and the hellacious "This Night (Ain't Fit for Nothing but Drinkin')."

Stoney Edwards: *Mississippi You're On My Mind* (Capitol). Edwards is a hard country singer in the Frizzell-Haggard mold who also happens to be black and (unlike Charlie Pride and the few other black country singers) has never shied away from that fact; he's simply weaved it into what he does along with other aspects of his background (son of a bootlegger, for example). He is also illiterate, though a songwriter with a rare knack for pinning his subject down fully ("The Cute Little Waitress" and "A Two Dollar Toy"). He picked appropriate covers like "Hank and Lefty Raised My Country Soul" (self-explanatory), "Jeweldene Turner (The World Needs to Hear You Sing)" (country gospel singer goes to Broadway), and "She's My Rock" (a love song that doesn't cloy). This 1975 album was easily his best—it reprised a few old hits while introducing the new ones, and though it has since fallen out of print, it's not that hard to find in bargain bins. Capitol should take the rest of his hits (especially "Poor Folks Stick Together" from 1971 and "Blackbird (Hold Your Head High)" from later in 1975) and program them into this album to produce a true "greatest hits" LP.

Stoney Edwards: *No Way to Drown a Memory* (Canadian Boot). This 1981 effort doesn't have quite the kick of his earlier Capitol efforts, but it does have the advantage of being easier to find. And Stoney's smoky, grainy voice is still probing on originals like "Reverend Leroy" and on outside material like "I Just Want You to Make Me Over" and "Because It Isn't You" (both from the inimitable Tommy Collins) or "One Bar at a Time." Edwards has lost none of his melodic touch, either, though he could find better material than "Fightin' Side of Me" and "Rose Colored Glasses" to fill out the album.

Famous Duets (Power Pak/Gusto). For a throw-together, this is quality stuff. Few of these teams lasted long (the exceptions are Johnny and Joanie Mosby, Carl and Pearl Butler, and Lulu Belle and Scotty), and not all are well matched (Jean Shepard blows Red Sovine out of the studio on "Jackson"), but this is the only way you'll ever get to hear Cowboy Copas and Dottie West pledging their love on "Loose Talk," or George Jones and Jeanette Hicks on "Yearning."

Red Foley: *The Red Foley Story* (MCA). Foley sang a variety of material during his decade-plus near the top of the charts, and though the hits stopped coming in 1959, he continued working right up until his death in 1969. With his intimate baritone, it's surprising he didn't try more pop, but he did sing hymns, narrative ballads, novelties, tearjerkers, country boogie, even some blues and R & B. Though the something-for-everyone approach didn't always work to his advantage, these re-recordings run the gamut. Too soft for some tastes, but his family-style fare resulted in his being elected to the Hall of Fame in 1967.

Larry Gatlin: *Greatest Hits, Volume 1* (Columbia). Gatlin writes and sings a slick and often superficial style of modern Nashville music that isn't half as smart as he thinks it is. But at its best ("Statues Without

Hearts," for example) it's smarter than most. Those three-part harmonies add a touch of sparkle, too.

Don Gibson: *Rockin' Rollin' Don Gibson* (German Bear Family). Gibson's fusion of pop rockabilly with the Nashville Sound is not really rockin' and rollin', but it was important, effective, and innovative, which is why it's discussed at length earlier in this section. This import, however, is currently the only place you can find in-print versions of that sound.

Mickey Gilley: *Greatest Hits* (Epic). He may be little more than a piano-playing clone for his illustrious cousin Jerry Lee Lewis, but for a brief period in the mid-seventies, Gilley was delivering on his country ballads while the Killer withered away. His interpretations of "Room Full of Roses," "Window Up Above," and "Fraulein," among others, are all admirable extensions of the Nashville Sound, and often left in ragged edges that Music City would have smoothed over.

Mickey Gilley: *Gilley's Smokin'* (Columbia). Primarily a singles artist, Gilley actually made comparisons to his cousin Jerry Lee seem less far-fetched with this 1976 album. Its highlight was "Don't the Girls All Get Prettier at Closing Time," a rocking slice of barroom lore. But "There's a Song on the Jukebox" and Vic McAlpin's standard "How's My Ex Treating You" hold up well, too. "Bring It On Home to Me," "My Babe," and "Lawdy Miss Clawdy" are credible rock and R & B covers, while "I'll Fly Away," the gospel standard, is a helluva way to end such an album.

Mickey Gilley: *Greatest Hits, Vol. II* (Columbia). No real surprises here, but with contemporary material like "Honky Tonk Wine" and "Overnight Sensation," as well as a pretty good Jerry Lee rip in "#1 Rock 'n' Roll C & W Boogie Blues Man," this marks Gilley's last hurrah before he slogged off into pop and professional urban cowboyism.

Lloyd Green: *Ten Shades of Green* (Mid-Land). It's hard to believe Green's played on as many records as the liner notes claim, because the artists he's backed have such disparate styles. On his own, as he is on this all-instrumental album, he proves himself one of the bluesiest of steel guitarists, and Nashville in the sixties (when Green was at his peak as a session man) didn't have a lot of use for bluesmen.

Jack Greene: *Greatest Hits* (MCA). This former Texas Troubador did his boss proud when he went solo in the mid-sixties, for "There Goes My Everything" is a country angst in its highest form and the follow-ups drove the point home. Getting all those songs from Dallas Frazier didn't hurt.

Tom T. Hall: *Greatest Hits* (Mercury). This has a couple of too-easy family-of-man songs in "One Hundred Children" and "I Washed My Face in the Morning Dew," and a too-easy religious song in "Me and Jesus." But everything else is first-rate early Hall, including "Homecoming," the story of an ambivalent country near-star visiting his father, and "Ballad of Forty Dollars," in which a gravedigger ruminates sardonically on the funeral procession of a man who died owing him money.

Tom T. Hall: *Greatest Hits, Vol. III* (Mercury). Thin by Hall's original standards, but leagues above *Vol. II.* "Faster Horses (The Cowboy and the Poet)" is as close as Hall ever came to an "outlaw" song, and "Fox on the Run" is the best of his bluegrass experiments. "I Can't Dance" and "She Gave Her Heart to Jethro" are vintage Hall, and "Turn It On, Turn It On, Turn It On" ("it" being the electric chair) ranks with his very best stories. Meanwhile, keep an eye on the bargain bins for such early, now-deleted Hall albums as *Tom T. Hall, I Witness Life,* and *Homecoming.*

Freddie Hart: *The Best of Freddie Hart* (MCA). Before he sapped out entirely in the mid-seventies, Hart was a journeyman Nashville balladeer who sounded like a weird mating of Webb Pierce, Freddy Fender, and Slim Whitman. He didn't have a bundle of hits during the mid-sixties (when he was on Kapp), but this is filled out with standards carefully chosen.

John Hughey: *On and Off Stage* (Chimer). Nashville's most acrobatic pedal steel guitarist turns in an instrumental album of songs ranging from Leon McAuliffe's "Pan Handle Rag" and Fred Rose's "Deep Water" to new Nashville fare like Linda Hargrove's "Let It Shine" and Jessi Colter's "I'm Not Lisa," with stops in between for mainstream writers like Conway Twitty (his regular employer) and Connie Smith.

Ferlin Husky: *The Hits of Ferlin Husky* (Capitol). Husky's soft, introspective brand of country-pop brought him hits steadily from 1955 right up into the seventies. This out-of-print album collects the best of them, including the two that will be forever associated with him, "Gone" and "Wings of a Dove."

Stonewall Jackson: *Greatest Hits* (Columbia). Stonewall's hype stems from the fact that he's the first artist ever to successfully audition for the Opry without benefit of a major label behind him. Supposedly, he just drove his truck up to the Opry offices from Georgia in 1956, sang for the boss, and was signed on the spot. The major label soon followed—his first hit for Columbia was "Life to Go," in 1958, and it immediately established him as a purist country singer still able to work within the Nashville mold. In 1959 he had his sole crossover success with "Waterloo," a novelty song likening a bad romance to the military battle. Among the other hits on this out-of-print gem are "Don't Be Angry," "A Wound Time Can't Erase," and "I Washed My Hands in Muddy Water."

Stonewall Jackson: *The Great Old Songs* (Columbia Limited Edition). Is Stonewall Jackson for real? Imagine a commercial country singer in the sixties recording Nashville updates of songs like "Knoxville Girl" and "Mother the Queen of My Heart"—and getting away with it.

Wanda Jackson: *The Best of Wanda Jackson* (Capitol). In 1961, Wanda switched to honky-tonk-influenced country, and with "Right or Wrong" proved she could handle the form as well as she did rockabilly. Her rockabilly strong-mindedness was especially useful when she was cutting admonitions like "Tears Will Be the Chaser for Your Wine," and though her best years were behind her by the mid-sixties (which is happily when this album ends), she continued enjoying modest hits until the early seventies, when she was born again and became a gospel singer.

Sonny James: *The Best of Sonny James* (Capitol). The make-out ballad "Teen Love" is as good a job as Nashville ever did of co-opting the teen market after rockabilly swaggered forth. Nothing else here is quite as convincing, but this takes James up into the mid-sixties and his formula still hasn't ossified.

Waylon Jennings: *Best of Waylon Jennings* (RCA). Is this a man in search of a style or did he really mean the likes of "MacArthur Park" and "The Days of Sand and Shovels"? I think the truth is a combination of both, but when he leans into material like "Only Daddy That'll Walk the Line," I stop wondering and just listen.

Johnny and Jack: *Here's Johnny and Jack* (Vocalion). Johnny Wright (who married Kitty Wells) and Jack Anglin teamed up in 1938. By 1948 they had joined the Opry, and throughout the fifties they enjoyed a string of hits (now all out of print) on RCA. Unlike most duet acts, they changed with the times; when they recorded these sides for Decca in the early sixties, they even used a bass-heavy, countrified version of the Bo Diddley beat. The duo was torn apart when Jack was killed in a car wreck on his way to Patsy Cline's funeral in 1963.

George Jones: *My Country* (Musicor). George's 1965–71 stint with Musicor was not his most memorable, but this double album of twenty songs has little filler. He's still writing some of his own best songs ("Small Town Laboring Man," "My Favorite Lies"). Dallas Frazier, who supplied seven more, never did George wrong either; Jones even did a whole album of Frazier songs without repeating any of these. Pappy Daily's production leaves much to be desired, but if you run across this out-of-print set in the bargain bins, don't hesitate.

George Jones: *George Jones Sings the Songs of Dallas Frazier* (Musicor). During the sixties, Frazier was writing some of the deepest honky-tonk in Nashville. Though he had a fondness for novelty songs, he also had a taste for the apocalyptic or the macabre that was fascinating in its own right. And when he sat down to dash off a ready-made, he produced wonders like "The Honky Tonk Downstairs." Jones, meanwhile, was continuing to grow as a vocalist, and if he was often saddled with lame bands and production, he sure did his best to overcome. Also out of print, and also worth looking for real hard.

George Jones: *Burn the Honky Tonk Down* (Rounder Special Series). During the Musicor years, Pappy Daily overrecorded Jones horrendously. Yet there was plenty of wheat among the chaff, as this reissue of singles-that-didn't-do-as-well-as-they-should-have and selected album cuts demonstrates. Most significantly, it contains some of his last truly great up-tempo performances, for once he signed with Epic, George turned increasingly to a slow and more considered groove that better fitted his mature voice.

George Jones: *The Battle* (Epic). Jones and Sherrill mark his separation from Tammy with a breaking-up ballad that uses military percussion to accent lyrics likening the situation to a state of war. "Baby, There's Nothing Like You" gives him plenty of room to stretch out, and his version of David Allan Coe's "I Still Sing the Old Songs" makes no bones about where his allegiances really lie. One of George's all-time great album covers, too.

George Jones: *Alone Again* (Epic). This 1976 set was the first of the "old George" albums Sherrill did, taking him back to the basics, sans schlocky overdubs. Even the material referred back to George's honky-tonking days, the two most astonishing being ("a man can be a drunk sometimes, but . . .") "A Drunk Can't Be a Man" and "Stand on My Own Two Knees." In the latter George illustrates how much he's grown by informing his woman that he no longer need crawl to her, he can stand on his own two knees. Nobody else could have pulled that off, believe me. For novelty's sake, there's "Her Name Is . . ." and George digs down for tailor-made songs like "Ain't Nobody Gonna Miss Me," "I'm All She's Got," "Over Something Good," and "Right Now I'd Come Back and Melt in Her Arms." Welcome back, George.

George Jones: *All-Time Greatest Hits, Vol. 1* (Epic). In 1977, right around the time George was being lionized by the outlaws and his cult was beginning to grow into a mass audience, Billy Sherrill got the bright idea of taking him into the studio and recutting some of his past master-pieces with minimal, back-to-the-roots production. Normally, such re-recordings don't work so well, but this one did. For the most part, Sherrill made good on his promise—only an extraneous female chorus mars some of these songs—and George had added new vocal tricks since recording the originals, so he had little trouble holding up his end of the deal. The slower songs work best; "Walk Through This World with Me" borders on the mystical. But up-tempo war-horses like "The Race Is On" and "Why Baby Why" survive, too.

George Jones: *Bartender's Blues* (Epic). George strains too frequently on this one, but that's understandable, given his condition and the material he's got to work with. As much as the Epic publicity machine has stayed revved up for him, the company has kept very few of his albums in print. This is one of them, so it must be a good seller. And if the title song is pretty pale for George (having James Taylor sing with him grates), the follow-up, the 1978 "I'll Just Take It Out in Love," is a big improvement. And the filler is better than usual—especially "Leaving Love All Over the Place," which is one of the more audacious novelties he's cut in recent years.

George Jones: *My* Very *Special Guests* (Epic). The much-vaunted 1979 duets album turned out to be a mixed bag, predictably enough. For one thing, George, whose health was worse than ever during the two-year period it took to record this, was undoubtedly more inclined than usual to let Billy take care of everything; I'll bet the ranch George had no input on most of the material here, but just showed up and sang what-ever Sherrill gave him. For another, his voice is failing on some cuts, which even Sherrill can't camouflage. Finally, you don't have to hear tape splices to be able to tell when the two participants in a duet were actually singing together in the studio at the same time; on this album, vocals were overdubbed separately. For all that, the highlights are a surprise—Linda Ronstadt acquits herself handsomely on "I've Turned You to Stone," and Elvis Costello, though hardly in George's league as a singer, turns in the album's other top-flight song in "Stranger in the House." "Will the Circle Be Unbroken," with Pop and Mavis Staples builds inexorably. The only outright clinkers are "I Still Hold Her Body (but I Think I've Lost Her Mind)" with Dennis and Ray (of Dr. Hook) and "Bartender's Blues," an imitation-George lyric by (and with) James Taylor.

George Jones: *I Am What I Am* (Epic). By the end of 1982 this album had spent more than two years on the charts, not bad for a "comeback" album, which is what it was supposed to be. It's not just that "He Stopped Loving Her Today" lets him put an old ghost to rest, so to speak; or that "I've Aged 20 Years in 5" and "If Drinkin' Don't Kill Me" speak to his recent past as eloquently as "Bone Dry" mocks it; or even that the filler, like "Brother to the Blues," is the kind of record other artists would kill for. It's also that George himself, fresh out of the detox ward, took on the project with such apparent calm and confidence; all the Jones vocal technique is here, and is more awesome than ever, but it's all sort of taken-for-granted, too. He sounds like it's the first time that he really understood just how great he is, and he was thus determined not to let down anyone, including himself.

George Jones and Tammy Wynette: *Golden Ring* (Epic). As a rule, their duet albums exploited the hit-plus-filler formula even more rigidly than did their respective solo albums. In fact, George and Tammy often sound like they're going through the musical equivalent of fulfilling marital duties. But this 1976 effort, when all was lost but George wasn't quite prepared to face it yet, puts more on the line than the others.

The Kendalls: *The Best of the Kendalls* (Ovation). This duet team is not husband and wife, but father and daughter. The fact that they sing mainly cheating songs ("Heaven's Just a Sin Away" is still their best and, not coincidentally, their most suggestive) has raised a few eyebrows. But what *really* makes the difference is that since they came along in 1977 they've stuck to hard country, and they're the most traditional team since Porter and Dolly. They're still going strong, though not quite up to the standards of their first three years, as documented on this out-of-print album for a now-defunct label.

Brenda Lee: *The Brenda Lee Story—Her Greatest Hits* (MCA). When Brenda surfaced in the late fifties as Little Miss Dynamite (she was a four-foot eleven-inch teen with a brassy voice), she was considered rock 'n' roll primarily because there was no other category to accommodate her. In retrospect, it's easy to see that she was always aiming for the middle of the road, filling the role of Patsy Cline for kids. She was at her best on ballads like "I'm Sorry" (1960) though she later moved more toward country. This concentrates more on her early period, and for once the label does it without rerecordings.

Jerry Lee Lewis: *The Country Hall of Fame, Vol. 1* (Smash/Mercury). The Killer cut many many country albums for this label, some of them absolutely superb, and there is no discernible logic as to what remains in print. But I'm not about to knock this late-sixties album, in which a rejuvenated Jerry Lee takes on standards as diverse as "Sweet Dreams," "Born to Lose," "Mom and Dad Waltz," "I'm So Lonesome I Could Cry," and "Jambalya," and makes each a pledge of allegiance to country music.

Jerry Lee Lewis: *Jerry Lee Lewis Sings the Country Hall of Fame Hits, Volume II* (Mercury). This is mid-period Killer, stretching out on his favorite country standards, something he did effortlessly and flawlessly. This budget-line reissue is a good start, but where's the rest of Jerry Lee's pivotal Nashville work?

Jerry Lee Lewis and Linda Gail Lewis: *Together* (Smash/Mercury). This is one of the sweatiest, most suggestive duet albums ever made, and who cares if it's his *sister* he's singing with. Linda Gail was as rough as female country singers got in the late sixties and early seventies, which is undoubtedly part of the reason her own career never took off; the other part is that she was often stuck with material so inappropriate to her down-home voice that the results were comical. But on this out-of-print album she certainly holds her own with Jerry Lee, which is more than most people do.

Jerry Lee Lewis: *The Best of Jerry Lee Lewis, Volume II* (Mercury). The Jerry Lee of the seventies continued to sing his pretty country songs, but they were more modern ("Middle Age Crazy"). With 1972's "Chantilly Lace" he also returned to rocking, while "Who's Gonna Play This Old Piano" and "Boogie Woogie Country Man" are both the kind of self-aggrandizement that he pulled off with such aplomb even when everything else was going sour. Meanwhile, "Sweet Georgia Brown" goes so fast that by the end of the song he's not making a whit of sense, and only Jerry Lee Lewis could get a hit doing something like that.

Jerry Lee Lewis: *Jerry Lee Lewis* (Warner Bros.). After moving to a new label in 1979, the Killer cut loose with this album of autumnal rockabilly just before commencing on another of his extended tailspins. For once, the voice, attitude, and piano chops are all willing *and* able, and the material is superb, including a fitting new anthem in "Rockin' My Life Away."

Jerry Lee Lewis: *The Best of Jerry Lee Lewis Featuring "39 and Holding"* (Warner Bros.). Jerry Lee's stint with his new label lasted barely two years, and after that compelling debut, the albums went downhill, slowly but perceptibly. This pulls together the best of them, though, and it's an impressive package. His reading of the Roger Miller/Bill Anderson song "When Two Worlds Collide" is particularly apt for him.

And if his voice is a little frayed, that only adds conviction to middle-age songs like "39 and Holding" and "I Wish I Was 18 Again," a type of material that is becoming something of a specialty with him.

Hank Locklin: *The Best of Hank Locklin* (RCA). Locklin's Irish tenor kept him on the charts from 1949 to 1971; though "Please Help Me, I'm Falling" was his sole No. 1, "Send Me the Pillow You Dream On" is nearly as well known. He's so sentimental you might not be able to take him for long, but this out-of-print album is the best place to start (and for most, to finish).

Hank Locklin: *20 Of the Best Of Hank Locklin* (British RCA). The alternative is this import, which may prove to be a little *too* much Locklin to all but the most teary-eyed.

Charlie Louvin: *Best of Charlie Louvin* (Capitol). Charlie was somewhat lost without Ira, but for much of the sixties he put together a modest string of hits that provided a compatible marriage between tradition and the Nashville mainstream.

Loretta Lynn: *You Ain't Woman Enough* (MCA). This early in her career (1966) Loretta still has plenty of energy for albums; though sometimes the production makes them sound like rush jobs even when they weren't, Loretta prevails. This is one of her most somber, with songs like "These Boots Are Made for Walking," "The Darkest Day," and "Talking to the Wall" joining the title classic to enforce moods of anger, frustration, and determination.

Loretta Lynn: *Don't Come Home A' Drinkin' (with Lovin' on Your Mind)* (MCA). This is her best getting-even album, what with the 1966 title song plus "The Shoe Goes On the Other Foot Tonight" and "The Devil Gets His Due." But Loretta is still too much of a "girl singer" to let herself take the upper hand all the way through, so she compensates with "Tomorrow Never Comes" and "There Goes My Everything."

Loretta Lynn: *Loretta Lynn Writes 'Em and Sings 'Em* (MCA). A 1970 collection of recent singles and album cuts thrown together by her record company *solely* because she wrote 'em, this is nonetheless one of her most powerful albums. Unfortunately, contractual disputes have kept her from writing much since then. "I Know How" is Loretta at her sexiest, "You Wanna Give Me a Lift" is Loretta at her sassiest, and the others are all in the same league.

Loretta Lynn: *One's On the Way* (MCA). Side one has enough emotional peaks and valleys to qualify as her best-rounded album side ever, the highlights being the unforgettable title song and "L-O-V-E Love," a lecture about bad language that Loretta co-wrote. It's also nice to know that this middle-aged woman can still get a thrill on "Blueberry Hill." Side two doesn't give her quite as much to dig into, but overall, this album certainly justifies her selection in 1972 as the first-ever female CMA Entertainer of the Year.

Loretta Lynn: *I Remember Patsy* (MCA). That's Patsy Cline, who befriended the new girl in town when Loretta first came to Nashville. Loretta's choice of Cline hits for this 1977 tribute is predictable enough, but she connects with each one. And on "Why Can't He Be You" she does much more than that. But wouldn't the seven-minutes-plus "conversation" that ends the LP have worked better as liner notes?

Loretta Lynn and Conway Twitty: *We Only Make Believe* (MCA). This is their first album of duets and the 1971 pairing is still tentative. But the remake of Conway's title song offers a taste of what's to come; "After the Fire Has Gone" hints at the emotional peaks they're capable of and "Take Me," "Hangin' On," "Working Girl," and "Pickin' Wild Mountain Berries" are all classy fillers.

Loretta Lynn and Conway Twitty: *The Very Best of Loretta Lynn and Conway Twitty* (MCA). This team's best albums were the early ones, but their best singles came later on, and this album never does quite reconcile that; both *We Only Make Believe* (1971) and *Honky Tonk Heroes* (1978) are represented with three songs each, with eight more cuts spread among their other six albums. But once they hit their stride as singles artists, they were terrific, especially tear-jerk overkill like "The Letter" (1976) and "As Soon as I Hang Up the Phone" (1974), both with recitations that pull every trick to pull heartstrings. "You're the Reason Our Kids Are Ugly," meanwhile, is an insult-swapping novelty song you'll just have to hear for yourself.

Barbara Mandrell: *The Best of Barbara Mandrell* (Columbia). In her earliest incarnation (1969–75), Barbara specialized in taking the sting out of soul classics like "Show Me" and "Do Right Woman, Do Right Man." But she was at her most popular when she was at her most suggestive ("Midnight Oil"), though for my money she was at her best when she was impatient to get down with her hubby ("Tonight My Baby's Coming Home") and not her outside man. How Billy Sherrill, who produced these sides, ever let her get away remains a mystery; the mind shudders when it imagines what *that* team could be concocting today.

Barbara Mandrell: *The Best of Barbara Mandrell* (MCA). The years 1975–78 were transitional. She's still covering can't-miss R & B songs

("Woman to Woman" and "Married but Not to Each Other") for the bread-and-butter hits, but she's not too proud to sing an (unintentionally) hilarious weeper like "Standing Room Only": "You must think my bed's a bus stop/The way you come and go."

Roger Miller: *Best of Roger Miller* (Mercury). These are his "covers" hits, and while Miller could pick 'em—he found "Me and Bobby McGee" in 1969—I miss the craziness. He's a good singer here; with his own material, he's great.

Ronnie Milsap: *Where My Heart Is* (RCA). Milsap brought R & B roots to his 1973 country debut, which is probably why the band sounds less flaccid, and his voice less creamy, than it did on subsequent albums. He left those roots fast, which makes the depth on this album all the more impressive. Not too many people could put out an album, let alone a debut album, with definitive readings of songs from Dan Penn (co-writer on "I Hate You"), Merle Haggard ("Branded Man"), Dallas Frazier and Doodle Owens ("Brothers, Strangers and Friends"), and Hillman Hall ("Pass Me By"). And those aren't necessarily even the hits.

Ronnie Milsap: *Live* (RCA). Right around the time he was transforming himself from a gutsy country balladeer to crooning wimp, Milsap went to the Opry Auditorium and cut this live album. It includes material from the old Milsap and the new one, as well as songs he never recorded on any of his studio albums. From here on out, he's been the musical equivalent of a have-a-nice-day button, though I will give him credit for being the only man in Nashville who consistently comes up with credible songs about happy marriages.

Willie Nelson: *Diamonds in the Rough* (Delta). On first arriving in Nashville, Willie went to someone else's recording session to pitch some songs. When the star never showed, Nelson took advantage of the sidemen assembled to make demos of the songs. This was in 1961, and they remained unheard by the public until 1977, when they were assembled for a small-label double album. If the musicianship is ragged, it fits perfectly with Willie's voice and these songs of psychic battering. Willie's own Lone Star label then boiled the double album down to a single album called *Face of a Fighter*, which was deleted when the label's distribution deal with Phonogram fell through. Now the single album has been picked up by this Texas indie, and if you're smart, you'll act while it's still available.

Willie Nelson: *Best of Willie Nelson* (Liberty). An early-sixties album cut in Hollywood, which means not enough of the right kind of country (no steel guitar, for example) and too much of the wrong kind of pop (the Anita Kerr Singers are almost as prominent as Willie). But it also contains seminal versions of "Funny How Time Slips Away," "Crazy," "Undo the Right," and the like—as well as neglected classics like "Darkness on the Face of the Earth."

Willie Nelson: *Live* (RCA). The band is too limp—they're still trying to pass as Nashville pros, methinks. But the concert format allows Willie to stray vocally, and even if the material is usually crammed into medleys, he gives eccentric readings to most of the best songs from his sixties RCA period. Added bonus: "I Gotta Get Drunk," which makes a laughingstock of all those drinking-compulsion songs.

Willie Nelson: *Yesterday's Wine* (RCA). Willie's first serious attempt at a concept album, this follows on "imperfect man" from the cradle to the grave. Though the emphasis is on the man's spiritual life, the stand-out track is the tongue-in-cheek profanity of "Me and Paul."

Norma Jean: *The Best of Norma Jean* (RCA). It's a measure of the role of the "girl singer" in country music that Norma Jean Beasler was never regarded as anything more than an appendage of Porter Wagoner, on whose show she preceded Dolly Parton. Between 1964 and 1967 the Oklahoma woman turned out a series of singles that, while never as popular as Porter's own, matched the boss with heart, hurtin', and cheatin' songs like "Let's Go All the Way," "Conscience Keep an Eye on Me," "Jackson Ain't a Very Big Town," "You Changed Everything About Me but My Name," and "You're Driving Me Out of My Mind." And occasionally, as on "The Shirt" (1966), she could be every bit as perverse as him, which is no small achievement. This is now out of print, but I'd put Norma Jean in a league with Loretta, Dolly, and Tammy any day.

Dolly Parton: *Coat of Many Colors* (RCA). On this 1971 album, Dolly starts coming into her own as a Personality. There's no small amount of nostalgia here, but there's much more happening than *just* nostalgia— notably, streaks of mysticism and sexual ambiguity that suggest she's already trying to reconcile her strict Calvinist background with the looser mores of the pop crowd she'll soon be pursuing. This transitional album catches her at her songwriting apex: The title tune weaves the biblical story of Joseph into her own story.

Dolly Parton: *My Tennessee Home* (RCA). This 1973 album begins with a recitation of the first letter Dolly wrote home after arriving in Nashville in 1964 and ends with "Down on Music Row," a summary of what happened when she got there. The other songs are all about growing up in that isolated section of east Tennessee. Now too much nostalgia can be an oppressive (and counterproductive) thing, and certain parts of this album do ring hollow. But that she can pull it off at all says something about both her tenacity and her talent. Also her mountain soul.

Dolly Parton: *Jolene* (RCA). Mostly upbeat, verging-on-pop Dolly, with one whole side of originals. Not a great album, but her last consistently good one. Ouch—it's from all the way back in 1974.

Johnny Paycheck: *Greatest Hits* (Epic). Paycheck is such a great all-around country singer that he can adapt himself to most any context, even Billy Sherrill's country goo. Which is just what Johnny does here, during his first comeback (from drugs and liquor) period of 1971–75, when he is singing all love songs not wholly suited to him. But "Someone to Give My Love To," with its hypnotic band track and Johnny's intense vocal is one of the landmark heart songs of that era, and "She's All I Got" and the gospel "Let's All Go Down to the River" (a duet with Jody Miller) aren't too far behind.

Charlie Pride: *Best of Charlie Pride* (RCA). Technically speaking, Pride is as good a country singer as there's been the last couple of decades. In truth, he's *too* smooth, but he sure can hit those notes. And he sounds best when he's produced by Jack Clement, which is the case on "The Snakes Crawl at Night" and too few others of these hits from the second half of the sixties. "All I Have to Offer You (Is Me)" remains his best poor-boy song, though.

Charlie Pride: *The Best of Charlie Pride, Vol. 2* (RCA). Because Pride is so slick, and so determined to eliminate all the black characteristics he can from his voice, his success often depends on the producer and the song more than anything else. The production here is all Jack Clement, and "Is Anybody Goin' to San Antone" and "Kiss an Angel Good Morning" pack a solid one-two punch that makes the early seventies his most fruitful period.

Charlie Pride: *The Best of Charlie Pride, Vol. III* (RCA). Pride's last gasp before turning to dreck was the 1974 "Mississippi Cotton Picking Delta Town," which asserted his blackness as no previous record had. That's here along with "I Don't Deserve a Mansion," but the rest of the album barely carries its weight.

Jerry Reed: *The Best of Jerry Reed* (RCA). It wasn't through his roles in Burt Reynolds movies that Jerry Reed cultivated the image of redneck nut. He did it earlier than that, in the late sixties and early seventies, when he was running up a string of smart(ass) novelty hits like "Amos Moses" and "Tupelo Mississippi Flash" (say hello, Elvis). Too bad this album has to include some of his more conventional hits, too, because they're nowhere near as inspired. Too bad, also, that the emphasis on singing and image-mongering overshadows almost completely his talents as a guitarist. Still, the essential Jerry Reed survives.

Del Reeves: *Looking at the World Through a Windshield* (United Artists). Reeves considered himself primarily a romantic crooner, but I'll take this collection of late-sixties trucking songs any day, especially the title tune (which is full of deceptive wordplays). His romantic ballads are just too plain. Virtually all his work, including this, is now out of print.

Jim Reeves: *The Best of Jim Reeves* (RCA). Though a native of east Texas, Reeves learned to wash that Lone Star grit out of his voice early on, and it served him well. Described as containing "a touch of velvet," it was a deep, soothing voice that was one of the first to enjoy a muted Nashville Sound backing. Reeves sang lyrics that wouldn't be out of place in a honky-tonk, but he was quick to move into a country-pop vein on his records; though he'd had several previous hits, the 1957 "Four Walls" was his first step in this direction. This also contains his other biggest hit, "He'll Have to Go" (1959), and others that kept Reeves at the top of the charts until his death in a 1964 airplane crash.

Jim Reeves: *The Best of Jim Reeves, Vol. II* (RCA). Though the Reeves cult—if a following as large as his can be thus described—is built around the mellifluous stylings of the songs on Volume I, hard-core country fans may actually prefer this. It has its fair share of schmaltz, but several of these songs predate his 1957 pop breakthrough, and actually qualify as pretty decent hard country. Which perhaps makes this more representative of the compleat Jim Reeves, though that's not what his mind-boggling popularity, which continues growing to this day, is based on.

Jim Reeves: *The Best of Jim Reeves, Vol. III* (RCA). If these are the original backing tracks (see next item), then there's little pretense here toward presenting Reeves as a country artist. The steel guitar and fiddle have been eliminated and the orchestra lays the slush on thick. But there's still some country left in Reeves' grainy voice despite the pure countrypolitan production, and on at least one track ("Pride Goes Before a Fall"), that's enough.

The Best of Jim Reeves, Vol. IV (RCA). On which the widow Mary and the revisionist corporation erase the old backing tracks from cuts from the late fifties and early sixties and replace them with a shiny new orchestra. And you know what? Some of this doesn't sound substantially different from records released when he was still alive. Some stellar material here, even if it's been sabotaged.

Jim Reeves: *The Abbot Recordings, Vol. 1* (British RCA). Before he hooked up with a major, Reeves recorded for a Texas indie. Here are seventeen of those sides, some of which he later rerecorded for RCA; they show just how pliable his voice was, and how close to the Nashville Sound he was from the beginning, but they also reveal more honky-tonk roots than you might expect.

Jim Reeves: *The Abbot Recordings, Vol. 2* (British RCA). Ditto, only this includes twenty cuts, some of them being released for the first time. For gluttons only.

Jeannie C. Riley: *Greatest Hits* (Plantation). Sure, "Harper Valley P.T.A." was one of the most spirited singles of the late sixties, as well as a breakthrough for modern topical country songs. And Jeannie's subsequent bad-girl image and tell-it-like-it-is delivery were almost as much fun as the actual music. But one problem with winning such resounding success on your first try is that you spend the rest of your career trying to match it. That's what she does here—most of these follow-ups failed to hit the Top 10, and the sexiest ones were rarely the best. She—or her producers, as the born-again Jeannie would now like us to believe—was trying too hard, straining for effect. A little goes a long way, and this is just enough.

Marty Robbins: *Marty's Greatest Hits* (Columbia). Since emerging in 1953, Robbins applied his high, clear, smooth, romantic tenor to a variety of material. Later in his career, in fact, he seemed to be spreading himself thin. Though his preference is clearly for love songs, this album of early hits runs the gamut from rockabilly ballads ("White Sport Coat" and "Singing the Blues") to countrified pop ("The Story of My Life" and "The Last Time I Saw My Heart," both from the team of Hal David and Burt Bacharach) to country ("The Blues Country Style") to blues ("Knee Deep in the Blues") to Hawaiian ("Aloha Oe"). He was probably the most adaptable singer in Nashville in the fifties, though this collection of hits gives inexplicably short shrift to the country songs which, after all, were his specialty.

Marty Robbins: *More Great Hits* (Columbia). This one puts more emphasis on the western Marty Robbins, reprising Spanish-flavored hits like "El Paso." He's as smooth as ever, but it still sells him short, as too few of these songs were actual hits. And there's no album that pulls together the bona fide hits from this period.

Marty Robbins: *Greatest Hits, Vol. 4* (Columbia). For some reason, the best records on *Vol. 3* are repeated here, and this has a couple more in the same league. With the 1976 "El Paso City," Marty recaptured that

Spanish magic from old hits like "Devil Woman" (which, though it was a hit in 1962, finally winds up here). With "My Woman, My Woman, My Wife," the kind of blind-love song that can't miss in Nashville, he tips his hand as to his true current directions. Still, the pipes are as crystal clear as ever.

Marty Robbins: *Country and Western Classics: Marty Robbins* (Time-Life). This three-record boxed set is easily the best overview of his entire career, with all the key hits, some notable misses, and some previously unreleased sides as a bonus. It shows indisputably that his late, overly mawkish ballads were of a piece with his earliest sides, though the latter sound "wetter" and thus more effective. And no matter how great his reputation as Mr. Teardrop, his gunslinger western ballads hold up better than anything else he ever did. He died in 1982, shortly after being elected to the Hall of Fame.

Johnny Rodriguez: *Introducing Johnny Rodriguez* (Mercury). When Rodriguez broke through in late 1972, he was touted as "the Next Big Thing"—a Mexican-American who sang in Spanish and English with a voice full of throbbing sincerity, a traditionalist with obvious "right" roots (mostly Frizzell and Haggard), and a young man with sex appeal to boot. He soon became a victim of indecision, indirection, and changing trends—the Next Big Thing happened outside the country mainstream, ironically enough, in the Texas Rodriguez had just fled. But that in no way diminished the impact or gracefulness of this, his debut album, which to this day sounds like one of the last hurrahs of the Nashville Sound—concise, compact, full of strong tunes, with a Jerry Kennedy production that goes light on all the extras.

Johnny Rodriguez: *The Greatest Hits of Johnny Rodriguez* (Mercury). Johnny never could recapture the clarity and sexiness of his 1972 debut, though many of the singles that followed ("Ridin' My Thumb to Mexico" and "That's the Way Love Goes" from 1973, "Just Get Up and Close the Door" from 1975, "I Couldn't Be Me Without You" from 1976) maintain the fervor. He held onto his roots (cutting oldies like "Faded Love" and "Born to Lose"), but this collection of hard country (sometimes sweetened) proved to be his last focused work.

Jean Shepard: *The Best of Jean Shepard* (Capitol). Jean was telling-it-like-it-was from the woman's point of view as early as 1953, and her 1955 debut hit, "Satisfied Mind," is one of the most compelling songs from that era. Her sobbing, compressed voice was well suited to Nashville's idea of a honky-tonk woman, and she enjoyed hits off and on for the next two decades. Though it is now out of print, this collects the best of the early ones.

Jean Shepard: *The First Lady of Country Music* (German Master-piece). Here's more of the same, all from the mid-fifties, and with a clarity and purposefulness too many country women of that era lacked.

Cal Smith: *The Best of Cal Smith* (MCA). Here's another former Texas Troubador who sounds somewhat like a higher-pitched version of his mentor, though Cal also owes a debt to Merle Haggard and other modern purists. This was unfortunately compiled before Smith had peaked (with "The Lord Knows I'm Drinking" in 1973 and "Country Bumpkin" in 1974), but there're faithful readings of "I'll Sail My Ship Alone" and "Silver Dew on the Bluegrass Tonight," as well as some early Gary Stewart songs and Willie Nelson's unheralded "So Much to Do."

Carl Smith: *Greatest Hits* (Columbia). Though his work is now out of print, Smith was one of the most successful at surviving the post-Hank Williams era and the onslaught of rock 'n' roll. He did it by melding a smooth vocal style to a basic honky-tonk band sound, and hits such as "Hey, Joe" and "There She Goes" established a dominance in the fifties that lasted into the early seventies.

Connie Smith: *The Best of Connie Smith* (RCA). Along with Loretta, Tammy, and Dolly, Connie gets my vote for top Nashville "girl singer" of the sixties, though her career hasn't sustained. She had a big, rich voice that sobbed and tore like she got her heart broken daily—which, judging from the songs, she might have. After being discovered by Bill Anderson, her first record, the 1964 "Once a Day," went to No. 1 and set the tone for subsequent releases: "Now I only cry once a day . . . every day . . . all day long." These mid-sixties sides pack a wallop that makes this out-of-print album worth searching for.

Connie Smith: *The Best of Connie Smith, Volume II* (RCA). With "Cry, Cry, Cry," "Burning a Hole in My Mind," "Run Away Little Tears," and "Only for Me," she's as magnetic as ever, her voice a little huskier, and her songs a little more introspective. But she still sounds like she's been around. Her career slowly trailed off after this, mainly because after being born again in the early seventies, she devoted herself to family instead of music; after a while, she wouldn't sing anything but gospel. This is also out of print.

Connie Smith: *"If It Ain't Love" and Other Great Dallas Frazier Songs* (RCA). This is also deleted, though it's only one of the most enduring duet albums of all time. It's not *all* duets, mind you, but Frazier helps out on three of these songs he wrote, and his roughness goes well with Connie's polish; even when he's not singing with her, his presence is felt, and that's the mark of a great writer. The title song was one of the great up-tempo country hits of the early seventies, and though she's cut a memorable song or two since, this marks the end of the line for her.

Hank Snow: *The Best of Hank Snow, Vol. II* (RCA). Though it's been allowed to slip out of print, this is the last of the essential Hank Snow; in fact, "Golden Rocket" is more like quintessential Hank Snow.

Billie Jo Spears: *The Singles Album* (Liberty). On mid-seventies hits like "Silver Wings and Golden Rings" or "Blanket on the Ground," Billie Jo usually plays the woman-in-waiting, though her voice has enough bite to make you think she won't stay that way forever.

Joe Stampley: *The Very Best of Joe Stampley* (MCA). Stampley is the kind of country singer who gives the word "journeyman" a good name. He has no real image or truly distinctive style, and his influences (especially, this early in his career, Conway Twitty) are apparent, but give him a good song and he'll do right by it. "Soul Song," "If You Touch Me (You've Got to Love Me)," "Too Far Gone" to name just three of his early-seventies hits, are better than good, and this is an unassuming little album that'll grow on you.

Joe Stampley: *Greatest Hits* (Epic). These hits from the mid-seventies move closer to honky-tonk and even (on "Sheik of Chicago," his salute to Chuck Berry) country-rock, but Stampley proves himself Mr. Reliable with everything. Again, no fireworks, but unadorned country singing from the heart, which is in increasingly short supply these days.

Joe Stampley: *Biggest Hits* (Epic). One in a rather cynical series of Columbia/Epic reissues that is really much more random than the title implies. In Stampley's case, there's little overlap with his true *Greatest Hits* compilation on Epic, because most of the songs here are from later (1978–81) in his career. During this phase, his novelty songs were even more novel and his drinking and cheating songs even more dramatic. And Stampley was one of the few who turned increasingly toward harder country as he matured.

The Statler Brothers: *The World of the Statler Brothers* (Columbia). While working for Johnny Cash in the mid-sixties, the Statlers perfected a chipper vocal group style best typified by "Flowers on the Wall," a novelty song that exhaustively mocked post-divorce *ennui*. This double album covers that era just as exhaustively.

The Statler Brothers: *The Best of the Statler Brothers* (Mercury). Some of these hits were originally cut for Columbia a good half decade before the early-seventies versions appearing here, and some of this music is just too mindlessly perky anyhow. But that's what some people like about the Statlers. Me, I like what I like because I'm not certain on some cuts whether they're really singing about nostalgia, which is supposedly their forte, or whether they're singing about dashed hopes; that's because sometimes they're not sure either, and when that happens, the slick facades come down and we're looking at the kind of nagging doubts that make modern country go.

The Statler Brothers as Lester "Roadhog" Moran and His Cadillac Cowboys: *Alive at the Johnny Mack Brown High School* (Mercury). This here is blasphemy, these people singing famous and favorite country songs that are all wrong because they're out of tune or the singers don't do harmony right or stuff like that and it's all supposed to be a funny joke too but I don't know. It's in the format of an old radio show and I can't see why anybody would want to do something like this to good old country music, but somebody did. I'm not one to spread rumors but I heard tell it might be the Statler Brothers under a phony name.

Mel Street: *The Very Best of Mel Street* (Capitol). Mel Street looks a little like Bobby Bare and sings in an ingratiating baritone. He's obsessed with devils, angels, and cheating, but anyone who still writes songs like "Borrowed Angel" in the seventies isn't faking it.

Mel Tillis: *Mel Tillis' Greatest Hits* (MCA). Tillis came to Music City primarily as a writer, but by the mid-sixties he was cutting records that struck a nice balance between the Nashville Sound and honky-tonk. Nothing flashy about the man, but he does have keen taste for the fine points of both domestic drama ("Who's Julie," in which a wife hears her husband talking in his sleep about another woman) and of the Bigger Picture ("Ruby, Don't Take Your Love to Town," in which an impotent Vietnam vet begs with his wife not to give up on him).

Mel Tillis: *The Best of Mel Tillis and the Statesiders* (Polydor). There were occasional descents into sludge, but on most of his releases between 1970 and 1975, when these songs were all hits, Tillis was helping people like Conway Twitty to keep the Nashville mainstream honest. Though he was a dark horse, his victory as 1976 Entertainer of the Year doesn't seem nearly so implausible after hearing the sides leading up to it. They embrace vague social consciousness and/or poor-boy blues ("Sawmill"), late-night misery ("Midnight, Me and the Blues"), honky-tonk ups and downs ("The Arms of a Fool" and especially the thumping "I Ain't Never"), and such gamey subjects as prostitution ("Commercial Affection"). Most are set to a shuffling beat that Tillis slides into naturally.

Mel Tillis: *The Very Best of Mel Tillis* (MCA). Back with MCA for the second half of the decade, Tillis proved his Entertainer of the Year award was no fluke. He may be a journeyman, but he's one with absolute mastery of the idiom, and he sells neither it nor himself short. "Good Woman Blues" was about as traditional as mainstream country could get during this era, and "What Did I Promise Her Last Night" is about as frank as mainstream country could get. As time passes, Tillis sounds more and more like the real thing, and one of the last of them.

Mel Tillis: *Greatest Hits* (Warner Bros.). His two-year stint with Elektra (which later merged with Warners' country division) was generally disappointing. But "Your Body Is an Outlaw" is not to be missed.

Tompall and The Glaser Brothers: *Greatest Hits* (Polydor). From 1966 through 1973, Tompall Glaser and his brothers Jim and Chuck were adapting brother harmonies to the Nashville Sound. It helped that Jack Clement was their producer, and also that, unlike the Statlers, their chief competition, they weren't addicted to novelty songs. With firm roots in the past, this is as hip as Nashville got back then.

Ernest Tubb and Loretta Lynn: *The Ernest Tubb–Loretta Lynn Story* (MCA). Ernest was one of Loretta's first patrons in Music City, and from 1964–69 they combined for four hits and two albums (repackaged here as a twofer). Their voices didn't match real well, but both of them were all personality when they sang together. They were thus especially effective on songs like "Who's Gonna Take the Garbage Out" that were designed to draw a laugh.

Tanya Tucker: *Greatest Hits* (Columbia). Tanya Tucker was thirteen when Billy Sherrill got ahold of her in 1972, and Billy knew just what to do with her and her booming, Brenda Lee-like voice. He simply paired that nubile innocence with the raciest material he could find—the woman gone slowly insane in "Delta Dawn," the murderous husband of "Blood Red and Goin' Down," the long-lost father of "What's Your Mama's Name," the anxious lover of "Would You Lay With Me (in a Field of Stone)," and especially the protagonist of "No Man's Land," a rape victim who turns frigid and who, years later, as a nurse, allows her attacker to die in his prison cell rather than treat him. This was American Gothic's last stand in country music, for my money, and those who claim Tanya sounded so good singing these only because she was too young to know what they were about either missed the whole decade or isn't really listening.

Tanya Tucker: *Greatest Hits* (MCA). Tanya began floundering after she left Sherrill and moved to a new label in the mid-seventies, but with

"San Antonio Stroll," "I Don't Believe My Heart Can Stand Another You," and "It's a Cowboy Lovin' Night," she struck the appropriate balance between waif and woman.

Conway Twitty: *Greatest Hits, Vol. 1* (MCA). Wherein Conway wages some of his mightiest battles against the Big G. We're talking about Guilt, as in "The Image of Me" and the definitive "How Much More Can She Stand." Subtheme: old loves he's never been able to forget, as in "Hello Darlin' " and "Fifteen Years Ago."

Conway Twitty: *Hello Darlin'* (MCA). This is the best of Conway's early hard-country albums, with a satisfying blend of originals and standards by the likes of Dallas Frazier and Fred Rose.

Conway Twitty: *Honky Tonk Angel* (MCA). Prime mid-period (1974) Conway, with the contradictions between his yearning for security and his wandering eyes raised to new heights.

Conway Twitty: *I've Already Loved You in My Mind* (MCA). Conway doesn't write nearly as often as he should, judging from this mid-seventies album of mostly originals. "Come See About Me" *(not* the Jr. Walker R & B hit) is white soul at its most searing.

Conway Twitty: *The High Priest of Country Music* (MCA). From the same era, but this one makes it not on the strength of the originals so much as on the way Conway manages to pump fresh blood into such overworked contemporary favorites as "Touch the Hand," "Amanda," and "Before the Next Teardrop Falls." Coming from anyone else, this would have been a throwaway.

Porter Wagoner: *The Best of Porter Wagoner* (RCA). Porter arrived in Nashville in 1955, a green Missouri farm boy, and from his first record, "A Satisfied Mind," he was in his element. Before he went into semiretirement in the mid-seventies, he was being called "the last of the hillbillies," and the tag fit. Who else would have bothered to cut "Uncle Pen"? Who else could have gotten excited by the likes of "Company's Comin' " or "Y'all Come," two songs expressing country life as people *wished* it to be more than it really was? What could be more quintessentially Porter than "Sorrow on the Rocks," "Skid Row Joe," "Misery Loves Company," and "I've Enjoyed as Much of This as I Can Stand"? Porter sings them all with sincerity and unbridled emotions, and each becomes a psychodrama of its own. Out of print now, but you can bet that when he's more safely in the distant past, they'll be reissuing his stuff as examples of what Nashville was like at its best.

Porter Wagoner: *The Best of Porter Wagoner, Vol. II* (RCA). This covers Porter from 1966 to his demise in the seventies. It includes homilies like "Pastor's Absent on Vacation," oldies like "Ole Slew-Foot," shameless tearjerkers like "Little Boy's Prayer" or "Men With Broken Hearts," novelties like "When You're Hot You're Hot," morality tales like "The Cold Hard Facts of Life" and "The Carroll County Accident." It summarizes all that was great about country music before country music became self-conscious. Because everything he did is out of print in America, I've limited my discussion of Porter to these two albums, but the man was tireless, and, if you ever see them, don't hesitate also to pick up such gems as *A Slice of Life—Songs Happy 'n' Sad, The Porter Wagoner Show, In Person, The Thin Man From West Plains,* or *Down in the Alley.*

Porter Wagoner: *20 of the Best of Porter Wagoner* (British RCA). Finally, a reissue from Porter's peak years, even if it's an import. It has mainly the same songs as the two Wagoner LPs listed above, but has the added bonus of being in print, albeit more expensive.

Porter Wagoner: *Down Home Country* (Accord). This recently released budget-line reissue is short on hits and hard to find, but "Crumbs from Another Man's Table" and "Devil's Alley" both show off Porter's dark side as well as anything he ever sang.

Porter Wagoner and Dolly Parton: *Sweet Harmony* (RCA Special Products/Pair). This is another budget-line special that duplicates some of the material on their in-print album of hits. It's also a double album, though, which proves that there's plenty more where the first collection came from.

Bill Walker: *Greatest Hits* (Columbia). Mexican-tinged ballads from the sixties, sort of like a huskier Marty Robbins, but with some acrobatic performances nonetheless. Now out of print.

Gene Watson: *The Best of Gene Watson* (Capitol). Watson was out of step with the seventies, a mainstream country singer just coming up. Since Nashville had very little use for mainstream country singers anymore, he's lucky to have lasted as long as he did. He's never achieved the stature of a Moe Bandy, and he probably never will; like a Joe Stampley, though, he's getting along okay anyhow. With efforts like "You Could Know as Much About a Stranger" or "Shadows on the Wall," he deserves to.

Gene Watson: *The Best of Gene Watson, Vol. 2* (Capitol). Watson sounds a little like Conway Twitty and a little more like any number of others. Because he has these identity problems, he's usually only as good as his next song. These are even better than those on Vol. 1, which enables Watson (and too few others) to carry the hard-country torch into the eighties. Here's hoping he never runs out of writers.

Kitty Wells: *The Kitty Wells Story* (MCA). Rerecordings, naturally, but Kitty's austere, nasal voice cuts through these Nashville Sound arrangements time and again. One of the few country singers actually born in Nashville (as Muriel Deason, in 1918), she shocked the country music world in 1952 with "It Wasn't God Who Made Honky Tonk Angels," the first hit by a woman to explain the facts of life to men. Later hits were less bold, but no less affecting, leading to her election to the Hall of Fame in 1976.

Kitty Wells: *The Golden Years* (Rounder Special Series). After her breakthrough with "It Wasn't God Who Made Honky Tonk Angels," Kitty herself got a sudden attack of conservatism and retreated into more ordinary "girl singer" songs. This album concentrates on the years 1953–58 and includes duets with Red Foley, Roy Acuff, Webb Pierce, and Johnny and Jack. Kitty's thin, weathered voice sounds just right with virtually any kind of material, though, and songs like "There's Poison in Your Heart" and "I Don't Claim to Be an Angel" make clear the retreat wasn't total. These are the original recordings, too.

Kitty Wells: *Country Hall of Fame* (British MCA Coral). This covers the same era as the previous two and then some; there's only a little overlap in material, and these are original versions, which makes it more desirable than *Story* for aficionados.

Kitty Wells and Red Foley: *Golden Favorites* (MCA). Kitty cut duets with numerous men, though Foley was one of the more anomalous. You'd think his slick expansiveness and her thin rawness would never mix, but they do, and he doesn't drown her out. This includes most of the hits they cut together between 1954 and 1969.

Dottie West: *The Best of Dottie West* (RCA). Her current output is so contrived that it's hard to believe there was a time when Dottie was a real trailblazer, writing and singing her own hits in what was fundamentally a man's world. Since this album is out of print, her legacy is hurting, but from 1963, when she first signed with the label, up into the early seventies, she turned out catchy, vital tunes that brought an unpretentious touch of class to the increasingly standardized Nashville Sound.

The Wilburn Brothers: *A Portrait* (MCA). In the end, Doyle and Teddy Wilburn might prove most important as businessmen. But during the sixties they were one of the last brother teams to make a go of it; they did so by cannily mixing old and new songs with state-of-the-art Nashville production, and this double album offers just what the title says.

Hank Williams, Jr.: *Greatest Hits* (Polydor). As a mainstream Nashville artist, Hank, Jr., had nothing to be ashamed of. In 1966 he wrote his first real song, "Standing in the Shadows" (of you-know-who) and revealed right off that he was a natural singer with a full, virile tone and a good feel for the blues. This offers enough hard-core country to convince anyone that had he chosen to stay on this course, Hank, Jr., might one day have been rated up there with Haggard, Jones, and the very best. The problem is he would never have been rated up there with Hank, Sr., and what he's doing today gets around that issue entirely.

Hank Williams, Jr.: *Greatest Hits, Volume II* (Polydor). With his convincing reading of Slim Harpo's "Raining in My Heart" and Fats Domino's "Ain't That a Shame," this veers more toward the R & B side of Hank, Jr., that had been there (albeit well disguised) since the beginning. Unfortunately, the latter is saddled by the accompaniment of the Mike Curb Congregation—but then, part of the reason Hank, Jr., left Nashville in the first place is that he couldn't keep his producer off his records.

Tammy Wynette: *Your Good Girl's Gonna Go Bad* (Epic). I prefer this edging-toward-stardom album to any early Tammy because both the material and the arrangements give her more room than she usually gets. If she doesn't always use that room to best advantage, you can still hear her working at it on such songs as "Don't Come Home A' Drinkin' (with Lovin' on Your Mind)," "Don't Touch Me," "There Goes My Everything," "Walk Through This World With Me," "I Wound Easy (but I Heal Fast)," and "Almost Persuaded." Can you imagine her tackling a repertoire that multifaceted today?

Tammy Wynette: *Stand By Your Man* (Epic). Which is not to suggest that the triumphant Tammy doesn't sound, uh, *triumphant,* where the earlier Tammy sounded uncertain. "My Arms Stay Open Late" sounds inviting enough, while "If I Were a Little Girl" is one of those children-songs (as opposed to children's songs) Tammy turns up once in a while that states her case better than adult-songs.

Faron Young: *Best of Faron Young* (Mercury). In the sixties, Faron Young eased himself effortlessly into the Nashville Sound. He began doing so with "The Yellow Bandana" in 1963, the year he left Capitol and the honky-tonk sound, and by the time he cut "Wine Me Up," this album's other highlight in 1969, the process was complete. This is now out of print.

BAKERSFIELD

Whed it was at its peak, there were few alternatives to the Nashville Sound. Country music went soft, and became easy listening, rather than dancing and drinking music. In Bakersfield, they remained faithful to the older honky-tonk styles, and in the process gave country music a much-needed shot of adrenaline. At one time, Bakersfield was even considered a serious threat to the Nashville industry. But it was too small to make good on that threat, and later it became too diffuse. Still, Bakersfield helped keep Nashville honest, and for a while there, people talked about a Bakersfield Sound the way they'd previously talked about the Nashville Sound.

The city of Bakersfield was scratched out of the parched, hard, central California earth at the foot of the Tehachapi Mountains. One hundred miles (and seemingly several worlds) north of Los Angeles, Bakersfield leads into central California's harsh, arid San Joaquin Valley. It's fit for oil and cotton and very little else.

The town boomed when refugees from the Oklahoma dust bowl began arriving in the thirties. As World War II created thousands of new jobs in the oil fields there, poor whites continued flocking in from Texas and Oklahoma. Bakersfield began looking like a hobo jungle and a boom town simultaneously.

As such, it was wide open. Merle Haggard recalls that during his teen-age years there seemed to be a bar, gambling den, or whorehouse on just about every corner. There was good money floating around, and very little else to spend it on. The music that grew in such an environment had to be as durable as the hard-working men who picked up their paychecks on Friday and jammed the clubs to drink, fight, and hustle women. Country music from the Southwest had always been tougher (and more danceable) than country music from the Southeast, and there was very little room for subtlety in the Bakerfield country that surfaced in the mid-fifties via men like Tommy Collins and Wynn Stewart and peaked a decade later with Buck Owens and Merle Haggard.

In Bakersfield, instruments were tuned to a high, shrill pitch. Guitars crackled and steel guitars shrieked. Bakersfield put fiddles and high harmony voices where Nashville put string sections and vocal choirs. Bakersfield lead singers had to shout to be heard over the clatter of their own bands, but when they did a ballad, they went heavy on the tears and the twang. This was emotional stuff, and it could get messy, but that was much of the attraction; it was as if honky-tonk music had never gone away.

But it didn't last long. Buck Owens built a business empire out of himself and his fellow Bakersfield artists, but his own records petered out in the early seventies. Merle Haggard's didn't, but by then he was well into his own individualistic style, and he owed no allegiances to any sound or movement. Singers like Red Simpson came and went after a few good singles. Nashville sighed a huge sigh of relief and went back about its business—but not before first injecting a dose of Bakersfield raunch back into the Nashville Sound.

Buck Owens: *Country Music* (Time-Life).

In the early sixties, when Nashville was at its softest, George Jones, Ray Price, and Buck Owens were the only men consistently keeping the faith. Buck represented the California end of the honky-tonk continuum, but his Texas roots were for real, and the only thing wrong with this "greatest hits" repackaging is that it doesn't go far enough.

He was born Alvis Edgar Owens, the son of a Sherman, Texas, sharecropper in 1929. When he was eight, the family moved to Arizona; he quit school in the ninth grade to work, and by the time he was seventeen he was playing lead guitar on a KTYL show out of Mesa, Arizona. At twenty, he was on the road with various small-time bands, having learned guitar, mandolin, steel guitar, saxophone, piano, and drums.

In 1951 he moved to Bakersfield and formed the Schoolhouse Playboys, his first band; he blew sax and trumpet with them, and cut some rockabilly sides under the name Corky Jones. But soon he was getting session work in Los Angeles as a guitarist. That led to a gig as lead guitarist and warm-up singer for Tommy Collins, which in 1957 led to a contract with Capitol. Two years later, his "Second Fiddle" went to No. 24 and Buck was on his way.

By 1970, owing to his aggressive business practices, Bakersfield was known within the industry as "Buckersfield." Owens had a publishing house and a booking agency that gave him a virtual stranglehold on most of the town's artists. But he'd also sold $40 million worth of albums by then, and racked up nineteen No. 1 country singles—most of which he wrote, a few of which have since become standards—recorded country and pop alike.

His band, the Buckaroos, was probably the hardest-hitting unit of the sixties. Bassist Doyle Holly cut a few records under his own name, while steel player Tom Brumley (the son of gospel songwriter Albert Brumley, best known for "I'll Fly Away" and "Turn Your Radio On") followed in the footsteps of Ralph Mooney's high, screaming style that laid the groundwork for country-rock at the end of the decade. Foremost was Don Rich, an incisive lead guitarist and fiddler who also provided the high harmony voice.

This album contains a measly nine songs, all released between 1960 and 1970; it's not much, but it's all there is to go on. Blame rests squarely with one Buck Owens, who owns his own catalog and thus caused all his great Capitol sides to go out of print when he moved over to Warner Bros. in 1976.

Owens ignored almost completely the drinking side of honky-tonk to concentrate on the travails of love—or, more specifically, of divorce. The album opens with "Above and Beyond," in which his rather flat country tenor is put to use wooing a young woman while the fiddle and steel add moral support. The song has a galloping beat that became an Owens trademark and often veered close to rock 'n' roll. It's the only song here he didn't write or co-write, and it's followed by "Love's Gonna Live Here," which finds our man already divorced and looking to get his life back together.

Buck phrases them both so thickly he recalls no one except maybe George Jones. His is an unvarnished country style that leaves him standing naked in many of his songs—he could be absolutely guileless. But while his voice swoops up and around the beat, it sometimes also retains a hint of incredulity that gave other songs a double edge. "Together Again," with the crying steel echoing his voice and then repeating the melody line with a slight twist, sounds infinitely sad, when the exact opposite is true.

As a writer, he was quick and clever. Buck had a rare gift for snatching a slang phrase out of popular usage and turning it into his own password. "Act Naturally" takes the everyman's fantasy of being a movie star and converts it into a real-life weeper about a classic loser, "the biggest fool that ever hit the big time." "I've Got a Tiger by the Tail" finds Buck with a younger woman who's wearing him out, though it's hard to be sure whether he's bragging or complaining. "Waitin' in Your Welfare Line" was his most shameless ever. He takes one of the major public issues of the time (1966), puts it to a beat halfway between western swing and a Texas shuffle, and milks it for all he can, using poverty-program buzz words as metaphors for his own love-starved condition, rhyming "Cadillac" with "by heck," and winding up with the plea "Gimme a handout!"

Shameless and then some, actually. But this *is* the man who once made a solemn "Pledge to Country Music" in which he vowed to sing no song that wasn't country and then came out a few weeks later with Chuck Berry's rocking "Memphis." This *is* the man who once advertised in the newspapers for a new wife. And this *is* the man who married his fiddler Jana Jae (who'd joined the band when Don Rich was killed in a 1973 motorcycle wreck) and then tried to divorce her within days on the grounds that she was insane, when in fact the only problem was that he had cold feet—which he admitted after she went into hiding to figure things out, and he bought full-page newspaper ads begging her to come back because he'd changed his mind again. That's Buck for you.

Not long into the seventies, Buck's songwriting slipped drastically, and his records began sounding contrived; gimmicks that would once have been amusing were now annoying. He began slipping down the charts accordingly, but at the same time, he found other avenues. Today he's best known for having been the co-host of "Hee-Haw," a show which perfectly fits his cornball ways, and he continues collecting royalties on many of these very same songs, some of which have been recorded by forty or more other artists.

Merle Haggard and the Strangers: *Best of Merle Haggard* (Capitol).

In the beginning, Merle Haggard was perhaps not sure who he was, but he was sure what he wanted to be—a country singer and nothing but. It doesn't denigrate the best of his early work to note that these are largely conventional drinking, heartbreak, and novelty songs rather than the more personal material that made him famous. These songs *do* also follow out of his life experiences, though in less obvious ways, and they set up the personal work to follow. And with the prison songs that close out the early days covered in this album, he begins moving toward the more starkly autobiographical.

Haggard's parents fled from Oklahoma to Bakersfield Hoover camps at the height of the Depression. His father converted an abandoned refrigerator car alongside the Southern Pacific tracks in Oildale into a home; Merle was born there in 1937. His father was a fiddler, though his mother, a strict Church of Christ member, frowned on secular music. When Merle was nine, his father died. Merle was soon going to juvenile halls and then jails for petty thefts, bad checks, breaking and entering, and similar crimes. Finally, in 1957, he was sentenced to six months to fifteen years in San Quentin; he did time in solitary, a few cells down from the condemned Caryl Chessman before straightening out and winning a discharge.

Sensing that he had a future in music and probably nowhere else, he went from prison directly into the flourishing Bakersfield club scene. He worked first as a sideman, most prominently for Wynn Stewart, and then began recording on Fuzzy Owens' Tally label, a local indie. There was one flop before "Sing a Sad Song" charted in 1963; "Sam Hill," a novelty, made noise in 1964, and then in 1965 "(My Friends Are Gonna

Be) Strangers" hit the country Top 10. At this point, Capitol bought out Tally (which is how those records made it onto this album), and Merle graduated to the national label.

"Strangers" is extraordinary in its bitter paranoia; Haggard even suggests he should be tarred and feathered for having believed in the woman who deserted him. If it's in other respects a standard weeper, it still makes clear both the depths of feeling he can reach and his potential to galvanize. Haggard idolized Jimmie Rodgers, Bob Wills, Lefty Frizzell, and Bing Crosby, and their influence is prominent in his early work. Frizzell's spirit is most conspicuous, particularly in Merle's vibrato and in the way he slides around words. Haggard has the truest Okie twang ever developed by a native Californian.

Much of his early recording success should be credited to the Strangers, Haggard's band, which accompanied him both on the road and in the studio (then an unusual situation in country music). Roy Nichols and James Burton alternated on lead guitar, with Glen Campbell on rhythm and harmony vocals. Glen D. Hardin played piano and the pioneering Ralph Mooney was on steel. The band didn't play with as much kick as Buck Owens' Buckaroos, but that merely pointed out more basic differences between the extroverted Owens and the contemplative Haggard. Merle's band was more relaxed and more intricate, lending the music a folkish flavor.

Into 1966, Hag was still singing drinking and cheating songs almost exclusively. "Swinging Doors" and "The Bottle Let Me Down" have since become barroom perennials. Now and then he'd do something unusual enough to hint at future directions—Tommy Collins' "High on a Hilltop" uses the gospel form and gospel imagery to describe a woman who's succumbed to the fast life in the city.

Good as all these records were, they were conservative embellishments on standard C & W. This makes sense. First off, Haggard was just out of prison, anxious to make good without making waves. Secondly, he's always been by nature a genuinely conservative man, respectful of tradition. Had he not come up with the prison songs that gave him his first public image, he might have gotten lost in the country mainstream.

Liz Anderson, who'd written "Strangers," gave him "I'm a Lonesome Fugitive" in 1966, and he took it to the top of the charts. He then revealed his prison record, which he'd been keeping secret for fear of backlash from his fans, and wrote follow-ups in "Branded Man" and "Sing Me Back Home" (which he wrote for a friend on San Quentin's death row). These songs weren't as personal or as rich in detail as most of his later work, but they were a start in that direction. As he matured, his songs became both more personal and more universal. From here on out, there would be no mistaking him for anyone else.

Merle Haggard and the Strangers: *Best of the Best of Merle Haggard* (Capitol).

During this phase (which ended in 1971) of his career, Haggard consolidated old ground with some of his most memorable love songs. He also headed simultaneously down two distinct paths which finally brought him national recognition.

"Today I Started Loving You Again" is his most adult and most complicated heart song; inexplicably, it was not a hit single. "Silver Wings" extends country's traveling motif to take in airplanes, and is brooding but free of self-pity. Both songs utilize melodies that broaden tradition without uprooting, though something should be done about the string section that nearly subverts "Silver Wings" (and several others here). Haggard's experiments with strings, oddly enough, began right around the same time he started integrating old-time country fiddle into the Strangers; he stretched himself both ways at once, a typical move for him.

Most of the other songs fall into one of two related categories. The first is flatly autobiographical—especially "Hungry Eyes" and "Mama Tried," both of which deal with Haggard's rearing by a widowed mother both strict and forgiving, but totally unable to cope as a single parent. The former conjures up a canvas-covered cabin in a labor camp, and then expands outward to confront the notion that there will always be an upper class and an under class; he also dwells on the way dreams and drive diminish with age (a problem he's faced periodically in his own career). "Mama Tried" relies on chugging rhythms and a biting, bluesy guitar as Haggard tells the story of a "one and only rebel child" who "turned twenty-one in prison, doin' life without parole."

Then there's the songs that got Haggard labeled "poet of the working man," a piece of press puffery that applies anyhow. "Workin' Man Blues" may present a common dilemma—a man hates his job but can't quit because he has to support a family and is too proud for welfare— but nobody before Haggard had drawn those strands together so clearly. In this case, the man's solace is a few beers at the end of the workday. Another version of that life is found in Dean Holloway's "No Reason to Quit," a mysterious song in which a man ostracized from society drinks his life away for reasons never expressed. It could be a woman, or just general dissatisfactions, but there's a strong sense of futility as he mopes, "I could sober up tomorrow and face my friends again/But I've got no reason to quit."

Haggard's voice has deepened for these sides, and the Strangers sound has opened up more. The guitarists move to the front of the band. Burton's opening lick on "Workin' Man Blues" is a grabber, while on songs like "Every Fool Has a Rainbow," he and/or Roy Nichols play elegant, note-bending solos so desolate they can dominate even those awful strings.

With so much growth evident on so many different fronts, it's ironic that it took a simpleton's anthem like "Okie from Muskogee" to make Haggard a household name. It was a joke, Haggard always swore, written in about twenty minutes one day as the bus rolled through Oklahoma and a highway sign noting the distance to Muskogee prompted one of the band members to crack, "I bet they don't smoke marijuana in Muskogee." The rest of the lines followed quickly from that remark, each one being meant to top the last. Indeed, it *sounds* like it was dashed off in about twenty minutes; as with other Haggard songs, you get the feeling he couldn't wait to finish it and move on to the next thing. That no one perceived it as a joke is at least partly due to the fact that Hag sang it without a trace of irony or humor; at a time (1969) when American society seemed to be irreparably polarized, with some talking about revolution and others about concentration camps, nobody had any trouble figuring out "Okie."

The song was of a piece with Haggard's autobiographical work and his blue-collar anthems. As an ex-con who'd made good when given another chance, Haggard had reason to believe the American Dream. But his self-righteous streak (which also causes him to equate welfare with loss of masculinity) blinds him to anything else. The actual song form adds to his problems. As interviews have shown, Haggard is an articulate, thoughtful man, with complex feelings about these issues. But when those views are forced into simple little rhyming verses for a song, all he's got are one-dimensional buzz words and slogans, which make his "jokes" sound awfully threatening.

Though he sometimes seemed to relish (and play right into) the way "Okie" could incite people, Haggard himself quickly came to fear the virulent feelings he'd tapped into with this song. It's true that he followed up with "Fightin' Side of Me"—which, no hedging here, was totally calculated—but then he backed off. There were fence-mending songs like "The Farmer's Daughter" (included here) and "Big Time Annie's Square." Merle pointed out that at the same time he was writing "Okie" and "Fightin' Side," he was also writing "Irma Jackson," a song of interracial love his record company wound up refusing to release until several years had passed. (They figured it would damage his image, which was just what he wanted to do.) Ultimately, he was as confused as everybody else during this era; the reactionary patriotic songs were indeed a part of Merle Haggard, but there was much more to the man, he kept insisting. It would be a while before anyone believed him.

Merle Haggard and the Strangers: *Someday We'll Look Back*
(Capitol).

After "Okie from Muskogee," Merle Haggard could have had it made. He wouldn't even have had to continue doing patriotic anthems, as long as he gave his large new audience what it wanted: safe music that didn't challenge basic assumptions. They wanted a spokesman, someone with easy answers that would reinforce their prejudices. Instead, true to his restless and inquisitive personal history, Haggard gave them an album that asked hard questions.

Released in 1971, *Someday We'll Look Back* is a cry—more like a weary, but determined, sigh, actually—from a cornered man. To deal with celebrity, with life under the magnifying glass, Haggard delves into his past. It's not a retreat so much as it's a refueling, though; this is not just simple nostalgia for simpler times. There's an honest effort to explain where Merle Haggard came from and why his values mean so much to him. His assertion that the world isn't easily divided into black and white, but also contains many shades of gray, may seem obvious to many, but it came as a shock to those who found an entire world view in "Okie" and "Fightin' Side."

The two growing-up songs are the obvious starting point. "California Cottonfields" was written not by Haggard but by Dallas Frazier and Peanut Montgomery. Frazier was born in Oklahoma and moved to central California with his parents as a boy. His background thus wasn't identical to Haggard's own but it was close enough, and this song about a Promised Land that seldom makes good on its vows packs in as much telling imagery and detail as Haggard's own best work. "Tulare Dust," a Haggard original, is a straightforward narrative of "life like it is" for the poor cotton pickers who migrated from Oklahoma; it asks no favors and pulls no punches.

By the time Haggard recorded this album, he'd already done his tributes to Jimmie Rodgers and to Bob Wills, and it was clear that he was as fascinated by their times as he was by their music. That's more explicit on these two cuts in particular, but really on this whole album. There's a bluesy, Depression-era atmosphere in this music; the Strangers have now become the most versatile band in country music, expanding to include more dobro and harp here, putting more emphasis on piano there, working in a banjo or mandolin in other places. The additional instruments bring more than depth to the music; they bring a sense of history, too.

Roger Miller's "Train of Life" is not the most original metaphor, but Haggard makes it work by arranging it so it sounds like something Jimmie Rodgers might have done. "The Only Trouble with Me" would be an ordinary Haggard-style blues were it not for the way the musicians pass solos around with such snap; this gives us a look at how Haggard's been absorbing Bob Wills into his own music. If on the tribute album he sought to reproduce Wills' sound, here he's trying to match Wills' ethos.

Haggard offers a little of everything he's ever done before and a few things he hasn't. The title song has warmth counteracting the sentimentality, and gives steel player Norman Hamlet, a relative newcomer to the group, one of his first chances to strut. "One Sweet Hello" is a honky-tonk ballad. "One Row at a Time," by Red Lane and Dottie West, is another hard-luck story Haggard might as well have written himself. "I'd Rather Be Gone" finds him facing up to the end of a relationship with neither bitterness nor self-pity. "Carolyn" is one of Tommy Collins' most effective ballads, and the album's only big production number; for once, the strings complement the band, adding drama rather than serving no purpose except to make the record more palatable for air play. "Huntsville" is his first prison song in some time.

And on "Big Time Annie's Square," Haggard seeks rapprochement of sorts with the people he so roundly condemned on "Okie." On "Farmer's Daughter," his previous peace-making gesture, he did so more or less against his will, but this time it's different. The singer goes from small-town Oklahoma to Los Angeles in search of an old girl friend who's become an acid-head. They somehow get along fine though he doesn't become a hippie himself. Nobody has to change to accommodate anyone else; he learns to accept her and her friends and they learn to accept him.

Now this is all tongue-in-cheek, and in real life things probably wouldn't work out like that. But as a fantasy about mutual respect, it's a big step for Haggard. It also helps to drive home this album's key point, because the man in this song doesn't fit into small-town Oklahoma any more than he does in cosmopolitan L.A. He's a perpetual outsider. And whatever benefits accrued from his flirtations with politics and mass popularity, Merle Haggard is himself a perpetual outsider. On this album, he makes it seem like the only thing he can be and still tell the truth.

Merle Haggard and the Strangers: *Serving 190 Proof* (MCA).

In 1979, at the age of forty-one, Merle Haggard underwent what he later described as "male menopause," and the result was this album. On record, anyhow, it seemed to be the first time in eight years he was even trying; the only albums after *Someday We'll Look Back* that did him justice were compilations put together by Capitol execs after he left the label.

But records can deceive, for Haggard didn't go stale in the seventies. His live show changed continually, and kept getting better as the decade wore on; that seemed to be what he cared about most at the time. At first, Haggard and the Strangers had trouble adapting to the western swing direction he took after cutting his Bob Wills tribute album. Two Texas Playboys alumni (guitarist Eldon Shamblin and electric mandolinist Tiny Moore) were added to his show, and that helped; in time, he and his other musicians were trading hot solos among themselves like they'd been doing it from day one. This improvisational approach best suits Haggard's own moodiness. He thrives on disorganization, and much of what's been interpreted as his "politics" is really his simple refusal to be pinned down. Try to pin him and he'll slip away faster than a steel player and a guitarist can trade eight bars. As he used his success to indulge himself more in this manner, rather than knuckling under to record-company schedules and image-making ploys, his records suffered from lack of attention.

But he's made his best records when something was eating at him, and in 1979, Hag was once again in that position. Some of it was tangible; his career was standing still and his marriage was up in the air. But some he couldn't quite put his finger on, and that's the stuff that gnawed most. If this album's "message" could be summed up in one sentence, it would go something like this: I'm sick and tired of what I'm doing, but I don't know anything else so I guess I'll keep doing it anyhow.

That's what he says in "Footlights," which opens the album, and it's believable despite the traces of self-pity in his voice. That's because his singing is mostly virile, full of a painful kind of resolve, and at the same time it sounds like it's coming from a wax-museum statue. Which is what the song is about, naturally. This is some of his most powerful singing in years, and there's more of it in songs like "Heaven Was a Drink of Wine." There he toys with the last word of each line until he's made it sink in, and this recharges an otherwise ordinary song.

But if that song is about going over the edge, most of the others are about wanting to and being unable. On "Driftwood," a modern western song like nobody else has written, and on "Red Bandana," he rues his inability to change. Admittedly, he uses that to his advantage. "Driftwood" suggests he must leave his woman because it's the best way to spare hurting her, but when the tables are turned on him in "I Must Have Done Something Wrong," he doesn't find that a very legit explanation.

Elsewhere, though, he owns up, piling contradictions on top of previous contradictions, and thereby adding to the turmoil already spread across the grooves. "I Can't Get Away," which follows "Driftwood," is its opposite; the confession here is that he's "running away from life," not that he's driven to run against his will. On "I Didn't Mean to Love You," he admits that for all his running, he really *is* stuck.

The western swing influence permeates this album, but there's not a swing cut on it. Tracks like "My Own Kind of Hat" or "I Didn't Mean to Love You" illustrate how seamlessly he's worked the feel of Wills' thirties swing into his own seventies country. Haggard is well past imitation by now; instead, he's doing what Wills did in the first place, which is to take the best of the various musics around him and reshape it all into his own image. The solos have an improvisational, in-concert feel (check out the fiddle and sax on "I Must Have Done Something Wrong"), and the soloists often say as much with what they leave out as with what they play.

This sounds and feels like an acoustic album, so masterfully has Haggard created his mood. It's not. "Got Lonely Too Early This Morning," for one, has a bigger and harder beat than normal for Haggard, and there's an uncharacteristically fuzzy electric guitar throughout the song. But there *is* more acoustic music than he usually plays, because acoustic instruments not only better evoke the aging process he's dealing with, they also signify the isolation he's feeling. The relative quietness of most of this album suggests the solitary brooding behind the songs.

The two that close the album are exceptions. "Sing a Family Song" advocates retreat into nostalgia, while "Roses in the Winter" is a Presleyesque devotional ballad. But given all that's preceded them, even Haggard's desire to leave the album on a note of optimism seems mainly to reinforce despair.

Supplementary Albums

Tommy Collins: *This Is Tommy Collins* (Capitol). Though he wrote numerous novelties, Collins was arguably the most driven of the Bakersfield honky-tonkers. But he had a fine understanding of what makes people change, and he was one of the town's leading writers. His own thin, quizzical voice does his songs as much justice as anybody else's, and it's too bad that this album is now in print only in Japan (under the title *Tommy Collins*). For all his ups and downs through the fifties and sixties, the man never entirely lost his sense of humor.

Dallas Frazier: *Elvira* (Capitol). A blues-loving Okie transplanted to central California and later to Nashville, Frazier was an unruly singer, which is a compliment. But Music City apparently didn't think so, because though he wrote countless sixties hits, he recorded rarely and was never promoted. His inordinate fondness for novelty songs can be irksome, and this album has its share, but it also has a number of songs that have become popular in other versions by other artists.

Dallas Frazier: *Singing My Songs* (RCA). If you want to know where Johnny Darrell got "The Son of Hickory Hollers Tramp," where Merle Haggard got "California Cottonfields," where Jack Greene got "There Goes My Everything," or where Charley Pride got "All I Have to Offer You Is Me," you've come to the right place. This is out of print (as are all his albums), but still turns up fairly regularly.

Merle Haggard and the Strangers: *Sing a Sad Song* (Capitol). The re-packaged version of Hag's 1964 debut album. Recommended primarily to diehards, because it shows a few unmistakable influences he hasn't talked much about—Johnny Cash, Ernest Tubb, and George Jones.

Merle Haggard and the Strangers: *Swinging Doors* (Capitol). The title song and "The Bottle Let Me Down" are two of his grimmest drinking songs, and the hurting songs here really do hurt: 1966 must not have been a very happy year for him. At the same time, this could do with one less novelty song.

Merle Haggard and the Strangers: *Pride In What I am* (Capitol). "I Think We're Living in the Good Old Days" is the tip-off for this, his best early (1968) album. The songwriting is more personal, and the populist songs are taking on more of a sociopolitical bent; he's delving into the Depression-era motifs that will later become a running theme with him.

Merle Haggard and the Strangers: *Same Train, A Different Time* (Capitol). Recorded around the same time as *Pride,* this two-record tribute to Jimmie Rodgers goes even deeper into the Depression, and he attacks these songs with rare ebullience. Though it's slowed down by his between-songs narrations, this is still the best of Hag's several tribute albums; if this be nostalgia, give me more.

Merle Haggard and the Strangers: *Okie from Muskogee* (Capitol). Ever notice how on live albums from this era (this one's 1970), the band always plays worse and Haggard always sings better than in the studio? Here, Merle gets an Okie pin and key to the city, and demonstrates his ambivalence toward the title song by prefacing it with petty digs and then singing it with pathos. And debuts a brand-new one called "Billy Overcame His Size," a subject dear to short-guy Hag's heart.

Merle Haggard and the Strangers: *Tribute to the Best Damn Fiddle Player in the World* (Capitol). The 1970 album that predated the western swing revival by half a decade. Haggard didn't need to rediscover Bob Wills, because he'd never really forgotten him, and he gets some of the original Playboys to join him for good measure. He swings more woodenly than he would a few years later, but we're talking about a man who taught himself fiddle in just three months so he could play this music, and it took him a little longer to really get the hang of it.

Merle Haggard and the Strangers: *Hag* (Capitol). Four hit singles, none of them among his best, but no obvious filler, either. His first studio album after all those live ones exploiting "Okie from Muskogee," this one successfully marked time in 1971 until *Someday We'll Look Back.*

Merle Haggard and the Strangers: *Let Me Tell You About a Song* (Capitol). This 1972 set is another concept album of sorts, with Haggard trying to explain why these songs are so meaningful to him, and how they help shape his own music. Hag's narrations don't offer the insights promised, but the songs and performances are still worth talking about.

Merle Haggard and the Strangers: *I Love Dixie Blues . . . So I Recorded "Live" in New Orleans* (Capitol). The Dixieland horn section sounds tacked on, but this provides Merle with a vehicle to sing aching slow blues like "Emptiest Arms in the World" and to offer yet another music-appreciation lesson with Emmett Miller's "Big Bad Bill (Is Sweet William Now)."

Merle Haggard and the Strangers: *It's Not Love (But It's Not Bad)* (Capitol). Amid all the concepts he's tossing around in the early seventies, this 1973 set comes off modest. In fact, it's a straightforward hard-country album with a bundle of probing Haggard originals, and covers mostly written by Tommy Collins and Hank Cochran. And in the country music world of 1973, there's nothing modest about either the title song or the reading he gives it.

Merle Haggard and the Strangers: *A Working Man Can't Get No Where Today* (Capitol). By 1977, Haggard had moved to a new label, and Capitol was releasing this album of outtakes that was better than his current stuff. The title song is a blues, as is most of the rest of the album. Appropriately, then, this also includes "I'm a White Boy," in which Hag fights his racial confusion to a draw.

Merle Haggard and the Strangers: *Songs I'll Always Sing* (Capitol). A double album that collects material from his first decade, roughly the period covered by the first three albums discussed at length earlier. If you were to want just one Haggard album, this would be the one. But you'd still be missing too much.

Merle Haggard and the Strangers: *The Way It Was in '51* (Capitol). In which Merle and Capitol wave good-bye to each other once more, with feeling. The title song is Haggard's salute to Hank Williams and Lefty Frizzell. The rest of that side is Frizzell covers culled mostly from old albums, while side two is Williams songs of the same origins. I give the Lefty side the edge, not just because Haggard always had more affinity with Frizzell, but also because it features more slow songs of the type Merle sings best.

Merle Haggard and the Strangers: *Eleven Winners* (Capitol). These are "greatest hits" from the mid-seventies, when his albums were often weak. If you've been following my advice so far, you'll already have many of these songs. But the horny "Old Man from the Mountain" comes from his otherwise-disappointing *30th Album.* "If We Make It Through December" probably expresses his "politics" as well as anything he's written, and the bitter "It's All in the Movies" does the same for his world-weary cynicism.

Merle Haggard and the Strangers: *Rainbow Stew/Live at Anaheim Stadium* (MCA). Recorded in 1980, when the Strangers were at their hottest, this is Merle's best live album. Material covers his entire career, with a couple of new ones thrown in for good measure, and the three drinking songs that open the album are much tougher here than in their original, studio versions. "Rainbow Stew" is Merle at his most sardonic, and "Fiddle Breakdown" runs wild.

Merle Haggard: *The Best Of Merle Haggard* (MCA). This covers the second half of the seventies, when Hag released very few consistently good albums. But he still knew how to craft a succinct hit single, and taken together, these tell you everything you need to know about this phase of his recording career, even if they barely hint at his power as a live performer.

Merle Haggard and the Strangers: *Big City* (Epic). Uh-oh . . . here it is the end of 1981, and Haggard, on a new label, suddenly has something new to say again, which he does with crispness and authority. That must mean he's restless again, too.

Buck Owens: *The Best of Buck Owens* (Capitol). Geez, take a look at that serious, somber fellow on the cover. Good thing that once you get inside to the actual music, it's the same old bubbling Buck—complete with such instant classics as "Excuse Me (I Think I've Got a Heartache)," "Under the Influence of Love," and "Under Your Spell Again." Dear Buck, please get this stuff back in print—it's simply too good to go unknown for much longer.

Buck Owens: *The Best of Buck Owens, Vol. 2* (Capitol). While you're at it, include the mid-sixties stuff, which is often less catchy but still country like nobody else—you know, songs like "I Don't Care" and "My Heart Skips a Beat."

Buck Owens: *The Best of Buck Owens, Vol. 3* (Capitol). By the late sixties the Owens sound has become a predictable formula, and he makes some efforts to bust out of it. Given the right material, he does so without sacrificing any of the wigged-out charm that makes him so appealing in the first place. Needless to say, this is also out of print.

Red Simpson: *I'm a Truck* (Capitol). For a while there in the sixties and early seventies, Red was the West Coast's answer to Dave Dudley. He had the burly voice and he had the mystique down cold. Then, in 1971, he weirded out with the title tune from this album. It is basically a talking blues, told from the point of view of the truck. ("There'd be no truck drivers if it weren't for us trucks.") The truck complains about how the driver lets a VW van full of hippies overtake him, and waxes psychosexual over the mud flaps on a pretty female (?) truck. *Real* sick, but done intentionally in that spirit, and it proved to be Red's first, and last, Top 10 hit. The album itself was thrown together by pulling truckers' anthems from his two previous (and now-deleted) albums, *Roll, Truck, Roll* and *Truck Drivin' Fool*.

Wynn Stewart: *The Songs of Wynn Stewart* (Capitol). Stewart peaked in the late sixties, around the same time as Merle Haggard, and between Hag's ascendance and Buck Owen's already-firm grip on the upper rungs of the charts, he was overlooked. He may not have been as consistent as either, but at his best, he was their equal as a writer. He was also a bluesy singer when he wanted to be. Like all his albums, this one is now out of print, though not impossible to find.

Wynn Stewart: *You Don't Care What Happens to Me* (Capitol). Did Wynn Stewart have the honky-tonk blues? Well, aside from the title song, one of the tracks on this album is "I Bought the Shoes That Just Walked Out on Me."

Leona Williams: *San Quentin's First Lady* (MCA). Here's a neat twist on the live prison album, even if it's now out of print. Shortly after she married Merle Haggard and joined his show, Leona accompanied him to San Quentin and cut her own album of mostly prison songs, with suitably bluesy backing from the Strangers. The concert was on New Year's Day, 1976, and Leona has such an unimpeachably down-home voice by today's standards that she hasn't had a solo album out since. But you'd better believe the inmates appreciated this one.

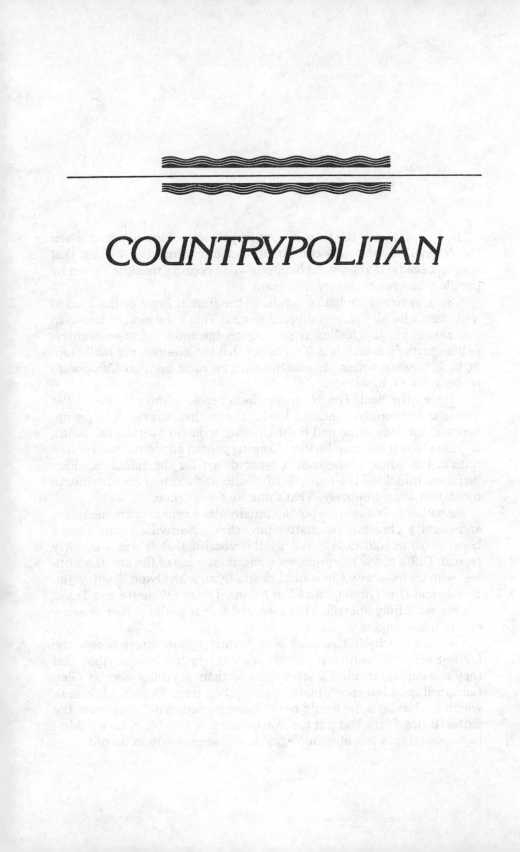

COUNTRYPOLITAN

The temptation is to say that countrypolitan is what happens when the Nashville Sound gets completely out of control. But it's not that simple, because it's also what happens when country music is played by people who aren't country musicians.

Such as television house bands, or the Boston Pops, or the kind of musicians who play on commercial jingles. That's the kind of musician you always get the feeling is playing on the most extreme countrypolitan records, even when it turns out that the sidemen are really top-flight L.A. session men (as was the case on most of Glen Campbell's records, for example).

Here's the deal. The Nashville Sound took country music all the way uptown; countrypolitan, a kissin' cousin that was rising to prominence at the same time and is threatening today to overrun the industry, then took it one step further. Countrypolitan added not just orchestration, but whole orchestras; it went direct for the mindless, shiny surface of middle-of-the-road (MOR) music, and scorned country instrumentation almost entirely. That's one key difference.

Another is that countrypolitan usually also scorns country melodies, and country phrasing. No matter how slick a Nashville Sound record became, you could usually tell by the vocalist that it was a country record. Think of the top producers, and then some of the artists identified with them—Patsy Cline and Loretta Lynn with Owen Bradley, Jim Reeves and Don Gibson with Chet Atkins, Tammy Wynette and Tanya Tucker with Billy Sherrill. That essential *tear* is in the voices of every one of those singers.

What's usually in the voice of a countrypolitan singer is only the faintest echo of country phrasing. It's hard to tell beyond that that they're country at all; it's sensed more than anything else. If Glen Campbell sounded much like a country boy from Delight, Arkansas, which is what he is, he would never have landed that TV series in the sixties. If Roy Clark had put too much twang in his guitar, he wouldn't have gotten into the biggest Vegas showcases as early as he did.

What's most frustrating about all this is that some of these people are extremely talented. Clark is a great guitarist, but you'd never know it from listening to his ostentatious version of "Malaguena." Campbell is also a fine guitarist, and he hardly plays it at all anymore. Ray Price can still be a moving singer, but he lets his orchestras distract from his voice.

You may have gathered by now that I'm down on countrypolitan. You're right. I think it's lowest-common-denominator stuff, and part of the reason I'm discussing so little of it is that I don't think much will last. Oh, I realize that the impulse toward this stuff has always been in country music, from Vernon Dalhart through George Morgan and Eddy Arnold. I realize also that this seems to be the current direction of the largest single segment of the industry. But it's still music designed to go in one ear and out the other, the most pleasantly escapist sounds modern producers and musicians can create. And while it will always be around as a form—will continue growing, in fact, particularly in economically grim times—individual singers and songs won't last in the way that Ernest Tubb or Loretta Lynn or Merle Haggard have lasted, in a way that "T for Texas" or "Your Cheatin' Heart" or "Blues Eyes Crying in the Rain" have lasted.

So you'll find no Kenny Rogers herein, no Mac Davis, no Olivia Newton-John. Nor will you find such closely related species as John Denver, Alabama, or the Oak Ridge Boys. But there are, on the other hand, a few who have done something special with the form, have breathed so much soul and personality into it that they can't be denied.

Charlie Rich: *The Best of Charlie Rich* (Epic).

For Charlie Rich, timing has always been a big problem in the record biz. Or maybe for the record biz, timing has always been a big problem when it comes to dealing with Rich. Throughout his checkered career, it's been a happy coincidence when his best work also sold well, and this album offers yet another example of that. These are the songs that immediately preceded his 1973 triumph with "Behind Closed Doors." With their city savvy and country horse sense, they comprise everything a countrypolitan album can be—but none except "I Take It On Home" (1972) reached the Top 10. Yet this compilation, an attempt by his record company to salvage four years worth of near-misses, is far more soulful than the much bigger records that began with "Behind Closed Doors."

Rich never fit in. Born in 1934 in Colt, Arkansas, he grew up in small-town Arkansas digging Dave Brubeck, Miles Davis, Count Basie, and especially Stan Kenton at a time when his peers were into country and R & B. When he was signed to Phillips International (the Sun subsidiary), Sam Phillips declared he had more talent than Elvis. Sam was referring mainly to Charlie's voice, which was similar to Elvis' though with a little more rasp and classic blues feeling, but he also considered Charlie's instrumental skills. Rich played a complex, brittle piano style based on gospel, but with the jazz inflections he picked up listening to his idols. At Sun, Rich was a utility man—he wrote and arranged, played piano and sang, for others as well as for his own records. He even had a 1959 hit with "Lonely Weekends," though there were numerous other Sun/Phillips singles just as good that went nowhere.

When he moved to Smash in the early sixties, his personal preferences became more clear. Rich came on like a white Ray Charles, but his version of gospel, jazz, and blues was also shot through with country. His two albums (which yielded one hit with the 1965 novelty "Mohair Sam" while towering efforts like "I Can't Go On" went unnoticed) were full of hip rhythms and driving horn charts, and Rich's voice continued growing into a wondrous instrument in its own right.

But nobody knew how to market him, and his heavy drinking further plagued his career. His talents were undeniable, but he also had a natural aversion to stardom, which was apparently a carry-over from his strict Missionary Baptist Church upbringing. So he kicked from label to label, cutting songs drawn from blues, pop, and country alike, in various incompatible settings. Finally, he signed to Epic, and was turned over to producer Billy Sherrill, who, whatever else you care to say about him, appreciates a great voice. Their first record together was "Set Me Free," a soul ballad with recitation, that charted in 1968.

In groping toward a viable formula, they tried a little of everything. Rich's range seemed unlimited. Just consider the leap from his version of Jimmy Reed's "Big Boss Man" to his version of Frank Sinatra's "Nice 'n' Easy," with its rolling electric piano, to "I Do My Swinging at Home," a straightforward gospel progression that begins a hymn to drinking and ends up a hymn to his wife.

Her name is Margaret Ann Rich, and she's been with Charlie through thick and thin. She's a compelling songwriter herself, with concern for the small, revealing detail and an unflinching emotional stance that's a worthy counterpoint to Charlie's own. Margaret Ann wrote "Life's Little Ups and Downs," which could be the story of their relationship, and it's easily one of the truest songs about working-class frustrations ever written. Disguised as an everyday slice-of-life story, it's really a parable about dashed hopes, love, and loyalty—and bad timing —full of unorthodox rhyming: "Like ponies on a merry-go-round/And no one grabs the brass ring every time/But she don't mind/She wears a gold ring on her finger/And it's mine."

"July 12, 1939" is a narrative told from the point of view of a young man held responsible for the rape of a girl that was actually committed by another youth whose rich family bought his way out of it. It has a murky city beat and a lilting country-blues bounce; Rich sings it with a sadness and resignation that also rises from a basic mixture of country and blues feelings.

These two songs succeed where countrypolitan usually falls flat. They tell engaging stories, utilizing both city sophistication and country simplicity. The words are chosen carefully, for maximum impact, and the music really does weld together the best of both worlds. It's not a case of country knuckling under to city, like most music in this genre.

"Sittin' and Thinkin' " could be a conventional honky-tonker (several other artists have cut it that way), but Rich makes it deeper and more disturbing. "Daddy Don't You Walk So Fast" also has many elements of a standard weeper, right down to the prominence of the pedal steel, but Rich's drawn-out phrasing is pure city; he could be a cabaret singer.

So what happened next? Sherrill got too good at what he was doing, and Rich let him get away with it. Sherrill took off the rough edges, honed in on the crooner in Rich's voice at the expense of the bluesman, and chose drecky song after drecky song to match. After "Behind Closed Doors" became a huge crossover hit, there was no more real life in Rich's follow-ups, only confection. Maybe that's what really made it successful. Who can be sure? The people who first discovered Rich with "Behind Closed Doors" in 1973 may henceforth have gotten what they wanted from him, but they were settling for so much less than what he had to offer. That's yet another case of bad timing, no?

Anne Murray: *Country* (Capitol).

A funny thing happened to Anne Murray in 1970 on her way to becoming a Canadian MOR star: She became an American country star as well. And as the selections on this compilation indicate, she was able to inject her smart brand of suburban heart and soul into both forms.

Though her musical background was in classical piano and Italian arias, she was not entirely without country credentials. She was born (in 1946) and raised in the coal-mining town of Springhill, Nova Scotia, and though the accents weren't the same, the atmosphere wasn't all that different from the coal-mining towns of Kentucky. As Anne has recalled in interviews, "Country music was always big there, though I wasn't so aware of it."

Music wasn't her first career anyhow. When she graduated from the University of New Brunswick with a degree in physical education, she became a high school gym teacher. And though she was also a regular on "Singalong Jubilee," a television show out of Halifax, she remained at her teaching job even after her initial Canadian hits.

In 1968 she recorded her first album, *What About Me*. (The title song, which became an American hit in 1972, is included here.) It was produced by Brian Ahern, then the musical director for "Singalong Jubilee" and today the husband and producer of Emmylou Harris. He *was* aware of country music already, it appears, and the album was enough of a Canadian success to win Anne a shot with Capitol records in the States.

Her first release was "Snowbird," by Canadian writer Gene MacLellan. She'd seen him singing the song on Canadian TV and was attracted to its light, scurrying melody, but, she quickly adds, "I had no idea it was a country tune." Strictly speaking, of course, it isn't—that melody has virtually nothing to do with traditional tunes. But the increasingly sophisticated country audience heard it that way even if

Anne didn't. They made it a country hit as well as a pop hit in both the
States and Canada. Once she got over the initial surprise, she and Ahern
began aiming her records more consciously at that market, often looking to Nashville for material, and the tactic worked. Sometimes songs
would break pop and then cross over to country, and other times the
process was reversed, but nearly everything she did scored equally in
both markets. By 1974 she'd had enough success with country songs
that Capitol could assemble this collection from old singles and album
cuts and have it sound as cogent as any album made up exclusively of
greatest hits, including the one later released on her. By then, she was
making regular appearances on Glen Campbell's American television
show, and playing with him regularly in Las Vegas.

It takes no genius to see where her country appeal comes from.
Strictly MOR singers tend to have pleasant voices that lack depth and
are instantly forgettable; they aim low so they don't run the risk of
failing. But Murray's thick contralto has an unusual amount of character, resonance, and vitality; she also keeps a lot of her emotion festering
under the surface, as do all good singers, so while she appears superfi-
cially to have the unqualified warmth and cheerfulness of your basic
MOR singer, a dark side emerges in Anne Murray that other MOR
singers would suppress at all costs.

That's where the country material comes in, because it serves that
side so well. Though the phrasing on her 1974 hit "He Thinks I Still
Care" (the George Jones song, with a gender switch) is far from pure
country, for example, she still "worries" words in the middle of lines to
create an effect nearly as emotional as the original. And though John D.
Loudermilk's "Break My Mind" was never a hit for Murray in the
bubblegum rock arrangement we have here, she "worries" words at the
ends of lines in a way that adds extra immediacy and pathos to a song
that had plenty of both to begin with.

As for Ahern, his productions are models of the countrypolitan
form. The steel guitar is more prominent than you'd expect, a fiddle
cuts through the string section here and there; the feel is more Nashville than Toronto. But he improves on Nashville in some ways; his
string arrangements are a big improvement over anything from Music
City because they really are an organic part of the song, thought out in
relation to the other voices and instruments rather than tacked on as a
way of gussying things up for radio.

Admittedly, not all these songs are country as much as they are
country-influenced (Gordon Lightfoot, Kenny Loggins, MacLellan). But
Murray herself is more country-influenced than she is country, too, so
she wears them well. She's really the only effective countrypolitan
singer coming from the MOR side of the fence. Shortly after the six-year

period covered here, she and Ahern quit working together. She's been unable since then to find anyone else quite so suitable, and the result has been a softening of her sound and her spunk that brings her more in line with standard MOR. Perhaps that was inevitable, given music directions generally as the seventies progressed, but before she began conforming, Anne Murray was an intriguing example of the difference between pop art and pop artifice.

Crystal Gayle: *Classic Crystal* (Liberty).

Crystal Gayle may be Loretta Lynn's "little sister," but they don't have much in common musically. Where Loretta and other country singers use background voices, strings, and additional noncountry instruments to "sweeten" their records, theoretically making them more acceptable to noncountry fans, Crystal's records are almost *all* sweetening, with just enough hint of country to make them inviting to country fans. In her early years, at least, her voice retained identifiable country elements, and her songs have always been exquisite. But success and homogenization increased alongside each other in her work; this album of early hits stops almost right at the point where she ceases to be interesting, or even country in any sense save that her records still sell in the country market. This is countrypolitan taken to the maximum.

As she's always opined, it's unrealistic to expect her to sound hard country, like Loretta, when she isn't even from the country. She was born Brenda Gail Webb in Paintsville, Kentucky, in 1951, the last of eight kids, and Loretta was already married and out of the house. Crystal (whose stage name, given to her by Loretta, is taken from a southern hamburger chain) was raised mostly in Wabash, Indiana, where the family moved in 1955. She grew up admiring Patsy Cline and Brenda Lee, who walked the line between pop and country, as well as Leslie Gore and Peter, Paul, and Mary, who had nothing to do with country. In the summer she often went on the road with Loretta, sometimes singing a song as a "special guest."

That got her a record contract, but it was with Loretta's label, which saddled her with Loretta's producer and a smarmy variation on the Nashville Sound. There followed a handful of minor—very minor—hits between 1970 and 1973. Once she got off on her own, she hooked up with producer Allen Reynolds to chart a new course.

The sound they devised relied on harp, French horn, and violins as much as it did on fiddle and pedal steel. It came to be called "Reynolds rock," presumably because it uses amplified instruments and has a light, loping beat—for other than that, it bears little relation to rock. (Crystal even called her backup band Peace and Quiet, and I can't think of anything more antithetical to rock than that.) Reynolds' backing tracks were unusually plush, even for these modern times, but he was most skillful at setting off Crystal's voice on a cushion of electric keyboards, or soft horns, or oozing strings. With "Wrong Road Again," the third single from her 1974 debut album *Crystal Gayle*, the sound, er, crystallized, and she had her first Top 10 hit.

Written by Reynolds, "Wrong Road Again" piles strings on top of strings, but at the bottom of it all is his version of the Johnny Cash beat, as well as a convincing quiver in Crystal's voice. It's clearly based on country music, which was true of most of her hits prior to "Don't It Make My Brown Eyes Blue."

Within very strict limits, Buddy Spicher plays some amazingly dextrous fiddle breaks behind Crystal; though he's often swamped by strings, it's inspiring to hear him slice through at the end of something like "Ready for the Times to Get Better." The same holds for Lloyd Green's steel and dobro. Crystal's voice carries a few traces of Loretta, but she's more reminiscent of Tammy Wynette, or even Tanya Tucker, in her phrasing and timbre. Her song themes remain constant, and can be summarized in a sentence: No matter what, I love you. Crystal Gayle is vulnerable, fragile—it figures that one of her first songs she sang as a child was Marion Worth's "Shake Me I Rattle (Squeeze Me I Cry)"—but she aims to please at any cost. Occasionally she's wistful, but there's apparently not a rancorous bone in her body. What better stance for a middle-of-the-road singer?

For Crystal, the transitional records were "You Never Miss a Real Good Thing (Till He Says Goodbye)" and "I'll Get Over You," her first two No. 1 hits, both from 1976. The former has chunks of fiddle and something close to a blues guitar, but the strings simply take over, building to a glitzy peak, while electric keyboards work especially well at providing small diversions. Spicher and Green are prominent on the latter, but ultimately they're overwhelmed; it's as if Crystal and Reynolds are letting country step out a little more on these two tracks so they can say good-bye and give it a proper burial.

"Don't It Make My Brown Eyes Blue," with its brushed drums and swank piano intro, marks the conclusive departure. The strings dominate; the melody is sultry; Crystal phrases so that a word like "blue" metamorphoses into "ooh" without a hint of country vibrato. She is a lounge singer.

Since then, she's become more studied, more formal, no matter what kind of songs or production. This album has three cuts from 1978, and if "Talking in Your Sleep" and "Why Have You Left the One You Left Me For" renew hope that the strictly pop Crystal might still have appeal, "When I Dream" represents the first nadir. This is a heart song with some of the most perfect lyrics ever written, and Crystal and

Reynolds blow it badly. It's not so much the increasingly lush instrumentation, though that's bad enough. It's how ordinary (how hackneyed) the "drama" is in both the singing and the arrangement. Crystal phrases so carefully, articulates each syllable with such precision, that she sounds like she's going through a prepared speech. And the instruments don't "set off" anything so much as they put the whole song, the whole emotion, under glass. Where this team had once made elegant countrypolitan seem like a distinct possibility, the most recent songs point out too many contradictions in their approach. But it was fine while it lasted.

Supplementary Albums

Chet Atkins: *A Legendary Performer, Vol. 1* (RCA). This goes all the way back to the late forties, when Chet was supposed to be RCA's answer to Merle Travis. Unfortunately, it continues all the way up to the late seventies, when he was RCA's answer to "Who's the biggest purveyor of schlock you can think of?" Whatever the case, in offering at least *some* old Atkins, it lets us see, as none of his other RCA albums do, just why he's always been so highly regarded. Plus, you can hear a Nashville Sound developing and mutating into countrypolitan.

Chet Atkins *The Atkins String Company: The Night Atlanta Burned* (RCA). Now here's the kind of project that enhances Chet's reputation. When he was a teen-ager, Nashville writer John D. Loudermilk met a hobo who owned a mandocello that had survived the burning of the Atlanta Conservatory of Music when General Sherman's troops roared through; the man also remembered fragments of a composition for mandolin orchestra that he played for Loudermilk. Loudermilk carried the music around in his head until the mid-seventies, when he took it to Atkins. Chet then put together a "country chamber ensemble" (violin, viola, mandolin, additional guitar) to play a fleshed-out version. The result is both stirring and soothing, with a timeless quality lacking in all Chet's slick, quick commercial albums; it brings back the Civil War era with dignity, respect, remorse, and majesty.

Chet Atkins and Les Paul: *Chester and Lester* (RCA). For someone who usually packs his music in ice before he puts it on album, Atkins sounds remarkably loose and spontaneous here. On most of his duet albums, he's been the boss, but this time guitar whiz Les Paul sets the pace, and in rising to the occasion, Chet shows more of himself than usual.

Glen Campbell: *Greatest Hits* (Capitol). These are some of the records that put countrypolitan on the map—"Gentle On My Mind" (still his best), "Wichita Lineman," "By the Time I Get to Phoenix," "Galveston," "Dreams of the Everyday Housewife." During this 1966–69 span, his arrangements were usually controlled enough to avoid orchestral overkill, his melodic flair was unbeatable, and his voice, while it was not what you could call bluesy, conveyed real sorrow and longing.

Glen Campbell: *The Best of Glen Campbell* (Capitol). It's too bad that about half these songs are also on *Greatest Hits.* Well into the midseventies, Campbell was still recording credible countrypolitan wish fulfillments like "Country Boy (You Got Your Feet in L.A.)" and "Rhinestone Cowboy," both of which are included here.

Roy Clark: *Greatest Hits, Vol. 1* (MCA). There's only a few in reality—"Yesterday When I Was Young" and "I Never Picked Cotton," which tells it like it is for Roy—and Clark is primarily an entertainer, not a recording artist. Still, throw in "Yesterday When I Was Young" for sensitivity, "Roy's Guitar Boogie" for chops, and any of a number of novelty songs for cheap kicks and you do indeed have the best of Roy circa the late sixties and early seventies.

Roy Clark/Gatemouth Brown: *Makin' Music* (MCA). This is not countrypolitan, but it shows what Clark is really capable of. Here, he's paired off with black multi-instrumentalist Clarence "Gatemouth" Brown (who, along with T-Bone Walker, invented Texas-style electric blues guitar in the forties). In the mid-seventies, Brown went more-or-less country, which meant basically that he played blues on country instruments or country on blues instruments. He's thus a perfect foil for Clark on this sleek but jumping collection of boogie, blues, and swing. This is what countrypolitan *could* be if it remembered music from the other side of the city.

Roy Clark: **Live From Austin City Limits** (Churchill). Because the audience for the TV show at which this was recorded is ostensibly younger and funkier, Roy shoots from the hip more often with his guitar. Not all the time, mind you, but often enough to make a difference.

Crystal Gayle: *Crystal Gayle* (Liberty). With nonfiller filler like Marshall Chapman's "A Woman's Heart (Is a Handy Place to Be)" and Dolly Parton's "You" among the 1974–75 hits, "Wrong Road Again" and "This Is My Year for Mexico," Crystal and Reynolds turn out an album meatier than her usual fare.

Crystal Gayle: *Crystal* (Liberty). Little more than a year later they are turning out the last album they did together that still sounded like they were reaching rather than holding ground.

Donna Fargo: *The Best of Donna Fargo* (MCA). Donna has just enough hard times in her voice that she makes all those "happiest girl" bromides sound like something she had to fight for. For that reason alone, she was a head above the others back around 1972–74, when the best of these hits were cut.

Bobbie Gentry: *Bobbie Gentry's Greatest* (Capitol). Bobbie had a southern Gothic hit in 1967 that no one will forget ("Ode to Billie Joe"), married rich, and got the hell out of the business. Since it's unlikely she'd ever again match the impact of that one record, I figure she's a smart woman for not even trying. (I'm ignoring "Louisiana Man" and "Fancy," the two ineffectual follow-up hits, because this album does, too.)

Brenda Lee: *Greatest Country Hits* (MCA). She started so young that sometimes it seems like she's been around forever, but Brenda has aged gracefully from teen belter to Nashville country singer to country-politan singer, and if something like "The Cowgirl and the Dandy" might seem just a little *too* much of a fairy tale for a voice still this gritty, "Big Four Poster Bed" and "He's My Rock" indicate that she's not reluctant to fire some reality into a musical form that's mostly about escapism.

Ronnie Milsap: *Greatest Hits* (RCA). This begins with his 1973 hard-country hits, and runs up to 1980, by which time "It Was Almost Like a Song" had made him an MOR star. There's too much experience and inner strength in that voice to rule him out entirely, but I sure prefer the early, more modest hits to the later monoliths. Two guesses, though, which Milsap has prevailed.

Anne Murray: *A Country Collection* (Capitol). Once her record company stumbled onto the fact that Anne had a large country following, it began pulling the country covers from previous LPs and making whole new albums out of them. This one, of late-seventies material, is not as consistently strong as *Country*, but that's only because of the songs, not the way she sings them.

Anne Murray: *Greatest Hits* (Capitol). Murray is not only the best MOR interpreter of country, she's wonderful with Beatles songs like "You Won't See Me" and even the imitation-Beatles Monkees hit "Daydream Believer" (written by John Stewart, who at least has *some* country roots). There's little overlap in songs between this and her country compilations, but the way she glides through these pop songs is just as impressive.

Dolly Parton: *9 to 5 and Odd Jobs* (RCA). A throwaway, you call it, designed to capitalize on the hit theme from Dolly's 1980 movie with Jane Fonda and Lily Tomlin. Ha! This just happens to be the most listenable album she's made since going pop; her taste is broad enough to include Woody Guthrie's migrant-workers ballad "Deportee," for one thing. But in rushing through this, Dolly manages to restrain herself from oversinging *or* overproducing for the only time during this phase in her career. More rush jobs, please.

Dolly Parton: *Greatest Hits* (RCA). The countrypolitan Dolly comes off so sure of herself that you think she knows just what she's doing. But if she does, why doesn't she wind up recording more "Two Doors Down" and "Do I Ever Cross Your Mind" (both included here) and less "Great Balls of Fire" (thankfully excluded), to name just one of her frequent atrocities? Can't she tell the difference? As it is, this album does make a reasonably good case for her as pop singer—which is more than the albums these songs were taken from can claim. Stripped of all her excesses, and served up in small doses, a winning personality is still there to carry the day—which surprised me, because until this came out in 1982, I was sure that she'd lost it for good. Now I'm only three quarters sure.

Ray Price: *The Best of Ray Price* (Columbia). Price really is a brilliant late-night ballad singer, so his move to countrypolitan shouldn't have turned out as badly as it did. His problem is that he just doesn't know when to leave well enough alone; he uses huge orchestras because their size wows listeners, not because they do anything musically to enhance his voice or material. Most of the time, they sound grafted on—the songs seem to have a layer of country vocal, a layer of rhythm section, a layer of horns, a layer of strings, etc. When it comes together just right, as on his reading of Kristofferson's "For the Good Times," Price is at the top of the idiom. But that performance and "The Lonesomest Lonesome" are the exceptions, not the rule.

Eddie Rabbitt: *The Best of Eddie Rabbitt* (Warner Bros.). In which we follow the 1976–79 rise and fall of a good man who went bad and made more money that way. Early Rabbitt hits such as "Drinkin' My Baby (Off My Mind)" and "Two Dollars in the Jukebox" had kick to them, but as soon as he established his name, he moved toward countrypolitan preciousness. That's where this album ends, and that's where he wallows today. Too bad.

Charlie Rich: *The Fabulous Charlie Rich* (Epic). Though it's now out of print, this was the greatest album Rich cut with Billy Sherrill, the songs ranging from "I Almost Lost My Mind" and "Bright Lights, Big City" to

"Life's Little Ups and Downs" and "Sittin' and Thinkin' " to "July 12, 1939." Each of them gets a fully committed reading from Charlie, the variety is stunning, and the sound is countrypolitan primarily because in retrospect this represents the first big step in the direction he ultimately took.

Charlie Rich: *Greatest Hits* (Epic). "Behind Closed Doors" still sounds convincing, a genuinely erotic song about marital bliss, which is a subject most Nashville singers treat so unrealistically you know they're really indulging in wishful thinking. But what followed that initial breakthrough didn't have a fraction of the soul, even if "The Most Beautiful Girl" and "Every Time You Touch Me (I Get High)" are state-of-the-art countrypolitan. Me, I listen to Charlie Rich for the soul, not for the technical proficiency of his producer.

Charlie Rich: *Silver Linings* (Epic). Rich always said that once he was successful he would use his clout to do projects he'd wanted to try but couldn't. This heartfelt 1976 album of gospel songs was the only time he made good on that vow, especially with "The Milky White Way." But it's now out of print.

CONTEMPORARY COUNTRY

Contemporary country is a catch-all phrase that refers to no particular sound, style, or place; it refers to the variety of musics that came about as a reaction to the Nashville Sound and the system of record production that prevailed in Music City. The vagueness of the term is indicative, depending on your point of view, of either the healthy diversity spawned in the seventies or of the continuing fragmentation and loss of identity in country music.

The term includes country-rock singers like Emmylou Harris who draw their base audience from the rock market but also have followings in country. (It doesn't include acts like the Eagles or Poco who played country-rock without reaching the country audience.) It includes southern rockers like Charlie Daniels who work both fields. Most important, it includes the new breed of country artist who broke through in the mid-seventies alongside, or on the coattails of, Willie Nelson and Waylon Jennings. These artists were generally identified with Austin, Texas, whether they came from there or just played there frequently, and they've been called everything from "outlaws" to "progressive country." (While the former term stuck the longest, it's hard to call a man like Willie an outlaw when he's selling more records and making more money than anyone else in the business. Still, as a marketing device, it's hard to beat.)

This wasn't always so. Throughout the sixties, Nelson was a successful Nashville songwriter whose own albums went nowhere. The Nashville Sound managed to camouflage everything that was unique in the man's music. He was part of a circle of songwriters in similar straits; occasionally, one of them busted loose, like Roger Miller did in the mid-sixties, or like Kris Kristofferson did in the early seventies.

Kristofferson, a former Rhodes Scholar who wrote florid, wordy songs that dealt largely with male vulnerability, was the first definite sign that new winds were blowing in Nashville. With his long hair, calculatedly scruffy dress, and flagrant marijuana use, he was an affront to polyester-suited, (ostensibly) drug-free Nashville. But his songs were recorded by rock and country artists alike, and his own albums were soon selling big in both markets.

In December 1972, after his Nashville house burned down, Nelson moved back to his home state of Texas. In Austin, a college town with a long history of good live music and relatively libertarian attitudes toward sex and drugs, he found a new audience. It was made up of young people who'd grown up on rock but gotten burned out on the beat and volume. They were now listening to a brand of music that was based in part on honky-tonk traditions and in part on the country-rock and singer-songwriter schools of Los Angeles. The local heroes were people like Michael Murphey and Jerry Jeff Walker, but Willie was the first authentic country singer to tap this market. He became something embarrassingly close to a deity in Texas, the man who united hippie and redneck, and he could seemingly do no wrong.

Back in Nashville, Waylon Jennings was entering into a partnership with Tompall Glaser, who ran a recording studio in the heart of Music Row. Jennings was another unmalleable singer whose music was aborted by Nashville production values. Like Nelson, he was trying to wrest control of his music away from the producers and executives. With Tompall's help, he succeeded. Tompall was doing the same thing with *his* solo recordings, too. (Tompall had previously been lead singer of Tompall and the Glaser Brothers, a mainstream brother trio popular in the sixties.)

That control meant an artist could name his own producer, or produce his own records, if he wanted. He picked his own songs and used his road band in the studio so he could get his true sound instead of the sound-alike Nashville music produced by the session pickers. Willie, Waylon, Tompall, Bobby Bare, and a handful of others started putting out records that sounded like nothing else in country music.

They weren't particularly "progressive" though—unless you consider the sound of the forties and fifties to be progressive in the seventies. What these men really did was strip away all the overdubs and orchestras and background singers in favor of stark, simple albums of country music. They were infatuated with the cowboy mythos of the old West—that's in part where the "outlaw" moniker came from—but their songs were also highly personal, semipoetic, clearly influenced by urban singer-songwriters.

Nashville resisted their every innovation. After all, if a singer could start getting hit records without using Nashville studios, producers, and pickers, that would put an end to the patriarchal Nashville recording industry. Which is, for a while at least, what appeared to be happening. At first radio wouldn't go near the new "outlaw" sounds. The musicians had trouble getting bookings outside central Texas, where Willie continued expanding his base through his annual Fourth of July picnics (three-day country music festivals patterned after the rock bashes of 1967–70, and spotlighting both new and old country talent). The media began taking notice, and the word started spreading.

In 1975, Willie did *Red-Headed Stranger,* an album so sparsely produced his record company tried to block its release. It sold like a pop album. The next year RCA released an anthology of nothing-special cuts by Willie, Waylon, Tompall, and Jessi Colter (Waylon's wife) called *Wanted! The Outlaws.* It became the first country album ever to go platinum—meaning it sold more than one million copies. That made things official—"outlaws" had arrived. And where country was once strictly a singles market, with albums being made up of a couple of hits plus ten pieces of filler material, it was now, like rock, an album market. That meant much bigger money.

Elements of rock, meanwhile, had been moving closer to country. The L.A. country-rock scene, inspired first by the Byrds' *Sweetheart of the Rodeo* and Bob Dylan's *Nashville Skyline,* was now producing singers who broke on the pop charts and crossed over to country while Willie and Waylon were doing just the opposite. Foremost among them were Linda Ronstadt and Emmylou Harris; Emmylou had first won notice singing harmony with Gram Parsons, the doomed avatar of the L.A. country-rock movement. Parsons was a Georgian who'd come to L.A. in the midst of the psychedelic boom and worked with the Byrds briefly during their country-rock phase. He then formed the Flying Burrito Brothers, the first of the full-time country-rock groups, before going solo in the early seventies. He died in 1973 after consuming too much of everything bad he could get his hands on, so he never saw how great his influence had been. But L.A. country-rock dominated pop music for much of the seventies.

Down south, various rock bands were synthesizing blues and country into a fluid new music. The best of these bands—the Allman Brothers Band, Lynyrd Skynyrd—rocked too hard for the country charts, but they had a huge influence on southern rockers who did cross over (among them Charlie Daniels, the Marshall Tucker Band, and the Amazing Rhythm Aces).

Before long country "outlaws"—Steve Young, Guy Clark, Delbert McClinton, Billy Joe Shaver, Lee Clayton, David Allen Coe, and many more—were all over the place. That first wave of album releases was remarkably strong; clearly, these were people with something to say who'd been held back too long. But it turned out that most had only one good album in them and they soon went soft and pretentious. The poseurs arrived in no time, singing the praises of the Lone Star State, Lone Star beer, Lone Star women, Lone Star cowboys, Lone Star boots and belt buckles, Lone Star anything. Austin remained a good town for live music for several more years, but there was never a serious attempt to build an alternative country music industry there. Next time anyone looked around, Billy Sherrill was producing "outlaw" albums on some of his singers, and everything had once again been reduced to product. The formula was different, but it was still a formula; the main difference now was that people dressed funnier and took different drugs.

Or was it? The most talented ones lasted, the foremost example being Willie himself. He is now an icon in American popular music, and can record absolutely anything he wants and know it will sell. He's also a movie star. Several others have continued their careers with varying degrees of success. Waylon still does well, though not as well as he used to, and his music has suffered badly ever since he started believing his own publicity blurbs. He and Tompall had a falling-out that stunned the whole movement, and Tompall is now back singing with his brothers. Gary Stewart has been a disappointment, Joe Ely hangs on, and David Allen Coe won't go away. Rosanne Cash and her husband, Rodney Crowell, have both proved themselves important new artists. So the music is still there—it's just that the buzz, the sense of a community of rebels fighting the establishment and winning, is gone.

Roger Miller: *Golden Hits* (Mercury).

Roger Miller was one of a kind, and there'll never be another album even remotely similar to this one. He came well disguised, too—why, when he started out, in the late fifties and early sixties, his career was following the same course as that of any number of other marginal country artists. His biggest success was as a writer; George Jones, Ernest Tubb, Jim Reeves, and Ray Price all cut his songs. He was also a sideman who'd worked for Price, Faron Young, even Minnie Pearl. Unable to solidify his position in Music City, he moved back and forth several times between Nashville and Texas (he'd been born in Fort Worth in 1936, but was raised in Oklahoma).

The songs he wrote for others were standard (though excellent) honky-tonkers. In the early sixties, when he began recording on his own for RCA, he cut similar material in a style closer to Ray Price than to anybody else. But Miller's lyrics and his interpretation of the Price shuffle were quirky; his records were denser than Price's classics, the beat more pronounced, and his singing was frantic. He was on his way to the sound that would make him famous, but he was only halfway there.

Meanwhile, he was writing curious little ditties way too off-the-wall for anyone to record. The only time they were even heard was when Miller and his roaring buddies got a head full of pills and whiskey and decided that since they were too high to sleep, they might as well pull out the acoustic guitars and bring up the sun swapping songs. Those buddies were other writers getting nowhere as performers—men like Willie Nelson and Hank Cochran—and around Nashville they were infamous and then some.

Finally, in 1964, Miller got a chance to record some of these songs. The results were a revelation. At a time when Nashville was settling comfortably and profitably into assembly-line production, Miller entered the studio with just four other men, all of them playing acoustic instruments. The plan was to capture the loose, informal atmosphere

Miller created when he sat around the living room playing these songs for friends.

It worked, and in the course of putting down sides like "Dang Me" and "Chug-a-Lug" in one take each, a new sound emerged. Defining it is not easy, for it came from deepest left field, but with its odd chording and scat-like singing, it owes something to pre-bop jazz as well as to Ray Price and similar country balladeers. The lyrics are full of outrageous puns and wordplays that brought new wit and verbal sophistication to country music. And Miller's melodies seemed to distill a century's worth of American tunes going all the way back to Stephen Foster. Look at it this way: Roger Miller recorded these sides a full ten years or more before the other albums listed in this section. He was that far ahead of everybody else, and during his peak he won so many Grammys that the rules were changed to make sure nobody else could again so dominate. He was also hosting his own network variety show, and this at a time when country artists were considered too insignificant to even *appear* on TV as a guest on someone else's show.

Innovative as his music was, Miller attracted the most attention for his lyrics. He was cocksure and on top of the world, the fast-talker who had an appropriate wisecrack for every occasion from drinking to death. And if words should fail Miller, he would simply improvise some ludicrous, nonverbal scatting that carried the song until he could think up a new line.

Miller has said that his chief influence was not another musician but Brother Dave Gardner, a freewheeling southern topical comedian who peaked in the sixties. Brother Dave cheerfully admitted that many of his routines were induced by massive intakes of amphetamines, and they sound like it. Some is racist vitriol, while other bits are acutely on-target swipes at southerners and northerners, hipsters and rednecks. But Brother Dave was so full of ideas he couldn't tell the good ones from the bad ones; he just spewed it all out and let it work people up. And he seemed to derive more glee from the chaos he created than from the ideas themselves.

Miller, however, did edit himself, and while his humor was sometimes dry and black, he had none of Brother Dave's malice or self-importance. In "Kansas City Star," he mocks the archetypal big-fish-in-a-small-pond with both affection and insight. Though the song is about a local TV star, by the way, it's named after a newspaper, and Miller absorbed other ideas from the popular press, particularly the gaudy world of advertising; "You Can't Roller Skate in a Buffalo Herd" was inspired by a line in a magazine ad for a new camera.

Miller also took country's most hallowed conceits and playfully set them on their ears, stripping them of their mystique. As writer Paul

Hemphill has pointed out, the hobo had always been a tragic figure, forever at the whims of the economy, the weather, the railroad bulls, and the charity of strangers, always trying to stay one step ahead of whatever dogged him. In "King of the Road," Miller's hobo takes his own sweet time and goes where he pleases; he's happy to subsist on old cigars and he's proud to pay no union dues. When he needs a room or some spare change, work is easy to come by, and the rest of the time it's to be avoided like the plague. He is, in short, a bum—and damn proud of it.

After two years of nonstop hits with his own songs, Miller dried up overnight. For five years he didn't write a single new song (though for a while he continued having hits with outside material). He's been relatively silent for more than a decade, and insists that he's a lazy guy who'd like to keep it that way. His periodic—and unsuccessful—attempts at a comeback suggest he might really feel otherwise, but it's not like the man wasn't prepared for something like this; as he once told an overly enthusiastic audience that he was trying to shush, "No matter how big you get, the size of your funeral depends on the weather."

Willie Nelson: *Phases and Stages* (Atlantic).

Though *Shotgun Willie* was supposed to be the album that freed Willie Nelson from the Nashville assembly line, it turned out to be a slapdash affair. But on *Phases and Stages,* the 1974 follow-up, Willie turned the trick.

Nearly everything about the album represents a departure. It was recorded at Muscle Shoals, Alabama, using primarily the same session musicians who cut much of the great soul music of the late sixties and early seventies; it was produced by Jerry Wexler, who made his name working with R & B and soul artists from the fifties and sixties. The album is also rife with contradictions; it's got more jazz inflections than anything Nelson had done, yet it's also true to his Texas country roots (he was born in Abbott in 1933). Finally, this is a concept album that sounds good whether you're listening to the words or not.

Not that the words are anything to be ashamed of. The songs are all originals, and this album represents the last songwriting jag for Willie, who became so popular as an artist that he quit writing. The concept is a simple one, dealing with the end of a marriage. Side one is from the woman's point of view; it opens with her expressing disgust with the marriage and then follows her as she disavows her husband and returns to her mother. At the end of the side, she's contemplating a new romance. Side two tells the man's story as he comes home, sinks deeper into misery at being left, and finally starts pulling himself together.

Loss, guilt, self-pity, disillusionment, being too messed up to think straight, let alone act sensibly: These are common C & W themes, but handled uncommonly well. It figures that the oft-divorced Nelson would get the man's story down better, and most of the songs on that side ("Bloody Mary Morning," "I Still Can't Believe You're Gone," "Heaven and Hell," "Pick Up the Tempo") have indeed become standards. But his fed-up woman is more well rounded than you might expect, too, so Willie must have done his share of listening. As he himself has noted, his songs express only surface thoughts—but they have an immediacy that cuts right to the bone. Look at how few words he needs to fully convey the woman's rejuvenation: "Down at the corner beer joint/Dancing to the rock and roll/Her jeans fit a little bit tighter than they did before."

Wexler's production is appropriately terse, allowing the songs to go directly to the listener. For the first time, we hear Willie's songs as he most likely heard them in his head, without the strings and background choirs and other overdubs. But when he wants, Wexler can still haul out the extras; for "I Still Can't Believe You're Gone," he has Mike Lewis whip up the kind of big, swelling string arrangements that used to engulf the Mr. Pitifuls of soul music. This is one of the few such string arrangements in all of C & W—still—that isn't hack work.

The Muscle Shoals pickers may usually play soul music, but they're mostly white boys themselves, and they have no trouble fitting themselves around Willie. They've played so little country in the past that it all still sounds fresh to them, and they make it fresh to us, too. They're kept in line by two of country music's foremost instrumentalists: Johnny Gimble, the Texas swing fiddler, and John Hughey, Conway Twitty's steel player. In addition to Willie's own gut-string guitar, Pete Carr and Fred Carter, Jr., of Muscle Shoals provide stinging dobros and snappy guitar lines that lend jazz flavor to songs like "Sister's Coming Home/Down at the Corner Beer Joint," which sound like a face-off between Floyd Tillman and Symphony Sid, as well as "No Love Around," which sounds like a field holler. This jazz influence, heretofore a well-kept secret of Willie's, is his way of updating western swing instead of aping it, and shows off his uncanny ability to move forward by reaching backward. The solos spun off in "Bloody Mary Morning" come out of bluegrass, but also anticipate the "hot group" Willie would assemble nearly a decade later for *Somewhere Over the Rainbow*, his tribute to French guitarist Django Reinhardt.

Willie's voice is the glue holding together these seemingly disparate elements—flat and just behind the beat, it's so monochromatic that the tiniest inflections serve to open up each song. Pretty dramatic stuff for a guy who supposedly can't sing.

Willie Nelson: *Red Headed Stranger* (Columbia).

A turn-of-the-century preacher is left by his wife. He traces her and her lover to a saloon in Montana and shoots both of them dead before they can even react to his presence. He leaves with his wife's horse in tow behind his own, and though he has some misgivings about his deed, they aren't enough to stop him from wordlessly killing another woman who dares touch that horse a few days later in another town. The code of the West exonerates him again. He roams wild-eyed toward Denver, his bloodlust still not sated. But there he meets another woman, in whose company he finds fulfillment. He begins to renew his own life.

This is a stock story—as enduring as the old West itself and as superficial, melodramatic, and self-serving as anything that ever came out of Hollywood. It even has your standard tacked-on Hollywood happy ending. But the best Hollywood westerns—those of John Ford, for example—are able to keep pumping new vitality into these themes, and Willie Nelson does something similar. This music reverberates until Willie's character begins to seem like the archetypal American drifter, seeking salvation in love and/or violence. Concept albums—whether song cycles like this or tributes to other artists and genres—usually bring out the best in Nelson. They force him to organize and focus a train of thought otherwise likely to meander. And mystique-wise, it doesn't hurt in this case that Willie himself is both red-headed and highly nomadic.

Released in 1975, this album almost didn't come out at all. Scheduled to be Willie's first release for his new company, Columbia, it was recorded in Texas with nobody from the label present, and with Nelson producing. It was then previewed for Columbia's Nashville staff. Billy Sherrill, who was the top executive in that office and who as a producer had almost single-handedly made overproduction fashionable in country music, reportedly deemed the album unfit for public consumption. Willie countered by saying that if CBS released the album and it flopped, he would thereafter give up his autonomy and do whatever the label asked of him. The gamble paid off—not only did the album then yield the first mega-hit singles of his career in "Blue Eyes Crying in the Rain" and "Remember Me," but it eventually went platinum, then an unprecedented feat for a country artist.

Sherrill's objections are predictable enough. *Red Headed Stranger* tells its story through a series of songs held together by short instrumental passages that don't do much but advance the action (yet are played with too much verve to be considered strictly filler). But even by Willie's minimalist standards, this is a lean record. To a producer like Sherrill, who regards horns and string sections and background vocalists as emblems of class and sophistication, this must have seemed like a direct affront. But silence can be a potent musical tool in itself, and its uses in these mostly acoustic arrangements provide the story with menace and tension. The spaces in this music also conjure up the vast, endless southwestern plains as effectively as does Willie's own parched, grainy voice.

By the time Willie recorded this, he'd been out of Nashville and back in Texas for several years. He was already playing to the young new "outlaw" audience that puzzled (and angered) Sherrill and his ilk. This audience, Willie correctly perceived, was as much a folk audience as it was a rock and country audience. Its folkie side was particularly susceptible to the charms of storytelling and simple acoustic music, while its rocking side was impressed by suggestions of artiness. The real surprise was that the mainstream country audience was so quick to fall in line, too, but apparently it remembered (better than the industry did) how recently country music itself had in essence been folk music. This was one of those too-good-to-be-true pop situations in which the artist and audience reshape each other, and that's the real significance of *Red Headed Stranger.*

There're still flaws. The fact that the protagonist is a preacher isn't explored at all, and lines here and there muddle the story just enough that some people (myself included) first believed that the killings were psychotic fantasies taking place only in his mind. The narrator's refusal to comment on the action makes it seem like he approves of everything that happens. Willie sticks to delivering just the facts, ma'am. The story has no moral; there is nothing to learn from it, as there would be from a John Ford movie. But you must draw your own conclusions anyway. This was the first album to take "progressive" country away from the cultists and into the mass marketplace, so you can bet many people were doing just that.

Waylon Jennings: *Dreaming My Dreams* (RCA).

It took Waylon Jennings a long time to get what he was after musically, and almost as soon as he did, he turned it into self-parody. But this album was released in 1975, and represents his peak; it reveals more about Waylon Jennings than any previous work, and does so without trick mirrors. In terms of music alone, it's his most satisfying album —but Waylon has never been about music alone.

"I like to take another man's song and make it sound like I wrote it," he once told interviewer Michael Bane. In concert, at his best, Jennings always did that. He wrote very little himself, but the material he chose was all of a piece; it all fit together as if it was written just for him. The image—last of the cowboys, always moving on, looking back with a sweet mixture of pride, regret, and bravado—was always a little too pat; part of the reason it worked so well is that it was so easy to latch onto. But if it was overtly romanticized, it was also a genuine part of Waylon's west Texas heritage. (He was born in Littlefield in 1937, and grew up around music more western than country.)

But records were another story. For years he was mishandled by his RCA producers; when he finally got control over his albums, he usually dwelled on one aspect of the sound or image until he had run it into the ground. He never could capture the overall picture that came so naturally in concert. But Jack Clement, who is listed here as co-producer but clearly had the upper hand in shaping the album, knows how to pull things together.

It's not just the way Clement uses cellos and the like in addition to the usual violins to color a song—Cowboy Jack is, after all, the man who invented chamber country music for the releases on his short-lived JMI label and on his own solo album. Nor is it just the kind of wash he gets between acoustic and electric guitars on something like the bluesy "High Time (You Quit Your Low Down Ways)." It's those and more, for the Cowboy has taught Waylon understatement, and that's something Jennings badly needed to learn. Just in terms of the vocals, this is not only Waylon's most ambitious album, it's also his most subtle, which is no small accomplishment for a man so prone to excess. In addition, Cowboy has cleaned up the Jennings beat so it hits more directly at the gut.

The beat is right there on the first cut, "Are You Sure Hank Done It This Way." It's a choppy, bass-heavy beat conceived as a result of Waylon's late-fifties stint with Buddy Holly but hardened by infusions of Johnny Cash's sound. His own guitar is heavily strummed to second the beat when he plays rhythm, and snarls in "chicken-pickin' " style when he takes leads. For years Nashville producers did their best to muffle this sound by bringing in wind-up session hacks to play the "same old clippity-clop" as one disgruntled songwriter described the beat, on Waylon's records. As soon as he began recording with his road band, the Waylors, in the early seventies, Jennings began moving toward the trademark sound on his albums. Clement not only got him there once and for all, he made minor adjustments like adding the stoned, easy-rolling rhythm guitars that improve the atmosphere.

It's fitting that Waylon should kick off the album with "Are You Sure Hank Done It This Way" because that song so grimly catalogs the obstacles he had to overcome. There's the uniformity of the Nashville Sound alongside the uniforms country singers wore. There's the endless string of one-nighters, all the same. There's the condescension Nashville holds out to new artists as a form of encouragement, and the adulation for the Hank Williams hell-raising legacy now that Hank's safely dead and nobody has to deal with its consequences. Despite his bitterness, Jennings weaves it all into a personal triumph.

Two more tributes add depth to Waylon's own legacy and to that of the movement he helped spearhead. "Bob Wills Is Still the King" is a nice piece of chest-puffing throwaway (enough so that on his next album, when Waylon did a salute to his original patron Buddy Holly, he used the same melody). But "Waymore's Blues," the Jimmie Rodgers tribute, is inspired. It climaxes with a couplet first noted in 1908 though undoubtedly much older, popularized by Rodgers in 1930 and thereafter modified and reused by Gene Autry, Harmonica Frank, and others both black and white. It's a boast about not having to work because his name is written on the tail of his shirt, and it sums up the elusive freedom Rodgers pursued in his day that others seek in Jimmie's music. The song has a loopy, stream-of-consciousness, talking-blues lyric that further identifies Waylon with the rambling tradition.

The rest is just as unrestrained. The obligatory road song, "I've Been a Long Time Leaving (But I'll Be a Long Time Gone)" is not as forced as the title might indicate; the obligatory wonders-of-a-woman song, "I Recall a Gypsy Woman," is saved from ostentatiousness by Waylon's earthy vocals. "She's Looking Good" is dryly tender, rather than starry-eyed, and "Dreaming My Dreams" transcends schmaltz purely on the strength of Waylon's conviction.

Lastly, there's "Let's All Help the Cowboys (Sing the Blues)," a Clement original meant to mock his own image as Nashville's resident crazy-man genius. I mean, do cowboys *really* care about Shakespeare? Do they really look for IQ in a woman? I think not. Waylon thinks not, too, but he does like the conceit. This is the kind of song with which he'd later destroy his credibility. But this time, tongues planted firmly in cheek, he and Cowboy do it up right.

Gary Stewart: *Out of Hand* (RCA).

Gary Stewart first appeared in Nashville in 1967 as a songwriter, but he spent most of the next decade going back and forth between Music City and his home in Florida. (He was born in Jenkins, Kentucky, in 1944.) He was regarded as a promising singer, writer, and multi-instrumentalist who was more interested in having a good time than in building a career, ambivalent about the music business if not the music. But his breakthrough as a recording artist, when he finally got around to making it in 1975, marked the introduction of a new kind of honky-tonk hero.

Stewart knows all about bow-legged country girls and blustering men, empty beds and emptied bottles, wedding bands and wandering eyes. He'll be happy to tell you more than you need to know about drinking too much and going home with the wrong person—or worse yet, going home alone because the *right* person went home with the wrong person. Stewart knows how to find trouble—how to get into it and how to get out of it. This is his milieu, and these are his people, but Stewart differs in crucial ways from both the traditional and the new breed of country singers specializing in such matters.

And that's because however familiar it may all seem to him, Stewart doesn't labor to make us think he's really singing exclusively about his own life and hard times. The traditional honky-tonker would take a song like "She's Actin' Single (I'm Drinkin' Doubles)" and milk those lines for every drop of self-pity they're worth. But Stewart stands back a bit, sings it with a knowing wink and enough distance from the subject to let everyone in on the absurdity of it all. Get a load of this, he says, nudging you in the ribs: "My heart is breaking/Like those tiny bubbles . . ."

A generation or two after honky-tonk has peaked, Stewart can think of the form the way a son might think of a cantankerous, stubbornly reactionary father—with no small amount of respect, but also with some amusement. He shows his affection for honky-tonk by replacing guilt with glee.

Similarly, while most young singers who emerged in the mid-seventies treated a hard-core drinking lyric as though it were a manifesto of existential angst, Stewart portrays the barroom as the fool's court-of-last-resort it most often really is. Much of his best work thus has comic-book overtones, but even they serve to reveal deeper truths. The men in his songs are often vulnerable and unashamed of it, for example, and they don't use that vulnerability as a tool for manipulation. They usually take responsibility for their own mistakes without getting overbearingly maudlin about it. The women here are usually friends as well as lovers; men and women in his songs meet on terms far more equal than you'll find in any other barroom songs, which lends more credibility to the likes of "I See the Want To in Your Eyes" or "Out of Hand."

In too many respects, this debut is a straightforward Nashville production. But when Stewart later came up with a more personal sound, he lost something else in the process, and even the most uninspired Nashville production couldn't entirely sabotage his rollicking boisterous attack—or his unfettered mountain tenor, with its slithering vibrato and his whimsical phrasing. Anyhow, even here he plays little tricks with the Nashville formula, starting with the Allmanesque twin guitars of "Draggin' Shackles" and the skittering piano of "Country Red." The final result is a hell-raising whoop as fuzzy around the edges as an all-night drinking binge. Stewart is like Jerry Lee Lewis without the mean streak; he has nothing to prove, and makes not proving it sound like more fun than anything else he could possibly think of to do.

Hank Williams, Jr.: *Hank Williams, Jr., and Friends* (MGM).

In August of 1975, while on a hunting trip near the Great Divide at Missoula, Montana, Hank Williams, Jr., fell five hundred feet down a mountainside, scraping off most of his face. He was given little chance to live, but he did; in the eight months that followed, he had his mouth, palate, nose, and forehead rebuilt almost from scratch. Three months after his fall, his mother, the legendary Audrey Williams, died. Hank, Jr., came to the funeral looking, as one writer described him, "like death itself." The fires of the ghoulish Hank Williams myth were stoked as high as they'd been in nearly twenty-five years.

Though this album wasn't released until after his accident, it was recorded just before. At the time, Hank, Jr., was not only going through his second divorce (he was twenty-five), but he was trying to cast off the straitjacket he'd grown up in as the son of country music's most revered star. Even before his accident, this album makes clear, Hank, Jr., was in a turbulent state of mind, a man suffering great personal emptiness but determined to take control of his life for the first time ever.

He was born in 1949 in Shreveport, Louisiana, but was moved to Nashville when he was three months old, and he lived there all his life. He barely knew his father, who died when the boy was still three years old, but when he became a professional entertainer before he even entered his teens, Hank, Jr., sang only his father's songs. The idea that he himself might have something to say was apparently never considered by his mother or their business managers. So while he never had to worry about whether or not he would be a success, he had every reason, always, to worry about *why* he was. In addition, he had the Williams myth to live up to, a myth best summarized in a Faron Young song: "I'm gonna live fast, love hard, die young/And leave a beautiful memory." When he was drinking and drugging heavily, Hank, Jr., seemed determined to do just that. But by surviving the accident, he broke the script. And once this album—the country equivalent to John Lennon's primal scream LP—came out, it was clear that he had everything to live for. *Hank Williams, Jr., and Friends* is the most powerful country-rock album of the era. In 1982, Hank, Jr., set a new record by putting nine albums on the charts simultaneously, and the greatest irony of it all was that this one was not among them because his old record company, unable to cope with the image change, had let it go out of print immediately.

In retrospect, it's not surprising that as he matured and stepped out on his own, Hank, Jr., would enlist such southern rockers as Toy Caldwell (of the Marshall Tucker Band), Charlie Daniels and Chuck Leavell (of the Allman Brothers Band) to help him. Nor is it a complete surprise that he would turn to rock for inspiration. Hank, Jr., may have seemed like an old man because he'd been out there in front of the public for so long, but he's younger than any of the Rolling Stones, for example. No matter how insulated he was as a child, he must have had some affinity for rock all along because he grew up with it; he just never had an outlet for it, because of the limits imposed on him.

The mainstream Nashville stuff he'd recorded was nothing to sniffle at, either. He was always an emotive singer, less detached than most in the style, and his mainstream country records were state-of-the-art. But none stood out like the songs here. These are highly personal and intimate, but they are not at all obscure; they have the kind of simple eloquence that only the best songwriters articulate. Hank, Jr., threw away his previous Nashville cool to sing each of these as though . . . well, as though his life depended on it. And they're equally durable musically, laced as they are with incandescent southern guitar solos, instrumental interplay, and riffs. In one way or another, nearly every song is about fighting the sensation of feeling adrift, and they were all written by Hank, Jr., except three—Caldwell's "Losing You" and "Can't You See" (Hank, Jr., had the first cover on this oft-covered song) and Shel Silverstein/Vince Matthew's "On Susan's Floor."

Two of the songs, eerily enough, allude to circumstances similar to those that would soon put Hank, Jr., temporarily out of action. The startling imagery of "Montana Song" made that one unbearably ironic by the time it was finally released; in it, Hank, Jr., sings about fleeing to Montana for the winter and leaving his troubles behind, at the same time fantasizing that his recently parted lover will join him there. They will make love in a sleeping bag, sit on the Great Divide, "and look out on America and feel so free inside," lines he sings with aching wistfulness. They're not the only good lines he turns, either; in the western-flavored "Clovis, New Mexico," he describes a newfound lover so meticulously she really does come alive for us, taking on living dimensions women seldom are granted in pop songs.

The capper is "Living Proof," a mournful ballad about "living for two men," as he says after being confronted by an old drunk who tells him he'll never be as good as his father. Hank, Jr., swears he'll never let his own son become a musician and vows to quit singing sad songs because they hit too close to home. But therein lies much of his dilemma . . . still. Because the song that precedes "Living Proof" is a perfectly crafted honky-tonker called "Stoned at the Jukebox," which is not only as sad a song as Hank, Jr., ever wrote, but it quotes from one of his daddy's songs. Yet it's such a devastating performance that you wind up taking his word when he says he sings it to "get the hurtin' out." And you know he'll continue singing sad songs after all.

When it was released, this album sounded like the catharsis Hank, Jr., had been seeking for so long. And it definitely was a breakthrough, though subsequent albums have all contained more songs about his image and his father and the burdens he must bear—by now, he doth protest way too much. But the subject keeps gnawing away at him, and he keeps nagging back at it. *Hank Williams, Jr., and Friends* remains the strongest antidote, revealing a man born into a most unenviable situation and doing his best to come to grips with it, while still seeking out both elbow room and the comfort of friends and lovers. With this album, Hank, Jr., becomes his own man.

Jimmy Murphy: *Electricity* (Sugar Hill).

Some people would include this album with those from the Jimmie Rodgers era, since that's where you'll find Jimmy Murphy's roots. Others would put it in with rockabilly, because that's how Murphy's few singles in the early fifties were marketed, or honky-tonk, because he has such an affinity with Hank Williams and other high, lonesome singers of the pre-rockabilly era. Still others would argue for bluegrass, because Murphy takes some bluegrass-based guitar solos, his album utilizes basically bluegrass sidemen (Ricky Skaggs on mandolin, fiddle, vocal harmonies; Jerry Douglas of the Country Gentlemen on dobro), and it was released by a basically bluegrass label. I'm putting it in this category because Murphy's seamless blend of acoustic country musics is so "progressive," as the marketing boys still like to call contemporary country sometimes; because it's one of the freshest-sounding albums of the seventies; and because sometimes I feel like being just as contrary as Murphy does. And also because *I* can't figure out where else to put it either —more than anyone else listed in these Top 100 albums, Murphy confounds categorization. With the possible exception of Harry Choates, nobody else in the Top 100 is more obscure.

Richard K. Spottswood's liner notes provide biographical details. Born in 1925 in Republic, Alabama, a mining town near Birmingham, Jimmy grew up on equal doses of country (mainly Opry stars like Roy Acuff) and blues (Blind Boy Fuller, Leadbelly). Though as a teen-ager he played on a Birmingham radio station, he joined his father's brick masonry business upon graduation from high school. Then he made his way to Knoxville, Tennessee, where, while working with Archie Campbell, he fell in with Chet Atkins, who got him a contract with RCA. Recording with just acoustic guitar and bass in the honky-tonk era, Murphy stiffed. His next records, affectionate send-ups of rockabilly that were cut for Columbia in 1955, did no better. In the sixties he cut isolated sides for various regional labels; Spottswood tracked him down in the mid-seventies for this album, which was released in 1978. Many of these cuts are rerecordings of earlier Murphy songs.

His track record is thus both eclectic and marginal, which helps explain how he shaped, and was shaped by, his various musics—though this makes him no less inventive, for nobody else has done anything even remotely similar. For example, though rockabilly artists all cited Bill Monroe as a major influence, I was never before able to see many connections between the two musics besides fast tempos and the sheer soulfulness of the best singers. But Murphy's bright, ringing acoustic guitar lines provide a missing musical link.

It's in the actual songs, and in his irascible way of singing them, that Murphy's generation-straddling becomes most clear, and most entertaining. "Electricity" is his best-known song, covered by others in bluegrass and rockabilly alike, and any writer would have to be proud if he could put a fairly lengthy train of thought across so briefly, vividly, wittily, and conclusively as Murphy does when he sings, "Well, you can't see electricity/A-movin' on the line/How in the world can you doubt it/When you can see it shine/When you get salvation/The currents you can feel/You won't have to have nobody/To tell you that it's real." He next compares salvation to the true tone of good music, and you know he's a believer. But then he answers those who say religion isn't "real" by declaring it to be as real as T-bone steak, honey, molasses, and cake, and you know he's going to have his fun with the subject too, tweaking those who take their faith so seriously and so sternly that they strip it of its human virtues. "Wake Me Up Sweet Jesus" is breakneck newgrass, with fancy picking from both Skaggs and Douglas, but Murphy courts apocalyptic Christianity coyly rather than literally when he begs, "Wake me up when it's all over/Wake me up when the trumpets sound/Wake me up Sweet Jesus/When this old world is burnin' down."

In a secular vein, "We Live a Long Long Time" relentlessly mocks an old man—but it's the old man who's singing the song, and he's having a laugh on the younger friends and relatives who ridicule him. They're more uneasy about his impending death than he is; at least *he* has fond memories of his own younger, more rambunctious days. On "Mother Where Is Your Daughter Tonight" he sings, "Remember the night she started to stray/You failed to whip her and make her obey/Now she has fallen and has a bad name/The rest of her life she'll be living in shame." This sounds like a notion Roy Acuff would *still* be happy with, and Murphy clearly loves the music of that era. But his reading of the song is so deadpan that he (and the listener) become incredulous. He's amused that people *ever* thought like that, let alone that they still do, and he's fascinated that such bad ideas can be tied in with such good music.

Others are perhaps less ironic, but no less acute. "I Get a Longing to Hear Hank Sing the Blues" was written and first recorded well after Hank Williams had died. Thus, unlike most of those who wrote tribute songs, Murphy actually had time to reflect on what Williams really meant to him. He concluded that being left by his woman just isn't the same unless there's Hank Williams music there in the background orchestrating the departure, and that's a review I'm sure Hank would have appreciated. "Shanty Boat Blues," though first done by Jimmy Skinner, works as an apt tribute to the style and times of Jimmie Rodgers. "Louise" is a blues for Murphy's clear, chiming guitar and his seductive talking/singing voice. "I Always Get What I Don't Want" is world-weary blues. And just to show he could keep up with the modernists, Murphy includes "You Touched Me and Made Me Live Again," the kind of modern heart song that pays the bills in Nashville.

Jimmy Murphy was a cross between Doc Watson and Harmonica Frank, the kind of maverick there's increasingly less room for in the music business today. Since he died shortly after this album was released, I'm extra-glad he got to make it at all. I'm just sorry he couldn't have done it for a major label, so it might have gotten some of the promotion and public acclaim it deserves. You have to hear him to believe him.

Joe Ely: *Honky Tonk Masquerade* (MCA).

It's hard to get much more isolated than Lubbock, a town sitting alone on the flat, windswept west Texas plains, surrounded for miles by nothing but hardscrabble farms. In a town like that, you make your own entertainment, and the area has produced a disproportionately high number of crack musicians, Waylon Jennings and Buddy Holly above all. But it's also the kind of stifling town that curious, ambitious young men and women flee as soon as they can.

For years, despite a bad case of wanderlust, something kept calling Joe Ely back. He was born there in 1947, lived there nearly all his life, and in his albums he has captured the spirit of the town with such telltale clarity that he makes it sound familiar; he could be speaking about small towns everywhere. In the process he's conceived a singularly apt sound that's neither country nor rock (nor country-rock), but some unanticipated fusion of all three, with a few more styles thrown in for spice.

Ely's breed of country comes straight from the bars and dance halls, and is somehow both lyrical and rugged. Bluesman Elmore James' signature electric guitar riff (which itself derives from Robert Johnson) turns up in the middle of a traditional country blues number; a jarring hard-rock guitar solo shatters a country ballad, an accordion fits into a waltz or a rocker that may be influenced equally by both Mexican border music and Cajun music. The open rhythms of west Texas rockabilly (like Holly's) blend with the harder Memphis stuff of Carl Perkins. Jimmy Reed's laconic blues coexist alongside the frantic jump-blues of Wynonie Harris. There are strains of country music from Jimmie Rodgers to Bob Wills to Hank Williams to George Jones to Gram Parsons, and Ely also shares kinship with such seventies singer-songwriters as Jackson Browne. At the bottom of his music is a beat that separates it from all other country, while the rave-ups between steel guitarist Lloyd Maines and guitarist Jesse Taylor became another Ely trademark. Finally, there's his supple voice, which sings the weepers with a tear and a tug of the heart, and the boppers with flat-out roadhouse abandon.

Because he began recording in the mid-seventies, Ely was lumped in with the Austin acts. That was a mistake, because Ely has real roots, and most of the Austin groups didn't. So while they were patching together songs based on fake nostalgia, silly notions like cosmic cowboys, hippie ideals about personal freedom, and romanticized notions about macho and the old West, Ely was alone in Lubbock writing about what he saw around him, what had always been around him. Butch Hancock and Jimmie Dale Gilmore, two more Lubbock writers who'd once played with Ely in a country-folk group called the Flatlanders, also provided him with material.

Honky Tonk Masquerade is the richest of his albums, though all have much to recommend them. This one opens with a grabber of a guitar line, the drums kick in strong, and Ely jumps right into "Cornbread Moon" (see what I mean about unforgettable imagery?). Taylor's guitar and Ponti Bone's marvelous accordion flesh the song out harmonically, and the band slips gracefully in and out of the melodic themes.

The title song lays out the ambivalence men as well as women can feel about barroom mating rituals and one-night stands, which is an accomplishment in itself, but it does so through such everyday imagery —the light from a beer sign, a hand tugging on a shirt sleeve—that you wonder why nobody's done it before. Elsewhere, Ely shows a mystical streak: On "Because of the Wind" he likens the memory of a former lover to the west Texas winds and himself to the trees on the border that are bent by those winds. In Gilmore's strange "Tonight I Think I'm Gonna Go Downtown," the singer, abandoned by his woman, murmurs about how real the world used to be to him, and how it's no longer real to him at all. This has something to do with why she left him, though it's not clear what; nor is it clear what will happen when he gets downtown, probably because he doesn't know himself, but it all has the portent of a spiritual act. Or at least that's what he hopes for. Ponti Bone's mournful accordion lines, which would be taken by the fiddler in a more conventional country band, add to the mystery.

Hancock's "Boxcars" is built on train rhythms, but the song is about being stuck, about small-town *ennui* so paralyzing that all the singer can do is gaze at the trains leaving town, knowing he'll never be on one. On "West Texas Waltz," Hancock draws the environment much more affectionately—touch-dancing and ice cream are life's greatest pleasures, along with something else too good to even talk about—but that feeling of living in too small of a world is still there, too.

That's because those boundaries are often there in real life, and like the other songs on this album, "West Texas Waltz" captures life as it is really lived. Ely keeps the promises made (and then broken) by most progressive country singers. Roots are not something we get to choose; we take what we're issued and do the best we can with them. Ely's own may seem limited—and limiting—but he confronts that and makes the most out of them anyhow.

Supplementary Albums

Amazing Rhythm Aces: *Stacked Deck* (MCA). When this 1975 debut was released, the Aces looked like they'd become the most versatile southern rock group of all, with crossover potential every which way. "Third Rate Romance," the single that led the way, was tough, smart, and sensitive all at once, and leader Russell Smith's other originals offered almost as much. They never could match it again, but this still stands as one of the signposts of the southern rock era.

John Anderson: *John Anderson* (Warner Bros.). Auspicious 1980 debut from a young—amazingly young, considering—Lefty Frizzell acolyte who knows what cheating songs are for. But he also likes semitopical material like "Havin' Hard Times" and he has a sense of humor.

John Anderson: *2* (Warner Bros.). This follow-up makes more explicit his debt to Frizzell with a knowing version of "I Love You a Thousand Ways" and proves he can also handle spiffy new songs like Billy Joe Shaver's "I'm Just an Old Chunk of Coal (But I'm Gonna Be a Diamond Someday)." Not quite the surprise his debut was, but still country music with few frills.

John Anderson: *Wild & Blue* (Warner Bros.). Anderson keeps looking like he'll fade away, but he never quite does it. By the time he cut this 1982 album he was starting to seem predictable enough—one Lefty tribute, one stringed-out schmaltz waltz with Emmylou guesting, etc. But side two lives up to the album title better than the title song itself does—though just when John shows he can boogie with "Swingin'," he brings in some backup singers who let all the air out of the song. In other words, still somewhat schizophrenic, but if Anderson would just concentrate on the barroom heartbreak he does best, he could wipe out the last of my doubts (or would going hard-core get him run out of the business these days?).

Bobby Bare: *Greatest Hits* (RCA). These sides represent the seventies Bare, who was a most unusual case. He was the first to win artistic control over his own albums—the first, for that matter, to record albums per se, rather than just throwing together a bunch of songs. So he was very much in tune with new movements sweeping Nashville, though he still didn't identify totally with the so-called outlaws; mostly, he just kept going his own way, and one of the results was that he may have been the last man in town to remain friendly with Waylon Jennings *and* Chet Atkins. His music retained a folkie flavor, but he recorded mostly novelty songs, too many of them by Shel Silverstein (all but one of these is written or co-written by Silverstein, but at least this is the cream of the crop). But when he recorded something other than novelties, it usually failed to sell as much. Since there was always a large dose of humor in his earlier, more serious songs, it follows that there would be a serious point to most of these novelties. As always, Bare gets way under your skin. And while this is the only stuff still in print from this era, search the bargain bins for albums like *Cowboys and Daddys*, which took the bullshit out of all those western themes the outlaws were overdoing during this same time.

Bobby Bare: *Encore* (Columbia). Not exactly a "greatest hits" set, but an amusing compilation of Bare album cuts from 1978–81. The emphasis is on novelty songs, as it was for this phase of his career in general, but give him a solid country song like "I Can Almost See Houston from Here," and Bare will still come up with an interpretation that shames the many others who've also recorded it.

Bobby Bare: *As Is* (Columbia). In the midst of a string of erratic albums, Bare tossed off this 1981 sleeper. It's the ideal Bobby Bare formula, really: Give him a batch of good songs and just turn him loose. No concepts here, nothing cutesy, just ten slices-of-life produced to perfection by Rodney Crowell.

Delia Bell: *Delia Bell* (Warner Bros.). How, you might ask, did an album as retrograde as this get released in 1983? Well, Delia has a powerful patron in Emmylou Harris, who produces this set with enviable common sense. Delia comes off the bluegrass circuit, but this isn't a bluegrass or even newgrass album by any stretch of the imagination. It's the same fusion of acoustic and electric, traditional and modernist, that Ricky Skaggs uses so effectively. Like him, Delia brings mountain music into the urban eighties. Emmylou describes her as having a voice like that of the hypothetical daughter of Hank Williams and Kitty Wells, and that description is good enough for me.

Jimmy Buffett: *Havana Daydreamin'* (MCA). Buffett is one of those singer-songwriters who built up cult followings in pop and around the fringes of country before finally busting out all over with the 1977 "Margaritaville," which faithfully translated the Jerry Jeff Walker style into something the masses could appreciate. Because Buffett was once a journalist, he wrote literate songs; because he was a Southerner, who wrote of southern people and places, his initial audience came mostly from below the Mason-Dixon Line. Because he was a sailor, many songs had nautical themes, dealing with pirates, smuggling, banana republics, and the like in ways that had surface appeal no matter how romanticized they became; because he was also a rogue, many were irreverent and witty. All of this, including the fanatical cult, was well established before this 1976 album came along, but the big money hadn't arrived yet. I've always considered Buffett something of an overachiever, a talented folk-rocker capable of providing small pleasures who arrived at just the right time—when southern pride, wordy singer-songwriters, and absorption in beer 'n' drugs as a way of life were all peaking. But I do think this album has tender, intelligent moments, as well as moments of compassion ("Woman Goin' Crazy on Caroline Street," about a burned-out barfly), low humor ("My Head Hurts, My Feet Stink and I Don't Love Jesus," a hangover song done as gospel music), and keepin'-on-keepin'-on ("Kick It In, Second Wind," which refuses to look at the musician's life as a hardship).

Johnny Bush and the Bandoleros: *Live from Texas* (Delta). Bush is one of the best interpreters of Willie Nelson's honky-tonk classics. He doesn't have quite the vocal power on this 1981 album that he had in his prime, but he still packs a wallop, the band is superb, and the rushed tempos that mark most of these performances don't sound like mistakes so much as they sound like signs of real life, the sound track to a rip-snorting night in a Texas barroom.

Carlene Carter: *Musical Shapes* (Warner Bros.). Maybe it makes sense that the best country-rock or rockabilly album to come out of the new wave movement would be by the sassy daughter of Carl Smith and June Carter Cash, the stepdaughter of Johnny Cash. But does it make sense that it was cut mostly in England, and produced by an Englishman (her husband, Nick Lowe)? Or that the sidemen are almost all English pub-rock veterans? Or that it didn't sell for beans though nothing else (except Joe Ely) is even in its league?

Rosanne Cash: *Seven Year Ache* (Columbia). Rosanne's 1980 debut had its moments, but was patchy. This follow-up, however, established her clearly as one of the major new artists of the eighties, and a writer of a mature new kind of country love song—romanticism with a hard edge. Bobby Bare described her as having a "wet" voice, which also explains part of the appeal, as does the country-with-a-beat music.

Rosanne Cash: *Somewhere in the Stars* (Columbia). Success, in the form of *Seven Year Ache*, was good to Rosanne Cash. It toughened her up in important ways and loosened her up in others. (Or does all that have to do with the arrival of her first child, as she maintains in interviews?) The rock here rocks harder, the country sounds brighter, and the jazzy pop, her one real weakness, is less conspicuous.

Guy Clark: *Old No. 1* (RCA). Others had hits with his material all along, but it took Guy Clark more than a half decade's worth of albums (for another label) to break through as a recording artist himself. Still, this 1975 debut remains leagues above anything he's done since. Clark represents the folk-oriented end of the new country singer-songwriter spectrum; he has a good eye for detail, a good ear for how people normally talk, a sense of history, and a voice grainy enough to make you think he's been kicking around Texas forever.

Marshall Chapman: *Me, I'm Feelin' Free* (Epic). In 1977, at the height of outlaw-mania, this husky-voiced woman came on enough like one of the boys to make some people uncomfortable, and enough like one of the girls to make the others hot. These are almost all smoky, sensuous country ballads, tough but full of heart, and they made the other women singing in Nashville (as well as most of the men) sound like anachronisms. Oh, yeah, by the way—it flopped, and quickly went out of print.

Lee Clayton: *Border Affair* (Capitol). Clayton, who probably didn't even realize what he was setting off when he wrote "Ladies Love Outlaws," was one of the artsiest of the new Nashville singers and writers, and it was to his detriment; the songs were often overwrought, the productions overburdened. But when he lightened up and went for more basic, more muscular music, as he did on this 1978 album, he lived up to his underground reputation. "If You Can Touch Her at All" became something of a standard love song, and "Tequila Is Addictive" should have become a standard roaring song.

Jack Clement: *All I Want to Do in Life* (Elektra). Nashville's resident eccentric sounds more like the town's only True Believer on this, his first (and last, so far) solo album after twenty years in the business as a writer and producer. The songs—"Gone Girl," "We Must Believe in Magic," "When I Dream," "Good Hearted Woman," "All I Want to Do in Life," "You Ask Me To," I can hardly stop listing them all—are like a primer for the new Nashville writing of the mid-seventies. But as familiar as they are, Cowboy Jack sings them with a guilelessness and quiet intensity that makes them all seem new again. This is brilliant late-night music, full of muted horns and weird percussion effects over a beat derived from Don Williams (who once recorded for Clement). Released in 1978 and deleted from the catalog not much later, this will make a True Believer out of you, too, if you can find it.

David Allan Coe: *Once Upon a Rhyme* (Columbia). I know it's uncool, and given his output since, it's no longer even justifiable, but for a while there, I sorta liked David Allan Coe. Once he got over his early, Newbury-derived attacks of poesy and his rock-derived attacks of Meaningful Social Commentary (you can hear most of that on his SSS albums), and before he pumped up an image as Nashville's only murderer and graduate of Death Row, he had a knack for writing songs more complex or daring than most, but still clearly linked to the country tradition. On this 1975 album he pays more homage to that tradition with "Fraulein" even as he extends it with "Would You Lay with Me (in a Field of Stone)," dramatizes it with "Another Pretty Country Song," and sends it up with "You Never Even Called Me By My Name."

David Allan Coe: *Greatest Hits* (Columbia). Coe's braggadocio turned into a creepy megalomania that undercut everything he did. Later, it would turn again into a bitterness and self-pity all out of proportion to his situation, which, after all, he did bring on himself. "Willie, Waylon and Me" and "Longhaired Redneck" mark the beginning of the end for him as a vital artist, but the rest showcases Coe as a challenging singer and writer.

Jessi Colter: *Jessi* (Capitol). "I'm Not Lisa" is easily the best thing she ever did, but the rest of her debut album was too pristine. This 1976 follow-up establishes her as the mystic-lover who's a match for any good-timin' man. In the process, she rocks out pretty good, too.

Commander Cody and His Lost Planet Airmen: *Lost in the Ozone* (MCA). Cody and crew were the first country-rock band that really mattered, the first gang of hippies to actually get out there and open concerts for Merle Haggard in those polarized years around 1970–71, the first to apply marijuana-and-beer consciousness to music and create such goofs as "Wine Do Yer Stuff," "Seeds and Stems (Again)" and the title song. Billy C. Farlow handled the rockabilly vocals, Bill Kirchen or John Tichy usually sang the country weepers, and the Commander himself grunted a novelty song or two. They were never such great musicians, but they were everything barroom music was ever meant to be.

Commander Cody and His Lost Planet Airmen: *Hot Licks, Cold Steel and Truckers Favorites* (MCA). Yes, along with all their other tongue-in-cheekisms—and the whole country-rock field could use 'em, believe me—the good Commander and his men were into trucks. But of course. And here they came up with five beauties, including the is-he-serious-or-not "Mama Hated Diesels," complete with a real tearjerker of a recitation, and the sorry "Semi-Truck" ("Well here I sit / All by myself I'm alone with a broken heart / I took three bennies / And my semi-truck won't start"). They also pull off a James Brown-country fusion riff in "Watch My .38," along with the usual sloppy, spirited, unpretentious takes on western swing, Cajun, and fifties rock 'n' roll.

Commander Cody and His Lost Planet Airmen: *Live from Deep in the Heart of Texas* (MCA). So you've got this cheesy little bar band everybody likes, right, and you can't get a radio station to play 'em since their fluke novelty hit ("Hot Rod Lincoln") of a couple of years earlier. And most people seem to think that the reason is because they don't make good records; they're primarily a live band and that's that. So you take them down to Austin and record them live at Armadillo World Headquarters, which in 1973–74 is where all these hip new country fans go, and you got yourself a hit, right? Well, not exactly. This is a great live album, from the jumping rockabilly of "Good Rockin' Tonight" to the cowboy crooning on "Sunset on the Sage" (complete with whistling break) to the careening "Too Much Fun," which is as close to a spiritual statement as Billy C. will ever make. These guys still sound like a bunch of acid-addled slobs from the Midwest, even if they live in Berkeley and spend most of their time on the road. And they've got that whole pre-rock era sewed up, whether it be jump-blues or boogie or R & B they're filtering through their mock-country sensibility. But it *still* wasn't enough to build their audience appreciably, and the effort took the wind right out of them. After this, they tried to make a few standard L.A. country-rock albums, and found they weren't slick enough. So they broke up. Some of those L.A. cowboy albums are also still in print, but don't bother.

Rodney Crowell: *Ain't Living Long Like This* (Warner Bros.). Crowell plays the best kind of country-rock. The music is both lean and muscular, strong-minded but full of country pathos, and Crowell's songs are ambitious lyrically and distinctive musically. He writes great originals like "Leaving Louisiana in the Broad Daylight" and "I Ain't Living Long Like This," and has equally impeccable taste in covers like Dallas Frazier's "Elvira" and William Trader's "(Now and Then, There's) A Fool Such as I." After Joe Ely, he's probably the most challenging male artist to have emerged in recent years (1978). So how come his material winds up on the charts only in bloodless versions by the Oak Ridge Boys?

Rodney Crowell: *Rodney Crowell* (Warner Bros.). "Till I Gain Control Again," an ultramodern hurtin' song, and "Old Pipeliner," an old boogie double entendre, define the parameters of this set, which is not up to his debut but is still fresher than anything else coming out of Nashville in 1982.

Hazel Dickens: *Hard Hitting Songs for Hard Hit People* (Rounder). Dickens is that modern-day rarity, the urban folkie with honest folk roots: She fled the coal-mining country of West Virginia for New England. Along the way, she lost her older brother to black lung disease, which is perhaps why these Reaganomics ballads (which are as diverse as the *a cappella* "Beautiful Hills of Galilee," Hazel's own "Old Calloused Hands" and "Scraps From Your Table," and "Busted," the country song made famous by Ray Charles) have so much more resonance, conviction, and depth than the work of other contemporary artists. And most amazingly, she does it in studios from Massachusetts to New York to Virginia to Tennessee, with sidemen ranging from Buddy Spicher, Lloyd Green, et al. (on the Nashville sides) to garden-variety folkies. This is the most modern country-folkie-whatever album in years.

Joe Ely: *Joe Ely* (MCA). Ely's 1977 debut brought country eclecticism to such unprecedented heights that at first it sounded like a noble try that still came out cluttered and off center. Now it sounds like a real breakthrough.

Joe Ely: *Down on the Drag* (MCA). Songs: A cut below par for Ely, though nothing to be ashamed of. Singing: More subtle, takes getting used to. Playing: The usual solid support from this resourceful band, though the production and the mix nearly capsize them. Prognosis: Ely's holding on through 1979, but maybe it's time to start finding something new.

The Joe Ely Band: *Live Shots* (MCA). Touring England with punk standard-bearers the Clash in 1980, Ely's country-rock (or whatever you call it) got more rambunctious. It did not suffer in the process, not even the most tender ballads. New (for Ely) songs: Buddy Holly's "Midnight Shift" and an extended, gleefully erotic "Black Snake Moan." The American version, released a year after the British, includes a bonus EP with Ely's new lineup, in which Smokey Joe Miller on sax replaces Lloyd Maines on steel.

Joe Ely: *Musta Notta Gotta Lotta* (South Coast/MCA). Ely's first stab at out-and-out rockabilly is forced enough that it almost conceals what's so unique about him. It takes longer for these songs to kick in, but when they do, they can stand beside most of his (and Butch Hancock's) earlier ones. And the new (1981) music brought a new stage show that was white hot.

Narvel Felts: *The Very Best of Narvel Felts* (MCA). Felts broke through with "Drift Away" on the Cinnamon label in 1973, and was snapped up by ABC (since merged into MCA) in 1975. His first album for the label was a gem. Produced by Johnny Morris and recorded at Muscle Shoals, it pitted Felts' trembling vibrato/falsetto on drawn-out ballads like "Reconsider Me" and "Funny How Time Slips Away." He was basically an R & B singer cutting adult rockabilly songs and he really did synthesize them both into something new and different. Why he didn't last longer I still haven't figured out except that he came along when Nashville was at its most wide-open, and the possibilities there quickly closed off to nearly everyone. At any rate, this gathers the highlights of his mid-seventies career into one heart-tugging album.

Freddy Fender: *Before the Next Teardrop Falls* (MCA). This "Chicano Elvis" from the Rio Grande Valley had been a Texas legend nearly two decades before legendary producer Huey Meaux got ahold of him in 1975, paired him with the sentimental title song, and made him the brightest new hope in country music. Freddy's high, pinched vibrato could make him sound as sincere singing "How Much Is that Doggie in the Window" (did just that, in fact) as he was singing "Wasted Days and Wasted Nights," his hymn to barrio betrayal. Meaux, meanwhile, made stereo records that sounded mono, and mixed up the instrumentation just enough to set Freddy off from the Nashville crowd without making him sound *too* progressive to get the air play that would be hard to come by for a Chicano.

The Best of Freddy Fender (MCA). Meaux and Fender wore out their formula pretty fast. Each album was the same—a countrified Gulf Coast R & B cover, a pop standard, a couple of country standards, a new song or two, a Mexican song. For a while there, Freddy gave them all his best, which was plenty, but the albums were undeniably thin and predictable. Singles never failed to connect, though, and here they all are through 1976. "Livin' It Down" is honky-tonk pathos at its most self-deprecating, and "Sugar Coated Love" flashes those R & B roots.

Flying Burrito Brothers: *Gilded Palace of Sin* (A&M). Face it, the Burritos were never the band they were cracked up to be, which is much of the reason Gram Parsons deserted them so early on. But their 1969 debut had its moments, both of humor and of horror, and is generally regarded as their best.

Flying Burrito Brothers: *Last of the Red-Hot Burritos* (A&M). I prefer this one, thanks, though the emphasis in this country-rock synthesis is definitely on the *rock*. Chris Hillman seems to be the chief force behind this edition of the Burritos, which plays with bluegrass-like speed and momentum.

Kinky Friedman: *Sold American* (Vanguard). When he surfaced out of Austin with this 1973 debut, Kinky's Texas Jewboy schtick appeared to be a long-overdue spit in the face of much that was wrong with Nashville—particularly its exclusivism and straitlaced white Protestantism, which were inseparable. It was just plain *fun* to hear somebody equate Jews with cowboys ("Ride 'Em Jewboy") as rugged individualists; "The Ballad of Charles Whitman" seemed to clear foul air in a therapeutic way; and "Sold American" was a great song about how we use up our heroes. The essential meanness of "Get Your Biscuits in the Oven and Your Buns in the Bed" was thus easier to overlook. But boy, did Kinky get tedious fast—a full decade later and he's still doing exactly the same stuff, a one-joke comic time has long since passed by. Today, his unreasoned hostility has become so vast (and so pointless) that I now suspect the real reason he wrote "The Ballad of Charles Whitman" is that he thought Charlie was a funny guy. To some extent, this album is a quaint period piece, and some of it isn't as funny as it used to be—but "Sold American" is still a great song, even if it's now about Kinky himself, and it's not the only one that scores a bull's-eye.

Tompall Glaser: *Tompall* (Polydor). He is the forgotten third of the original "outlaw" triumvirate that included Willie and Waylon, so it's sadly appropriate that his least innovative solo album (from 1974) be the only one still widely available. Still, you can hear Tompall just getting his legs, working toward his new style, on these eleven Shel Silverstein songs, including "Put Another Log on the Fire," the tongue-in-cheek ode to male chauvinism that proved to be Glaser's biggest solo hit. Eleven Shel Silverstein songs may be too many for some people, myself usually included, but with tunes like "Old New Orleans Custom," this is one of Shel's most diverse batches, and there's real meat among the cutesy.

Tompall Glaser of the Glaser Brothers: *Charlie* (MGM). Of the four solo albums he made, this 1973 debut is hands down the best. Certainly it formalizes his split from the Nashville musical and social scene, and it does so by denouncing those scenes explicitly. You might even say it was the first bona fide "outlaw" album, and the title song should have become a standard.

Tompall Glaser: *The Great Tompall and His Outlaw Band* (MGM). The first of two albums he recorded with his salt-and-pepper band, including blues guitarist Mel Brown, and an introduction to what became the Tompall "style," with a good balance between old songs ("The Wild Side of Life" and "We Live in Two Different Worlds") and new ("The Hunger" and "West Canterbury Subdivision Blues"). The new ones are as ambitious as the new Nashville got, and Tompall takes apart the old ones and rebuilds them almost from scratch, relying on stinging dobro and electric guitar. There's a solid dance beat—Tompall called this music "discobilly"—and elements of everything from western swing to New Orleans R & B to rockabilly. Tompall moans, groans, and slurs through these songs in a husky voice you'll either love or hate.

Tompall Glaser: *Tompall Glaser and His Outlaw Band* (ABC). Side one is absolutely unbeatable—a rockabilly ("You Can Have Her"), a country standard ("Release Me"), a white blues ("Tennessee Blues"), Tompall's cowboy ballad to woo back the estranged Waylon ("Come Back Shane"), and one of those new Nashville tunes that defies classification ("It'll Be Her"). Tompall sings like he's facedown on the barroom floor at sunrise.

Butch Hancock: *West Texas Waltzes and Dust-Blown Tractor Tunes* (Rainlight). Butch is the man who provides Joe Ely with some of his best tunes, and what's surprising is how few of them Butch bothers to record himself. This 1978 album's "West Texas Waltz" was cut by Ely but it's the only one here, and we're talking about two very different sounds anyhow. Hancock accompanies himself with just guitar and harmonica, and between that fact and songs like "They Say It's a Good Land" and "I Grew Up to Be a Stranger," one is left to conclude that Lubbock, Texas, has bred its own version of Woody Guthrie.

Butch Hancock: *1981: A Spare Odyssey* (Rainlight). Nobody combines folkie mysticism and country fatalism quite like Hancock does. He's also a more compelling performer when he's playing solo acoustic, which he is for this 1981 album, apparently inspired by a trip to Stonehenge. You can question his country credentials—I mean, would George Jones be inspired to write a song by a trip to Stonehenge?—but stuff like "I Wish You Were Here with Me Tonight" ought to shoot down your objections pretty quickly.

Butch Hancock: *Firewater Seeks Its Own Level* (Rainlight). Also from 1981, and also recorded live at the Alamo, then the leading folk club in Austin, Texas. This one uses additional electric instrumentalists and reprises old favorites like "One Road More" or "The Wind's Dominion" (recorded previously by Hancock) as well as "If You Were a Bluebird" and "I Keep Wishin' for You" (known best in their versions by Ely). Hancock remains as unpretentious a folkie as you'd ever hope to meet.

Linda Hargrove: *Blue Jean Country Queen* (Elektra). Hargrove came to Nashville as a writer, session guitarist, and country-rock singer in the early seventies, but had her best luck later on Capitol, when her recordings moved closer to the Nashville mainstream. This 1974 album—her second, and now out of print—is one of the more endearing country-rock fusions to come out of Music City, and it went nowhere. Without being Pollyanna, it's full of humor, optimism, and good spirits; had she cut the exact same album in Los Angeles with L.A. musicians, she'd probably have gotten a hit out of it.

Emmylou Harris: *Profile—The Best of Emmylou Harris* (Warner Bros.). There are certain types of tradition-oriented songs on which Emmylou's thin, tense, and tiny voice suffices, but when she's doing material from the fifties or later, which is what she does most of the time, to me she sounds just plain feeble. I know she's wildly popular and there are hundreds of thousands of people for whom she can do no wrong, but I can't help it—with only a couple of exceptions, I think that as a solo star she makes a terrific harmony singer.

Waylon Jennings: *Honky Tonk Heroes* (RCA). This 1973 collection of modern-day cowboy songs (all but one of them written by Billy Joe Shaver) cemented Waylon's new persona. It also provided a focus for the outlaw movement, then in its infancy and still a genuine grass-roots rebellion against the Nashville bad guys. Shaver was the most literate new country writer since Kris Kristofferson, and though his songs were sometimes too diffuse, he was twice as funky.

Waylon Jennings: *This Time* (RCA). In 1974, Waylon snuck in through the back door with this meditative album of low-key, late-night music. It's his most underrated, though it could use a little less Willie Nelson.

Waylon Jennings: *Wanted! The Outlaws* (RCA). Though it was released in 1976 under Waylon's name apparently for contractual reasons, this album is by Waylon, his wife, Jessi Colter, Willie Nelson, and Tompall Glaser. Better (or identical) versions of most of these songs exist on other albums; only Tompall's astonishing interpretation of Jimmie Rodgers' "T for Texas" is not expendable. But as a marketing device, this is the album that put "outlaw" on the map, and it remains an acceptable sampler of those heady early days.

Waylon Jennings: *Waylon Live* (RCA). All the hits of the early seventies, with that crackling west Texas band unencumbered by any of the niceties of the recording studios. It's one of country music's best live albums, showing a side of Waylon in 1976 that even his best studio work misrepresented.

Waylon Jennings and Willie Nelson: *Waylon and Willie* (RCA). Actually, some Waylon, some Willie, *and* some Waylon and Willie. The solo cuts are better than the duets, and this works best as another sampler for the uninitiated or as a souvenir for the diehard fan. Here it is 1978 and already their schtick is starting to wear thin.

Waylon Jennings: *Greatest Hits* (RCA). This could be subtitled " 'What I Did During the Seventies,' by Waylon Jennings." Worth it for the choice cuts that appeared on otherwise-deficient albums ("Amanda" and "Lonesome, On'ry and Mean," to name two), but I sure could do without the posturing that had taken over by the end of the decade ("I've Always Been Crazy," to name one).

Waylon Jennings: *It's Only Rock & Roll* (RCA). "Lucille (You Don't Do Your Daddy's Will)," the old Little Richard barrelhouse rocker, is done here as a slow ballad full of deep pain, misgivings, and resignation. You're likely to not even recognize the song, so completely does Waylon transform it—but when he was at his peak, Waylon's forte was taking somebody else's song and making it wholly his own. There're a couple of throwaways here, and Waylon's voice is not always up to the task, but coming in 1983, after years of consistently disappointing albums, this one puts him back on the right track.

Kris Kristofferson: *Songs of Kristofferson* (Monument). It must embarrass Kristofferson that seven of these twelve songs come from his first two albums and that the only one of the five remaining that's even remotely inspired is the gospel song "Why Me." Or does it? As soon as he found success he lit out for Hollywood, and it's been a decade since he appeared interested in music. That said, I should also point out that his first album in particular did indeed stretch country music in new directions, even if the songs were invariably a little too wordy. I'm probably most partial to the leaner ones like "Help Me Make It Through the Night." And having said *that,* I'd like to add that every good song he's ever written has been done a zillion times better by someone else. As a singer, he's embarrassingly inept, and he's no better as an arranger. He's just a good-looking man who has a way with words. And knows how to exploit himself. But sometimes I *still* have to marvel at how he pulled it all off with such a flimsy foundation to build on.

Delbert McClinton: *Victim of Life's Circumstances* (ABC). This 1975 album was one of the dark horses of the whole progressive country movement, but went out of print fast. McClinton is greasy and compulsive, but basically just out for good times, though it gets him in trouble with women (single and otherwise), the husbands of married women, various other denizens of the barroom, and the law—and not necessarily in that order. He writes tough songs with vivid imagery (the judge who "halfway closed one eye" before sentencing him, for example) and mixes horns with his pedal steel. Unlike the other Texas types, though, McClinton also likes crotch-grinding rhythms, which is one of the main reasons that after this album he switched to white R & B. He didn't hit until a good five years after this album, and a few of these songs can be found on an MCA "best of," which is mostly R & B. Meanwhile, Emmylou Harris made a hit out of "Two More Bottles of Wine," and there's plenty more here just crying to be covered.

Rick Nelson: *The Decca Years* (MCA). Between 1963 and 1972, Rick Nelson recorded a series of soft, seductive country-rock records that had a lot more to do with defining that form than most people remember; his musicians were among the most highly regarded pickers to emerge from L.A. "Garden Party" is the record most people will remember, but in general, Rick seemed better suited to this form than to the pop-rockabilly he'd been doing earlier.

Roger Miller: *Dang Me* (Mercury). The acoustic, small-group debut album that launched him. The title song and "Chug-a-lug" are the hits, but "It Takes All Kinds to Make a World" is Miller with one of his favorite self-images, that of the cosmic loser, and "Private John Q." and "Squares Make the World Go Round" offer typically serio-comic philosophizing.

Tracy Nelson: *Mother Earth Presents Tracy Nelson Country* (Mercury). One of the first (1970), and still one of the best, of the country-rock albums, even if it's long been out of print. Tracy Nelson understood the dodgy relationship between modern country and modern R & B better than anybody, and showed real vision in choosing both her songs and her sidemen.

Willie Nelson: *The Troublemaker* (Columbia). Willie and friends sing traditional gospel music, recorded in 1972 but not released until 1976, when he was so big he called his own shots. Willie doesn't approach gospel as stiffly as most country stars; he sees it instead as the opportunity for a loose, spirited sing-along.

Willie Nelson: *To Lefty From Willie* (Columbia). A debt paid in full (in 1977) to some of Willie's Texas roadhouse roots. He doesn't even try to capture the vibrato-laden sound of Lefty Frizzell's original versions, but his own dry baritone gets the point across just the same.

Willie Nelson: *Stardust* (Columbia). In which the small-town Texas boy claims a group of old Tin Pan Alley standards as his own in 1977— which, of course, he makes them. And in introducing his pop tastes to country fans, he introduces his country self to the world at large.

Willie Nelson: *Willie Nelson Sings Kristofferson* (Columbia). And sings it a whole lot better than Kristofferson ever did (or is it even necessary to point that out?). On this 1979 album, songs of an artificially induced weariness become songs of experience and wisdom.

Willie Nelson: *Pretty Paper* (Columbia). For some reason, all of these Christmas tunes sound like kiddie songs (including, of course, the ones that really are). Which in 1979 leaves him very few markets left to conquer.

Willie Nelson: *Somewhere Over the Rainbow* (Columbia). Only a cynic could call this *Stardust, 1981*. Sure, he's back to pop standards—and not as hardy a batch as on the prior pop album, either—but the smaller, hotter, Django Reinhardt-inspired band gets more of the emphasis this time than Willie's voice *or* the songs. Snappy.

Willie Nelson: *Greatest Hits (And Some That Will Be)* (Columbia). This 1981 double album assembles material from every phase of Willie's years with Columbia, which means it has hit singles from uneventful sets like *The Sound in Your Mind* and his *Willie and Family Live* album, as well as the best-known songs from triumphs like *Stardust*. Best of all, it takes the two originals from the *Honeysuckle Rose* film fiasco, "On the Road Again" and "Angel Flying Too Close to the Ground," and gives them a more appropriate context.

Gram Parsons: *Gram Parsons* (Shiloh). This reissue of the fabled International Submarine Band's sole album, produced by Lee Hazelwood, shows leader Gram Parsons groping toward his early conception of "cosmic American music," as he called it, or "white soul," as Don Everly labeled it. His vehicles were mostly country standards, and in retrospect were performed quite awkwardly. But it does retain a certain charm.

Gram Parsons: *GP* (Reprise). Gram's 1971 solo debut was closer to his aims than the Burritos' *Gilded Palace of Sin,* but still somewhat tentative. He has great taste in covers (Tompall Glaser's "Streets of Baltimore" especially, but also his overhaul of the J. Geils Band's "Cry One More Time") and a couple of his originals ("The New Soft Shoe" and "How Much I've Lied") match up, too. As one largely unimpressed with him the first time around, I have to concede how much better he sounds now—probably because once his followers reduced country-rock to light, frothy feelin'-good music, Gram's own commitment to the mystery, pain, and unquenchable yearnings of real country music became that much more admirable.

Gram Parsons: *Grievous Angel* (Reprise). This is better. One of Gram's problems had been that he seemed to be attracted solely to the pain in country music; in 1972 that's still here in abundance, but his version of Tom T. Hall's "I Can't Dance" offers some comic relief. Emmylou Harris is more prominent now, too, and proves herself a haunting background singer, though barely tolerable on leads; their version of "Love Hurts" goes right for the heart, and "In My Hour of Darkness" couldn't have been a better sign-off if Gram had planned it that way. Yet this still falls short in vital areas; as a singer, Gram is too much of a folkie, and as a writer, he's too one-dimensional. Because nobody really matched him anyhow, it makes me wonder if there was something about country-rock that made it such a limited form (though I can't see why that has to be), or if it just attracted musicians with limited talents.

Gram Parsons and the Fallen Angels: *Live 1973* (Sierra). Really sloppy, and not always in a particularly charming way. But what do you know, turns out Gram never really lost the sense of humor he brought to the Burritos, he just put it aside for his solo studio albums. It's restored here enough to save you from thinking he bled all over the stage every time out, and the material comprises a best-of with added bonuses like "California Cottonfields" (from Merle Haggard), "Six Days on the Road" (from Dave Dudley), and "Drug Store Truck Driving Man" (from the Byrds when they included Gram Parsons). Erratic like all his work—he was simply too scattered to ever fully live up to his potential—but the failings were eminently human, and humane; he just never could find a way to make traditional country morality compatible with contemporary hip, urban life.

John Austin Paycheck: *11 Months and 29 Days* (Epic). The "outlaw" Johnny Paycheck emerged in 1976, after the "Mr. Lovemaker" phase of his career had bottomed out and it became necessary to launch yet another comeback. But the title song, which refers to a jail sentence, is a Jimmy Reed-styled blues that should have done much better than it did, and "I've Seen Better Days" establishes Johnny as one of the masterful ballad singers of contemporary country. "The Woman Who Put Me Here" shows he never lost his touch for the straight honky-tonkers, either.

Johnny Paycheck: *Slide Off Your Satin Sheets* (Epic). Hey, I know Johnny's supposed to be real modern now (1977), but the title song sounds to me just like one of those fifties country ballads about the poor-but-good man who gives meaning to the life of a rich woman who has everything she could possibly want except love. Class consciousness lives on in country music—it just got more overtly sexual. And "I'm the Only Hell (Mama Ever Raised)" is the kind of mindless boast Paycheck made so entertaining until he began believing it himself. "You're Still on My Mind" pays old debts to his George Jones sound-alike days, while "I Did the Right Thing" (he went back to his wife and straightened out his life) does not exactly jibe with the rest, but that's Johnny for you. A strange but admirably consistent LP.

Johnny Paycheck: *Greatest Hits, Vol. II* (Epic). So what if he ran his "outlaw" schtick into the ground. One of Paycheck's greatest charms is that sooner or later he'll run *everything* into the ground, and veteran Johnny-watchers like myself will always hang around long enough to watch him belly-flop once again off the deep end. "Take This Job and Shove It" was certainly *the* anthem of the late seventies, and "Colorado Cool-Aid" was one of the more twisted paeans to casual violence, so at least he went out in style. He'll be the last to find out, but he's been self-parody since this 1978 turning point.

John Prine: *Pink Cadillac* (Asylum). In the most willfully perverse takeoff on rockabilly since I don't know when, Prine sounds like Bob-Dylan-meets-Elvis-Presley after an all-night Hycodan cough syrup bash. Produced primarily by Knox and Jerry Phillips, with ultrarare assistance from their illustrious father, Sam, this 1979 album is murky and barely comprehensible, but it retains the primal power of its sources.

Redneck Mothers (RCA). I'm a sucker for concepts like the one behind this late-seventies patchwork. RCA pulls together whatever it can find in the vaults that uses the word "redneck" in the title, or that implies it, or that simply builds a good enough case for the joys of excessive drinking. Johnny Russell's "Rednecks, White Socks and Blue Ribbon Beer," in which the singer boasts about being a slob, is one of the peaks of the genre. But the absolute pinnacle is Vernon Oxford's bodacious, tongue-in-cheek "Redneck! (The Redneck National Anthem)," which sports a honking band and gets in the last word through such deathless lines as "I love those dancehall women and those grinding honky-tonk bands/I groove on Waylon and Willie/I was born with a six-pack in my hand." Who can resist?

Linda Ronstadt: *Different Drum* (Capitol). The early Linda was much more uneven than the later Linda, and often more tantalizing for just that reason. You never knew for sure what she'd do next, and it didn't always work; but when it did, it carried a jolt her later work usually lacked. This "greatest hits" sampler from her early days (the seven years that began in 1967 with the Stone Poneys debut) offers at least two prime examples in her wonderfully blowsy reading of Bob Dylan's "I'll Be Your Baby Tonight" and the heartbreaking "Long Long Time." But the near-misses (the title song, "Some of Shelly's Blues" and more) show lots of promise.

Linda Ronstadt: *Heart Like a Wheel* (Capitol). This is the 1974 album on which Linda established her formula—a couple of obscure (but not *too* obscure) rock oldies, some contemporary singer-songwriter stuff, a country standard or two, an unlikely R & B oldie. Her singing is sure, Peter Asher's production is sure, and they would continue to milk the format for a long, long time.

Linda Ronstadt: *Greatest Hits* (Asylum). "Long Long Time" and "Different Drum" turn up on LP for the umpteenth time, but the rest of this is Linda's mid-seventies triumphs, most of them state-of-the art country-rock arrangements of rock oldies (two from Buddy Holly work better than the cover of "Heat Wave," that's for sure) or contemporary L.A. stuff like "Desperado" and "Love Has No Pride."

Linda Ronstadt: *Greatest Hits, Volume Two* (Asylum). This one rocks more than its predecessor, and not always with optimum results (the big exception being "How Do I Make You"). She still does Buddy Holly ("It's So Easy") better than anyone else, but she owes Roy Orbison an apology for her massacre of "Blue Bayou."

Billy Joe Shaver: *I'm Just an Old Chunk of Coal, But I'm Gonna Be a Diamond Someday* (Columbia). Billy Joe's most revered work is on out-of-print albums on Monument and Capricorn, but I'm one of the few who thinks his later stuff, cut around the turn of the decade, is superior. For one thing, he's much less under the spell of Kristofferson;

he's more clear-headed about what he's saying, and about how he wants to say it. With age, he grew both simpler and tougher, and if the title song is the most eloquent example here, the rest of the album holds up pretty well, too.

Billy Joe Shaver: *Billy Joe Shaver* (Columbia). Some new versions of old songs—including the great "Bottom Dollar," which I've always thought was overlooked among his work because it's more like a good direct song than like the bad, abstruse "poetry" his fans prefer. As he ages, which he definitely is doing, Shaver sings more like Jerry Lee Lewis, oddly enough.

Silver Meteor (Briar). An anthology of early-seventies country-rock, Los Angeles style. There's an obscure, terrific side by the Everly Brothers (backed by the Byrds) in "I'm On My Way Home Again," and nearly half the album is filled out by the rock-bluegrass fusion Clarence White was recording for a solo album at the time of his death in 1973.

Ricky Skaggs: *Waitin' for the Sun to Shine* (Epic). His 1981 major-label debut, which includes smart reworkings of bluegrass ("Don't Get Above Your Raising") and honky-tonk ("So Round, So Firm, So Fully Packed") standards alike, still sounds fresher than everything else he's done, even though it's less celebrated—eclectic in the best sense, steady, unpretentious, beautifully crafted, and quietly soulful country-with-roots in an era that needs some.

Ricky Skaggs: *Highways & Heartaches* (Epic). Skaggs does better than most outside the bluegrass ghetto because rather than doing something cheap and easy (like simply playing electrified bluegrass) he weds the ethos and ancient hurts of bluegrass to a lean, largely honky-tonk backing. "Don't Let Your Sweet Love Die" shows how effective this strategy can be, though whether such an approach can carry him through many albums remains to be seen.

Hank Snow: *#104—Still Movin' On* (RCA). What happens when the Nashville establishment goes outlaw? Well, Hank Snow tried it in 1977 in a desperate attempt to save a sagging career, and with Chuck Glaser producing, he succeeded artistically though not commercially. It's a bluesy album with pedal steel and electric guitar playing off mandolin and dobro, with Buddy Spicher's fiddle getting lots of space, too. Hank's updates of "Breakfast with the Blues," "Trouble in Mind," "Trying to Get My Baby Off My Mind," and even "I'm Still Movin' On" (revised lyrics courtesy Shel Silverstein) are as convincing as anything revivified by younger "outlaws" themselves. But Hank had image problems to overcome that they didn't. So this went out of print in no time.

Gary Stewart: *You're Not the Woman You Used to Be* (MCA). Stewart reportedly hates these recordings because they're so primitive, barely more than demos done when he was working primarily as a writer and still searching for his own style. MCA tossed the package out onto the market after Gary hit with RCA, and yes, the singing is sometimes tentative and the band could use a little more rehearsal time. But it's still as vibrant as anything he's done, and story-songs like "Sweet-Tater and Cisco" and "The Snuff Queen" are among his funniest. He can relax, too; it's out of print.

Gary Stewart: *Steppin' Out* (RCA). A primer of the kinds of music he likes best, with a bluegrass cut, a shimmering bottleneck stomper, and some honky-tonk and country ballads. He's already getting too self-conscious—this is only 1976—but the moves toward rock are welcome, because that's a natural for him.

Gary Stewart: *Your Place or Mine* (RCA). This 1977 album flaunts the most cohesive band sound he ever got in the studio; harmonically, these session men can sound surprisingly like the Nashville cats who backed Bob Dylan on *Blonde on Blonde*, and they hit some rocking grooves as well. Some of these songs are a little too arch for him, but he cuts them down to size.

Gary Stewart: *Greatest Hits* (RCA). Some of which aren't nearly as great as his non-hits and album cuts. This is an acceptable introduction to the man, but *Out of Hand* and *Your Place or Mine* are more consistent; this not only charts his meteoric rise, but it unintentionally documents his premature decline as well. After about three years, his performances started sounding indifferent, or like set pieces he was oversinging or doing by rote.

George Strait: *Strait Country* (MCA). Strait's 1981 debut was the best shot of straight-ahead Texas honky-tonk since Moe Bandy came along, though he can be diffident enough as a singer that I have to wonder how long he'll last. Still, his taste is exquisite, and I have to tip my hat to anyone trying to crack country music in the eighties with songs like "Unwound" (which is what the girl once wrapped around his finger has just become), "She's Playin' Hell (Trying to Get Me to Heaven)," and— my favorite phrase in years—("every time you throw dirt on that girl you . . .") "Lose a Little Ground."

Joe Sun: *The Best of Joe Sun* (Warner Bros.). In the late seventies, Joe Sun emerged as one of the honky-tonk hopes for the future; he even got Johnny Cash's endorsement. I've always found his smoky voice and diffuse arrangements hard to take for long because the emotional range is so stunted. But I can see what it is about him others like—he sounds like nobody but Joe Sun—and for most of this album, I can even agree with them.

Billy Swan: *I Can Help* (Monument). The neo-rockabilly title song was the one-off hit single of 1974 and this album slapped together to capitalize on it is an ingenious update of the Memphis beat, as filtered through more recent influences from the Beatles and Motown.

Billy Swan: *Rock 'n' Roll Moon* (Monument). His 1975 follow-up rocked even harder, behind such material as "(You Just) Woman Handled My Mind" and "Ubangi Stomp," but as "Everything's the Same (Ain't Nothin' Changed)" shows, Swan was not at all your basic macho rocker. Instead, his urgent, nervous vocals made him sound cautious and outreaching simultaneously, which reflects a truly seventies schizophrenia. But his equanimity was admirable, as was his sense of roots: "Got You On My Mind" is a Cookie and the Cupcakes Louisiana shuffle that flows like a bayou inlet easing toward the Gulf of Mexico.

Billy Swan: *Billy Swan* (Monument). This is the album on which Swan pulled everything together—brilliant, iconoclastic songs, quirky arrangements, white-hot singing and musicianship. Released in 1976, it sounds like nothing that came before it and nobody—including Swan—has made anything like it since. "Just Want to Taste Your Wine" is one of the most peculiar takes ever on the triangle theme, and the band burns. Swan's originals—especially those co-written with Dennis Linde—are magnanimous, and even the rather obvious covers ("Blue Suede Shoes") come back to life.

Billy Swan: *Billy Swan at His Best* (Columbia). Swan was called "progressive rockabilly" for lack of a better term, but these 1974–76 cuts (a distressingly small number of them were actually hits) do their roots proud, even if they leave them fast to light out for a harder-to-pin-down southern roadhouse sound. Until the newly revived Monument gets the previous three back in print, this is all we have.

James Talley: *Got No Bread, No Milk, No Money, But We Sure Got a Lot of Love* (Capitol). Talley was an anomaly in the cynical seventies, a genuine populist with much education, a love for history, an activist streak, and true country roots. He probably couldn't have happened anywhere else except in the remarkably open Nashville scene of the mid-seventies, and he barely happened there. (He made this album on his own, trading his skills as a construction worker for free studio time, and when the album made some noise, Capitol then picked it up.) With its recollections of growing up in Oklahoma and its western-flavored music, it made a great Bicentennial album. Like all his work, it's now out of print.

James Talley: *Tryin' Like the Devil* (Capitol). With this follow-up album, Talley turns his attention toward the working class and connects on the title song, "Forty Hours," and "Are They Gonna Make Us Outlaws Again," any of which could have become an anthem. At the same time, he's more bluesy (the eternal "Deep Country Blues" and "Nothin' But the Blues").

The Marshall Tucker Band: *Greatest Hits* (Warner Bros.). Marshall Tucker did the unexpected just often enough to set them apart from your run-of-the-mill southern country-rockers; in Toy Caldwell they had a reliable songwriter ("Can't You See," "Heard It in a Love Song") and they could boogie, though never too frenetically. Lotsa cowboys, rambling men, and rambling cowboy men, but don't blame Toy—they come with the genre, and this is far superior to simpleton stuff like the Charlie Daniels boogies.

Townes Van Zandt: *Live at the Old Quarter, Houston, Texas* (Tomato). Yet another of those legendary Texas singer-songwriters whose reputation turns out to be much greater than his accomplishments. (They've got a *lot* of them down there, but it's a big state, you know.) Van Zandt has cut at least half a dozen albums since the late sixties, but they're all impossible to find. I'm including this one to stand for his *oeuvre*, if you will, for several reasons. As his most recent album, it's probably less rare than the others. As a live album in which he accompanies himself, it really does showcase his songs, which is what he is about; on his studio albums stock arrangements often subverted his intents. As a double album, it offers quantity. And as an added bonus, it flaunts his sense of humor, whereas studio albums always flaunt his sense of impending doom (not that the two can't go together; it's just that they never did until now). Good luck finding it. (And good luck, Townes.)

Jerry Jeff Walker: *A Man Must Carry On* (MCA). Walker (along with Michael Murphey, who is just plain lame) symbolized the new breed of singer-songwriter coming out of Austin in the mid-seventies, though from his albums it was always hard to figure out why. They were so spotty and so sloppy (as opposed to casual, which is what they were *supposed* to be) that they hid many of his virtues. Really, his reputation stemmed from his wildness as much as anything else: Jerry Jeff was everybody's favorite pet nut. Until, that is, this 1977 double album came along. And then some previously unnoticed (because they'd been done so poorly the first time around) songs snapped into focus, some of the old favorites got dusted off and spruced up, his rock rocked harder and his folk was folksy. Undoubtedly, the recent death of Jerry Jeff's friend Hondo Crouch, who pretty much *was* Luckenback, Texas, for years, and to whom this album is dedicated, had a lot to do with the way Jerry Jeff shaped up. For the first time on album, Jerry Jeff sounds as though something matters to him, and his frayed, world-weary voice makes a lot more sense in this context. Now if only somebody would go back and compile a "best of" from the one or two remaining good cuts on his other MCA albums, we might begin to see that sometimes Walker did have more to offer than a drunken clown show, and that sometimes he *was* able to tell the difference between laid-back and out-to-lunch.

Don Williams: *Greatest Hits* (MCA). As a collection of 1972–75 songs, this is a staggering album. But somehow, it doesn't quite hold up; emotions that are supposed to be standing naked sound like posturing—or reverse posturing, to be more precise. But those are minor quibbles when the songs in question are along the lines of "Amanda," "She's in Love with a Rodeo Man," "The Ties That Bind," "I Recall a Gypsy Woman," and other early hits.

Don Williams: *The Best of Don Williams, Vol. II* (MCA). Williams keeps everything so low-key that he *makes* you concentrate on his music, the way someone who speaks very softly makes you listen more closely. For that reason, he can also wear thin; after the initial glow wore off his sound, his albums became less rewarding. But this volume covers his peak years of 1975–78, when Wayland Holyfield and Bob McDill were giving him songs like "Some Broken Hearts Never Mend," "(Turn Out the Light and) Love Me Tonight," " 'Til All the Rivers Run Dry," "Rake and Rambling Man," and "You're My Best Friends." These are all direct sentiments, expressed simply, and the intimate backing of the band, complete with strings, combines with Williams' muffled baritone to create warmth and empathy. Williams' recurring suggestion that the emotional problems men and women struggle through are not all that different is a shocking admission coming from a male country singer.

Hank Williams, Jr.: *The New South* (Warner Bros.). This 1977 album is the first Hank recorded after fully recovering from his fall, and is easily the most underrated of his "progressive" LPs. He touches every base here, with autobiography in "Feelin' Better," Hank-tribute in "Montgomery in the Rain," a Hank-cover in "You're Gonna Change (Or I'm Gonna Leave)," a Dixie-tribute in the title song, a Hank-and-Dixie tribute in "Long Way to Hollywood," honky-tonk and bluegrass standards in "How's My Ex Treating You," and "Uncle Pen" and more. The music has a beat—thank producers Waylon Jennings and Richie Albright—and bluesy feel—thank those steel and slide guitars. Hank, Jr.'s vocals are tattered and optimistic both, with plenty of bite.

Hank Williams, Jr.: ***Whiskey Bent and Hell Bound*** (Warner Bros.). Hank, Jr., is the most maddeningly uneven country singer alive today, and part of the reason it's so maddening is that his good stuff is *really good.* This 1979 album is more consistent than most for several reasons—it's bluesy and very southern without being blustery and empty-headed southern chauvinism (*à la* Charlie Daniels and sometimes Hank, Jr.), the self-pity is at least about something specific, and the Hank-song doesn't grate.

Hank Williams, Jr.: *Greatest Hits* (Warner Bros.). The albums are often spotty because they are experimental, and because given that much space, he can't resist indulging himself. The singles, however, are successful for just the opposite reason—Hank, Jr., goes into the studio thinking small, and in this remarkable collection of hits from the late seventies and early eighties, he fashions a very distinctive sound that really is a fusion of country and rock in which neither takes a back seat. Some people complain about his casual attitude toward violence, his Dixie chauvinism, his obsession with his father, his antiurban bias, but to me, all these songs are about something important and none take cheap shots. That makes Hank, Jr., the last of the troubadors, a modern version of an ancient musical phenomenon, and his singing is still improving. Even when he misses he's provocative, and I defy you to name anyone who's put out a "hits" collection during this period anywhere near this diverse and anywhere near this engaging.

Steve Young: *Renegade Picker* (RCA). Young was one of the best writers of the mid-seventies Nashville renaissance; his "Lonesome, On'ry and Mean" became a theme song for Waylon Jennings, his "Renegade Picker" became a theme song for himself. Covering songs like Rodney Crowell's "Home Sweet Home (Revisited)" and John D. Loudermilk's "Tobacco Road" puts his own southern roots up front, for Young is a master at evoking a specific time and place. His tendency to oversing—clearly unnecessary when you have a baritone as husky as his—might have held him back, for he had no chart success at all and this 1976 debut quickly slipped out of print.

APPENDIX

Addresses are provided for domestic record companies only. For all imports, the only complete mail-order service in America is Down Home Music, 10341 San Pablo Ave., El Cerrito, Calif. 94530. In addition to imports, Down Home also stocks the small, independent American labels whose records will be hard to find outside specialty stores in most of the country, and they carry the major-label releases as well; in other words, if Down Home doesn't have it, it probably can't be had. Their current catalog lists thousands of country albums; write for details.

In many instances, corporate sales or mergers have resulted in change-of-label affiliations for artists. All in-print records listed in this book are assigned their current label affiliations, regardless of the company which may originally have released them. Out-of-print records appearing on such labels, however, are still listed with the original company, as that's the logo they'll appear under in the cut-out bins, bargain racks, etc. A very few domestic labels don't reveal their address, because they are reissuing material that still belongs to a major label; such practices are technically illegal, but the majors usually look the other way (unless the artist involved is a top seller) because the cost for pursuing legal action is usually more than it's worth. At any rate, most such labels can be ordered through Down Home; as for the rest, you're on your own.

Accord Records
141 E. 63rd St.
New York, N.Y. 10021

ACM
see Old Homestead

Adelphi Records
P.O. Box 7688
Silver Spring, Md. 20907

AFM (American Folk Music
  Archive and Research Center)
see JEMF

A & M Records
1416 N. LaBrea Ave.
Hollywood, Calif. 90028

Arhoolie/Old Timey Records
10341 San Pablo Ave.
El Cerrito, Calif. 94530

Asylum Records
see Elektra

Atlantic Records
75 Rockefeller Plaza
New York, N.Y. 10019

Biograph/Historical/Melodeon
  Records
16 River St.
Chatham, N.Y. 12037

Blind Pig Records
208 S. 1st St.
Ann Arbor, Mich. 48103

Capitol/EMI-America/Liberty
  Records
1750 N. Vine St.
Hollywood, Calif. 90028

Chimer Records
see Mid-Land

Churchill Records
32255 S. Norwood
Tulsa, Okla. 74135

Club of Spades/Longhorn Records
P.O. Box 1995
Studio City, Calif. 91604

CMH Records
P.O. Box 39439
Los Angeles, Calif. 90039

Columbia/Epic Records
51 W. 52nd St.
New York, N.Y. 10019

Coral Records
see MCA

Country Turtle
P.O. Box 417
Cathedral Station
New York, N.Y. 10025

County/Rebel Records
P.O. Box 191
Floyd, Va. 24901

Cowboy Carl Records
P.O. Box 116
Park Forest, Ill. 60466

D Records
3409 Brinkman St.
Houston, Tex. 77018

Delta Records
P.O. Box 225
Nacogdoches, Tex. 75961

Elektra/Asylum Records
666 5th Ave.
New York, N.Y. 10022

Epic Records
see Columbia

Feathers Records
P.O. Box 37251
Cincinnati, O. 45222

1st Generation Records
809 18th Ave. South
Nashville, Tenn. 37203

Flying Fish Records
1304 Schubert
Chicago, Ill. 60614

Folk-Legacy Records
Sharon Mountain Rd.
Sharon, Conn. 06069

Folkways Records
43 W. 61st St.
New York, N.Y. 10023

Gusto/King/Starday/Power Pak
  Records
1900 Elm Hill Pike
Nashville, Tenn. 37210

Historical Records
see Biograph

JEMF/AFM Records
John Edwards Memorial
  Foundation
Folklore and Mythology Center
University of California
Los Angeles, Calif. 90024

June Appal Recordings
P.O. Box 743
Whitesburg, Ky. 41858

Kaleidoscope Records
P.O. Box O
El Cerrito, Calif. 94530

King Records
see Gusto

Liberty Records
see Capitol

Library of Congress Records
Motion Picture, Broadcasting and
  Recorded Sound Division
Library Of Congress
Washington, D.C. 20540

Little Darlin' Records
42 Music Square West
Nashville, Tenn. 37203

Longhorn Records
see Club Of Spades

Lovely Records
325 Spring St.
New York, N.Y. 10013

Melodeon Records
see Biograph

Mark 56 Records
P.O. Box 1
Anaheim, Calif. 92805

MCA/Coral/Vocalion Records
Universal City Plaza
Universal City, Calif. 91608

Mercury/Polydor Records
PolyGram Records
910 7th Ave.
New York, N.Y. 10019

Mid-Land Records
Scotty's Music
9535 Midland Blvd.
Overland, Mo. 63114

Monument Records
21 Music Square East
Nashville, Tenn. 37203

Morning Star Records
Shanachie Record Corp.
Dolebrook Park
Ho-Ho-Kus, N.J. 07423

Old Dominion Records
P.O. Box 27
Gallatin, Tenn. 37066

Old Homestead/ACM Records
P.O. Box 100
Brighton, Mich. 48116

Old Timey Records
see Arhoolie

Origin Jazz Library
330 California #302
Santa Monica, Calif. 90403

Picadilly Records
1st American
73 Marion
Seattle, Wash. 98104

Plantation Records
see Sun

Polydor Records
see Mercury

Power Pak Records
see Gusto

Publisher's Central Bureau
Dept. 176
1 Champion Ave.
Avenal, N.J. 07001

Puritan Records
P.O. Box 946
Evanston, Ill. 60204

Rainlight Records
Drawer 810
Clarendon, Tex. 79226

Rambler/Western Records
Mutual Music Corp.
254 Scott St.
San Francisco, Calif. 94117

RCA Records
1133 Avenue of the Americas
New York, N.Y. 10036

Rebel Records
see County

Reprise Records
see Warner Bros.

Ridge Runner Records
Richey Records
P.O. Box 12937
Ft. Worth, Tex. 76116

Rock-a-Billy Records
P.O. Box 295
Walls, Miss. 38680

Rounder Records
186 Willow Ave.
Somerville, Mass. 02144

Shasta Records
4720 Forman Ave.
North Hollywood, Calif. 91602

Shiloh Records
415 N. El Camino Real
San Clemente, Calif. 92672

Sierra Records
P.O. Box 5853
Pasadena, Calif. 91107

Smithsonian Institution
Division of Performing Arts
Washington, D.C. 20560

Solid Smoke Records
P.O. Box 22372
San Francisco, Calif. 94122

Starday Records
see Gusto

Steel Guitar Record Club
Pedal Steel Guitar Products
P.O. Box 931
Concord, Calif. 94522

Sugar Hill Records
P.O. Box 4040
Duke Station
Durham, N.C. 27706

Sun/Plantation Records
MOM Music
P.O. Box 12711
Nashville, Tenn. 37212

Texas Rose Records
P.O. Box 545
Sugarland, Tex. 77478

Time-Life Records
777 Duke St.
Alexandria, Va. 22314

Vanguard Recording Society
71 W. 23rd St.
New York, N.Y. 10010

Vetco Records
5825 Vine St.
Cincinnati, O. 45216

Vocalion Records
see MCA

Voyager Recordings
424 35th Ave.
Seattle, Wash. 98122

Warner Bros./Reprise Records
4000 Warner Blvd.
Burbank, Calif. 91505

Western Records
see Rambler

INDEX

ACKNOWLEDGMENTS

Ideally, I owe a tip of the hat to everyone who's played a role in my career of ten years or so as a country music journalist and critic, but that's impossible. The list of those who in some way contributed directly to this book is long enough, and I apologize to anyone I've overlooked.

My agents, Diana Price and Joyce Frommer, took care of business efficiently and tastefully, while my editor, James Raimes, showed remarkable sensitivity and flexibility when I presented him with a manuscript much longer than he'd originally bargained for. All three were also crucial in getting me started when I had my own initial doubts, and their continuing enthusiasm—even after we hit waters more troubled than anticipated—helped carry me through the entire project.

Rich Kienzle, who knows this stuff so well it sometimes embarrasses me, read most of the manuscript, and caught more than a few factual errors. Rich also pointed me toward some key records I was unaware of, and gave me tapes of others I was unable to locate on my own. Jeff Nesin, John Swenson, and Billy Altman also loaned me records, while Doug Green, Doug Tuchman, Peter Guralnick, Greil Marcus, and Gary Rice all turned me on to records I should have known about but didn't.

Ronnie Pugh and the staff of the Country Music Foundation Library and Media Center in Nashville fielded many frantic phone calls about discographical information; when they didn't have the facts on hand, they were always able to steer me to a source that did. The library's files were also useful during my preliminary research; aside from them, I relied most heavily on Joel Whitburn's *Top Country & Western Records*, his annual collations of the *Billboard* charts, for additional discographical data.

Record company publicists or officers who provided promotional records and/or vital information include Lynn Kellerman at MCA, Jill Baum at the Smithsonian Institution, Bob Merlis at Warner Bros., Jenelle Holland at Gusto, Maureen O'Connor at Capitol, David Freeman at County/Rebel, Bill Givens at Origin Jazz Library, Sim Myers at

RCA, Mike Hyland at Monument, Marilyn Laverty and Paula Batson at Columbia, Eliot Hubbard at Epic, Chris Strachwitz at Arhoolie/Old Timey, Sherry Ring at PolyGram, Dotty Kenul at Elektra/Asylum, Paul Wells at CMH, Katie Valk at Solters, Roskin and Friedman Public Relations, John Delgatto at Sierra, the late Norman E. Pierce at Rambler/ Western, Paul Martin at Sun/Plantation, Arnold Caplin at Biograph/ Historical, David Stallings at Delta, John Holland at Folk-Legacy, Carl Schneider at Cowboy Carl, Margaret Dawson at Time-Life, DeWitt Scott at Mid-Land, and Moe Asch at Folkways.

Margot Core of Rounder Records' New York office did a Herculean job of guiding me through the labyrinth of small indie and import labels that Rounder distributes, and was successful in procuring records for me from many of them when I had struck out on my own. Mark Warren of Down Home Music filled my special orders promptly and patiently.

When I desperately needed peace and quiet to get over the roughest part of the job, Leonard Kamsler and Steve Lyles allowed me to hole up in their weekend house in upstate New York for ten days. Betsy Farren typed the final manuscript.

Finally, I'd like to add a few more words about the late Lester Bangs. He was my friend and colleague for thirteen years, and he influenced and inspired me in more ways than I could begin to list. Lester was the one who most strongly encouraged me to do this book in the first place. About halfway through, when the project once again seemed bigger than I and I was completely stymied, he came over to visit for the afternoon; our marathon conversation dealt with various other traumas and triumphs both of us were currently experiencing, but he used much of the time to help set me back on course to continue the book. That night, he died, leaving a huge hole in the lives of all of us he touched, either personally or through his own writing, with his raving, raging humanity. So here's to you, Lester.